CONTEMPORARY MORAL PROBLEMS

EIGHTH EDITION

James E. White
St. Cloud State University

THOMSON
™
WADSWORTH

Australia • Canada • Mexico • Singapore • Spain • United Kingdom • United States

THOMSON

™

WADSWORTH

Publisher: Holly J. Allen
Philosophy Editor: Steve Wainwright
Assistant Editors: Lee McCracken, Barbara Hillaker
Editorial Assistant: John Gahbauer
Technology Project Manager: Julie Aguilar
Marketing Manager: Worth Hawes
Marketing Assistant: Andrew Keay
Advertising Project Manager: Laurel Anderson
Executive Art Director: Maria Epes
Print/Media Buyer: Lisa Claudeanos

Permissions Editor: Chelsea Junget
Production Service: Matrix Productions
Copy Editor: Cheryl Smith
Cover Designer: Yvo Riezebos
Cover Image: *Ancient Landscape,* 1982,
  by George Dannatt (Getty Images)
Compositor: International Typesetting
  and Composition
Text and Cover Printer: Malloy Incorporated

Printed in the United States of America
1 2 3 4 5 6 7 08 07 06 05 04

For more information about our products, contact us at:
Thomson Learning Academic Resource Center
1-800-423-0563
For permission to use material from this text or product,
submit a request online at **http://www.thomsonrights.com**.
Any additional questions about permissions can be submitted
by email to **thomsonrights@thomson.com**.

Library of Congress Control Number: 2004111476
ISBN 0-534-58430-6

Thomson Wadsworth
10 Davis Drive
Belmont, CA 94002-3098
USA

Asia
Thomson Learning
5 Shenton Way #01-01
UIC Building
Singapore 068808

Australia/New Zealand
Thomson Learning
102 Dodds Street
Southbank, Victoria 3006
Australia

Canada
Nelson
1120 Birchmount Road
Toronto, Ontario M1K 5G4
Canada

Europe/Middle East/Africa
Thomson Learning
High Holborn House
50/51 Bedford Row
London WC1R 4LR
United Kingdom

Latin America
Thomson Learning
Seneca, 53
Colonia Polanco
11560 Mexico D.F.
Mexico

Spain/Portugal
Paraninfo
Calle Magallanes, 25
28015 Madrid, Spain

Contents

Preface

The eighth edition has been extensively revised from the previous edition; it has eighteen new readings and 24 new problem cases. Three chapters have new topics. The new topics are the duty to die (in Chapter 3), liberty (in Chapter 6), and consumption (in Chapter 8). Abortion, euthanasia, capital punishment, sexuality, marriage, drugs, animals, the environment, war, and terrorism continue to be topics of interest. The chapter on ethical theories provides a basic theoretical background for the readings; many of them assume or apply a moral theory such as utilitarianism, Kant's theory, Rawls' theory, or natural law theory.

The choice of particular readings for each topic was influenced by a variety of considerations. First, there was an attempt to find readings of high quality. All the readings have been previously published. Many of the readings are considered to be classics, such as Mary Anne Warren's "On the Moral and Legal Status of Abortion" and Peter Singer's "Famine, Affluence, and Morality." Other readings were chosen for their historical importance—for example, the Supreme Court decisions on abortion and capital punishment. There was an attempt to balance the readings, to allow different and conflicting points of view to be expressed. Thus, in the chapter on abortion, we see a variety of viewpoints, from Noonan's strict pro-life position to Warren's radical pro-choice view. But the readings also were chosen to be read together; they respond to one another as in a conversation. This is seen in the abortion chapter, where the articles can be read as replying to one another.

Suitability for students was another important consideration. The book is intended to be an introductory-level textbook that can be read and understood by most college or junior college students. But finding the right level can be difficult, as most practicing teachers know. No doubt some will find the book too easy, and others will say it is too hard. For those who need it, several student aids have been provided:

1. Chapter Introductions. With the exception of the first chapter, on ethical theories, each chapter introduction is divided into three sections: factual background, the readings, and philosophical issues. The emphasis on factual background continues in this edition; an attempt has been made to provide accurate and up-to-date information on each topic. Next, there are brief summaries of the readings, and finally a discussion of the main philosophical issues.

2. Reading Introductions. An author biography and a brief summary of the author's main arguments and conclusions precede each reading.

3. Study Questions. Two types of study questions follow each reading. First are rather detailed and pedestrian review questions that test the student's grasp of the main points in the reading. These are intended for students wanting help in following the text. Second are more difficult discussion questions that probe deeper into the subject. These are aimed at the student who has understood the reading and is ready to discuss it.

4. Problem Cases. The problem cases at the end of each chapter require the student to apply the arguments and theories discussed in the chapter to hard cases, either actual or hypothetical. This case study method, as it is called in law schools and business schools, can produce lively discussion and is a good way to get students to think about the issues. The problem cases also can be assigned as short paper topics or used for essay tests.

5. Suggested Readings. Instead of going to the library, I have come to rely on the Internet for information, using Google as my search engine. For factual information I include some useful websites. But the Internet is not a substitute for printed books and articles, which constitute the bulk of the annotated suggestions for further reading.

In revising the book for the eighth edition, I have benefited from the help and advice of many people. Lee McCracken, editor at Wadsworth, got me started with reviews and planning. Barbara Seefeldt helped with photocopying and other office work. Elena White gave suggestions and did some proofreading. Professor Myron Anderson loaned books. Professor Matthias Steup offered support and encouragement. Professor Frederick W. Thomas provided updates on authors. Aaron Downey and Joshua Barnes at Matrix Productions did the production coordination and permissions. John Larson emailed cartoons for comic relief. Finally, I am grateful to the following reviewers for their thoughtful advice and criticisms: Patrick D. Dinsmore, University of Portland; Richard Galvin, Texas Christian University; Robert Hambourger, North Carolina State University; Richard Hanley, University of Delaware; and Eddy Nahmias, Florida State University.

Chapter 1

Ethical Theories

Introduction

This chapter presents the basic moral theories that are the background for the subsequent readings in the book. For the sake of discussion, we can divide the theories into five types: theory of the right, theory of the good, virtue theory, social contract theory, and feminist theory.

Theory of the Right

A theory of the right tries to tell us what is morally right and what is morally wrong. Such a theory is obviously relevant to moral problems in the book, such as abortion, euthanasia, capital punishment, and war and terrorism.

Theories of the right are usually subdivided into two types: teleological and deontological theories. Teleological theories focus on consequences; they can be said to be forward looking. Deontological theories do not do this but, rather, look backward at some nonconsequential feature, such as a motive or God's commands. One standard teleological theory is ethical egoism, the view that everyone ought to act in his or her rational self-interest. This view is often defended by an appeal to psychological egoism, the thesis that, as a matter of fact, everyone does act in a self-interested way. But if this is so, then it is impossible for us to act unselfishly; all we can do is act selfishly. It seems to follow that ethical egoism is the only option available to us.

James Rachels attacks both psychological and ethical egoism. He argues that psychological egoism is false and confused. It is false because people do act unselfishly, and in ways contrary to self-interest. It is confused because it fails to distinguish between selfishness and self-interest, it falsely assumes that every action is done either from self-interest or from other-regarding motives, and it ignores the fact that concern for one's own welfare is compatible with concern for the welfare of others.

As for ethical egoism, Rachels admits that it is not logically inconsistent and that it cannot be decisively refuted. But he thinks there are considerations that count very strongly against it. Most people do care about others; genuine egoists who really do not care about others are rare. And saying that an action will benefit others is giving a complete and sufficient reason for doing it. No further reason needs to be given.

Perhaps the most famous and widely discussed teleological theory is utilitarianism. The standard formulation of this theory is presented by John Stuart Mill. The most basic principle of utilitarianism is the Principle of Utility, which Mill states as follows: "Actions are right in proportion as they tend to promote happiness, wrong as they tend to produce the reverse of happiness." But what is happiness? Mill's answer is that happiness (or what is good) is pleasure and the absence of pain. Here Mill adopts a standard theory of the good, called hedonism, the view that the good is pleasure. We will examine this theory and alternatives to it in the next section.

In considering the happiness or unhappiness (or the good or evil) produced, utilitarianism counts everyone equally. But who counts? The answer of Mill and his followers is radical and important: We should consider everyone who is capable of suffering, including nonhuman animals. In Chapter 7 we see Peter Singer and others arguing that it is wrong to discriminate against animals. This is in sharp contrast to the conventional view (defended by John T. Noonan in Chapter 2 and Roger Scruton in Chapter 7) that only human beings count, or at least human beings count more than nonhumans.

Now let us turn to the other main kind of theory of the right, deontological theory. One popular view is the divine command theory, discussed by John Arthur. As Arthur explains it, the divine command theory says that an act is right if and because God commands it, and wrong if and because God forbids it. According to this view God is the source of morality because without God there would be no right or wrong. Just as a legislator enacts laws, God commands moral rules. According to Arthur, defenders of the divine command theory such as F. C. Copleston often add the claim that the objective difference between right and wrong rests on the existence of God as the foundation of morality. No doubt this theory is accepted by millions of religious people, but few philosophers are willing to defend it. One problem is that many philosophers think that morality can be founded on something other than God's commands, such as reason, human nature, culture, or natural sentiments. Another objection is that "right" and "commanded by God" do not mean the same thing. People in other cultures, in Japan and China for example, use moral concepts without understanding them as references to God's commands. It goes without saying that atheists will not accept the theory, but Arthur thinks that even theists should reject it because of the possibility that God might change the moral commands. Suppose tomorrow God commands us to be cruel. Since on the theory something is right just because God commands it, cruelty is now morally right. This would be like a legistature changing the law. Arthur thinks this is just absurd. It is absurd to think that the greatest atrocities might be morally right if God were to command them. This point is similar to the famous question posed by Socrates in Plato's dialogue *Euthyphro:* Is something holy (or right) because God commands it, or does God command it because it is holy (or right)? As Arthur demonstrates in his discussion, this question raises some fundamental difficulties for the divine command theory. On the first alternative, morality seems arbitrary, since God could command anything at all and make it right. On the second alternative, God is not the source of morality after all, since it seems that God has to discover what is right rather than legislating it.

An influential deontological theory in Christian thought is the *natural law theory* of Saint Thomas Aquinas. On this view, God created the world following a divine plan that Aquinas calls the eternal law. According to this plan, everything in nature has a purpose—for example, eyes are designed for seeing and rain falls in order to nourish plants. The divine plan includes values; it includes a natural law that tells us what is right and what is good. This natural law can be discerned by humans using the natural light of reason, which humans have because they are made in the image of the rational God. The most basic precept of the natural law is the self-evident truth that one ought to do good and avoid evil. But what is good and what is evil?

Aquinas equates goodness with what is in accord with natural inclinations, and evil as that which is opposed by natural inclinations. For example, humans have a basic natural inclination to preserve life and to avoid death. This implies that actions that preserve life are right, and those that do not, such as abortion, suicide, euthanasia, capital punishment, and war, are wrong. Another basic instinct is the animal inclination to engage in sexual intercourse. But since the natural purpose of sex is reproduction, non-reproductive sex such as masturbation is wrong. (For a clear exposition of the natural law view of sex, see the Vatican Declaration on Sexual Ethics in Chapter 5.)

Few people outside the Catholic Church appeal to natural law theory. One problem is that modern science does not explain things in terms of purposes or values. The eye was not designed for seeing; it is simply the result of a long period of evolution and natural selection. Or at least that is the explanation given in biology. Rain does not fall in order to nourish plants. It falls because of the law of gravity. The laws of science merely describe what happens; they do not ascribe purposes or values to anything. Another problem is the equation of natural inclination with good and unnatural inclination with evil. Male humans have a natural inclination to be aggressive and to dominate females, but are these natural tendencies good? Feminists such as Mary Daly do not think so. (Daly's views are explained in the Jean Grimshaw reading.) Many people find celibacy to be unnatural, since it is opposed by natural desires, yet the Church teaches that total abstinence from sex is good, not evil. Finally, how do we know what the natural law says? Any rational person is supposed to be able to discern the natural law, but we find that rational people do not agree about values. Is it possible that some rational people are deceived when they try to discern the moral law? How can we be sure we are perceiving the true moral law, assuming there is such a thing? Even Catholics who accept natural law theory do not agree about everything. For example, some are pacifists who find war immoral, while others justify war using the just war theory. (For a discussion of pacifism just war theory see Chapter 9.)

Unlike Aquinas, David Hume denies that reason can tell us what is right and what is good. Hume argues that morality cannot be derived from reason. According to Hume, if you consider, for example, a case of intentional murder, you will find that the wrongness of murder is not found in your reasoning about objective facts or relations of ideas, but simply in your sentiment, in your feelings of disapproval of murder. The view that moral judgments are based on subjective feelings of approval or disapproval is called *ethical subjectivism*. Strictly speaking, this is a view about the factual basis of morality, not a deontological theory that tells us what is right. In the fifth reading, Shaw calls such a theory a *meta-ethical theory*. It tells us what morality is based on as a matter of fact, not what morality ought to be. In a famous passage, Hume suggests that it is a mistake to argue from "is" to "ought," that is, to argue that because something is the case, that therefore it ought to be the case. But Aquinas seems to make this very mistake when he says that what is natural ought to be done, for example, that since reproductive sex is natural, it ought to be done. It should be noted that Hume did have views about what ought to be done. He recommended following a sentiment of benevolence toward all humans. But he did not think that people ought to do this because they do have such a sentiment. The fact that people have such a sentiment only shows that acting benevolently is possible.

Hume's views are controversial. Some philosophers have maintained that arguing from "is" to "ought" is acceptable in some cases. For example, in the reading Mill claims that the only proof that can be given that happiness is desirable is that people desire it. Happiness is good because everyone wants it. Clearly Mill is arguing from a fact to a value, but is this a mistake? A problem with Hume's theory about morality is that it implies that people cannot be mistaken in their moral judgments. If moral judgments are just expressions of feeling, the equivalent of approving or disapproving of something, then as long as they are sincere, people cannot be mistaken when making a moral judgment. But it seems obvious to William H. Shaw that people such as sadists or Nazis can be mistaken in their moral judgments. A related problem is that Hume's theory doesn't seem to give an adequate account of moral disagreements. If the abortion controversy amounts to different people having different feelings about abortion, with some approving and others disapproving, then they do not really have a substantive disagreement. They are not contradicting each other. They just have different feelings. This hardly seems like a satisfactory account of the disagreement. After all, both sides defend their position using arguments and reasoning. They appeal to facts. No doubt emotions play a role in the controversy, but it is not just about feelings.

A deontological theory that takes moral disagreements seriously is *ethical relativism*. William H. Shaw distinguishes between two types of ethical relativism, cultural and individual. Cultural ethical relativism is the view that what is right is whatever a culture says is right. If our culture says that homosexuality is wrong, then it is wrong in our society. But if ancient Greek culture said that homosexuality is right, then it was right in that society. Individual ethical relativism is the view that what is right is whatever an individual thinks is right. Sometimes this popular view is expressed in the slogan that "Morality is just a matter of opinion," with the implication that one opinion is just as good as another.

Shaw rejects both types of ethical relativism. Like Hume's theory, the individual type makes moral judgments infallible, and this cannot be right in Shaw's view. Surely there is a difference between merely thinking something is right and its actually being right. Furthermore, the theory fails to provide an adequate account of ethical debate and disagreement, and it doesn't allow for moral deliberation.

Cultural ethical relativism has a different set of problems according to Shaw. First, it doesn't allow for valid moral criticism of other societies, for example, the slave society of the American South in the 19th century or Nazi Germany. Second, it is not clear how it should be applied. Is abortion wrong if 51 percent of the people in a society disapprove of it, and does the wrong flip-flop to right if the approval rate goes up to 51 percent? Is a culture defined by geography or class or what? Are the Hell's Angels a separate culture? Third, and most decisive in Shaw's view, is the fact that societies can make moral mistakes; they can say something is right when it is really wrong. To use Shaw's example, a society that approves of the torture of children is making a moral mistake, for in Shaw's view the torture of children is clearly wrong no matter what a society says.

The most influential deontological theory is Immanuel Kant's theory. Kant believes that by pure reasoning we can discover one supreme moral principle that is binding on all rational beings. By "pure reasoning" he means reasoning that does not appeal to anything else, such as religious faith or popular opinion; it is like reasoning in geometry and mathematics. The category of "rational beings" excludes animals in Kant's view (see his reading in Chapter 7); it includes not just human beings but also God and angels. The supreme moral principle uncovered by pure reasoning is called the *categorical imperative* because it commands absolutely, as distinguished from hypothetical imperatives that command only if you have certain desires.

Kant formulates the categorical imperative in several different ways, but commentators usually focus on two distinct versions. The first one is that you should "act only on that maxim through which you can at the same time will that it should become a universal law." This principle gives you a way of deciding whether an act is wrong or not. You ask yourself what rule you would be following if you did something; this rule is the "maxim" of your act. If you are not willing to have this rule become a universal law that everyone follows, then the act is wrong. To take one of Kant's examples, suppose you want to borrow money and not pay it back. To get the money you have to promise to pay it back even though you have no intention of doing so. The maxim of your act, then, would be something like this: "Whenever I believe myself short of money, I will borrow money and promise to pay it back, though I know that this will never be done." According to Kant, this maxim could never be a universal law because it contradicts itself. If everyone followed this maxim, then the very practice of promising would be impossible because nobody would believe a promise. These considerations show that such false promising is wrong.

Many philosophers have thought that this first formulation of the categorical imperative is problematic. One problem is that you can formulate the rule under which an act falls in different ways. Some of these rules could be made universal and others not. To go back to borrowing money, suppose you need to borrow money to pay for expensive cancer treatment to save your infant son's life. You do not have health insurance, and Medicaid will not cover the treatment. To get the money, you promise to pay it back even though you know you cannot do so. Now the maxim of your act is something like this: "Whenever I need money to save my baby's life, then I will borrow money from the bank and promise to pay it back, even though I know this will never be done because I will never have that much money." Would you be willing to have this be a universal law? If so, would it destroy the practice of promising?

Another objection attacks Kant's notion of perfect duty, the idea that there are duties that admit no exceptions. The objection is that there are always possible exceptions, exceptions that arise when there is a conflict between duties. Suppose, for example, that there is a conflict between the duty to not lie and the duty to not harm others. A terrorist asks you for a loaded gun to use in killing innocent hostages. You know where there is a gun handy, but should you tell the truth? It seems obvious enough that you should not tell the truth in this case because the duty to not harm others overrides the duty to not lie.

Kant formulated the categorical imperative in a second way, which some commentators find more plausible. This second formulation, called the *formula of the end in itself,* recommends that you "act in such a way that you always treat humanity, whether in your own person or in the person of any other, never simply as a means, but always at the same time as an end." Treating others as a mere means is to engage them in an activity to which they could not, in principle, consent—for example, a deception. Treating people as ends in themselves requires that we treat them not only as mere means, but that we help them with their projects and activities. This gives us a duty to help or a duty of beneficence, but this duty is only imperfect. That is, it is a duty that cannot always be satisfied, but requires us to exercise judgment and discretion.

Kant's theory has had an important impact on three of the moral problems covered in the book. First, Kant is a stern defender of capital punishment. In the reading in Chapter 4, Kant condemns the "serpent-windings of utilitarianism" and insists that the only appropriate punishment for murderers is death. They must be paid back for their crimes, and the consequences of the punishment are irrelevant. Kant is one of the main sources of the retributive theory of punishment, which holds that guilty people should be punished and that the punishment should fit the crime. Second, according to Kant, we do not have any direct duties toward animals. (See the reading in Chapter 7.) We have only indirect duties based on the effect the treatment of animals has on the treatment of humans. We should not be cruel to animals because this makes us likely to be cruel to humans. Animals are not subjects of direct moral concern because they are not rational beings. Kant's view, then, stands in sharp contrast to the utilitarians such as Mill and Singer, who believe that animals do have the status of moral subjects who deserve moral consideration. Third, there is the abortion controversy. Kant does not discuss abortion. But it seems clear that fetuses are not rational beings, and thus an implication of Kant's view is that they have no more moral status than animals. This is similar to the position that Mary Anne Warren takes in Chapter 2.

Theory of the Good

A theory of the good tries to tell us what is good and what is bad. Teleological theories seem to require some theory of the good in order to evaluate consequences. We noted previously that Mill accepts hedonism, the theory that the good is pleasure. Hedonism is usually defended by making two important distinctions. First, there is a distinction between intrinsic and instrumental value. Something has intrinsic value if it is good or bad in itself apart from its use or consequences. By contrast, something has instrumental value if it is good or bad depending on how it is used. Hedonists allow that things such as knowledge and beauty can be instrumentally good but insist that only pleasure is intrinsically good. Similarly, things such as ignorance and ugliness can be instrumentally bad, but hedonists claim that only pain is intrinsically bad.

Critics of Mill and hedonism argue, however, that other things besides pleasure can be intrinsically good—for example, unexperienced beauty that is not instrumentally good because no one experiences it. And things besides pain can be intrinsically bad—for example, the injustice of punishing an innocent person. Indeed, the fact that utilitarianism does not seem to give a satisfactory account of retributive or distributive justice is seen as a serious defect. This has led modern philosophers to formulate theories of justice that are independent of utilitarianism—for example, Rawls's theory of justice in the readings for this chapter. Another criticism of hedonism (which can be found in the reading by Aristotle) is that pleasure is an appropriate goal for animals but not for humans. According to Aristotle, the highest good for humans is found in contemplation because this involves the use of reason, and reasoning is what humans are naturally suited to do. The reply that Mill makes in the reading rests on the second distinction made by hedonists, a distinction between higher and lower pleasures. Roughly, higher pleasures involve the use of the intellect, whereas lower pleasures involve the senses. The higher pleasures are better than the lower pleasures, Mill argues, because the person who has experienced both will prefer the higher pleasures. Whether this is true or not is a matter of debate. In any event, Mill's view about the good life turns out to be not much different from Aristotle's view; on both views intellectual activities have a central role.

There are alternatives to hedonism. One is Kant's position that the only thing that is good without qualification is the good will, the desire to do one's duty for its own sake. Kant denied, by the way, that pleasure is always intrinsically good. He thought that the pleasure of a wicked person is not good; for example, in Kant's view the pleasure the sadist gets from torturing others is both instrumentally and intrinsically evil.

Another main source of alternatives to hedonism is religion. The monotheistic religions (Judaism, Christianity, and Islam) agree that the highest good involves God in some way. It might be obedience to God's will (emphasized in Islam), or love of God (recommended by Jesus), or a mystical union with God in this life, or a beatific vision of God in heaven. Aristotle says that the highest good for humans is found in the contemplation of God. Although we will not be concerned with religion as such, there is no doubt that religion has played an important role in ethics. Arthur discusses some of the connections between ethics and religion in the reading. We have already discussed the divine command theory, which is tacitly adopted in the monotheistic religions. (There are, of course, religions that do not worship God—for example, Buddhism, Taoism, and Confucianism.) Other religious doctrines come up in various contexts. In Chapter 2, Noonan mentions ensoulment, the doctrine that the immortal soul enters the fetus (or technically, the zygote) at the moment of conception. Traditionally, philosophers have defended our lack of moral concern for animals by maintaining that animals do not have souls (although it should be mentioned that in Hinduism and Jainism, animals are believed to have souls; indeed, some of them have the reincarnated souls of humans!).

Virtue Theory

Virtue theory is included in this chapter because it offers an important alternative to the theories that dwell on moral rightness and duty. The classical source of virtue theory is Aristotle. Aristotle makes several important points about virtues. First, there is a distinction between intellectual and moral virtue. Intellectual virtue involves the use of what is best in humans—namely, reasoning—and the highest form of reasoning is self-sufficient, pure contemplation of God. Moral virtues involve a mean between the extremes of excess and deficiency. This is sometimes called the *doctrine of the golden mean*. To use one of Aristotle's examples, courage is a mean between the excess of foolhardiness and the deficiency of cowardliness.

Second, Aristotle claims that some actions do not involve any means but are always wrong. This is an important point, for if there are such actions, then it seems to follow that some of the theories we have just discussed are problematic. Consider, for example, the action of torturing a small child to death. As Shaw suggests in the reading, it seems obvious that this is wrong even if a person or a culture believes it is right, and even if God commands it, and even if it produces good consequences for others or the person doing the torturing. If so, then egoism, cultural relativism, the divine command theory, and utilitarianism all have a serious problem.

Social Contract Theory

Many of the readings in the book do not appeal to virtues or to duties, but to rights. We find references to the rights of fetuses, newborn infants, the terminally ill, animals, and even the environment. Most often mentioned are the rights to life and liberty.

The traditional basis for moral rights is that they are created by God. John Locke and Thomas Jefferson talk about humans being endowed by their Creator with certain basic rights that are inalienable, that cannot be taken away by other people or the government. But most philosophers today do not want to make God the source of rights; they want a different foundation. The traditional secular view that is used to provide a foundation for rights is the *social contract theory* of Thomas Hobbes and Jean Jacques Rousseau. According to this theory, it is in everyone's self-interest to live together in a society rather than alone in a state of nature. Life in a state of nature would be short, nasty, and brutish. But to live in a society, people must agree to follow certain rules (don't steal, don't murder, etc.), and these rules imply corresponding rights. Every citizen tacitly makes such an agreement (the social contract) to get the benefits of living in society. Without this social contract, society would be impossible.

John Rawls's theory of justice is a type of social contract theory. We are asked to imagine what rules free, rational, and informed people would accept for a society. To make sure that the contractors are fair and unbiased, we are to imagine them operating under a "veil of ignorance" that hides from them personal facts such as their gender, race, and class. The rules such contractors would accept in the hypothetical original position, according to Rawls, are a principle giving people an equal right to liberty and a principle concerning social and economic inequalities.

Feminist Theory

In general, feminist theory is critical of the male theories discussed so far. They display a male bias that ignores the experience of women and contributes to the oppression of women in a male-dominated society. According to Jean Grimshaw, the male preoccupation with war, politics, and capitalistic economic domination has harmed women and the natural environment, and part of the blame can be placed on the male theories that are used to justify the violence and destruction. For example, the emphasis on the value of freedom we find in Mill, Rawls, Kant, and the other male philosophers is of little help to poor and oppressed women who lack basic necessities such as food, shelter, and medical care. The justice perspective of

Kant, Rawls, and other male philosophers is irrelevant to the experience of women who care for children. The experience of these women involves emotions such as love and not reasoning about abstract principles such as the categorical imperative. But what is the feminist alternative to the male theories? Grimshaw discusses the idea of a female ethic, that is, moral thinking and moral theory that is unique to women and superior to male thinking and theories. According to feminists such as Carol Gilligan and Nel Noddings, for example, women do not tend to appeal to abstract rules and principles in the same sort of way as men; rather they appeal to concrete and detailed knowledge of the situation, and they are more likely to consider the personal relationships involved. Sara Ruddick argues that the activity of mothering generates a concept of virtue that is the basis for a critique of the male values of contermporary life such as the militarism we see in the United States. Caroline Whitbeck argues that the practices of caring for others can provide an acceptable ethical model of mutual realization, which is an alternative to the competitive and individualistic model we see in male-dominated society.

A problem with the feminists theories is that they seem to apply to the private world of domestic life, where women care for children, and not to the male-dominated public world of war, politics, and the market. Male theorists argue that when it comes to the marketplace and war, for example, the feminist ethic of caring does not make sense. The very concept of the market or war precludes the sort of caring or mothering behavior recommended by the feminists. Grimshaw replies that there is no clear distinction between the public male world of the market and the private female world of domestic relations. Women work outside the home, and men have a domestic role. But she admits that the distinction between the public and the private has shaped social reality, and explains the differences between men and women in their moral thinking. This is not to say, however, that the experiences of women in the private domestic world cannot provide a valuable source of criticism of the male-dominated public world and a basis for reform.

Egoism and Moral Scepticism

JAMES RACHELS

James Rachels (1941–2003) was University Professor of Philosophy at the University of Alabama at Birmingham. He was the author of *The End of Life: Euthanasia and Morality* (1986), *Created from Animals: The Moral Implications of Darwinism* (1991), *The Elements of Moral Philosophy* (4e, 2002), and *Can Ethics Provide*

Source: James Rachels, "Egoism and Moral Skepticism," from *A New Introduction to Philosophy*, ed. Steven M. Cahn (Harper & Row, 1971). Reprinted with permission.

Answers? And Other Essays in Moral Philosophy (1997). In addition, he published more than 60 articles in philosophy.

Rachels examines psychological egoism and ethical egoism, two popular views used to attack conventional morality. Psychological egoism holds that all human actions are self-interested, whereas ethical egoism says that all actions ought to be self-interested. After discussing two arguments used to defend psychological egoism, Rachels concludes that it is both false and confused. Although he is unable to decisively refute ethical egoism, he finds that it has serious problems. Genuine egoists are rare, and that it is a fundamental fact of human psychology that humans care about others and not just about themselves.

1. OUR ORDINARY THINKING about morality is full of assumptions that we almost never question. We assume, for example, that we have an obligation to consider the welfare of other people when we decide what actions to perform or what rules to obey; we think that we must refrain from acting in ways harmful to others, and that we must respect their rights and interests as well as our own. We also assume that people are in fact capable of being motivated by such considerations, that is, that people are not wholly selfish and that they do sometimes act in the interests of others.

Both of these assumptions have come under attack by moral sceptics, as long ago as by Glaucon in Book II of Plato's *Republic*. Glaucon recalls the legend of Gyges, a shepherd who was said to have found a magic ring in a fissure opened by an earthquake. The ring would make its wearer invisible and thus would enable him to go anywhere and do anything undetected. Gyges used the power of the ring to gain entry to the Royal Palace where he seduced the Queen, murdered the King, and subsequently seized the throne. Now Glaucon asks us to determine that there are two such rings, one given to a man of virtue and one given to a rogue. The rogue, of course, will use his ring unscrupulously and do anything necessary to increase his own wealth and power. He will recognize no moral constraints on his conduct, and, since the cloak of invisibility will protect him from discovery, he can do anything he pleases without fear of reprisal. So, there will be no end to the mischief

he will do. But how will the so-called virtuous man behave? Glaucon suggests that he will behave no better than the rogue: "No one, it is commonly believed, would have such iron strength of mind as to stand fast in doing right or keep his hands off other men's goods, when he could go to the market-place and fearlessly help himself to anything he wanted, enter houses and sleep with any woman he chose, set prisoners free and kill men at his pleasure, and in a word go about among men with the powers of a god. He would behave no better than the other; both would take the same course."[1] Moreover, why shouldn't he? Once he is freed from the fear of reprisal, why shouldn't a man simply do what he pleases, or what he thinks is best for himself? What reason is there for him to continue being "moral" when it is clearly not to his own advantage to do so?

These sceptical views suggested by Glaucon have come to be known as *psychological egoism* and *ethical egoism* respectively. Psychological egoism is the view that all men are selfish in everything that they do, that is, that the only motive from which anyone ever acts is self-interest. On this view, even when men are acting in ways apparently calculated to benefit others, they are actually motivated by the belief that acting in this way is to their own advantage, and if they did not believe this, they would not be doing that action. Ethical egoism is, by contrast,

1 *The Republic of Plato*, translated by F. M. Cornford (Oxford, 1941), p. 45.

a normative view about how men *ought* to act. It is the view that, regardless of how men do in fact behave, they have no obligation to do anything except what is in their own interests. According to the ethical egoist, a person is always justified in doing whatever is in his own interests, regardless of the effect on others.

Clearly, if either of these views is correct, then "the moral institution of life" (to use Butler's well-turned phrase) is very different than what we normally think. The majority of mankind is grossly deceived about what is, or ought to be, the case, where morals are concerned.

2. Psychological egoism seems to fly in the face of the facts. We are tempted to say: "Of course people act unselfishly all the time. For example, Smith gives up a trip to the country, which he would have enjoyed very much, in order to stay behind and help a friend with his studies, which is a miserable way to pass the time. This is a perfectly clear case of unselfish behavior, and if the psychological egoist thinks that such cases do not occur, then he is just mistaken." Given such obvious instances of "unselfish behavior," what reply can the egoist make? There are two general arguments by which he might try to show that all actions, including those such as the one just outlined, are in fact motivated by self-interest. Let us examine these in turn:

A. The first argument goes as follows. If we describe one person's action as selfish, and another person's action as unselfish, we are overlooking the crucial fact that in both cases, assuming that the action is done voluntarily, *the agent is merely doing what he most wants to do.* If Smith stays behind to help his friend, that only shows that he wanted to help his friend more than he wanted to go to the country. And why should he be praised for his "unselfishness" when he is only doing what he most wants to do? So, since Smith is only doing what he wants to do, he cannot be said to be acting unselfishly.

This argument is so bad that it would not deserve to be taken seriously except for the fact that so many otherwise intelligent people have been taken in by it. First, the argument rests on the premise that people never voluntarily do anything except what they want to do. But this is patently false; there are at least two classes of actions that are exceptions to this generalization. One is the set of actions which we may not want to do, but which we do anyway as a means to an end which we want to achieve; for example, going to the dentist in order to stop a toothache, or going to work every day in order to be able to draw our pay at the end of the month. These cases may be regarded as consistent with the spirit of the egoist argument, however, since the ends mentioned are wanted by the agent. But the other set of actions are those which we do, not because we want to, nor even because there is an end which we want to achieve, but because we feel ourselves *under an obligation* to do them. For example, someone may do something because he has promised to do it, and thus feels obligated, even though he does not want to do it. It is sometimes suggested that in such cases we do the action because, after all, we want to keep our promises; so, even here, we are doing what we want. However, this dodge will not work: if I have promised to do something, and if I do not want to do it, then it is simply false to say that I want to keep my promise. In such cases we feel a conflict precisely because we do *not* want to do what we feel obligated to do. It is reasonable to think that Smith's action falls roughly into this second category: he might stay behind, not because he wants to, but because he feels that his friend needs help.

But suppose we were to concede, for the sake of the argument, that all voluntary action is motivated by the agent's wants, or at least that Smith is so motivated. Even if this were granted, it would not follow that Smith is acting selfishly or from self-interest. For if Smith wants to do something that will help his friend, even when it means forgoing his own enjoyments, that is precisely what makes him *un*selfish. What else could unselfishness be, if not wanting to help others?

Another way to put the same point is to say that it is the *object* of a want that determines whether it is selfish or not. The mere fact that I am acting on *my* wants does not mean that I am acting selfishly; that depends on *what it is* that I want. If I want only my own good, and care nothing for others, then I am selfish; but if I also want other people to be well-off and happy, and if I act on *that* desire, then my action is not selfish. So much for this argument.

B. The second argument for psychological egoism is this. Since so-called unselfish actions always produce a sense of self-satisfaction in the agent,[2] and since this sense of satisfaction is a pleasant state of consciousness, it follows that the point of the action is really to achieve a pleasant state of consciousness, rather than to bring about any good for others. Therefore, the action is "unselfish" only at a superficial level of analysis. Smith will feel much better with himself for having stayed to help his friend—if he had gone to the country, be would have felt terrible about it—and that is the real point of the action. According to a well-known story, this argument was once expressed by Abraham Lincoln:

> Mr. Lincoln once remarked to a fellow-passenger on an old-time mud-coach that all men were prompted by selfishness in doing good. His fellow-passenger was antagonizing this position when they were passing over a corduroy bridge that spanned a slough. As they crossed this bridge they espied an old razor-backed sow on the bank making a terrible noise because her pigs had got into the slough and were in danger of drowning. As the old coach began to climb the hill, Mr. Lincoln called out, "Driver, can't you stop just a moment?" Then Mr. Lincoln jumped out, ran back, and lifted the little pigs out of the mud and water and placed them on the bank. When he returned, his companion remarked: "Now, Abe, where does selfishness come in on this little episode?"

> "Why, bless your soul, Ed, that was the very essence of selfishness. I should have had no peace of mind all day had I gone on and left that suffering old sow worrying over those pigs. I did it to get peace of mind, don't you see?"[3]

This argument suffers from defects similar to the previous one. Why should we think that merely because someone derives satisfaction from helping others this makes him selfish? Isn't the unselfish man precisely the one who *does* derive satisfaction from helping others, while the selfish man does not? If Lincoln "got peace of mind" from rescuing the piglets, does this show him to be selfish, or, on the contrary, doesn't it show him to be compassionate and good-hearted? (If a man were truly selfish, why should it bother his conscience that *others* suffer—much less pigs?) Similarly, it is nothing more than shabby sophistry to say, because Smith takes satisfaction in helping his friend, that he is behaving selfishly. If we say this rapidly, while thinking about something else, perhaps it will sound all right; but if we speak slowly, and pay attention to what we are saying, it sounds plain silly.

Moreover, suppose we ask *why* Smith derives satisfaction from helping his friend. The answer will be, it is because Smith cares for him and wants him to succeed. If Smith did not have these concerns, then he would take no pleasure in assisting him; and these concerns, as we have already seen, are the marks of unselfishness, not selfishness. To put the point more generally: if we have a positive attitude toward the attainment of some goal, then we may derive satisfaction from attaining that goal. But the *object* of our attitude is *the attainment of that goal;* and we must want to attain the goal *before* we can find any satisfaction in it. We do not, in other words, desire some sort of "pleasurable consciousness" and then try to figure out how to achieve it; rather, we desire all sorts of different

---

2 Or, as it is sometimes said, "It gives him a clear conscience," or "He couldn't sleep at night if he had done otherwise," or "He would have been ashamed of himself for not doing it," and so on.

3 Frank C. Sharp, *Ethics* (New York, 1928), pp. 74–75. Quoted from the Springfield (Ill.) *Monitor* in the *Outlook*, vol. 56, p. 1059.

things—money, a new fishing-boat, to be a better chess-player, to get a promotion in our work, etc.—and because we desire these things, we derive satisfaction from attaining them. And so, if someone desires the welfare and happiness of another person, he will derive satisfaction from that; but this does not mean that this satisfaction is the object of his desire, or that he is in any way selfish on account of it.

It is a measure of the weakness of psychological egoism that these insupportable arguments are the ones most often advanced in its favor. Why, then, should anyone ever have thought it a true view? Perhaps because of a desire for theoretical simplicity: In thinking about human conduct, it would be nice if there were some simple formula that would unite the diverse phenomena of human behavior under a single explanatory principle, just as simple formulae in physics bring together a great many apparently different phenomena. And since it is obvious that self-regard is an overwhelmingly important factor in motivation, it is only natural to wonder whether all motivation might not be explained in these terms. But the answer is clearly No; while a great many human actions are motivated entirely or in part by self-interest, only by a deliberate distortion of the facts can we say that all conduct is so motivated. This will be clear, I think, if we correct three confusions which are commonplace. The exposure of these confusions will remove the last traces of plausibility from the psychological egoist thesis.

The first is the confusion of selfishness with self-interest. The two are clearly not the same. If I see a physician when I am feeling poorly, I am acting in my own interest but no one would think of calling me "selfish" on account of it. Similarly, brushing my teeth, working hard at my job, and obeying the law are all in my self-interest but none of these are examples of selfish conduct. This is because selfish behavior is behavior that ignores the interests of others, in circumstances in which their interests ought not to be ignored. This concept has a definite evaluative flavor; to call someone "selfish" is not just

to describe his action but to condemn it. Thus, you would not call me selfish for eating a normal meal in normal circumstances (although it may surely be in my self-interest); but you would call me selfish for hoarding food while others about are starving.

The second confusion is the assumption that every action is done *either* from self-interest or from other-regarding motives. Thus, the egoist concludes that if there is no such thing as genuine altruism then all actions must be done from self-interest. But this is certainly a false dichotomy. The man who continues to smoke cigarettes, even after learning about the connection between smoking and cancer, is surely not acting from self-interest, not even by his own standards—self-interest would dictate that he quit smoking at once—and he is not acting altruistically either. He *is*, no doubt, smoking for the pleasure of it, but all that this shows is that undisciplined pleasure-seeking and acting from self-interest are very different. This is what led Butler to remark that "The thing to be lamented is, not that men have so great regard to their own good or interest in the present world, for they have not enough."[4]

The last two paragraphs show (*a*) that it is false that all actions are selfish, and (*b*) that it is false that all actions are done out of self-interest. And it should be noted that these two points can be made, and were, without any appeal to putative examples of altruism.

The third confusion is the common but false assumption that a concern for one's own welfare is incompatible with any genuine concern for the welfare of others. Thus, since it is obvious that everyone (or very nearly everyone) does desire his own well-being, it might be thought that no one can really be concerned with others. But again, this is false. There is no inconsistency

4 *The Works of Joseph Butler*, edited by W. E. Gladstone (Oxford, 1896), vol. II, p. 26. It should be noted that most of the points I am making against psychological egoism were first made by Butler. Butler made all the important points; all that is left for us is to remember them.

in desiring that everyone, including oneself *and* others, be well-off and happy. To be sure, it may happen on occasion that our own interests conflict with the interests of others, and in these cases we will have to make hard choices. But even in these cases we might sometimes opt for the interests of others, especially when the others involved are our family or friends. But more importantly, not all cases are like this: sometimes we are able to promote the welfare of others when our own interests are not involved at all. In these cases not even the strongest self-regard need prevent us from acting considerately toward others.

Once these confusions are cleared away, it seems to me obvious enough that there is no reason whatever to accept psychological egoism. On the contrary, if we simply observe people's behavior with an open mind, we may find that a great deal of it is motivated by self-regard, but by no means all of it; and that there is no reason to deny that "the moral institution of life" can include a place for the virtue of beneficence.[5]

3. The ethical egoist would say at this point, "Of course it is possible for people to act altruistically, and perhaps many people do act that way—but there is no reason why they *should* do so. A person is under no obligation to do anything except what is in his own interests."[6] This is really quite a radical doctrine. Suppose I have an urge to set fire to some public building (say, a department store) just for the fascination of watching the spectacular blaze: according to this view, the fact that several people might be burned to death provides no reason whatever why I should not do it. After all, this only concerns

their welfare, not my own, and according to the ethical egoist the only person I need think of is myself.

Some might deny that ethical egoism has any such monstrous consequences. They would point out that it is really to my own advantage not to set the fire—for, if I do that I may be caught and put into prison (unlike Gyges, I have no magic ring for protection). Moreover, even if I could avoid being caught it is still to my advantage to respect the rights and interests of others, for it is to my advantage to live in a society in which people's rights and interests are respected. Only in such a society can I live a happy and secure life; so, in acting kindly toward others, I would merely be doing my part to create and maintain the sort of society which it is to my advantage to have.[7] Therefore, it is said, the egoist would not be such a bad man; he would be as kindly and considerate as anyone else, because he would see that it is to his own advantage to be kindly and considerate.

This is a seductive line of thought, but it seems to me mistaken. Certainly it is to everyone's advantage (including the egoist's) to preserve a stable society where people's interests are generally protected. But there is no reason for the egoist to think that merely because *he* will not honor the rules of the social game, decent society will collapse. For the vast majority of people are not egoists, and there is no reason to think that they will be converted by his example—especially if he is discreet and does not unduly flaunt his style of life. What this line of reasoning shows is not that the egoist himself must act benevolently, but that he must encourage *others* to do so. He must take care to conceal from public view his own self-centered method of decision-making, and urge others to act on precepts very different from those on which he is willing to act.

The rational egoist, then, cannot advocate that egoism be universally adopted by everyone. For he wants a world in which his own

5 The capacity for altruistic behavior is not unique to human beings. Some interesting experiments with rhesus monkeys have shown that these animals will refrain from operating a device for securing food if this causes other animals to suffer pain. See Masserman, Wechkin, and Terris, "'Altruistic' Behavior in Rhesus Monkeys," *The American Journal of Psychiatry*, vol. 121 (1964), 584–585.

6 I take this to be the view of Ayn Rand, in so far as I understand her confusing doctrine.

7 Cf. Thomas Hobbes, *Leviathan* (London, 1651), chap. 17.

interests are maximized; and if other people adopted the egoistic policy of pursuing their own interests to the exclusion of his interests, as he pursues his interests to the exclusion of theirs, then such a world would be impossible. So he himself will be an egoist, but he will want others to be altruists.

This brings us to what is perhaps the most popular "refutation" of ethical egoism current among philosophical writers—the argument that ethical egoism is at bottom inconsistent because it cannot be universalized.[8] The argument goes like this:

To say that any action or policy of action is *right* (or that it *ought* to be adopted) entails that it is right for *anyone* in the same sort of circumstances. I cannot, for example, say that it is right for me to lie to you, and yet object when you lie to me (provided, of course, that the circumstances are the same). I cannot hold that it is all right for me to drink your beer and then complain when you drink mine. This is just the requirement that we be consistent in our evaluations; it is a requirement of logic. Now it is said that ethical egoism cannot meet this requirement because, as we have already seen, the egoist would not want others to act in the same way that he acts. Moreover, suppose he *did* advocate the universal adoption of egoistic policies: he would be saying to Peter, "You ought to pursue your own interests even if it means destroying Paul"; and he would be saying to Paul, "You ought to pursue your own interests even if it means destroying Peter." The attitudes expressed in these two recommendations seem clearly inconsistent—he is urging the advancement of Peter's interest at one moment, and countenancing their defeat at the next. Therefore, the argument goes, there is no way to maintain the doctrine of

ethical egoism as a consistent view about how we ought to act. We will fall into inconsistency whenever we try.

What are we to make of this argument? Are we to conclude that ethical egoism has been refuted? Such a conclusion, I think, would be unwarranted; for I think that we can show, contrary to this argument, how ethical egoism can be maintained consistently. We need only to interpret the egoist's position in a sympathetic way: we should say that he has in mind a certain kind of world which he would prefer over all others; it would be a world in which his own interests were maximized, regardless of the effects on other people. The egoist's primary policy of action, then, would be to act in such a way as to bring about, as nearly as possible, this sort of world. Regardless of however morally reprehensible we might find it, there is nothing *inconsistent* in someone's adopting this as his ideal and acting in a way calculated to bring it about. And if someone did adopt this as his ideal, then he would not advocate universal egoism; as we have already seen, he would want other people to be altruists. So, if he advocates any principles of conduct for the general public, they will be altruistic principles. This would not be inconsistent; on the contrary, it would be perfectly consistent with his goal of creating a world in which his own interests are maximized. To be sure, he would have to be deceitful; in order to secure the good will of others, and a favorable hearing for his exhortations to altruism, he would have to pretend that he was himself prepared to accept altruistic principles. But again, that would be all right; from the egoist's point of view, this would merely be a matter of adopting the necessary means to the achievement of his goal—and while we might not approve of this, there is nothing inconsistent about it. Again, it might be said: "He advocates one thing, but does another. Surely *that's* inconsistent." But it is not; for what he advocates and what he does are both calculated as means to an end (the *same* end, we might note); and as such,

8 See, for example, Brian Medlin, "Ultimate Principles and Ethical Egoism," *Australasian Journal of Philosophy,* vol. 35 (1957), 111–118; and D. H. Monro, *Empiricism and Ethics* (Cambridge, 1967), chap. 16.

he is doing what is rationally required in each case. Therefore, contrary to the previous argument, there is nothing inconsistent in the ethical egoist's view. He cannot be refuted by the claim that he contradicts himself.

Is there, then, no way to refute the ethical egoist? If by "refute" we mean show that he has made some *logical* error, the answer is that there is not. However, there is something more that can be said. The egoist challenge to our ordinary moral convictions amounts to a demand for an explanation of why we should adopt certain policies of action, namely policies in which the good of others is given importance. We can give an answer to this demand, albeit an indirect one. The reason one ought not to do actions that would hurt other people is: other people would be hurt. The reason one ought to do actions that would benefit other people is: other people would be benefited. This may at first seem like a piece of philosophical sleight-of-hand, but it is not. The point is that the welfare of human beings is something that most of us value *for its own sake,* and not merely for the sake of something else. Therefore, when *further* reasons are demanded for valuing the welfare of human beings, we cannot point to anything further to satisfy this demand. It is not that we have no reason for pursuing these policies, but that our reason *is* that these policies are for the good of human beings.

So: if we are asked "Why shouldn't I set fire to this department store?" one answer would be "Because if you do, people may be burned to death." This is a complete, sufficient reason which does not require qualification or supplementation of any sort. If someone seriously wants to know why this action shouldn't be done, that's the reason. If we are pressed further and asked the sceptical question "But why shouldn't I do actions that will harm others?" we may not know what to say—but this is because the questioner has included in his question the very answer we would like to give: "Why shouldn't you do actions that will harm

others? Because, doing those actions would harm others."

The egoist, no doubt, will not be happy with this. He will protest that *we* may accept this as a reason, but *he* does not. And here the argument stops: there are limits to what can be accomplished by argument, and if the egoist really doesn't care about other people—if he honestly doesn't care whether they are helped or hurt by his actions—then we have reached those limits. If we want to persuade him to act decently toward his fellow humans, we will have to make our appeal to such other attitudes as he does possess, by threats, bribes, or other cajolery. That is all that we can do.

Though some may find this situation distressing (we would like to be able to show that the egoist is just *wrong*), it holds no embarrassment for common morality. What we have come up against is simply a fundamental requirement of rational action, namely, that the existence of reasons for action always depends on the prior existence of certain attitudes in the agent. For example, the fact that a certain course of action would make the agent a lot of money is a reason for doing it only if the agent wants to make money; the fact that practicing at chess makes one a better player is a reason for practicing only if one wants to be a better player; and so on. Similarly, the fact that a certain action would help the agent is a reason for doing the action only if the agent cares about his own welfare, and the fact that an action would help others is a reason for doing it only if the agent cares about others. In this respect ethical egoism and what we might call ethical altruism are in exactly the same fix: both require that the agent *care* about himself, or about other people, before they can get started.

So a nonegoist will accept "It would harm another person" as a reason not to do an action simply because he cares about what happens to that other person. When the egoist says that he does *not* accept that as a reason, he is saying something quite extraordinary. He is saying that he has no affection for friends or family, that he never feels pity or compassion, that he is the sort of person who can look on scenes of human misery with complete indifference, so long as he is not the one suffering. Genuine egoists, people who really don't care at all about anyone other than themselves, are rare. It is important to keep this in mind when thinking about ethical egoism; it is easy to forget just how fundamental to human psychological makeup the feeling of sympathy is. Indeed, a man without any sympathy at all would scarcely be recognizable as a man; and that is what makes ethical egoism such a disturbing doctrine in the first place.

4. There are, of course, many different ways in which the sceptic might challenge the assumptions underlying our moral practice. In this essay I have discussed only two of them, the two put forward by Glaucon in the passage that I cited from Plato's *Republic*. It is important that the assumptions underlying our moral practice should not be confused with particular judgments made within that practice. To defend one is not to defend the other. We may assume—quite properly, if my analysis has been correct—that the virtue of beneficence does, and indeed should, occupy an important place in "the moral institution of life"; and yet we may make constant and miserable errors when it comes to judging when and in what ways this virtue is to be exercised. Even worse, we may often be able to make accurate moral judgments, and know what we ought to do, but not do it. For these ills, philosophy alone is not the cure.

Review Questions

1. Explain the legend of Gyges. What questions about morality are raised by the story?
2. Distinguish between psychological and ethical egoism.
3. Rachels discusses two arguments for psychological egoism. What are these arguments, and how does he reply to them?
4. What three commonplace confusions does Rachels detect in the thesis of psychological egoism?
5. State the argument for saying that ethical egoism is inconsistent. Why doesn't Rachels accept this argument?
6. According to Rachels, why shouldn't we hurt others, and why should we help others? How can the egoist reply?

Discussion Questions

1. Has Rachels answered the question raised by Glaucon, namely, "Why be moral?" If so, what exactly is his answer?
2. Are genuine egoists rare, as Rachels claims? Is it a fact that most people care about others, even people they don't know?
3. Suppose we define ethical altruism as the view that one should always act for the benefit of others and never in one's own self-interest. Is such a view immoral or not?

Religion, Morality, and Conscience

JOHN ARTHUR

What is morality? Does it need religion in some way? Or is it purely social? In this essay, John Arthur first discusses, and rejects, three ways morality has been thought to depend on religion: that without religious motivation people could not be expected to do the right thing; that religion is necessary to provide guidance to people in their search for the correct course of action; and that religion is essential for there even to be a right and wrong. Arthur then considers another conception of morality, suggested by John Dewey, which claims "morality is social." He concludes with some brief comments on the importance of these reflections for moral deliberation and for education.

John Arthur is professor of philosophy and director of the Program in Philosophy, Politics, and Law at Binghampton University. He is the author of *Words That Bind* (1995) and *The Unfinished Constitution* (1989). For his picture and publications, and a link to his home page, see http://philosophy.binghamton.edu/deptmembers/Arthur.htm.

MY FIRST AND PRIME CONCERN in this paper is to explore the connections, if any, between morality and religion. I will argue that although there are a variety of ways the two can be connected, in fact religion is not necessary for morality. Despite the lack of any logical or other necessary connection, I will claim, there remain important respects in which the two are related. In the concluding section I will discuss the notion of moral conscience, and then look briefly at the various respects in which morality is "social" and the implications of that idea for moral education. First, however, I want to say something about the subjects: Just what are we referring to when we speak of morality and of religion?

1. MORALITY AND RELIGION

A useful way to approach the first question—the nature of morality—is to ask what it would mean for a society to exist without a social moral code. How would such people think and behave? What would that society look like? First, it seems clear that such people would never feel guilt or resentment. For example, the notions that I ought to remember my parents' anniversary, that he has a moral responsibility to help care for his children after the divorce, that she has a right to equal pay for equal work, and that discrimination on the basis of race is unfair would be absent in such a society. Notions of duty, rights, and obligations would not be present, except perhaps in the legal sense; concepts of justice and fairness would also be foreign to these people. In short, people would have no tendency to evaluate or criticize the behavior of others, nor to feel remorse about their own behavior. Children would not be taught to be ashamed when they steal or hurt others, nor would they be allowed to complain when others treat them badly. (People might, however, feel regret at a decision that didn't turn out as they had hoped; but that would only be because their expectations were frustrated, not because they feel guilty.)

Such a society lacks a moral code. What, then, of religion? Is it possible that a society such as

Source: John Arthur, "Religion, Morality, and Conscience," from *Morality and Moral Controversies* 4th ed., ed. John Arthur (Prentice Hall, 1996), pp. 21–28. Reprinted with permission.

the one I have described would have religious beliefs? It seems clear that it is possible. Suppose every day these same people file into their place of worship to pay homage to God (they may believe in many gods or in one all-powerful creator of heaven and earth). Often they can be heard praying to God for help in dealing with their problems and thanking Him for their good fortune. Frequently they give sacrifices to God, sometimes in the form of money spent to build beautiful temples and churches, other times by performing actions they believe God would approve, such as helping those in need. These practices might also be institutionalized, in the sense that certain people are assigned important leadership roles. Specific texts might also be taken as authoritative, indicating the ways God has acted in history and His role in their lives or the lives of their ancestors.

To have a moral code, then, is to tend to evaluate (perhaps without even expressing it) the behavior of others and to feel guilt at certain actions when we perform them. Religion, on the other hand, involves beliefs in supernatural power(s) that created and perhaps also control nature, the tendency to worship and pray to those supernatural forces or beings, and the presence of organizational structures and authoritative texts. The practices of morality and religion are thus importantly different. One involves our attitudes toward various forms of behavior (lying and killing, for example), typically expressed using the notions of rules, rights, and obligations. The other, religion, typically involves prayer, worship, beliefs about the supernatural, institutional forms, and authoritative texts.

We come, then, to the central question: What is the connection, if any, between a society's moral code and its religious practices and beliefs? Many people have felt that morality is in some way dependent on religion or religious truths. But what sort of "dependence" might there be? In what follows, I distinguish various ways in which one might claim that religion is necessary for morality, arguing against those who claim morality depends in some way on religion. I will

also suggest, however, some other important ways in which the two are related, concluding with a brief discussion of conscience and moral education.

2. RELIGIOUS MOTIVATION AND GUIDANCE

One possible role which religion might play in morality relates to motives people have. Religion, it is often said, is necessary so that people will DO right. Typically, the argument begins with the important point that doing what is right often has costs: refusing to shoplift or cheat can mean people go without some good or fail a test; returning a billfold means they don't get the contents. Religion is therefore said to be necessary in that it provides motivation to do the right thing. God rewards those who follow His commands by providing for them a place in heaven or by ensuring that they prosper and are happy on earth. He also punishes those who violate the moral law. Others emphasize less self-interested ways in which religious motives may encourage people to act rightly. Since God is the creator of the universe and has ordained that His plan should be followed, they point out, it is important to live one's life in accord with this divinely ordained plan. Only by living a moral life, it is said, can people live in harmony with the larger, divinely created order.

The first claim, then, is that religion is necessary to provide moral motivation. The problem with that argument, however, is that religious motives are far from the only ones people have. For most of us, a decision to do the right thing (if that is our decision) is made for a variety of reasons: "What if I get caught? What if somebody sees me—what will he or she think? How will I feel afterwards? Will I regret it?" Or maybe the thought of cheating just doesn't arise. We were raised to be a decent person, and that's what we are—period. Behaving fairly and treating others well is more important than whatever we might gain from stealing or cheating, let alone seriously harming another person.

So it seems clear that many motives for doing the right thing have nothing whatsoever to do with religion. Most of us, in fact, do worry about getting caught, being blamed, and being looked down on by others. We also may do what is right just because it's right, or because we don't want to hurt others or embarrass family and friends. To say that we need religion to act morally is mistaken; indeed, it seems to me that many of us, when it really gets down to it, don't give much of a thought to religion when making moral decisions. All those other reasons are the ones that we tend to consider, or else we just don't consider cheating and stealing at all. So far, then, there seems to be no reason to suppose that people can't be moral yet irreligious at the same time.

A second argument that is available for those who think religion is necessary to morality, however, focuses on moral guidance and knowledge rather than on people's motives. However much people may want to do the right thing, according to this view, we cannot ever know for certain what is right without the guidance of religious teaching. Human understanding is simply inadequate to this difficult and controversial task; morality involves immensely complex problems, and so we must consult religious revelation for help.

Again, however, this argument fails. First, consider how much we would need to know about religion and revelation in order for religion to provide moral guidance. Besides being aware that there is a God, we'd also have to think about which of the many religions is true. How can anybody be sure his or her religion is the right one? But even if we assume the Judeo-Christian God is the real one, we still need to find out just what it is He wants us to do, which means we must think about revelation.

Revelation comes in at least two forms, and not even all Christians agree on which is the best way to understand revelation. Some hold that revelation occurs when God tells us what he wants by providing us with His words: The Ten Commandments are an example. Many even believe, as evangelist Billy Graham once said, that the entire Bible was written by God using thirty-nine secretaries. Others, however, doubt that the "word of God" refers literally to the words God has spoken, but believe instead that the Bible is an historical document, written by human beings, of the events or occasions in which God revealed himself. It is an especially important document, of course, but nothing more than that. So on this second view, revelation is not understood as *statements* made by God but rather as His *acts,* such as leading His people from Egypt, testing Job, and sending His son as an example of the ideal life. The Bible is not itself revelation, it's the historical account of revelatory actions.

If we are to use revelation as a moral guide, then, we must first know what is to count as revelation—words given us by God, historical events, or both? But even supposing that we could somehow answer those questions, the problems of relying on revelation are still not over since we still must interpret that revelation. Some feel, for example, that the Bible justifies various forms of killing, including war and capital punishment, on the basis of such statements as "An eye for an eye." Others, emphasizing such sayings as "Judge not lest ye be judged" and "Thou shalt not kill," believe the Bible demands absolute pacifism. How are we to know which interpretation is correct? It is likely, of course, that the answer people give to such religious questions will be influenced in part at least by their own moral beliefs; if capital punishment is thought to be unjust, for example, then an interpreter will seek to read the Bible in a way that is consistent with that moral truth. That is not, however, a happy conclusion for those wishing to rest morality on revelation, for it means that their understanding of what God has revealed is itself dependent on their prior moral views. Rather than revelation serving as a guide for morality, morality is serving as a guide for how we interpret revelation.

So my general conclusion is that far from providing a short-cut to moral understanding, looking to revelation for guidance often creates more questions and problems. It seems wiser under the circumstances to address complex moral problems like abortion, capital punishment, and affirmative action directly, considering the pros and cons of each side, rather than to seek answers through the much more controversial and difficult route of revelation.

3. THE DIVINE COMMAND THEORY

It may seem, however, that we have still not really gotten to the heart of the matter. Even if religion is not necessary for moral motivation or guidance, it is often claimed, religion is necessary in another more fundamental sense. According to this view, religion is necessary for morality because without God there could BE no right or wrong. God, in other words, provides the foundation or bedrock on which morality is grounded. This idea was expressed by Bishop R. C. Mortimer:

> God made us and all the world. Because of that He has an absolute claim on our obedience. . .
> From [this] it follows that a thing is not right simply because we think it is. It is right because God commands it.[1]

What Bishop Mortimer has in mind can be seen by comparing moral rules with legal ones. Legal statutes, we know, are created by legislatures; if the state assembly of New York had not passed a law limiting the speed people can travel, then there would be no such legal obligation. Without the statutory enactments, such a law simply would not exist. Mortimer's view, the *divine command theory*, would mean that God has the same sort of relation to moral law as the legislature has to statutes it enacts: without God's commands there would be no moral rules, just as without a legislature there would be no statutes.

Defenders of the divine command theory often add to this a further claim, that only by assuming God sits at the foundation of morality can we explain the objective difference between right and wrong. This point was forcefully argued by F. C. Copleston in a 1948 British Broadcasting Corporation radio debate with Bertrand Russell.

Copleston: . . . The validity of such an interpretation of man's conduct depends on the recognition of God's existence, obviously. . . . Let's take a look at the Commandant of the [Nazi] concentration camp at Belsen. That appears to you as undesirable and evil and to me too. To Adolph Hitler we suppose it appeared as something good and desirable. I suppose you'd have to admit that for Hitler it was good and for you it is evil.

Russell: No, I shouldn't go so far as that. I mean, I think people can make mistakes in that as they can in other things. If you have jaundice you see things yellow that are not yellow. You're making a mistake.

Copleston: Yes, one can make mistakes, but can you make a mistake if it's simply a question of reference to a feeling or emotion? Surely Hitler would be the only possible judge of what appealed to his emotions.

Russell: . . . You can say various things about that; among others, that if that sort of thing makes that sort of appeal to Hitler's emotions, then Hitler makes quite a different appeal to my emotions.

Copleston: Granted. But there's no objective criterion outside feeling then for condemning the conduct of the Commandant of Belsen, in your view. . . . The human being's idea of the content of the moral law depends certainly to a large extent on education and environment, and a man has to use his reason in assessing the validity of the actual moral ideas of his social group. But the possibility of criticizing the accepted moral code presupposes that there is an objective standard, that there is an ideal moral order, which imposes itself. . . . It implies the existence of a real foundation of God.[2]

Against those who, like Bertrand Russell, seek to ground morality in feelings and attitudes, Copleston argues that there must be a more solid foundation if we are to be able to claim truly that the Nazis were evil. God, according to Copleston, is able to provide the objective basis for the distinction, which we all know to exist, between right and wrong. Without divine commands at the root of human obligations, we

1 R. C. Mortimer, *Christian Ethics* (London: Hutchinson's University Library, 1950), pp. 7–8.

2 This debate was broadcast on the Third Program of the British Broadcasting Corporation in 1948.

would have no real reason for condemning the behavior of anybody, even Nazis. Morality, Copleston thinks, would then be nothing more than an expression of personal feeling.

To begin assessing the divine command theory, let's first consider this last point. Is it really true that only the commands of God can provide an objective basis for moral judgments? Certainly many philosophers have felt that morality rests on its own perfectly sound footing, be it reason, human nature, or natural sentiments. It seems wrong to conclude, automatically, that morality cannot rest on anything but religion. And it is also possible that morality doesn't have any foundation or basis at all, so that its claims should be ignored in favor of whatever serves our own self-interest.

In addition to these problems with Copleston's argument, the divine command theory faces other problems as well. First, we would need to say much more about the relationship between morality and divine commands. Certainly the expressions "is commanded by God" and "is morally required" do not *mean* the same thing. People and even whole societies can use moral concepts without understanding them to make any reference to God. And while it is true that God (or any other moral being for that matter) would tend to want others to do the right thing, this hardly shows that being right and being commanded by God are the same thing. Parents want their children to do the right thing, too, but that doesn't mean parents, or anybody else, can make a thing right just by commanding it!

I think that, in fact, theists should reject the divine command theory. One reason is what it implies. Suppose we were to grant (just for the sake of argument) that the divine command theory is correct, so that actions are right just because they are commanded by God. The same, of course, can be said about those deeds that we believe are wrong. If God hadn't commanded us not to do them, they would not be wrong.

But now notice this consequence of the divine command theory. Since God is all-powerful, and since right is determined solely by His commands, is it not possible that He might change the rules and make what we now think of as wrong into right? It would seem that according to the divine command theory the answer is "yes": it is theoretically possible that tomorrow God would decree that virtues such as kindness and courage have become vices while actions that show cruelty and cowardice will henceforth be the right actions. (Recall the analogy with a legislature and the power it has to change law.) So now rather than it being right for people to help each other out and prevent innocent people from suffering unnecessarily, it would be right (God having changed His mind) to create as much pain among innocent children as we possibly can! To adopt the divine command theory therefore commits its advocate to the seemingly absurd position that even the greatest atrocities might be not only acceptable but morally required if God were to command them.

Plato made a similar point in the dialogue *Euthyphro*. Socrates is asking Euthyphro what it is that makes the virtue of holiness a virtue, just as we have been asking what makes kindness and courage virtues. Euthyphro has suggested that holiness is just whatever all the gods love.

Socrates: Well, then, Euthyphro, what do we say about holiness? Is it not loved by all the gods, according to your definition?
Euthyphro: Yes.
Socrates: Because it is holy, or for some other reason?
Euthyphro: No, because it is holy.
Socrates: Then it is loved by the gods because it is holy: it is not holy because it is loved by them?
Euthyphro: It seems so.
Socrates: . . . Then holiness is not what is pleasing to the gods, and what is pleasing to the gods is not holy as you say, Euthyphro. They are different things.
Euthyphro: And why, Socrates?
Socrates: Because we are agreed that the gods love holiness because it is holy: and that it is not holy because they love it.[3]

---

3 Plato, *Euthyphro*, trans. H. N. Fowler (Cambridge, MA: Harvard University Press, 1947).

This raises an interesting question. Why, having claimed at first that virtues are merely what is loved (or commanded) by the gods, would Euthyphro contradict this and agree that the gods love holiness *because* it's holy, rather than the reverse? One likely possibility is that Euthyphro believes that whenever the gods love something, they do so with good reason, not without justification and arbitrarily. To deny this and say that it is merely the gods' love that makes holiness a virtue would mean that the gods have no basis for their attitudes, that they are arbitrary in what they love. Yet—and this is the crucial point—it's far from clear that a religious person would want to say that God is arbitrary in that way. If we say that it is simply God's loving something that makes it right, then what sense would it make to say God wants us to do right? All that could mean, it seems, is that God wants us to do what He wants us to do; He would have no reason for wanting it. Similarly, "God is good" would mean little more than "God does what He pleases." The divine command theory therefore leads us to the results that God is morally arbitrary, and that His wishing us to do good or even God's being just mean nothing more than that God does what He does and wants whatever He wants. Religious people who reject that consequence would also, I am suggesting, have reason to reject the divine command theory itself, seeking a different understanding of morality.

This now raises another problem, however. If God approves kindness because it is a virtue and hates the Nazis because they were evil, then it seems that God discovers morality rather than inventing it. So haven't we then identified a limitation on God's power, since He now, being a good God, must love kindness and command us not to be cruel? Without the divine command theory, in other words, what is left of God's omnipotence?

But why, we may ask, is such a limitation on God unacceptable? It is not at all clear that God really can do anything at all. Can God, for example, destroy Himself? Or make a rock so heavy that He cannot lift it? Or create a universe which was never created by Him? Many have thought that God cannot do these things, but also that His inability to do them does not constitute a serious limitation on His power since these are things that cannot be done at all: to do them would violate the laws of logic. Christianity's most influential theologian, Thomas Aquinas, wrote in this regard that "whatever implies contradiction does not come within the scope of divine omnipotence, because it cannot have the aspect of possibility. Hence it is more appropriate to say that such things cannot be done than that God cannot do them."[4]

How, then, ought we to understand God's relationship to morality if we reject the divine command theory? Can religious people consistently maintain their faith in God the Creator and yet deny that what is right is right because He commands it? I think the answer to this is "yes." Making cruelty good is not like making a universe that wasn't made, of course. It's a moral limit on God rather than a logical one. But why suppose that God's limits are only logical?

One final point about this. Even if we agree that God loves justice or kindness because of their nature, not arbitrarily, there still remains a sense in which God could change morality even having rejected the divine command theory. That's because if we assume, plausibly, I think, that morality depends in part on how we reason, what we desire and need, and the circumstances in which we find ourselves, then morality will still be under God's control since God could have constructed us or our environment very differently. Suppose, for instance, that he created us so that we couldn't be hurt by others or didn't care about freedom. Or perhaps our natural environment were created differently, so that all we have to do is ask and anything we want is given to us. If God had created either nature or us that way, then it seems likely our morality might also be different in important ways from the one we now

---

4 Thomas Aquinas, *Summa Theologica*, Part I, Q. 25, Art. 3.

think correct. In that sense, then, morality depends on God whether or not one supports the divine command theory.

4. "MORALITY IS SOCIAL"

I have argued here that religion is not necessary in providing moral motivation or guidance, and that the religious person should not subscribe to the divine command theory's claim that God is necessary for there to be morality. In this last section, I want first to look briefly at how religion and morality sometimes *do* influence each other. Then I will consider briefly the important ways in which morality might correctly be thought to be "social."

Nothing I have said so far means that morality and religion are independent of each other. But in what ways are they related, assuming I am correct in claiming morality does not *depend* on religion? First, of course, we should note the historical influence religions have had on the development of morality as well as on politics and law. Many of the important leaders of the abolitionist and civil rights movements were religious leaders, as are many current members of the pro-life movement. The relationship is not, however, one-sided: morality has also influenced religion, as the current debate within the Catholic Church over the role of women, abortion, and other social issues shows. In reality, then, it seems clear that the practices of morality and religion have historically each exerted an influence on the other.

But just as the two have shaped each other historically, so, too, do they interact at the personal level. I have already suggested how people's understanding of revelation, for instance, is often shaped by morality as they seek the best interpretations of revealed texts. Whether trying to understand a work of art, a legal statute, or a religious text, interpreters regularly seek to understand them in the best light—to make them as good as they can be, which requires that they bring moral judgment to the task of religious interpretation and understanding.

The relationship can go the other direction as well, however, as people's moral views are shaped by their religious training and their current religious beliefs. These relationships are often complex, hidden even from ourselves, but it does seem clear that our views on important moral issues, from sexual morality and war to welfare and capital punishment, are often influenced by our religious outlook. So not only are religious and moral practices and understandings historically linked, but for many religious people the relationship extends to the personal level—to their understanding of moral obligations as well as their sense of who they are and their vision of who they wish to be.

Morality, then, is influenced by religion (as is religion by morality), but morality's social character extends deeper even than that, I want to argue. First, of course, the existence of morality assumes that we possess a socially acquired language within which we think about our choices and which alternatives we ought to follow. Second, morality is social in that it governs relationships among people, defining our responsibilities to others and theirs to us. Morality provides the standards we rely on in gauging our interactions with family, lovers, friends, fellow citizens, and even strangers. Third, morality is social in the sense that we are, in fact, subject to criticism by others for our actions. We discuss with others what we should do, and often hear from them concerning whether our decisions were acceptable. Blame and praise are a central feature of morality.

While not disputing any of this, John Dewey has suggested another important sense in which morality is social. Consider the following comments about the origins of morality and conscience taken from an article he titled "Morality Is Social":

> In language and imagination we rehearse the responses of others just as we dramatically enact other consequences. We foreknow how others will act, and the foreknowledge is the beginning of judgment passed on action. We know *with* them; there is conscience. An assembly is

formed within our breast which discusses and appraises proposed and performed acts. The community without becomes a forum and tribunal within, a judgment-seat of charges, assessments and exculpations. Our thoughts of our own actions are saturated with the ideas that others entertain about them. . . . Explicit recognition of this fact is a prerequisite of improvement in moral education. . . . Reflection is morally indispensable.[5]

So in addition to the three points I already mentioned, Dewey also wants to make another, and in some ways more important suggestion about morality's social character. This fourth idea depends on appreciating the fact that to think from the moral point of view, as opposed to the selfish one, for instance, demands that we reject our private, subjective perspective in favor of the perspective of others, envisioning how they might respond to various choices we might make. Far from being private and unrelated to others, moral conscience is in that sense "public." To consider a decision from the moral perspective requires envisioning what Dewey terms an "assembly of others" that is "formed within our breast." In that way, conscience cannot even be distinguished from the social: conscience invariably brings with it, or constitutes, the perspective of the other. "Is this right?" and "What would this look like were I to have to defend it to others?" are not separate questions.[6]

It is important not to confuse Dewey's point here, however. He is *not* saying that what is right is finally to be determined by the reactions of actually existing other people, or even by the reaction of society as a whole. To the contrary,

what is right, and accords with the true dictates of conscience, might in fact not meet the approval of others. Conscience is "social" not in the sense that morality is determined by surveying what others in society think. Understood as the voice of an "assembly" of others within each of us, conscience cannot be reduced to the expected reaction of any existing individual or group. But what then does Dewey mean? The answer is that the assembly Dewey is describing is not an actual one but instead an hypothetical, "ideal" one; the actual "community without" is transformed into a "forum and tribunal within, a judgment seat of charges, assessments and exculpations." Only through the powers of imagination can we exercise our moral powers, envisioning with the powers of judgment what conscience requires.

Morality is therefore *inherently* social, in a variety of ways. It depends on socially learned language, is learned from interactions with others, and governs our interactions with others in society. But it also demands, as Dewey put it, that we know "with" others, envisioning for ourselves what their points of view would require along with our own. Conscience demands we occupy the positions of others.

Viewed in this light, God might play a role in moral reflection and conscience. That is because it is unlikely a religious person would wish to exclude God from the "forum and tribunal" that constitutes conscience. Rather, for the religious person conscience would almost certainly include the imagined reaction of God along with the reactions of others who might be affected by the action. So it seems that for a religious person morality and God's will cannot be separated, though the connection between them is not as envisioned by the divine command theory.

This leads to my final point, about moral education. If Dewey is correct, then it seems clear there is an important sense in which morality not only can be taught but must be. Besides early moral training, moral thinking depends on our ability to imagine others' reactions and to imaginatively put ourselves into their shoes.

5 John Dewey, "Morality Is Social," in *The Moral Writings of John Dewey,* rev. ed., ed. James Gouinlock (Amherst, NY: Prometheus Books, 1994), pp. 182–4.

6 Obligations to animals raise an interesting problem for this conception of morality. Is it wrong to torture animals only because other *people* could be expected to disapprove? Or is it that the animal itself would disapprove? Or, perhaps, that duties to animals rest on sympathy and compassion while human moral relations are more like Dewey describes, resting on morality's inherently social nature and on the dictates of conscience viewed as an assembly of others?

"What would somebody (including, perhaps, God) think if this got out?" expresses more than a concern with being embarrassed or punished; it is also the voice of conscience and indeed of morality itself. But that would mean, thinking of education, that listening to others, reading about what others think and do, and reflecting within ourselves about our actions and whether we could defend them to others are part of the practice of morality itself. Morality cannot exist without the broader, social perspective introduced by others, and this social nature ties it, in that way, with education and with public discussion, both actual and imagined. "Private" moral reflection taking place independently of the social world would be no moral reflection at all; and moral education is not only possible, but essential.

Review Questions

1. According to Arthur, how are morality and religion different?
2. Why isn't religion necessary for moral motivation?
3. Why isn't religion necessary as a source of moral knowledge?
4. What is the divine command theory? Why does Arthur reject this theory?
5. According to Arthur, how are morality and religion connected?
6. Dewey says that morality is social. What does this mean, according to Arthur?

Discussion Questions

1. Has Arthur refuted the divine command theory? If not, how can it be defended?
2. If morality is social, as Dewey says, then how can we have any obligations to nonhuman animals? (Arthur mentions this problem and some possible solutions to it in footnote 6.)
3. What does Dewey mean by moral education? Does a college ethics class count as moral education?

The Natural Law

SAINT THOMAS AQUINAS

Saint Thomas Aquinas (1225–1274) was one of the most important Christian philosophers. He was declared a saint in 1323, and in 1567 he was named an Angelic Doctor of the Roman Catholic Church, giving his teachings a special authority. Our reading is taken from his Treatise on Law, which is Questions 90–97 of the *Summa Theologia*, a vast work containing 22 volumes.

Aquinas sees the world as the creation of a supremely rational being, God, who has made everything according to a divine plan, an eternal law governing everything. God rules the world according to the eternal law. This divine law gives everything a role or purpose: Eyes are designed for seeing; rain falls in order to nourish plants, and so on. Humans are made in the image of God; they are rational as God is rational, although to a lesser degree. Because they are rational, humans are endowed with the light of natural reason that enables them to discern the eternal law, which includes the natural law. The natural law is the moral law that tells us what is right and good. According to Aquinas, the most basic precept of the natural law is the self-evident truth that good ought to be done, and evil ought to be avoided. All the precepts of the natural moral law are derived from this fundamental principle. But what is good and what is evil? Aquinas goes on to say that because good is an end, all things to which humans have a natural inclination are good. He mentions three such natural inclinations: the inclination to preserve human life, animal inclinations for sexual intercourse, education of the young, and so on, and a general inclination to good, which includes knowing the truth, avoiding offense to others, and so on. Aquinas does not attempt to give an exhaustive list of the precepts of the natural law; presumably it is up to us to add to the list using the natural light of reason.

WHETHER THERE IS IN US A NATURAL LAW?

. . . A *GLOSS ON ROM.* ii. 14 (*When the Gentiles, who have not the law, do by nature those things that are of the law*) comments as follows: *Although they have no written law, yet they have the natural law, whereby each one knows, and is conscious of, what is good and what is evil.*

I answer that, As we have stated above, law, being a rule and measure, can be in a person in two ways: in one way, as in him that rules and measures; in another way, as in that which is ruled and measured, since a thing is ruled and measured in so far as it partakes of the rule or measure. Therefore, since all things subject to divine providence are ruled and measured by the eternal law, as was stated above, it is evident that all things partake in some way in the eternal law, in so far as, namely, from its being imprinted on them, they derive their respective inclinations to their proper acts and ends. Now among all others, the rational creature is subject to divine providence in a more excellent way, in so far as it itself partakes of a share of providence, by being provident both for itself and for others. Therefore it has a share of the eternal reason, whereby it has a natural inclination to its proper act and end; and this participation of the eternal law in the rational creature is called the natural law. Hence the Psalmist, after saying (*Ps. iv. 6*): *Offer*

up the sacrifice of justice, as though someone asked what the works of justice are, adds: *Many say, Who showeth us good things?* in answer to which question he says: *The light of Thy countenance, O Lord, is signed upon us.* He thus implies that the light of natural reason, whereby we discern what is good and what is evil, which is the function of the natural law, is nothing else than an imprint on us of the divine light. It is therefore evident that the natural law is nothing else than the rational creature's participation of the eternal law. . . .

WHETHER THERE IS HUMAN LAW?

. . . Now it is to be observed that the same procedure takes place in the practical and in the speculative reason, for each proceeds from principles to conclusions, as was stated above. Accordingly, we conclude that, just as in the speculative reason, from naturally known indemonstrable principles we draw the conclusions of the various sciences, the knowledge of which is not imparted to us by nature, but acquired by the efforts of reason, so too it is that from the precepts of the natural law, as from common and indemonstrable principles, the human reason needs to proceed to the more particular determination of certain matters. These particular determinations, devised by human reason, are called human laws, provided that the other essential conditions of law be observed, as was stated above. . . .

WHETHER THE NATURAL LAW CONTAINS SEVERAL PRECEPTS, OR ONLY ONE?

. . . As was stated above, the precepts of the natural law are to the practical reason what the first principles of demonstrations are to the speculative reason, because both are self-evident principles. Now a thing is said to be self-evident in two ways: first, in itself; secondly, in relation to us. Any proposition is said to be self-evident in itself, if its predicate is contained in the notion of the subject; even though it may happen that to one who does not know the definition of the subject, such a proposition is not self-evident. For instance, this proposition, *Man is a rational being,* is, in its very nature, self-evident, since he who says *man,* says *a rational being;* and yet to one who does not know what a man is, this proposition is not self-evident. Hence it is that, as Boethius says, certain axioms or propositions are universally self-evident to all; and such are the propositions whose terms are known to all, as, *Every whole is greater than its part, and, Things equal to one and the same are equal to one another.* But some propositions are self-evident only to the wise, who understand the meaning of the terms of such propositions. Thus to one who understands that an angel is not a body, it is self-evident that an angel is not circumscriptively in a place. But this is not evident to the unlearned, for they cannot grasp it.

Now a certain order is to be found in those things that are apprehended by men. For that which first falls under apprehension is *being,* the understanding of which is included in all things whatsoever a man apprehends. Therefore the first indemonstrable principle is that *the same thing cannot be affirmed and denied at the same time,* which is based on the notion of *being* and *not-being:* and on this principle all others are based, as is stated in *Metaph.* iv. Now as *being* is the first thing that falls under the apprehension

absolutely, so *good* is the first thing that falls under the apprehension of the practical reason, which is directed to action (since every agent acts for an end, which has the nature of good). Consequently, the first principle in the practical reason is one founded on the nature of good, viz., that *good is that which all things seek after.* Hence this is the first precept of law, that *good is to be done and promoted, and evil is to be avoided.* All other precepts of the natural law are based upon this; so that all the things which the practical reason naturally apprehends as man's good belong to the precepts of the natural law under the form of things to be done or avoided.

Since, however, good has the nature of an end, and evil, the nature of the contrary, hence it is that all those things to which man has a natural inclination are naturally apprehended by reason as being good, and consequently as objects of pursuit, and their contraries as evil, and objects of avoidance. Therefore, the order of the precepts of the natural law is according to the order of natural inclinations. For there is in man, first of all, an inclination to good in accordance with the nature which he has in common with all substances, inasmuch, namely, as every substance seeks the preservation of its own being, according to its nature; and by reason of this inclination, whatever is a means of preserving human life, and of warding off its obstacles, belongs to the natural law. Secondly, there is in man an inclination to things that pertain to him more specially, according to that nature which he has in common with other animals; and in virtue of this inclination, those things are said to belong to the natural law *which nature has taught to all animals,* such as sexual intercourse, the education of offspring and so forth. Thirdly, there is in man an inclination to good according to the nature of his reason, which nature is proper to him. Thus man has a natural inclination to know the truth about God, and to live in society; and in this respect, whatever pertains to this inclination belongs to the natural law: *e.g.,* to shun ignorance, to avoid offending those among whom one has to live, and other such things regarding the above inclination.

Review Questions

1. Distinguish between the eternal law and the natural law. How are they related?
2. What are the precepts of the natural law? Specifically what should we do, and what should we avoid?

Discussion Questions

1. Do you agree that everything in the world has a purpose? If so, can you discern it using reason alone?
2. Are all natural inclinations good? Why or why not?
3. Does the natural law tell you what to do in a particular situation? Explain your answer.

Morality Is Based on Sentiment

DAVID HUME

David Hume (1711–1776), the great Scottish philosopher and historian, wrote his most famous work, *A Treatise of Human Nature,* before he was 24 years old. His other important philosophical work, the *Dialogues Concerning Natural Religion,* was published posthumously.

Hume argues that moral judgments are not based on reason but on sentiment, feelings of approval or disapproval. According to Hume, reason deals with relations of ideas or matters of fact. But an examination of common moral evils reveals neither relations of ideas nor matters of fact, but only sentiment. He uses three examples to support his argument: incest, murder, and ingratitude. Why is it that incest in humans is wrong, while the very same action in animals is not? There is no difference in the relations of ideas or in the basic facts. The only difference is that we disapprove of incest in humans and not in animals. Hume finds this argument to be entirely decisive. Or consider a deliberate murder. Is the wrongness of murder to be found in any objective fact or any reasoning about relations of ideas? Hume thinks not. The wrongness is a matter of fact, but it is the fact that you disapprove of intentional murder. Examine the crime of ingratitude. Is the crime an observable fact? Is it found in relations of ideas? No, it is found in the mind of the person who is ungrateful; specifically, it is a feeling of ill-will or indifference. Hume's conclusion is that morality is determined by sentiment, not reasoning.

Source: From David Hume, *A Treatise of Human Nature* (1740), bk. 3, pt. 1, sec. 1; and *An Inquiry Concerning the Principle of Morals* (1751), app. 1.

THOSE WHO AFFIRM THAT VIRTUE is nothing but a conformity to reason; that there are eternal fitnesses and unfitnesses of things, which are the same to every rational being that considers them; that the immutable measures of right and wrong impose an obligation, not only on human creatures, but also on the Deity himself: All these systems concur in the opinion, that morality, like truth, is discern'd merely by ideas, and by their juxta-position and comparison. In order, therefore, to judge of these systems, we need only consider, whether it be possible, from reason alone, to distinguish betwixt moral good and evil, or whether there must concur some other principles to enable us to make that distinction.

If morality had naturally no influence on human passions and actions, 'twere in vain to take such pains to inculcate it; and nothing wou'd be more fruitless than that multitude of rules and precepts, with which all moralists abound. Philosophy is commonly divided into *speculative* and *practical;* and as morality is always comprehended under the latter division, 'tis supposed to influence our passions and actions, and to go beyond the calm and indolent judgments of the understanding. And this is confirm'd by common experience, which informs us, that men are often govern'd by their duties, and are deter'd from some actions by the opinion of injustice, and impell'd to others by that of obligation.

Since morals, therefore, have an influence on the actions and affections, it follows, that they cannot be deriv'd from reason; and that because reason alone, as we have already prov'd, can never have any such influence. Morals excite passions, and produce or prevent actions. Reason of itself is utterly impotent in this particular. The rules of morality, therefore, are not conclusions of our reason. . . .

But to make these general reflexions more clear and convincing, we may illustrate them by some particular instances, wherein this character of moral good or evil is the most universally acknowledged. . . .

I would fain ask any one, why incest in the human species is criminal, and why the very same action, and the same relations in animals have not the smallest moral turpitude and deformity? If it be answer'd, that this action is innocent in animals, because they have not reason sufficient to discover its turpitude; but that man, being endow'd with that faculty, which *ought* to restrain him to his duty, the same action instantly becomes criminal to him; should this be said, I would reply, that this is evidently arguing in a circle. For before reason can perceive this turpitude, the turpitude must exist; and consequently is independent of the decisions of our reason, and is their object more properly than their effect. According to this system, then, every animal, that has sense, and appetite, and will; that is, every animal must be susceptible of all the same virtues and vices, for which we ascribe praise and blame to human creatures. All the difference is, that our superior reason may serve to discover the vice or virtue, and by that means may augment the blame or praise: But still this discovery supposes a separate being in these moral distinctions, and a being, which depends only on the will and appetite, and which, both in thought and reality, may be distinguish'd from the reason. Animals are susceptible of the same relations, with respect to each other, as the human species, and therefore wou'd also be susceptible of the same morality, if the essence of morality consisted in these relations. Their want of a sufficient degree of reason may hinder them from perceiving the duties and obligations of morality, but can never hinder these duties from existing; since they must antecedently exist, in order to their being perceiv'd. Reason must find them, and can never produce them. This argument deserves to be weigh'd, as being, in my opinion, entirely decisive.

Nor does this reasoning only prove, that morality consists not in any relations, that are the objects of science; but if examin'd, will prove with equal certainty, that it consists not in any *matter of fact,* which can be discover'd by the understanding. This is the *second* part of our argument; and if it can be made evident, we may conclude, that morality is not an object of reason.

But can there be any difficulty in proving, that vice and virtue are not matters of fact, whose existence we can infer by reason? Take any action allow'd to be vicious: Wilful murder, for instance. Examine it in all lights, and see if you can find that matter of fact, or real existence, which you call *vice*. In which-ever way you take it, you find only certain passions, motives, volitions and thoughts. There is no other matter of fact in the case. The vice entirely escapes you, as long as you consider the object. You never can find it, till you turn your reflexion into your own breast, and find a sentiment of disapprobation, which arises in you, towards this action. Here is a matter of fact; but 'tis the object of feeling, not of reason. It lies in yourself, not in the object. So that when you pronounce any action or character to be vicious, you mean nothing, but that from the constitution of your nature you have a feeling or sentiment of blame from the contemplation of it. Vice and virtue, therefore, may be compar'd to sounds, colours, heat and cold, which, according to modern philosophy, are not qualities in objects, but perceptions in the mind: And this discovery in morals, like that other in physics, is to be regarded as a considerable advancement of the speculative sciences; tho', like that too, it has little or no influence on practice. Nothing can be more real, or concern us more, than our own sentiments of pleasure and uneasiness; and if these be favourable to virtue, and unfavourable to vice, no more can be requisite to the regulation of our conduct and behaviour.

I cannot forbear adding to these reasonings an observation, which may, perhaps, be found of some importance. In every system of morality, which I have hitherto met with, I have always remark'd, that the author proceeds for some time in the ordinary way of reasoning, and establishes the being of a God, or makes observations concerning human affairs; when of a sudden I am surpriz'd to find, that instead of the usual copulations of propositions, *is,* and *is not,* I meet with no proposition that is not connected with an *ought,* or an *ought not.* This change is imperceptible; but is, however, of the last consequence.

For as this *ought,* or *ought not,* expresses some new relation or affirmation, 'tis necessary that it shou'd be observ'd and explain'd; and at the same time that a reason should be given, for what seems altogether inconceivable, how this new relation can be a deduction from others, which are entirely different from it. But as authors do not commonly use this precaution, I shall presume to recommend it to the readers; and am persuaded, that this small attention wou'd subvert all the vulgar systems of morality, and let us see, that the distinction of vice and virtue is not founded merely on the relations of objects, nor is perceiv'd by reason. . . .

Examine the crime of *ingratitude,* for instance; which has place, wherever we observe good-will, expressed and known, together with good-offices performed, on the one side, and a return of ill-will or indifference, with ill-offices or neglect on the other: anatomize all these circumstances, and examine, by your reason alone, in what consists the demerit or blame. You never will come to any issue or conclusion.

Reason judges either of *matter of fact* or of *relations.* Enquire then, *first,* where is that matter of fact which we here call *crime;* point it out; determine the time of its existence; describe its essence or nature; explain the sense or faculty to which it discovers itself. It resides in the mind of the person who is ungrateful. He must, therefore, feel it, and be conscious of it. But nothing is there, except the passion of ill-will or absolute indifference. You cannot say that these, of themselves, always, and in all circumstances, are crimes. No, they are only crimes when directed towards persons who have before expressed and displayed good-will towards us. Consequently, we may infer, that the crime of ingratitude is not any particular individual *fact;* but arises from a complication of circumstances, which, being presented to the spectator, excites the *sentiment* of blame, by the particular structure and fabric of his mind.

This representation, you say, is false. Crime, indeed, consists not in a particular *fact,* of whose reality we are assured by *reason;* but it consists in certain *moral relations,* discovered by reason, in the same manner as we discover by reason the truths of geometry or algebra. But what are the relations, I ask, of which you here talk? In the case stated above, I see first good-will and good-offices in one person; then ill-will and ill-offices in the other. Between these, there is a relation of *contrariety*. Does the crime consist in that relation? But suppose a person bore me ill-will or did me ill-offices; and I, in return, were indifferent towards him, or did him good-offices. Here is the same relation of *contrariety;* and yet my conduct is often highly laudable. Twist and turn this matter as much as you will, you can never rest the morality on relation; but must have recourse to the decisions of sentiment.

When it is affirmed that two and three are equal to the half of ten, this relation of equality I understand perfectly. I conceive, that if ten be divided into two parts, of which one has as many units as the other; and if any of these parts be compared to two added to three, it will contain as many units as that compound number. But when you draw thence a comparison to moral relations, I own that I am altogether at a loss to understand you. A moral action, a crime, such as ingratitude, is a complicated object. Does the morality consist in the relation of its parts to each other? How? After what manner? Specify the relation: be more particular and explicit in your propositions, and you will easily see their falsehood.

No, say you, the morality consists in the relation of actions to the rule of right; and they are denominated good or ill, according as they agree or disagree with it. What then is this rule of right? In what does it consist? How is it determined? By reason, you say, which examines the moral relations of actions. So that moral relations are determined by the comparison of action to a rule. And that rule is determined by considering the moral relations of objects. Is not this fine reasoning?

All this is metaphysics, you cry. That is enough; there needs nothing more to give a strong presumption of false-hood. Yes, reply I, here are metaphysics surely; but they are all on your side, who advance an abstruse hypothesis, which can never be made intelligible, nor quadrate with any particular instance or illustration. The hypothesis which we embrace is plain. It maintains that morality is determined by sentiment. It defines virtue to be *whatever mental action or quality gives to a spectator the pleasing sentiment of approbation;* and vice the contrary. We then proceed to examine a plain matter of fact, to wit, what actions have this influence. We consider all the circumstances in which these actions agree, and thence endeavour to extract some general observations with regard to these sentiments. If you call this metaphysics, and find anything abstruse here, you need only conclude that your turn of mind is not suited to the moral sciences.

Review Questions

1. According to Hume, how do morals have an influence on action?
2. Explain Hume's argument about incest.
3. What is Hume's point about "is" and "ought"?
4. How does Hume explain ingratitude?

Discussion Questions

1. Suppose I say, "I disapprove of abortion, but it is not wrong." Does this make any sense? Why or why not?
2. Some philosophers have claimed that arguing from facts to values is not always a mistake. Can you construct an acceptable argument with a fact as a premise and a value as a conclusion? For example, what about Mill's argument that if something is desired, then it is desirable?

Ethical Relativism

WILLIAM H. SHAW

William H. Shaw teaches philosophy at San Jose State University. He is the author of *Marx's Theory of History* (1978), *Contemporary Ethics: Taking Account of Utilitarianism* (1999), and the editor of *Social and Personal Ethics* (5e 2004) and *Business Ethics* (5e 2005).

Shaw discusses normative ethical relativism that tells us what is right and wrong. There are two kinds of normative ethical relativism. First, *cultural* ethical relativism makes right and wrong relative to one's culture. What is right is what one's culture says is right, and what is wrong is what one's culture says is wrong. For example, if Catholic Spain condemns abortion, then it is wrong (in that culture). But if abortion is approved in Japan, then it is right (in that culture). Second, *individual* ethical relativism says that right and wrong are relative to the individual's opinion, what she thinks is right and wrong. If an individual thinks something is right, then it is right (for her); and if she thinks something is wrong, then it is wrong (for her).

Shaw quickly dismisses individual ethical relativism. It collapses the common distinction between merely thinking something is right and its actually being right. It makes ethical debate pointless, and fails to explain how moral deliberation is possible.

Shaw takes cultural ethical relativism more seriously, but in the end he finds it to be false. It does not allow valid moral criticism. For example, we cannot truly say that slavery in a slave society like that of the American South in the 19th century was immoral and unjust. It is not clear how it should be applied, and worst of all, it flies in the face of Shaw's certainty that some things are wrong even if a society accepts them. For example, Shaw claims it is clear that a society that applauded the random torture of children would be immoral, even if it thought such a practice were right. If a society can make moral mistakes like this, then cultural ethical relativism is false.

1. ETHICAL RELATIVISM

THE PEOPLES AND SOCIETIES of the world are diverse; their institutions, fashions, ideas, manners, and mores vary tremendously. This is a simple truth. Sometimes an awareness of this

Source: William H. Shaw, "Relativism and Objectivity in Ethics," from *Morality and Moral Controversies*, ed. John Arthur (Prentice-Hall, 1981) pp. 31–38, 46–50. Used by permission.

diversity and of the degree to which our own beliefs and habits mirror those of the culture around us stimulates self-examination. In the realm of ethics, familiarity with strikingly different cultures has led many people to suppose that morality itself is relative to particular societies, that right and wrong vary from culture to culture.

This view is generally called "ethical relativism"; it is the normative theory that what is right is what the culture says is right. What is right in one place may be wrong in another, because the only criterion for distinguishing right from wrong—the only ethical standard for judging an action—is the moral system of the society in which the act occurs. Abortion, for example, is condemned as immoral in Catholic Spain, but practiced as a morally neutral form of birth control in Japan. According to the ethical relativist, then, abortion is wrong in Spain but morally permissible in Japan. The relativist is not saying merely that the Spanish believe abortion is abominable and the Japanese do not; that is acknowledged by everyone. Rather, the ethical relativist contends that abortion is immoral in Spain because the Spanish believe it to be immoral and morally permissible in Japan because the Japanese believe it to be so. There is no absolute ethical standard, independent of cultural context, no criterion of right and wrong by which to judge other than that of particular societies. In short, morality is relative to society.

A different sort of relativist might hold that morality is relative, not to the culture, but to the individual. The theory that what is right and wrong is determined by what a person thinks is right and wrong, however, is not very plausible. The main reason is that it collapses the distinction between thinking something is right and its actually being right. We have all done things we thought were right at the time, but later decided were wrong. Our normal view is that we were mistaken in our original thinking; we believed the action to have been right, but it was not. In the relativist view under consideration, one would have to say that the action in question was originally right, but later wrong as our thinking changed—surely a confused and confusing thing to say! Furthermore, if we accept this view, there would be no point in debating ethics with anyone, for whatever he thought right would automatically be right for him, and whatever we thought right would be right for us. Indeed, if right were determined solely by what we took to be right, then it would not be at all clear what

we are doing when we try to decide whether something is right or wrong in the first place—since we could never be mistaken! Certainly this is a muddled doctrine. Most likely its proponents have meant to emphasize that each person must determine for himself as best he can what actually is right or to argue that we ought not to blame people for acting according to their sincere moral judgments. These points are plausible, and with some qualifications, perhaps everyone would accept them, but they are not relativistic in the least.

The theory that morality is relative to society, however, is more plausible, and those who endorse this type of ethical relativism point to the diverseness of human values and the multiformity of moral codes to support their case. From our own cultural perspective, some seemingly "immoral" moralities have been adopted: polygamy, homosexuality, stealing, slavery, infanticide, and the eating of strangers have all been tolerated or even encouraged by the moral system of one society or another. In light of this, the ethical relativist feels that there can be no nonethnocentric standard by which to judge actions. We feel the individuals in some remote tribe are wrong to practice infanticide, while other cultures are scandalized that we eat animals. Different societies have different rules; what moral authority other than society, asks the relativist, can there be? Morality is just like fashion in clothes, beauty in persons, and legality in action—all of which are relative to, and determined by, the standards of a particular culture.

In some cases this seems to make sense. Imagine that Betty is raised in a society in which one is thought to have a special obligation to look after one's maternal aunts and uncles in their old age, and Sarah lives in a society in which no such obligation is supposed. Certainly we are inclined to say that Betty really does have an obligation that Sarah does not. Sarah's culture, on the other hand, may hold that if someone keeps a certain kind of promise to you, you owe him or her a favor, or that children are not required to tell the truth to adults. Again, it seems plausible that different sorts of obligations arise in Sarah's society; in her society, promisees really do owe their promisors and children are not wrong to lie, whereas this might not be so in other cultures.

Ethical relativism explains these cases by saying that right and wrong are determined solely by the standards of the society in question, but there are other, nonrelativistic ways of accounting for these examples. In Betty's society, people live with the expectation that their sister's offspring will look after them; for Betty to behave contrary to this institution and to thwart these expectations may produce bad consequences—so there is a reason to think she has this obligation other than the fact that her society thinks she has it. In Sarah's world, on the other hand, no adult expects children to tell the truth; far from deceiving people, children only amuse them with their tall tales. Thus, we are not required to be ethical relativists in order to explain why moral obligations may differ according to the social context. And there are other cases in which ethical relativism seems implausible. Suppose Betty's society thinks that it is wicked to engage in intercourse on Sundays. We do not believe it wrong of her to do so just because her society thinks such conduct is impermissible. Or suppose her culture thinks that it is morally reprehensible to wear the fur of rare animals. Here we may be inclined to concur, but if we think it is wrong of her to do this, we do not think it so because her society says so. In this example and the previous one, we look for some reason why her conduct should be considered immoral. The fact that her society thinks it so is not enough.

Ethical relativism undermines any moral criticism of the practices of other societies as long as their actions conform to their own standards. We cannot say that slavery in a slave society like that of the American South of the 19th century was immoral and unjust as long as that society held it to be morally permissible. Slavery was right for them, although it is wrong for us today. To condemn slave owners as immoral, says the relativist, is to attempt to extend the standards of our society illegitimately to another culture. But this is not the way we usually think. Not only do we wish to say that a society is mistaken if it thinks that slavery (or cannibalism, cruelty, racial bigotry) is morally permissible, but we also think we have justification for so saying and are not simply projecting ethnocentrically the standards of our own culture. Indeed, far from mirroring those standards in all our moral judgments, we sometimes criticize certain principles or practices accepted by our own society. None of this makes sense from the relativist's point of view. People can be censured for not living up to their society's moral code, but that is all; the moral code itself cannot be criticized. Whatever a society takes to be morally right really is right for it. Reformers who campaign against the "injustices" of their society are only encouraging people to be immoral—that is, to depart from the moral standards of their society—unless or until the majority of society agrees with the reformers. The minority can never be right in moral matters; to be right it must become the majority.

This raises some puzzles for the theory of ethical relativism. What proportion of a society must believe, say, that abortion is permissible for it to be morally acceptable in that society—90 percent? 75 percent? 51 percent? If the figure is set high (say 75 percent) and only 60 percent of the society condone abortion, then it would not be permissible; yet it would seem odd for the relativist to say that abortion was therefore wrong, given that a majority of the population believes otherwise. Without a sufficient majority either way, abortion would be neither morally permissible nor impermissible. On the other hand, if the figure is set lower, then there will be frequent moral flip-flops. Imagine that last year abortion was thought wrong by 51 percent of the populace, but this year only 49 percent are of that opinion; that means, according to the relativist, that it was wrong last year, but is now morally permissible—and things may change again. Surely, though, something is wrong with majority rule in matters of morality. In addition one might wonder what is to count, for the relativist, as a society. In a large and heterogeneous nation like the United States, are right and wrong determined by the whole country; or do smaller societies like Harlem, San Francisco, rural Iowa, or the Chicano community in Los Angeles set their own moral standards? But if these are cohesive enough to count as morality-generating societies, what about such "societies" as outlaw bikers, the drug culture, or the underworld? And what, then, does the relativist say about conflicts between these group moralities or between them and the morality of the overall society? Since an individual may be in several overlapping "societies" at the same time, he may well be receiving conflicting moral instructions—all of which, it would seem, are correct according to the relativist.

These are all questions the relativist must answer if he is to make his theory coherent. To raise them is not to refute relativism, of course, since the relativist may be able to explain satisfactorily what he means by "society," how its standards relate to those of other groups, and what is to count as moral approval by a given society. However the relativist attempts to refine his theory, he will still be maintaining that what is right is determined by what the particular society, culture, or group takes to be right and that this is the only standard by which an individual's actions can be judged. Not only does the relativist neglect to give us a reason for believing that a society's own views about morality are conclusive as to what is actually right and wrong, but also his theory does not square with our understanding of morality and the nature of ethical discourse. By contending that the moralities of different societies are all equally valid, the relativist holds that there can be no nonethnocentric ground for preferring one moral code to another, that one cannot speak of moral progress. Moralities may change, but they do not get better or worse. If words mean anything, however, it seems clear that a society that applauded the random torture of children would be immoral, even if it thought such a practice were right. It would simply be mistaken, and disastrously so. Since this is the case, ethical relativism must be false as a theory of normative ethics.

Review Questions

1. Explain Shaw's distinction between the two types of ethical relativism.
2. Why does he reject the second type, the theory that makes morality relative to the individual?
3. Shaw thinks the theory that morality is relative to society is more plausible. Why?
4. According to Shaw, what are the problems facing cultural ethical relativism? Why does he think it is false?

Discussion Questions

1. Does Shaw suceed in refuting both types of ethical relativism? Does the relativist have any reply?
2. Is religion relative to society? Shaw suggests that you will be a Baptist if born in Tennessee, a Jew if born in Tel Aviv, and a Muslim if born in Tehran. If so, what does this imply about the nature of religion?
3. Consider Mill's principle of liberty: You should be free to do whatever you want as long as you don't harm others. Is this an acceptable moral principle? Why or why not?
4. Shaw says that if it is going to work, a moral code has to be acceptable to everyone. But how could there be such a code if there are fundamental disagreements in morality? Is there any way to get agreement?

Utilitarianism

JOHN STUART MILL

John Stuart Mill (1806–1873) was one of the most important and influential British philosophers. His most important works in ethics are *On Liberty* (1859) and *Utilitarianism* (1861), from which the reading is taken.

Mill sets forth the basic principles of utilitarianism, including the Principle of Utility (or the Greatest Happiness Principle) and the hedonistic principle that happiness is pleasure. He explains the theory by replying to various objections and concludes with an attempt to prove the Principle of Utility.

THE CREED which accepts as the foundation of morals, Utility, or the Greatest Happiness Principle, holds that actions are right in proportion as they tend to promote happiness, wrong as they tend to produce the reverse of happiness. By happiness is intended pleasure, and the absence of pain; by unhappiness, pain, and the privation of pleasure. To give a clear view of the moral standard set up by the theory, much more requires to be said; in particular, what things it includes in the ideas of pain and pleasure; and to what extent this is left an open question. But these supplementary explanations do not affect the theory of life on which this theory of morality is grounded—namely, that pleasure, and freedom from pain, are the only things desirable as ends; and that all desirable things (which are as numerous in the utilitarian as in any other scheme) are desirable either for the pleasure inherent in themselves, or as means to the promotion of pleasure and the prevention of pain.

Now, such a theory of life excites in many minds, and among them in some of the most estimable in feeling and purpose, inveterate dislike. To suppose that life has (as they express it) no higher end than pleasure—no better and nobler object of desire and pursuit—they designate as utterly mean and groveling; as a doctrine worthy only of swine, to whom the followers of Epicurus were, at a very early period, contemptuously likened; and modern holders of the doctrine are occasionally made the subject of equally polite comparison by its German, French, and English assailants.

When thus attacked, the Epicureans have always answered, that it is not they, but their accusers, who represent human nature in a degrading light; since the accusation supposes human beings to be capable of no pleasures except those of which swine are capable. If this supposition were true, the charge could not be gainsaid, but would then be no longer an imputation; for if the sources of pleasure were precisely the same to human beings and to swine, the rule of life which is good enough for the one would be good enough for the other. The comparison of the Epicurean life to that of beasts is felt as degrading, precisely because a beast's pleasures do not satisfy a human being's conceptions of happiness. Human beings have faculties more elevated than the animal appetites, and when once made conscious of them, do not regard anything as happiness which does not include their gratification. I do not, indeed, consider the Epicureans to have been by any means faultless in drawing out their scheme of consequences from the utilitarian principle. To do this in any sufficient manner, many Stoic, as well as Christian elements require to be included.

Source: John Stuart Mill, from *Utilitarianism* (1861), chapters 12 and 17.

But there is no known Epicurean theory of life which does not assign to the pleasures of the intellect, of the feelings and imagination, and of the moral sentiments, a much higher value as pleasures than to those of mere sensation. It must be admitted, however, that utilitarian writers in general have placed the superiority of mental over bodily pleasures chiefly in the greater permanency, safety, uncostliness, etc., of the former—that is, in their circumstantial advantages rather than in their intrinsic nature. And on all these points utilitarians have fully proved their case; but they might have taken the other and, as it may be called, higher ground, with entire consistency. It is quite compatible with the principle of utility to recognize the fact, that some *kinds* of pleasure are more desirable and more valuable than others. It would be absurd that while, in estimating all other things, quality is considered as well as quantity, the estimation of pleasures should be supposed to depend on quantity alone.

If I am asked, what I mean by difference of quality in pleasures, or what makes one pleasure more valuable than another, merely as a pleasure, except its being greater in amount, there is but one possible answer. Of two pleasures, if there be one to which all or almost all who have experience of both give a decided preference, irrespective of any feeling of moral obligation to prefer it, that is the more desirable pleasure. If one of the two is, by those who are competently acquainted with both, placed so far above the other that they prefer it, even though knowing it to be attended with a greater amount of discontent, and would not resign it for any quantity of the other pleasure which their nature is capable of, we are justified in ascribing to the preferred enjoyment a superiority in quality, so far outweighing quantity as to render it, in comparison, of small account.

Now it is an unquestionable fact that those who are equally acquainted with, and equally capable of appreciating and enjoying, both, do give a most marked preference to the manner of existence which employs their higher faculties.

Few human creatures would consent to be changed into any of the lower animals, for a promise of the fullest allowance of a beast's pleasures; no intelligent human being would consent to be a fool, no instructed person would be an ignoramus, no person of feeling and conscience would be selfish and base, even though they should be persuaded that the fool, the dunce, or the rascal is better satisfied with his lot than they are with theirs. They would not resign what they possess more than he for the most complete satisfaction of all the desires which they have in common with him. If they ever fancy they would, it is only in cases of unhappiness so extreme, that to escape from it they would exchange their lot for almost any other, however undesirable in their own eyes. A being of higher faculties requires more to make him happy, is capable probably of more acute suffering, and certainly accessible to it at more points, than one of an inferior type; but in spite of these liabilities, he can never really wish to sink into what he feels to be a lower grade of existence. We may give what explanation we pleasure of this unwillingness; we may attribute it to pride, a name which is given indiscriminately to some of the most and to some of the least estimable feelings of which mankind are capable; we may refer it to the love of liberty and personal independence, an appeal to which was with the Stoics one of the most effective means for the inculcation of it; to the love of power, or to the love of excitement, both of which do really enter into and contribute to it: but its most appropriate appellation is a sense of dignity, which all human beings possess in one form or other, and in some, though by no means in exact, proportion to their higher faculties, and which is so essential a part of the happiness of those in whom it is strong, that nothing which conflicts with it could be, otherwise than momentarily, an object of desire to them. Whoever supposes that this preference takes place at a sacrifice of happiness—that the superior being, in anything like equal circumstances, is not happier than the inferior—confounds the two very different ideas, of happiness, and content. It is indisputable that the being whose capacities of enjoyment are low, has the greatest chance of having them fully satisfied; and a highly endowed being will always feel that any happiness which he can look for, as the world is constituted, is imperfect. But he can learn to bear its imperfections, if they are at all bearable; and they will not make him envy the being who is indeed unconscious of the imperfections, but only because he feels not at all the good which those imperfections qualify. It is better to be a human being dissatisfied than a pig satisfied; better to be Socrates dissatisfied than a fool satisfied. And if the fool, or the pig, are of a different opinion, it is because they only know their own side of the question. The other party to the comparison knows both sides.

It may be objected, that many who are capable of the higher pleasures, occasionally, under the influence of temptation, postpone them to the lower. But this is quite compatible with a full appreciation of the intrinsic superiority of the higher. Men often, from infirmity of character, make their election for the nearer good, though they know it to be the less valuable; and this no less when the choice is between two bodily pleasures, than when it is between bodily and mental. They pursue sensual indulgence to the injury of health, though perfectly aware that health is the greater good. It may be further objected, that many who begin with youthful enthusiasm for everything noble, as they advance in years sink into indolence and selfishness. But I do not believe that those who undergo this very common change, voluntarily choose the lower description of pleasures in preference to the higher. I believe that before they devote themselves exclusively to the one, they have already become incapable of the other. Capacity for the nobler feelings is in most natures a very tender plant, easily killed, not only by hostile influences, but by mere want of sustenance; and in the majority of young persons it speedily dies away if the occupations to which their position in life has devoted them, and the society into which it has thrown them, are not favourable to keeping that higher capacity in exercise. Men lose their high aspirations as they lose their intellectual tastes, because they have not time or opportunity for indulging them; and they addict themselves to inferior pleasures, not because they deliberately prefer them, but because they are either the only ones to which they have access or the only ones which they are any longer capable of enjoying. It may be questioned whether any one who has remained equally susceptible to both classes of pleasures, ever knowingly and calmly preferred the lower; though many, in all ages, have broken down in an ineffectual attempt to combine both.

From this verdict of the only competent judges, I apprehend there can be no appeal. On a question which is the best worth having of two pleasures, or which of two modes of existence is the most grateful to the feelings, apart from its moral attributes and from its consequences, the judgment of those who are qualified by knowledge of both, or, if they differ, that of the majority among them, must be admitted as final. And there needs be the less hesitation to accept this judgment respecting the quality of pleasures, since there is no other tribunal to be referred to even on the question of quantity. What means are there of determining which is the acutest of two pains, or the intensest of two pleasurable sensations, except the general suffrage of those who are familiar with both? Neither pains nor pleasures are homogeneous, and pain is always heterogeneous with pleasure. What is there to decide whether a particular pleasure is worth purchasing at the cost of a particular pain, except the feelings and judgment of the experienced? When, therefore, those feelings and judgment declare the pleasures derived from the higher faculties to be preferable *in kind,* apart from the question of intensity, to those of which the animal nature, disjoined from the higher faculties, is susceptible, they are entitled on this subject to the same regard.

I have dwelt on this point, as being a necessary part of a perfectly just conception of Utility or Happiness, considered as the directive rule of human conduct. But it is by no means an indispensable condition to the acceptance of the utilitarian stand; for that standard is not the agent's own greatest happiness, but the greatest amount of happiness altogether; and if it may possibly be doubted whether a noble character is always the happier for its nobleness, there can be no doubt that it makes other people happier, and that the world in general is immensely a gainer by it. Utilitarianism, therefore, could only attain its end by the general cultivation of nobleness of character, even if each individual were only benefited by the nobleness of others, and his own, so far as happiness is concerned, were a sheer deduction from the benefit. But the bare enunciation of such an absurdity as this last, renders refutation superfluous.

According to the Greatest Happiness Principle, as above explained, the ultimate end, with reference to and for the sake of which all other things are desirable (whether we are considering our own good or that of other people), is an existence exempt as far as possible from pain, and as rich as possible in enjoyments, both in point of quantity and quality; the test of quality, and the rule for measuring it against quantity, being the preference felt by those who in their opportunities of experience, to which must be added their habits of self-consciousness and self-observation, are best furnished with the means of comparison. This, being, according to the utilitarian opinion, the end of human action, is necessarily also the standard of morality; which may accordingly be defined, the rules and precepts for human conduct, by the observance of which an existence such as has been described might be, to the greatest extent possible, secured to all mankind; and not to them only, but, so far as the nature of things admits, to the whole sentient creation. . . .

I must again repeat what the assailants of utilitarianism seldom have the justice to acknowledge, that the happiness which forms the utilitarian standard of what is right in conduct, is not the agent's own happiness, but that of all concerned. As between his own happiness and that of others, utilitarianism requires him to be as strictly impartial as a disinterested and benevolent spectator. In the golden rule of Jesus of Nazareth, we read the complete spirit of the ethics of utility. To do as you would be done by, and to love your neighbor as yourself, constitute the ideal perfection of utilitarian morality. As the means of making the nearest approach to this ideal, utility would enjoin, first, that laws and social arrangements should place the happiness, or (as, speaking practically it may be called) the interest, of every individual, as nearly as possible in harmony with the interest of the whole; and secondly that education and opinion, which have so vast a power over human character, should so use that power as to establish in the mind of every individual an indissoluble association between his own happiness and the good of the whole; especially between his own happiness and the practice of such modes of conduct, negative and positive, as regard for the universal happiness prescribes; so that not only he may be unable to conceive the possibility of happiness to himself, consistently with conduct opposed to the general good, but also that a direct impulse to promote the general good may be in every individual one of the habitual motives of action, and the sentiments connected therewith may fill a large and prominent place in every human being's sentient existence. If the impugners of the utilitarian morality represented it to their own minds in this its true character, I know not what recommendation possessed by any other morality they could possibly affirm to be wanting to it; what more beautiful or more exalted developments of human nature any other ethical system can be supposed to foster, or what springs of action, not accessible to the utilitarian, such systems rely on for giving effect to their mandates. . . .

OF WHAT SORT OF PROOF THE PRINCIPLE OF UTILITY IS SUSCEPTIBLE

It has already been remarked, that questions of ultimate ends do not admit of proof, in the ordinary acceptation of the term. To be incapable of proof by reasoning is common to all first principles; to the first premises of our knowledge, as well as to those of our conduct. But the former, being matters of fact, may be the subject of a direct appeal to the faculties which judge of fact—namely, our senses, and our internal consciousness. Can an appeal be made to the same faculties on questions of practical ends? Or by what other faculty is cognizance taken of them?

Questions about ends, in other words, question what things are desirable. The utilitarian doctrine is, that happiness is desirable, and the only thing desirable, as an end; all other things being only desirable as means to that end. What ought to be required of this doctrine—what conditions is it requisite that the doctrine should fulfil—to make good its claim to be believed?

The only proof capable of being given that an object is visible, is that people actually see it. The only proof that a sound is audible, is that people hear it: and so of the other sources of our experience. In like manner, I apprehend, the sole evidence it is possible to produce that anything is desirable, is that people do actually desire it. If the end which the utilitarian doctrine proposes to itself were not, in theory and in practice, acknowledged to be an end, nothing could ever convince any person that it was so. No reason can be given why the general happiness is desirable, except that each person, so far as he believes it to be attainable, desires his own happiness. This, however, being a fact, we have not only all the proof which the cases admits of, but all which it is possible to require, that happiness is a good: that each person's happiness is a good to that person, and the general happiness, therefore, a good to the aggregate of all persons. Happiness has made out its title as one of the ends of conduct, and consequently one of the criteria of morality.

But it has not, by this alone, proved itself to be the sole criterion. To do that, it would seem, by the same rule, necessary to show, not only that people desire happiness, but that they never desire anything else. Now it is palpable that they do desire things which, in common language, are decidedly distinguished from happiness. They

desire, for example, virtue, and the absence of vice, no less really than pleasure and the absence of pain. The desire of virtue is not as universal, but it is as authentic a fact, as the desire of happiness. And hence the opponents of the utilitarian standard deem that they have a right to infer that there are other ends of human action besides happiness, and that happiness is not the standard of approbation and disapprobation.

But does the utilitarian doctrine deny that people desire virtue, or maintain that virtue is not a thing to be desired? The very reverse. It maintains not only that virtue is to be desired, but that it is to be desired disinterestedly, for itself. Whatever may be the opinion of utilitarian moralists as to the original conditions by which virtue is made virtue; however they may believe (as they do) that actions and dispositions are only virtuous because they promote another end than virtue; yet this being granted, and it having been decided, form considerations of this description, what *is* virtuous, they not only place virtue at the very head of the things which are good as means to the ultimate end, but they also recognise as a psychological fact that possibility of its being, to the individual, a good in itself, without looking to any end beyond it; and hold, that the mind is not in a right state, not in a state conformable to Utility, not in the state most conducive to the general happiness, unless it does love virtue in this manner—as a thing desirable in itself, even although, in the individual instance, it should not produce those other desirable consequences which it tends to produce, and on account of which it is held to be virtue. This opinion is not, in the smallest degree, a departure from the Happiness principle. The ingredients of happiness are very various, and each of them is desirable in itself, and not merely when considered as swelling an aggregate. The principle of utility does not mean that any given pleasure, as music, for instance, or any given exemption from pain, as for example health, is to be looked upon as means to a collective something termed happiness, and to be desired on that account. They are desired and desirable in and for themselves; besides being means, they are a part of the end. Virtue, according to the utilitarian doctrine, is not naturally and originally part of the end, but it is capable of becoming so; and in those who love it disinterestedly it has become so, and is desired and cherished, not as a means to happiness, but as a part of their happiness.

To illustrate this farther, we may remember that virtue is not the only thing, originally a means, and which if it were not a means to anything else, would be and remain indifferent, but which by association with what it is a means to, comes to be desired for itself, and that too with the utmost intensity. What, for example, shall we say of the love of money? There is nothing originally more desirable about money than about any heap of glittering pebbles. Its worth is solely that of the things which it will buy; the desires for other things than itself, which it is a means of gratifying. Yet the love of money is not only one of the strongest moving forces of human life, but money is, in many cases, desired in and for itself; the desire to possess it is often stronger than the desire to use it, and goes on increasing when all the desires which point to ends beyond it, to be compassed by it, are falling off. It may, then, be said truly, that money is desired not for the sake of an end, but as part of the end. From being a means to happiness, it has come to be itself a principal ingredient of the individual's conception of happiness. The same may be said of the majority of the great objects of human life—power, for example, or fame; except that to each of these there is a certain amount of immediate pleasure annexed, which has at least the semblance of being naturally inherent in them; a thing which cannot be said of money. Still, however, the strongest natural attraction, both of power and of fame, is the immense aid they give to the attainment of our other wishes; and it is the strong association thus generated between them and all our objects of desire, which gives to the direct desire of them the intensity it often assumes, so as in some characters to surpass in strength all other desires. In these cases the means have become a part of the end, and a more important part of it than any of the things which they are means to.

What was once desired as an instrument for the attainment of happiness, has come to be desired for its own sake. In being desired for its own sake it is, however, desired as *part* of happiness. The person is made, or thinks he would be made, happy by its mere possession; and is made unhappy by failure to obtain it. The desire of it is not a different thing from the desire of happiness, any more than the love of music, or the desire of health. They are included in happiness. They are some of the elements of which the desire of happiness is made up. Happiness is not an abstract idea, but a concrete whole; and these are some of its parts. And the utilitarian standard sanctions and approves their being so. Life would be a poor thing, very ill provided with sources of happiness, if there were not this provision of nature, by which things originally indifferent, but conducive to, or otherwise associated with, the satisfaction of our primitive desires, become in themselves sources of pleasure more valuable than the primitive pleasures, both in permanency, in the space of human existence that they are capable of covering, and even in intensity.

Virtue, according to the utilitarian conception, is a good of this description. There was no original desire of it, or motive to it, save its conduciveness to pleasure, and especially to protection from pain. But through the association thus formed, it may be felt a good in itself, and desired as such with as great intensity as any other good; and with this difference between it and the love of money, of power, or of fame, that all of these may, and often do, render the individual noxious to the other members of the society to which he belongs, whereas there is nothing which makes him so much a blessing to them as the cultivation of the disinterested love of virtue. And consequently, the utilitarian standard, while it tolerates and approves those other acquired desires, up to the point beyond which they would be more injurious to the general happiness than promotive of it, enjoins and requires the cultivation of the love of virtue up to the greatest strength possible, as being above all things important to the general happiness.

It results from the preceding considerations, that there is in reality nothing desired except happiness. Whatever is desired otherwise than as a means to some end beyond itself, and ultimately to happiness, is desired as itself a part of happiness, and is not desired for itself until it has become so. Those who desire virtue for its own sake, desire it either because the consciousness of it is a pleasure, or because the consciousness of being without it is a pain, or for both reasons united; as in truth the pleasure and pain seldom exist separately, but almost always together, the same person feeling pleasure in the degree of virtue attained, and pain in not having attained more. If one of these gave him no pleasure, and the other no pain, he would not love or desire virtue, or would desire it only for the other benefits which it might produce to himself or to persons whom he cared for. . . .

Review Questions

1. State and explain the Principle of Utility. Show how it could be used to justify actions that are conventionally viewed as wrong, such as lying and stealing.
2. How does Mill reply to the objection that epicureanism is a doctrine worthy only of swine?
3. How does Mill distinguish between higher and lower pleasures?
4. According to Mill, whose happiness must be considered?
5. Carefully reconstruct Mill's proof of the Principle of Utility.

Discussion Questions

1. Is happiness nothing more than pleasure, and the absence of pain? What do you think?
2. Does Mill convince you that the so-called higher pleasures are better than the lower ones? What about the person of experience who prefers the lower pleasures over the higher ones?
3. Mill says, "In the golden rule of Jesus of Nazareth, we read the complete spirit of the ethics of utility." Is this true or not?
4. Many commentators have thought that Mill's proof of the Principle of Utility is defective. Do you agree? If so, then what mistake or mistakes does he make? Is there any way to reformulate the proof so that it is not defective?

The Categorical Imperative

IMMANUEL KANT

Immanuel Kant (1724–1804), a German, was one of the most important philosophers of all time. He made significant contributions to all areas of philosophy. He wrote many books; the most important ones are *Critique of Pure Reason, Prolegomena*

Source: Immanuel Kant, "The Categorical Imperative," from *The Moral Law: Kant's Groundwork of the Metaphysic of Morals,* trans. H. J. Paton (New York: Barnes & Noble, Inc., 1948).

to *All Future Metaphysics, Critique of Practical Reason, Critique of Judgment,* and *The Foundations of the Metaphysics of Morals,* from which the reading is taken.

Kant believes that our moral duty can be formulated in one supreme rule, the categorical imperative, from which all our duties can be derived. Although he says that there is just one rule, he gives different versions of it, and two of them seem to be distinct. He arrives at the supreme rule or rules by considering the nature of the good will and duty.

THE GOOD WILL

IT IS IMPOSSIBLE to conceive anything at all in the world, or even out of it, which can be taken as good without qualification, except a *good will.* Intelligence, wit, judgment, and any other *talents* of the mind we may care to name, or courage, resolution, and constancy of purpose, as qualities of *temperament,* are without doubt good and desirable in many respects; but they can also be extremely bad and hurtful when the will is not good which has to make use of these gifts of nature, and which for this reason has the term "*character*" applied to its peculiar quality. It is exactly the same with *gifts of fortune.* Power, wealth, honour, even health and that complete well-being and contentment with one's state which goes by the name of "*happiness,*" produce boldness, and as a consequence often overboldness as well, unless a good will is present by which their influence on the mind—and so too the whole principle of action—may be corrected and adjusted to universal ends; not to mention that a rational and impartial spectator can never feel approval in contemplating the uninterrupted prosperity of a being graced by no touch of a pure and good will, and that consequently a good will seems to constitute the indispensable condition of our very worthiness to be happy.

Some qualities are even helpful to this good will itself and can make its task very much easier. They have none the less no inner unconditioned worth, but rather presuppose a good will which sets a limit to the esteem in which they are rightly held and does not permit us to regard them as absolutely good. Moderation in affections and passions, self-control, and sober reflexion are not only good in many respects: they may even seem to constitute part of the *inner* worth of a person. Yet they are far from being properly described as good without qualification (however unconditionally they have been commended by the ancients). For without the principles of a good will they may become exceedingly bad; and the very coolness of a scoundrel makes him, not merely more dangerous, but also immediately more abominable in our eyes than we should have taken him to be without it.

THE GOOD WILL AND ITS RESULTS

A good will is not good because of what it effects or accomplishes—because of its fitness for attaining some proposed end: it is good through its willing alone—that is, good in itself. Considered in itself it is to be esteemed beyond comparison as far higher than anything it could ever bring about merely in order to favour some inclination or, if you like, the sum total of inclinations. Even if, by some special disfavour of destiny or by the niggardly endowment of stepmotherly nature, this will is entirely lacking in power to carry out its intentions; if by its utmost effort it still accomplishes nothing, and only good will is left (not, admittedly, as a mere wish, but as the straining of every means so far as they are in our control); even then it would still shine like a jewel for its own sake as something which has its full value in itself. Its usefulness or fruitlessness can neither add to, nor subtract from, this value. Its usefulness would be merely, as it were, the setting which enables us to handle it better in our ordinary dealings or to attract the attention of those not yet sufficiently expert, but not to commend it to experts or to determine its value. . . .

THE GOOD WILL AND DUTY

We have now to elucidate the concept of a will estimable in itself and good apart from any further end. This concept, which is already present in a sound natural understanding and requires not so much to be taught as merely to be clarified, always holds the highest place in estimating the total worth of our actions and constitutes the condition of all the rest. We will therefore take up the concept of *duty*, which includes that of a good will, exposed, however, to certain subjective limitations and obstacles. These, so far from hiding a good will or disguising it, rather bring it out by contrast and make it shine forth more brightly.

THE MOTIVE OF DUTY

I will here pass over all actions already recognized as contrary to duty, however useful they may be with a view to this or that end; for about these the question does not even arise whether they could have been done *for the sake of duty* inasmuch as they are directly opposed to it. I will also set aside actions which in fact accord with duty, yet for which men have *no immediate inclination,* but perform them because impelled to do so by some other inclination. For there it is easy to decide whether the action which accords with duty has been done *from duty* or from some purpose of self-interest. This distinction is far more difficult to perceive when the action accords with duty and the subject has in addition an *immediate* inclination to the action. For example, it certainly accords with duty that a grocer should not overcharge his inexperienced customer; and where there is much competition a sensible shopkeeper refrains from so doing and keeps to a fixed and general price for everybody so that a child can buy from him just as well as anyone else. Thus people are served *honestly;* but this is not nearly enough to justify us in believing that the shopkeeper has acted in this way from duty or from principles of fair dealing; his interests required him to do so. We cannot assume him to have in addition an immediate inclination towards his customers, leading him, as it were out of love, to give no man preference over another in the matter of price. Thus the action was done neither from duty nor from immediate inclination, but solely from purposes of self-interest.

On the other hand, to preserve one's life is a duty, and besides this every one has also an immediate inclination to do so. But on account of this the often anxious precautions taken by the greater part of mankind for this purpose have no inner worth, and the maxim of their action is without moral content. They do protect their lives *in conformity with duty,* but not *from the motive of duty.* When on the contrary, disappointments and hopeless misery have quite taken away the taste for life; when a wretched man, strong in soul and more angered at his fate than faint-hearted or cast down, longs for death and still preserves his life without loving it—not from inclination or fear but from duty; then indeed his maxim has a moral content.

To help others where one can is a duty, and besides this there are many spirits of so sympathetic a temper that, without any further motive of vanity or self-interest, they find an inner pleasure in spreading happiness around them and can take delight in the contentment of others as their own work. Yet I maintain that in such a case an action of this kind, however right and however amiable it may be, has still no genuinely moral worth. It stands on the same footing as other inclinations—for example, the inclination for honour, which if fortunate enough to hit on something beneficial and right and consequently honourable, deserves praise and encouragement, but not esteem; for its maxim lacks moral content, namely, the performance of such actions, not from inclination, but *from duty.* Suppose then that the mind of this friend of man were overclouded by sorrows of his own which extinguished all sympathy with the fate of others, but that he still had power to help those in distress, though no longer stirred by the need of others because sufficiently occupied with his own; and suppose that, when no longer moved by any inclination, he tears himself out of this deadly insensibility and does the action without any inclination for the sake of duty alone; then for the first time his action has its genuine moral worth. Still further: if nature had implanted little sympathy in this or that man's heart; if (being in other respects an honest fellow) he were cold in temperament and indifferent to the sufferings of others—perhaps because, being endowed with the special gift of patience and robust endurance in his own sufferings, he assumed the like in others or even demanded it; if such a man (who would in truth not be the worth product of nature) were not exactly fashioned by her to be a philanthropist, would he not still find in himself a source from which he might draw a worth far higher than any that a good-natured temperament can have? Assuredly he would. It is precisely in this that the worth of character begins to show—a moral worth and beyond all comparison the highest—namely, that he does good, not from inclination, but from duty. . . .

Thus the moral worth of an action does not depend on the result expected from it, and so too does not depend on any principle of action that needs to borrow its motive from this expected result. For all these results (agreeable states and even the promotion of happiness in others) could have been brought about by other causes as well, and consequently their production did not require the will of a rational being, in which, however, the highest and unconditioned good can alone be found. Therefore nothing but the *idea of the law* in itself, *which admittedly is present only in a rational being*—so far as it, and not an expected result, is the ground determining the will—can constitute that preeminent good which we call moral, a good which is already present in the person acting on this idea and has not to be awaited merely from the result.

THE CATEGORICAL IMPERATIVE

But what kind of law can this be the thought of which, even without regard to the results expected from it, has to determine the will if this is to be called good absolutely and without qualification? Since I have robbed the will of every inducement that might arise for it as a consequence of obeying any particular law, nothing is left but the conformity of actions to universal law as such, and this alone must serve the will as its principle. That is to say, I ought never to act except in such a way *that I can also will that my maxim should become a universal law.* Here bare conformity to universal law as such (without having as its base any law prescribing particular actions) is what serves the will as its principle, and must so serve it if duty is not to be everywhere an empty delusion and a chimerical concept. The ordinary reason of mankind also agrees with this completely in its practical judgements and always has the aforesaid principle before its eyes. . . .

When I conceive a *hypothetical imperative* in general, I do not know beforehand what it will contain—until its condition is given. But if I conceive a *categorical imperative,* I know at once what it contains. For since besides the law this imperative contains only the necessity that our maxim[1] should conform to this law, while the law, as we have seen, contains no condition to limit it, there remains nothing over to which the maxim has to conform except the universality of a law as such; and it is this conformity alone that the imperative properly asserts to be necessary.

There is therefore only a single categorical imperative and it is this: *"Act only on that maxim through which you can at the same time will that it should become a universal law."*

Now if all imperatives of duty can be derived from this one imperative as their principle, then even although we leave it unsettled whether what we call duty may not be an empty concept, we

---

1 A *maxim* is a subjective principle of action and must be distinguished from an *objective principle*—namely, a practical law. The former contains a practical rule determined by reason in accordance with the conditions of the subject (often his ignorance or against his inclinations): it is thus a principle on which the subject *acts.* A law, on the other hand, is an objective principle valid for every rational being; and it is a principle on which he *ought to act*—that is, an imperative.

shall still be able to show at least what we understand by it and what the concept means. . . .

ILLUSTRATIONS

We will now enumerate a few duties, following their customary division into duties towards self and duties towards others and into perfect and imperfect duties.[2]

1. A man feels sick of life as the result of a series of misfortunes that has mounted to the point of despair, but he is still so far in possession of his reason as to ask himself whether taking his own life may not be contrary to his duty to himself. He now applies the test "Can the maxim of my action really become a universal law of nature?" His maxim is "From self-love I make it my principle to shorten my life if its continuance threatens more evil than it promises pleasure." The only further question to ask is whether this principle of self-love can become a universal law of nature. It is then seen at once that a system of nature by whose law the very same feeling whose function (*Bestimmung*) is to stimulate the furtherance of life should actually destroy life would contradict itself and consequently could not subsist as a system of nature. Hence this maxim cannot possibly hold as a universal law of nature and is therefore entirely opposed to the supreme principle of all duty.

2. Another finds himself driven to borrowing money because of need. He well knows that he will not be able to pay it back; but he sees too that he will get no loan unless he gives a firm promise to pay it back within a fixed time. He is inclined to make such a promise; but he has still

enough conscience to ask "Is it not unlawful and contrary to duty to get out of difficulties in this way?" Supposing, however, he did resolve to do so, the maxim of his action would run thus: "Whenever I believe myself short of money, I will borrow money and promise to pay it back, though I know that this will never be done." Now this principle of self-love or personal advantage is perhaps quite compatible with my own entire future welfare; only there remains the question "Is it right?" I therefore transform the demand of self-love into a universal law and frame my question thus: "How would things stand if my maxim became a universal law?" I then see straight away that this maxim can never rank as a universal law of nature and be self-consistent, but must necessarily contradict itself. For the universality of a law that every one believing himself to be in need can make any promise he pleases with the intention not to keep it would make promising, and the very purpose of promising, itself impossible, since no one would believe he was being promised anything, but would laugh at utterances of this kind as empty shams.

3. A third finds in himself a talent whose cultivation would make him a useful man for all sorts of purposes. But he sees himself in comfortable circumstances, and he prefers to give himself up to pleasure rather than to bother about increasing and improving his fortunate natural aptitudes. Yet he asks himself further "Does my maxim of neglecting my natural gifts, besides agreeing in itself with my tendency to indulgence, agree also with what is called duty?" He then sees that a system of nature could indeed always subsist under such a universal law, although (like the South Sea Islanders) every man should let his talents rust and should be bent on devoting his life solely to idleness, indulgence, procreation, and, in a word, to enjoyment. Only he cannot possibly *will* that this should become a universal law of nature or should be implanted in us as such a law by a natural instinct. For as a rational being he necessarily wills that all his powers should be developed,

---

2 It should be noted that I reserve my division of duties entirely for a future *Metaphysic of Morals* and that my present division is therefore put forward as arbitrary (merely for the purpose of arranging my examples). Further, I understand here by a perfect duty one which allows no exception in the interests of inclination, and so I recognize among *perfect duties*, not only outer ones, but also inner. This is contrary to the accepted usage of the schools, but I do not intend to justify it here, since for my purpose it is all one whether this point is conceded or not.

since they serve him, and are given him, for all sorts of possible ends.

4. Yet a *fourth* is himself flourishing, but he sees others who have to struggle with great hardships (and whom he could easily help); and he thinks, "What does it matter to me? Let every one be as happy as Heaven wills or as he can make himself; I won't deprive him of anything; I won't even envy him; only I have no wish to contribute anything to his well-being or to his support in distress!" Now admittedly if such an attitude were a universal law of nature, mankind could get on perfectly well—better no doubt than if everybody prates about sympathy and goodwill, and even takes pains, on occasion, to practise them, but on the other hand cheats where he can, traffics in human rights, or violates them in other ways. But although it is possible that a universal law of nature could subsist in harmony with this maxim, yet it is impossible to *will* that such a principle should hold everywhere as a law of nature. For a will which decided in this way would be in conflict with itself, since many a situation might arise in which the man needed love and sympathy from others, and in which, by such a law of nature sprung from his own will, he would rob himself of all hope of the help he wants for himself. . . .

THE FORMULA
OF THE END IN ITSELF

The will is conceived as a power of determining oneself to action *in accordance with the idea of certain laws*. And such a power can be found only in rational beings. Now what serves the will as a subjective ground of its self-determination is an *end;* and this, if it is given by reason alone, must be equally valid for all rational beings. What, on the other hand, contains merely the ground of the possibility of an action whose effect is an end is called a *means*. . . .

Now I say that man, and in general every rational being, *exists* as an end in himself, *not merely as a means* for arbitrary use by this or that will: he must in all his actions, whether they are directed to himself or to other rational beings, always be viewed *at the same time as an end*. All the objects of inclination have only a conditioned value; for if there were not these inclinations and the needs grounded on them, their object would be valueless. Inclinations themselves, as sources of needs, are so far from having an absolute value to make them desirable for their own sake that it must rather be the universal wish of every rational being to be wholly free from them. Thus the value of all objects that can *be produced* by our action is always conditioned. Beings whose existence depends, not on our will, but on nature, have none the less, if they are non-rational beings, only a relative value as means and are consequently called *things*. Rational beings, on the other hand, are called *persons* because their nature already marks them out as ends in themselves—that is, as something which ought not to be used merely as a means—and consequently imposes to that extent a limit on all arbitrary treatment of them (and is an object of reverence). Persons, therefore, are not merely subjective ends whose existence as an object of our actions has a value *for us:* they are *objective ends*—that is, things whose existence is in itself an end, and indeed an end such that in its place we can put no other end to which they should serve *simply* as means; for unless this is so, nothing at all of *absolute* value would be found anywhere. But if all value were conditioned—that is, contingent—then no supreme principle could be found for reason at all.

If then there is to be a supreme practical principle and—so far as the human will is concerned—a categorical imperative, it must be such that from the idea of something which is necessarily an end for every one because it is an *end in itself* it forms an *objective* principle of the will and consequently can serve as a practical law. The ground of this principle is: *Rational nature exists as an end in itself*. This is the way in which a man necessarily conceives his own existence: it is therefore so far a *subjective* principle of human actions. But it is also the way in which every other rational being conceives his existence on the same rational ground which is valid also for me; hence it is at the same time an *objective* principle, from which, as a supreme practical ground, it must be possible to derive all laws for the will. The practical imperative will therefore be as follows: *Act in such a way that you always treat humanity, whether in your own person or in the person of any other, never simply as a means, but always at the same time as an end....*

Review Questions

1. Explain Kant's account of the good will.
2. Distinguish between hypothetical and categorical imperatives.
3. State the first formulation of the categorical imperative (using the notion of a universal law), and explain how Kant uses this rule to derive some specific duties toward self and others.
4. State the second version of the categorical imperative (using the language of means and end), and explain it.

Discussion Questions

1. Are the two versions of the categorical imperative just different expressions of one basic rule, or are they two different rules? Defend your view.
2. Kant claims that an action that is not done from the motive of duty has no moral worth. Do you agree or not? If not, give some counterexamples.
3. Some commentators think that the categorical imperative (particularly the first formulation) can be used to justify nonmoral or immoral actions. Is this a good criticism?

Happiness and Virtue

ARISTOTLE

Aristotle (384–322 B.C.E.) made important contributions to all areas of philosophy, including the formulation of traditional logic. Along with his teacher Plato, he is regarded as one of the founders of Western philosophy.

Aristotle argues that all human beings seek happiness, and that happiness is not pleasure, honor, or wealth, but an activity of the soul in accordance with virtue. Virtue is of two kinds: moral and intellectual. Moral virtue comes from training and habit, and generally is a state of character that is a mean between the vices of excess and deficiency. For example, Aristotle portrays the virtue of courage as a mean between the extremes of rashness (an excess) and cowardice (a deficiency). Intellectual virtue produces the most perfect happiness and is found in the activity of reason or contemplation.

Source: Extracts from "Ethica Nicomachea", Volume 9 *Ethics,* translated by W. D. Ross in *The Oxford Translation of Aristotle* (Oxford University Press, 1925) Reprinted by permission of Oxford University Press.

OUR DISCUSSION WILL BE ADEQUATE if it has as much clearness as the subject-matter admits of, for precision is not to be sought for alike in all discussions, any more than in all the products of the crafts. Now fine and just actions, which political science investigates, admit of much variety and fluctuation of opinion, so that they may be thought to exist only by convention, and not by nature. And goods also give rise to a similar fluctuation because they bring harm to many people; for before now men have been undone by reason of their wealth, and others by reason of their courage. We must be content, then, in speaking of such subjects and with such premisses to indicate the truth roughly and in outline, and in speaking about things which are only for the most part true and with premisses of the same kind to reach conclusions that are no better. In the same spirit, therefore, should each type of statement be received; for it is the mark of an educated man to look for precision in each class of things just so far as the nature of the subject admits; it is evidently equally foolish to accept probable reasoning from a mathematician and to demand from a rhetorician scientific proofs.

Now each man judges well the things he knows, and of these he is a good judge. And so the man who has been educated in a subject is a good judge of that subject, and the man who has received an all-round education is a good judge in general. Hence a young man is not a proper hearer of lectures on political science; for he is inexperienced in the actions that occur in life, but its discussions start from these and are about these; and, further, since he tends to follow his passions, his study will be vain and unprofitable, because the end aimed at is not knowledge but action. And it makes no difference whether he is young in years or youthful in character; the defect does not depend on time, but on his living, and pursuing each successive object, as passion directs. For to such persons, as to the incontinent, knowledge brings no profit; but to those who desire and act in accordance with a rational principle knowledge about such matters will be of great benefit.

These remarks about the student, the sort of treatment to be expected, and the purpose of the inquiry, may be taken as our preface.

Let us resume our inquiry and state, in view of the fact that all knowledge and every pursuit aims at some good, what it is that we say political science aims at and what is the highest of all goods achievable by action. Verbally there is very general agreement; for both the general run of men and people of superior refinement say that it is happiness, and identify living well and doing well with being happy; but with regard to what happiness is they differ, and the many do not give the same account as the wise. For the former think it is some plain and obvious thing, like pleasure, wealth, or honour; they differ, however, from one another—and often even the same man identifies it with different things, with health when he is ill, with wealth when he is poor; but, conscious of their ignorance, they admire those who proclaim some great ideal that is above their comprehension. Now some thought that apart from these many goods there is another which is self-subsistent and causes the goodness of all these as well. To examine all the opinions that have been held were perhaps somewhat fruitless; enough to examine those that are most prevalent or that seem to be arguable. . . .

Let us, however, resume our discussion from the point at which we digressed. To judge from the lives that men lead, most men, and men of the most vulgar type, seem (not without some ground) to identify the good, or happiness, with pleasure; which is the reason why they love the life of enjoyment. For there are, we may say, three prominent types of life—that just mentioned, the political, and thirdly the contemplative life. Now the mass of mankind are evidently quite slavish in their tastes, preferring a life suitable to beasts, but they get some ground for their view from the fact that many of those in high places share the tastes of Sardanapallus. A consideration of the prominent types of life shows that people of superior refinement and of active disposition identify happiness with honour;

for this is, roughly speaking, the end of the political life. But it seems too superficial to be what we are looking for, since it is thought to depend on those who bestow honour rather than on him who receives it, but the good we divine to be something proper to a man and not easily taken from him. Further, men seem to pursue honour in order that they may be assured of their goodness; at least it is by men of practical wisdom that they seek to be honoured, and among those who know them, and on the ground of their virtue; clearly, then, according to them, at any rate, virtue is better. And perhaps one might even suppose this to be, rather than honour, the end of the political life. But even this appears somewhat incomplete; for possession of virtue seems actually compatible with being asleep, or with life-long inactivity, and, further, with the greatest sufferings and misfortunes; but a man who was living so no one would call happy, unless he were maintaining a thesis at all costs. But enough of this; for the subject has been sufficiently treated even in the current discussions. Third comes the contemplative life, which we shall consider later.

The life of money-making is one undertaken under compulsion, and wealth is evidently not the good we are seeking; for it is merely useful and for the sake of something else. And so one might rather take the aforenamed objects to be ends; for they are loved for themselves. But it is evident that not even these are ends; yet many arguments have been thrown away in support of them. . . .

Let us again return to the good we are seeking, and ask what it can be. It seems different in different actions and arts; it is different in medicine, in strategy, and in the other arts likewise. What then is the good of each? Surely that for whose sake everything else is done. In medicine this is health, in strategy victory, in architecture a house, in any other sphere something else, and in every action and pursuit the end; for it is for the sake of this that all men do whatever else they do. Therefore, if there is an end for all that we do, this will be the good achievable by action,

and if there are more than one, these will be the goods achievable by action.

So the argument has by a different course reached the same point; but we must try to state this even more clearly. Since there are evidently more than one end, and we choose some of these (e.g. wealth, flutes, and in general instruments) for the sake of something else, clearly not all ends are final ends; but the chief good is evidently something final. Therefore, if there is only one final end, this will be what we are seeking, and if there are more than one, the most final of these will be what we are seeking. Now we call that which is in itself worthy of pursuit more final than that which is worthy of pursuit for the sake of something else, and that which is never desirable for the sake of something else more final than the things that are desirable both in themselves and for the sake of that other thing, and therefore we call final without qualification that which is always desirable in itself and never for the sake of something else.

Now such a thing happiness, above all else, is held to be; for this we choose always for itself and never for the sake of something else, but honour, pleasure, reason, and every virtue we choose indeed for themselves (for if nothing resulted from them we should still choose each of them), but we choose them also for the sake of happiness, judging that by means of them we shall be happy. Happiness, on the other hand, no one chooses for the sake of these, nor, in general, for anything other than itself. . . .

Presumably, however, to say that happiness is the chief good seems a platitude, and a clearer account of what it is is still desired. This might perhaps be given, if we could first ascertain the function of man. For just as for a fluteplayer, a sculptor, or any artist, and, in general, for all things that have a function or activity, the good and the 'well' is thought to reside in the function, so would it seem to be for man, if he has a function. Have the carpenter, then, and the tanner certain functions or activities, and has man none? Is he born without a function? Or as eye, hand, foot, and in general each of the parts evidently has a function, may one lay it down that man similarly has a function apart from all these? What then can this be? Life seems to be common even to plants, but we are seeking what is peculiar to man. Let us exclude, therefore, the life of nutrition and growth. Next there would be a life of perception, but *it* also seems to be common even to the horse, the ox, and every animal. There remains, then, an active life of the element that has a rational principle; of this, one part has such a principle in the sense of being obedient to one, the other in the sense of possessing one and exercising thought. And, as "life of the rational element" also has two meanings, we must state that life in the sense of activity is what we mean; for this seems to be the more proper sense of the term. Now if the function of man is an activity of soul which follows or implies a rational principle, and if we say "a so-and-so" and "a good so-and-so" have a function which is the same in kind, e. g. a lyre-player and a good lyre-player, and so without qualification in all cases, eminence in respect of goodness being added to the name of the function (for the function of a lyre-player is to play the lyre, and that of a good lyre-player is to do so well): if this is the case, [and we state the function of man to be a certain kind of life, and this to be an activity or actions of the soul implying a rational principle, and the function of a good man to be the good and noble performance of these, and if any action is well performed when it is performed in accordance with the appropriate excellence: if this is the case,] human good turns out to be activity of soul in accordance with virtue, and if there are more than one virtue, in accordance with the best and most complete.

But we must add "in a complete life." For one swallow does not make a summer, nor does one day; and so too one day, or a short time, does not make a man blessed and happy. . . .

We must consider it, however, in the light not only of our conclusion and our premises, but also of what is commonly said about it; for with a true view all the data harmonize, but with a false one the facts soon clash. Now goods have

been divided into three classes, and some are described as external, others as relating to soul or to body; we call those that relate to soul most properly and truly goods, and psychical actions and activities we class as relating to soul. Therefore our account must be sound, at least according to this view, which is an old one and agreed on by philosophers. It is correct also in that we identify the end with certain actions and activities; for thus it falls among goods of the soul and not among external goods. Another belief which harmonizes with our account is that the happy man lives well and does well; for we have practically defined happiness as a sort of good life and good action. The characteristics that are looked for in happiness seem also, all of them, to belong to what we have defined happiness as being. For some identify happiness with virtue, some with practical wisdom, others with a kind of philosophic wisdom, others with these, or one of these, accompanied by pleasure or not without pleasure; while others include also external prosperity. Now some of these views have been held by many men and men of old, others by a few eminent persons; and it is not probable that either of these should be entirely mistaken, but rather that they should be right in at least some one respect or even in most respects.

With those who identify happiness with virtue or some one virtue our account is in harmony; for to virtue belongs virtuous activity. But it makes, perhaps, no small difference whether we place the chief good in possession or in use, in state of mind or in activity. For the state of mind may exist without producing any good result, as in a man who is asleep or in some other way quite inactive, but the activity cannot; for one who has the activity will of necessity be acting, and acting well. And as in the Olympic Games it is not the most beautiful and the strongest that are crowned but those who compete (for it is some of these that are victorious), so those who act win, and rightly win, the noble and good things in life.

Their life is also in itself pleasant. For pleasure is a state of *soul,* and to each man that which he is said to be a lover of is pleasant; e. g. not only is a horse pleasant to the lover of horses, and a spectacle to the lover of sights, but also in the same way just acts are pleasant to the lover of justice and in general virtuous acts to the lover of virtue. Now for most men their pleasures are in conflict with one another because these are not by nature pleasant, but the lovers of what is noble find pleasant the things that are by nature pleasant; and virtuous actions are such, so that these are pleasant for such men as well as in their own nature. Their life, therefore, has no further need of pleasure as a sort of adventitious charm, but has its pleasure in itself. For, besides what we have said, the man who does not rejoice in noble actions is not even good; since no one would call a man just who did not enjoy acting justly, nor any man liberal who did not enjoy liberal actions; and similarly in all other cases. If this is so, virtuous actions must be in themselves pleasant. But they are also *good* and *noble,* and have each of these attributes in the highest degree, since the good man judges well about these attributes; his judgment is such as we have described. Happiness then is the best, noblest, and most pleasant thing in the world. . . .

Yet evidently, as we said, it needs the external goods as well; for it is impossible, or not easy, to do noble acts without the proper equipment. In many actions we use friends and riches and political power as instruments; and there are some things the lack of which takes the lustre from happiness, as good birth, goodly children, beauty; for the man who is very ugly in appearance or ill-born or solitary and childless is not very likely to be happy, and perhaps a man would be still less likely if he had thoroughly bad children or friends or had lost good children or friends by death. As we said, then, happiness seems to need this sort of prosperity in addition; for which reason some identify happiness with good fortune, though others identify it with virtue.

For this reason also the question is asked, whether happiness is to be acquired by learning or by habituation or some other sort of training, or comes in virtue of some divine providence or again by chance. Now if there is *any* gift of the gods to men, it is reasonable that happiness should be god-given, and most surely god-given of all human things inasmuch as it is the best. But this question would perhaps be more appropriate to another inquiry; happiness seems, however, even if it is not god-sent but comes as a result of virtue and some process of learning or training, to be among the most god-like things; for that which is the prize and end of virtue seems to be the best thing in the world, and something godlike and blessed.

It will also on this view be very generally shared; for all who are not maimed as regards their potentiality for virtue may win it by a certain kind of study and care. But if it is better to be happy thus than by chance, it is reasonable that the facts should be so, since everything that depends on the action of nature is by nature as good as it can be, and similarly everything that depends on art or any rational cause, and especially if it depends on the best of all causes. To entrust to chance what is greatest and most noble would be a very defective arrangement.

The answer to the question we are asking is plain also from the definition of happiness; for it has been said to be a virtuous activity of soul, of a certain kind. Of the remaining goods, some must necessarily pre-exist as conditions of happiness, and others are naturally co-operative and useful as instruments. And this will be found to agree with what we said at the outset; for we stated the end of political science to be the best end, and political science spends most of its pains on making the citizens to be of a certain character, viz. good and capable of noble acts.

It is natural, then, that we call neither ox nor horse nor any other of the animals happy; for none of them is capable of sharing in such activity. For this reason also a boy is not happy; for he is not yet capable of such acts, owing to his age; and boys who are called happy are being congratulated by reason of the hopes we have for them. For there is required, as we said, not only complete virtue but also a complete life, since many changes occur in life, and all manner of chances, and the most prosperous may fall into great misfortunes in old age, as is told of Priam in the Trojan Cycle; and one who has experienced such chances and has ended wretchedly no one calls happy. . . .

Since happiness is an activity of soul in accordance with perfect virtue, we must consider the nature of virtue; for perhaps we shall thus see better the nature of happiness. . . .

Virtue, then, being of two kinds, intellectual and moral, intellectual virtue in the main owes both its birth and its growth to teaching (for which reason it requires experience and time), while moral virtue comes about as a result of habit. . . . From this it is also plain that none of the moral virtues arises in us by nature; for nothing that exists by nature can form a habit contrary to its nature. For instance the stone which by nature moves downwards cannot be habituated to move upwards, not even if one tries to train it by throwing it up ten thousand times; nor can fire be habituated to move downwards, nor can anything else that by nature behaves in one way be trained to behave in another. Neither by nature, then, nor contrary to nature do the virtues arise in us; rather we are adapted by nature to receive them, and are made perfect by habit. . . .

We must, however, not only describe virtue as a state of character, but also say what sort of state it is. We may remark, then, that every virtue or excellence both brings into good condition the thing of which it is the excellence and makes the work of that thing be done well; e. g. the excellence of the eye makes both the eye and its work good; for it is by the excellence of the eye that we see well. Similarly the excellence of the horse makes a horse both good in itself and good at running and at carrying its rider and at awaiting the attack of the enemy. Therefore, if this is true in every case, the virtue of man also will be the state of character which makes a man good and which makes him do his own work well.

How this is to happen we have stated already, but it will be made plain also by the following

consideration of the specific nature of virtue. In everything that is continuous and divisible it is possible to take more, less, or an equal amount, and that either in terms of the thing itself or relatively to us; and the equal is an intermediate between excess and defect. By the intermediate in the object I mean that which is equidistant from each of the extremes, which is one and the same for all men; by the intermediate relatively to us that which is neither too much nor too little—and this is not one, nor the same for all. For instance, if ten is many and two is few, six is the intermediate, taken in terms of the object; for it exceeds and is exceeded by an equal amount; this is intermediate according to arithmetical proportion. But the intermediate relatively to us is not to be taken so; if ten pounds are too much for a particular person to eat and two too little, it does not follow that the trainer will order six pounds; for this also is perhaps too much for the person who is to take it, or too little—too little for Milo, too much for the beginner in athletic exercises. The same is true of running and wrestling. Thus a master of any art avoids excess and defect, but seeks the intermediate and chooses this—the intermediate not in the object but relatively to us.

If it is thus, then, that every art does its work well—by looking to the intermediate and judging its works by this standard (so that we often say of good works of art that it is not possible either to take away or to add anything, implying that excess and defect destroy the goodness of the works of art, while the mean preserves it; and good artists, as we say, look to this in their work), and if, further, virtue is more exact and better than any art, as nature also is, then virtue must have the quality of aiming at the intermediate. I mean moral virtue; for it is this that is concerned with passions and actions, and in these there is excess, defect, and the intermediate. For instance, both fear and confidence and appetite and anger and pity and in general pleasure and pain may be felt both too much and too little, and in both cases not well; but to feel them at the right times, with reference to the right objects, towards the right people, with the right motive, and in the right way, is what is both intermediate and best, and this is characteristic of virtue. Similarly with regard to actions also there is excess, defect, and the intermediate. Now virtue is concerned with passions and actions, in which excess is a form of failure, and so is defect, while the intermediate is praised and is a form of success; and being praised and being successful are both characteristics of virtue. Therefore virtue is a kind of mean, since, as we have seen, it aims at what is intermediate.

Again, it is possible to fail in many ways (for evil belongs to the class of the unlimited, as the Pythagoreans conjectured, and good to that of the limited), while to succeed is possible only in one way (for which reason also one is easy and the other difficult—to miss the mark easy, to hit it difficult); for these reasons also, then, excess and defect are characteristic of vice, and the mean of virtue;

> For men are good in but one way, but bad in many.

Virtue, then, is a state of character concerned with choice, lying in a mean, i. e. the mean relative to us, this being determined by a rational principle, and by that principle by which the man of practical wisdom would determine it. Now it is a mean between two vices, that which depends on excess and that which depends on defect; and again it is a mean because the vices respectively fall short of or exceed what is right in both passions and actions, while virtue both finds and chooses that which is intermediate. Hence in respect of its substance and the definition which states its essence virtue is a mean, with regard to what is best and right an extreme.

But not every action nor every passion admits of a mean; for some have names that already imply badness, e. g. spite, shamelessness, envy, and in the case of actions adultery, theft, murder; for all of these and suchlike things imply by their names that they are themselves bad, and not the excesses or deficiencies of them. It is not possible, then, ever to be right with regard to

them; one must always be wrong. Nor does goodness or badness with regard to such things depend on committing adultery with the right woman, at the right time, and in the right way, but simply to do any of them is to go wrong. It would be equally absurd, then, to expect that in unjust, cowardly, and voluptuous action there should be a mean, an excess, and a deficiency; for at that rate there would be a mean of excess and of deficiency, an excess of excess, and deficiency of deficiency. But as there is no excess and deficiency of temperance and courage because what is intermediate is in a sense an extreme, so too of the actions we have mentioned there is no mean nor any excess and deficiency, but however they are done they are wrong; for in general there is neither a mean of excess and deficiency, nor excess and deficiency of a mean.

We must, however, not only make this general statement, but also apply it to the individual facts. For among statements about conduct those which are general apply more widely, but those which are particular are more genuine, since conduct has to do with individual cases, and our statements must harmonize with the facts in these cases. We may take these cases from our table. With regard to feelings of fear and confidence courage is the mean; of the people who exceed, he who exceeds in fearlessness has no name (many of the states have no name), while the man who exceeds in confidence is rash, and he who exceeds in fear and falls short in confidence is a coward. With regard to pleasures and pains—not all of them, and not so much with regard to the pains—the mean is temperance, the excess self-indulgence. Persons deficient with regard to the pleasures are not often found; hence such persons also have received no name. But let us call them "insensible."

With regard to giving and taking of money the mean is liberality, the excess and the defect prodigality and meanness. In these actions people exceed and fall short in contrary ways; the prodigal exceeds in spending and falls short in taking, while the mean man exceeds in taking and falls short in spending. (At present we are giving a mere outline or summary, and are satisfied with this; later these states will be more exactly determined.) With regard to money there are also other dispositions—a mean, magnificence (for the magnificent man differs from the liberal man; the former deals with large sums, the latter with small ones), and excess, tastelessness, and vulgarity, and a deficiency, niggardliness; these differ from the states opposed to liberality. . . .

That moral virtue is a mean, then, and in what sense it is so, and that it is a mean between two vices, the one involving excess, the other deficiency, and that it is such because its character is to aim at what is intermediate in passions and in actions, has been sufficiently stated. Hence also it is no easy task to be good. For in everything it is no easy task to find the middle, e.g. to find the middle of a circle is not for every one but for him who knows; so, too, any one can get angry—that is easy—or give or spend money; but to do this to the right person, to the right extent, at the right time, with the right motive, and in the right way, *that* is not for every one, nor is it easy; wherefore goodness is both rare and laudable and noble. . . .

If happiness is activity in accordance with virtue, it is reasonable that it should be in accordance with the highest virtue; and this will be that of the best thing in us. Whether it be reason or something else that is this element which is thought to be our natural ruler and guide and to take thought of things noble and divine, whether it be itself also divine or only the most divine element in us, the activity of this in accordance with its proper virtue will be perfect happiness. That this activity is contemplative we have already said.

Now this would seem to be in agreement both with what we said before and with the truth. For, firstly, this activity is the best (since not only is reason the best thing in us, but the objects of reason are the best of knowable objects); and, secondly, it is the most continuous, since we can contemplate truth more continuously than we can do anything. And we think happiness has

pleasure mingled with it, but the activity of philosophic wisdom is admittedly the pleasantest of virtuous activities; at all events the pursuit of it is thought to offer pleasures marvellous for their purity and their enduringness, and it is to be expected that those who know will pass their time more pleasantly than those who inquire. And the self-sufficiency that is spoken of must belong most to the contemplative activity. For while a philosopher, as well as a just man or one possessing any other virtue, needs the necessaries of life, when they are sufficiently equipped with things of that sort the just man needs people towards whom and with whom he shall act justly, and the temperate man, the brave man, and each of the others is in the same case, but the philosopher, even when by himself, can contemplate truth, and the better the wiser he is; he can perhaps do so better if he has fellow-workers, but still he is the most self-sufficient. And this activity alone would seem to be loved for its own sake; for nothing arises from it apart from the contemplating, while from practical activities we gain more or less apart from the action. And happiness is thought to depend on leisure; for we are busy that we may have leisure, and make war that we may live in peace. Now the activity of the practical virtues is exhibited in political or military affairs, but the actions concerned with these seem to be unleisurely. Warlike actions are completely so (for no one chooses to be at war, or provokes war, for the sake of being at war; any one would seem absolutely murderous if he were to make enemies of his friends in order to bring about battle and slaughter); but the action of the statesman is also unleisurely, and—apart from the political action itself—aims at despotic power and honours, or at all events happiness, for him and his fellow citizens—a happiness different from political action, and evidently sought as being different. So if among virtuous actions political and military actions are distinguished by nobility and greatness, and these are unleisurely and aim at an end and are not desirable for their own sake, but the activity of reason, which is contemplative, seems both to be superior in serious worth and to aim at no end beyond itself, and to have its pleasure proper to itself (and this augments the activity), and the self-sufficiency, leisureliness, unweariedness (so far as this is possible for man), and all the other attributes ascribed to the supremely happy man are evidently those connected with this activity, it follows that this will be the complete happiness of man, if it be allowed a complete term of life (for none of the attributes of happiness is *in*complete).

But such a life would be too high for man; for it is not in so far as he is man that he will live so, but in so far as something divine is present in him; and by so much as this is superior to our composite nature is its activity superior to that which is the exercise of the other kind of virtue. If reason is divine, then in comparison with man, the life according to it is divine in comparison with human life. But we must not follow those who advise us, being men, to think of human things, and, being mortal, of mortal things, but must, so far as we can, make ourselves immortal, and strain every nerve to live in accordance with the best thing in us; for even if it be small in bulk, much more does it in power and worth surpass everything. This would seem, too, to be each man himself, since it is the authoritative and better part of him. It would be strange, then, if he were to choose not the life of his self but that of something else. And what we said before will apply now; that which is proper to each thing is by nature best and most pleasant for each thing; for man, therefore, the life according to reason is best and pleasantest, since reason more than anything else is man. This life therefore is also the happiest.

But in a secondary degree the life in accordance with the other kind of virtue is happy; for the activities in accordance with this befit our human estate. Just and brave acts, and other virtuous acts, we do in relation to each other, observing our respective duties with regard to contracts and services and all manner of actions and with regard to passions; and all of these seem to be typically human. Some of them seem even to arise from the body, and virtue of character to be in many ways bound up with the passions. Practical wisdom, too, is linked to virtue of character, and this to practical wisdom, since the principles of practical wisdom are in accordance with the moral virtues and rightness in morals is in accordance with practical wisdom. Being connected with the passions also, the moral virtues must belong to our composite nature; and the virtues of our composite nature are human; so, therefore, are the life and the happiness which correspond to these. The excellence of the reason is a thing apart; we must be content to say this much about it, for to describe it precisely is a task greater than our purpose requires. It would seem, however, also to need external equipment but little, or less than moral virtue does. Grant that both need the necessaries, and do so equally, even if the statesman's work is the more concerned with the body and things of that sort; for there will be little difference there; but in what they need for the exercise of their activities there will be much difference. The liberal man will need money for the doing of his liberal deeds, and the just man too will need it for the returning of services (for wishes are hard to discern, and even people who are not just pretend to wish to act justly); and the brave man will need power if he is to accomplish any of the acts that correspond to his virtue, and the temperate man will need opportunity; for how else is either he or any of the others to be recognized? It is debated, too, whether the will or the deed is more essential to virtue, which is assumed to involve both; it is surely clear that its perfection involves both; but for deeds many things are needed, and more, the greater and nobler the deeds are. But the man who is contemplating the truth needs no such thing, at least with a view to the exercise of his activity; indeed they are, one may say, even hindrances, at all events to his contemplation; but in so far as he is a man and lives with a number of people, he chooses to do virtuous acts; he will therefore need such aids to living a human life.

But that perfect happiness is a contemplative activity will appear from the following consideration as well. We assume the gods to be above all other beings blessed and happy; but what sort of actions must we assign to them? Acts of justice? Will not the gods seem absurd if they make contracts and return deposits, and so on? Acts of a brave man, then, confronting dangers and running risks because it is noble to do so? Or liberal acts? To whom will they give? It will be strange if they are really to have money or anything of the kind. And what would their temperate acts be? Is not such praise tasteless, since they have no bad appetites? If we were to run through them all, the circumstances of action would be found trivial and unworthy of gods. Still, every one supposes that they *live* and therefore that they are active; we cannot suppose them to sleep like Endymion. Now if you take away from a living being action, and still more production, what is left but contemplation? Therefore the activity of God, which surpasses all others in blessedness, must be contemplative; and of human activities, therefore, that which is most akin to this must be most of the nature of happiness.

This is indicated, too, by the fact that the other animals have no share in happiness, being completely deprived of such activity. For while the whole life of the gods is blessed, and that of men too in so far as some likeness of such activity belongs to them, none of the other animals is happy, since they in no way share in contemplation. Happiness extends, then, just so far as contemplation does, and those to whom contemplation more fully belongs are more truly happy, not as a mere concomitant but in virtue of the contemplation; for this is in itself precious. Happiness, therefore, must be some form of contemplation.

But, being a man, one will also need external prosperity; for our nature is not self-sufficient for the purpose of contemplation, but our body also must be healthy and must have food and other attention. Still, we must not think that the man who is to be happy will need many things or great things, merely because he cannot be supremely happy without external goods; for self-sufficiency and action do not involve excess, and we can do noble acts without ruling earth and sea; for even with moderate advantages one can act virtuously (this is manifest enough; for private persons are thought to do worthy acts no less than despots—indeed even more); and it is enough that we should have so much as that; for the life of the man who is active in accordance with virtue will be happy. . . .

Review Questions

1. What is happiness, according to Aristotle? How is it related to virtue? How is it related to pleasure?
2. How does Aristotle explain moral virtue? Give some examples.
3. Is it possible for everyone in our society to be happy, as Aristotle explains it? If not, who cannot be happy?

Discussion Questions

1. Aristotle characterizes a life of pleasure as suitable for beasts. But what, if anything, is wrong with a life of pleasure?
2. Aristotle claims that the philosopher will be happier than anyone else. Why is this? Do you agree or not?

A Theory of Justice

JOHN RAWLS

John Rawls (1921–2002) was the James Bryant Conant University Professor Emeritus at Harvard University. He was the author of *Political Liberalism* (1993), *Collected Papers* (1999), *Lectures on the History of Moral Philosophy* (2000), *Justice As Fairness: A Restatement* (2001) and *The Law of Peoples* (2001). Our reading is taken from his well-known book, *A Theory of Justice* (1971).

Rawls's theory states that there are two principles of justice: The first principle involves equal basic liberties, and the second principle concerns the arrangement of social and economic inequalities. According to Rawls's theory, these are the principles that free and rational persons would accept in a hypothetical original position where there is a veil of ignorance hiding from the contractors all the particular facts about themselves.

THE MAIN IDEA
OF THE THEORY OF JUSTICE

MY AIM IS TO PRESENT a conception of justice which generalizes and carries to a higher level of abstraction the familiar theory of the social contract as found, say, in Locke, Rousseau, and Kant.[1] In order to do this we are not to think of the original contract as one to enter a particular society or to set up a particular form of government. Rather, the guiding idea is that the principles of justice for the basic structure of society are the object of the original agreement. They are the principles that free and rational persons concerned to further their own interests would accept in an initial position of equality as defining the fundamental terms of their association. These principles are to regulate all further agreements; they specify the kinds of social cooperation that can be entered into and the forms of government that can be established. This way of regarding the principles of justice I shall call justice as fairness.

Thus we are to imagine that those who engage in social cooperation choose together, in one joint act, the principles which are to assign basic rights and duties and to determine the division of social benefits. Men are to decide in advance how they are to regulate their claims against one another and what is to be the foundation charter of their society. Just as each person must decide by rational reflection what constitutes his good, that is, the system of ends which it is rational for him to pursue, so a group of persons must decide once and for all what is to count among them as just and unjust. The choice which rational men would make in this hypothetical

---

Source: Reprinted by permission of the publisher from *A Theory of Justice* by John Rawls, pp. 11–16, 60–65 Cambridge, Mass.: The Belknap Press of Harvard University Press. Copyright © 1971, 1999 by the President and Fellows of Harvard College. Footnotes renumbered.

1 As the text suggests, I shall regard Locke's *Second Treatise of Government*, Rousseau's *The Social Contract*, and Kant's ethical works beginning with *The Foundations of the Metaphysics of Morals* as definitive of the contract tradition. For all of its greatness, Hobbe's *Leviathan* raises special problems. A general historical survey is provided by J. W. Gough, *The Social Contract*, 2nd ed. (Oxford, The Clarendon Press, 1957), and Otto Gierke, *Natural Law and the Theory of Society*, trans. with an introduction by Ernest Barker (Cambridge, The University Press, 1934). A presentation of the contract view as primarily an ethical theory is to be found in G. R. Grice, *The Grounds of Moral Judgment* (Cambridge, The University Press, 1967).

situation of equal liberty, assuming for the present that this choice problem has a solution, determines the principles of justice.

In justice as fairness the original position of equality corresponds to the state of nature in the traditional theory of the social contract. This original position is not, of course, thought of as an actual historical state of affairs, much less as a primitive condition of culture. It is understood as a purely hypothetical situation characterized so as to lead to a certain conception of justice.[2] Among the essential features of this situation is that no one knows his place in society, his class position or social status, nor does any one know his fortune in the distribution of natural assets and abilities, his intelligence, strength, and the like. I shall even assume that the parties do not know their conceptions of the good or their special psychological propensities. The principles of justice are chosen behind a veil of ignorance. This ensures that no one is advantaged or disadvantaged in the choice of principles by the outcome of natural chance or the contingency of social circumstances. Since all are similarly situated and no one is able to design principles to favor his particular condition, the principles of justice are the result of a fair agreement or bargain. For given the circumstances of the original position, the symmetry of everyone's relations to each other, this initial situation is fair between individuals as moral persons, that is, as rational beings with their own ends and capable, I shall assume, of a sense of justice. The original position is, one might say, the appropriate initial status quo, and thus the fundamental agreements

reached in it are fair. This explains the propriety of the name "justice as fairness": it conveys the idea that the principles of justice are agreed to in an initial situation that is fair. The name does not mean that the concepts of justice and fairness are the same, any more than the phrase "poetry as metaphor" means that the concepts of poetry and metaphor are the same.

Justice as fairness begins, as I have said, with one of the most general of all choices which persons might make together, namely, with the choice of the first principles of a conception of justice which is to regulate all subsequent criticism and reform of institutions. Then, having chosen a conception of justice, we can suppose that they are to choose a constitution and a legislature to enact laws, and so on, all in accordance with the principles of justice initially agreed upon. Our social situation is just if it is such that by this sequence of hypothetical agreements we would have contracted into the general system of rules which defines it. Moreover, assuming that the original position does determine a set of principles (that is, that a particular conception of justice would be chosen), it will then be true that whenever social institutions satisfy these principles those engaged in them can say to one another that they are cooperating on terms to which they would agree if they were free and equal persons whose relations with respect to one another were fair. They could all view their arrangements as meeting the stipulations which they would acknowledge in an initial situation that embodies widely accepted and reasonable constraints on the choice of principles. The general recognition of this fact would provide the basis for a public acceptance of the corresponding principles of justice. No society can, of course, be a scheme of cooperation which men enter voluntarily in a literal sense; each person finds himself placed at birth in some particular position in some particular society, and the nature of this position materially affects his life prospects. Yet a society satisfying the principles of justice as fairness comes as close as a society can to being a voluntary scheme,

---

2 Kant is clear that the original agreement is hypothetical. See *The Metaphysics of Morals,* pt. I (*Rechtslehre*), especially §47, 52; and pt. II of the essay "Concerning the Common Saying: This May Be True in Theory but It Does Not Apply in Practice," in *Kant's Political Writings,* ed. Hans Reiss and trans. by H. B. Nisbet (Cambridge, The University Press, 1970), pp. 73–87. See Georges Vlachos, *La Pensée politique de Kant* (Paris, Presses Universitaires de France, 1962), pp. 326–335; and J. G. Murphy, *Kant: The Philosophy of Right* (London, Macmillan, 1970), pp. 109–112, 133–136, for a further discussion.

for it meets the principles which free and equal persons would assent to under circumstances that are fair. In this sense its members are autonomous and the obligations they recognize self-imposed.

One feature of justice as fairness is to think of the parties in the initial situation as rational and mutually disinterested. This does not mean that the parties are egoists, that is, individuals with only certain kinds of interests, say in wealth, prestige, and domination. But they are conceived as not taking an interest in one another's interests. They are to presume that even their spiritual aims may be opposed, in the way that the aims of those of different religions may be opposed. Moreover, the concept of rationality must be interpreted as far as possible in the narrow sense, standard in economic theory, of taking the most effective means to given ends. I shall modify this concept to some extent . . . but one must try to avoid introducing into it any controversial ethical elements. The initial situation must be characterized by stipulations that are widely accepted.

In working out the conception of justice as fairness one main task clearly is to determine which principles of justice would be chosen in the original position. To do this we must describe this situation in some detail and formulate with care the problem of choice which it presents. . . . It may be observed, however, that once the principles of justice are thought of as arising from an original agreement in a situation of equality, it is an open question whether the principle of utility would be acknowledged. Offhand it hardly seems likely that persons who view themselves as equals, entitled to press their claims upon one another, would agree to a principle which may require lesser life prospects for some simply for the sake of a greater sum of advantages enjoyed by others. Since each desires to protect his interests, his capacity to advance his conception of the good, no one has a reason to acquiesce in an enduring loss for himself in order to bring about a greater net balance of satisfaction. In the absence of strong and lasting benevolent impulses, a rational man would not accept a basic structure merely because it maximized the algebraic sum of advantages irrespective of its permanent effects on his own basic rights and interests. Thus it seems that the principle of utility is incompatible with the conception of social cooperation among equals for mutual advantage. It appears to be inconsistent with the idea of reciprocity implicit in the notion of a well-ordered society. Or, at any rate, so I shall argue.

I shall maintain instead that the persons in the initial situation would choose two rather different principles: the first requires equality in the assignment of basic rights and duties, while the second holds that social and economic inequalities, for example inequalities of wealth and authority, are just only if they result in compensating benefits for everyone, and in particular for the least advantaged members of society. These principles rule out justifying institutions on the grounds that the hardships of some are offset by a greater good in the aggregate. It may be expedient but it is not just that some should have less in order that others may prosper. But there is no injustice in the greater benefits earned by a few provided that the situation of persons not so fortunate is thereby improved. The intuitive idea is that since everyone's well-being depends upon a scheme of cooperation without which no one could have a satisfactory life, the division of advantages should be such as to draw forth the willing cooperation of everyone taking part in it, including those less well situated. Yet this can be expected only if reasonable terms are proposed. The two principles mentioned seem to be a fair agreement on the basis of which those better endowed, or more fortunate in their social position, neither of which we can be said to deserve, could expect the willing cooperation of others when some workable scheme is a necessary condition of the welfare of all.[3] Once we decide to look for a conception of justice that nullifies the accidents

3 For the formulation of this intuitive idea I am indebted to Allan Gibbard.

of natural endowment and the contingencies of social circumstance as counters in quest for political and economic advantage, we are led to these principles. They express the result of leaving aside those aspects of the social world that seem arbitrary from a moral point of view.

The problem of the choice of principles, however, is extremely difficult. I do not expect the answer I shall suggest to be convincing to everyone. It is, therefore, worth noting from the outset that justice as fairness, like other contract views, consists of two parts: (1) an interpretation of the initial situation and of the problem of choice posed there, and (2) a set of principles which, it is argued, would be agreed to. One may accept the first part of the theory (or some variant thereof), but not the other, and conversely. The concept of the initial contractual situation may seem reasonable although the particular principles proposed are rejected. To be sure, I want to maintain that the most appropriate conception of this situation does lead to principles of justice contrary to utilitarianism and perfectionism, and therefore that the contract doctrine provides an alternative to these views. . . .

A final remark. Justice as fairness is not a complete contract theory. For it is clear that the contract idea can be extended to the choice of more or less an entire ethical system, that is, to a system including principles for all the virtues and not only for justice. Now for the most part I shall consider only principles of justice and others closely related to them; I make no attempt to discuss the virtues in a systematic way. Obviously if justice as fairness succeeds reasonably well, a next step would be to study the more general view suggested by the name "rightness as fairness." But even this wider theory fails to embrace all moral relationships, since it would seem to include only our relations with other persons and to leave out of account how we are to conduct ourselves toward animals and the rest of nature. I do not contend that the contract notion offers a way to approach these questions which are certainly of the first importance;

and I shall have to put them aside. We must recognize the limited scope of justice as fairness and of the general type of view that it exemplifies. How far its conclusions must be revised once these other matters are understood cannot be decided in advance. . . .

TWO PRINCIPLES OF JUSTICE

I shall now state in a provisional form the two principles of justice that I believe would be chosen in the original position. In this section I wish to make only the most general comments, and therefore the first formulation of these principles is tentative. As we go on I shall run through several formulations and approximate step by step the final statement to be given much later. I believe that doing this allows the exposition to proceed in a natural way.

The first statement of the two principles reads as follows.

> First: Each person is to have an equal right to the most extensive basic liberty compatible with a similar liberty for others.
>
> Second: Social and economic inequalities are to be arranged so that they are both (a) reasonably expected to be to everyone's advantage, and (b) attached to positions and offices open to all. . . .

By way of general comment, these principles primarily apply, as I have said, to the basic structure of society. They are to govern the assignment of rights and duties and to regulate the distribution of social and economic advantages. As their formulation suggests, these principles presuppose that the social structure can be divided into two more or less distinct parts, the first principle applying to the one, the second to the other. They distinguish between those aspects of the social system that define and secure the equal liberties of citizenship and those that specify and establish social and economic inequalities. The basic liberties of citizens are, roughly speaking, political liberty (the right to vote and to be eligible for public office) together with freedom of speech and assembly; liberty of conscience and freedom of thought; freedom of the person along with the right to hold (personal) property; and freedom from arbitrary arrest and seizure as defined by the concept of the rule of law. These liberties are all required to be equal by the first principle, since citizens of a just society are to have the same basic rights.

The second principle applies, in the first approximation, to the distribution of income and wealth and to the design of organizations that make use of differences in authority and responsibility, or chains of command. While the distribution of wealth and income need not be equal, it must be to everyone's advantage, and at the same time, positions of authority and offices of command must be accessible to all. One applies the second principle by holding positions open, and then, subject to this constraint, arranges social and economic inequalities so that everyone benefits.

These principles are to be arranged in a serial order with the first principle prior to the second. This ordering means that a departure from the institutions of equal liberty required by the first principle cannot be justified by, or compensated for, by greater social and economic advantages. The distribution of wealth and income, and the hierarchies of authority, must be consistent with both the liberties of equal citizenship and equality of opportunity.

It is clear that these principles are rather specific in their content, and their acceptance rests on certain assumptions that I must eventually try to explain and justify. A theory of justice depends upon a theory of society in ways that will become evident as we proceed. For the present, it should be observed that the two principles (and this holds for all formulations) are a special case of a more general conception of justice that can be expressed as follows.

> All social values—liberty and opportunity, income and wealth, and the bases of self-respect—are to be distributed equally unless an unequal distribution of any, or all, of these values is to everyone's advantage.

Injustice, then, is simply inequalities that are not to the benefit of all. Of course, this conception is extremely vague and requires interpretation.

As a first step, suppose that the basic structure of society distributes certain primary goods, that is, things that every rational man is presumed to want. These goods normally have a use whatever a person's rational plan of life. For simplicity, assume that the chief primary goods at the disposition of society are rights and liberties, powers and opportunities, income and wealth. . . . These are the social primary goods. Other primary goods such as health and vigor, intelligence and imagination, are natural goods; although their possession is influenced by the basic structure, they are not so directly under its control. Imagine, then, a hypothetical initial arrangement in which all the social primary goods are equally distributed: everyone has similar rights and duties, and income and wealth are evenly shared. This state of affairs provides a benchmark for judging improvements. If certain inequalities of wealth and organizational powers would make everyone better off than in this hypothetical starting situation, then they accord with the general conception.

Now it is possible, at least theoretically, that by giving up some of their fundamental liberties men are sufficiently compensated by the resulting social and economic gains. The general conception of justice imposes no restrictions on what sort of inequalities are permissible; it only requires that everyone's position be improved. We need not suppose anything so drastic as consenting to a condition of slavery. Imagine instead that men forego certain political rights when the economic returns are significant and their capacity to influence the course of policy by the exercise of these rights would be marginal in any case. It is this kind of exchange which the two principles as stated rule out; being arranged in serial order they do not permit exchanges between basic liberties and economic and social gains. The serial ordering of principles expresses an underlying preference among primary social goods. When this preference is rational so likewise is the choice of these principles in this order.

In developing justice as fairness I shall, for the most part, leave aside the general conception of justice and examine instead the special case of the two principles in serial order. The advantage of this procedure is that from the first the matter of priorities is recognized and an effort made to find principles to deal with it. One is led to attend throughout to the conditions under which the acknowledgment of the absolute weight of liberty with respect to social and economic advantages, as defined by the lexical order of the two principles, would be reasonable. Offhand, this ranking appears extreme and too special a case to be of much interest; but there is more justification for it than would appear at first sight. Or at any rate, so I shall maintain. . . . Furthermore, the distinction between fundamental rights and liberties and economic and social benefits marks a difference among primary social goods that one should try to exploit. It suggests an important division in the social system. Of course, the distinctions drawn and the ordering proposed are bound to be at best only approximations. There are surely circumstances in which they fail. But it is essential to depict clearly the main lines of a reasonable conception of justice; and under many conditions anyway, the two principles in serial order may serve well enough. When necessary we can fall back on the more general conception.

The fact that the two principles apply to institutions has certain consequences. Several points illustrate this. First of all, the rights and liberties referred to by these principles are those which are defined by the public rules of the basic structure. Whether men are free is determined by the rights and duties established by the major institutions of society. Liberty is a certain pattern of social forms. The first principle simply requires that certain sorts of rules, those defining basic liberties, apply to everyone equally and that they allow the most extensive liberty compatible with a like liberty for all. The only reason for circumscribing the rights defining liberty and making men's freedom less extensive than it might otherwise be is that these equal rights as institutionally defined would interfere with one another.

Another thing to bear in mind is that when principles mention persons, or require that everyone gain from an inequality, the reference is to representative persons holding the various social positions, or offices, or whatever, established by the basic structure. Thus in applying the second principle I assume that it is possible to assign an expectation of well-being to representative individuals holding these positions. This expectation indicates their life prospects as viewed from their social station. In general, the expectations of representative persons depend upon the distribution of rights and duties throughout the basic structure. When this changes, expectations change. I assume, then, that expectations are connected: by raising the prospects of the representative man in one position we presumably increase or decrease the prospects of representative men in other positions. Since it applies to institutional forms, the second principle (or rather the first part of it) refers to the expectations of representative individuals. As I shall discuss below, neither principle applies to distributions of particular goods to particular individuals who may be identified by their proper names. The situation where someone is considering how to allocate certain commodities to needy persons who are known to him is not within the scope of the principles. They are meant to regulate basic institutional arrangements. We must not assume that there is much similarity from the standpoint of justice between an administrative allotment of goods to specific persons and the appropriate design of society. Our common sense institutions for the former may be a poor guide to the latter.

Now the second principle insists that each person benefit from permissible inequalities in the basic structure. This means that it must be reasonable for each relevant representative man defined by this structure, when he views it as a going concern, to prefer his prospects with the inequality to his prospects without it. One is not allowed to justify differences in income or organizational powers on the ground that the disadvantages of those in one position are outweighed by the greater advantages of those in another. Much less can infringements of liberty be counterbalanced in this way. Applied to the basic structure, the principle of utility would have us maximize the sum of expectations of representative men (weighed by the number of persons they represent, on the classical view); and this would permit us to compensate for the losses of some by the gains of others. Instead, the two principles require that everyone benefit from economic and social inequalities. It is obvious, however, that there are indefinitely many ways in which all may be advantaged when the initial arrangement of equality is taken as a benchmark. How then are we to choose among these possibilities? The principles must be specified so that they yield a determinate conclusion. I now turn to this problem. . . .

Review Questions

1. Carefully explain Rawls's conception of the original position.
2. State and explain Rawls's first principle of justice.
3. State and explain the second principle. Which principle has priority such that it cannot be sacrificed?

Discussion Questions

1. On the first principle, each person has an equal right to the most extensive basic liberty as long as this does not interfere with a similar liberty for others. What does this allow people to do? Does it mean, for example, that people have a right to engage in homosexual activities as long as they don't interfere with others? Can people produce and view pornography if it does not restrict anyone's freedom? Are people allowed to take drugs in the privacy of their homes?
2. Is it possible for free and rational persons in the original position to agree upon different principles than those given by Rawls? For example, why wouldn't they agree to an equal distribution of wealth and income rather than an unequal distribution? That is, why wouldn't they adopt socialism rather than capitalism? Isn't socialism just as rational as capitalism?

The Idea of a Female Ethic

JEAN GRIMSHAW

Jean Grimshaw teaches in the Department of Humanities, Bristol Polytechnic. She is the author of *Feminist Philosophers: Women's Perspectives on Philosophical Traditions* (1986), and *Philosophy and Feminist Thinking* (1996).

Source: Grimshaw, Jean, "The Idea of a Female Ethic," from *A Companion to Ethics,* ed. Peter Singer (Blackwell, 1991), pp. 491–499. Reprinted by permission of Blackwell Publishers, Inc.

Grimshaw explains the development of the idea of a female ethic, beginning in the eighteenth century. According to Rousseau, for example, women can be virtuous only as wives and mothers. This view was attacked by Mary Wollstonecraft, who argued that virtue should be the same for men and women. Nevertheless, contemporary feminist thought has remained attracted to the idea that there are specific female virtues, and even that women are morally superior to men. For example, Mary Daly claims that women are less aggressive and more cooperative than men. Carol Gilligan argues that women reason differently than men about moral issues. Sara Ruddick bases female virtue on mothering. Nel Noddings argues that morality should be centered on caring, not abstract rules. Grimshaw concludes with a discussion and critique of the distinction between a public sphere of war and politics dominated by men and a private sphere of home and family occupied by women.

QUESTIONS ABOUT GENDER have scarcely been central to mainstream moral philosophy this century. But the idea that virtue is in some way *gendered,* that the standards and criteria of morality are different for women and men, is one that has been central to the ethical thinking of a great many philosophers. It is to the eighteenth century that we can trace the beginnings of those ideas of a 'female ethic,' of 'feminine' nature and specifically female forms of virtue, which have formed the essential background to a great deal of feminist thinking about ethics. The eighteenth century, in industrializing societies, saw the emergence of the concern about questions of femininity and female consciousness that was importantly related to changes in the social situation of women. Increasingly, for middle class women, the home was no longer also the workplace. The only route to security (of a sort) for a woman was a marriage in which she was wholly economically dependent, and for the unmarried woman, the prospects were bleak indeed. At the same time, however, as women were becoming increasingly dependent on men in practical and material terms, the eighteenth century saw the beginnings of an idealization of family life and the married state that remained influential throughout the nineteenth century. A sentimental vision of the subordinate but virtuous and idealized wife and mother, whose specifically female virtues both defined and underpinned the 'private' sphere of domestic life, came to dominate

a great deal of eighteenth and nineteenth-century thought.

The idea that virtue is gendered is central, for example, to the philosophy of Rousseau. In *Emile,* Rousseau argued that those characteristics which would be faults in men are virtues in women. Rousseau's account of female virtues is closely related to his idealized vision of the rural family and simplicity of life which alone could counteract the evil manners of the city, and it is only, he thought, as wives and mothers that women can become virtuous. But their virtue is also premised on their dependence and subordination within marriage; for a woman to be independent, according to Rousseau, or for her to pursue goals whose aim was not the welfare of her family, was for her to lose those qualities which would make her estimable and desirable.

It was above all Rousseau's notion of virtue as 'gendered' that Mary Wollstonecraft attacked in her *Vindication of the Rights of Woman.* Virtue, she argued, should mean the same thing for a woman as for a man, and she was a bitter critic of the forms of 'femininity' to which women were required to aspire, and which, she thought, undermined their strength and dignity as human beings. Since the time of Wollstonecraft, there has always been an important strand in feminist thinking which has viewed with great suspicion, or rejected entirely, the idea that there are specifically female virtues. There are very good reasons for this suspicion. The idealization of female virtue, which perhaps reached its apogee in the effusions of many nineteenth-century male Victorian writers such as Ruskin, has usually been premised on female subordination. The 'virtues' to which it was thought that women should aspire often reflect this subordination—a classic example is the 'virtue' of selflessness, which was stressed by a great number of Victorian writers.

Despite this well-founded ambivalence about the idea of 'female virtue,' however, many women in the nineteenth century, including a large number who were concerned with the question of women's emancipation, remained attracted to the idea, not merely that there were specifically female virtues, but sometimes that women were morally superior to men, and to the belief that society could be morally transformed through the influence of women. What many women envisaged was, as it were, an *extension* throughout society of the 'female values' of the private sphere of home and family. But, unlike many male writers, they used the idea of female virtue as a reason for women's entry into the 'public' sphere rather than as a reason for their being restricted to the 'private' one. And in a context where any sort of female independence was so immensely difficult to achieve, it is easy to see the attraction of any view which sought to re-evaluate and affirm those strengths and virtues conventionally seen as 'feminine.'

The context of contemporary feminist thought is of course very different. Most of the formal barriers to the entry of women into spheres other than the domestic have been removed, and a constant theme of feminist writing in the last twenty years has been a critique of women's restriction to the domestic role or the 'private' sphere. Despite this, however, the idea of 'a female ethic' has remained very important within feminist thinking. A number of concerns underlie the continued interest within feminism in the idea of a 'female ethic.' Perhaps most important is concern about the violent and destructive consequences to human life and to the planet of those fields of activity which have been largely male-dominated, such as war, politics, and capitalist economic domination. The view that the frequently destructive nature of these things is at least in part *due* to the fact that they are male-dominated is not of course new; it was common enough in many arguments for female suffrage at the beginning of the twentieth century. In some contemporary feminist thinking this has been linked to a view that many forms of aggression and destruction are closely linked to the nature of 'masculinity' and the male psyche.

Such beliefs about the nature of masculinity and about the destructive nature of male spheres of activity are sometimes linked to 'essentialist' beliefs about male and female nature. Thus, for example, in the very influential work of Mary Daly, all the havoc wreaked on human life and the planet tends to be seen as an undifferentiated result of the unchanging nature of the male psyche, and of the ways in which women themselves have been 'colonized' by male domination and brutality. And contrasted with this havoc, in Daly's work, is a vision of an uncorrupted female psyche which might rise like a phoenix from the ashes of male-dominated culture and save the world. Not all versions of essentialism are quite as extreme or vivid as that of Daly; but it is not uncommon (among some supporters of the peace movement for example) to find the belief that women are 'naturally' less aggressive, more gentle and nurturing, more cooperative, than men.

Such essentialist views of male and female nature are of course a problem if one believes that the 'nature' of men and women is not something that is monolithic or unchanging, but is, rather, socially and historically constructed. And a great deal of feminist thinking has rejected any form of essentialism. But if one rejects the idea that any differences between male and female values and priorities can be ascribed to a fundamental male and female 'nature,' the question then arises as to whether the idea of a 'female ethic' can be spelled out in a way that avoids essentialist assumptions. The attempt to do this is related to a second major concern of feminist thinking. This concern can be explained as follows. Women themselves have constantly tended to be devalued or inferiorized (frequently at the same time as being idealized). But this devaluation has not simply been of women themselves—their nature, abilities and characteristics. The 'spheres' of activity with which they have particularly been associated have also been devalued. Again, paradoxically, they have also been idealized. Thus home, family, the domestic virtues, and women's role in the physical and emotional care of others have constantly been praised to the skies and seen as the bedrock of social life. At the same time, these things are commonly seen as a mere 'backdrop' to the more 'important' spheres of male activity, to which no self-respecting man could allow himself to be restricted; and as generating values which must always take second place if they conflict with values or priorities from elsewhere.

The second sort of approach to the idea of a 'female ethic' results, then, both from a critique of essentialism, and from an attempt to see whether an alternative approach to questions about moral reasoning and ethical priorities can be derived from a consideration of those spheres of life and activity which have been regarded as paradigmatically female. Two things, in particular, have been suggested. The first is that there *are* in fact common or typical differences in the ways in which women and men think or reason about moral issues. This view of course, is not new. It has normally been expressed, however, in terms of a *deficiency* on the part of women; women are incapable of reason, of acting on principles; they are emotional, intuitive, too personal, and so forth. Perhaps, however, we might recognize *difference* without ascribing *deficiency;* and maybe a consideration of female moral reasoning can highlight the problems in the male forms of reasoning which have been seen as the norm?

The second important suggestion can be summarized as follows. It starts from the assumption that specific social practices generate their own vision of what is 'good' or what is to be especially valued, their own concerns and priorities, and their own criteria for what is to be seen as a

'virtue.' Perhaps, then, the social practices, especially those of mothering and caring for others, which have traditionally been regarded as female, can be seen as generating ethical priorities and conceptions of 'virtue' which should not only not be devalued but which can also provide a corrective to the more destructive values and priorities of those spheres of activity which have been dominated by men.

In her influential book *In A Different Voice: Psychological Theory and Women's Development* (1982) Carol Gilligan argued that those who have suggested that women typically reason differently from men about moral issues are right; what is wrong is their assumption of the inferiority or deficiency of female moral reasoning. The starting point for Gilligan's work was an examination of the work of Lawrence Kohlberg on moral development in children. Kohlberg attempted to identify 'stages' in moral development, which could be analysed by a consideration of the responses children gave to questions about how they would resolve a moral dilemma. The 'highest' stage, the stage at which, in fact, Kohlberg wanted to say that a specifically *moral* framework of reasoning was being used, was that at which moral dilemmas were resolved by an appeal to rules and principles, a logical decision about priorities, in the light of the prior acceptance of such rules or principles.

A much quoted example of Kohlberg's method, discussed in detail by Gilligan, is the case of two eleven-year-old children, 'Jake' and 'Amy.' Jake and Amy were asked to respond to the following dilemma; a man called Heinz has a wife who is dying, but he cannot afford the drug she needs. Should he steal the drug in order to save his wife's life? Jake is clear that Heinz *should* steal the drug; and his answer revolves around a resolution of the rules governing life and property. Amy, however, responded very differently. She suggested that Heinz should go and talk to the druggist and see if they could not find some solution to the problem. Whereas Jake sees the situation as needing mediation through systems of logic or law, Amy, Gilligan suggests, sees a need for mediation through communication in relationships.

It is clear that Kohlberg's understanding of morality is based on the tradition that derives from Kant and moves through the work of such contemporary philosophers as John Rawls and R. M. Hare. The emphasis in this tradition is indeed on rules and principles, and Gilligan is by no means the only critic to suggest that any such understanding of morality will be bound to misrepresent women's moral reasoning and set up a typically male pattern of moral reasoning as a standard against which to judge women to be deficient. Nel Noddings, for example, in her book *Caring: A Feminine Approach to Ethics and Moral Education* (1984), argues that a morality based on rules or principles is in itself inadequate, and that it does not capture what is distinctive or typical about female moral thinking. She points out how, in a great deal of moral philosophy, it has been supposed that the moral task is, as it were, to abstract the 'local detail' from a situation and see it as falling under a rule or principle. Beyond that, it is a question of deciding or choosing, in a case of conflict, how to order or rank one's principles in a hierarchy. And to rank as a *moral* one, a principle must be universalizable; that is to say, of the form 'Whenever X, then do Y'. Noddings argues that the posing of moral dilemmas in such a way misrepresents the nature of moral decision making. Posing moral issues in the 'desert-island dilemma' form, in which only the 'bare bones' of a situation are described, usually serves to conceal rather than to reveal the sorts of questions to which only situational and contextual knowledge can provide an answer, and which are essential to moral judgement in the specific context.

But Noddings wants to argue, like Gilligan, not merely that this sort of account of morality is inadequate in general, but that women are less likely than men even to attempt to justify their moral decisions in this sort of way. Both of them argue that women do not tend to appeal to rules and principles in the same sort of way as men; that they are more likely to appeal to concrete and detailed knowledge of the situation, and to consider the dilemma in terms of the relationships involved.

Gilligan and Noddings suggest, therefore, that there are, as a matter of fact, differences in the ways in which women and men reason about moral issues. But such views of difference always pose great difficulties. The nature of the evidence involved is inevitably problematic; it would not be difficult to find two eleven-year-old children who reacted quite differently to Heinz's dilemma; and appeals to 'common experience' of how women and men reason about moral issues can always be challenged by pointing to exceptions or by appealing to different experience.

The question, however, is not just one of empirical difficulty. Even if there *were* some common or typical differences between women and men, there is always a problem about how such differences are to be described. For one thing, it is questionable whether the sort of description of moral decision making given by Kohlberg and others really does adequately represent its nature. Furthermore, the view that women do not act on principle, that they are intuitive and more influenced by 'personal' considerations, has so often been used in contexts where women have been seen as deficient that it is as well to be suspicious of any distinction between women and men which seems to depend on this difference. It might, for example, be the case, not so much that women and men *reason differently* about moral issues, but that their ethical priorities differ, as that what is regarded as an important principle by women (such as maintaining relationships) is commonly seen by men as a *failure* of principle.

At best then, I think that the view that women 'reason differently' over moral issues is difficult to spell out clearly or substantiate; at worst, it runs the risk of recapitulating old and oppressive dichotomies. But perhaps there is some truth in the view that women's ethical *priorities* may commonly differ from those of men? Again, it is not easy to see how this could be very clearly established, or what sort of evidence would settle the question; but if it is correct to argue that ethical priorities will emerge from life experiences and from the ways these are socially articulated, then maybe one might assume that, given that the life experiences of women are commonly very different from those of men, their ethical priorities will differ too? Given, for instance, the experience of women in pregnancy, childbirth and the rearing of children, might there be, for example, some difference in the way they will view the 'waste' of those lives in war. (This is not an idea that is unique to contemporary feminism; it was, for example, suggested by Olive Schreiner in her book *Woman and Labour*, which was published in 1911.)

There have been a number of attempts in recent feminist philosophy to suggest that the practices in which women engage, in particular the practices of childcare and the physical and emotional maintenance of other human beings, might be seen as generating social priorities and conceptions of virtue which are different from those which inform other aspects of social life. Sara Ruddick, for example, in an article entitled 'Maternal thinking' (1980) argues that the task of mothering generates a conception of virtue which might provide a resource for a critique of those values and priorities which underpin much contemporary social life—including those of militarism. Ruddick does not want to argue that women can simply enter the public realm 'as mothers' (as some suffragist arguments earlier in the twentieth century suggested) and transform it. She argues, nevertheless, that women's experience as mothers is central to their ethical life, and to the ways in which they might articulate a critique of dominant values and social mores. Rather similarly, Caroline Whitbeck has argued that the practices of caring for others, which have motherhood at their centre, provide an ethical model of the 'mutual realization of people' which is very different from the competitive and individualistic norms of much social life (Whitbeck, 1983).

There are, however, great problems in the idea that female practices can generate an autonomous

or coherent set of 'alternative' values. Female practices are always socially situated and inflected by things such as class, race, material poverty or well-being, which have divided women and which they do not all share. Furthermore, practices such as childbirth and the education and rearing of children have been the focus of constant ideological concern and struggle; they have not just been developed by, women in isolation from other aspects of the culture. The history of childcare in the 20th century, for example, has constantly been shaped by the (frequently contradictory) interventions both of 'experts' in childcare (who have often been male) and by the state. Norms of motherhood have also been used in ways that have reinforced classist and racist assumptions about the 'pathology' of working-class or black families. They have been used, too, by women themselves, in the service of such things as devotion to Hitler's 'Fatherland' or the bitter opposition to feminism and equal rights in the USA. For all these reasons, if there is any usefulness at all in the idea of a 'female ethic,' I do not think it can consist in appealing to a supposedly autonomous realm of female values which can provide a simple corrective or alternative to the values of male-dominated spheres of activity.

Nevertheless, it is true that a great deal of the political theory and philosophy of the last two hundred years *has* operated with a distinction between the 'public' and 'private' spheres, and that the 'private' sphere has been seen as the sphere of women. But that which is opposed to the 'world' of the home, of domestic virtue and female self-sacrifice, is not just the 'world' of war, or even of politics, it is also that of the 'market.' The concept of 'the market' defines a realm of 'public' existence which is contrasted with a private realm of domesticity and personal relations. The structure of individuality presupposed by the concept of the market is one which requires an instrumental rationality directed towards the abstract goal of production and profit, and a pervasive self-interest. The concept of 'the market' precludes altruistic behaviour, or the taking of the well-being of another as the goal of one's activity.

The morality which might seem most appropriate to the marketplace is that of utilitarianism, which, in its classic forms, proposed a conception of happiness as distinct from the various activities which lead to this, of instrumental reason, and of an abstract individuality, as in the 'felicific calculus' of Bentham, for example, whereby all subjects of pain or happiness are to be counted as equal and treated impersonally. But, as Ross Poole has argued, in 'Morality, masculinity and the market' (1985), utilitarianism was not really able to provide an adequate morality, mainly because it could never provide convincing reasons why individuals should submit to a duty or obligation that was not in their interests in the short term. It is Kantianism, he suggests, that provides a morality that is more adequate to the market. Others have to figure in one's scheme of things not just as means to an end, but as agents, and the 'individual' required by the market must be assumed to be equipped with a form of rationality that is not purely instrumental, and to be prepared to adhere to obligations and constraints that are experienced as duty rather than inclination. The sphere of the market, however, is contrasted with the 'private' sphere of domestic and familial relations. Although of course men participate in this private sphere, it is the sphere in which female identity is found, and this identity is constructed out of care and nurturance and service for others. Since these others are known and particular, the 'morality' of this sphere cannot be universal or impersonal; it is always 'infected' by excess, partiality and particularity.

The first important thing to note about this contrast between the public sphere of the market and the private sphere of domestic relations is that it does not, and never has, corresponded in any simple way to reality. Thus working-class women have worked outside the home since the earliest days of the Industrial Revolution, and the exclusive association of women with the domestic and private sphere has all but disappeared. Secondly, it is important to note that the moral-

ity of the marketplace and of the private sphere exist in a state of tension with each other. The marketplace could not exist without a sphere of domestic and familial relations which 'supported' its own activities; yet the goals of the marketplace may on occasion be incompatible with the demands of the private sphere. The 'proper' complementarity between them can only exist if the private sphere is subordinate to the public sphere, and that subordinacy has often been expressed by the dominance of men in the household as well as in public life. The practical subordinacy of the private sphere is mirrored by the ways in which, in much moral and political philosophy and social thought, the immediate and personal morality of the private sphere is seen as 'inferior' to that which governs the exigencies of public life.

Furthermore, although, ideologically, the public and private spheres are seen as separate and distinct, in practice the private sphere is often governed by constraints and requirements deriving from the public sphere. A clear example of this is the ways in which views on how to bring up children and on what the task of motherhood entailed have so often been derived from broader social imperatives, such as the need to create a 'fit' race for the task of ruling an empire, or the need to create a disciplined and docile industrial workforce.

The distinction between the public and the private has nevertheless helped to shape reality, and to form the experiences of people's lives. It is still commonly true, for example, that the tasks of the physical and emotional maintenance of other people largely devolve upon women, who often bear this responsibility as well as that of labour outside the home. And the differences between male and female experience which follow from these things allow us to understand both why there may well often be differences between women and men in their perception of moral issues or moral priorities, and why these differences can never be summed up in the form of generalizations about women and men. Women and men commonly participate both in domestic and familial relations and in the world of labour and the marketplace. And the constraints and obligations experienced by individuals in their daily lives may lead to acute tensions and contradictions which may be both practically and morally experienced. (A classic example of this would be the woman who faces an acute conflict between the 'impersonal' demands of her situation at work, as well as her own needs for activity outside the home, and the needs or demands of those such as children or aged parents whose care cannot easily be fitted into the requirements of the workplace.)

If ethical concerns and priorities arise from different forms of social life, then those which have emerged from a social system in which women have so often been subordinate to men must be suspect. Supposedly 'female' values are not only the subject of little agreement among women; they are also deeply mired in conceptions of 'the feminine' which depend on the sort of polarization between 'masculine' and 'feminine' which has itself been so closely related to the subordination of women. There is no autonomous realm of female values, or of female activities which can generate 'alternative' values to those of the public sphere; and any conception of a 'female ethic' which depends on these ideas cannot, I think, be a viable one.

But to say this is not necessarily to say that the lives and experiences of women cannot provide a source for a critique of the male-dominated public sphere. Experiences and perspectives which are articulated by gender cannot be sharply demarcated from those which are also articulated along other dimensions, such as race and class; and there is clearly no consensus among

women as to how a critique of the priorities of the 'public' world might be developed. Nevertheless taking seriously the experiences and perspectives of women—in childbirth and childcare for example—whilst not immediately generating any consensus about how things might be changed, generates crucial forms of questioning of social and moral priorities. It is often remarked, for example, that if men had the same sort of responsibility for children that women have, or if women had the same sorts of power as men to determine such things as priorities in work, or health care, or town planning, or the organization of domestic labour, many aspects of social life might be very different.

We cannot know in advance exactly what sorts of changes in moral and social priorities might result from radical changes in such things as the sexual division of labour or transformed social provision for the care of others; or from the elimination of the many forms of oppression from which women and men alike suffer. No appeal to current forms of social life can provide a blueprint. Nor should women be seen (as they are in some forms of feminist thinking) as 'naturally' likely to espouse different moral or social priorities from men. Insofar as there are (or might be) differences in female ethical concerns, these can only emerge from, and will need to be painfully constructed out of, changes in social relationships and modes of living; and there is every reason to suppose that the process will be conflictual. But there is every reason, too, to suppose that in a world in which the activities and concerns which have traditionally been regarded as primarily female were given equal value and status, moral and social priorities would be very different from those of the world in which we live now.

References

M. Daly, *Gyn/Ecology: The Metaethics of Radical Feminism* (Boston: Beacon Press, 1978).

C. Gilligan, *In a Different Voice: Psychological Theory and Women's Development* (Cambridge, Mass.: Harvard University Press, 1982).

L. Kohlberg, *The Philosophy of Moral Development* (San Francisco: Harper and Row, 1981).

N. Noddings, *Caring: A Feminine Approach to Ethics and Education* (Berkeley: University of California Press, 1978).

R. Poole, 'Morality, masculinity and the market,' *Radical Philosophy,* 39 (1985).

J. J. Rousseau, *Emile* (London: Dent, Everyman's Library, 1974).

S. Ruddick, 'Maternal thinking,' *Feminist Studies,* 6, (Summer 1980).

O. Schreiner, *Woman and Labour* (1911); (London: Virago, 1978).

C. Whitbeck, 'A different reality; feminist ontology,' *Beyond Domination,* ed. C. Gould (Totowa, NJ: Rowman and Allanheld, 1983).

M. Wollstonecraft, *A Vindication of the Rights of Woman* (Harmondsworth: Pelican, 1975).

Review Questions

1. How does Grimshaw explain the development of the idea of a female ethic?
2. According to Grimshaw, what was Rousseau's view of women's virtue? Why did Wollstonecraft attack this view?
3. How does Grimshaw describe contemporary feminist thought? What are its main features?
4. Explain Mary Daly's view. How are men and women different?
5. According to Grimshaw, what is the second major concern of feminist thinking? What are the two suggestions of this concern?
6. Explain Carol Gilligan's work on women's moral reasoning.
7. What is Nel Nodding's view of female moral thinking?
8. Why does Sara Ruddick think that mothering is central to morality?
9. Distinguish between the public and private spheres. Why does Grimshaw attack this distinction?

Discussion Questions

1. Are women morally superior to men? Why or why not?
2. Do men and women have an essential nature? If so, what is it? If not, why not?
3. Do men and women think differently about moral issues? Explain your answer.
4. Is mothering or caring for others an acceptable basis for morality? Why or why not?
5. Is there a clear distinction between the public and private spheres or not? Explain your view.

Problem Cases

1. The Myth of Gyges' Ring

(The myth about Gyges is found in Book II of Plato's *Republic*. The story is told by Glaucon, who is having an argument with Socrates and his companions.) Gyges is a poor shepherd who one day finds a magic ring, a ring that makes the wearer invisible, so that the wearer can go anywhere and do anything undetected. Gyges uses the ring to his advantage. He goes into the royal palace, seduces the queen, murders the king, and seizes the throne. Just how he does all this is not explained; apparently the ring has other powers besides making the wearer invisible.

Now suppose there are two such rings. One is given to a wicked man and another to a virtuous man. No doubt the wicked man will act like Gyges. He will commit crimes to gain wealth and power, and since he cannot be caught and punished, he will do this without being constrained by morality, by considerations of right and wrong. But what will the virtuous man do? Glaucon argues that the virtuous man will behave no better than the wicked man. If he can commit crimes like stealing and killing with no fear of punishment, then why wouldn't he do them? Why should he care about morality? Why should he worry about what is right and wrong?

How would you reply to Glaucon? Why should you care about morality if you can do whatever you want without getting caught and punished? Why be moral?

2. A Lost Wallet

You are taking a walk in Central Park in New York City. It is very early in the morning. Nobody else is around at the moment. Off the path and under a tree you see a black object. You go over and pick it up. It is an expensive-looking wallet. You open it up and find credit cards, a driver's license, and various other cards including a business card with a business address, e-mail address, fax number, and telephone number. Apparently the wallet belongs to a vice president at Merrill Lynch named Parker Borg. There is money, too, lots of one hundred dollar bills. You look around, but there is nobody in sight. You count the money. It adds up to $1500 in cash. You could take the money and leave the wallet where you found it. Maybe Parker Borg will come looking for it. You could call him up and tell him you found his wallet. If he is grateful, maybe he will give you a reward. Or you could just put the wallet back where you found it and forget about it. What would you do? Explain your choice.

3. Lying

Many philosophers have held that lying is morally wrong. Kant thought that lying is "a crime of man against his own person" and should be avoided at all costs. St. Augustine said that when regard for truth has broken down, then everything is open to doubt, and little by little lies grow in size. On the other hand, Nietzsche thought that "lying is a necessity of life" and is "part of the terrifying and problematic character of existence." Goethe asserted that lying is part of human nature; truth is not.

Certainly, lying seems to be very common in our society. As the saying goes, people tell lies in love and war. There are professions that seem to require lying, such as espionage agents and politicians. Or at least these people cannot stay in business very long if they tell the whole truth and nothing but the truth. Consider the list of public figures caught lying in recent years: Representative Gary A. Condit, Democrat of California, lied about his affair with Chandra Ann Levy. President Bill Clinton lied under oath about his relationship with Monica Lewinsky, and then argued that distorting the truth in testimony is not necessarily illegal. Edmund Morris, the author of a so-called biography of President Ronald Reagan, lied about his participation in Reagan's life. The Nobel Prize winner Rigoberta Menchu lied about her life in Guatemala. The historian Joseph J. Ellis lied about his heroic service in Vietnam. Jayson Blair, the New York Times reporter, wrote more than 600 articles with misleading information and false quotes. George W. Bush lied when he said (in his state of the union speech) that Iraq had tried to buy yellowcake uranium from Africa to make nuclear weapons. Dick Cheney lied when he said there was no doubt that Saddam Hussein was building a nuclear device. The list goes on and on with no end in sight. But is lying always wrong? Is it wrong to give people misleading information? Explain your view.

4. The Colt Sporter and Handguns

The Colt Sporter is one of the most popular semiautomatic assault rifles. A semi-automatic weapon fires one bullet with each pull of the trigger, as distinguished from a fully automatic weapon, which fires a stream of bullets with one trigger pull. Fully automatic weapons are banned by the federal government, but semiautomatic weapons are legal in most states. In 1993, a Connecticut law banned thirty kinds of semiautomatic guns, including the Colt Sporter. The Sporter is made by Colt's Manufacturing Company, based in Hartford, Connecticut. Even though it looks just like a Colt-made M16 (a standard military weapon), Colt officials say the Sporter is made for target practice and hunting. Furthermore, the Colt officials insist that people have a right to own and use rifles such as the Sporter. Critics claim that the Sporter can be converted into a fully automatic weapon and that it is used mostly in urban gang and drug shootings.

Do citizens have a right to own and use semiautomatic weapons? What about fully automatic weapons? What is your position?

Most gun owners have handguns, not semiautomatic or fully automatic weapons. It is estimated that there are 70 million handguns owned by private citizens in the United States. Those who support more gun control or even the elimination of all these guns point to statistics. Each year about 39,000 Americans are killed with guns: There are 19,000 suicides, 18,000 homicides, and some 2,000 people killed in gun accidents. In addition, there are about 40,000 injuries from accidents with guns each year, and probably millions of crimes committed using guns. By contrast, countries with strict handgun control have much lower rates of homicide. In 1990, there were 87 people killed by handguns in Japan, 13 in Sweden, 10 in Australia, and 22 in Great Britain.

Given these facts, why not have strict gun control in the United States? What would Mill say? How about Kant?

The opposition to gun control comes mainly from the National Rifle Association and its members. The NRA defends each person's right to own and use handguns in self-defense. The NRA claims that the homicide statistics are inflated and that the most important statistic is that there are 645,000 defensive uses of handguns each year. As for accidental deaths and injuries, the NRA solution is to teach principles of safe use of weapons.

Do you agree with the NRA position? Why or why not?

5. A New Drug

Suppose you are a poor and uneducated person from Chicago. Your only chance for success in life is through athletics, particularly distance running. You have trained hard, and you have placed high in 10-kilometer and marathon races, but you have never won a major race. You need to be just a little faster to win. In one month, there is the Chicago Marathon, with a cash prize of $100,000 for the winner. There is a good chance that the winner will also get a lucrative contract with a major shoe company, such as Nike. A friend who is an athletic trainer tells you she has obtained a limited supply of a new drug that dramatically improves endurance by preventing the buildup of lactic acid in the muscles. The drug is the result of genetic research on human growth hormones, and thus far it has been tested on animals with no bad side effects. It seems to be much safer and more effective than steroids or the human growth hormones used by some runners. Your friend offers you a month's supply of the drug. She assures you that it is not on the list of banned drugs and that it will not show up on drug tests, or at least the drug tests currently used. In return for giving you the drug, your friend wants $5,000, but only if you win the race and collect the $100,000 cash prize. If you do not win, you owe her nothing.

Should you take the drug or not? Why or why not?

6. The Equal Rights Amendment

This amendment was originally proposed by Alice Paul in 1923, just three years after women in the United States received the right to vote. It was approved by Congress in 1971, but it has not been ratified by the required three-fourths of the state legislatures and is now considered dead. The proposed amendment reads as follows:

Section 1. Equality of rights under the law shall not be denied or abridged by the United States or by any state on account of sex.

Section 2. This amendment shall take effect two years after the date of ratification.

Should this amendment be ratified or not? Why or why not?

Suggested Readings

1. James Rachels, *The Elements of Moral Philosophy,* 3rd ed. (New York: McGraw-Hill Companies, 1999), is a good introduction to the standard moral theories. *A Companion to Ethics,* ed. Peter Singer (Oxford: Basil Blackwell Ltd, 1991) is a useful anthology that includes short articles on egoism, natural law theory, relativism, subjectivism, utilitarianism, Kantian ethics, virtue theory, and rights theory. A reliable source of on-line information on philosophers, terms, and theories, with essays written by experts, is the Stanford Encyclopedia of Philosophy (http://plato.stanford.edu).
2. Joseph Butler makes the classical attack on egoism in *Fifteen Sermons upon Human Nature* (London: Society for Promoting Christain Knowledge, 1970). Ayn Rand explains and defends egoism in *The Virtue of Selfishness* (New York: Signet, 1964). Paul W. Taylor argues that ethical egoism contains an inconsistency in *Principles of Ethics: An Introduction* (Belmont, CA: Wadsworth, 1975).
3. *The Divine Command Theory of Ethics,* ed. Paul Helm (Oxford: Oxford University Press, 1979), contains several articles on the divine command theory. Robert M. Adams defends the theory in "A Modified Divine Command Theory of Ethical Wrongness," in *The Virtue of Faith* (Oxford: Oxford University Press, 1987). Philip L. Quinn gives a sophisticated

defense and explanation of the theory using deontic logic in *Divine Commands and Moral Requirements* (Oxford: Clarendon Press, 1978). Kai Nielsen, *Ethics without God* (Buffalo, NY: Prometheus Books, 1990), argues that ethics can exist without belief in God.

4. John Finnis, *Natural Law and Natural Rights* (Oxford: Clarendon Press, 1980), gives a sophisticated defense of natural law theory; basically Finnis argues that following natural law is necessary for human flourishing. J. Budziszewski, *Written on the Heart: The Case for Natural Law* (Chicago: Intervarsity Press, 1997), explains and defends natural law theory as it is found in Aristotle, Aquinas, and Locke. Anthony J. Lisska, *Aquinas's Theory of Natural Law: An Analytical Reconstuction* (Oxford: Oxford University Press, 1998), argues that the problem with natural theory is its assumption that all humans have a common nature or essence.

5. James Baillie, *Hume on Morality* (London: Routledge, 2000), gives a clear and well-organized introduction to Hume's moral philosophy. J.L. Mackie, *Hume's Moral Theory* (London: Routledge Kegan & Paul, 1980), presents a classic discussion of Hume's views on morality. *The Is-Ought Problem*, ed. W. D. Hudson (Macmillan, 1969) is a collection of papers on Hume's famous problem on reasoning from "is" to "ought."

6. *Ethical Relativism,* ed. John Ladd (Belmont, CA: Wadsworth, 1973), has readings on cultural relativism. James Rachels criticizes cultural relativism and subjectivism in *The Elements of Moral Philosophy* (New York: Random House, 1993). William H. Shaw dismisses subjectivism as implausible and raises objections to cultural relativism in "Relativism and Objectivity in Ethics," in *Morality and Moral Controversies,* ed. John Arthur (Englewood Cliffs, N.J.: Prentice-Hall, 1981), pp. 31–50. J. L. Mackie presents a subjectivist theory in *Ethics* (Harmondsworth, U.K.: Penguin, 1977). Gilbert Harman defends a version of relativism in *The Nature of Morality: An Introduction to Ethics* (Oxford: Oxford University Press, 1977).

7. J. J. C. Smart defends utilitarianism and Bernard Williams attacks it in J. J. C. Smart and Bernard Williams, *Utilitarianism: For and Against* (Cambridge: Cambridge University Press, 1973). *Utilitarianism and Beyond,* ed. A. Sen and Bernard Williams (Cambridge: Cambridge University Press, 1973), is a collection of articles on utilitarianism. *Ethics,* ed. Peter Singer (Oxford: Oxford University Press, 1994), has a selection of classical and modern readings on utilitarianism.

8. Kant's work on ethics is difficult. A good place to begin is his *Lectures on Ethics,* trans. Louis Infield (New York: Harper & Row, 1963). His ethical theory is developed in *Critique of Practical Reason,* trans. Lewis White Beck (New York: Bobbs-Merrill, 1956); *The Metaphysical Elements of Justice,* trans. John Ladd (New York: Bobbs-Merrill, 1965); and *The Metaphysical Principles of Virtue,* trans. James Ellington (New York: Bobbs-Merrill, 1964). For commentaries on Kant's moral philosophy, see H. J. Paton, *The Categorical Imperative* (New York: Harper & Row, 1967), and H. B. Acton, *Kant's Moral Philosophy* (New York: Macmillan, 1970).

9. W. D. Ross explains Aristotle's ethics in his *Aristotle* (New York: Meridian Books, 1959), chapter 7. John M. Cooper defends Aristotelian ethics in *Reason and the Human Good in Aristotle* (Cambridge, MA: Harvard University Press, 1975). For articles on virtue theory by classical and contemporary philosophers, see *Vice and Virtue in Everyday Life,* 3rd ed., ed. Christina Sommers and Fred Sommers (San Diego: Harcourt Brace Jovanovich, 1993). James Rachels raises objections to virtue theory in *The Elements of Moral Philosophy* (New York: McGraw-Hill, 1993). Peter Geach discusses classical virtues such as courage in *The Virtues* (Cambridge: Cambridge University Press, 1977).

10. *Human Rights,* ed. Ellen Paul, Fred Mill, and Jeffrey Paul (Oxford: Blackwell, 1948), is a collection of articles on rights. Another anthology on rights is *Theories of Rights,* ed. Jeremy

Waldron (Oxford: Oxford University Press, 1984). Ronald Dworkin, *Taking Rights Seriously* (Cambridge, MA: Harvard University Press, 1977), argues that the basis of rights in the Constitution of the United States is the Kantian idea of treating people with dignity as members of the moral community. Judith Jarvis Thomson, in *The Realm of Rights* (Cambridge, MA: Harvard University Press, 1990), develops a systematic theory of the nature and foundation of rights. John Locke's classical theory of God-given natural rights is found in his *Two Treatises* (1690).

11. The classical formulations of the social contract theory are Thomas Hobbes's *Leviathan* (1651), John Locke's *The Second Treatise of Government* (1690), and Jean-Jacques Rousseau's *The Social Contract* (1762).

12. Since it first appeared in 1971, Rawls's theory of justice has been widely discussed. One of the first books on the theory to appear was Brian Barry, *The Liberal Theory of Justice* (Oxford: Oxford University Press, 1973). Another useful critical discussion is Robert Paul Wolff, *Understanding Rawls* (Princeton: Princeton University Press, 1977). The journal *Ethics* devoted its entire July 1989 issue to a symposium on developments in the Rawlsian theory of justice.

13. Feminist theory has been much discussed in recent years. A big anthology that covers the application of feminist theory to current issues such as affirmative action, abortion, reproductive technology, meat-eating, militarism, and environmentalism is *Living with Contradictions*, ed. Allison M. Jaggar (Boulder, CO: Westview Press, Inc., 1994). Another recent collection of readings on feminist theory and its applications is *Woman and Values*, 2nd ed., ed. Marilyn Pearsall (Belmont, CA: Wadsworth, 1993). For a comprehensive introduction to different feminist theories, see *Feminist Thought*, ed. Rosemarie Tong (Boulder, CO: Westview Press, 1989). Another comprehensive anthology is *Feminism and Philosophy*, ed. Nancy Tuana and Rosemarie Tong (Boulder, CO: Westview Press, 1995). This book covers liberal, Marxist, radical, psychoanalytic, socialist, ecological, phenomenological, and postmodern feminist perspectives.

Chapter 2

Abortion

Introduction

Factual Background

Abortion is usually defined as the intentional termination of pregnancy. Although the term *fetus* is often used to describe the prenatal organism from conception to birth, the prenatal organism is, strictly speaking, an embryo until the eighth week and a zygote when it is a fertilized egg. In the future, no doubt, it will be possible to terminate pregnancy at any stage without causing the fetus to die; the fetus could be kept alive in an artificial womb. Then the decision to terminate pregnancy would be separate from the decision about the life of the fetus. But given the present state of medical technology, the decision to terminate pregnancy is also a decision to kill the fetus or let it die.

In 2000, an estimated 1.31 million abortions were performed in the United States, down from 1.4 million in 1994. From 1973 through 1994, more than 31 million legal abortions were obtained in the United States. In 2000, 21 out of every 1,000 women aged 15 to 44 had an abortion, making it one of the most common surgical procedures in the country. It is estimated that 46 million abortions occur worldwide each year; about 26 million of these abortions are legal, and about 20 million women have abortions in countries where abortion is restricted or prohibited by law. (For sources of statistics on abortion, see the Suggested Readings at the end of the chapter.)

In the United States, about 52 percent of the women obtaining abortions each year are younger than age 25, and about 20 percent of them are teenagers. Never-married women obtain two-thirds of all abortions. Three-fourths of the women having abortions say that having a baby would interfere with work, school, or other responsibilities. About two-thirds say that they cannot afford a child. About 13,000 women have abortions each year because they became pregnant after rape or incest.

Before the U.S. Supreme Court decision in *Roe v. Wade* in 1973, the number of illegal abortions in the United States was 1.2 million a year. After the *Roe* decision made abortion legal, the number of abortions increased to 1.4 million a year in 1994 and then decreased to 1.31 million in 2000. The latest figures show that the number of abortions in the United States continues to decrease.

When performed by a qualified doctor, abortion is a reasonably safe procedure. Fewer than 1 percent of all abortion patients experience complications such as infection or hemorrhage requiring a blood transfusion. The risk of death from abortion increases with length of pregnancy, however, with 1 death for every 600,000 abortions at 8 or fewer weeks to 1 death per 8,000 at 20 or more weeks. But the risk of death from childbirth is 10 times as high as that associated with all abortions.

The law has treated abortion differently at different times. As Justice Blackmun notes in the first reading, English common law did not treat abortion before "quickening" as a criminal offense. "Quickening," or the first movement of the fetus, usually occurs between the sixteenth and eighteenth weeks of pregnancy. This traditional view of abortion was widely accepted up to the mid-nineteenth century, but it was rejected in 1828, when Connecticut made abortion before quickening a crime.

Other states followed the example of Connecticut, and by the 1960s most states had laws restricting abortion. All fifty states and the District of Columbia, however, allowed abortion to save the life of the mother, and Colorado and New Mexico permitted abortion to prevent serious harm to the mother.

These laws restricting abortion were overturned by the Supreme Court in the landmark *Roe* decision in 1973. In this case, the Court ruled that restrictive abortion laws, except in certain narrowly defined circumstances, are unconstitutional. In a companion case, *Doe v. Bolton* (1973), the Court held further that a state may not unduly burden a woman's right to abortion by prohibiting or limiting her access to the procedure. These decisions made abortion before viability legally available to women who could afford it and who could find a doctor willing to perform the procedure. It is not accurate to say, as critics do, that the Court legalized "abortion on demand." In fact, the Court has allowed a number of restrictions on the abortion right, as we shall see.

The decision has been very controversial, and it has been repeatedly challenged. Opponents of the decision have proposed to amend the Constitution with the Human Life bill, which affirms that human life begins at conception and that every human life has intrinsic worth and equal value under the Constitution. As Justice Blackman notes in the reading, the Constitution says that the bearers of rights are "persons" and not "human lives."

A legal challenge to the decision was the case of *Webster v. Reproductive Health Services* (1989). In a 5-to-4 decision, the Court did not overturn *Roe* but allowed as constitutional certain restrictions placed on abortion by a Missouri law, namely, (1) banning the use of public funds for abortion and abortion counseling, (2) banning abortions in public hospitals and clinics, and (3) forbidding public employees to assist in the performance of an abortion.

The next challenge to *Roe* was the case of *Planned Parenthood v. Casey* (1992). In a complicated and controversial decision that left people on both sides of the issue unsatisfied, the Court again reaffirmed the essential holding of *Roe* that a woman has a right to abortion. However, it permitted states to impose further restrictions on abortion, provided they do not impose an undue burden on the woman. The majority of the present Supreme Court has indicated that they do not intend to reconsider the basic abortion right, but given the ongoing controversy about abortion, it seems likely that it will be revisited by the Court in the future.

Many states have passed laws banning partial-birth abortions, and in November 2003, President Bush signed into law the Partial-Birth Abortion Act Ban of 2003, which carries two-year prison terms for doctors who perform the procedure. The federal law is being contested in the courts, and the issue is expected to reach the Supreme Court. Just what the law bans is a matter of controversy. Defenders insist that the law only prohibits a rare and unnecessary procedure called intrauterine cranial decompression, which involves crushing the skull of the infant. Opponents of the law argue that it also prohibits a common procedure called intact dilation and evacuation, which is typically performed in the first or second trimester before viability, and thus is protected under *Roe*. This procedure is sometimes necessary to protect the woman's life or health. (For more on partial-birth abortion, see the second Problem Case.)

The Readings

With the exception of the excerpt from *Roe,* the readings are not concerned with the legal aspects of the abortion controversy, but instead concentrate on the moral problem of whether abortion is wrong or not. There are at least three views of the matter: (1) the pro-life view, (2) the pro-choice view, and (3) moderate views. Let us consider each in turn.

The pro-life view is that abortion is wrong, or almost always wrong, because it is the killing of an innocent person, or at least a potentially innocent person. It seems more accurate to call this the "anti-abortion" view rather than a "pro-life" view, because defenders of this view are rarely in favor of preserving all life, including the lives of murderers or those engaging in an unjust war or, for that matter, the lives of animals. Nevertheless, those who hold this view prefer the label "pro-life" rather than "anti-abortion" so I will continue to refer to it as the "pro-life" view.

The representatives of the pro-life view in the readings are Noonan and Marquis. Although they are both opposed to abortion, they are willing to grant some exceptions. Noonan mentions the cases of ectopic pregnancy and cancer in the uterus. The most common form of ectopic pregnancy (where the fetus is not in the usual position) is tubal pregnancy; in this condition the zygote does not descend to the uterus but remains lodged in the fallopian tube. The mother will die if the abortion is not performed in this situation, and there is no hope for the survival of the zygote at the present stage of medical technology. Noonan grants that abortion is not wrong in this case, and so does Marquis, because he allows abortion to save the mother's life. In addition, Marquis mentions as exceptions cases of rape, when the fetus is anencephalic (partially or completely lacking a brain), and when the abortion is performed during the first fourteen days after conception. Given the number of these exceptions he allows himself at the outset, it is tempting to say that Marquis is really a moderate rather than strictly pro-life, but because his emphasis is on the claim that abortion is seriously wrong, I will put him in the pro-life camp.

It is worth noting that those adopting the pro-life view do not agree about when a human being with rights comes into existence. Marquis puts it at fourteen days—before that time, twinning can occur, producing more than one human being. Noonan accepts the standard Catholic position that human life begins at conception because at conception there is the full human genetic code. (But this is not quite right. According to medical textbooks, DNA sets from the egg and sperm do not immediately merge. The complete genetic coding that is the result of the combination of the DNA from the egg and sperm does not exist until the ovum divides after it has been fertilized.)

The pro-choice view is that abortion is morally permissible whenever the mother chooses it. It would not be fair to call this the "pro-abortion" view, because those who hold it do not believe that every mother ought to get an abortion; they merely defend the option to have one. Perhaps it would be better to call it the "pro-abortion-choice" view, because defenders of this view certainly do not endorse any and all choices, including the choice to murder innocent adult humans. With these qualifications in mind, I will continue to refer to the view in question as "pro-choice."

Instead of viewing the fetus as a person with rights, or as a potential person, the pro-choice view defended by Mary Anne Warren in her essay adopts the Kantian view that only rational beings are persons with a moral status, and because fetuses are not rational, self-conscious beings, they have no moral status, or at least not the moral status of persons. She takes seriously the fact that in the later stages of development the fetus resembles a person, and she seems to accept this as a reason for not killing it. Thus she holds that an early abortion is preferable to a late one. But Warren's position is that in the early stages of development, when the fetus does not resemble a person, abortion should be permitted whenever the mother chooses it.

Those who defend the pro-choice view do not agree about infanticide. In a classic article (see the Suggested Readings), Michael Tooley argues that there is no moral difference between abortion and infanticide; both are morally acceptable in his view. Warren does not agree. She gives several reasons for making a moral distinction between abortion and infanticide. One important difference, she says, is that the fetus can pose a threat to the woman's life or health, whereas the newborn infant cannot pose such a threat because the mother can put it up for adoption or place it in foster care.

The Supreme Court decision in *Roe,* and the readings by Judith Jarvis Thomson and Elizabeth Harman, represent what I am calling the moderate view. Moderates agree in rejecting both the pro-life and the pro-choice views. Generally speaking, moderates are willing to morally allow abortions in some cases and not others, but they give different reasons for doing so.

Thomson does not think that a newly fertilized ovum is a person, and she rejects the slippery slope argument for saying that the fetus is a person from the moment of conception. But she is not inclined to draw a dividing line in development of the fetus, a line demarking the point at which it becomes a person. Instead she takes a different approach. Suppose we grant the conservative premise that the fetus is a person from the moment of conception. It does not follow, she argues, that abortion is never permitted. Take a case of rape, for example. The woman's rights, her right to self-defense and her right to control her own body, are strong enough to justify an abortion when pregnancy is due to rape. But a woman also has a duty of decency generated by a principle Thomson calls Minimally Decent Samaritanism, and this duty rules out abortion in some cases. To use Thomson's example, it would be indecent for a woman in her seventh month of pregnancy to get an abortion just to avoid postponing a trip abroad.

Harman is concerned to defend a very liberal view of abortions of early fetuses, but she does not defend late abortions. That is why I am classifying her as a moderate. She defines an early fetus as one that has no intrinsic properties conferring moral status, and she thinks it is plausible to hold that an early fetus lacks any conscious experience. This suggests that conscious experience is an intrinsic property that confers moral status, implying that a late abortion after the fetus is conscious is morally problematic. But the abortion of the fetus before it is conscious requires no justification at all. This is because an early fetus that dies while it is still an early fetus has no moral status. Harman argues that the moral status of the early fetus is not determined by its intrinsic properties but by its actual future, and specifically by The Actual Future Principle, which says that an early fetus that becomes a person has a moral status, but an early fetus that dies while still an early fetus has none. Interesting enough, she concludes that an early abortion is morally insignificant, but the decision to *fail* to abort is morally significant. Before failing to abort, a women should deliberate seriously and recognize her responsibility for the creation of a person.

Harman seems to accept consciousness as a morally significant dividing line in the development of the fetus. The majortity decision in *Roe* also takes a dividing-line position. That is, Justice Blackmun tries to draw a line in the development of the fetus before which abortion is justified and after which it is much harder to justify. Unlike Harman, the dividing line adopted by Justice Blackmun in the *Roe* decision is viability. Viability occurs when the fetus is capable of surviving outside the womb. Just when this occurs is the subject of debate. Justice Blackmun puts viability at the twenty-eighth week of pregnancy, but many doctors say it occurs at twenty-four weeks or perhaps as early as twenty weeks. In any case, Justice Blackmun holds that abortion is legal before viability but that after viability the state may impose restrictions or even proscribe it except when it is necessary to save the life or health of the mother.

Noonan objects to lines drawn in the development of the fetus separating what is a person and what is not a person. These lines, he argues, are always arbitrary and inadequate. For example, viability is a shifting point. The development of artificial incubation will make the fetus viable at any time, even shortly after conception. Furthermore, the time at which the fetus is viable varies according to circumstances such as its weight, age, and race.

Opponents of dividing lines also use what are called slippery slope arguments; that is, they argue that a line cannot be securely drawn at any point in the development of the fetus because such a line inevitably slides down the slope of development to conception. They insist that the only place to draw the line is at conception. Thomson rejects this argument as invalid. The conclusion does not follow. It is like arguing that because an acorn develops into an oak tree, therefore an acorn is an oak tree.

Philosophical Issues

How can we resolve the moral issue about the wrongness of abortion? Most writers agree that settling this issue requires solving some very difficult problems in ethics. One is formulating an acceptable principle about the wrongness of killing. Such a principle is relevant not only in the abortion controversy but also in dealing with questions about euthanasia, capital punishment, war, and killing nonhuman animals. But it is hard to find a moral principle about killing that does not have scope problems—that is, that is not too broad or too narrow or subject to counterexamples. For example, the principle that it is wrong to take a human life is obviously too broad because it makes it wrong to kill a human cancer-cell culture (which is both human and living). The alternative principle that it is wrong to kill a human being is too narrow; it doesn't seem to apply to the fetus in the early stages of development. The Kantian principle that it is wrong to kill persons or rational beings has similar problems; for example, it doesn't seem to apply to newborn infants or the retarded or the mentally ill.

In his reading, Don Marquis suggests that "killing someone is wrong, in general, when it deprives her of a future like ours." This principle forbids killing someone because it inflicts on the victim the loss of a future containing valuable experiences, activities, projects, and enjoyments. But this principle seems to have scope problems similar to those of the other principles about killing. It may be too broad because it seems to imply that killing nonhuman animals such as pigs is wrong, and this is very problematic in our meat-eating society. (See the discussion of animals rights in Chapter 7.) Marquis's principle may be too narrow, as well, for it seems to imply that active euthanasia of those facing unhappy or meaningless lives, such as the mentally ill or the severely retarded or the incurably diseased, is not wrong, and this is surely debatable.

Another focus of the debate about abortion has been the nature and status of the fetus. Is it a person or not, and how do we tell if a living being is a person or not? One common approach to these problems is to search for a criterion of personhood—that is, some one feature, such as human genetic coding or rationality, that is both a necessary and a sufficient condition for being a person. Utilitarians, for example, say that consciousness is the criterion for personhood or moral standing, whereas followers of Kant, such as Warren, hold that rationality is essential. (Warren adds five other features—sentience, emotionality, the capacity to communicate, self-awareness, and moral agency—but these seem to be built into the concept of rationality.) Noonan thinks that human genetic coding is the criterion for personhood.

Marquis argues in his reading that these criteria for personhood have scope problems, problems like the ones plaguing the principles about killing we just discussed. For example, the genetic criterion is too broad because it includes human cancer cells that are biologically human but not persons. Warren's criterion, on the other hand, is too narrow because it excludes from the class of persons infants, the severely retarded, and some of the mentally ill.

In an important article listed in the Suggested Readings, Jane English makes a different objection to the search for a criterion of personhood. The search is doomed from the outset because the concept of person has fuzzy borders; that is, there are borderline cases in which we cannot say whether a living being is a person or not, and the fetus constitutes just such a case.

Marquis argues that the moral status of the fetus is not based on properties such as consciousness, but rather the potentiality of the fetus. If it has a future like ours, it is wrong to kill it. Harman does not agree. In "The Potentiality Problem" (see the Suggested Readings), Harman takes the position that consciousness does give a being moral status, and this means that both cats and conscious babies have this status. But the potentiality of the non-conscious embryo does not by itself confer any moral status on the embryo. According to her Actual Future Principle, it is the actual future of the fetus that determines its moral status. If the fetus dies in an abortion, then it has no actual future as a person, and it has no moral status at all. On the other hand, if the fetus does have an actual future as a person, then it does have a moral status as a subject of care and concern.

If we cannot conclusively determine the nature and moral status of the fetus, then how can we answer the moral question about abortion? Thomson's tactic is to shift the focus of debate from the status of the fetus to the rights of the pregnant woman. She argues that even if the fetus is a person with a right to life, it still does not follow that abortions are never justified. The rights of the mother can outweigh those of the fetus. These rights include the mother's right to life, her right to self-defense, and the right to control her own body.

Thomson has been criticized for relying too heavily on puzzling imaginary cases, such as the case of the famous violinist who is plugged into another person who has been kidnapped. Is this case really analogous to a case of rape? The case of the famous violinist involves failing to save a life, a life that someone else could save instead, but abortion involves taking a life that cannot be saved by another person. Another person could offer to be plugged into the violinist, but another woman could not take over the pregnancy of the raped woman. Thomson asks us what we would say or think in such cases; that is, she appeals to our moral intuitions. But we cannot assume that everyone will have the same intuitions, particularly when we are dealing with strange cases and a difficult subject like abortion. Those who are pro-life and those who are pro-choice will no doubt have different intuitions.

Excerpts from *Roe v. Wade* (1973)

THE U.S. SUPREME COURT

Harry B. Blackmun (1909–1999) was an associate justice of the U.S. Supreme Court. He was appointed to the Court in 1970 and retired in 1994.

Byron R. White was appointed to the Supreme Court in 1962 and retired in 1993.

In the case of *Roe v. Wade*, a pregnant single woman challenged a Texas abortion law making abortion (except to save the mother's life) a crime punishable by a prison sentence of two to five years. ("Jane Roe" was a pseudonym for Norma McCorvey, a woman who now says she is pro-life.) By a 7-to-2 vote, the Court ruled that the Texas law was unconstitutional.

Source: U.S. Supreme Court, *Roe v. Wade* (1973).

The reading includes excerpts from the majority opinion, written by Justice Blackmun, and from the dissenting opinion, written by Justice White.

After an interesting survey of historical views of abortion, Justice Blackmun argues that the abortion decision is included in the right of personal privacy. But this right is not absolute; it must yield at some point to the state's legitimate interest in protecting potential life, and this interest becomes compelling at the point of viability.

In his dissenting opinion, Justice White claims that the Court has no constitutional basis for its decision and that it incorrectly values the convenience of the mother more than the existence and development of human life.

IT PERHAPS IS NOT GENERALLY APPRECIATED that the restrictive criminal abortion laws in effect in a majority of States today are of relatively recent vintage. Those laws, generally proscribing abortion or its attempt at any time during pregnancy except when necessary to preserve the pregnant woman's life, are not of ancient or even of common-law origin. Instead, they derive from statutory changes effected, for the most part, in the latter half of the 19th century.

ANCIENT ATTITUDES

These are not capable of precise determination. We are told that at the time of the Persian Empire, abortifacients were known and that criminal abortions were severely punished. We are also told, however, that abortion was practiced in Greek times as well as in the Roman Era, and that "it was resorted to without scruple." The Ephesian, Soranos, often described as the greatest of the ancient gynecologists, appears to have been generally opposed to Rome's prevailing free abortion practices. He found it necessary to think first of the life of the mother, and he resorted to abortion when, upon this standard, he felt the procedure advisable. Greek and Roman law afforded little protection to the unborn. If abortion was prosecuted in some places, it seems to have been based on a concept of a violation of the father's right to his offspring. Ancient religion did not bar abortion.

THE HIPPOCRATIC OATH

What then of the famous Oath that has stood so long as the ethical guide of the medical profession and that bears the name of the great Greek (460(?)–377(?) B.C.E.), who has been described as the Father of Medicine, the "wisest and the greatest practitioner of his art," and the "most important and most complete medical personality of antiquity," who dominated the medical schools of his time, and who typified the sum of the medical knowledge of the past? The Oath varies somewhat according to the particular translation, but in any translation the content is clear: "I will give no deadly medicine to anyone if asked, nor suggest any such counsel; and in like manner I will not give to a woman a pessary to produce abortion," or "I will neither give a deadly drug to anybody if asked for it, nor will I make a suggestion to this effect. Similarly, I will not give to a woman an abortive remedy."

Although the Oath is not mentioned in any of the principal briefs in this case or in *Doe v. Bolton, post,* p. 179, it represents the apex of the development of strict ethical concepts in medicine, and its influence endures to this day. Why did not the authority of Hippocrates dissuade abortion practice in his time and that of Rome? The late Dr. Edelstein provides us with a theory: The Oath was not uncontested even in Hippocrates' day; only the Pythagorean school of philosophers frowned upon the related act of suicide. Most Greek thinkers, on the other hand, commended abortion, at least prior to viability. See Plato, Republic, V, 461; Aristotle, Politics, VII, 1335b 25. For the Pythagoreans, however, it was a matter of dogma. For them the embryo was animate from the moment of conception, and abortion meant destruction of a living being. The abortion clause of the Oath, therefore, "echoes Pythagorean doctrines," and "[i]n no other stratum of Greek opinion were such views held or proposed in the same spirit of uncompromising austerity."

Dr. Edelstein then concludes that the Oath originated in a group representing only a small segment of Greek opinion and that it certainly was not accepted by all ancient physicians. He points out that medical writings down to Galen (130–200 C.E.) "give evidence of the violation of almost every one of its injunctions." But with the end of antiquity a decided change took place. Resistance against suicide and against abortion became common. The Oath came to be popular. The emerging teachings of Christianity were in agreement with the Pythagorean ethic. The Oath "became the nucleus of all medical ethics" and "was applauded as the embodiment of truth." Thus, suggests Dr. Edelstein, it is "a Pythagorean manifesto and not the expression of an absolute standard of medical conduct."

This, it seems to us, is a satisfactory and acceptable explanation of the Hippocratic Oath's apparent rigidity. It enables us to understand, in historical context, a long-accepted and revered statement of medical ethics.

THE COMMON LAW

It is undisputed that at common law, abortion performed *before* "quickening"—the first recognizable movement of the fetus *in utero*, appearing usually from the 16th to the 18th week of pregnancy—was not an indictable offense. The absence of a common-law crime for pre-quickening abortion appears to have developed from a confluence of earlier philosophical, theological, and civil and canon law concepts of when life begins. These disciplines variously approached the question in terms of the point at which the embryo or fetus became "formed" or recognizably human, or in terms of when a "person" came into being, that is, infused with a "soul" or "animated." A loose consensus evolved in early English law that these events occurred at some point between conception and live birth. This was "mediate animation." Although Christian theology and the canon law came to fix the point of animation at 40 days for a male and 80 days for a female, a view that persisted until the 19th century, there was otherwise little agreement about the precise time of formation or animation. There was agreement, however, that prior to this point the fetus was to be regarded as part of the mother, and its destruction, therefore, was not homicide. Due to continued uncertainty about the precise time when animation occurred, or to the lack of any empirical basis for the 40–80-day view, and perhaps to Aquinas' definition of movement as one of the two first principles of life, Bracton focused upon quickening as the critical point. The significance of quickening was echoed by later common-law scholars and found its way into the received common law in this country.

Whether abortion of a *quick* fetus was a felony at common law, even a lesser crime, is still disputed. Bracton, writing early in the 13th century, thought it homicide. But the later and predominant view, following the great common-law scholars, has been that it was, at most, a lesser offense. In a frequently cited passage, Coke took the position that abortion of a woman "quick with childe" is "a great misprision, and no murder." Blackstone followed, saying that while abortion after quickening had once been considered manslaughter (though not murder), "modern law" took a less severe view. A recent review of the common-law precedents argues, however, that those precedents contradict Coke and that even post-quickening abortion was never established as a common-law crime. This is of some importance because while most American courts ruled, in holding or dictum, that abortion of an unquickened fetus was not criminal under their received common law, others followed Coke in stating that abortion of a quick fetus was a "misprision," a term they translated to mean "misdemeanor." That their reliance on Coke on this aspect of the law was uncritical and, apparently in all the reported cases, dictum (due probably to the paucity of common-law prosecutions for post-quickening abortion), makes it now appear doubtful that abortion was ever firmly established as a common-law crime even with respect to the destruction of a quick fetus. . . .

THE AMERICAN LAW

In this country, the law in effect in all but a few States until mid-19th century was the pre-existing English common law. Connecticut, the first State to enact abortion legislation, adopted in 1821 that part of Lord Ellenborough's Act that related to a woman "quick with child." The death penalty was not imposed. Abortion before quickening was made a crime in that State only in 1860. In 1828, New York enacted legislation that, in two respects, was to serve as a model for early anti-abortion statutes. First, while barring destruction of an unquickened fetus as well as a quick fetus, it made the former only a misdemeanor, but the latter second-degree manslaughter. Second, it incorporated a concept of therapeutic abortion by providing that an abortion was excused if it "shall have been necessary to preserve the life of such mother, or shall have been advised by two physicians to be necessary for such purpose." By 1840, when Texas had received the common law, only eight American States had statutes dealing with abortion. It was not until after the War Between the States that legislation began generally to replace the common law. Most of these initial statutes dealt severely with abortion after quickening but were lenient with it before quickening. Most punished attempts equally with completed abortions. While many statutes included the exception for an abortion thought by one or more physicians to be necessary to save the mother's life, that provision soon disappeared and the typical law required that the procedure actually be necessary for that purpose.

Gradually, in the middle and late 19th century the quickening distinction disappeared from the statutory law of most States and the degree of the offense and the penalties were increased. By the end of the 1950s, a large majority of the jurisdictions banned abortion, however and whenever performed, unless done to save or preserve the life of the mother. The exceptions, Alabama and the District of Columbia, permitted abortion to preserve the mother's health. Three States permitted abortions that were not "unlawfully" performed or that were not "without lawful justification," leaving interpretation of those standards to the courts. In the past several years, however, a trend toward liberalization of abortion statutes has resulted in adoption, by about one-third of the States, of less stringent laws, most of them patterned after the ALI Model Penal Code, § 230.3.

It is thus apparent that common law, at the time of the adoption of our Constitution, and throughout the major portion of the 19th century, viewed abortion with less disfavor than most American statutes currently in effect. Phrasing it another way, a woman had a substantially broader right to terminate a pregnancy than she does in most states today. At least with respect to the early stage of pregnancy and very possibly without such a limitation, the opportunity to make this choice was present in this country well into the 19th century. Even later, the law continued for some time to treat less punitively an abortion procured in early pregnancy. . . .

Three reasons have been advanced to explain historically the enactment of criminal abortion laws in the 19th century and to justify their continued existence.

It has been argued occasionally that these laws were the product of a Victorian social concern to discourage illicit sexual conduct. Texas, however, does not advance this justification in the present case, and it appears that no court or commentator has taken the argument seriously.

The appellants and *amici* contend, moreover, that this is not a proper state purpose at all and suggest that, if it were, the Texas statutes are overbroad in protecting it since the law fails to distinguish between married and unwed mothers.

A second reason is concerned with abortion as a medical procedure. When most criminal abortion laws were first enacted, the procedure was a hazardous one for the woman. This was particularly true prior to the development of antisepsis. Antiseptic techniques, of course were based on discoveries by Lister, Pasteur, and others first announced in 1867, but were not generally accepted and employed until about the turn of the century. Abortion mortality was high. Even after 1900, and perhaps until as late as the development of antibiotics in the 1940's, standard modern techniques such as dilation and curettage were not nearly so safe as they are today. Thus, it has been argued that a State's real concern in enacting a criminal abortion law was to protect the pregnant woman, that is, to restrain her from submitting to a procedure that placed her life in serious jeopardy.

Modern medical techniques have altered this situation. Appellants and various *amici* refer to medical data indicating that abortion in early pregnancy, that is, prior to the end of the first trimester, although not without its risk, is now relatively safe. Mortality rates for women undergoing early abortions, where the procedure is legal, appear to be as low as or lower than the rates for normal childbirth. Consequently, any interest of the State in protecting the women from an inherently hazardous procedure, except when it would be equally dangerous for her to forgo it, has largely disappeared. Of course, important state interests in the areas of health and medical standards do remain. The State has a legitimate interest in seeing to it that abortion, like any other medical procedure, is performed under circumstances that insure maximum safety for the patient. This interest obviously extends at least to the performing physician and his staff, to the facilities involved, to the availability of after-care, and to adequate provision for any complication or emergency that might arise. The prevalence of high mortality rates at illegal "abortion mills" strengthens, rather than weakens, the State's interest in regulating the conditions under which abortions are performed. Moreover, the risk to the woman increases as her pregnancy continues. Thus the State retains a definite interest in protecting the woman's own health and safety when an abortion is proposed at a late stage of pregnancy.

The third reason is the State's interest— some phrase it in terms of duty—in protecting prenatal life. Some of the argument for this justification rests on the theory that a new human life is present from the moment of conception. The State's interest and general obligation to protect life then extends, it is argued, to prenatal life. Only when the life of the pregnant mother herself is at stake, balanced against the life she carries within her, should the interest of the embryo or fetus not prevail. Logically, of course, a legitimate state interest in this area need not stand or fall on acceptance of the belief that life begins at conception or at some other point prior to live birth. In assessing the State's interest, recognition may be given to the less rigid claim that as long as at least *potential* life is involved, the State may assert interests beyond the protection of the pregnant woman alone.

Parties challenging state abortion laws have sharply disputed in some courts the contention that a purpose of these laws, when enacted, was to protect prenatal life. Pointing to the absence of legislative history to support the contention, they claim that most state laws were designed solely to protect the woman. Because medical advances have lessened this concern, at least with respect to abortion in early pregnancy, they argue that with respect to such abortions the laws can no longer be justified by any state interest. There is some scholarly support for this view of original purpose. The few state courts called upon to interpret their laws in the late 19th and early 20th centuries did focus on the State's interest in protecting the woman's health rather than in preserving the embryo and fetus. Proponents of this view point out that in many States, including Texas, by statute or judicial interpretation, the pregnant woman herself could not be prosecuted for self-abortion or for cooperating in an abortion performed upon her by another. They claim that adoption of the "quickening" distinction through received common law and state statutes tacitly recognizes the greater health hazards inherent in late abortion and impliedly repudiates the theory that life begins at conception.

It is with these interests, and the weight to be attached to them, that this case is concerned.

The Constitution does not explicitly mention any right of privacy. In a line of decisions, however, going back perhaps as far as *Union Pacific R. Co. v. Botsford,* 141 U.S. 250, 251 (1891), the Court has recognized that a right of personal privacy, or a guarantee of certain areas or zones of privacy does exist under the Constitution. In carrying contexts, the Court or individual justices have, indeed, found at least the roots of that right in the First Amendment, in the Fourth and Fifth Amendments, in the penumbras of the Bill of Rights, in the Ninth Amendment, or in the concept of liberty guaranteed by the first section of the Fourteenth Amendment. These decisions make it clear that only personal rights that can be deemed "fundamental" or "implicit in the concept of ordered liberty," are included in this guarantee of personal privacy. They also make it clear that the right has some extension to activities relating to marriage, procreation, contraception, family relationships, and child rearing and education.

This right of privacy, whether it be founded in the Fourteenth Amendment's concept of personal liberty and restrictions upon state action, as we feel it is, or, as the District Court determined, in the Ninth Amendment's reservation of rights to the people, is broad enough to encompass a woman's decision whether or not to terminate her pregnancy. The detriment that the State would impose upon the pregnant woman by denying this choice altogether is apparent. Specific and direct harm medically diagnosable even in early pregnancy may be involved. Maternity, or additional offspring, may force upon the woman a distressful life and future. Psychological harm may be imminent. Mental and physical health may be taxed by child care. There is also the distress, for all concerned, associated with the unwanted child, and there is the problem of bringing a child into a family already unable, psychologically and otherwise, to care for it. In other cases, as in this one, the additional difficulties and continuing stigma of unwed motherhood may be involved. All these are factors the woman and her responsible physician necessarily will consider in consultation.

On the basis of elements such as these, appellant and some *amici* argue that the woman's right is absolute and that she is entitled to terminate her pregnancy at whatever time, in whatever way, and for whatever reason she alone chooses. With this we do not agree. Appellant's arguments that Texas either has no valid interest at all in regulating the abortion decision, or no interest strong enough to support any limitation upon the woman's sole determination, are unpersuasive. The Court's decisions recognizing a right of privacy also acknowledge that some state regulation in areas protected by that right is appropriate. As noted above, a State may properly assert important interests in safeguarding health, in maintaining medical standards, and in protecting potential life. At some point in pregnancy, these respective interests become sufficiently compelling to sustain regulation of the factors that govern the abortion decision. The privacy right involved, therefore, cannot be said to be absolute. In fact, it is not clear to us that the claim asserted by some *amici* that one has an unlimited right to do with one's body as one pleases bears a close relationship to the right of privacy previously articulated in the Court's decisions. The Court has refused to recognize an unlimited right of this kind in the past.

We, therefore, conclude that the right of personal privacy includes the abortion decision, but that this right is not unqualified and must be considered against important state interests in regulation.

We note that those federal and state courts that have recently considered abortion law challenges have reached the same conclusion.

Although the results are divided, most of these courts have agreed that the right of privacy, however based, is broad enough to cover the abortion decision, that the right, nonetheless, is not absolute and is subject to some limitations; and that at some point the state interests as to protection of health, medical standards, and prenatal life, become dominant. We agree with this approach.

Where certain "fundamental rights" are involved, the Court has held that regulation limiting these rights may be justified only by a "compelling state interest," and that legislative enactments must be narrowly drawn to express only the legitimate state interests at stake.

In the recent abortion cases, cited above, courts have recognized these principles. Those striking down state laws have generally scrutinized the State's interests in protecting health and potential life, and have concluded that neither interest justified broad limitations on the reasons for which a physician and his pregnant patient might decide that she should have an abortion in the early stages of pregnancy. Courts sustaining state laws have held that the State's determinations to protect health or prenatal life are dominant and constitutionally justifiable.

The District Court held that the appellee failed to meet his burden demonstrating that the Texas statute's infringement upon Roe's rights was necessary to support a compelling state interest, and that, although the appellee presented "several compelling justifications for state presence in the area of abortions," the statutes outstripped these justifications and swept "far beyond any areas of compelling state interest." Appellant and appellee both contest that holding. Appellant, as has been indicated, claims an absolute right that bars any state imposition of criminal penalties in the area. Appellee argues that the State's determination to recognize and protect prenatal life from and after conception constitutes a compelling state interest. As noted above, we do not agree fully with either formulation.

A. The appellee and certain *amici* argue that the fetus is a "person" within the language and meaning of the Fourteenth Amendment. In support of this, they outline at length and in detail the well-known facts of fetal development. If this suggestion of personhood is established, the appellant's case, of course, collapses, for the fetus' right to life would then be guaranteed specifically by the Amendment. The appellant conceded as much on reargument. On the other hand, the appellee conceded on reargument that no case could be cited that holds that a fetus is a person within the meaning of the Fourteenth Amendment.

The Constitution does not define "person" in so many words. Section 1 of the Fourteenth Amendment contains three references to "person." In nearly all these instances, the use of the word is such that it has application only postnatally. None indicates, with any assurance, that it has any possible pre-natal application.

All this, together with our observation, *supra,* that throughout the major portion of the 19th century prevailing legal abortion practices were far freer than they are today, persuades us that the word "person," as used in the Fourteenth Amendment, does not include the unborn. This is in accord with the results reached in those few cases where the issue has been squarely presented. Indeed, our decision in *United States v. Vuitch,* 402 U.S. 62 (1971), inferentially is to the same effect, for we there would not have indulged in statutory interpretation favorable to abortion in specified circumstances if the necessary consequence was the termination of life entitled to Fourteenth Amendment protection.

This conclusion, however, does not of itself fully answer the contentions raised by Texas, and we pass on to other considerations.

B. The pregnant woman cannot be isolated in her privacy. She carried an embryo and, later, a fetus, if one accepts the medical definitions of the developing young in the human uterus. See Dorland's Illustrated Medical Dictionary 478–479, 547 (24th ed. 1965). The situation therefore is inherently different from marital intimacy, or bedroom possession of obscene material, or marriage, or procreation, or education, with which *Eisenstadt* and *Griswold, Stanley, Loving, Skinner,* and *Pierce* and *Meyer* were respectively concerned. As we have intimated above, it is reasonable and appropriate for a State to decide that at some point in time another interest, that of health of the mother or that of potential human life, becomes significantly involved. The woman's privacy is no longer sole and any right of privacy she possesses must be measured accordingly.

Texas urges that, apart from the Fourteenth Amendment, life begins at conception and is present throughout pregnancy, and that, therefore, the State has a compelling interest in protecting that life from and after conception. We need not resolve the difficult question of when life begins. When those trained in the respective disciplines of medicine, philosophy, and theology are unable to arrive at any consensus, the judiciary, at this point in the development of man's knowledge, is not in a position to speculate as to the answer.

It should be sufficient to note briefly the wide divergence of thinking on this most sensitive and difficult question. There has always been strong support for the view that life does not begin until live birth. This was the belief of the Stoics. It appears to be the predominant, though not the unanimous, attitude of the Jewish faith. It may be taken to represent also the position of a large

segment of the Protestant community, insofar as that can be ascertained; organized groups that have taken a formal position on the abortion issue have generally regarded abortion as a matter for the conscience of the individual and her family. As we have noted, the common law found greater significance in quickening. Physicians and their scientific colleagues have regarded that event with less interest and have tended to focus either upon conception, upon live birth, or upon the interim point at which the fetus becomes "viable," that is, potentially able to live outside the mother's womb, albeit with artificial aid. Viability is usually placed at about seven months (28 weeks) but may occur earlier, even at 24 weeks. The Aristotelian theory of "mediate animation," that held sway throughout the Middle Ages and the Renaissance in Europe, continued to be official Roman Catholic dogma until the 19th century, despite opposition to this "ensoulment" theory from those in the Church who would recognize the existence of life from the moment of conception. The latter is now, of course, the official belief of the Catholic Church. As one brief *amicus* discloses, this is a view strongly held by many non-Catholics as well, and by many physicians. Substantial problems for precise definition of this view are posed, however, by new embryological data that purport to indicate that conception is a "process" over time, rather than an event, and by new medical techniques such as menstrual extraction, the "morning-after" pill, implantation of embryos, artificial insemination, and even artificial wombs.

In areas other than criminal abortion, the law has been reluctant to endorse any theory that life, as we recognize it, begins before live birth or to accord legal rights to the unborn except in narrowly defined situations and except when the rights are contingent upon live birth. For example, the traditional rule of tort law denied recovery for prenatal injuries even though the child was born alive. That rule has been changed in almost every jurisdiction. In most States, recovery is said to be permitted only if the fetus was viable, or at least quick, when the injuries were sustained, though few courts have squarely so held. In a recent development, generally opposed by the commentators, some States permit the parents of a stillborn child to maintain an action for wrongful death because of prenatal injuries. Such an action, however, would appear to be one to vindicate the parents' interest and is thus consistent with the view that the fetus, at most, represents only the potentiality of life. Similarly, unborn children have been recognized as acquiring rights or interests by way of inheritance or other devolution of property, and have been represented by guardians *ad litem*. Perfection of the interests involved, again, has generally been contingent upon live birth. In short, the unborn have never been recognized in the law as persons in the whole sense.

In view of all this, we do not agree that, by adopting one theory of life, Texas may override the rights of the pregnant woman that are at stake. We repeat, however, that the State does have an important and legitimate interest in preserving and protecting the health of the pregnant woman, whether she be a resident of the State or a nonresident who seeks medical consultation and treatment there, and that it has still *another* important and legitimate interest in protecting the potentiality of human life. These interests are separate and distinct. Each grows in substantiality as the woman approaches term and, at a point during pregnancy, each becomes "compelling."

With respect to the State's important and legitimate interest in the health of the mother, the "compelling" point, in the light of present medical knowledge, is at approximately the end of the first trimester. This is so because of the now-established medical fact, referred to above, that until the end of the first trimester mortality in abortion may be less than mortality in normal childbirth. It follows that, from and after this point, a State may regulate the abortion procedure to the extent that the regulation reasonably relates to the preservation and protection of maternal health. Examples of permissible state regulation in this area are requirements as to the qualifications of the person who is to perform the abortion; as to the licensure of that person; as to the facility in which the procedure is to be performed, that is, whether it must be a hospital or may be a clinic or some other place of less-than-hospital status; as to the licensing of the facility; and the like.

This means, on the other hand, that, for the period of pregnancy prior to this "compelling" point, the attending physician, in consultation with his patient, is free to determine, without regulation by the State, that, in his medical judgment, the patient's pregnancy should be terminated. If that decision is reached, the judgment may be effectuated by an abortion free of interference by the State.

With respect to the State's important and legitimate interest in potential life, the "compelling" point is at viability. This is so because the fetus then presumably has the capability of meaningful life outside the mother's womb. State regulation protective of fetal life after viability thus has both logical and biological justifications. If the State is interested in protecting fetal life after viability, it may go so far as to proscribe abortion during that period, except when it is necessary to preserve the life or health of the mother.

To summarize and to repeat:

1. A state criminal abortion statute of the current Texas type, that excepts from criminality only a *lifesaving* procedure on behalf of the mother, without regard to pregnancy stage and without recognition of the other interests involved, is violative of the Due Process Clause of the Fourteenth Amendment.

   (a) For the stage prior to approximately the end of the first trimester, the abortion decision and its effectuation must be left to the medical judgment of the pregnant woman's attending physician.

(b) For the stage subsequent to approximately the end of the first trimester, the State, in promoting its interest in the health of the mother, may, if it chooses, regulate the abortion procedure in ways that are reasonably related to maternal health.

(c) For the stage subsequent to viability, the State in promoting its interest in the potentiality of human life may, if it chooses, regulate, and even proscribe, abortion except where it is necessary, in appropriate medical judgment, for the preservation of the life or health of the mother.

2. The State may define the term "physician" as it has been employed in the preceding paragraphs of this Part XI of this opinion, to mean only a physician currently licensed by the State, and may proscribe any abortion by a person who is not a physician as so defined.

In *Doe v. Bolton, post,* p. 179, procedural requirements contained in one of the modern abortion statutes are considered. That opinion and this one, of course, are to be read together.

This holding, we feel, is consistent with the relative weights of the respective interests involved, with the lessons and examples of medical and legal history, with the lenity of the common law, and with the demands of the profound problems of the present day. The decision leaves the State free to place increasing restrictions on abortion as the period of pregnancy lengthens, so long as those restrictions are tailored to the recognized state interests. The decision vindicates the right of the physician to administer medical treatment according to his professional judgment up to the points where important state interests provide compelling justifications for intervention. Up to those points, the abortion decision in all its aspects is inherently, and primarily, a medical decision, and basic responsibility for it must rest with the physician. If an individual practitioner abuses the privilege of exercising proper medical judgment, the usual remedies, judicial and intra-professional, are available.

MR. JUSTICE WHITE, DISSENTING

At the heart of the controversy in these cases are those recurring pregnancies that pose no danger whatsoever to the life or health of the mother but are nevertheless unwanted for any one or more of a variety of reasons—convenience, family planning, economics, dislike of children, the embarrassment of illegitimacy, etc. The common claim before us is that for any one of such reasons, or for no reason at all, and without asserting or claiming any threat to life or health, any woman is entitled to an abortion at her request if she is able to find a medical advisor willing to undertake the procedure.

The Court for the most part sustains this position: During the period prior to the time the fetus becomes viable, the Constitution of the United States values the convenience, whim or caprice of the putative mother more than the life or potential life of the fetus; the Constitution, therefore, guarantees the right to an abortion as against any state law or policy seeking to protect the fetus from an abortion not prompted by more compelling reasons of the mother.

With all due respect, I dissent. I find nothing in the language or history of the Constitution to support the Court's judgment. . . . As an exercise of raw judicial power, the Court perhaps has authority to do what it does today; but in my view its judgment is an improvident and extravagant exercise of the power of judicial review which the Constitution extends to this Court.

The Court apparently values the convenience of the pregnant mother more than the continued existence and development of the life or potential life which she carries. . . .

It is my view, therefore, that the Texas statute is not constitutionally infirm because it denies abortions to those who seek to serve only their convenience rather than to protect their life or health. . . .

Review Questions

1. Justice Blackmun discusses three reasons for the enactment of criminal abortion laws. Why doesn't he accept these reasons?
2. Where does the Constitution guarantee a right of privacy, according to Justice Blackmun?
3. Is the fetus a person in the legal sense according to Justice Blackmun?
4. According to Justice Blackmun, when is the *compelling* point in the state's interest in the health of the mother?
5. When, according to Justice Blackmun, is the *compelling* point in the state's interest in potential life?
6. Explain Justice Blackmun's conclusions.
7. What are Justice White's objections?

Discussion Questions

1. What is the right to privacy? Try to define it.
2. What do you think is properly included in the right to privacy, and what is properly excluded?
3. Do you think that the fetus has any legal rights or any moral rights? Defend your view.
4. Justice White complains that Justice Blackmun's opinion allows a woman to get an abortion "without asserting or claiming any threat to life or health" provided she is able to find a doctor willing to undertake the procedure. Do you think that women should be allowed to get such abortions? Explain your answer. Do you believe that doctors have any obligation to perform such abortions? Why or why not?

An Almost Absolute Value in History

JOHN T. NOONAN, JR.

John T. Noonan, Jr., was a judge for the United States Court of Appeals for the Ninth Circuit (in San Francisco), and is professor emeritus of law at the University of California, Berkeley. His books include *Contraception: A History of Its Treatment by the Catholic Theologians and Canonists* (1970), *Persons and Masks of the Law* (1976), and *The Lustre of Our Country: The American Experience of Religious Freedom* (1998).

Noonan begins with the question: How do you determine the humanity of a being? The answer he defends is what he says is the view of traditional Christian

Source: John T. Noonan, Jr., "An Almost Absolute Value in History," reprinted by permission of the publisher from *The Morality of Abortion,* John T. Noonan, Jr., ed. (Cambridge, Mass.: Harvard University Press), pp. 51–59. Copyright © 1970 by the President and Fellows of Harvard College.

theology, namely, that you are human if you are conceived by human parents. This view is compared with other alleged criteria of humanity, such as viability, experience, feelings of adults, sensations of adults, and social visibility. Each of these is rejected as inadequate and arbitrary. In his defense of the traditional view, Noonan does not appeal to the medieval theory of ensoulment, that is, the theory that the soul enters the body at conception. Instead, he rests his case on the fact that at conception the fetus (or strictly speaking, the zygote) receives the full genetic code of a human being. He assumes that anything with human genetic coding is a human being with rights equal to those of other humans. It follows that the fetus is a human being with rights from the moment of conception. Once this assumption has been granted, we can see that abortion is morally wrong except in rare cases where it is necessary to save the mother's life.

THE MOST FUNDAMENTAL QUESTION involved in the long history of thought on abortion is: How do you determine the humanity of a being? To phrase the question that way is to put in comprehensive humanistic terms what the theologians either dealt with as an explicitly theological question under the heading of "ensoulment" or dealt with implicitly in their treatment of abortion. The Christian position as it originated did not depend on a narrow theological or philosophical concept. It had no relation to theories of infant baptism.[1] It appealed to no special theory of instantaneous ensoulment. It took the world's view on ensoulment as that view changed from Aristotle to Zacchia. There was, indeed, theological influence affecting the theory of ensoulment finally adopted, and, of course, ensoulment itself was a theological concept, so that the position was always explained in theological terms. But the theological notion

of ensoulment could easily be translated into humanistic language by substituting "human" for "rational soul"; the problem of knowing when a man is a man is common to theology and humanism.

If one steps outside the specific categories used by the theologians, the answer they gave can be analyzed as a refusal to discriminate among human beings on the basis of their varying potentialities. Once conceived, the being was recognized as man because he had man's potential. The criterion for humanity, thus, was simple and all-embracing: if you are conceived by human parents, you are human.

The strength of this position may be tested by a review of some of the other distinctions offered in the contemporary controversy over legalizing abortion. Perhaps the most popular distinction is in terms of viability. Before an age of so many months, the fetus is not viable, that is, it cannot be removed from the mother's womb and live apart from her. To that extent, the life of the fetus is absolutely dependent on the life of the mother. This dependence is made the basis of denying recognition to its humanity.

There are difficulties with this distinction. One is that the perfection of artificial incubation may make the fetus viable at any time: it may be removed and artificially sustained. Experiments with animals already show that such a procedure

1 According to Glanville William (*The Sanctity of Human Life*) "The historical reason for the Catholic objection to abortion is the same as for the Christian Church's historical opposition to infanticide: the horror of bringing about the death of an unbaptized child." This statement is made without any citation of evidence. As had been seen, desire to administer baptism could, in the Middle Ages, even be urged as a reason for procuring an abortion. It is highly regrettable that the American Law Institute was apparently misled by Williams' account and repeated after him the same baseless statement. See American Law Institute, *Model Penal Code: Tentative Draft No. 9* (1959), p. 148, n. 12.

is possible. This hypothetical extreme case relates to an actual difficulty: there is considerable elasticity to the idea of viability. Mere length of life is not an exact measure. The viability of the fetus depends on the extent of its anatomical and functional development. The weight and length of the fetus are better guides to the state of its development than age, but weight and length vary. Moreover, different racial groups have different ages at which their fetuses are viable. Some evidence, for example, suggests that Negro fetuses mature more quickly than white fetuses. If viability is the norm, the standard would vary with race and with many individual circumstances.

The most important objection to this approach is that dependence is not ended by viability. The fetus is still absolutely dependent on someone's care in order to continue existence; indeed a child of one or three or even five years of age is absolutely dependent on another's care for existence; uncared for, the older fetus or the younger child will die as surely as the early fetus detached from the mother. The unsubstantial lessening in dependence at viability does not seem to signify any special acquisition of humanity.

A second distinction has been attempted in terms of experience. A being who has had experience, has lived and suffered, who possesses memories, is more human than one who has not. Humanity depends on formation by experience. The fetus is thus "unformed" in the most basic human sense.

This distinction is not serviceable for the embryo which is already experiencing and reacting. The embryo is responsive to touch after eight weeks and at least at that point is experiencing. At an earlier stage the zygote is certainly alive and responding to its environment. The distinction may also be challenged by the rare case where aphasia has erased adult memory: has it erased humanity? More fundamentally, this distinction leaves even the older fetus or the younger child to be treated as an unformed inhuman thing. Finally, it is not clear why experience as such confers humanity. It could be

argued that certain central experiences such as loving or learning are necessary to make a man human. But then human beings who have failed to love or to learn might be excluded from the class called man.

A third distinction is made by appeal to the sentiments of adults. If a fetus dies, the grief of the parents is not the grief they would have for a living child. The fetus is an unnamed "it" till birth, and is not perceived as personality until at least the fourth month of existence when movements in the womb manifest a vigorous presence demanding joyful recognition by the parents.

Yet feeling is notoriously an unsure guide to the humanity of others. Many groups of humans have had difficulty in feeling that persons of another tongue, color, religion, sex, are as human as they. Apart from reactions to alien groups, we mourn the loss of a ten-year-old boy more than the loss of his one-day-old brother or his 90-year-old grandfather. The difference felt and the grief expressed vary with the potentialities extinguished, or the experience wiped out; they do not seem to point to any substantial difference in the humanity of baby, boy, or grandfather.

Distinctions are also made in terms of sensation by the parents. The embryo is felt within the womb only after about the fourth month. The embryo is seen only at birth. What can be neither seen nor felt is different from what is tangible. If the fetus cannot be seen or touched at all, it cannot be perceived as man.

Yet experience shows that sight is even more untrustworthy than feeling in determining humanity. By sight, color became an appropriate index for saying who was a man, and the evil of racial discrimination was given foundation. Nor can touch provide the test; a being confined by sickness, "out of touch" with others, does not thereby seem to lose his humanity. To the extent that touch still has appeal as a criterion, it appears to be a survival of the old English idea of "quickening"—a possible mistranslation of the Latin *animatus* used in the canon law. To that extent touch as a criterion seems to be dependent on the Aristotelian notion of ensoulment, and to fall when this notion is discarded.

Finally, a distinction is sought in social visibility. The fetus is not socially perceived as human. It cannot communicate with others. Thus, both subjectively and objectively, it is not a member of society. As moral rules are rules for the behavior of members of society to each other, they cannot be made for behavior toward what is not yet a member. Excluded from the society of men, the fetus is excluded from the humanity of men.[2]

By force of the argument from the consequences, this distinction is to be rejected. It is more subtle than that founded on an appeal to physical sensation, but it is equally dangerous in its implications. If humanity depends on social recognition, individuals or whole groups may be dehumanized by being denied any status in their society. Such a fate is fictionally portrayed in *1984* and has actually been the lot of many men in many societies. In the Roman empire, for example, condemnation to slavery meant the practical denial of most human rights; in the Chinese Communist world, landlords have been classified as enemies of the people and so treated as nonpersons by the state. Humanity does not depend on social recognition, though often the failure of society to recognize the prisoner, the alien, the heterodox as human has led to the destruction of human beings. Anyone conceived by a man and a woman is human. Recognition of this condition by society follows a real event in the objective order, however imperfect and halting the recognition. Any attempt to limit humanity to exclude some group runs the risk of furnishing authority and precedent for excluding other groups in the name of the consciousness or perception of the controlling group in the society.

A philosopher may reject the appeal to the humanity of the fetus because he views "humanity" as a secular view of the soul and because he doubts the existence of anything real and objective which can be identified as humanity. One answer to such a philosopher is to ask how he reasons about moral questions without supposing that there is a sense in which he and the others of whom he speaks are human. Whatever group is taken as the society which determines who may be killed is thereby taken as human. A second answer is to ask if he does not believe that there is a right and wrong way of deciding moral questions. If there is such a difference, experience may be appealed to: to decide who is human on the basis of the sentiment of a given society has led to consequences which rational men would characterize as monstrous.

The rejection of the attempted distinctions based on viability and visibility, experience and feeling, may be buttressed by the following considerations: Moral judgments often rest on distinctions, but if the distinctions are not to appear arbitrary *fiat,* they should relate to some real difference in probabilities. There is a kind of continuity in all life, but the earlier stages of the elements of human life possess tiny probabilities of development. Consider, for example, the spermatozoa in any normal ejaculate: there are about 200,000,000 in any single ejaculate, of which one has a chance of developing into a zygote. Consider the oocytes which may become ova: there are 100,000 to 1,000,000 oocytes in a female infant, of which a maximum of 390 are ovulated. But once spermatozoon and ovum meet and the conceptus is formed, such studies as have been made show that roughly in only 20 percent of the cases will spontaneous abortion occur. In other words, the chances are about 4 out of 5 that this new being will develop. At this stage in the life of the being there is a sharp shift in probabilities, an immense jump in potentialities. To make a distinction between the rights of spermatozoa and the rights of the fertilized ovum is to respond to

---

2 . . . Thomas Aquinas gave an analogous reason against baptizing a fetus in the womb: "As long as it exists in the womb of the mother, it cannot be subject to the operation of the ministers of the Church as it is not known to men" (*In sententias Petri Lombardi* 4.6 1.1.2).

an enormous shift in possibilities. For about twenty days after conception the egg may split to form twins or combine with another egg to form a chimera, but the probability of either event happening is very small.

It may be asked, What does a change in biological probabilities have to do with establishing humanity? The argument from probabilities is not aimed at establishing humanity but at establishing an objective discontinuity which may be taken into account in moral discourse. As life itself is a matter of probabilities, as most moral reasoning is an estimate of probabilities, so it seems in accord with the structure of reality and the nature of moral thought to found a moral judgment on the change in probabilities at conception. The appeal to probabilities is the most commonsensical of arguments; to a greater or smaller degree all of us base our actions on probabilities, and in morals, as in law, prudence and negligence are often measured by the account one has taken of the probabilities. If the chance is 200,000,000 to 1 that the movement in the bushes into which you shoot is a man's, I doubt if many persons would hold you careless in shooting; but if the chances are 4 out of 5 that the movement is a human being's, few would acquit you of blame. Would the argument be different if only one out of ten children conceived came to term? Of course this argument would be different. This argument is an appeal to probabilities that actually exist, not to any and all states of affairs which may be imagined.

The probabilities as they do exist do not show the humanity of the embryo in the sense of a demonstration in logic any more than the probabilities of the movement in the bush being a man demonstrate beyond all doubt that the being is a man. The appeal is a "buttressing" consideration, showing the plausibility of the standard adopted. The argument focuses on the decisional factor in any moral judgment and assumes that part of the business of a moralist is drawing lines. One evidence of the nonarbitrary character of the line drawn is the difference of probabilities on either side of it. If a spermatozoon is destroyed, one destroys a being which had a chance of far less than 1 in 200 million of developing into a reasoning being, possessed of the genetic code, a heart and other organs, and capable of pain. If a fetus is destroyed, one destroys a being already possessed of the genetic code, organs, and sensitivity to pain, and one which had an 80 percent chance of developing further into a baby outside the womb who, in time, would reason.

The positive argument for conception as the decisive moment of humanization is that at conception the new being receives the genetic code. It is this genetic information which determines his characteristics, which is the biological carrier of the possibility of human wisdom, which makes him a self-evolving being. A being with a human genetic code is man.

This review of current controversy over the humanity of the fetus emphasizes what a fundamental question the theologians resolved in asserting the inviolability of the fetus. To regard the fetus as possessed of equal rights with other humans was not, however, to decide every case where abortion might be employed. It did decide the case where the argument was that the fetus should be aborted for its own good. To say a being was human was to say it had a destiny to decide for itself which could not be taken from it by another man's decision. But human beings with equal rights often come in conflict with each other, and some decision must be made as to whose claims are to prevail. Cases of conflict involving the fetus are different only in two respects: the total inability of the fetus to speak for itself and the fact that the right of the fetus regularly at stake is the right to life itself.

The approach taken by the theologians to these conflicts was articulated in terms of "direct" and "indirect." Again, to look at what they were doing from outside their categories, they may be said to have been drawing lines or "balancing values." "Direct" and "indirect" are spatial metaphors; "line-drawing" is another. "To weigh" or "to balance" values is a metaphor of a more complicated mathematical sort hinting at the process which goes on in moral judgments. All the metaphors suggest that, in the moral judgments made, comparisons were necessary, that no value completely controlled. The principle of double effect was no doctrine fallen from heaven, but a method of analysis appropriate where two relative values were being compared. In Catholic moral theology, as it developed, life even of the innocent was not taken as an absolute. Judgments on acts affecting life issued from a process of weighing. In the weighing, the fetus was always given a value greater than zero, always a value separate and independent from its parents. This valuation was crucial and fundamental in all Christian thought on the subject and marked it off from any approach which considered that only the parents' interests needed to be considered.

Even with the fetus weighed as human, one interest could be weighed as equal or superior: that of the mother in her own life. The casuists between 1450 and 1895 were willing to weigh this interest as superior. Since 1895, that interest was given decisive weight only in the two special cases of the cancerous uterus and the ectopic pregnancy. In both of these cases the fetus itself had little chance of survival even if the abortion were not performed. As the balance was once struck in favor of the mother whenever her life was endangered, it could be so struck again. The balance reached between 1895 and 1930 attempted prudentially and pastorally to forestall a multitude of exceptions for interests less than life.

The perception of the humanity of the fetus and the weighing of fetal rights against other human rights constituted the work of the moral analysts. But what spirit animated their abstract judgments? For the Christian community it was the injunction of Scripture to love your neighbor as yourself. The fetus as human was a neighbor; his life had parity with one's own. The commandment gave life to what otherwise would have been only rational calculation.

The commandment could be put in humanistic as well as theological terms: Do not injure your fellow man without reason. In these terms, once the humanity of the fetus is perceived, abortion is never right except in self-defense. When life must be taken to save life, reason alone cannot say that a mother must prefer a child's life to her own. With this exception, now of great rarity, abortion violates the rational humanist tenet of the equality of human lives.

For Christians the commandment to love had received a special imprint in that the exemplar proposed of love was the love of the Lord for his disciples. In the light given by this example, self-sacrifice carried to the point of death seemed in the extreme situations not without meaning. In the less extreme cases, preference for one's own interests to the life of another seemed to express cruelty or selfishness irreconcilable with the demands of love.

Review Questions

1. According to Noonan, what is the simple Christian criterion for humanity?
2. Noonan discusses five distinctions (starting with viability) used by defenders of abortion. Explain Noonan's critique of these distinctions.
3. State and explain Noonan's argument from probabilities.
4. What is Noonan's positive argument for saying that conception is "the decisive moment of humanization"?
5. In Noonan's view, why does the fetus have rights equal to those of other human beings?
6. According to Noonan, how do Christian theologians resolve conflicts of rights such as that between the mother's right to life and the fetus's right to life?

7. According to the traditional view defended by Noonan, in which cases does the fetus's right to life outweigh the mother's right to life?

Discussion Questions

1. Consider the following objection to Noonan's claim that "a being with a human genetic code is a man." A human cell also is a being with a human genetic code, but obviously it is not a man in the sense of being a human being; therefore, Noonan's claim is false. How could Noonan respond to this objection?
2. Is it possible for a nonhuman being—for example an angel or an intelligent alien being—to have rights equal to those of human beings? Defend your answer.
3. Noonan admits that abortion can be justified by appealing to the right of self-defense. Does this right justify an abortion in a case of rape? Why or why not?

A Defense of Abortion

JUDITH JARVIS THOMSON

Judith Jarvis Thomson is professor of philosophy at Massachusetts Institute of Technology and author of *Rights, Restitution, and Risk* (1986), *Acts and Other Events* (1977), *The Realm of Rights* (1990), and *Goodness and Advice* (2001). For her picture and a complete list of her publications see http://web.mit.edu/philos/www.thomson.html

Thomson does not believe that the fetus is a person from the moment of conception, and she rejects the slippery slope argument for saying this. The newly fertilized ovum is no more a person than an acorn is an oak tree. But suppose we grant, just for the sake of argument, that the fetus is a person from the moment of conception. What follows from that assumption? It does not follow, she argues, that abortion is never justified. Appealing to a series of imaginary examples such as being kidnapped and plugged into a famous violinist, she tries to convince us that the woman's rights such as the right to control her own body are strong enough to justify abortion in at least some cases. These are cases of rape, threat to life, or when the woman has taken reasonable precautions to not get pregnant. But she does not argue that abortion is justified in any case. There is a moral requirement to be a Minimally Decent Samaritan (as she puts it), and this makes a late abortion wrong if it is done just for the sake of convenience. To use her example, it would be wrong for a woman in her seventh month of pregnancy to get an abortion just to avoid the nuisance of postponing a trip abroad.

Source: Judith Jarvis Thomson, "A Defense of Abortion," from *Philosophy & Public Affairs* 1, 1 (Fall 1971): 47–66. Copyright © 1971 by Princeton University Press, Reprinted by permission of Blackwell Publishing.

MOST OPPOSITION TO abortion relies on the premise that the fetus is a human being, a person, from the moment of conception. The premise is argued for, but, as I think, not well. Take, for example, the most common argument. We are asked to notice that the development of a human being from conception through birth into childhood is continuous; then it is said that to draw a line, to choose a point in this development and say "before this point the thing is not a person, after this point it is a person" is to make an arbitrary choice, a choice for which in the nature of things no good reason can be given. It is concluded that the fetus is, or anyway that we had better say it is, a person from the moment of conception. But this conclusion does not follow. Similar things might be said about the development of an acorn into an oak tree, and it does not follow that acorns are oak trees, or that we had better say they are. Arguments of this form are sometimes called "slippery slope arguments"—the phrase is perhaps self-explanatory—and it is dismaying that opponents of abortion rely on them so heavily and uncritically.

I am inclined to agree, however, that the prospects for "drawing a line" in the development of the fetus look dim. I am inclined to think also that we shall probably have to agree that the fetus has already become a human person well before birth. Indeed, it comes as a surprise when one first learns how early in its life it begins to acquire human characteristics. By the tenth week, for example, it already has a face, arms and legs, fingers and toes; it has internal organs, and brain activity is detectable.[1] On the other hand, I think that the premise is false, that the fetus is not a person from the moment of

conception. A newly fertilized ovum, a newly implanted clump of cells, is no more a person than an acorn is an oak tree. But I shall not discuss any of this. For it seems to me to be of great interest to ask what happens if, for the sake of argument, we allow the premise. How, precisely, are we supposed to get from there to the conclusion that abortion is morally impermissible? Opponents of abortion commonly spend most of their time establishing that the fetus is a person, and hardly any time explaining the step from there to the impermissibility of abortion. Perhaps they think the step too simple and obvious to require much comment. Or perhaps instead they are simply being economical in argument. Many of those who defend abortion rely on the premise that the fetus is not a person, but only a bit of tissue that will become a person at birth; and why pay out more arguments than you have to? Whatever the explanation, I suggest that the step they take is neither easy nor obvious, that it calls for closer examination than it is commonly given, and that when we do give it this closer examination we shall feel inclined to reject it.

I propose, then, that we grant that the fetus is a person from the moment of conception. How does the argument go from here? Something like this, I take it. Every person has a right to life. So the fetus has a right to life. No doubt the mother has a right to decide what shall happen in and to her body; everyone would grant that. But surely a person's right to life is stronger and more stringent than the mother's right to decide what happens in and to her body, and so outweighs it. So the fetus may not be killed; an abortion may not be performed.

It sounds plausible. But now let me ask you to imagine this. You wake up in the morning and find yourself back to back in bed with an unconscious violinist. A famous unconscious violinist. He has been found to have a fatal kidney ailment, and the Society of Music Lovers has canvassed all the available medical records and found that you alone have the right blood type to help. They have therefore kidnapped

---

1 Daniel Callahan, *Abortion: Law, Choice and Morality* (New York, 1970), p. 373. This book gives a fascinating survey of the available information on abortion. The Jewish tradition is surveyed in David M. Feldman, *Birth Control in Jewish Law* (New York, 1968), Part 5, the Catholic tradition in John T. Noonan, Jr., "An Almost Absolute Value in History," in *The Morality of Abortion*, ed. John T. Noonan, Jr. (Cambridge, Mass., 1970).

you, and last night the violinist's circulatory system was plugged into yours, so that your kidneys can be used to extract poisons from his blood as well as your own. The director of the hospital now tells you, "Look, we're sorry the Society of Music Lovers did this to you—we would never have permitted it if we had known. But still, they did it, and the violinist now is plugged into you. To unplug you would be to kill him. But never mind, it's only for nine months. By then he will have recovered from his ailment, and can safely be unplugged from you." Is it morally incumbent on you to accede to this situation? No doubt it would be very nice of you if you did, a great kindness. But do you *have* to accede to it? What if it were not nine months, but nine years? Or longer still? What if the director of the hospital says, "Tough luck, I agree, but you've now got to stay in bed, with the violinist plugged into you, for the rest of your life. Because remember this. All persons have a right to life, and violinists are persons. Granted you have a right to decide what happens in and to your body, but a person's right to life outweighs your right to decide what happens in and to your body. So you cannot ever be unplugged from him." I imagine you would regard this as outrageous, which suggests that something really is wrong with that plausible-sounding argument I mentioned a moment ago.

In this case, of course, you were kidnapped; you didn't volunteer for the operation that plugged the violinist into your kidneys. Can those who oppose abortion on the ground I mentioned make an exception for a pregnancy due to rape? Certainly. They can say that persons have a right to life only if they didn't come into existence because of rape; or they can say that all persons have a right to life, but that some have less of a right to life than others, in particular, that those who came into existence because of rape have less. But these statements have a rather unpleasant sound. Surely the question of whether you have a right to life at all, or how

much of it you have, shouldn't turn on the question of whether or not you are the product of a rape. And in fact the people who oppose abortion on the ground I mentioned do not make this distinction, and hence do not make an exception in case of rape.

Nor do they make an exception for a case in which the mother has to spend the nine months of her pregnancy in bed. They would agree that would be a great pity, and hard on the mother; but all the same, all persons have a right to life, the fetus is a person, and so on. I suspect, in fact, that they would not make an exception for a case in which, miraculously enough, the pregnancy went on for nine years, or even the rest of the mother's life.

Some won't even make an exception for a case in which continuation of the pregnancy is likely to shorten the mother's life; they regard abortion as impermissible even to save the mother's life. Such cases are nowadays very rare, and many opponents of abortion do not accept this extreme view. All the same, it is a good place to begin: a number of points of interest come out in respect to it.

1. Let us call the view that abortion is impermissible even to save the mother's life "the extreme view." I want to suggest first that it does not issue from the argument I mentioned earlier without the addition of some fairly powerful premises. Suppose a woman has become pregnant, and now learns that she has a cardiac condition such that she will die if she carries the baby to term. What may be done for her? The fetus, being a person, has a right to life, but as the mother is a person too, so has she a right to life. Presumably they have an equal right to life. How is it supposed to come out that an abortion may not be performed? If mother and child have an equal right to life, shouldn't we perhaps flip a coin? Or should we add to the mother's right to life her right to decide what happens in and to her body, which everybody seems to be ready to grant—the sum of her rights now outweighing the fetus' right to life?

The most familiar argument here is the following. We are told that performing the abortion would be directly killing[2] the child, whereas doing nothing would not be killing the mother, but only letting her die. Moreover, in killing the child, one would be killing an innocent person, for the child has committed no crime, and is not aiming at his mother's death. And then there are a variety of ways in which this might be continued. (1) But as directly killing an innocent person is always and absolutely impermissible, an abortion may not be performed. Or (2) as directly killing an innocent person is murder, and murder is always and absolutely impermissible, an abortion may not be performed.[3] Or (3) as one's duty to refrain from directly killing an innocent person is more stringent than one's duty to keep a person from dying, an abortion may not be performed. Or (4) if one's only options are directly killing an innocent person or letting a person die, one must prefer letting the person die, and thus an abortion may not be performed.[4]

Some people seem to have thought that these are not further premises which must be added if the conclusion is to be reached, but that they follow from the very fact that an innocent person has a right to life.[5] But this seems to me to be a mistake, and perhaps the simplest way to show this is to bring out that while we must certainly grant that innocent persons have a right to life, the theses in (1) through (4) are all false. Take (2), for example. If directly killing an innocent person is murder, and thus is impermissible, then the mother's directly killing the innocent person inside her is murder, and thus is impermissible. But it cannot seriously be thought to be murder if the mother performs an abortion on herself to save her life. It cannot seriously be said that she *must* refrain, that she *must* sit passively by and wait for her death. Let us look again at the case of you and the violinist. There you are, in bed with the violinist, and the director of the hospital says to you, "It's all most distressing, and I deeply sympathize, but you see this is putting an additional strain on your kidneys, and you'll be dead within the month. But you *have* to stay where you are all the same. Because unplugging you would be directly killing an innocent violinist, and that's murder, and that's impermissible." If anything in the world is true, it is that you do not commit murder, you do not do what is impermissible, if you reach around to your back and unplug yourself from that violinist to save your life.

The main focus of attention in writings on abortion has been on what a third party may or may not do in answer to a request from a woman for an abortion. This is in a way understandable.

2 The term "direct" in the arguments I refer to is a technical one. Roughly, what is meant by "direct killing" is either killing as an end in itself, or killing as a means to some end, for example, the end of saving someone else's life. See note 5 for an example of its use.

3 Cf. *Encyclical Letter of Pope Pius XI on Christian Marriage,* St. Paul Editions (Boston, n.d.), p. 32: "however much we may pity the mother whose health and even life is gravely imperiled in the performance of the duty alloted to her by nature, nevertheless what could ever be a sufficient reason for excusing in any way the direct murder of the innocent? This is precisely what we are dealing with here." Noonan (*The Morality of Abortion,* p. 43) reads this as follows: "What cause can ever avail to excuse in any way the direct killing of the innocent? For it is a question of that."

4 The thesis in (4) is in an interesting way weaker than those in (1), (2), and (3): they rule out abortion even in cases in which both mother *and* child will die if the abortion is not performed. By contrast, one who held the view expressed in (4) could consistently say that one needn't prefer letting two persons die to killing one.

5 Cf. The following passage from Pius XII, *Address to the Italian Catholic Society of Midwives:* "The baby in the maternal breast has the right to life immediately from God. Hence there is no man, no human authority, no science, no medical, eugenic, social, economic or moral 'indication' which can establish or grant a valid juridical ground for a direct deliberate disposition of an innocent human life, that is, a disposition which looks to its destruction either as an end or as a means to another end perhaps in itself not illicit. The baby, still not born, is a man in the same degree and for the same reason as the mother" (quoted in Noonan, *The Morality of Abortion,* p. 45).

Things being as they are, there isn't much a woman can safely do to abort herself. So the question asked is what a third party may do, and what the mother may do, if it is mentioned at all, is deduced, almost as an afterthought, from what it is concluded that third parties may do. But it seems to me that to treat the matter in this way is to refuse to grant to the mother that very status of person which is so firmly insisted on for the fetus. For we cannot simply read off what a person may do from what a third party may do. Suppose you find yourself trapped in a tiny house with a growing child. I mean a very tiny house, and a rapidly growing child—you are already up against the wall of the house and in a few minutes you'll be crushed to death. The child on the other hand won't be crushed to death; if nothing is done to stop him from growing he'll be hurt, but in the end he'll simply burst open the house and walk out a free man. Now I could well understand it if a bystander were to say, "There's nothing we can do for you. We cannot choose between your life and his, we cannot be the ones to decide who is to live, we cannot intervene." But it cannot be concluded that you too can do nothing, that you cannot attack it to save your life. However innocent the child may be, you do not have to wait passively while it crushes you to death. Perhaps a pregnant woman is vaguely felt to have the status of house, to which we don't allow the right of self-defense. But if the woman houses the child, it should be remembered that she is a person who houses it.

I should perhaps stop to say explicitly that I am not claiming that people have a right to do anything whatever to save their lives. I think, rather, that there are drastic limits to the right of self-defense. If someone threatens you with death unless you torture someone else to death, I think you have not the right, even to save your life, to do so. But the case under consideration here is very different. In our case there are only two people involved, one whose life is threatened, and one who threatens it. Both are innocent: the one who is threatened is not threatened because of any fault, the one who threatens does not threaten because of any fault. For this reason we may feel that we bystanders cannot intervene. But the person threatened can.

In sum, a woman surely can defend her life against the threat to it posed by the unborn child, even if doing so involves its death. And this shows not merely that the theses in (1) through (4) are false; it shows also that the extreme view of abortion is false, and so we need not canvass any other possible ways of arriving at it from the argument I mentioned at the outset.

2. The extreme view could of course be weakened to say that while abortion is permissible to save the mother's life, it may not be performed by the third party, but only by the mother herself. But this cannot be right either. For what we have to keep in mind is that the mother and the unborn child are not like two tenants in a small house which has, by an unfortunate mistake, been rented to both: the mother *owns* the house. The fact that she does adds to the offensiveness of deducing that the mother can do nothing from the supposition that third parties can do nothing. But it does more than this: it casts a bright light on the supposition that third parties can do nothing. Certainly it lets us see that a third party who says "I cannot choose between you" is fooling himself if he thinks this is impartiality. If Jones has found and fastened on a certain coat, which he needs to keep him from freezing, but which Smith also needs to keep him from freezing, then it is not impartiality that says "I cannot choose between you" when Smith owns the coat. Women have said again and again "This body is *my* body!" and they have reason to feel angry, reason to feel that it has been like shouting into the wind. Smith, after all, is hardly likely to bless us if we say to him, "Of course it's your coat, anybody would grant that it is. But no one may choose between you and Jones who is to have it." . . .

3. Where the mother's life is not at stake, the argument I mentioned at the outset seems to have a much stronger pull. "Everyone has a right to life, so the unborn person has a right to

life." And isn't the child's right to life weightier than anything other than the mother's own right to life, which she might put forward as ground for an abortion?

This argument treats the right to life as if it were unproblematic. It is not, and this seems to me to be precisely the source of the mistake.

For we should now, at long last, ask what it comes to, to have a right to life. In some views having a right to life includes having a right to be given at least the bare minimum one needs for continued life. But suppose that what in fact *is* the bare minimum a man needs for continued life is something he has no right at all to be given? If I am sick unto death, and the only thing that will save my life is the touch of Henry Fonda's cool hand on my fevered brow, then all the same, I have no right to be given the touch of Henry Fonda's cool hand on my fevered brow. It would be frightfully nice of him to fly in from the West Coast to provide it. It would be less nice, though no doubt well meant, if my friends flew out to the West Coast and carried Henry Fonda back with them. But I have no right at all against anybody that he should do this for me. Or again, to return to the story I told earlier, the fact that for continued life that violinist needs the continued use of your kidneys does not establish that he has a right to be given the continued use of your kidneys. He certainly has no right against you that *you* should give him continued use of your kidneys. For nobody has any right to use your kidneys unless you give him such a right; and nobody has the right against you that you shall give him this right—if you do allow him to go on using your kidneys, this is kindness on your part, and not something he can claim from you as his due. Nor has he any right against anybody else that *they* should give him continued use of your kidneys. Certainly he had no right against the Society of Music Lovers that they should plug him into you in the first place. And if you now start to unplug yourself, having learned that you will otherwise have to spend nine years in bed with him, there is nobody in the world who must try to prevent

you, in order to see to it that he is given something he has a right to be given.

Some people are rather stricter about the right to life. In their view, it does not include the right to be given anything, but amounts to, and only to, the right not to be killed by anybody. But here a related difficulty arises. If everybody is to refrain from killing that violinist, then everybody must refrain from doing a great many different sorts of things. Everybody must refrain from slitting his throat, everybody must refrain from shooting him—and everybody must refrain from unplugging you from him. But does he have a right against everybody that they shall refrain from unplugging you from him? To refrain from doing this is to allow him to continue to use your kidneys. It could be argued that he has a right against us that *we* should allow him to continue to use your kidneys. That is, while he had no right against us that we should give him the use of your kidneys, it might be argued that he anyway has a right against us that we shall not now intervene and deprive him of the use of your kidneys. I shall come back to third-party interventions later. But certainly the violinist has no right against you that *you* shall allow him to continue to use your kidneys. As I said, if you do allow him to use them, it is a kindness on your part, and not something you owe him.

The difficulty I point to here is not peculiar to the right to life. It reappears in connection with all the other natural rights; and it is something which an adequate account of rights must deal with. For present purposes it is enough just to draw attention to it. But I would stress that I am not arguing that people do not have a right to life—quite to the contrary, it seems to me that the primary control we must place on the acceptability of an account of rights is that it should turn out in that account to be a truth that all persons have a right to life. I am arguing only that having a right to life does not guarantee having either a right to be given the use of or a right to be allowed continued use of another person's body—even if one needs it for life itself.

So the right to life will not serve the opponents of abortion in the very simple and clear way in which they seem to have thought it would.

4. There is another way to bring out the difficulty. In the most ordinary sort of case, to deprive someone of what he has a right to is to treat him unjustly. Suppose a boy and his small brother are jointly given a box of chocolates for Christmas. If the older boy takes the box and refuses to give his brother any of the chocolates, he is unjust to him, for the brother has been given a right to half of them. But suppose that, having learned that otherwise it means nine years in bed with that violinist, you unplug yourself from him. You surely are not being unjust to him, for you gave him no right to use your kidneys, and no one else can have given him any such right. But we have to notice that in unplugging yourself, you are killing him; and violinists, like everybody else, have a right to life, and thus in the view we were considering just now, the right not to be killed. So here you do what he supposedly has a right you shall not do, but you do not act unjustly to him in doing it.

The emendation which may be made at this point is this: the right to life consists not in the right not to be killed, but rather in the right not to be killed unjustly. This runs a risk of circularity, but never mind: it would enable us to square the fact that the violinist has a right to life with the fact that you do not act unjustly toward him in unplugging yourself, thereby killing him. For if you do not kill him unjustly, you do not violate his right to life, and so it is no wonder you do him no injustice.

But if this emendation is accepted, the gap in the argument against abortion stares us plainly in the face: it is by no means enough to show that the fetus is a person, and to remind us that all persons have a right to life—we need to be shown also that killing the fetus violates its right to life, i.e., that abortion is unjust killing. And is it?

I suppose we may take it as a datum that in a case of pregnancy due to rape the mother has not given the unborn person a right to the use of her body for food and shelter. Indeed, in what pregnancy could it be supposed that the mother has given the unborn person such a right? It is not as if there were unborn persons drifting about the world, to whom a woman who wants a child says "I invite you in."

But it might be argued that there are other ways one can have acquired a right to the use of another person's body than by having been invited to use it by that person. Suppose a woman voluntarily indulges in intercourse, knowing of the chance it will issue in pregnancy, and then she does become pregnant; is she not in part responsible for the presence, in fact the very existence, of the unborn person inside her? No doubt she did not invite it in. But doesn't her partial responsibility for its being there itself give it a right to the use of her body?[6] If so, then her aborting it would be more like the boy's taking away the chocolates, and less like your unplugging yourself from the violinist—doing so would be depriving it of what it does have a right to, and thus would be doing it an injustice.

And then, too, it might be asked whether or not she can kill it even to save her own life: If she voluntarily called it into existence, how can she now kill it, even in self-defense?

The first thing to be said about this is that it is something new. Opponents of abortion have been so concerned to make out the independence of the fetus, in order to establish that it has a right to life, just as its mother does, that they have tended to overlook the possible support they might gain from making out that the fetus is *dependent* on the mother, in order to establish that she has a special kind of responsibility for it, a responsibility that gives it rights against her which are not possessed by any independent person—such as an ailing violinist who is a stranger to her.

On the other hand, this argument would give the unborn person a right to its mother's

---

6 The need for a discussion of this argument was brought home to me by members of the Society for Ethical and Legal Philosophy, to whom this paper was originally presented.

body only if her pregnancy resulted from a voluntary act, undertaken in full knowledge of the chance a pregnancy might result from it. It would leave out entirely the unborn person whose existence is due to rape. Pending the availability of some further argument, then, we would be left with the conclusion that unborn persons whose existence is due to rape have no right to the use of their mothers' bodies, and thus that aborting them is not depriving them of anything they have a right to and hence is not unjust killing.

And we should also notice that it is not at all plain that this argument really does go even as far as it purports to. For there are cases and cases, and the details make a difference. If the room is stuffy, and I therefore open a window to air it, and a burglar climbs in, it would be absurd to say, "Ah, now he can stay, she's given him a right to the use of her house—for she is partially responsible for his presence there, having voluntarily done what enabled him to get in, in full knowledge that there are such things as burglars, and that burglars burgle." It would be still more absurd to say this if I had had bars installed outside my windows, precisely to prevent burglars from getting in, and a burglar got in only because of a defect in the bars. It remains equally absurd if we imagine it is not a burglar who climbs in, but an innocent person who blunders or falls in. Again, suppose it were like this: people-seeds drift about in the air like pollen, and if you open your windows, one may drift in and take root in your carpets or upholstery. You don't want children, so you fix up your windows with fine mesh screens, the very best you can buy. As can happen, however, and on very, very rare occasions does happen, one of the screens is defective; and a seed drifts in and takes root. Does the person-plant who now develops have a right to the use of your house? Surely not—despite the fact that you voluntarily opened your windows, you knowingly kept carpets and upholstered furniture, and you knew that screens were sometimes defective. Someone may argue that you are responsible for its

rooting, that it does have a right to your house, because after all you *could* have lived out your life with bare floors and furniture, or with sealed windows and doors. But this won't do—for by the same token anyone can avoid a pregnancy due to rape by having a hysterectomy, or anyway by never leaving home without a (reliable!) army.

It seems to me that the argument we are looking at can establish at most that there are *some* cases in which the unborn person has a right to the use of its mother's body, and therefore *some* cases in which abortion is unjust killing. There is room for much discussion and argument as to precisely which, if any. But I think we should sidestep this issue and leave it open, for at any rate the argument certainly does not establish that all abortion is unjust killing.

5. There is room for yet another argument here, however. We surely must all grant that there may be cases in which it would be morally indecent to detach a person from your body at the cost of his life. Suppose you learn that what the violinist needs is not nine years of your life, but only one hour: all you need do to save his life is to spend one hour in that bed with him. Suppose also that letting him use your kidneys for that one hour would not affect your health in the slightest. Admittedly you were kidnapped. Admittedly you did not give anyone permission to plug him into you. Nevertheless it seems to me plain you *ought* to allow him to use your kidneys for that hour—it would be indecent to refuse.

Again, suppose pregnancy lasted only an hour, and constituted no threat to life or health. And suppose that a woman becomes pregnant as a result of rape. Admittedly she did not voluntarily do anything to bring about the existence of a child. Admittedly she did nothing at all which would give the unborn person a right to the use of her body. All the same it might well be said, as in the newly emended violinist story, that she *ought* to allow it to remain for that hour—that it would be indecent in her to refuse.

Now some people are inclined to use the term "right" in such a way that it follows from the fact that you ought to allow a person to use your body for the hour he needs, that he has a right to use your body for the hour he needs, even though he has not been given that right by any person or act. They may say that it follows also that if you refuse, you act unjustly toward him. This use of the term is perhaps so common that it cannot be called wrong; nevertheless it seems to me to be an unfortunate loosening of what we would do better to keep a tight rein on. Suppose that box of chocolates I mentioned earlier had not been given to both boys jointly, but was given only to the older boy. There he sits, stolidly eating his way through the box, his small brother watching enviously. Here we are likely to say "You ought not to be so mean. You ought to give your brother some of those chocolates." My own view is that it just does not follow from the truth of this that the brother has any right to any of the chocolates. If the boy refuses to give his brother any, he is greedy, stingy, callous—but not unjust. I suppose that the people I have in mind will say it does follow that the brother has a right to some of the chocolates, and thus that the boy does act unjustly if he refuses to give his brother any. But the effect of saying this is to obscure what we should keep distinct, namely the difference between the boy's refusal in this case and the boy's refusal in the earlier case, in which the box was given to both boys jointly, and in which the small brother thus had what was from any point of view clear title to half.

A further objection to so using the term "right" that from the fact that A ought to do a thing for B, it follows that B has a right against A that A do it for him, is that it is going to make the question of whether or not a man has a right to a thing turn on how easy it is to provide him with it; and this seems not merely unfortunate, but morally unacceptable. Take the case of Henry Fonda again. I said earlier that I had no right to the touch of his cool hand on my fevered brow, even though I needed it to save my life. I said it would be frightfully nice of him to fly in from the West Coast to provide me with it, but that I

had no right against him that he should do so. But suppose he isn't on the West Coast. Suppose he has only to walk across the room, place a hand briefly on my brow—and lo, my life is saved. Then surely he ought to do it, it would be indecent to refuse. Is it to be said "Ah, well, it follows that in this case she has a right to the touch of his hand on her brow, and so it would be an injustice in him to refuse"? So that I have a right to it when it is easy for him to provide it, though no right when it's hard? It's rather a shocking idea that anyone's rights should fade away and disappear as it gets harder and harder to accord them to him.

So my own view is that even though you ought to let the violinist use your kidneys for the one hour he needs, we should not conclude that he has a right to do so—we should say that if you refuse, you are, like the boy who owns all the chocolates and will give none away, self-centered and callous, indecent in fact, but not unjust. And similarly, that even supposing a case in which a woman pregnant due to rape ought to allow the unborn person to use her body for the hour he needs, we should not conclude that he has a right to do so; we should conclude that she is self-centered, callous, indecent, but not unjust, if she refuses. The complaints are no less grave; they are just different. However, there is no need to insist on this point. If anyone does wish to deduce "he has a right" from "you ought," then all the same he must surely grant that there are cases in which it is not morally required of you that you allow that violinist to use your kidneys, and in which he does not have a right to use them, and in which you do not do him an injustice if you refuse. And so also for mother and unborn child. Except in such cases as the unborn person has a right to demand it—and we were leaving open the possibility that there may be such cases—nobody is morally *required* to make large sacrifices, of health, of all other interests and concerns, of all other duties and commitments, for nine years, or even for nine months, in order to keep another person alive. . . .

6. My argument will be found unsatisfactory on two counts by many of those who want to regard abortion as morally permissible. First, while I do argue that abortion is not impermissible, I do not argue that it is always permissible. There may well be cases in which carrying the child to term requires only Minimally Decent Samaritanism of the mother, and this is a standard we must not fall below. I am inclined to think it a merit of my account precisely that it does *not* give a general yes or a general no. It allows for and supports our sense that, for example, a sick and desperately frightened fourteen-year-old schoolgirl, pregnant due to rape, may *of course* choose abortion, and that any law which rules this out is an insane law. And it also allows for and supports our sense that in other cases resort to abortion is even positively indecent. It would be indecent in the woman to request an abortion, and indecent in a doctor to perform it, if she is in her seventh month, and wants the abortion just to avoid the nuisance of postponing a trip abroad. The very fact that the arguments I have been drawing attention to treat all cases of abortion, or even all cases of abortion in which the mother's life is not at stake, as morally on a par ought to have made them suspect at the outset.

Secondly, while I am arguing for the permissibility of abortion in some cases, I am not arguing for the right to secure the death of the unborn child. It is easy to confuse these two things in that up to a certain point in the life of the fetus it is not able to survive outside the mother's body; hence removing it from her body guarantees its death. But they are importantly different. I have argued that you are not morally required to spend nine months in bed, sustaining the life of that violinist; but to say this is by no means to say that if, when you unplug yourself, there is a miracle and he survives, you then have a right to turn round and slit his throat. You may detach yourself even if this costs him his life; you have no right to be guaranteed his death, by some other means, if unplugging yourself does not kill him. There are some people who will feel dissatisfied by this feature of my argument. A woman may be utterly devastated by the thought of a child, a bit of herself, put out for adoption and never seen or heard of again. She may therefore want not merely that the child be detached from her, but more, that it die. Some opponents of abortion are inclined to regard this as beneath contempt—thereby showing insensitivity to what is surely a powerful source of despair. All the same, I agree that the desire for the child's death is not one which anybody may gratify, should it turn out to be possible to detach the child alive.

At this place, however, it should be remembered that we have only been pretending throughout that the fetus is a human being from the moment of conception. A very early abortion is surely not the killing of a person, and so is not dealt with by anything I have said here.

Review Questions

1. What are "slippery slope arguments," and why does Thomson reject them?
2. Explain the example about the famous violinist.
3. What is the "extreme view," and what argument is used to defend it? How does Thomson attack this argument?
4. What is the point of the example about the tiny house and the growing child?
5. Why do women say, "This body is *my* body"? Do they say this?
6. Explain the example about "Henry Fonda's cool hand on my fevered brow."
7. What is the point of the example about people-seeds taking root in the carpet?
8. What are Thomson's conclusions? When is abortion justified and when is it not justified?

Discussion Questions

1. Is the case of the famous violinist really analogous to a case of pregnancy caused by rape?
2. What are the limits to the right to self-defense? Do these limits apply to abortion in cases of rape?
3. What obligations do we have to people who have a right to life? Do we have an obligation, for example, to take care of them and feed them?
4. Does a woman who is accidentally pregnant have a right to get an abortion?

On the Moral and Legal Status of Abortion

MARY ANNE WARREN

Mary Anne Warren is professor of philosophy at San Francisco State University. Her books include *The Nature of Woman* (1980), *Gendercide* (1985), and *Moral Status* (2000).

In the first part of her article, Warren argues that Thomson's argument about the famous violinist proves that abortion is justified in cases of rape but fails to demonstrate that abortion is permissible when pregnancy is not due to rape and is not life threatening. Warren thinks that more argument is needed to show the permissibility of abortion in those cases.

In the second part, Warren begins by distinguishing between two senses of the term *human being,* a genetic sense and a moral sense. She criticizes Noonan for not providing an argument for saying that whatever is genetically human is also morally human. Then she suggests six criteria for personhood: sentience, emotionality, reason, the capacity to communicate, self-awareness, and moral agency. She claims that the fetus has none of these characteristics of a person in the early stages of development, and thus it is not a person with moral rights in those stages. The fact that a late-term fetus resembles a person is taken seriously by Warren, and she recommends that women wanting an abortion get one before the third trimester. But she is not impressed by an appeal to the fetus's potential for becoming a person because she thinks that the rights of an actual person—namely, the mother— will always outweigh the rights of a merely potential person when they conflict. Warren concludes with a reply to the objection that her view justifies infanticide. She argues that there are several reasons why infanticide is more difficult to justify than abortion.

Source: Mary Anne Warren, "On the Moral and Legal Status of Abortion," from *Ethics in Practice,* ed. Hugh LaFollette, pp. 79–90. Copyright © 1997 Blackwell Publishers. Reprinted with permission.

FOR OUR PURPOSES, abortion may be defined as the act a woman performs in deliberately terminating her pregnancy before it comes to term, or in allowing another person to terminate it. Abortion usually entails the death of a fetus.[1] Nevertheless, I will argue that it is morally permissible, and should be neither legally prohibited nor made needlessly difficult to obtain, e.g., by obstructive legal regulations.[2]

Some philosophers have argued that the moral status of abortion cannot be resolved by rational means.[3] If this is so then liberty should prevail; for it is not a proper function of the law to enforce prohibitions upon personal behavior that cannot clearly be shown to be morally objectionable, and seriously so. But the advocates of prohibition believe that their position is objectively correct, and not merely a result of religious beliefs or personal prejudices. They argue that the humanity of the fetus is a matter of scientific fact, and that abortion is therefore the moral equivalent of murder, and must be prohibited in all or most cases. (Some would make an exception when the woman's life is in danger, or when the pregnancy is due to rape or incest; others would prohibit abortion even in these cases.)

In response, advocates of a right to choose abortion point to the terrible consequences of prohibiting it, especially while contraception is still unreliable, and is financially beyond the reach of much of the world's population. Worldwide, hundreds of thousands of women die each year from illegal abortions, and many more suffer from complications that may leave them injured or infertile. Women who are poor, under-age, disabled, or otherwise vulnerable, suffer most from the absence of safe and legal abortion. Advocates of choice also argue that to deny a woman access to abortion is to deprive her of the right to control her own body—a right so fundamental that without it other rights are often all but meaningless.

These arguments do not convince abortion opponents. The tragic consequences of prohibition leave them unmoved, because they regard the deliberate killing of fetuses as even more tragic. Nor do appeals to the right to control one's own body impress them, since they deny that this right includes the right to destroy a fetus. We cannot hope to persuade those who equate abortion with murder that they are mistaken, unless we can refute the standard antiabortion argument: that because fetuses are human beings, they have a right to life equal to that of any other human being. Unfortunately, confusion has prevailed with respect to the two important questions which that argument raises: (1) Is a human fetus really a human being at all stages of prenatal development? and (2) If so, what (if anything) follows about the moral and legal status of abortion?

John Noonan says that "the fundamental question in the long history of abortion is: How do you determine the humanity of a being?"[4] His antiabortion argument is essentially that of the Roman Catholic Church. In his words,

> . . . it is wrong to kill humans, however poor, weak, defenseless, and lacking in opportunity to develop their potential they may be. It is therefore morally wrong to kill Biafrans. Similarly, it is morally wrong to kill embryos.[5]

Noonan bases his claim that fetuses are human beings from the time of conception upon what he calls the theologians' criterion of humanity:

1 Strictly speaking, a human conceptus does not become a fetus until the primary organ systems have formed, at about six to eight weeks gestational age. However, for simplicity I shall refer to the conceptus as a fetus at every stage of its prenatal development.

2 The views defended in this article are set forth in greater depth in my book *Moral Status*, (Oxford University Press, 2000).

3 For example, Roger Wertheimer argues, in "Understanding the Abortion Argument," *Philosophy and Public Affairs*, 1 (Fall, 1971), that the moral status of abortion is not a question of fact, but only of how one responds to the facts.

4 John Noonan, "Abortion and the Catholic Church: A Summary History," *Natural Law Forum*, 12 (1967), p. 125.

5 John Noonan, "Deciding Who Is Human," *Natural Law Forum*, 13 (1968), p. 134.

that whoever is conceived of human beings is a human being. But although he argues at length for the appropriateness of this criterion of humanity, he does not question the assumption that if a fetus is a human being then abortion is almost always immoral.[6]

Judith Thomson has questioned this assumption. She argues that, even if we grant the antiabortionist the claim that a fetus is a human being with the same right to life as any other human being, we can still demonstrate that women are not morally obliged to complete every unwanted pregnancy.[7] Her argument is worth examining, because if it is sound it may enable us to establish the moral permissibility of abortion without having to decide just what makes an entity a human being, or what entitles it to full moral rights. This would represent a considerable gain in the power and simplicity of the pro-choice position.

Even if Thomson's argument does not hold up, her essential insight—that it requires *argument* to show that if fetuses are human beings then abortion is murder—is a valuable one. The assumption that she attacks is invidious, for it requires that in our deliberations about the ethics of abortion we must ignore almost entirely the needs of the pregnant woman and other persons for whom she is responsible. This will not do; determining what moral rights a fetus has is only one step in determining the moral status of abortion. The next step is finding a just solution to conflicts between whatever rights the fetus has, and the rights and responsibilities of the woman who is unwillingly pregnant.

My own inquiry will also have two stages. In Section I, I consider whether abortion can be

shown to be morally permissible even on the assumption that a fetus is a human being with a strong right to life. I argue that this cannot be established, except in special cases. Consequently, we cannot avoid facing the question of whether or not a fetus has the same right to life as any human being.

In Section II, I propose an answer to this question, namely, that a fetus is not a member of the moral community—the set of beings with full and equal moral rights. The reason that a fetus is not a member of the moral community is that it is not yet a person, nor is it enough like a person in the morally relevant respects to be regarded the equal of those human beings who are persons. I argue that it is personhood, and not genetic humanity, which is the fundamental basis for membership in the moral community. A fetus, especially in the early stages of its development, satisfies none of the criteria of personhood. Consequently, it makes no sense to grant it moral rights strong enough to override the woman's moral rights to liberty, bodily integrity, and sometimes life itself. Unlike an infant who has already been born, a fetus cannot be granted full and equal moral rights without severely threatening the rights and well-being of women. Nor, as we will see, is a fetus's *potential* personhood a threat to the moral permissibility of abortion, since merely potential persons do not have a moral right to become actual—or none that is strong enough to override the fundamental moral rights of actual persons.

I

Judith Thomson argues that, even if a fetus has a right to life, abortion is often morally permissible. Her argument is based upon an imaginative analogy. She asks you to picture yourself waking up one day, in bed with a famous violinist, who is a stranger to you. Imagine that you have been kidnapped, and your bloodstream connected to that of the violinist, who has an ailment that will kill him unless he is permitted to share your kidneys for nine months.

6 Noonan deviates from the current position of the Roman Catholic Church in that he thinks that abortion is morally permissible when it is the only way of saving the woman's life. See "An Almost Absolute Value in History," in *Contemporary Issues in Bioethics,* edited by Tom L. Beauchamp and LeRoy Walters (Belmont, California: Wadsworth, 1994), p. 283.

7 Judith Jarvis Thomson, "A Defense of Abortion," *Philosophy and Public Affairs,* 1:1 (Fall, 1971), pp. 173–8.

No one else can save him, since you alone have the right type of blood. Consequently, the Society of Music Lovers has arranged for you to be kidnapped and hooked up. If you unhook yourself, he will die. But if you remain in bed with him, then after nine months he will be cured and able to survive without further assistance from you.

Now, Thomson asks, what are your obligations in this situation? To be consistent, the antiabortionist must say that you are obliged to stay in bed with the violinist: for violinists are human beings, and all human beings have a right to life.[8] But this is outrageous; thus, there must be something very wrong with the same argument when it is applied to abortion. It would be extremely generous of you to agree to stay in bed with the violinist; but it is absurd to suggest that your refusal to do so would be the moral equivalent of murder. The violinist's right to life does not oblige you to do whatever is required to keep him alive; still less does it justify anyone else in forcing you to do so. A law which required you to stay in bed with the violinist would be an unjust law, since unwilling persons ought not to be required to be Extremely Good Samaritans, i.e., to make enormous personal sacrifices for the sake of other individuals towards whom they have no special prior obligation.

Thomson concludes that we can grant the antiabortionist his claim that a fetus is a human being with a right to life, and still hold that a pregnant woman is morally entitled to refuse to be an Extremely Good Samaritan toward the fetus. For there is a great gap between the claim that a human being has a right to life, and the claim that other human beings are morally obligated to do whatever is necessary to keep him alive. One has no duty to keep another human being alive *at great personal cost*, unless one has somehow contracted a special obligation toward that individual; and a woman who is pregnant may have done nothing that

morally obliges her to make the burdensome personal sacrifices necessary to preserve the life of the fetus.

This argument is plausible, and in the case of pregnancy due to rape it is probably conclusive. Difficulties arise, however, when we attempt to specify the larger range of cases in which abortion can be justified on the basis of this argument. Thomson considers it a virtue of her argument that it does not imply that abortion is *always* morally permissible. It would, she says, be indecent for a woman in her seventh month of pregnancy to have an abortion in order to embark on a trip to Europe. On the other hand, the violinist analogy shows that, "a sick and desperately frightened fourteen-year-old schoolgirl, pregnant due to rape, may *of course* choose abortion, and that any law which rules this out is an insane law."[9] So far, so good; but what are we to say about the woman who becomes pregnant not through rape but because she and her partner did not use available forms of contraception, or because their attempts at contraception failed? What about a woman who becomes pregnant intentionally, but then re-evaluates the wisdom of having a child? In such cases, the violinist analogy is considerably less useful to advocates of the right to choose abortion.

It is perhaps only when a woman's pregnancy is due to rape, or some other form of coercion, that the situation is sufficiently analogous to the violinist case for our moral intuitions to transfer convincingly from the one case to the other. One difference between a pregnancy caused by rape and most unwanted pregnancies is that only in the former case is it perfectly clear that the woman is in no way responsible for her predicament. In the other cases, she *might* have been able to avoid becoming pregnant, e.g., by taking birth control pills (more faithfully), or insisting upon the use of high-quality condoms, or even avoiding heterosexual intercourse altogether throughout her fertile years. In contrast, if you are suddenly kidnapped by strange music

8 Ibid., p. 174.

9 Ibid., p. 187.

lovers and hooked up to a sick violinist, then you are in no way responsible for your situation, which you could not have foreseen or prevented. And responsibility does seem to matter here. If a person behaves in a way which she could have avoided, and which she knows might bring into existence a human being who will depend upon her for survival, then it is not entirely clear that if and when that happens she may rightly refuse to do what she must in order to keep that human being alive.

This argument shows that the violinist analogy provides a persuasive defense of a woman's right to choose abortion only in cases where she is in no way morally responsible for her own pregnancy. In all other cases, the assumption that a fetus has a strong right to life makes it necessary to look carefully at the particular circumstances in order to determine the extent of the woman's responsibility, and hence the extent of her obligation. This outcome is unsatisfactory to advocates of the right to choose abortion, because it suggests that the decision should not be left in the woman's own hands, but should be supervised by other persons, who will inquire into the most intimate aspects of her personal life in order to determine whether or not she is entitled to choose abortion.

A supporter of the violinist analogy might reply that it is absurd to suggest that forgetting her pill one day might be sufficient to morally oblige a woman to complete an unwanted pregnancy. And indeed it is absurd to suggest this. As we will see, a woman's moral right to choose abortion does not depend upon the extent to which she might be thought to be morally responsible for her own pregnancy. But once we allow the assumption that a fetus has a strong right to life, we cannot avoid taking this absurd suggestion seriously. On this assumption, it is a vexing question whether and when abortion is morally justifiable. The violinist analogy can at best show that aborting a pregnancy is a deeply tragic act, though one that is sometimes morally justified.

My conviction is that an abortion is not always this deeply tragic, because a fetus is not yet a person, and therefore does not yet have a strong moral right to life. Although the truth of this conviction may not be self-evident, it does, I believe, follow from some highly plausible claims about the appropriate grounds for ascribing moral rights. It is worth examining these grounds, since this has not been adequately done before.

II

The question we must answer in order to determine the moral status of abortion is: How are we to define the moral community, the set of beings with full and equal moral rights? What sort of entity has the inalienable moral rights to life, liberty, and the pursuit of happiness? Thomas Jefferson attributed these rights to all *men*, and he may have intended to attribute them *only* to men. Perhaps he ought to have attributed them to all human beings. If so, then we arrive, first, at Noonan's problem of defining what makes an entity a human being, and second, at the question which Noonan does not consider: What reason is there for identifying the moral community with the set of all human beings, in whatever way we have chosen to define that term?

On the Definition of "Human"

The term "human being" has two distinct, but not often distinguished, senses. This results in a slide of meaning, which serves to conceal the fallacy in the traditional argument that, since (1) it is wrong to kill innocent human beings, and (2) fetuses are innocent human beings, therefore (3) it is wrong to kill fetuses. For if "human being" is used in the same sense in both (1) and (2), then whichever of the two senses is meant, one of these premises is question-begging. And if it is used in different senses then the conclusion does not follow.

Thus, (1) is a generally accepted moral truth,[10] and one that does not beg the question about abortion, only if "human being" is used to mean something like "a full-fledged member of the moral community, who is also a member of the human species." I will call this the *moral* sense of "human being." It is not to be confused with what I will call the *genetic* sense, i.e., the sense in which any individual entity that belongs to the human species is a human being, regardless of whether or not it is rightly considered to be an equal member of the moral community. Premise (1) avoids begging the question only if the moral sense is intended; while premise (2) avoids it only if what is intended is the genetic sense.

Noonan argues for the classification of fetuses with human beings by pointing, first, to the presence of the human genome in the cell nuclei of the human conceptus from conception onwards; and secondly, to the potential capacity for rational thought.[11] But what he needs to show, in order to support his version of the traditional antiabortion argument, is that fetuses are human beings in the moral sense—the sense in which all human beings have full and equal moral rights. In the absence of any argument showing that whatever is genetically human is also morally human—and he gives none—nothing more than genetic humanity can be demonstrated by the presence of human chromosomes in the fetus's cell nuclei. And, as we will see, the strictly potential capacity for rational thought can at most show that the fetus may later *become* human in the moral sense.

Defining the Moral Community

Is genetic humanity sufficient for moral humanity? There are good reasons for not defining the moral community in this way. I would suggest that the moral community consists, in the first instance, of all *persons,* rather than all genetically human entities.[12] It is persons who invent moral rights, and who are (sometimes) capable of respecting them. It does not follow from this that only persons can have moral rights. However, persons are wise not to ascribe to entities that clearly are not persons moral rights that cannot in practice be respected without severely undercutting the fundamental moral rights of those who clearly are.

What characteristics entitle an entity to be considered a person? This is not the place to attempt a complete analysis of the concept of personhood; but we do not need such an analysis to explain why a fetus is not a person. All we need is an approximate list of the most basic criteria of personhood. In searching for these criteria, it is useful to look beyond the set of people with whom we are acquainted, all of whom are human. Imagine, then, a space traveler who lands on a new planet, and encounters organisms unlike any she has ever seen or heard of. If she wants to behave morally toward these organisms, she has somehow to determine whether they are people and thus have full moral rights, or whether they are things that she need not feel guilty about treating, for instance, as a source of food.

How should she go about making this determination? If she has some anthropological background, she might look for signs of religion, art, and the manufacturing of tools, weapons, or shelters, since these cultural traits have frequently been used to distinguish our human ancestors from prehuman beings, in what seems to be closer to the moral than the genetic sense of "human being." She would be right to take

10 The principle that it is always wrong to kill innocent human beings may be in need of other modifications, e.g., that it may be permissible to kill innocent human beings in order to save a larger number of equally innocent human beings; but we may ignore these complications here.
11 Noonan, "Deciding Who Is Human," p. 135.

12 From here on, I will use "human" to mean "genetically human," since the moral sense of the term seems closely connected to, and perhaps derived from, the assumption that genetic humanity is both necessary and sufficient for membership in the moral community.

the presence of such traits as evidence that the extraterrestrials were persons. It would, however, be anthropocentric of her to take the absence of these traits as proof that they were not, since they could be people who have progressed beyond, or who have never needed, these particular cultural traits.

I suggest that among the characteristics which are central to the concept of personhood are the following:

1. *Sentience*—the capacity to have conscious experiences, usually including the capacity to experience pain and pleasure;

2. *Emotionality*—the capacity to feel happy, sad, angry, loving, etc.;

3. *Reason*—the capacity to solve new and relatively complex problems;

4. *The capacity to communicate,* by whatever means, messages of an indefinite variety of types; that is, not just with an indefinite number of possible contents, but on indefinitely many possible topics;

5. *Self-awareness*—having a concept of oneself, as an individual and/or as a member of a social group; and finally

6. *Moral agency*—the capacity to regulate one's own actions through moral principles or ideals.

It is difficult to produce precise definitions of these traits, let alone to specify universally valid behavioral indications that these traits are present. But let us assume that our explorer knows approximately what these six characteristics mean, and that she is able to observe whether or not the extraterrestrials possess these mental and behavioral capacities. How should she use her findings to decide whether or not they are persons?

An entity need not have *all* of these attributes to be a person. And perhaps none of them is absolutely necessary. For instance, the absence of emotion would not disqualify a being that was personlike in all other ways. Think, for instance, of two of the *Star Trek* characters, Mr. Spock (who is half human and half alien), and Data (who is an android). Both are depicted as lacking the capacity to feel emotion; yet both are sentient, reasoning, communicative, self-aware moral agents, and unquestionably persons. Some people are unemotional; some cannot communicate well; some lack self-awareness; and some are not moral agents. It should not surprise us that many people do not meet all of the criteria of personhood. Criteria for the applicability of complex concepts are often like this: none may be logically necessary, but the more criteria that are satisfied, the more confident we are that the concept is applicable. Conversely, the fewer criteria are satisfied, the less plausible it is to hold that the concept applies. And if none of the relevant criteria are met, then we may be confident that it does not.

Thus, to demonstrate that a fetus is not a person, all I need to claim is that an entity that has *none* of these six characteristics is not a person. Sentience is the most basic mental capacity, and the one that may have the best claim to being a necessary (though not sufficient) condition for personhood. Sentience can establish a claim to moral considerability, since sentient beings can be harmed in ways that matter to them; for instance, they can be caused to feel pain, or deprived of the continuation of a life that is pleasant to them. It is unlikely that an entirely insentient organism could develop the other mental and behavioral capacities that are characteristic of persons. Consequently, it is odd to claim that an entity that is not sentient, and that has never been sentient, is nevertheless a person. Persons who have permanently and irreparably lost all capacity for sentience, but who remain biologically alive, arguably still have strong moral rights by virtue of what they have been in the past. But small fetuses, which have not yet begun to have experiences, are not persons yet and do not have the rights that persons do.

The presumption that all persons have full and equal basic moral rights may be part of the very concept of a person. If this is so, then the concept of a person is in part a moral one; once we have admitted that X is a person, we have implicitly committed ourselves to recognizing X's right to be treated as a member of the moral community.[13] The claim that X is a *human being* may also be voiced as an appeal to treat X decently; but this is usually either because "human being" is used in the moral sense, or because of a confusion between genetic and moral humanity.

If 1–6 are the primary criteria of personhood, then genetic humanity is neither necessary nor sufficient for personhood. Some genetically human entities are not persons, and there may be persons who belong to other species. A man or woman whose consciousness has been permanently obliterated but who remains biologically alive is a human entity who may no longer be a person; and some unfortunate humans, who have never had any sensory or cognitive capacities at all, may not be people either. Similarly, an early fetus is a human entity which is not yet a person. It is not even minimally sentient, let alone capable of emotion, reason, sophisticated communication, self-awareness, or moral agency.[14] Thus, while it may be greatly valued as a future child, it does not yet have the claim to moral consideration that it may come to have later.

Moral agency matters to moral status, because it is moral agents who invent moral rights, and who can be obliged to respect them. Human beings have become moral agents from social necessity. Most social animals exist well enough, with no evident notion of a moral right. But human beings need moral rights, because we are not only highly social, but also sufficiently clever and self-interested to be capable of undermining our societies through violence and duplicity. For human persons, moral rights are essential for peaceful and mutually beneficial social life. So long as some moral agents are denied basic rights, peaceful existence is difficult, since moral agents justly resent being treated as something less. If animals of some terrestrial species are found to be persons, or if alien persons come from other worlds, or if human beings someday invent machines whose mental and behavioral capacities make them persons, then we will be morally obliged to respect the moral rights of these nonhuman persons—at least to the extent that they are willing and able to respect ours in turn.

Although only those persons who are moral agents can participate directly in the shaping and enforcement of moral rights, they need not and usually do not ascribe moral rights only to themselves and other moral agents. Human beings are social creatures who naturally care for small children, and other members of the social community who are not currently capable of moral agency. Moreover, we are all vulnerable to the temporary or permanent loss of the mental capacities necessary for moral agency. Thus, we have self-interested as well as altruistic reasons for extending basic moral rights to infants and other sentient human beings who have already been born, but who currently lack some of these other mental capacities. These human beings, despite their current disabilities, are persons and members of the moral community.

But in extending moral rights to beings (human or otherwise) that have few or none of the morally significant characteristics of persons, we need to be careful not to burden human moral agents with obligations that they cannot possibly fulfill, except at unacceptably great cost to their own well-being and that of those they care about. Women often cannot complete unwanted pregnancies, except at intolerable mental, physical, and economic cost to themselves and their families. And heterosexual intercourse is too important a part of the social lives of most men and women to be reserved for times when pregnancy is an acceptable outcome.

13 Alan Gewirth defends a similar claim, in *Reason and Morality* (University of Chicago Press, 1978).
14 Fetal sentience is impossible prior to the development of neurological connections between the sense organs and the brain, and between the various parts of the brain involved in the processing of conscious experience. This stage of neurological development is currently thought to occur at some point in the late second or early third trimester.

Furthermore, the world cannot afford the continued rapid population growth which is the inevitable consequence of prohibiting abortion, so long as contraception is neither very reliable nor available to everyone. If fetuses were persons, then they would have rights that must be respected, even at great social or personal cost. But given that early fetuses, at least, are unlike persons in the morally relevant respects, it is unreasonable to insist that they be accorded exactly the same moral and legal status.

Fetal Development and the Right to Life

Two questions arise regarding the application of these suggestions to the moral status of the fetus. First, if indeed fetuses are not yet persons, then might they nevertheless have strong moral rights based upon the degree to which they *resemble* persons? Secondly, to what extent, if any, does a fetus's potential to *become* a person imply that we ought to accord to it some of the same moral rights? Each of these questions requires comment.

It is reasonable to suggest that the more like a person something is—the more it appears to meet at least some of the criteria of personhood—the stronger is the case for according it a right to life, and perhaps the stronger its right to life is. That being the case, perhaps the fetus gradually gains a stronger right to life as it develops. We should take seriously the suggestion that, just as "the human individual develops biologically in a continuous fashion . . . the rights of a human person . . . develop in the same way."[15]

A seven-month fetus can apparently feel pain, and can respond to such stimuli as light and sound. Thus, it may have a rudimentary form of consciousness. Nevertheless, it is probably not as conscious, or as capable of emotion, as even a very young infant is; and it has as yet little or no capacity for reason, sophisticated intentional communication, or self-awareness. In these respects, even a late-term fetus is arguably less like a person than are many nonhuman animals. Many animals (e.g., large-brained mammals such as elephants, cetaceans, or apes) are not only sentient, but clearly possessed of a degree of reason, and perhaps even of self-awareness. Thus, on the basis of its resemblance to a person, even a late-term fetus can have no more right to life than do these animals.

Animals may, indeed, plausibly be held to have some moral rights, and perhaps rather strong ones.[16] But it is impossible in practice to accord full and equal moral rights to all animals. When an animal poses a serious threat to the life or well-being of a person, we do not, as a rule, greatly blame the person for killing it; and there are good reasons for this species-based discrimination. Animals, however intelligent in their own domains, are generally not beings with whom we can reason; we cannot persuade mice not to invade our dwellings or consume our food. That is why their rights are necessarily weaker than those of a being who can understand and respect the rights of other beings.

But the probable sentience of late-term fetuses is not the only argument in favor of treating late abortion as a morally more serious matter than early abortion. Many—perhaps most—people are repulsed by the thought of needlessly aborting a late-term fetus. The late-term fetus has features which cause it to arouse in us almost the same powerful protective instinct as does a small infant.

This response needs to be taken seriously. If it were impossible to perform abortions early in pregnancy, then we might have to tolerate the mental and physical trauma that would be occasioned by the routine resort to late abortion. But where early abortion is safe, legal, and readily available to all women, it is not unreasonable to

---

15 Thomas L. Hayes, "A Biological View," *Commonweal*, 85 (March 17, 1967), pp. 677–8; cited by Daniel Callahan, in *Abortion: Law, Choice, and Morality* (London: Macmillan, 1970).

16 See, for instance, Tom Regan, *The Case for Animal Rights* (Berkeley: University of California Press, 1983).

expect most women who wish to end a pregnancy to do so prior to the third trimester. Most women strongly prefer early to late abortion, because it is far less physically painful and emotionally traumatic. Other things being equal, it is better for all concerned that pregnancies that are not to be completed should be ended as early as possible. Few women would consider ending a pregnancy in the seventh month in order to take a trip to Europe. If, however, a woman's own life or health is at stake, or if the fetus has been found to be so severely abnormal as to be unlikely to survive or to have a life worth living, then late abortion may be the morally best choice. For even a late-term fetus is not a person yet, and its rights must yield to those of the woman whenever it is impossible for both to be respected.

Potential Personhood and the Right to Life

We have seen that a presentient fetus does not yet resemble a person in ways which support the claim that it has strong moral rights. But what about its *potential,* the fact that if nurtured and allowed to develop it may eventually become a person? Doesn't that potential give it at least some right to life? The fact that something is a potential person may be a reason for not destroying it; but we need not conclude from this that potential people have a strong right to life. It may be that the feeling that it is better not to destroy a potential person is largely due to the fact that potential people are felt to be an invaluable resource, not to be lightly squandered. If every speck of dust were a potential person, we would be less apt to suppose that all potential persons have a right to become actual.

We do not need to insist that a potential person has no right to life whatever. There may be something immoral, and not just imprudent, about wantonly destroying potential people, when doing so isn't necessary. But even if a potential person does have some right to life, that right could not outweigh the right of a woman to obtain an abortion; for the basic moral rights of an actual person outweigh the rights of a merely potential person, whenever the two conflict. Since this may not be immediately obvious in the case of a human fetus, let us look at another case.

Suppose that our space explorer falls into the hands of an extraterrestrial civilization, whose scientists decide to create a few thousand new human beings by killing her and using some of her cells to create clones. We may imagine that each of these newly created women will have all of the original woman's abilities, skills, knowledge, and so on, and will also have an individual self-concept; in short, that each of them will be a bona fide (though not genetically unique) person. Imagine, further, that our explorer knows all of this, and knows that these people will be treated kindly and fairly. I maintain that in such a situation she would have the right to escape if she could, thus depriving all of these potential people of their potential lives. For her right to life outweighs all of theirs put together, even though they are all genetically human, and have a high probability of becoming people, if only she refrains from acting.

Indeed, I think that our space traveler would have a right to escape even if it were not her life which the aliens planned to take, but only a year of her freedom, or only a day. She would not be obliged to stay, even if she had been captured because of her own lack of caution—or even if she had done so deliberately, knowing the possible consequences. Regardless of why she was captured, she is not obliged to remain in captivity for *any* period of time in order to permit merely potential people to become actual people. By the same token, a woman's rights to liberty and the control of her own body outweigh whatever right to life a fetus may have merely by virtue of its potential personhood.

The Objection from Infanticide

One objection to my argument is that it appears to justify not only abortion, but also infanticide. A newborn infant is not much more personlike than a nine-month fetus, and thus it might appear that if late-term abortion is sometimes justified, then infanticide must also sometimes be justified. Yet most people believe that infanticide is a form of murder, and virtually never justified.

This objection is less telling than it may seem. There are many reasons why infanticide is more difficult to justify than abortion, even though neither fetuses nor newborn infants are clearly persons. In this period of history, the deliberate killing of newborns is virtually never justified. This is in part because newborns are so close to being persons that to kill them requires a very strong moral justification—as does the killing of dolphins, chimpanzees, and other highly personlike creatures. It is certainly wrong to kill such beings for the sake of convenience, or financial profit, or "sport." Only the most vital human needs, such as the need to defend one's own life and physical integrity, can provide a plausible justification for killing such beings.

In the case of an infant, there is no such vital need, since in the contemporary world there are usually other people who are eager to provide a good home for an infant whose own parents are unable or unwilling to care for it. Many people wait years for the opportunity to adopt a child, and some are unable to do so, even though there is every reason to believe that they would be good parents. The needless destruction of a viable infant not only deprives a sentient human being of life, but also deprives other persons of a source of great satisfaction, perhaps severely impoverishing *their* lives.

Even if an infant is unadoptable (e.g., because of some severe physical disability), it is still wrong to kill it. For most of us value the lives of infants, and would greatly prefer to pay taxes to support foster care and state institutions for disabled children, rather than to allow them to be killed or abandoned. So long as most people feel this way, and so long as it is possible to provide care for infants who are unwanted, or who have special needs that their parents cannot meet without assistance, it is wrong to let any infant die who has a chance of living a reasonably good life.

If these arguments show that infanticide is wrong, at least in today's world, then why don't they also show that late-term abortion is always wrong? After all, third-trimester fetuses are almost as personlike as infants, and many people value them and would prefer that they be preserved. As a potential source of pleasure to some family, a fetus is just as valuable as an infant. But there is an important difference between these two cases: once the infant is born, its continued life cannot pose any serious threat to the woman's life or health, since she is free to put it up for adoption or to place it in foster care. While she might, in rare cases, prefer that the child die rather than being raised by others, such a preference would not establish a right on her part.

In contrast, a pregnant woman's right to protect her own life and health outweighs other people's desire that the fetus be preserved—just as, when a person's life or health is threatened by an animal, and when the threat cannot be removed without killing the animal, that person's right to self-defense outweighs the desires of those who would prefer that the animal not be killed. Thus, while the moment of birth may mark no sharp discontinuity in the degree to which an infant resembles a person, it does mark the end of the mother's right to determine its fate. Indeed, if a late abortion can be safely performed without harming the fetus, she has in most cases no right to insist upon its death, for the same reason that she has no right to insist that a viable infant be killed or allowed to die.

It remains true that, on my view, neither abortion nor the killing of newborns is obviously a form of murder. Perhaps our legal system is correct in its classification of infanticide as murder, since no other legal category adequately expresses the force of our disapproval of this action. But some moral distinction remains, and it has important consequences. When a society cannot possibly care for all of the children who are born, without endangering the survival of adults and older children, allowing some infants to die may be the best of a bad set of options. Throughout history, most societies—from those that lived by gathering and hunting to the highly civilized Chinese, Japanese, Greeks, and Romans—have permitted infanticide under such unfortunate circumstances, regarding it as a necessary evil. It shows a lack of understanding to condemn these societies as morally benighted for this reason alone, since in the absence of safe and effective means of contraception and abortion, parents must sometimes have had no morally better options.

CONCLUSION

I have argued that fetuses are neither persons nor members of the moral community. Furthermore, neither a fetus's resemblance to a person, nor its potential for becoming a person, provides an adequate basis for the claim that it has a full and equal right to life. At the same time, there are medical as well as moral reasons for preferring early to late abortion when the pregnancy is unwanted.

Women, unlike fetuses, are undeniably persons and members of the human moral community. If unwanted or medically dangerous pregnancies never occurred, then it might be possible to respect women's basic moral rights, while at the same time extending the same basic rights to fetuses. But in the real world such pregnancies do occur—often despite the woman's best efforts to prevent them. Even if the perfect contraceptive were universally available, the continued occurrence of rape and incest would make access to abortion a vital human need. Because women are persons, and fetuses are not, women's rights to life, liberty, and physical integrity morally override whatever right to life it may be appropriate to ascribe to a fetus. Consequently, laws that deny women the right to obtain abortions, or that make safe early abortions difficult or impossible for some women to obtain, are an unjustified violation of basic moral and constitutional rights.

Review Questions

1. According to Warren, what is the standard anti-abortion argument, and what is the standard pro-choice response?
2. What objection does Warren make to Thomson's argument about the famous violinist?
3. Warren distinguishes between two senses of the term *human being*. What are these two senses?
4. What are the characteristics of a person, according to Warren? Why isn't the fetus a person?
5. Besides saying that the fetus is not a person, what other reasons does Warren give for allowing abortions?
6. Warren grants that there are two problems with her account of the moral status of the fetus. What are these two problems, and how does she respond to them?

Discussion Questions

1. What is the moral status of a brain-dead human who is biologically alive but permanently unconscious? What is Warren's view? What do you think?
2. Explain Warren's position on the moral status of nonhuman animals. Do you agree with her? Why or why not?
3. Warren believes that there can be nonhuman persons—for example, alien beings, androids, and even robots—who think and act like humans. Are these beings persons with moral rights? Explain your position.
4. Do the rights of an actual person always outweigh the rights of a merely potential person? Can you think of any counterexamples?

An Argument that Abortion Is Wrong

DON MARQUIS

Don Marquis is professor of philosophy at the University of Kansas. For his picture and a list published articles see www.ku.edu/^philos/faculty/dmarquis.htm.

Marquis wants to show why abortion is seriously wrong, but he begins by granting a number of cases in which it is not wrong, including cases of rape, of abortion during the first fourteen days after conception, of threat to the woman's life, and an anencephalic fetus. After showing why the standard arguments fail to resolve the debate about abortion, he proceeds to his own argument: that abortion is wrong for the same reason that killing us is wrong. It is wrong because it deprives the fetus of a "future like ours," a future having valuable experiences, activities, projects, and enjoyments.

THE PURPOSE OF THIS ESSAY is to set out an argument for the claim that abortion, except perhaps in rare instances, is seriously wrong.[1] One reason for these exceptions is to eliminate from consideration cases whose ethical analysis should be controversial and detailed for clear-headed opponents of abortion. Such cases include abortion after rape and abortion during the first fourteen days after conception when there is an argument that the fetus is not definitely an individual. Another reason for making these exceptions is to allow for those cases in which the permissibility of abortion is compatible with the argument of this essay. Such cases include abortion when continuation of a pregnancy endangers a woman's life and abortion when the fetus is anencephalic. When I speak of the wrongness of abortion in this essay, a reader should presume the above qualifications. I mean by an abortion an action intended to bring about the death of a fetus for the sake of the woman who carries it. (Thus, as is standard on the literature on this subject, I eliminate spontaneous abortions from consideration.) I mean by a fetus a developing human being from the time of conception to the time of birth. (Thus, as is standard, I call embryos and zygotes, fetuses.)

The argument of this essay will establish that abortion is wrong for the same reason as killing a reader of this essay is wrong. I shall just assume, rather than establish, that killing you is seriously wrong. I shall make no attempt to offer a complete ethics of killing. Finally, I shall make no attempt to resolve some very fundamental and difficult general philosophical issues into which this analysis of the ethics of abortion might lead.

WHY THE DEBATE OVER ABORTION SEEMS INTRACTABLE

Symmetries that emerge from the analysis of the major arguments on either side of the abortion debate may explain why the abortion debate seems intractable. Consider the following standard anti-abortion argument: Fetuses are both human and alive. Humans have the right to life. Therefore, fetuses have the right to life.

Source: Don Marquis, "An Argument that Abortion Is Wrong," from *Ethics in Practice,* ed. Hugh LaFollette, pp. 91–102. Copyright © 1997 Blackwell Publishers. Reprinted with permission.

1 This essay is an updated version of a view that first appeared in the *Journal of Philosophy* (1989). This essay incorporates attempts to deal with the objections of McInerney (1990), Norcross (1990), Shirley (1995), Steinbock (1992), and Paske (1994) to the original version of the view.

Of course, women have the right to control their own bodies, but the right to life overrides the right of a woman to control her own body. Therefore, abortion is wrong.

Thomson's View

Judith Thomson (1971) has argued that even if one grants (for the sake of argument only) that fetuses have the right to life, this argument fails. Thomson invites you to imagine that you have been connected while sleeping, bloodstream to bloodstream, to a famous violinist. The violinist, who suffers from a rare blood disease, will die if disconnected. Thomson argues that you surely have the right to disconnect yourself. She appeals to our intuition that having to be in bed with a violinist for an indefinite period is too much for morality to demand. She supports this claim by noting that the body being used is *your* body, not the violinist's body. She distinguishes the right to life, which the violinist clearly has, from the right to use someone else's body when necessary to preserve one's life, which it is not at all obvious the violinist has. Because the case of pregnancy is like the case of the violinist, one is no more morally obligated to remain attached to a fetus than to remain attached to the violinist.

It is widely conceded that one can generate from Thomson's vivid case the conclusion that abortion is morally permissible when a pregnancy is due to rape (Warren, 1973, p. 49; and Steinbock, 1992, p. 79). But this is hardly a general right to abortion. Do Thomson's more general theses generate a more general right to an abortion? Thomson draws our attention to the fact that in a pregnancy, although a fetus uses a woman's body as a life-support system, a pregnant woman does not use a fetus's body as a life-support system. However, an opponent of abortion might draw our attention to the fact that in an abortion the life that is lost is the fetus's, not the woman's. This symmetry seems to leave us with a stand-off.

Thomson points out that a fetus's right to life does not entail its right to use someone else's body to preserve its life. However, an opponent of abortion might point out that a woman's right to use her own body does not entail her right to end someone else's life in order to do what she wants with her body. In reply, one might argue that a pregnant woman's right to control her own body doesn't come to much if it is wrong for her to take any action that ends the life of the fetus within her. However, an opponent of abortion can argue that the fetus's right to life doesn't come to much if a pregnant woman can end it when she chooses. The consequence of all of these symmetries seems to be a stand-off. But if we have the stand-off, then one might argue that we are left with a conflict of rights: a fetal right to life versus the right of a woman to control her own body. One might then argue that the right to life seems to be a stronger right than the right to control one's own body in the case of abortion because the loss of one's life is a greater loss than the loss of the right to control one's own body in one respect for nine months. Therefore, the right to life overrides the right to control one's own body and abortion is wrong. Considerations like these have suggested to both opponents of abortion and supporters of choice that a Thomsonian strategy for defending a general right to abortion will not succeed (Tooley, 1972; Warren, 1973; and Steinbock, 1992). In fairness, one must note that Thomson did not intend her strategy to generate a general moral permissibility of abortion.

Do Fetuses Have the Right to Life?

The above considerations suggest that whether abortion is morally permissible boils down to the question of whether fetuses have the right to life. An argument that fetuses either have or lack the right to life must be based upon some general criterion for having or lacking the right to life. Opponents of abortion, on the one hand, look around for the broadest possible plausible criterion, so that fetuses will fall under it. This explains why classic arguments against abortion appeal to the criterion of being human (Noonan, 1970; Beckwith, 1993). This criterion appears plausible: The claim that all humans, whatever their race, gender, religion or *age,* have the right to life seems evident enough. In addition, because the fetuses we are concerned with do not, after all, belong to another species, they are clearly human. Thus, the syllogism that generates the conclusion that fetuses have the right to life is apparently sound.

On the other hand, those who believe abortion is morally permissible wish to find a narrow, but plausible, criterion for possession of the right to life so that fetuses will fall outside of it. This explains, in part, why the standard pro-choice arguments in the philosophical literature appeal to the criterion of being a person (Feinberg, 1986; Tooley, 1972; Warren, 1973; Benn, 1973; Engelhardt, 1986). This criterion appears plausible: The claim that only persons have the right to life seems evident enough. Furthermore, because fetuses neither are rational nor possess the capacity to communicate in complex ways nor possess a concept of self that continues through time, no fetus is a person. Thus, the syllogism needed to generate the conclusion that no fetus possesses the right to life is apparently sound. Given that no fetus possesses the right to life, a woman's right to control her own body easily generates the general right to abortion. The existence of two apparently defensible syllogisms which support contrary conclusions helps to explain why partisans on both sides of the abortion dispute often regard their opponents as either morally depraved or mentally deficient.

Which syllogism should we reject? The anti-abortion syllogism is usually attacked by attacking its major premise: the claim that whatever is biologically human has the right to life. This premise is subject to scope problems because the class of the biologically human includes too much: human cancer-cell cultures are biologically human, but they do not have the right to life. Moreover, this premise also is subject to moral-relevance problems: the connection the biological and the moral is merely assumed. It is

hard to think of a good *argument* for such a connection. If one wishes to consider the category of "human" a moral category, as some people find it plausible to do in other contexts, then one is left with no way of showing that the fetus is fully human without begging the question. Thus, the classic anti-abortion argument appears subject to fatal difficulties.

These difficulties with the classic anti-abortion argument are well known and thought by many to be conclusive. The symmetrical difficulties with the classic pro-choice syllogism are not as well recognized. The pro-choice syllogism can be attacked by attacking its major premise: Only persons have the right to life. This premise is subject to scope problems because the class of persons includes too little: infants, the severely retarded, and some of the mentally ill seem to fall outside the class of persons as the supporter of choice understands the concept. The premise is also subject to moral-relevance problems: Being a person is understood by the pro-choicer as having certain psychological attributes. If the pro-choicer questions the connection between the biological and the moral, the opponent of abortion can question the connection between the psychological and the moral. If one wishes to consider "person" a moral category, as is often done, then one is left with no way of showing that the fetus is not a person without begging the question.

Pro-choicers appear to have resources for dealing with their difficulties that opponents of abortion lack. Consider their moral-relevance problem. A pro-choicer might argue that morality rests on contractual foundations and that only those who have the psychological attributes of persons are capable of entering into the moral contract and, as a consequence, being a member of the moral community. [This is essentially Engelhardt's (1986) view.] The great advantage of this contractarian approach to morality is that it seems far more plausible than any approach the anti-abortionist can provide. The great disadvantage of this contractarian approach to morality is that it adds to our earlier scope problems by leaving it unclear how we can have the duty not to inflict pain and suffering on animals.

Contractarians have tried to deal with their scope problems by arguing that duties to some individuals who are not persons can be justified even though those individuals are not contracting members of the moral community. For example, Kant argued that, although we do not have direct duties to animals, we "must practice kindness towards animals, for he who is cruel to animals becomes hard also in his dealings with men" (Kant, 1963, p. 240). Feinberg argues that infanticide is wrong, not because infants have the right to life, but because our society's protection of infants has social utility. If we do not treat infants with tenderness and consideration, then when they are persons they will be worse off and we will be worse off also (Feinberg, 1986, p. 271).

These moves only stave off the difficulties with the pro-choice view; they do not resolve them. Consider Kant's account of our obligations to animals. Kantians certainly know the difference between persons and animals. Therefore, no true Kantian would treat persons as she would treat animals. Thus, Kant's defense of our duties to animals fails to show that Kantians have a duty not to be cruel to animals. Consider Feinberg's attempt to show that infanticide is wrong even though no infant is a person. All Feinberg really shows is that it is a good idea to treat with care and consideration the infants we intend to keep. That is quite compatible with killing the infants we intend to discard. This point can be supported by an analogy with which any pro-choicer will agree. There are plainly good reasons to treat with care and consideration the fetuses we intend to keep. This is quite compatible with aborting those fetuses we intend to discard. Thus, Feinberg's account of the wrongness of infanticide is inadequate.

Accordingly, we can see that a contractarian defense of the pro-choice personhood syllogism fails. The problem arises because the contractarian cannot account for our duties to individuals who are not persons, whether these individuals are animals or infants. Because the pro-choicer wishes to adopt a narrow criterion for the right to life so that fetuses will not be included, the scope of her major premise is too narrow. Her problem is the opposite of the problem the classic opponent of abortion faces.

The argument of this section has attempted to establish, albeit briefly, that the classic anti-abortion argument and the pro-choice argument favored by most philosophers both face problems that are mirror images of one another. A stand-off results. The abortion debate requires a different strategy.

THE "FUTURE LIKE OURS" ACCOUNT OF THE WRONGNESS OF KILLING

Why do the standard arguments in the abortion debate fail to resolve the issue? The general principles to which partisans in the debate appeal are either truisms most persons would affirm in the absence of much reflection, or very general moral theories. All are subject to major problems. A different approach is needed.

Opponents of abortion claim that abortion is wrong because abortion involves killing someone like us, a human being who just happens to be very young. Supporters of choice claim that ending the life of a fetus is not in the same moral category as ending the life of an adult human being. Surely this controversy cannot be resolved in the absence of an account of what it is about killing us that makes killing us wrong. On the one hand, if we know what property we possess that makes killing us wrong, then we can ask whether fetuses have the same property. On the other hand, suppose that we do not know what it is about us that makes killing us wrong. If this is so, we do not understand even easy cases in which killing is wrong. Surely, we will not understand the ethics of killing fetuses, for if we do not understand easy cases, then we will not understand hard cases. Both pro-choicer and anti-abortionist agree that it is obvious that it is wrong to kill us. Thus, a discussion of what it is about us that makes killing us not only wrong, but seriously wrong, seems to be the right place to begin a discussion of the abortion issue.

Who is primarily wronged by a killing? The wrong of killing is not primarily explained in terms of the loss to the family and friends of the victim. Perhaps the victim is a hermit. Perhaps one's friends find it easy to make new friends. The wrong of killing is not primarily explained in terms of the brutalization of the killer. The great wrong to the victim explains the brutalization, not the other way around. The wrongness of killing us is understood in terms of what killing does to us. Killing us imposes on us the misfortune of premature death. That misfortune underlies the wrongness.

Premature death is a misfortune because when one is dead, one has been deprived of life. This misfortune can be more precisely specified. Premature death cannot deprive me of my past life. That part of my life is already gone. If I die tomorrow or if I live thirty more years my past life will be no different. It has occurred on either alternative. Rather than my past, my death deprives me of my future, of the life that I would have lived if I had lived out my natural life span.

The loss of a future biological life does not explain the misfortune of death. Compare two scenarios: In the former I now fall into a coma from which I do not recover until my death in thirty years. In the latter I die now. The latter scenario does not seem to describe a greater misfortune than the former.

The loss of our future conscious life is what underlies the misfortune of premature death. Not any future conscious life qualifies, however. Suppose that I am terminally ill with cancer. Suppose also that pain and suffering would dominate my future conscious life. If so, then death would not be a misfortune for me.

Thus, the misfortune of premature death consists of the loss to us of the future goods of consciousness. What are these goods? Much can

be said about this issue, but a simple answer will do for the purposes of this essay. The goods of life are whatever we get out of life. The goods of life are those items toward which we take a "pro" attitude. They are completed projects of which we are proud, the pursuit of our goals, aesthetic enjoyments, friendships, intellectual pursuits, and physical pleasures of various sorts. The goods of life are what makes life worth living. In general, what makes life worth living for one person will not be the same as what makes life worth living for another. Nevertheless, the list of goods in each of our lives will overlap. The lists are usually different in different stages of our lives.

What makes the goods of my future good for me? One possible, but wrong, answer is my desire for those goods now. This answer does not account for those aspects of my future life that I now believe I will later value, but about which I am wrong. Neither does it account for those aspects of my future that I will come to value, but which I don't value now. What is valuable to the young may not be valuable to the middle-aged. What is valuable to the middle-aged may not be valuable to the old. Some of life's values for the elderly are best appreciated by the elderly. Thus it is wrong to say that the value of my future to me is just what I value now. What makes my future valuable to me are those aspects of my future that I will (or would) value when I will (or would) experience them, whether I value them now or not.

It follows that a person can believe that she will have a valuable future and be wrong. Furthermore, a person can believe that he will not have a valuable future and also be wrong. This is confirmed by our attitude toward many of the suicidal. We attempt to save the lives of the suicidal and to convince them that they have made an error in judgment. This does not mean that the future of an individual obtains value from the value that others confer on it. It means that, in some cases, others can make a clearer judgment of the value of a person's future *to that person* than the person herself. This often happens when one's judgment concerning the value of one's own future is clouded by personal tragedy. (Compare the views of McInerney, 1990, and Shirley, 1995.)

Thus, what is sufficient to make killing us wrong, in general, is that it causes premature death. Premature death is a misfortune. Premature death is a misfortune, in general, because it deprives an individual of a future of value. An individual's future will be valuable to that individual if that individual will come, or would come, to value it. We know that killing us is wrong. What makes killing us wrong, in general, is that it deprives us of a future of value. Thus, killing someone is wrong, in general, when it deprives her of a future like ours. I shall call this "an FLO."

ARGUMENTS IN FAVOR OF THE FLO THEORY

At least four arguments support this FLO account of the wrongness of killing.

The Considered Judgment Argument

The FLO account of the wrongness of killing is correct because it fits with our considered judgment concerning the nature of the misfortune of death. The analysis of the previous section is an exposition of the nature of this considered judgment. This judgment can be confirmed. If one were to ask individuals with AIDS or with incurable cancer about the nature of their misfortune, I believe that they would say or imply that their impending loss of an FLO makes their premature death a misfortune. If they would not, then the FLO account would plainly be wrong.

The Worst of Crimes Argument

The FLO account of the wrongness of killing is correct because it explains why we believe that killing is one of the worst of crimes. My being killed deprives me of more than does my being robbed or beaten or harmed in some other way because my being killed deprives me of all of the

value of my future, not merely part of it. This explains why we make the penalty for murder greater than the penalty for other crimes.

As a corollary the FLO account of the wrongness of killing also explains why killing an adult human being is justified only in the most extreme circumstances, only in circumstances in which the loss of life to an individual is outweighed by a worse outcome if that life is not taken. Thus, we are willing to justify killing in self-defense, killing in order to save one's own life, because one's loss if one does not kill in that situation is so very great. We justify killing in a just war for similar reasons. We believe that capital punishment would be justified if, by having such an institution, fewer premature deaths would occur. The FLO account of the wrongness of killing does not entail that killing is always wrong. Nevertheless, the FLO account explains both why killing is one of the worst of crimes and, as a corollary, why the exceptions to the wrongness of killing are so very rare. A correct theory of the wrongness of killing should have these features.

The Appeal to Cases Argument

The FLO account of the wrongness of killing is correct because it yields the correct answers in many life-and-death cases that arise in medicine and have interested philosophers.

Consider medicine first. Most people believe that it is not wrong deliberately to end the life of a person who is permanently unconscious. Thus we believe that it is not wrong to remove a feeding tube or a ventilator from a permanently comatose patient, knowing that such a removal will cause death. The FLO account of the wrongness of killing explains why this is so. A patient who is permanently unconscious cannot have a future that she would come to value, whatever her values. Therefore, according to the FLO theory of the wrongness of killing, death could not, *ceteris paribus,* be a misfortune to her. Therefore, removing the feeding tube or ventilator does not wrong her.

By contrast, almost all people believe that it is wrong, *ceteris paribus,* to withdraw medical treatment from patients who are temporarily unconscious. The FLO account of the wrongness of killing also explains why this is so. Furthermore, these two unconsciousness cases explain why the FLO account of the wrongness of killing does not include present consciousness as a necessary condition for the wrongness of killing.

Consider now the issue of the morality of legalizing active euthanasia. Proponents of active euthanasia argue that if a patient faces a future of intractable pain and wants to die, then, *ceteris paribus,* it would not be wrong for a physician to give him medicine that she knows would result in his death. This view is so universally accepted that even the strongest *opponents* of active euthanasia hold it. The official Vatican view (Sacred Congregation, 1980) is that it is permissible for a physician to administer to a patient morphine sufficient (although no more than sufficient) to control his pain even if she foresees that the morphine will result in his death. Notice how nicely the FLO account of the wrongness of killing explains this unanimity of opinion. A patient known to be in severe intractable pain is presumed to have a future without positive value. Accordingly, death would not be a misfortune for him and an action that would (foreseeably) end his life would not be wrong.

Contrast this with the standard emergency medical treatment of the suicidal. Even though the suicidal have indicated that they want to die, medical personnel will act to save their lives. This supports the view that it is not the mere *desire* to enjoy an FLO which is crucial to our understanding of the wrongness of killing. *Having* an FLO is what is crucial to the account, although one would, of course, want to make an exception in the case of fully autonomous people who refuse life-saving medical treatment. Opponents of abortion can, of course, be willing to make an exception for fully autonomous fetuses who refuse life support.

The FLO theory of the wrongness of killing also deals correctly with issues that have concerned philosophers. It implies that it would be wrong to kill (peaceful) persons from outer space who come to visit our planet even though they are biologically utterly unlike us. Presumably, if they are persons, then they will have futures that are sufficiently like ours so that it would be wrong to kill them. The FLO account of the wrongness of killing shares this feature with the personhood views of the supporters of choice. Classical opponents of abortion who locate the wrongness of abortion somehow in the biological humanity of a fetus cannot explain this.

The FLO account does not entail that there is another species of animals whose members ought not to be killed. Neither does it entail that it is permissible to kill any non-human animal. On the one hand, a supporter of animals' rights might argue that since some non-human animals have a future of value, it is wrong to kill them also, or at least it is wrong to kill them without a far better reason than we usually have for killing non-human animals. On the other hand, one might argue that the futures of non-human animals are not sufficiently like ours for the FLO account to entail that it is wrong to kill them. Since the FLO account does not specify which properties a future of another individual must possess so that killing that individual is wrong, the FLO account is indeterminate with respect to this issue. The fact that the FLO account of the wrongness of killing does not give a determinate answer to this question is not a flaw in the theory. A sound ethical account should yield the right answers in the obvious cases; it should not be required to resolve every disputed question.

A major respect in which the FLO account is superior to accounts that appeal to the concept of person is the explanation the FLO account provides of the wrongness of killing infants. There was a class of infants who had futures that included a class of events that were identical to the futures of the readers of this essay. Thus, reader, the FLO account explains why it was as wrong to kill you when you were an infant as it is to kill you now. This account can be generalized to almost all infants. Notice that the wrongness of killing infants can be explained in the absence of an account of what makes the future of an individual sufficiently valuable so that it is wrong to kill that individual. The absence of such an account explains why the FLO account is indeterminate with respect to the wrongness of killing non-human animals.

If the FLO account is the correct theory of the wrongness of killing, then because abortion involves killing fetuses and fetuses have FLOs for exactly the same reasons that infants have FLOs, abortion is presumptively seriously immoral. This inference lays the necessary groundwork for a fourth argument in favor of the FLO account that shows that abortion is wrong.

The Analogy with Animals Argument

Why do we believe it is wrong to cause animals suffering? We believe that, in our own case and in the case of other adults and children, suffering is a misfortune. It would be as morally arbitrary to refuse to acknowledge that animal suffering is wrong as it would be to refuse to acknowledge that the suffering of persons of another race is wrong. It is, on reflection, suffering that is a misfortune, not the suffering of white males or the suffering of humans. Therefore, infliction of suffering is presumptively wrong no matter on whom it is inflicted and whether it is inflicted on persons or nonpersons. Arbitrary restrictions on the wrongness of suffering count as racism or speciesism. Not only is this argument convincing on its own, but it is the only way of justifying the wrongness of animal cruelty. Cruelty toward animals is clearly wrong. (This famous argument is due to Singer, 1979.)

The FLO account of the wrongness of abortion is analogous. We believe that, in our own case and the cases of other adults and children, the loss of a future of value is a misfortune. It would be as morally arbitrary to refuse to acknowledge that the loss of a future of value to a fetus is wrong as to refuse to acknowledge that the loss of a future

of value to Jews (to take a relevant twentieth-century example) is wrong. It is, on reflection, the loss of a future of value that is a misfortune; not the loss of a future of value to adults or loss of a future of value to non-Jews. To deprive someone of a future of value is wrong no matter on whom the deprivation is inflicted and no matter whether the deprivation is inflicted on persons or nonpersons. Arbitrary restrictions on the wrongness of this deprivation count as racism, genocide or ageism. Therefore, abortion is wrong. This argument that abortion is wrong should be convincing because it has the same form as the argument for the claim that causing pain and suffering to non-human animals is wrong. Since the latter argument is convincing, the former argument should be also. Thus, an analogy with animals supports the thesis that abortion is wrong.

REPLIES TO OBJECTIONS

The four arguments in the previous section establish that abortion is, except in rare cases, seriously immoral. Not surprisingly, there are objections to this view. There are replies to the four most important objections to the FLO argument for the immorality of abortion.

THE POTENTIALITY OBJECTION

The FLO account of the wrongness of abortion is a potentiality argument. To claim that a fetus *has* an FLO is to claim that a fetus now has the potential to be in a state of a certain kind in the future. It is not to claim that all ordinary fetuses *will* have FLOs. Fetuses who are aborted, of course, will not. To say that a standard fetus has an FLO is to say that a standard fetus either will have or would have a life it will or would value. To say that a standard fetus would have a life it would value is to say that it will have a life it will value if it does not die prematurely. The truth of this conditional is based upon the nature of fetuses (including the fact that they naturally age) and this nature concerns their potential.

Some appeals to potentiality in the abortion debate rest on unsound inferences. For example, one may try to generate an argument against abortion by arguing that because persons have the right to life, potential persons also have the right to life. Such an argument is plainly invalid as it stands. The premise one needs to add to make it valid would have to be something like: "If Xs have the right to Y, then potential Xs have the right to Y." This premise is plainly false. Potential presidents don't have the rights of the presidency; potential voters don't have the right to vote.

In the FLO argument potentiality is not used in order to bridge the gap between adults and fetuses as is done in the argument in the above paragraph. The FLO theory of the wrongness of killing adults is based upon the adult's potentiality to have a future of value. Potentiality is in the argument from the very beginning. Thus, the plainly false premise is not required. Accordingly, the use of potentiality in the FLO theory is not a sign of an illegitimate inference.

The Argument from Interests

A second objection to the FLO account of the immorality of abortion involves arguing that even though fetuses have FLOs, nonsentient fetuses do not meet the minimum conditions for having any moral standing at all because they lack interests. Steinbock (1992, p. 5) has presented this argument clearly:

> Beings that have moral status must be capable of caring about what is done to them. They must be capable of being made, if only in a rudimentary sense, happy or miserable, comfortable or distressed. Whatever reasons we may have for preserving or protecting nonsentient beings, these reasons do not refer to their own interests. For without conscious awareness, beings cannot have interests. Without interests, they cannot have a welfare of their own. Without a welfare of their own, nothing can be done for their sake. Hence, they lack moral standing or status.

Medical researchers have argued that fetuses do not become sentient until after 22 weeks of gestation (Steinbock, 1992, p. 50). If they are correct, and if Steinbock's argument is sound, then we have both an objection to the FLO account of the wrongness of abortion and a basis for a view on abortion minimally acceptable to most supporters of choice.

Steinbock's conclusion conflicts with our settled moral beliefs. Temporarily unconscious human beings are nonsentient, yet no one believes that they lack either interests or moral standing. Accordingly, neither conscious awareness nor the capacity for conscious awareness is a necessary condition for having interests.

The counter-example of the temporarily unconscious human being shows that there is something internally wrong with Steinbock's argument. The difficulty stems from an ambiguity. One cannot *take* an interest in something without being capable of caring about what is done to it. However, something can be *in* someone's interest without that individual being capable of caring about it, or about anything. Thus, life support can be *in* the interests of a temporarily unconscious patient even though the temporarily unconscious patient is incapable of *taking* an interest in that life support. If this can be so for the temporarily unconscious patient, then it is hard to see why it cannot be so for the temporarily unconscious (that is, nonsentient) fetus who requires placental life support. Thus the objection based on interests fails.

The Problem of Equality

The FLO account of the wrongness of killing seems to imply that the degree of wrongness associated with each killing varies inversely with the victim's age. Thus, the FLO account of the wrongness of killing seems to suggest that it is far worse to kill a five-year-old than an 89-year-old because the former is deprived of far more than the latter. However, we believe that all persons have an equal right to life. Thus, it appears that the FLO account of the wrongness of killing entails an obviously false view (Paske, 1994).

However, the FLO account of the wrongness of killing does not, strictly speaking, imply that it is worse to kill younger people than older people. The FLO account provides an explanation of the wrongness of killing that is sufficient to account for the serious presumptive wrongness of killing. It does not follow that killings cannot be wrong in other ways. For example, one might hold, as does Feldman (1992, p. 184), that in addition to the wrongness of killing that has its basis in the future life of which the victim is deprived, killing an individual is also made wrong by the admirability of an individual's past behavior. Now the amount of admirability will presumably vary directly with age, whereas the amount of deprivation will vary inversely with age. This tends to equalize the wrongness of murder.

However, even if, *ceteris paribus,* it is worse to kill younger persons than older persons, there are good reasons for adopting a doctrine of the legal equality of murder. Suppose that we tried to estimate the seriousness of a crime of murder by appraising the value of the FLO of which the victim had been deprived. How would one go about doing this? In the first place, one would be confronted by the old problem of interpersonal comparisons of utility. In the second place, estimation of the value of a future would involve putting oneself, not into the shoes of the victim at the time she was killed, but rather into the shoes the victim would have worn had the victim survived, and then estimating from that perspective the worth of that person's future. This task seems difficult, if not impossible. Accordingly, there are reasons to adopt a convention that murders are equally wrong.

Furthermore, the FLO theory, in a way, explains why we do adopt the doctrine of the legal equality of murder. The FLO theory explains why we regard murder as one of the worst of crimes, since depriving someone of a future like ours deprives her of more than depriving her of anything else. This gives us a reason for making the punishment for murder very harsh, as harsh as is compatible with civilized society. One should not make the punishment for younger victims harsher than that. Thus, the doctrine of the equal legal right to life does not seem to be incompatible with the FLO theory.

The Contraception Objection

The strongest objection to the FLO argument for the immorality of abortion is based on the claim that, because contraception results in one less FLO, the FLO argument entails that contraception, indeed, abstention from sex when conception is possible, is immoral. Because neither contraception nor abstention from sex when conception is possible is immoral, the FLO account is flawed.

There is a cogent reply to this objection. If the argument of the early part of this essay is correct, then the central issue concerning the morality of abortion is the problem of whether fetuses are individuals who are members of the class of individuals whom it is seriously presumptively wrong to kill. The properties of being human and alive, of being a person, and of having an FLO are criteria that participants in the abortion debate have offered to mark off the relevant class of individuals. The central claim of this essay is that having an FLO marks off the relevant class of individuals. A defender of the FLO view could, therefore, reply that since, at the time of contraception, there is no individual to have an FLO, the FLO account does not entail that contraception is wrong. The wrong of killing is primarily a wrong to the individual who is killed; at the time of contraception there is no individual to be wronged.

However, someone who presses the contraception objection might have an answer to this reply. She might say that the sperm and egg are the individuals deprived of an FLO at the time of contraception. Thus, there are individuals whom contraception deprives of an FLO and if depriving an individual of an FLO is what makes killing wrong, then the FLO theory entails that contraception is wrong.

There is also a reply to this move. In the case of abortion, an objectively determinate individual is the subject of harm caused by the loss of an FLO. This individual is a fetus. In the case of contraception, there are far more candidates (see Norcross, 1990). Let us consider some possible candidates in order of the increasing number of individuals harmed: (1) The single harmed individual might be the combination of the particular sperm and the particular egg that would have united to form a zygote if contraception had not been used. (2) The two harmed individuals might be the particular sperm itself, and, in addition, the ovum itself that would have physically combined to form the zygote. (This is modeled on the double homicide of two persons who would otherwise in a short time fuse. (1) is modeled on harm to a single entity some of whose parts are not physically contiguous, such as a university.) (3) The many harmed individuals might be the millions of *combinations* of sperm and the released ovum whose (small) chances of having an FLO were reduced by the successful contraception. (4) The even larger class of harmed individuals (larger by one) might be the class consisting of all of the individual sperm in an ejaculate and, in addition, the individual ovum released at the time of the successful contraception. (1) through (4) are all candidates for being the subject(s) of harm in the case of successful contraception or abstinence from sex. Which should be chosen? Should we hold a lottery? There seems to be no non-arbitrarily

determinate subject of harm in the case of successful contraception. But if there is no such subject of harm, then no determinate thing was harmed. If no determinate thing was harmed, then (in the case of contraception) no wrong has been done. Thus, the FLO account of the wrongness of abortion does not entail that contraception is wrong.

CONCLUSION

This essay contains an argument for the view that, except in unusual circumstances, abortion is seriously wrong. Deprivation of an FLO explains why killing adults and children is wrong. Abortion deprives fetuses of FLOs. Therefore, abortion is wrong. This argument is based on an account of the wrongness of killing that is a result of our considered judgment of the nature of the misfortune of premature death. It accounts for why we regard killing as one of the worst of crimes. It is superior to alternative accounts of the wrongness of killing that are intended to provide insight into the ethics of abortion. This account of the wrongness of killing is supported by the way it handles cases in which our moral judgments are settled. This account has an analogue in the most plausible account of the wrongness of causing animals to suffer. This account makes no appeal to religion. Therefore, the FLO account shows that abortion, except in rare instances, is seriously wrong.

References

Beckwith, F. J., *Politically Correct Death: Answering Arguments for Abortion Rights* (Grand Rapids, Michigan: Baker Books, 1993).

Benn, S. I., "Abortion, infanticide, and respect for persons," *The Problem of Abortion,* ed. J. Feinberg (Belmont, California: Wadsworth, 1973), pp. 92–104.

Engelhardt, Jr., H. T., *The Foundations of Bioethics* (New York: Oxford University Press, 1986).

Feinberg, J., "Abortion," *Matters of Life and Death: New Introductory Essays in Moral Philosophy,* ed. T. Regan (New York: Random House, 1986).

Feldman, F., *Confrontations with the Reaper: A Philosophical Study of the Nature and Value of Death* (New York: Oxford University Press, 1992).

Kant, I., *Lectures on Ethics,* tr. L. Infeld (New York: Harper, 1963).

Marquis, D. B., "A future like ours and the concept of person: a reply to McInerney and Paske," *The Abortion Controversy: A Reader,* ed. L. P. Pojman and F. J. Beckwith (Boston: Jones and Bartlett, 1994), pp. 354–68.

———, "Fetuses, futures and values: a reply to Shirley," *Southwest Philosophy Review,* 11 (1995): 263–5.

———, "Why abortion is immoral," *Journal of Philosophy,* 86 (1989): 183–202.

McInerney, P., "Does a fetus already have a future like ours?," *Journal of Philosophy,* 87 (1990): 264–8.

Noonan, J., "An almost absolute value in history," in *The Morality of Abortion,* ed. J. Noonan (Cambridge, Massachusetts: Harvard University Press).

Norcross, A., "Killing, abortion, and contraception: a reply to Marquis," *Journal of Philosophy,* 87 (1990): 268–77.

Paske, G., "Abortion and the neo-natal right to life: a critique of Marquis's futurist argument," *The Abortion Controversy: A Reader,* ed. L. P. Pojman and F. J. Beckwith (Boston: Jones and Bartlett, 1994), pp. 343–53.

Sacred Congregation for the Propagation of the Faith, *Declaration on Euthanasia* (Vatican City, 1980).

Shirley, E. S., "Marquis' argument against abortion: a critique," *Southwest Philosophy Review,* 11 (1995): 79–89.

Singer, P., "Not for humans only: the place of nonhumans in environmental issues," *Ethics and Problems of the 21st Century,* ed. K. E. Goodpaster and K. M. Sayre (South Bend: Notre Dame University Press, 1979).

Steinbock, B., *Life Before Birth: The Moral and Legal Status of Embryos and Fetuses* (New York: Oxford University Press, 1992).

Thomson, J. J., "A defense of abortion," *Philosophy and Public Affairs,* 1 (1971): 47–66.

Tooley, M., "Abortion and infanticide," *Philosophy and Public Affairs,* 2 (1972): 37–65.

Warren, M. A., "On the moral and legal status of abortion," *Monist,* 57 (1973): 43–61.

Review Questions

1. What exceptions does Marquis allow to his claim that abortion is seriously wrong? Why does he make these exceptions?
2. What "symmetries" does Marquis find in the abortion debate? Why do these make the debate seem intractable?
3. Why is killing a person wrong, according to Marquis?
4. State and explain the four arguments Marquis uses to support his account of the wrongness of killing.
5. What is the potentiality objection, and how does Marquis respond to it?
6. State and explain Steinbock's argument from interests. How does Marquis reply?
7. What is the problem of equality? How does Marquis deal with it?
8. Explain the contraception objection and Marquis's reply.

Discussion Questions

1. There seem to be a number of cases in which the fetus does not have a "future like ours" besides the case of the anencephalic fetus that Marquis mentions. For example, the fetus can be deformed in other ways or have a genetic disease. Or perhaps the child will have abusive parents and a life full of suffering. Does Marquis have to grant that abortion is not wrong in all these cases where the fetus does not have a "future like ours"? Explain your answer.
2. Is the wrongness of killing a matter of degree, such that killing a person at the end of her life is not as wrong as killing a young person? Or is killing the old and the young equally wrong? What is Marquis's position on this? What do you think?

3. Is it wrong to kill nonhuman animals? Why doesn't Marquis take a position on this? What is your view?
4. In his reply to the contraception objection, Marquis assumes that the fetus is one individual. But when the zygote divides into twins there are two individuals, not one. Does twinning pose a problem for Marquis or not? Why or why not?

Creation Ethics: The Moral Status of Early Fetuses and the Ethics of Abortion

ELIZABETH HARMAN

Elizabeth Harman is assistant professor of philosophy at New York University. She is the author of "The Potentiality Problem," *Philosophical Studies,* May 2003. For her picture and publications see www.nyu.edu/gsus/dept/philo/faculty/harman.

Harman defends a very liberal view on the ethics of early abortion. This is the view that an early abortion requires no moral justification whatsoever. Why? On her Actual Future Principle, the moral status of the early fetus is determined by its actual future, by whether or not it becomes a person. An early fetus that becomes a person has some moral status, but an early fetus that is killed in an abortion will not become a person, and it has no moral status at all. She argues that her liberal view of early abortion is compatible with several attractive views: the view that the fetus is an object of caring, the view that the fetus should not be harmed, the feeling that an early miscarriage is upsetting, the claim that the abortion decision is unique, and the view that it is reasonable to regret an abortion. Along the way she replies to three objections. She concludes that allowing a pregnancy to continue deserves more serious moral consideration than having an abortion.

THERE HAS BEEN CONSIDERABLE discussion of the moral status of early fetuses and the ethics of the choice whether to abort a pregnancy. But one tenable view about the moral status of early fetuses has been regularly ignored. As a consequence, a very liberal view about the ethics of abortion is more attractive than has previously been thought.

Let us use the term "early fetus" as follows:

(1) "early fetus": a fetus before it has any intrinsic properties that themselves confer moral status on the fetus.

I assume that there is a nonnegligible period of time in which fetuses are early fetuses in my sense; it may be as short as a few weeks or as long as several months, depending on which intrinsic properties can themselves confer moral status. One plausible view says that an early fetus is a fetus before it has any conscious experience

I am indebted to the many people who provided comments on earlier drafts of this paper. In particular, I thank Paul Bassen, Sally Haslanger, Christine Korsgaard, Derek Parfit, Seada Shiffrin, Judith Jarvis Thomson, and the Editors of *Philosophy & Public Affairs.* Most importantly, I thank James Pryor and Sherri Roush. Versions of this paper were presented to Harvard Women in Philosophy, the MIT M.A.T.T.I. Group, and the Eastern Division of the APA; I thank the participants at these events.

Source: From *Philosophy & Public Affairs* 28, no. 4.

and before it can properly be described as the subject of experience.[1]

Consider a woman, Katherine, who is wrestling with the question whether early fetuses have moral status. Katherine contemplates the early fetuses that die in early abortions. She has the intuition that these early fetuses have no moral status; their deaths simply do not matter morally. She thinks that nothing morally significant happens in an early abortion, and that no moral justification whatsoever is required for an early abortion. However, then Katherine goes on to contemplate the early fetuses that are carried to term and that become persons. She thinks of a couple who wants to have a baby. A woman in the couple becomes pregnant, and the couple decides that she will carry the pregnancy to term. Very quickly, the couple starts to care about and to love the fetus, while it is still an early fetus. Katherine believes that such an early fetus is the appropriate object of love. This very thing, the early fetus, is the beginning stage of the child of this couple. Because it is itself the beginning of their child, their love for it seems appropriate. Because this early fetus is the kind of thing it is appropriate to love, Katherine believes that it has some moral status.

Katherine appears torn by two conflicting views of the moral status of early fetuses. She has the intuition that early fetuses that die in early abortions lack moral status; she generalizes to the view that all early fetuses lack moral status. She has the intuition that early fetuses that will become persons have some moral status; she generalizes to the view that all early fetuses have some moral status. It seems that Katherine must give up one of her intuitions. The situation seems this way because we all make the following assumption:

(2) For any two early fetuses at the same stage of development and in the same

health, either both have some moral status or neither does.

This assumption is left unquestioned not only by all philosophers who write about abortion, but by everyone who discusses abortion.

Claim (2) can be denied. Katherine can keep both of her intuitions while denying the corresponding generalizations. She can take the following view of the moral status of early fetuses:

(3) The Actual Future Principle: An early fetus that will become a person has some moral status. An early fetus that will die while it is still an early fetus has no moral status.

The Actual Future Principle says that an early fetus's actual future determines whether it has moral status. The Principle says that there are two significantly different kinds of early fetuses.[2] Early fetuses that die while they are still early fetuses go through their entire existence without any intrinsic properties that themselves confer moral status. But an early fetus that will become a person is a very different kind of thing: it will one day have the full moral status of a person, and that is a good reason to think it has some moral status now.[3]

---

1 Someone might believe that up until the moment of birth, or for some time after, an individual has no intrinsic properties that themselves confer moral status on it. While the arguments make about early fetuses might be put forward about fetuses at any stage of development or about young babies, they are not written with such applications in mind.

2 For simplicity, I will sometimes talk as if all early fetuses fall into these two categories. But there is a class of early fetuses not addressed by the Actual Future Principle: those early fetuses that will die after they have developed some intrinsic properties that themselves confer moral status but before they have become persons. I leave open to further discussion what a proponent of the Actual Future Principle should say about the moral status of these early fetuses.

3 Warren Quinn ("Abortion: Identity and Loss," *Philosophy & Public Affairs* 13, no. 1 [Winter 1984]: 24–54) makes the point that it is numerically one and the same individual which is a fetus and then later a person. However, Quinn neglects to recognize that this fact only applies to some fetuses. He claims that the fact that the person is "already present" (p. 40) in the fetus is reason to think that all early fetuses have some moral status. But this fact gives us no reason to think that fetuses that will not become persons have some moral status. The person is not "already present" in one of these fetuses; there is and will be no person to be so present. The Actual Future Principle recognizes the moral status of early fetuses that will become persons; it is precisely these early fetuses in which persons can be said to be already present.

Eric T. Olson ("Was I Ever a Fetus?" *Philosophy and Phenomenological Research* 57 [1997]: 95–110) points out that

I make the following assumption; I do not have the space to argue for it:

(4) If early abortion requires any moral justification whatsoever, then this is so because the early fetus that dies in the abortion has some moral status.[4]

Given (4), the Actual Future Principle implies the following view:

(5) The very liberal view on the ethics of abortion: Early abortion requires no moral justification whatsoever.[5]

Note that what I am calling "the very liberal view on the ethics of abortion" ("the very liberal view" for short) is much stronger than the common liberal view that early abortion is permissible but requires at least some justification, however minimal.

In this paper, I am concerned to establish four conclusions:

Conclusion 1: The Actual Future Principle is a tenable view of the moral status of early fetuses.

Conclusion 2: The very liberal view on the ethics of abortion is compatible with several attractive views with which it has seemed incompatible. Therefore, the very liberal view on the ethics of abortion is more attractive than has been thought.

These first two conclusions matter to everyone who cares about the moral status of early fetuses and the ethics of abortion. To the proponent of the very liberal view on abortion, Conclusion 2 is particularly welcome. But Conclusion 2 is also significant to those who think early abortion requires justification or cannot be justified,

---

contemporary philosophers commonly accept two incompatible views: that the criterion of identity for persons is psychological, and that we persons were once fetuses. It is clear that we do not bear the appropriate psychological relations to the fetuses that we commonly believe became us, so one of the views must give. I agree with Olson that it is the criterion of identity that must give. What we are is biological living organisms, with the same criteria of identity we would apply to other animals. Questions as to which future contingencies are as good as my own survival, and which future lives I should anticipate as my own, do turn on the appropriate psychological relations; but this is a distinct matter from the question what is identical with me. (See Derek Parfit, *Reasons and Persons* [Oxford: Clarendon Press, 1984].) A related point is this: it is a mistake to claim that I am essentially a person. I was once a fetus, and that fetus might never have become a person. Therefore, I am something that might never have been a person. I am something that is a person now, but I was not always a person—and I may well not always be a person in the future (i.e., if I end up in a vegetative state before dying).

4 It might be claimed that early abortion is wrong (or requires some moral justification) because the abortion deprives the fetus of its future. Peter K. McInerney ("Does a Fetus Already have a Future-Like-Ours?" *The Journal of Philosophy* 87 [1990]: 264–68) defends against this claim by appealing to the fact that fetuses lack "mental life" and cannot plan or "control" their futures, unlike persons (p. 266). McInerney claims that fetuses bear a different relation to their futures from persons, such that a person "already has" (p. 265) a future, though a fetus does not; therefore, a fetus is not deprived of its future by an abortion. Contra McInerney, I think we must accept that abortion deprives fetuses of possible futures that would be good. In this sense, abortion can be seen as a loss for the fetus—as bad for the fetus. However, this badness need not matter morally, because the fetuses in question lack moral status. (Interestingly, the reasons McInerney gives in support of his argument are reasons to think fetuses lack intrinsic properties that themselves confer moral status.) By contrast, smoking during a pregnancy that will be carried to term, is bad for the fetus and *therefore* matters morally, because the fetus has some moral status.

It might be claimed that early abortion requires some moral justification not because the early fetus that dies in the abortion has some moral status, but because the early fetus's life has intrinsic value. I take the following attitude toward this view: I don't think we should make a claim like "life has intrinsic value" unless we are forced to, unless we have good positive reasons to make such a claim or we find such a claim necessary to explain everything we want to explain. Ronald Dworkin (*Life's Dominion: An Argument about Abortion, Euthanasia, and Individual Freedom* [New York: Vintage, 1994]) claims than an advocate of a liberal view on abortion needs to posit that life has intrinsic value in order to explain why it is reasonable to regret an abortion; my argument for claim (13) below rejects Dworkin's argument.

5 It is consistent with the very liberal view on the ethics of abortion that some early abortions may require moral justification, when they have particular aspects that not every early abortion need have. The very liberal view merely claims that an action will never require moral justification simply in virtue of being an early abortion.

because Conclusion 2 says that their opponent's view is more attractive than they might have thought. My third conclusion is of more limited interest, in that my arguments can only be taken to argue from some views to this conclusion:

> *Conclusion 3:* The Actual Future Principle is the correct view of the moral status of early fetuses.

I provide arguments to bring someone from a moderate liberal view on abortion (held for particular reasons) to Conclusion 3. No argument is provided to bring someone from a conservative view about abortion to Conclusion 3. I state my fourth conclusion at the end of this article.

I take myself to have prima facie established Conclusion 1 by stating the Actual Future Principle. Below, I consider some objections to Conclusion 1. My argument for Conclusion 2 relies on Conclusion 1. The very liberal view has seemed incompatible with several attractive views precisely because it has seemed that a proponent of the very liberal view must hold that all early fetuses lack moral status. The tenability of the Actual Future Principle shows us that a proponent of the very liberal view need not say this. Conclusion 2 is established by my arguments for claims (6) through (9) and (13) below.

First:

(6) The very liberal view is compatible with the view that some early fetuses are the appropriate objects of caring attitudes such as love.

My discussion of Katherine's intuitions demonstrated that (6) is true. It is possible to have the view that early abortion requires no moral justification whatsoever because the early fetuses that die in early abortions have no moral status, while also having the view that some early fetuses have moral status and are the appropriate objects of caring attitudes.[6] This is so because we can see

that, as the Actual Future Principle holds, there are two significantly different kinds of early fetuses: those that die while they are still early fetuses, and those that will become persons.

Second:

(7) It is possible to give a good account of how the very liberal view is compatible with prohibitions on harming early fetuses that will become persons.

It might seem that the very liberal view is incompatible with our intuitions about our obligations not to harm some early fetuses. There is an existing account that responds to this worry without relying on the tenability of the Actual Future Principle; but it is a bad account. According to the existing account, we are prohibited from harming those early fetuses that will be carried to term not because of anything constitutive of the harming itself. It is not that these things, these early fetuses, are the kind of things we shouldn't harm. It is merely that there is a bad further consequence of harming these fetuses: in the future, a baby is born who suffers from fetal alcohol syndrome or some other bad effect of the earlier harming. This bad account may fail to address the worry expressed by those who challenge the liberal view. The worry may not simply be that the liberal view is incompatible with prohibitions on harming early fetuses. Rather, it may be that the liberal view is incompatible with its being the case that some early fetuses are the kind of things we are prohibited from harming. The worry is that the liberal view cannot appeal to the nature and status of these

---

6 It might be objected that we cannot really *love* something, such as an early fetus, that we know so little about. I do claim that we can love early fetuses; I claim that this is very common. While our love for early fetuses cannot reach the depth and complexity of our love for persons, it is real love directed at a particular individual. The couple knows that there is a living being in the womb of the pregnant woman, and they have attitudes toward that being. They are not merely anticipating loving their future child. The fact that the fetus is itself the beginning of their child is reason to love it now. Furthermore, the couple does know some things about the fetus: depending on how long into pregnancy fetuses are early fetuses in my sense (a point I have left open), the couple may be able to hear the fetus's heartbeat, see ultrasound pictures of it, and even feel it move.

early fetuses themselves in explaining why we are prohibited from harming them. The tenability of the Actual Future Principle allows us to satisfy this worry. The Actual Future Principle says precisely that some early fetuses have some moral status, thus they are the kind of things we are prohibited from harming. We are able to give a good account of the compatibility of the very liberal view and our intuitions about prohibitions on harming some early fetuses.

Third:

(8) The very liberal view is compatible with a reasonable view about miscarriages of early fetuses: a couple may be understandably upset about such a miscarriage, but it is inappropriate to mourn the death of the fetus.

It may seem that the very liberal view is incompatible with any reasonable view that takes seriously the badness of early miscarriages. Suppose that a woman in a couple becomes pregnant, and they decide to continue the pregnancy to term and raise the child. This couple starts to love the fetus while it is still an early fetus. Then the woman suffers an early miscarriage; the fetus dies. The couple's natural response is to mourn the death, treating it as the same kind of thing as the death of a person, something that is bad because it is bad for the subject who died. It seems that the very liberal view must say that this couple is being silly and irrational: because the deaths of early fetuses in early abortions lack moral significance, this death must lack moral significance as well.[7]

In fact, a proponent of the very liberal view can say the following. The couple is understandably upset by the death of the fetus; this is clear.

They loved a living being and then that being died; that is a traumatic event. While the fetus lived, the couple was rational to love the fetus, according to the Actual Future Principle, because they had a false belief. They thought that the fetus was the beginning stage of their child. They thought that the very living being in the woman's womb was identical with their child. If this had been true, then the fetus would have been the kind of thing that is the appropriate object of love: an attitude of love toward the fetus would have been warranted by (and appropriate given) the nature of the fetus. But as it turns out, the fetus was not the beginning of their child; its entire existence lacked any moment of consciousness or experience. It turns out that the fetus did not have any moral status. The couple rightly recognizes the miscarriage as a terrible thing that has happened to them; not only is it traumatic, but now they must start again in their attempt to have a child. However, they should also recognize that the death of the fetus should not be mourned—it should not be treated as the death of a morally significant being—because it turns out that the fetus lacked moral status.

Fourth:

(9) The very liberal view is compatible with an explanation of the unique position of a woman genuinely unsure whether she will abort her pregnancy.

A pregnant woman who is genuinely unsure whether she will abort her pregnancy is in a unique position; it is importantly unlike other cases of difficult choice between two alternatives. Any good account of the moral features of the choice whether to abort a pregnancy should account for the unique uncertainty of such a woman's situation; the very liberal view in combination with the Actual Future Principle does so. In other cases of difficult decision, it is natural to approach the decision by first recognizing what attitudes one ought to take toward the relevant elements of the situation and then deciding on the basis of these attitudes what to

---

7. Rosalind Hursthouse ("Virtue Theory and Abortion," *Philosophy & Public Affairs* 20, no. 3 [Summer 1991]: 223–46) argues that "proponents of the view that deliberate abortion is just like an appendectomy" run into inconsistency when faced with miscarriage: "to react to people's grief over miscarriage by saying, or even thinking, 'What a fuss about nothing!' would be callous and light-minded" (p. 238). My argument for claim (8) shows that proponents of the very liberal view need not react this way.

do. The pregnant woman cannot do this. She cannot first determine what attitude she ought to take toward the fetus and then decide whether to abort the pregnancy. The decision she makes will determine what attitude she ought to take. If she chooses abortion, then it turns out that the fetus is morally insignificant. If she chooses to continue the pregnancy, then the fetus is the beginning of her child, and she owes it her love. This circle may look like a defect of the Actual Future Principle. But in fact, I think it is the true situation of women genuinely unsure whether they will abort their pregnancies. Their choice is unique, because it determines a feature of their present situation. Most choices simply determine the future, but the choice whether to abort determines the present moral status of a living being.

I take my arguments for claims (6) through (9) above to have established Conclusion 2: the very liberal view on abortion is compatible with several attractive views with which it has seemed incompatible. These arguments have relied on Conclusion 1, which says that the Actual Future Principle is tenable. I will now consider three objections to Conclusion 1. I am not concerned here to defend the stronger claim that the Actual Future Principle is the correct view. But the Actual Future Principle may appear to be incoherent or to be plainly wrong on its face. I will consider three versions of this objection.

(10) First Objection: "Facts about a fetus's actual future can't determine its moral status, because something's moral status is determined by its 'nature.'"

The objector points out that one could bring up all sorts of facts to differentiate fetuses into categories and then assign different moral status to the various categories. For instance, we could stipulate that all early fetuses in North Carolina have some moral status, while those in South Carolina have none. This stipulation would be absurd because the facts appealed to don't play a role in what kind of thing each fetus is. The objector may propose the following

claim: a thing's present nature is solely determined by the intrinsic properties it now has. It does seem that a thing's present intrinsic properties are relevant to the kind of thing it is now; but other properties may be relevant as well. I propose: a thing's present nature is solely determined by the intrinsic properties it ever has. On this view of a thing's nature, the Actual Future Principle does appeal to facts about a fetus's nature in determining whether it has moral status. My proposal rules out many stipulations of fetuses' moral statuses (such as the Carolinas stipulation above), demonstrating that the Actual Future Principle is at least less arbitrary than these other stipulations.

Compare the Actual Future Principle to a possible revision of it: the Mother's Intention Principle states that an early fetus has some moral status if and only if the woman pregnant with it is planning to carry it to term. This principle preserves not only the liberal view on abortion and the rationality of caring attitudes toward early fetuses, but also the rationality of mourning the deaths of early fetuses in miscarriages. Despite some initial appeal, the Mother's Intention Principle must be rejected. Consider the case of a woman who is firmly decided on one day that she will abort her early pregnancy, but the next day is convinced by a friend's argument to carry her pregnancy to term; she firmly holds that intention for a week, then has a discussion with another friend and the next day has an abortion. According to the Mother's Intention Principle, the early fetus in question has no moral status on the first day, then has some moral status for a week, then for a day has no moral status again before it dies in the abortion. This is metaphysically absurd; these fluctuations in moral status do not correspond to any fluctuations in anything we might call the fetus's nature. The intentions of the woman who carries a fetus are weak, relational properties of that fetus; they are not among the facts that can determine what kind of thing it is. The Actual Future Principle does not require us to accept any similar metaphysical absurdity. Throughout each fetus's existence as an early fetus, the question whether it has moral status yields a single answer. It does not depend on the day of the week.

(11) Second Objection: "If the Actual Future Principle is true, then inaccessible facts determine a fetus's moral status. We can't ever know how to treat an early fetus, because we can't be sure of its moral status."

This objection neglects the fact that we often do know a fetus's over-whelmingly likely future. Whenever a woman is sure that she is going to abort her early pregnancy, and the means to have an abortion are within her reach, we can be confident that the early fetus lacks moral status. Whenever a woman has decided to continue her pregnancy, we can be confident that the early fetus has moral status. If future events occur as expected, we will have treated each of these fetuses as was appropriate and our attitudes toward them will have been appropriate to their moral statuses. But sometimes unexpected events occur. A woman who planned to continue her pregnancy may suffer a miscarriage; I discussed this case in arguing for (8) above. A woman who expected to be able to have an abortion may find herself unable to obtain one. In this case, it turns out that something we thought lacked moral status in fact had moral status. We have failed to love or care for this being, but more importantly we may have harmed it. The pregnant woman may have smoked while knowing she was pregnant, because she was planning to abort. Her choice to smoke was morally blameless in that, given the facts as she knew them, her action should not have harmed any other being with moral status. When she becomes unable to obtain an abortion, she will be upset by the fact that she has harmed a being with moral status, but she should not blame herself. The Actual Future Principle does not hold us to standards we cannot meet. Like all moral principles that give moral relevance to facts we may sometimes not know, the Principle merely implies that there may be situations in which it

turns out that we caused bad events without realizing we were doing so.[8]

Note that the case of the woman who smokes while she is planning to have an abortion is distinct from the case where we genuinely aren't sure what the early fetus's future will be. If a pregnant woman is considering having an abortion, but knows she may not choose to do so, it is morally impermissible for her to smoke. In any case where we are genuinely unsure of the facts of our situation, we should do the morally cautious thing.

The third objection says that the Actual Future Principle "plays a trick" in allowing our actions to determine whether these very actions are permissible:

(12) Third Objection: "According to the Actual Future Principle, you just can't lose! If you abort, then it turns out that the fetus you aborted was the kind of thing it's okay to abort. If you don't abort, then it turns out that the fetus was the kind of thing it's not okay to abort."

I have two responses to this objection. First, the objector is right that "you just can't lose" if you have an abortion. As I have argued, the Actual Future Principle implies the very liberal view on abortion. Therefore, according to the Actual Future Principle, no moral justification is required for an early abortion. Second, the objector's final

8 Suppose a woman, Julie, smokes during pregnancy, intending to abort and reasonably believing that she will be able to obtain an abortion. Then things occur such that Julie would have to go to extraordinary means to obtain an abortion. It might seem that Julie is obligated to go to those extraordinary means *because otherwise she will have done something wrong:* i.e., harmed the early fetus by smoking. I deny this. What Julie ought to do in this situation is no different from what she ought to do if the fetus had been similarly harmed by some accidental process (I am not here taking any stand on whether we have any obligations to abort damaged fetuses). The worry seems to presuppose the following principle: our present actions are constrained by the condition that we make it such that none of our earlier actions in fact caused morally relevant harm. I am not convinced of this principle.

claim is wrong. It is not the case that if you don't abort, then it turns out that the fetus was the kind of thing it's not okay to abort. It is true that the Actual Future Principle divides early fetuses into two different kinds of things and that it says that fetuses of one of these kinds have moral status while fetuses of the other kind do not. This does look awfully like the claim that fetuses of the first kind are the kind of thing it's not okay to kill, while fetuses of the second kind are the kind of thing it is okay to kill. That interpretation would be correct if the Actual Future Principle said that it is a necessary truth about each fetus whether it has moral status. But the Actual Future Principle does not say that. The Actual Future Principle does not say that a fetus that lacks moral status could not have had moral status; nor does it say that a fetus that has moral status could not have lacked moral status; clearly these are both possibilities. Rather, it says that each fetus has its status in virtue of facts about that fetus's actual life; these facts might have been different. If we do not abort an early fetus (and the fetus does not die in an early miscarriage), then it turns out that the fetus is the kind of thing that has moral status, according to the Actual Future Principle. It is not the case that this fetus is the kind of thing it would have been wrong (or at all morally problematic) to abort. If this fetus had been aborted, it would have turned out to be a different kind of thing, a kind of thing with no moral status.

According to the Actual Future Principle, early fetuses have their moral statuses contingently. Therefore, in morally evaluating events, one must be careful to evaluate actual events with respect to the actual moral statuses of the early fetuses involved; and one must evaluate *counterfactual* events with respect to the *counterfactual* moral statuses of the fetuses involved—the moral statuses the early fetuses would have had in that counterfactual situation. The objector's first claim evaluates an actual event with respect to the early fetus's actual moral status; that is right. But the objector's second claim evaluates a counterfactual

event with respect to the fetus's actual moral status, which it would not have had in that counterfactual event—this is where the objector goes wrong.[9]

I turn now to an independent consideration in support of Conclusion 2; this argument does not rely on the tenability of the Actual Future Principle. I will argue that:

(13) The liberal view on abortion is compatible with the rationality of two common experiences of women who have abortions: finding having an abortion very difficult (though the choice to abort is settled) and regretting an abortion (though one does not regret the choice to abort).

It is commonly thought that the very liberal view on abortion is incompatible with the rationality of women's finding having an abortion very difficult when the choice to abort is settled, and with women's regretting an abortion when they do not regret the choice to abort. I take it to be clear that such experiences are quite common. There is something upsetting and saddening about having an abortion, for many women, which is independent of uncertainty about the choice itself. It has seemed that the only way to explain these experiences is by saying that these women are recognizing their moral responsibility for a morally significant bad event, the death of the fetus. The very liberal view blocks this

---

9 Some may worry that the Actual Future Principle attributes implausible "godlike" powers to us, in that we can determine the moral status of other beings. However, there is nothing godlike about our ability to determine the future, so the worry must be that the future should not be relevant to something's moral status. I respond to this worry in discussing claim (10), but two further points are relevant. It may seem that *all beings* have their moral statuses simply in virtue of their present intrinsic properties. However, human beings at the end of their lives may plausibly be said to have their moral statuses in virtue of their pasts as well as their present states. Furthermore, some early fetuses (those that will become persons) are *unusual* in that their present intrinsic properties are much less morally significant than the intrinsic properties they will come to have; this is not true of persons, and it can explain why the moral statuses of early fetuses and persons would be determined differently.

explanation. It seems that a proponent of the very liberal view must say that women who regret their abortions are silly or irrational.[10] I will offer another explanation.

I explained the unique position of a woman genuinely unsure whether she would abort her pregnancy by the difference her choice makes to the fetus; I will explain the reasonableness of regret by the difference the woman's choice makes to the woman's own life. When a woman becomes pregnant, she sees vividly two very different possible futures. In one possibility, the woman's life continues largely as it has been: she aborts her pregnancy and there need be no disruption of her life. In the other possibility, the woman carries the pregnancy to term: she becomes a mother. It is likely that she raises the child, in which case she will come to love a living being that she has created, and most likely her child will love her back in a way she may be loved by no one else in her life. Becoming a mother changes a woman's life, and fundamentally changes who she is as a person. Pregnancy forces into a woman's mind the consciousness of what her life would become were she to continue the pregnancy—and that consciousness is vivid even if she is certain that she will not continue the pregnancy. A woman may regret an abortion because she regrets a lost possibility for her own life: the chance to become the woman she would have become if she had had a child at that time.

Claims (6) through (9) together with claim (13) establish Conclusion 2. It has seemed that the very liberal view is incompatible with the following attractive views: that some early fetuses are the appropriate objects of caring attitudes, that some early fetuses are the kind of things we

are prohibited from harming, that it is understandable to be upset by an early miscarriage, that the position of a woman genuinely unsure whether she will abort her pregnancy is unique, and that it is reasonable to regret an abortion when one does not regret the choice to abort. I have argued that the very liberal view is in fact compatible with these attractive views. I take it that many people who are attracted to the very liberal view on abortion adopt a moderate view instead, because they want to hold some of these attractive views. My arguments should convince these people to adopt the very liberal view and the Actual Future Principle in place of a moderate view; these are the people to whom my Conclusion 3 is addressed.

I will now argue for a fourth conclusion. I claim that virtually everyone who discusses pregnancy and abortion gets things fundamentally backwards. Most people believe that the choice whether to abort a pregnancy is a morally significant choice; I agree with this. But most people think that the choice between aborting and failing to abort is significant because aborting would be morally significant. They think that one ought to deliberate seriously and recognize one's moral responsibility before aborting. I deny that this is true. Because I hold the very liberal view on abortion, I believe that nothing morally significant happens in an early abortion.

However, the choice whether to abort a pregnancy is very morally significant. This is so because failing to abort a pregnancy is morally significant. Creating a person always involves occurrences of great moral weight.[11] Not only

---

10 Dworkin (in *Life's Dominion*) makes the very argument I have described (and will now reject). He poses the following rhetorical questions as challenges to the claim that nothing bad happens in an abortion: "Why should abortion raise any moral issue at all. . . . Why is abortion then not like a tonsillectomy? Why should a woman feel any regret after an abortion? Why should she feel more regret than after sex with contraception?" (p. 34).

11 Sarah Stroud ("Dworkin and Casey on Abortion," *Philosophy & Public Affairs* 25, no. 2 [Spring 1996]: 140–70) criticizes Dworkin's claim (in *Life's Dominion*) that the state has an interest in fostering moral deliberation and a recognition of moral responsibility for morally weighty actions such as having an abortion. Dworkin thinks this implies that the state can require women to think about alternatives to abortion, by imposing waiting periods and required distribution of information about such alternatives. Stroud points out that the same rationale could justify the state's legally mandating

does the pregnant woman's own life change, but her moral responsibility to others changes as well. She is committed to a lifetime of responsibility to the child; even if she makes an adoption plan for the child, she has a unique responsibility and relation to that person. Because it is so morally significant, *and because there is a morally insignificant alternative,* the creation of a person should not be undertaken lightly.[12] I claim:

parental or spousal consent of the continuation of a pregnancy or requiring that pregnant women read about the arguments for abortion. My claims go further than Stroud's. She merely points out that the moral weight some people stress about abortion also exists in the failure to abort; I deny that this moral weight is present in abortion.

12 Hugh LaFollette ("Licensing Parentism," in *Morality and Moral Controversies,* ed. John Arthur [Upper Saddle River, NJ: Prentice Hall, 1997], pp. 442–49) suggests that "the state should require all parents to be licensed" (p. 442). He argues that we presently regulate "any activity that is potentially harmful to others and requires certain demonstrated competence for its safe performance" (p. 443) such as driving a car or being a surgeon, and that parenting meets this criterion. LaFollette never comments on a central assumption of his suggestion: that creating a child is something

Conclusion 4: If the very liberal view on abortion is true, then: It is false that one ought to both deliberate seriously and recognize one's moral responsibility before aborting.[13] Furthermore, one ought to both deliberate seriously and recognize one's moral responsibility before failing to abort.

While there is nothing wrong with having an abortion on a whim, there is something gravely wrong with allowing a pregnancy to continue without moral deliberation.

that is chosen, that can be avoided, and that is thereby a candidate for regulation. His suggestion presupposes exactly what I here claim: that creation is something we choose, for which we are morally responsible.

13 I here deny the following claim: whenever someone has an early abortion, she ought to both deliberate seriously and recognize her moral responsibility for aborting. I am not myself making the stronger claim that it is never the case that one ought to deliberate seriously or recognize one's moral responsibility for a particular early abortion. This may be true of an abortion that has some features that not every early abortion need have. (See footnote 5.)

Review Questions

1. What is an early fetus? Explain the two conflicting views of the moral status of an early fetus.
2. What unquestioned assumption about an early fetus does Harman uncover?
3. State and explain Harman's Actual Future Principle. What does the principle say about early fetuses that die after attaining moral status?
4. State Harman's very liberal view on the ethics of early abortion. What three conclusions does she try to establish relating to this view?
5. Harman argues that the very liberal view is compatible with four attractive views. What are these views, and why are they compatible with the very liberal view according to Harman?
6. How does Harman respond to the objection that the moral status of the fetus is determined by its nature, not its actual future?
7. What is Harman's reply to the objection about the uncertainty of the fetus's moral status?
8. How does Harman reply to the objection that the Actual Future Principle plays a trick?
9. Explain the independent consideration in support of Conclusion 2.
10. State and explain Harman's fourth conclusion.

Discussion Questions

1. What intrinsic properties, if any, confer moral status on a fetus? Do these properties apply only to human fetuses? Why or why not?

2. A pregnant woman drinks heavily knowing full well that this causes fetal alcohol syndrome. But then she has an early abortion. Did she do anything wrong? What is Harman's view? What do you think?

3. Is an early miscarriage something bad? How does Harman view this? What is your view?

4. Harman argues that the abortion choice itself determines the moral status of the fetus. Can this be right? Why or why not?

5. Harman concludes that there is nothing morally wrong with having an early abortion on a whim. Do you agree? Why or why not?

6. Hugh LaFollette suggests that the state should require all parents to be licensed. Is this a good idea? Explain your view.

Problem Cases

1. Human Embryonic Stem Cell Research and Cloning. (For information on stem cell research and cloning see The National Institutes of Health website, www.nih.gov.)

Human embryonic stem cells are extracted from human embryos at a very early stage of development, when the embryos are as tiny as the tip of a sewing needle. These tiny clusters of about 200 cells are called blastocysts. Self-sustaining colonies of stem cells, called lines, are derived from the blastocysts, which are destroyed in the process.

Stem cells are unique in that they can theoretically grow into any of the body's more than 200 cell types. For example, they might grow into the nerve cells that secrete dopamine and be used to treat a person with Parkinson's disease. Scientists are eager to do research with stem cells because they believe stem cells will prove to be the building blocks for a new era of regenerative medicine. The cells may enable the body to heal itself from spinal cord injuries and various diseases such as Parkinson's disease, Alzheimer's disease, type 1 diabetes, and heart disease.

Where do researchers get the stem cells for their research? Currently they come from fertility clinics that have a surplus of blastocysts left over from in vitro fertilization. If not used, these blastocysts are usually discarded. The problem with stem cells from these surplus blastocysts is that they may be rejected by the patient receiving them.

A more promising approach is to use stem cells that are genetically matched to the patient. Advanced Cell Technology, a biotechnology company, is planning to do this using cloning techniques. The company wants to remove the nucleus from a female donor's egg, insert a cell from the skin of another donor or patient, and then stimulate the egg to reprogram the genes of the skin cell to start growing into a blastocyst. Then stem cells would be derived from the blastocyst.

What is the objection to stem cell research? The most common one is that harvesting stem cells from a blasocyst kills it, and this is seen as the equivalent of killing a human being. This is the position taken by Pope John Paul II, the U.S. Conference of Catholic Bishops, and abortion opponents. Others find it hard to believe that a tiny clump of cells in a petri dish is a human being with a right to life or that destroying it is the same as murdering a person.

More objections are raised in The President's Council on Bioethics statement on Huuman Cloning and Human Dignity, (www.bioethics.gov). The cloned embryos could be used to produce children and this is unethical because it crosses a line from sexual to asexual reproduction. The women who are egg donors undergo an unpleasant and risky procedure; they are being exploited for the sake of the research. The cloned embryo is a potential child that is not treated with proper respect; in research it is treated as a means to an end. Cloning of human embryos for research is a slippery slope that will lead to harvesting cloned children for their organs or tissues. (Michael Tooley defends the cloning of children for medical purposes in "The Moral Status of the Cloning of Humans," in *Biomedical Ethics Reviews: Human Cloning,* ed. James Humber and Robert Almeder, Humana Press, 1998, pp. 65–101).

There are a number of questions about this research to cure disease. Are early-stage embryos or blastocysts human lives or human beings with a right to life? Is destroying them murder? Should fertility clinics stop discarding unused blastocysts? If so, what should be done with them? What do you think of cloning embryos for research on disease? Is that morally objectionable? What about cloning human children?

2. The Partial-Birth Abortion Ban Act of 2003

This bill was signed into law by President Bush on November 5, 2003. (The full text of the new law can be found at www.theorator.com.) The law defines "partial-birth abortion" as "deliberately and intentionally vaginally delivering a living fetus" whose head or trunk past the navel is "outside the body of the mother" and then killing it. The law does not prohibit the procedure if it is deemed necessary to save the life of the mother. The woman receiving the abortion may not be prosecuted under the law, but the doctor who performs it (if not to save the life or health of the mother) may be fined and imprisoned for not more than two years, or both.

The language of the law criminalizes any abortion procedure in which the head or trunk of a living fetus is outside the woman's body. The law does not use exact medical terminology, and for that reason it is subject to interpretation. Defenders of the law say it prohibits a cruel and unnecessary procedure that kills an unborn baby, and use graphic pictures to illustrate what happens. Doctors who perform abortions claim the law prohibits a procedure that the American College of Obstetrics and Gynecology calls intact dilation and evacuation. This procedure is usually done between twenty and twenty-four weeks of pregnancy, when the fetus has grown too large to fit through the woman's cervix easily. If the procedure is done before viability as defined by the Supreme Court in *Roe v. Wade,* then it is protected under *Roe.* That is one of the reasons the bill is being challenged in the courts and will likely go to the Supreme Court, which may revisit the *Roe* decision.

What exactly takes place in the procedure? A doctor who has performed 200 such abortions describes it as follows: Twenty-four hours before the abortion, the woman's cervix is dilated through the use of laminaria, which are sterilized sticks of seaweed. The next day, the patient is given a local anesthetic and a sedative. Both the mother and the fetus are asleep during the procedure. The fetus is partly pulled out in a breach position, that is, with the feet first and the head remaining in the womb (thus the phrase "partial birth"). Then the skull of the fetus has to be crushed or perforated with forceps to get it out.

Doctors who perform the intact dilation and evacuation procedure claim that it is safer for the woman than a classic dilation and curetage (D & C), where the fetus is scraped out with a serrated forceps, dismembering and killing it in the process. The woman's uterus can be perforated by the forceps or by fragments of bone as the fetus disintegrates. It is much safer to manually pull out the fetus intact, the doctors say.

Many abortion providers say that the new law also prohibits D & C because the fetus may start to pass through the cervix while still alive. In that case, D & C seems to fit the law's description of a partial-birth abortion.

No reliable statistics exist on the use of the intact dilation and extraction procedure. Groups opposing the ban originally claimed there were between 450 and 500 a year, but the Catholic bishops estimate that there are between 800 and 2,000 a year.

No reliable statistics are available for abortions performed after viability as defined by *Roe*. Federal statistics define a late abortion as one performed between twenty and twenty-four weeks. About 86 percent of these so-called late abortions are done by some kind of dilation and evacuation procedure. About 15,000 late abortions are performed a year, about 1 percent of the 1.3 million abortions that occur in the United States each year.

Doctors who perform late abortions say that they are most often used on poor, young women choosing to end an unwanted pregnancy. But in some cases, they are done for medical reasons—for example, because the fetus is severely abnormal or the woman faces grave health risks.

In June 2004, a federal judge in San Francisco, Phillis J. Hamilton, ruled that the Partial Birth Abortion Ban Act is unconstitutional. First, she argued that the law places an undue burden on women seeking abortions because common abortion methods could violate the law. In *Planned Parenthood* (1992), the Supreme Court ruled that states cannot impose an undue burden on women seeking abortions. Second, she said that the language of the law is unconstitutionally vague. In particular, she objected to the terms "partial-birth abortion" and "overt act." Third, she ruled that the law is unconstitutional because it has no exception for abortions necessary to preserve the woman's health. Citing the testimony of medical experts, she said that the procedure in question is sometimes required to protect the woman's health.

When President Clinton vetoed the partial-birth abortion ban in 1996, he surrounded himself with five women who had obtained partial-birth abortions for medical reasons. Do you agree with President Clinton that partial-birth abortions should not be banned? Or do you agree with President Bush that the procedure should be banned? Explain your position.

3. The Unborn Victims of Violence Act of 2004

(The full text of the bill can be found at FindLaw, http://news.findlaw.com.) The bill passed the Senate by a single vote—49–50. It is also known as "Laci and Conner's Law," to honor the killing of Laci Peterson and her unborn son, Connor. The bill was signed into law by President George W. Bush on April 6, 2004.

The new law recognizes as a legal person any "child in utero" who is injured or killed during the commission of a violent federal crime. The law defines "child in utero" as "a member of the species homo sapiens, at any stage of development, who is carried in the womb." Anyone who injures or "causes the death" of a "child in utero" is subject to the same punishment "provided under Federal law for that conduct had that injury or death occurred to the unborn child's mother." In other words, the law doubles the penalty for anyone who harms or kills a fetus in the course of harming or killing a pregnant woman. There are two victims instead of one because the fetus at any state of development is a person too. But that is exactly what Justice Blackmun denied in the majority opinion in *Roe*. He specifically says that the word person, as used in the U.S. Constitution, does not include the unborn.

What does this mean for abortion? The new law seems to directly contradict the findings in *Roe*. However, the new law stipulates that "nothing in this section shall be construed to permit the prosecution . . . of any person for conduct relating to an abortion." But if killing a woman and her fetus is a double murder, then why isn't killing the fetus and not the woman a single murder? Doesn't the law imply that abortion is the murder of a person? Is this new law consistent? Of course the basic question is whether or not the fetus, at any stage of development, is a person. What do you think?

4. Plan B

(Reported by Gina Kolata in The *New York Times,* December 16 and 17, 2003.) If plan A—contraception—fails or is not used, then women who do not want to be pregnant can use Plan B, an emergency contraceptive that prevents unintended pregnancy. Plan B consists of two high-dose birth control pills; it is meant to be used within 72 hours after unprotected sexual intercourse. If used according to the directions, it can prevent nearly 90 percent of unintended pregnancies.

Although the so-called morning-after pill has been available by prescription only since the late 1990s, it has been largely unavailable and unused. (See the next Problem Case.) In December 2003, however, two expert advisory committees to the Food and Drug Administration (FDA) recommended that Plan B be sold over the counter.

The drug is being marketed by Barr Laboratories. The company says that extensive studies show that Plan B is safe. Side effects such as nausea and vomiting are limited and minor. There have been no deaths resulting from use of the drug, and there are no contraindications except allergies to the pills' ingredients, which are very rare. The company says it will provide detailed information to women on what the pills do and on how to use them. It wants to sell the drug in stories with pharmacies. The prescription drug now sells for $25 to $35.

Dr. James Trussell, an advisory committee member from Princeton University, who voted for the motion to make the drug available over the counter, said that Plan B would have an enormous impact in preventing unwanted pregnancies, second only to the introduction of birth control pills. It is estimated that the drug could prevent as many as half of the three million unintended pregnancies in the United States each year.

Opponents of the morning-after pill claim that over-the-counter sales will encourage irresponsible sexual behavior. Furthermore, they argue that women may not understand how the pill works. Although it usually acts by preventing ovulation, it also may prevent the fertilized egg from implanting in the uterus. If pregnancy begins with fertilization, as conservatives believe, then the pills could induce an early abortion. "The pill acts to prevent pregnancy by aborting a child," said Judy Brown, president of the American Life League, an anti-abortion group.

In May 2004, the acting director of the FDA's Center for Drug Evaluation and Research, Steven Galson, rejected the application for Plan B on the grounds that access to emergency contraception might harm young teenagers. He claimed the proponents of Plan B failed to supply data about the drug's impact on "the younger age group from 11 to 14, where we know there's a substantial amount of sexual activity."

But according to a report issued by the Centers for Disease Control and Prevention, www.cdc.gov., just 4 percent of girls have sexual intercourse before age 13. Furthermore, according to the Alan Guttmacher Institute, www.agi-usa.org., 7 out of 10 girls who have sex before the age of 13 do so involuntarily.

Should Plan B be sold over the counter? Should it be available without a prescription to girls under age 13? Would you be willing to have it sold to adult women? Explain your position.

5. *The Morning-After Pill*

(Discussed in "The Morning-After Pill," by Jan Hoffman, in *The New York Times Magazine,* January 10, 1993.) Depending on when a woman takes it, the morning-after pill prevents either fertilization (occurring up to eighteen hours after intercourse) or implantation of the fertilized egg in the lining of the uterus (occurring about a week or two after conception). Because pregnancy tests do not register positive until a day or two after implantation, a woman who takes the pill after intercourse will not know if she has prevented conception or implantation.

The drug most often used as a morning-after pill is Ovral. It is also used as a birth-control pill, and it was approved as such by the FDA (the Federal Food and Drug Administration) in 1968. Other lower-dose pills that can be used as morning-after pills are Lo/Ovral, Nordette, Levlen, Triphasil, and Tri Levlen. All these pills combine estrogen and progestin. They affect a woman's hormones in such a way that the egg cannot be fertilized; or if it is, it cannot become implanted in the lining of the uterus. Instead the egg is sloughed off during menstruation.

The morning-after pill can be effectively taken up to 72 hours after intercourse, and it reduces the likelihood of pregnancy to below 8 percent. (On her most fertile day, a woman's chance of becoming pregnant is at most about 25 percent.) Although it certainly reduces the chances of becoming pregnant, it is not completely effective because it does not prevent tubal pregnancies. The side effects of the morning-after pill include temporary nausea and breast tenderness, and it is not recommended for women who should not take oral contraceptives.

According to the *Times* article, the morning-after pill has been part of standard care for rape victims for more than a decade. Planned Parenthood affiliates have been offering it for about three years. Use of birth-control pills as morning-after pills has not received the approval of the FDA, largely because no drug company has sought approval, and without FDA approval they cannot be dispensed in federally supported Title X clinics that serve poor women.

Doctors estimate that by making the morning-after pill widely available, the number of unwanted pregnancies could be reduced by 1.7 million annually and the number of abortions could be reduced by 800,000 annually. Currently, there are about 3.5 million unwanted pregnancies per year in the United States and about 1.4 million abortions.

The morning-after pill raises several interesting questions:

Is preventing implantation an abortion, contraception, interception, or what?

Is the zygote or fertilized egg a person with rights before it becomes implanted?

The IUD (interuterine device) also prevents fertilization or implantation. Does using it amount to getting an abortion?

In the one or two weeks before implantation, many fertilized eggs are naturally sloughed off, and women don't usually think of this as miscarriage. So why should a woman think of preventing implantation as an abortion?

6. Mrs. Sherri Finkbine and Thalidomide

In 1962, Mrs. Sherri Finkbine, the mother of four normal children, became pregnant. During the pregnancy, Mrs. Finkbine had trouble sleeping, so without consulting her physician, she took some tranquilizers containing the drug thalidomide that her husband had brought back from a trip to Europe. In Europe, the sedative was widely used.

Later Mrs. Finkbine read that a number of severely deformed children had been born in Europe. These children's limbs failed to develop or developed in malformed ways; some were born blind and deaf or had seriously defective internal organs. The birth defects were traced to the use in pregnancy of a widely used tranquilizer whose active ingredient was thalidomide, the very tranquilizer that she had taken.

Mrs. Finkbine went to her physician, and he confirmed her fears. The tranquilizer did contain thalidomide, and she had a very good chance of delivering a seriously deformed baby. The physician recommended an abortion. Mrs. Finkbine then presented her case to the three-member medical board of Phoenix, and they granted approval for the abortion.

In her concern for other women who might have taken thalidomide, Mrs. Finkbine told her story to a local newspaper. The story made the front page, and it wasn't long before reporters had discovered and published Mrs. Finkbine's identity. She became the object of an intense anti-abortion campaign, and she was condemned as a murderer by the Vatican newspaper.

As a result of the controversy, the medical board decided that their approval for an abortion would not survive a court test because the Arizona statute at that time allowed abortion only to save the mother's life. So the board withdrew their approval.

Eventually Mrs. Finkbine found it necessary to get an abortion in Sweden. After the abortion, Mrs. Finkbine asked if the fetus was a boy or a girl. The doctor could not say because the fetus was too badly deformed.

Do you think that Mrs. Finkbine acted wrongly in having an abortion? Explain your answer.

Do you think that the government has a right to prohibit abortions in such cases? Why or why not?

Suggested Readings

1. The Alan Guttmacher Institute, www.agi-use.org, is a good source for statistics on all aspects of abortion and pregnancy. The Centers for Disease Control and Prevention, www.ckc.gov, provides national data, but focuses on the safety of abortion. The National Right to Life organization, www.nric.org, advocates the pro-life view. Another pro-life organization is the Pro-Life Action League, www.prolifeaction.org. The pro-choice view is defended on Naral Pro-Choice America, www.prochoiceamerica.org. For advocacy of women's rights see the Feminist Majority website, www.feminist.org.

2. Elizabeth Harman, "The Potentiality Problem," *Philosophical Studies* 114:1–2 (May 2003): 173–98, available online at her website, www.nyu.edu/gsas/dept/philo/faculty/harman, claims that the potentiality of the embryo does not give it moral status, but the consciousness of the fetus does give it some moral standing.

3. William J. Fitzpatrick, "Totipotency and the Moral Status of Embryos: New Problems for an Old Argument," *Journal of Social Philosophy* 35: 1 (Spring 2004): 108–22, critically examines the pro-life argument that appeals to totipotency, the potential to develop into a living organism when placed in a suitable environment. The sperm and egg do not have this property, but the zygote does.

4. Rosalind Hursthouse, "Virtue Theory and Abortion," *Philosophy & Public Affairs* 20:3 (1991): 223–46, applies virtue theory to the problem of abortion, and concludes that some abortions exhibit vices such as selfishness or callousness, but others display virtues such as modesty or humility.

5. Sally Markowitz, "Abortion and Feminism," *Social Theory and Practice* 16 (Spring 1990): 1–17, presents a feminist argument for abortion rights. Basically, her argument is that women should not have to endure an unwanted pregnancy in a sexist society where they are oppressed.

6. Michael Tooley, "Abortion and Infanticide," *Philosophy and Public Affairs* 2 (Fall 1972): 47–66, presents a classic defense of the pro-choice view that neither a fetus nor a new-born infant has a serious right to continued existence and that both abortion and infanticide are morally acceptable. Tooley also has a book titled *Abortion and Infanticide* (Oxford: Oxford University Press, 1974), in which he develops his position.

7. Celia Wolf-Devine, "Abortion and the "Feminine Voice,'" *Public Affairs Quarterly,* 3 (July 1989): 81–97, contends that the feminine voice in morality, the voice that cares for particular others, says that abortion is to be avoided.

8. Gary M. Atkinson, "The Morality of Abortion," *International Philosophy Quarterly* 14 (Spring 1974): 347–62, argues, like Tooley, that abortion and infanticide are morally equivalent, but he takes the argument a step further by claiming that each is equivalent to involuntary euthanasia. But because involuntary euthanasia is wrong, on Atkinson's view, it follows that abortion and infanticide are wrong too.

9. Jane English, "Abortion and the Concept of a Person," *Canadian Journal of Philosophy* 5:2 (October 1975): 233–43, argues that the question about whether the fetus is a person or not cannot be conclusively settled because the concept of person cannot be defined

in terms of necessary and sufficient conditions. English goes on to argue that even if the fetus is a person, the mother's right to self-defense is strong enough to justify abortions to avoid death or serious harm.

10. L. W. Sumner, "Abortion," in *Health Care Ethics,* ed. Donald VanDeVeer and Tom Regan (Philadelphia: Temple University Press, 1987), pp. 162–81, proposes a moderate view about the moral standing of the fetus: it acquires moral standing when it becomes sentient—that is, capable of feeling pleasure and pain. Before this dividing line in the development of the fetus (which occurs sometime in the second trimester), abortion is the moral equivalent of contraception, and after this line abortion is the moral equivalent of infanticide.

11. Susan Sherwin, "Abortion through a Feminist Ethics Lens," *Dialogue* 30 (1991): 327–42, presents a standard feminist view that freedom to choose abortion is essential for sexual and reproductive freedom, and without it, women will continue to be oppressed by men.

12. *Feminist Philosophies,* ed. Janet A. Kourany, James P. Sterba, and Rosemarie Tong (Englewood Cliffs, NJ: Prentice-Hall, 1992), has four feminist articles on abortion and reproduction, including "Abortion: Is a Woman a Person?" by Ellen Willis. Willis claims that pro-lifers view the woman as a mere womb and not as a person with rights.

13. Angela Davis, *Women, Race, and Class* (New York: Random House, 1981), chapter 12, discusses the abortion rights movement in the context of race, class, and the women's liberation movement.

14. Ronald Dworkin, "A Critical Review of Feminist Analyses of Abortion," *The New York Review of Books* (June 10, 1993), attacks Catharine MacKinnon, Robin West, Carol Gilligan, and other feminists who emphasize the unique relationship between the pregnant woman and the fetus.

15. Jim Stone, "Why Potentiality Matters," *Canadian Journal of Philosophy* 17 (December 1987): 815–30, argues that the fetus has a right to life because it is potentially an adult human being.

16. Louis P. Pojman and Francis J. Beckwith, eds., *The Abortion Controversy* (Belmont, CA: Wadsworth, 1988), is a comprehensive anthology that includes articles on the *Roe* decision, Thomson's appeal to the woman's right to her body, numerous articles about the personhood of the fetus, and feminist articles.

17. Alan Zaitchik, "Viability and the Morality of Abortion," *Philosophy and Public Affairs* 10:1 (1981): 18–24, defends the view that viability is a morally significant dividing line.

18. Tristram H. Engelhardt, Jr., "The Ontology of Abortion," *Ethics* 84 (April 1974): 217–34, maintains that the fetus is not a person until the later stages of pregnancy, but after viability it can be treated as if it were a person.

19. Peter Singer, *Practical Ethics*, 2nd ed. (Cambridge: Cambridge University Press, 1993), chapter 6, presents a utilitarian view of abortion. The version of utilitarianism that Singer accepts is called preference utilitarianism.

20. Sissela Bok, "Ethical Problems of Abortion," *Hastings Center Studies* 2 (January 1974): 33–52, rejects attempts to define humanity and suggests that various reasons for not getting an abortion become stronger as the fetus develops.

21. Daniel Callahan, *Abortion, Law, Choice and Morality* (New York: Macmillan, 1970), defends the moderate view that the fetus has what he calls a partial moral status.

22. Joel Feinberg and Barbara Baum Levenbook, "Abortion," in *Matters of Life and Death,* 3rd ed., ed. Tom Regan (New York: Random House, 1993), provide a sophisticated discussion of various issues connected to abortion and end up with a moderate position. But in a postscript they decide that a legal ban on abortion may be justified even if abortion is not generally morally wrong.

23. R. M. Hare, "Abortion and the Golden Rule," *Philosophy and Public Affairs* 4 (Spring 1975): 201–22, attacks those, such as Judith Jarvis Thomson, who appeal to moral intuition and uses the golden rule as a basic ethical principle to defend a moderate view of abortion.

24. Susan Nicholson, *Abortion and the Roman Catholic Church* (Knoxsville, TN: Religious Ethics, 1974), explains the position of the Catholic Church on abortion.

Chapter 3

Euthanasia and the Duty to Die

Introduction

Factual Background

Euthanasia is killing someone for the sake of mercy to relieve great suffering. But when a doctor helps an injured or ill person commit suicide, as Dr. Jack Kevorkian has done in 120 cases, it seems that there is little difference between doctor-assisted suicide and euthanasia. Singer makes this point in the readings.

Statistics on euthanasia and physician-assisted suicide are difficult to obtain in the United States. Other than Dr. Kevorkian, few doctors come forward to talk about something that is illegal in every state except Oregon. In one study, 36 percent of the doctors said they would write lethal prescriptions if it were legal, and 24 percent said they would administer lethal injections. Another study, reported in the *Journal of the American Medical Association* (August 12, 1998), found in telephone interviews of 355 oncologists that almost 16 percent had participated in euthanasia or physician-assisted suicide. A national survey found that nearly one in five doctors who care for very ill and dying people said that they had been asked for help in dying, either by delivering a lethal injection or by writing a prescription for lethal drugs, but only 5 percent admitted to administering a lethal injection, and only 3 percent said they had ever written the prescription.

Euthanasia and physician-assisted suicide have been socially accepted and openly practiced in the Netherlands for about twenty years. Until recently euthanasia in the Netherlands was technically illegal, but on April 10, 2001, the Netherlands became the first country in the world to pass a law decriminalizing voluntary euthanasia. The new legislation states that doctors must be convinced that the patient's request is voluntary and well considered and that the patient is facing unremitting and unbearable suffering. Doctors must have advised the patient of his or her situation and prospects and reached a firm conclusion that there is no reasonable alternative solution. The doctor must consult with at least one other independent physician. Also, the law allows minors aged twelve to sixteen to request euthanasia with consent of their parents. The strict conditions established under the law require that a commission that includes a doctor, a medical ethics expert, and a lawyer review each euthanasia case. Only legal residents of the Netherlands are eligible for the procedure. It is estimated that there are 5,000 cases of voluntary euthanasia or physician-assisted suicide in the Netherlands each year.

Oregon is the only state in the United States where doctor-assisted suicide for the terminally ill is legal. The state law, known officially as the Death with Dignity Act, took effect in November 1997. The law applies only to adults of sound mind who have, in the opinion of at least two doctors, less than six months to live. Doctors may prescribe but not administer the lethal dose. Those requesting death must fill out and sign a single-page form titled "Request for medication to end my life in a humane and dignified manner," and wait 15 days before receiving the medication. According to the Oregon Department of Human Services (http://www.dhs.state.org.us), 171 patients have died from physician-assisted suicide since the law took effect, with 42 dying in 2003. The median age was 73. The patients were ill with cancer, HIV/AIDS, or amyotrophic lateral schlerosis (ALS), which is often called Lou Gehrig's disease. Most patients used pentobarbital as their lethal medication.

In recent years ten states have passed bills making euthanasia or physician-assisted suicide illegal, and bills are pending in five more. In 1998, Michigan voters overwhelming (70% to 30%) rejected Proposal B, a ballot initiative that would have permitted doctors to administer lethal doses of medication to terminally ill patients. Previously, the state had outlawed assisted suicide for fifteen months in response to the practices of Dr. Kevorkian. In November 1998, CBS's "60 Minutes" aired a videotape showing Dr. Kevorkian giving a lethal injection to Thomas Youk, 52, who was suffering from Lou Gehrig's disease. Three days later, Michigan charged Dr. Kervorkian with first-degree murder. He was convicted of second-degree murder on April 13, 1999, and was sentenced to 10 to 25 years in prison. He will be eligible for parole in 2005.

In June 1997, the Supreme Court ruled that laws in New York and Washington making doctor-assisted suicide a crime were not unconstitutional. But the 9-to-0 decision was tentative, and some of the justices seemed to grant that some terminally ill people in intractable pain might be able to claim a constitutional right to a doctor's assistance in hastening their deaths. Justice Sandra Day O'Connor, for example, said that it was still an open question whether "a mentally competent person who is experiencing great suffering" that cannot otherwise be controlled has a constitutionally based "interest in controlling the circumstances of his or her imminent death."

The Readings

Discussions of euthanasia often distinguish between different types of euthanasia. Voluntary euthanasia is mercy killing with the consent of the terminally ill or suffering person. Many writers include physician-assisted suicide as a type of voluntary euthanasia, and Peter Singer seems to do this in his reading. Nonvoluntary euthanasia, by contrast, is mercy killing without the consent of the person killed, although the consent of others, such as parents or relatives, can be obtained. Writers who discuss nonvoluntary euthanasia usually have in mind the killing of those who are unable to give consent—for example, a comatose person such as Karen Quinlan or a defective infant. Obviously, such a person cannot commit suicide. There is another possibility, however, and that is the mercy killing of a person who is able to give consent but is not asked. If the person killed does not wish to die, it might be more accurate to call this involuntary euthanasia. This form of euthanasia is not discussed in the readings, but it may be safely assumed that all the authors in this book would consider it morally wrong.

A further distinction is often made between active and passive euthanasia, or between killing and letting a patient die for the sake of mercy. Just how this distinction should be drawn and whether the distinction should be made at all is a focus of debate in the readings. As James Rachels explains it in the reading, active euthanasia is taking a direct action designed to kill the patient, such as giving a lethal injection of morphine. Passive euthanasia, by contrast, is allowing the patient to die by withholding treatment—not performing lifesaving surgery on a defective infant, for example.

Rachels believes that this distinction has no moral significance and that using it leads to pointless suffering and confused moral thinking. Philippa Foot does not agree. She argues that the distinction has moral significance in many important cases. For example, she thinks there is a clear difference between a person sending starving people poisoned food, killing them by an action, and letting them die by not sending food. The difference is that in the first case the person is an agent of harm and in the second case the person is not an agent of harm. She goes on to discuss other interesting cases in which our moral intuitions seem to be that we should not kill one person to rescue five people, but it is allowable to let one person die in order to save five. But she admits that sometimes it might not be wrong to kill one person to save five, as in the much-discussed case of the runaway trolley, where there is a choice between killing one person or five standing on the track.

John Harris raises more problems for the distinction between killing and letting die in his discussion of the survival lottery. Suppose we can save two dying patients, Y and Z, by killing an innocent person, A. We take A's heart and give it to Y, who needs a new heart to survive, and we take A's lungs and give them to Z, who needs new lungs. No doubt we are guilty of killing an innocent person, but if we let Y and Z die by failing to perform the transplants, then are we still guilty—guilty of killing two innocent persons instead of one?

John Hardwig does not think the distinction between killing and letting die matters when it comes to the duty to die. He believes that this duty for the old and/or ill includes not just refusing life-prolonging medical treatment but also suicide. In his view, the basis of this duty to die is the burden the old and/or ill impose on their families. When the burden is too great, the old and/or ill person has a duty to kill herself or let herself die. To convince you of this, he presents a case of an 87-year-old woman dying of congestive heart failure with only six months to live. Even if the woman wants to live, and wants aggressive life-prolonging treatment, she has a duty to die. Why? Because in this case prolonging her life will impose too great a burden on her 55-year-old daughter, the only remaining family member, who will lose all her savings, her home, her job, and her career caring for her mother.

Felicia Ackerman (see the Suggested Readings) objects to Hardwig's failure to distinguish between killing and letting die. She agrees that the old and/or ill have a duty to not burden their families or society by demanding and receiving aggressive life-prolonging medical treatment. She notes that this view is widely accepted. But it is entirely another matter to claim that the old and/or ill have a duty to kill themselves to avoid imposing a burden on their families. She thinks this view is problematic, if only for the practical reason that it applies to a great many people.

Philosophical Issues

One basic issue is whether voluntary euthanasia and physician-assisted suicide are wrong or not. The standard view, presented by the AMA statement, is that both are wrong. The AMA statement quoted by Rachels says clearly that "the intentional termination of the life of one human being by another—mercy killing—is contrary to that for which the medical profession stands." Bonnie Steinbock defends the AMA statement against Rachels's attack. She says that the AMA statement does not rest on any distinction between active and passive euthanasia, as Rachels says. Both are wrong if they involve the intentional termination of life of one human being by another. The AMA statement does rest on an important distinction between ordinary and extraordinary means of treatment, however, because it allows the cessation of extraordinary means of treatment. But this is based on the patient's right to refuse treatment and does not assume any right to die.

Some doctors object to making voluntary active euthanasia legal. For example, Stephen G. Potts (see the Suggested Readings) argues that the legalized practice of voluntary active euthanasia would have a number of bad effects including the abandonment of hope, increased fear of hospitals and doctors, increased pressure on patients, and a slippery slope leading to nonvoluntary euthanasia and even involuntary euthanasia where undesirable people are killed without their consent. These potential bad effects mean that the burden of proof is on those who want to make euthanasia legal.

Susan M. Wolf (see the Suggested Readings) attacks euthanasia and physician-assisted suicide from a feminist point of view. Women in our sexist society have been socialized to be self-sacrificing, and this means that women will be more inclined to request death than men. If euthanasia and physician-assisted suicide are made legal, more women than men will die. She supports her view by pointing out that the first eight patients killed by Dr. Kevorkian were women.

Rachels and Singer take a different view. Rachels argues that in some cases active euthanasia is preferable to passive euthanasia because it reduces suffering. If there is a choice between a quick and painless death and prolonged suffering, and no other alternative, then Rachels would prefer a quick and painless death. Singer appeals to the principle of respect for autonomy. This principle tells us to allow rational agents to live their lives according to their decisions, and if they choose to die, they should be allowed to do so and even should be assisted in carrying out their decision.

Another important issue, as we have seen, is whether or not there is a morally significant difference between killing and letting a patient die, or between active and passive euthanasia, or between intentionally causing death and merely permitting death. Rachels attacks such distinctions, and Foot defends them. It seems obvious that most doctors make such distinctions; the statistics show that withholding or withdrawing lifesaving treatment is much more common than active euthanasia or physician-assisted suicide.

Another matter of controversy is the distinction between ordinary and extraordinary means of prolonging life. This distinction is found in the AMA statement that allows the cessation of the employment of extraordinary means to prolong the life of the body. Rachels thinks that the cessation of extraordinary means of treatment amounts to passive euthanasia because it is the intentional termination of life. But Steinbock suggests a response to this. She says that the reason for discontinuing extraordinary treatment is not to bring about the patient's death, but to avoid treatment that will cause more suffering than the disease and will have little hope of benefiting the patient. By contrast, cessation of ordinary means of treatment can be seen as neglect or even the intentional infliction of harm.

Although she does not explicitly discuss it, Steinbock seems to accept a traditional view about intentions called the *Doctrine of Double Effect*. (See the article by Philippa Foot cited in the Suggested Readings.) According to this doctrine, as long as the intended consequence of an act is good, a bad foreseen consequence (such as death) can be morally allowed, provided it is not intended and prevents a greater evil (such as great suffering). A common medical practice can be used to illustrate this. Suppose that a doctor gives a terminal cancer patient an overdose of morphine, that is, an amount sufficient to kill the patient. If the doctor intends only to reduce or eliminate the patient's pain and not to kill the patient, and if the death of the patient is not as bad as the patient's suffering, then according to the Doctrine of Double Effect the doctor's action is not wrong, even though the doctor foresees that the patient will die from the overdose.

This kind of reasoning seems fairly common among doctors. It seems to be suggested, for example, when the AMA statement says that it is intentional termination of life that is forbidden. Doesn't this allow for unintentional but foreseen death? In his legal defenses, Dr. Kevorkian repeatedly said that his only intention is to reduce or eliminate great suffering and not to cause death.

Critics of the Doctrine of Double Effect complain that no clear distinction can be made between the two effects, the intended one and the unintended but foreseen one. If Dr. Kevorkian intends to reduce the patient's suffering but also knows that the patient is getting a lethal dose of drugs when she turns the switch on the suicide machine, does it make sense to say that Dr. Kevorkian doesn't also intend to kill the patient with his machine?

Another important issue is whether or not old and/or ill people have a duty to die to avoid burdening their families. Hardwig thinks so, but Felicia Ackerman disagrees. Ackerman argues that family members have a strong obligation to care for each other. Consider again Hardwig's case of the 87-year-old woman dying of congestive heart failure. In Ackerman's view, much depends on the mother's relationship with her 55-year-old daughter. Suppose the mother made sacrifices for her daughter. She paid for the daughter's education so that the daughter could have a career. She gave her daughter money so that the daughter could buy a home. She cared for the daughter when she was a baby and child. All of these considerations suggest that the daughter has a duty to care for her ill mother. Furthermore, in this case the care is supposed to last for only six months. Why couldn't the daughter find another job?

Hardwig does not distinguish between cases of parents and children and cases involving married people. Ackerman thinks they are different. Children have a strong duty to care for their parents because the parents usually had a long period of caring for their children. Married people do not usually begin with a long period of one-sided caregiving, and unlike children, they freely enter into the arrangement. This gives married people the opportunity to agree upon caregiving duties.

Finally, there is the basic issue of how to make life-or-death decisions. One standard answer, given by Rachels, is to appeal to the quality of a person's life. If a person will have a bad life, then she should be allowed to end it; but if she will have a good life, then it is wrong to end it. But how do we distinguish between good and bad lives?

That is a classical problem that resists easy solution. Hedonists would say that a life full of pleasure is good and a life filled with suffering is bad. But Kant and many others would reject this view. It is not represented in the readings, but it is worth mentioning that the Christian view is that all life is sacred, all life is valuable, no matter how much suffering it contains.

Active and Passive Euthanasia

JAMES RACHELS

For biographical information on James Rachels, see the reading in Chapter 1.

Here Rachels attacks the distinction between active and passive euthanasia, and the doctrine apparently accepted by the American Medical Association that taking direct action to kill a patient (active euthanasia) is wrong, but withholding treatment and allowing a patient to die (passive euthanasia) is allowable. Rachels makes three criticisms of this doctrine. First, it results in unnecessary suffering for patients who die slowly and painfully rather than quickly and painlessly. Second, the doctrine leads to moral decisions based on irrelevant considerations. Third, the distinction between killing and letting die assumed by the doctrine is of no moral significance.

THE DISTINCTION BETWEEN active and passive euthanasia is thought to be crucial for medical ethics. The idea is that it is permissible, at least in some cases, to withhold treatment and allow a patient to die, but it is never permissible to take any direct action designed to kill the patient. This doctrine seems to be accepted by most doctors, and it is endorsed in a statement adopted by the House of Delegates of the American Medical Association on December 4, 1973:

> The intentional termination of the life of one human being by another—mercy killing—is contrary to that for which the medical profession stands and is contrary to the policy of the American Medical Association. The cessation

Source: James Rachels, "Active and Passive Euthanasia," from *The Elements of Moral Philosophy* (1986), pp. 90–103. Reprinted with the permission of The McGraw-Hill Companies.

of the employment of extraordinary means to prolong the life of the body when there is irrefutable evidence that biological death is imminent is the decision of the patient and/or his immediate family. The advice and judgment of the physician should be freely available to the patient and/or his immediate family.

However, a strong case can be made against this doctrine. In what follows I will set out some of the relevant arguments, and urge doctors to reconsider their views on this matter.

To begin with a familiar type of situation, a patient who is dying of incurable cancer of the throat is in terrible pain, which can no longer be satisfactorily alleviated. He is certain to die within a few days, even if present treatment is continued, but he does not want to go on living for those days since the pain is unbearable. So he asks the doctor for an end to it, and his family joins in the request.

Suppose the doctor agrees to withhold treatment, as the conventional doctrine says he may. The justification for his doing so is that the patient is in terrible agony, and since he is going to die anyway, it would be wrong to prolong his suffering needlessly. But now notice this. If one simply withholds treatment, it may take the patient longer to die, and so he may suffer more than he would if more direct action were taken and a lethal injection given. This fact provides strong reason for thinking that, once the initial decision not to prolong his agony has been made, active euthanasia is actually preferable to passive euthanasia, rather than the reverse. To say otherwise is to endorse the option that leads to more suffering rather than less, and is contrary to the humanitarian impulse that prompts the decision not to prolong his life in the first place.

Part of my point is that the process of being "allowed to die" can be relatively slow and painful, whereas being given a lethal injection is relatively quick and painless. Let me give a different sort of example. In the United States about one in 600 babies is born with Down's syndrome. Most of these babies are otherwise healthy—that is, with only the usual pediatric care, they will proceed to an otherwise normal infancy. Some, however, are born with congenital defects such as intestinal obstructions that require operations if they are to live. Sometimes, the parents and the doctor will decide not to operate, and let the infant die. Anthony Shaw describes what happens then:

> . . . When surgery is denied [the doctor] must try to keep the infant from suffering while natural forces sap the baby's life away. As a surgeon whose natural inclination is to use the scalpel to fight off death, standing by and watching a salvageable baby die is the most emotionally exhausting experience I know. It is easy at a conference, in a theoretical discussion, to decide that such infants should be allowed to die. It is altogether different to stand by in the nursery and watch as dehydration and

infection wither a tiny being over hours and days. This is a terrible ordeal for me and the hospital staff—much more so than for the parents who never set foot in the nursery.[1]

I can understand why some people are opposed to all euthanasia, and insist that such infants must be allowed to live. I think I can also understand why other people favor destroying these babies quickly and painlessly. But why should anyone favor letting "dehydration and infection wither a tiny being over hours and days"? The doctrine that says that a baby may be allowed to dehydrate and wither, but may not be given an injection that would end its life without suffering, seems so patently cruel as to require no further refutation. The strong language is not intended to offend, but only to put the point in the clearest possible way.

My second argument is that the conventional doctrine leads to decisions concerning life and death made on irrelevant grounds.

Consider again the case of the infants with Down's syndrome who need operations for congenital defects unrelated to the syndrome to live. Sometimes, there is no operation, and the baby dies, but when there is no such defect, the baby lives on. Now, an operation such as that to remove an intestinal obstruction is not prohibitively difficult. The reason why such operations are not performed in these cases is, clearly, that the child has Down's syndrome and the parents and doctor judge that because of that fact it is better for the child to die.

But notice that this situation is absurd, no matter what view one takes of the lives and potentials of such babies. If the life of such an infant is worth preserving, what does it matter if it needs a simple operation? Or, if one thinks it better that such a baby should not live on, what difference does it make that it happens to have an unobstructed intestinal tract? In either case, the matter

1 A. Shaw: "Doctor, Do We Have a Choice?" The *New York Times Magazine,* January 30, 1972, p. 54.

of life and death is being decided on irrelevant grounds. It is the Down's syndrome, and not the intestines, that is the issue. The matter should be decided, if at all, on that basis, and not be allowed to depend on the essentially irrelevant question of whether the intestinal tract is blocked.

What makes this situation possible, of course, is the idea that when there is an intestinal blockage, one can "let the baby die," but when there is no such defect there is nothing that can be done, for one must not "kill" it. The fact that this idea leads to such results as deciding life or death on irrelevant grounds is another good reason why the doctrine should be rejected.

One reason why so many people think that there is an important moral difference between active and passive euthanasia is that they think killing someone is morally worse than letting someone die. But is it? Is killing, in itself, worse than letting die? To investigate this issue, two cases may be considered that are exactly alike except that one involves killing whereas the other involves letting someone die. Then, it can be asked whether this difference makes any difference to the moral assessments. It is important that the cases be exactly alike, except for this one difference, since otherwise one cannot be confident that it is this difference and not some other that accounts for any variation in the assessments of the two cases. So, let us consider this pair of cases:

In the first, Smith stands to gain a large inheritance if anything should happen to his six-year-old cousin. One evening while the child is taking his bath, Smith sneaks into the bathroom and drowns the child, and then arranges things so that it will look like an accident.

In the second, Jones also stands to gain if anything should happen to his six-year-old cousin. Like Smith, Jones sneaks in planning to drown the child in his bath. However, just as he enters the bathroom Jones sees the child slip and hit his head and fall face down in the water. Jones is delighted; he stands by, ready to push the child's head back under if it is necessary, but it is not

necessary. With only a little thrashing about the child drowns all by himself, "accidentally," as Jones watches and does nothing.

Now Smith killed the child, whereas Jones "merely" let the child die. That is the only difference between them. Did either man behave better, from a moral point of view? If the difference between killing and letting die were in itself a morally important matter, one should say that Jones's behavior was less reprehensible than Smith's. But does one really want to say that? I think not. In the first place, both men acted from the same motive, personal gain, and both had exactly the same end in view when they acted. It may be inferred from Smith's conduct that he is a bad man, although that judgment may be withdrawn or modified if certain further facts are learned about him—for example, that he is mentally deranged. But would not the very same thing be inferred about Jones from his conduct? And would not the same further considerations also be relevant to any modification of this judgment? Moreover, suppose Jones pleaded, in his own defense, "After all, I didn't do anything except just stand there and watch the child drown. I didn't kill him; I only let him die." Again, if letting die were in itself less bad than killing, this defense should have at least some weight. But it does not. Such a "defense" can only be regarded as a grotesque perversion of moral reasoning. Morally speaking, it is no defense at all.

Now, it may be pointed out, quite properly, that the cases of euthanasia with which doctors are concerned are not like this at all. They do not involve personal gain or the destruction of normally healthy children. Doctors are concerned only with cases in which the patient's life is of no further use to him, or in which the patient's life has become or will soon become a terrible burden. However, the point is the same in these cases: the bare difference between killing and letting die does not, in itself, make a moral difference. If a doctor lets a patient die, for humane reasons, he is in the same moral position as if he had given the patient a lethal injection for humane reasons. If his decision was wrong—if, for example, the patient's illness was in fact curable—the decision would be equally regrettable no matter which method was used to carry it out. And if the doctor's decision was the right one, the method used is not in itself important.

The AMA policy statement isolates the crucial issue very well; the crucial issue is "the intentional termination of the life of one human being by another." But after identifying this issue, and forbidding "mercy killing," the statement goes on to deny that the cessation of treatment is the intentional termination of a life. This is where the mistake comes in, for what is the cessation of treatment, in these circumstances, if it is not "the intentional termination of the life of one human being by another"? Of course it is exactly that, and if it were not, there would be no point to it.

Many people will find this judgment hard to accept. One reason, I think, is that it is very easy to conflate the question of whether killing is, in itself, worse than letting die, with the very different question of whether most actual cases of killing are more reprehensible than most actual cases of letting die. Most actual cases of killing are clearly terrible (think, for example, of all the murders reported in the newspapers), and one hears of such cases every day. On the other hand, one hardly ever hears of a case of letting die, except for the actions of doctors who are motivated by humanitarian reasons. So one learns to think of killing in a much worse light than of letting die. But this does not mean that there is something about killing that makes it in itself worse than letting die, for it is not the bare difference between killing and letting die that makes the difference in these cases. Rather, the other factors—the murderer's motive of personal gain, for example, contrasted with the doctor's humanitarian motivation— account for different reactions to the different cases.

I have argued that killing is not in itself any worse than letting die; if my contention is right, it follows that active euthanasia is not any worse than passive euthanasia. What arguments can be given on the other side? The most common, I believe, is the following:

> The important difference between active and passive euthanasia is that, in passive euthanasia, the doctor does not do anything to bring about the patient's death. The doctor does nothing, and the patient dies of whatever ills already afflict him. In active euthanasia, however, the doctor does something to bring about the patient's death: he kills him. The doctor who gives the patient with cancer a lethal injection has himself caused his patient's death; whereas if he merely ceases treatment, the cancer is the cause of the death.

A number of points need to be made here. The first is that it is not exactly correct to say that in passive euthanasia the doctor does nothing, for he does do one thing that is very important: he lets the patient die. "Letting someone die" is certainly different, in some respects, from other types of action—mainly in that it is a kind of action that one may perform by way of not performing certain other actions. For example, one may let a patient die by way of not giving medication, just as one may insult someone by way of not shaking his hand. But for any purpose of moral assessment, it is a type of action nonetheless. The decision to let a patient die is subject to moral appraisal in the same way that a decision to kill him would be subject to moral appraisal: it may be assessed as wise or unwise, compassionate or sadistic, right or wrong. If a doctor deliberately let a patient die who was suffering from a routinely curable illness, the doctor would certainly be to blame for what he had done, just as he would be to blame if he had needlessly killed the patient. Charges against him would then be appropriate. If so, it would be no defense at all for him to insist that he didn't "do anything." He would have done something very serious indeed, for he let his patient die.

Fixing the cause of death may be very important from a legal point of view, for it may determine whether criminal charges are brought against the doctor. But I do not think that this notion can be used to show a moral difference between active and passive euthanasia. The reason why it is considered bad to be the cause of someone's death is that death is regarded as a great evil—and so it is. However, if it has been decided that euthanasia—even passive euthanasia—is desirable in a given case, it has also been decided that in this instance death is no greater an evil than the patient's continued existence. And if this is true, the usual reason for not wanting to be the cause of someone's death simply does not apply.

Finally, doctors may think that all of this is only of academic interest—the sort of thing that philosophers may worry about but that has no practical bearing on their own work. After all, doctors must be concerned about the legal consequences of what they do, and active euthanasia is clearly forbidden by the law. But even so, doctors should also be concerned with the fact that the law is forcing upon them a moral doctrine that may well be indefensible, and has a considerable effect on their practices. Of course, most doctors are not now in the position of being coerced in this matter, for they do not regard themselves as merely going along with what the law requires. Rather in statements such as the AMA policy statement that I have quoted, they are endorsing this doctrine as a central point of medical ethics. In that statement, active euthanasia is condemned not merely as illegal but as "contrary to that for which the medical profession stands," whereas passive euthanasia is approved. However, the preceding considerations suggest that there is really no moral difference between the two, considered in themselves (there may be important moral differences in some cases in their *consequences*, but, as I pointed out, these differences may make active euthanasia, and not passive euthanasia, the morally preferable option). So, whereas doctors may have to discriminate between active and passive euthanasia to satisfy the law, they should not do any more than that. In particular, they should not give the distinction any added authority and weight by writing it into official statements of medical ethics.

Review Questions

1. According to Rachels, what is the distinction between active and passive euthanasia?
2. Why does Rachels think that being allowed to die is worse in some cases than a lethal injection?
3. What is Rachels's second argument against the conventional doctrine?
4. According to Rachels, why isn't killing worse than letting die?

Discussion Questions

1. The AMA statement quoted by Rachels does not use the terminology of active and passive euthanasia. Furthermore, so-called passive euthanasia could be the intentional termination of life rejected by the AMA. Does the AMA really accept this distinction? Why or why not?
2. Is the distinction between killing and letting die morally relevant? What do you think?
3. Should the law be changed to allow active euthanasia or not? Defend your view.

The Intentional Termination of Life

BONNIE STEINBOCK

Bonnie Steinbock is chair and professor of philosophy at the University at Albany, SUNY. She is the author of *Life Before Birth* (1992), and the editor of *Legal and Ethical Issues in Human Reproduction* (2002). Her home page is at www.albany.edu/philosophy/steinbock.

Steinbock defends the AMA statement on euthanasia from the attack made by Rachels. She argues that the AMA statement does not make the distinction between active and passive euthanasia that Rachels attacks. According to Steinbock, the AMA statement rejects both active and passive euthanasia, but does permit the cessation of extraordinary means of treatment to prolong life. This is not the same as passive euthanasia. Cessation of extraordinary means can be done to respect the patient's right to refuse treatment or because continued treatment is painful. Neither reason is the same as letting the patient die. She grants, however, that in some cases the cessation of extraordinary means does amount to letting the patient die and that in some cases a quick and painless death may be preferable to letting a patient die slowly.

ACCORDING TO JAMES RACHELS[1] a common mistake in medical ethics is the belief that there is a moral difference between active and passive euthanasia. This is a mistake, [he] argues, because the rationale underlying the distinction between active and passive euthanasia is the idea that there is a significant moral difference between intentionally killing and letting die. . . . Whether the belief that there is a significant moral difference (between intentionally killing and intentionally letting die) is mistaken is not my concern here. For it is far from clear that this distinction *is* the basis of the doctrine of the American Medical Association which Rachels attacks. And if the killing/letting die distinction is not the basis of the AMA doctrine, then arguments showing that the distinction has no moral force do not, in themselves, reveal in the doctrine's adherents either "confused thinking" or "a moral point of view unrelated to the interests of individuals." Indeed, as we examine the AMA doctrine, I think it will become clear that it appeals to and makes use of a number of overlapping distinctions, which may have moral significance in particular cases, such as the distinction between intending and foreseeing, or between ordinary and extraordinary care. Let us then turn to the statement, from the House of Delegates of the American Medical Association, which Rachels cites:

> The intentional termination of the life of one human being by another—mercy-killing—is contrary to that for which the medical profession stands and is contrary to the policy of the American Medical Association. The cessation of the employment of extraordinary means to prolong the life of the body when there is irrefutable evidence that biological death is imminent is the decision of the patient and/or

Source: Bonnie Steinbock, "The Intentional Termination of Life," *Social Science & Medicine*, Vol 6, No. 1, 1979, pp. 59–64. Used by permission.

1 James Rachels. Active and passive euthanasia. *New Engl. J. Med.*, 292, 78–80, 1975.

his immediate family. The advice and judgment of the physician should be freely available to the patient and/or his immediate family.[2]

Rachels attacks this statement because he believes that it contains a moral distinction between active and passive euthanasia. . . .

I intend to show that the AMA statement does not imply support of the active/passive euthanasia distinction. In forbidding the intentional termination of life, the statement rejects both active and passive euthanasia. It does allow for ". . . the cessation of the employment of extraordinary means . . ." to prolong life. The mistake Rachels makes is in identifying the cessation of life-prolonging treatment with passive euthanasia, or intentionally letting die. If it were right to equate the two, then the AMA statement would be self-contradictory, for it would begin by condemning, and end by allowing, the intentional termination of life. But if the cessation of life-prolonging treatment is not always or necessarily passive euthanasia, then there is no confusion and no contradiction.

Why does Rachels think that the cessation of life-prolonging treatment is the intentional termination of life? He says:

> The AMA policy statement isolates the crucial issue very well: the crucial issue is "the intentional termination of the life of one human being by another." But after identifying this issue, and forbidding "mercy-killing," the statement goes on to deny that the cessation of treatment is the intentional termination of a life. That is where the mistake comes in, for what is the cessation of treatment, in these circumstances, if it is not "the intentional termination of the life of one human being by another"? Of course it is exactly that, and if it were not, there would be no point to it.[3]

However, there *can* be a point (to the cessation of life-prolonging treatment) other than an endeavor to bring about the patient's death, and so the blanket identification of cessation of

treatment with the intentional termination of a life is inaccurate. There are at least two situations in which the termination of life-prolonging treatment cannot be identified with the intentional termination of the life of one human being by another.

The first situation concerns the patient's right to refuse treatment. Rachels gives the example of a patient dying of an incurable disease, accompanied by unrelievable pain, who wants to end the treatment which cannot cure him but can only prolong his miserable existence. Why, they ask, may a doctor accede to the patient's request to stop treatment, but not provide a patient in a similar situation with the lethal dose? The answer lies in the patient's right to refuse treatment. In general, a competent adult has the right to refuse treatment, even where such treatment is necessary to prolong life. Indeed, the right to refuse treatment has been upheld even when the patient's reason for refusing treatment is generally agreed to be inadequate.[4] This right can be overridden (if, for example, the patient has dependent children) but, in general, no one may legally compel you to undergo treatment to which you have not consented. "Historically, surgical intrusion has always been considered a technical battery upon the person and one to be excused or justified by consent of the patient or justified by necessity created by the circumstances of the moment. . . ."[5]

At this point, it might be objected that if one has the right to refuse life-prolonging treatment, then consistency demands that one have the right to decide to end his life, and to obtain help in doing so. The idea is that the right to refuse treatment somehow implies a right to voluntary euthanasia, and we need to see why someone might think this. The right to refuse treatment has been considered by legal writers

2 Rachels, p. 78.
3 Rachels, pp. 79–80.

4 For example, *In re Yetter,* 62 Pa. D. & C. 2d 619, C.P., Northampton County Ct., 1974.
5 David W. Meyers, Legal aspects of voluntary euthanasia, *Dilemmas of Euthanasia* (edited by John Behnke and Sissela Bok), p. 56. Anchor Books, New York, 1975.

as an example of the right to privacy or, better, the right to bodily self-determination. You have the right to decide what happens to your own body, and the right to refuse treatment is an instance of that more general right. But if you have the right to determine what happens to your body, then should you not have the right to choose to end your life, and even a right to get help in doing so?

However, it is important to see that the right to refuse treatment is not the same as, nor does it entail, a right to voluntary euthanasia, even if both can be derived from the right to bodily self-determination. The right to refuse treatment is not itself a "right to die"; that one may choose to exercise this right even at the risk of death, or even *in order to die,* is irrelevant. The purpose of the right to refuse medical treatment is not to give persons a right to decide whether to live or die, but to protect them from the unwanted interferences of others. Perhaps we ought to interpret the right to bodily self-determination more broadly so as to include a right to die: but this would be a substantial extension of our present understanding of the right to bodily self-determination, and not a consequence of it. Should we recognize a right to voluntary euthanasia, we would have to agree that people have the right not merely to be left alone, but also the right to be killed. I leave to one side that substantive moral issue. My claim is simply that there can be a reason for terminating life-prolonging treatment other than "to bring about the patient's death."

The second case in which termination of treatment cannot be identified with intentional termination of life is where continued treatment has little chance of improving the patient's condition and brings greater discomfort than relief.

The question here is what treatment is appropriate to the particular case. A cancer specialist describes it in this way:

My general rule is to administer therapy as long as a patient responds well and has the potential for a reasonably good quality of life. But when all feasible therapies have been administered and a patient shows signs of rapid deterioration, the continuation of therapy can cause more discomfort than the cancer. From that time I recommend surgery, radiotherapy, or chemotherapy only as a means of relieving pain. But if a patient's condition should once again stabilize after the withdrawal of active therapy and if it should appear that he could still gain some good time, I would immediately reinstitute active therapy. The decision to cease anticancer treatment is never irrevocable, and often the desire to live will push a patient to try for another remission, or even a few more days of life.[6]

The decision here to cease anticancer treatment cannot be construed as a decision that the patient die, or as the intentional termination of life. It is a decision to provide the most appropriate treatment for that patient at that time. Rachels suggests that the point of the cessation of treatment is the intentional termination of life. But here the point of discontinuing treatment is not to bring about the patient's death, but to avoid treatment that will cause more discomfort than the cancer and has little hope of benefiting the patient. Treatment that meets this description is often called "extraordinary."[7] The concept is flexible, and what might be considered "extraordinary" in one situation might be ordinary in another. The use of a respirator to sustain a patient through a severe bout with a respiratory disease would be considered ordinary; its use to sustain the life of a severely brain damaged person in an irreversible coma would be considered extraordinary.

Contrasted with extraordinary treatment is ordinary treatment, the care of a doctor would normally be expected to provide. Failure to provide ordinary care constitutes neglect, and can even be construed as the intentional infliction of harm, where there is a legal obligation to provide

6 Ernest H. Rosenbaum, Md., *Living with Cancer,* p. 27. Praeger, New York, 1975.
7 Cf. H. Tristram Engelhardt, Jr., Ethical issues in aiding the death of young children, *Beneficent Euthanasia* (Edited by Marvin Kohl), Prometheus Books, Buffalo, N.Y. 1975.

care. The importance of ordinary/extraordinary care distinction lies partly in its connection to the doctor's intention. The withholding of extraordinary care should be seen as a decision not to inflict painful treatment on a patient without reasonable hope of success. The withholding of ordinary care, by contrast, must be seen as neglect. Thus, one doctor says, "We have to draw a distinction between ordinary and extraordinary means. We never withdraw what's needed to make a baby comfortable, we would never withdraw the care a parent would provide. We never kill a baby. . . . But we may decide certain heroic intervention is not worthwhile."[8]

We should keep in mind the ordinary/extraordinary care distinction when considering an example given by Rachels to show the irrationality of the active/passive distinction with regard to infanticide. The example is this: a child is born with Down's syndrome and also has an intestinal obstruction which requires corrective surgery. If the surgery is not performed, the infant will starve to death, since it cannot take food orally. This may take days or even weeks, as dehydration and infection set in. Commenting on this situation, Rachels says:

> I can understand why some people are opposed to all euthanasia, and insist that such infants must be allowed to live. I think I can also understand why other people favor destroying these babies quickly and painlessly. But why should anyone favor letting "dehydration and infection wither a tiny being over hours and days"? The doctrine that says that a baby may be allowed to dehydrate and wither, but may not be given an injection that would end its life without suffering, seems so patently cruel as to require no further refutation.[9]

Such a doctrine perhaps does not need further refutation; but this is not the AMA doctrine. For the AMA statement criticized by Rachels

allows only for the cessation of extraordinary means to prolong life when death is imminent. Neither of these conditions is satisfied in this example. Death is not imminent in this situation, any more than it would be if a normal child had an attack of appendicitis. Neither the corrective surgery to remove the intestinal obstruction, nor the intravenous feeding required to keep the infant alive until such surgery is performed, can be regarded as extraordinary means, for neither is particularly expensive, nor does either place an overwhelming burden on the patient or others. (The continued existence of the child might be thought to place an overwhelming burden on its parents, but that has nothing to do with the characterization of the means to prolong its life as extraordinary. If it had, then *feeding* a severely defective child who required a great deal of care could be regarded as extraordinary.) The chances of success if the operation is undertaken are quite good, though there is always a risk in operating on infants. Though the Down's syndrome will not be alleviated, the child will proceed to an otherwise normal infancy.

It cannot be argued that the treatment is withheld for the infant's sake, unless one is prepared to argue that all mentally retarded babies are better off dead. This is particularly implausible in the case of Down's syndrome babies who generally do not suffer and are capable of giving and receiving love, of learning and playing, to varying degrees.

In a film on this subject entitled, "Who Should Survive?", a doctor defended a decision not to operate, saying that since the parents did not consent to the operation, the doctors' hands were tied. As we have seen, surgical intrusion requires consent, and in the case of infants, consent would normally come from the parents. But, as their legal guardians, parents are required to provide medical care for their children, and failure to do so can constitute criminal neglect or even homicide. In general, courts have been understandably reluctant to recognize a parental right to terminate life-prolonging

---

8 B. D. Colen, *Karen Ann Quinlan: Living and Dying in the Age of Eternal Life*, p. 115. Nash, 1976.
9 Rachels, p. 79.

treatment.[10] Although prosecution is unlikely, physicians who comply with invalid instructions from the parents and permit the infant's death could be liable for aiding and abetting, failure to report child neglect, or even homicide. So it is not true that, in this situation, doctors are legally bound to do as the parents wish.

To sum up, I think that Rachels is right to regard the decision not to operate in the Down's syndrome example as the intentional termination of life. But there is no reason to believe that either the law or the AMA would regard it otherwise. Certainly the decision to withhold treatment is not justified by the AMA statement. That such infants have been allowed to die cannot be denied; but this, I think, is the result of doctors misunderstanding the law and the AMA position.

Withholding treatment in this case is the intentional termination of life because the infant is deliberately allowed to die; that is the point of not operating. But there are other cases in which that is not the point. If the point is to avoid inflicting painful treatment on a patient with little or no reasonable hope of success, this is not the intentional termination of life. The permissibility of such withholding of treatment, then, would have no implications for the permissibility of euthanasia, active or passive.

The decision whether or not to operate, or to institute vigorous treatment, is particularly agonizing in the case of children born with spina bifida, an opening in the base of the spine usually accompanied by hydrocephalus and mental retardation. If left unoperated, these children usually die of meningitis or kidney failure within the first few years of life. Even if they survive, all affected children face a lifetime of illness, operations and varying degrees of disability. The policy used to be to save as many as possible, but the trend now is toward selective treatment, based on the physician's estimate of the chances

of success. If operating is not likely to improve significantly the child's condition, parents and doctors may agree not to operate. This is not the intentional termination of life, for again the purpose is not the termination of the child's life but the avoidance of painful and pointless treatment. Thus, the fact that withholding treatment is justified does not imply that killing the child would be equally justified.

Throughout the discussion, I have claimed that intentionally ceasing life-prolonging treatment is not the intentional termination of life unless the doctor has, as his or her purpose in stopping treatment, the patient's death.

It may be objected that I have incorrectly characterized the conditions for the intentional termination of life. Perhaps it is enough that the doctor intentionally ceases treatment, foreseeing that the patient will die; perhaps the reason for ceasing treatment is irrelevant to its characterization as the intentional termination of life. I find this suggestion implausible, but am willing to consider arguments for it. Rachels has provided no such arguments: indeed, he apparently shares my view about the intentional termination of life. For when he claims that the cessation of life-prolonging treatment is the intentional termination of life, his reason for making the claim is that "if it were not, there would be no point to it." Rachels believes that the point of ceasing treatment, "in these cases," is to bring about the patient's death. If that were not the point, he suggests, why would the doctor cease treatment? I have shown, however, that there can be a point to ceasing treatment which is not the death of the patient. In showing this, I have refuted Rachels' reason for identifying the cessation of life-prolonging treatment with the intentional termination of life, and thus his argument against the AMA doctrine.

Here someone might say: Even if the withholding of treatment is not the intentional termination of life, does that make a difference, morally speaking? If the life-prolonging treatment may be withheld, for the sake of the child, may not an easy death be provided, for the sake of the

10 Cf. Norman L. Cantor, Law and the termination of an incompetent patient's life-preserving care. *Dilemmas of Euthanasia op. cit.,* pp. 69–105.

child, as well? The unoperated child with spina bifida may take months or even years to die. Distressed by the spectacle of children "lying around waiting to die," one doctor has written, "It is time that society and medicine stopped perpetuating the fiction that withholding treatment is ethically different from terminating a life. It is time that society began to discuss mechanisms by which we can alleviate the pain and suffering for those individuals whom we cannot help."[11]

I do not deny that there may be cases in which death is in the best interests of the patient. In such cases, a quick and painless death may be the best thing. However, I do not think that, once active or vigorous treatment is stopped, a quick death is always preferable to a lingering one. We must be cautious about attributing to defective children *our* distress at seeing them linger. Waiting for them to die may be tough on parents, doctors and nurses—it isn't necessarily tough on the child. The decision not to operate need not mean a decision to neglect, and it may be possible to make the remaining months of the child's life comfortable, pleasant and filled with love. If this alternative is possible, surely it is more decent and humane than killing the child. In such a situation, withholding treatment, foreseeing the child's death, is not ethically equivalent to killing the child, and we cannot move from the permissibility of the former to

11 John Freeman, Is there a right to die—quickly?, *J. Pediat.* 80. p. 905.

that of the latter. I am worried that there will be a tendency to do precisely that if active euthanasia is regarded as morally equivalent to the withholding of life-prolonging treatment.

CONCLUSION

The AMA statement does not make the distinction Rachels wishes to attack, i.e. that between active and passive euthanasia. Instead, the statement draws a distinction between the intentional termination of life, on the one had, and the cessation of the employment of extraordinary means to prolong life, on the other. Nothing said by Rachels shows that this distinction is confused. It may be that doctors have misinterpreted the AMA statement, and that this had led, for example, to decisions to allow defective infants slowly to starve to death. I quite agree with Rachels that the decisions to which they allude were cruel and made on irrelevant grounds. Certainly it is worth pointing out that allowing someone to die can be the intentional termination of life, and that it can be just as bad as, or worse than, killing someone. However, the withholding of life-prolonging treatment is not necessarily the intentional termination of life, so that if it is permissible to withhold life-prolonging treatment, it does not follow that, other things being equal, it is permissible to kill. Furthermore, most of the time, other things are not equal. In many of the cases in which it would be right to cease treatment, I do not think that it would also be right to kill.

Review Questions

1. According to Steinbock, what mistake does Rachels make in his interpretation of the AMA statement?
2. How does Steinbock understand the right to refuse treatment?
3. How does Steinbock distinguish between extraordinary and ordinary treatment?
4. What is Steinbock's view of the case of the child with Down's syndrome, and how does her view differ from that of Rachels?
5. What is Steinbock's view of the treatment of children with spina bifida?

6. Why does Steinbock think that she has refuted Rachels' attack against the AMA statement?
7. Explain Steinbock's conclusion.

Discussion Questions

1. In what cases can the right to refuse medical treatment be overridden and why?
2. Steinbock grants that in some cases "a quick and painless death may be the best thing." Can you think of any such cases? Why is death "the best thing" in such cases?

Killing and Letting Die

PHILIPPA FOOT

Philippa Foot is the Griffen Professor of Philosophy Emeritus at the University of California, Los Angeles, and an Honorary Fellow of Somerville College, Oxford. She is the author of *Moral Dilemmas* (2002), *Natural Goodness* (2001), and *Virtues and Vices* (1978), from which our reading is taken.

Foot argues that there is an important moral difference between killing and letting die. This distinction is best captured by saying that one person may or may not be the agent of harm that befalls another. She illustrates the distinction by comparing two cases. In Rescue I, we can save five and let one die, and in Rescue II we can kill one in order to save five. She thinks it would be wrong to kill one to save five, but not wrong to let one die in order to save five. On the other hand, she admits that in some cases, as in the runaway trolley example, it is not wrong to kill one to save five.

IS THERE A MORALLY RELEVANT distinction between killing and allowing to die? Many philosophers say that there is not, and further insist that there is no other closely related difference, as for instance that which divides act from omission, whichever plays a part in determining the moral character of an action. James Rachels has argued this case in his well-known article on active and passive euthanasia, Michael Tooley has argued it in his writings on abortion, and Jonathan Bennett argued it in the Tanner Lectures given in Oxford in 1980.[1] I believe that these people are mistaken, and this is what I shall try to show in this essay. I shall first consider the question in abstraction from any particular practical moral problem, and then I shall

Source: Philippa Foot, "Killing and Letting Die," in Joy L. Garfield and Patricia Hennessy, *Abortion: Moral and Legal Perspectives* (Amherst: The University of Massachusetts Press, 1984), pp. 177–185. Reprinted with the permission of the University of Massachusetts Press.

1 James Rachels, "Active and Passive Euthanasia," *New England Journal of Medicine* 292 (January 9, 1975): 78–80; Michael Tooley, "Abortion and Infanticide," *Philosophy and Public Affairs* 2, no. 1 (Fall 1972); Jonathan Bennett, "Morality and Consequences," in *The Tanner Lectures on Human Values,* vol. 2, ed. Sterling McMurrin (Cambridge: Cambridge University Press, 1981).

examine the implications my thesis may have concerning the issue of abortion.

The question with which we are concerned has been dramatically posed by asking whether we are as equally to blame for allowing people in Third World countries to starve to death as we would be for killing them by sending poisoned food? In each case it is true that if we acted differently—by sending good food or by not sending poisoned food—those who are going to die because we do not send the good food or do send the poisoned food would not die after all. Our agency plays a part in what happens whichever way they die. Philosophers such as Rachels, Tooley, and Bennett consider this to be all that matters in determining our guilt or innocence. Or rather they say that although related things are morally relevant, such as our reasons for acting as we do and the cost of acting otherwise, these are only contingently related to the distinction between doing and allowing. If we hold *them* steady and vary only the way in which our agency enters into the matter, no moral differences will be found. It is of no significance, they say, whether we kill others or let them die, or whether they die by our act or our omission. Whereas these latter differences may at first seem to affect the morality of action, we shall always find on further enquiry that some other difference—such as a difference of motive or cost—has crept in.

Now this, on the face of it, is extremely implausible. We are not inclined to think that it would be no worse to murder to get money for some comfort such as a nice winter coat than it is to keep the money back before sending a donation to Oxfam or Care. We do not think that we might just as well be called murderers for one as for the other. And there are a host of other examples which seem to make the same point. We may have to allow one person to die if saving him would mean that we could not save five others, as for instance when a drug is in short supply and he needs five times as much as each of them, but that does not mean that we could carve up one patient to get "spare parts" for five.

These moral intuitions stand clearly before us, but I do not think it would be right to conclude from the fact that these examples all seem to hang on the contrast between killing and allowing to die that this is precisely the distinction that is important from the moral point of view. For example, having someone killed is not strictly *killing* him, but seems just the same morally speaking; and on the other hand, turning off a respirator might be called killing, although it seems morally indistinguishable from allowing to die. Nor does it seem that the difference between 'act' and 'omission' is quite what we want, in that a respirator that had to be turned on each morning would not change the moral problems that arise with the ones we have now. Perhaps there is no locution in the language which exactly serves our purposes and we should therefore invent our own vocabulary. Let us mark the distinction we are after by saying that one person may or may not be 'the agent' of harm that befalls someone else.

When is one person 'the agent' in this special sense of someone else's death, or of some harm other than death that befalls him? This idea can easily be described in a general way. If there are difficulties when it comes to detail, some of these ideas may be best left unsolved, for there may be an area of indefiniteness reflecting the uncertainty that belongs to our moral judgments in some complex and perhaps infrequently encountered situations. The idea of agency, in the sense that we want, seems to be composed of two subsidiary ideas. First, we think of particular effects as the result of particular sequences, as when a certain fatal sequence leads to someone's death. This idea is implied in coroners' verdicts telling us what someone died of, and this concept is not made suspect by the fact that it is sometimes impossible to pick out a single fatal sequence—as in the lawyers' example of the man journeying into the desert who had two enemies, one of whom bored a hole in his water barrel while another filled it with brine. Suppose such complications absent. Then we can pick out the fatal sequence and go on to ask who initiated it. If the subject died by poisoning and it was I who put the poison into his drink, then I am the agent of his death; likewise if I shot him and he died of a bullet wound. Of course there are problems about fatal sequences which would have been harmless but for special circumstances, and those which although threatening would have run out harmlessly but for something that somebody did. But we can easily understand the idea that a death comes about through our agency if we send someone poisoned food or cut him up for spare parts, but not (ordinarily) if we fail to save him when he is threatened by accident or disease. Our examples are not problem cases from *this* point of view.

Nor is it difficult to find more examples to drive our original point home, and show that it is sometimes permissible to allow a certain harm to befall someone, although it would have been wrong to bring this harm on him by one's own agency, i.e., by originating or sustaining the sequence which brings the harm. Let us consider, for instance, a pair of cases which I shall call Rescue I and Rescue II. In the first Rescue story we are hurrying in our jeep to save some people—let there be five of them—who are imminently threatened by the ocean tide. We have not a moment to spare, so when we hear of a single person who also needs rescuing from some other disaster we say regretfully that we cannot rescue him, but must leave him to die. To most of us this seems clear, and I shall take it as clear, ignoring John Taurek's interesting if surprising argument against the obligation to save the greater number when we can.[2] This is Rescue I and with it I contrast Rescue II. In this second story we are again hurrying to the place where the tide is coming in in order to rescue the party of people, but this time it is relevant that the road is narrow and rocky. In this version the lone individual is trapped (do not ask me how) on the path. If we are to rescue the five we would have to drive over him. But can we do so?

2 John Taurek, "Should the Numbers Count?" *Philosophy and Public Affairs,* no. 4 (Summer 1977): 293–316.

If we stop he will be all right eventually: he is in no danger unless from us. But of course all five of the others will be drowned. As in the first story our choice is between a course of action which will leave one man dead and five alive at the end of the day and a course of action which will have the opposite result. And yet we surely feel that in one case we can rescue the five men and in the other we cannot. We can allow someone to die of whatever disaster threatens him if the cost of saving him is failing to save five; we cannot, however, drive over *him* in order to get to *them*. We cannot originate a fatal sequence, although we can allow one to run its course. Similarly, in the pair of examples mentioned earlier, we find a contrast between on the one hand refusing to give to one man the whole supply of a scarce drug, because we can use portions of it to save five, and on the other, cutting him up for spare parts. And we notice that we may not originate a fatal sequence even if the resulting death is in no sense our object. We could not knowingly subject one person to deadly fumes in the process of manufacturing some substance that would save many, even if the poisoning were a mere side effect of the process that save lives.

Considering these examples, it is hard to resist the conclusion that it makes all the difference whether those who are going to die if we act a certain way will die as a result of a sequence that we originate or of one that we allow to continue, it being of course something that did not *start* by our agency. So let us ask how this could be? If the distinction—which is roughly that between killing and allowing to die—*is* morally relevant, because it sometimes makes the difference between what is right and what is wrong, how does this work? After all, it cannot be a magical difference, and it does not satisfy anyone to hear that what we have is just an ultimate moral fact. Moreover, those who deny the relevance can point to cases in which it seems to make no difference to the goodness or badness of an action having a certain result, as, for example, that some innocent person dies, whether due to a sequence we originate or because of one we merely allow. And if the way the result comes about *sometimes* makes no difference, how can it ever do so? If it sometimes makes an action bad that harm came to someone else as a result of a sequence we *originated,* must this not always contribute some element of badness? How can a consideration be a reason for saying that an action is bad in one place without being at least a reason for saying the same elsewhere?

Let us address these questions. As to the route by which considerations of agency enter the process of moral judgment, it seems to be through its connection with different types of rights. For there are rights to noninterference, which form one class of rights; and there are also rights to goods or services, which are different. And corresponding to these two types of rights are, on the one hand, the duty not to interfere, called a 'negative duty,' and on the other the duty to provide the goods or services, called a 'positive duty.' These rights may in certain circumstances be overridden, and this can in principle happen to rights of either kind. So, for instance, in the matter of property rights, others have in ordinary circumstances a duty not to interfere with our property, though in exceptional circumstances the right is overridden, as in Elizabeth Anscombe's example of destroying someone's house to stop the spread of a fire.[3] And a right to goods or services depending, for example, on a promise will quite often be overridden in the same kind of case. There is, however, no guarantee that the special circumstances that allow one kind of right to be overridden will always allow the overriding of the other. Typically, it takes more to justify an interference than to justify the withholding of goods or services; and it is, of course, possible to think that nothing whatsoever will justify, for example, the infliction of torture or the deliberate killing of the innocent. It is not hard to find how all this connects with the morality of killing and allowing to die—and in general with harm which an

agent allows to happen and harm coming about through his agency, in my special sense having to do with originating or sustaining harmful sequences. For the violation of a right to noninterference consists in interference, which implies breaking into an existing sequence and initiating a new one. It is not usually possible, for instance, to violate that right to noninterference, which is at least part of what is meant by 'the right to life' by failing to save someone from death. So if, in any circumstances, the right to noninterference is the only right that exists, or if it is the only right special circumstances have not overridden, then it may not be permissible to initiate a fatal sequence, but it *may* be permissible to withhold aid.

The question now is whether we ever find cases in which the right to noninterference exists and is not overridden, but where the right to goods or services either does not exist or *is* here overridden. The answer is, of course, that this is quite a common case. It often happens that whereas someone's rights stand in the way of our interference, we owe him no *service* in relation to that which he would lose if we interfered. We may not deprive him of his property, though we do not have to help him secure his hold on it, in spite of the fact that the balance of good and evil in the outcome (counting his loss or gain and the cost to us) will be the same regardless of how they come about. Similarly, where the issue is one of life and death, it is often impermissible to kill someone—although special circumstances having to do with the good of others make it permissible, or even required, that we do not spend the time or resources needed to save his life, as for instance, in the story of Rescue I, or in that of the scarce drug.

It seems clear, therefore, that there are circumstances in which it makes all the difference, morally speaking, whether a given balance of good and evil came about through our agency (in our sense), or whether it was rather something we had the ability to prevent but, for good reasons, did not prevent. Of course, we often have a strict duty to prevent harm to others, or

3 G. E. M. Anscombe, "Modern Moral Philosophy," *Philosophy* 33 (1958): 1–19.

to ameliorate their condition. And even where they do not, strictly speaking, have a *right* to our goods or services, we should often be failing (and sometimes grossly failing) in charity if we did not help them. But, to reiterate, it may be right to allow one person to die in order to save five, although it would not be right to kill him to bring the same good to them.

How is it, then, that anyone has ever denied this conclusion, so sympathetic to our everyday moral intuitions and apparently so well grounded in a very generally recognized distinction between different types of rights? We must now turn to an argument first *given,* by James Rachels, and more or less followed by others who think as he does. Rachels told a gruesome story of a child drowned in a bathtub in two different ways: in one case someone pushed the child's head under water, and in the other he found the child drowning and did not pull him out. Rachels says that we should judge one way of acting as bad as the other, so we have an example in which killing is as bad as allowing to die. But how, he asks, can the distinction ever be relevant if it is not relevant here?[4]

Based on what has been said earlier, the answer to Rachels should be obvious. The reason why it is, in ordinary circumstance, "no worse" to leave a child drowning in a bathtub than to push it under, is that both charity and the special duty of care that we owe to children give us a positive obligation to save them, and we have no particular reason to say that it is "less bad" to fail in this than it is to be in dereliction of the negative duty by being the agent of harm. The level of badness is, we may suppose, the same, but because a different kind of bad action has been done, there is no reason to suppose that the two ways of acting will always give this same result. In other circumstances one might be worse than the other, or only one might be bad. And this last result is exactly what we find in circumstances that allow a positive but not a negative duty to be overridden.

Thus, it could be right to leave someone to die by the roadside in the story of Rescue I, though wrong to run over him in the story of Rescue II; and it could be right to act correspondingly in the cases of the scarce drug and the "spare parts."

Let me now consider an objection to the thesis I have been defending. It may be said that I shall have difficulty explaining a certain range of examples in which it seems permissible, and even obligatory, to make an intervention which jeopardizes people not already in danger in order to save others who are. The following case has been discussed. Suppose a runaway trolley is heading toward a track on which five people are standing, and that there is someone who can possibly switch the points, thereby diverting the trolley onto a track on which there is only one person. It seems that he should do this, just as the pilot whose plane is going to crash has a duty to steer, if he can, toward a less crowded street than the one he sees below. But the railway man then puts the one man newly in danger, instead of allowing the five to be killed. Why does not the one man's right to noninterference stand in his way, as one person's right to noninterference impeded the manufacture of poisonous fumes when this was necessary to save five?

The answer seems to be that this is a special case, in that we have here the *diverting* of a fatal sequence and not the starting of a new one. So we could not start a flood to stop a fire, even when the fire would kill more than the flood, but we could divert a flood to an area in which fewer people would be drowned.

A second and much more important difficulty involves cases in which it seems that the distinction between agency and allowing is inexplicably irrelevant. Why, I shall be asked, is it not morally permissible to allow someone to die deliberately in order to use his body for a medical procedure that would save many lives? It might be suggested that the distinction between agency and allowing is relevant when what is allowed to happen is itself aimed at. Yet this is not quite right, because there are cases in which it does make a difference whether one

4 Rachels, "Active and Passive Euthanasia."

originates a sequence or only allows it to continue, although the allowing is with deliberate intent. Thus, for instance, it may not be permissible to deprive someone of a possession which only harms him, but it may be reasonable to refuse to get it back for him if it is already slipping from his grasp.[5] And it is arguable that nonvoluntary passive euthanasia is sometimes justifiable although nonvoluntary active euthanasia is not. What these examples have in common is that *harm* is not in question, which suggests that the 'direct', i.e., deliberate, intention of *evil* is what makes it morally objectionable to allow the beggar to die. When this element is present it is impossible to justify an action by indicating that no *origination* of evil is involved. But this special case leaves no doubt about the relevance of distinguishing between originating an evil and allowing it to occur. It was never suggested that there will *always and everywhere* be a difference of permissibility between the two.

Having defended the moral relevance of the distinction which roughly corresponds to the contrast between killing and allowing to die, I shall now ask how it affects the argument between those who oppose and those who support abortion. The answer seems to be that this entirely depends on how the argument is supposed to go. The most usual defense of abortion lies in the distinction between the destruction of a fetus and the destruction of a human person, and neither side in *this* debate will have reason to refer to the distinction between being the agent of an evil and allowing it to come about. But this is not the only defense of abortion which is current at the present time. In an influential and widely read article, Judith Jarvis Thomson has suggested an argument for allowing abortion which depends on denying what I have been at pains to maintain.[6]

Thomson suggests that abortion can be justified, at least in certain cases, without the need to deny that the fetus has the moral rights of a human person. For, she says, no person has an absolute right to the use of another's body, even to save his life, and so the fetus, whatever its status, has no right to the use of the mother's body. *Her* rights override *its* rights, and justify her in removing it if it seriously encumbers her life. To persuade us to agree with her she invents an example, which is supposed to give a parallel, in which someone dangerously ill is kept alive by being hooked up to the body of another person, without that person's consent. It is obvious, she says, that the person whose body was thus being used would have no obligation to continue in that situation, suffering immobility or other serious inconvenience, for any length of time. We should not think of him as a murderer if he detached himself, and we ought to think of a pregnant woman as having the same right to rid herself of an unwanted pregnancy.

Thomson's whole case depends on this analogy. It is, however, faulty if what I have said earlier is correct. According to my thesis, the two cases must be treated quite differently because one involves the initiation of a fatal sequence and the other the refusal to save a life. It is true that someone who extricated himself from a situation in which his body was being used in the way a respirator or a kidney machine is used could, indeed, be said to kill the other person in detaching himself. But this only shows, once more, that the use of "kill" is not important: what matters is that the fatal sequence resulting in death is not initiated but is rather allowed to take its course. And although charity or duties of care could have dictated that the help be given, it seems perfectly reasonable to treat this as a case in which such presumptions are overridden by other rights—those belonging to the person whose body would be used. The cases of abortion is of course completely different. The fetus is not in jeopardy because it is in its mother's womb; it is merely dependent on her in the way children are dependent on their parents for food.

5 Cf. Philippa Foot, "Killing, Letting Die, and Euthanasia: A Reply to Holly Smith Goldman," *Analysis* 41, no. 4 (June 1981).
6 Judith Jarvis Thomson, "A Defense of Abortion," *Philosophy and Public Affairs* 1 (1971): 44.

An abortion, therefore, originates the sequence which ends in the death of the fetus, and the destruction comes about "through the agency" of the mother who seeks the abortion. If the fetus has the moral status of a human person then her action is, at best, likened to that of killing for spare parts or in Rescue II; conversely, the act of someone who refused to let his body to be used to save the life of the sick man in Thomson's story belongs with the scarce drug decision, or that of Rescue I.

It appears, therefore, that Thomson's argument is not valid, and that we are thrown back to the old debate about the moral status of the fetus, which stands as the crucial issue in determining whether abortion is justified.

Review Questions

1. Why does Foot find it extremely implausible to hold that there is no moral difference between killing and letting die?
2. How does Foot make out the distinction using the concept of the agent of harm?
3. Explain the cases of Rescue I and II. How do these cases support a moral distinction between killing and letting die?
4. Foot distinguishes between two different types of right, and two corresponding types of duty. How do these distinctions work in showing a moral difference between killing and letting die?
5. How does Foot respond to Rachels's example about the child drowned in the bathtub?
6. Explain the runaway trolley case.

Discussion Questions

1. Is killing a patient by turning off a respirator a case of killing or letting die? Explain your answer.
2. Do you agree that in the Rescue II case it would be wrong to kill one to save five? Why or why not?
3. What would you do in the runaway trolley case?
4. Is passive euthanasia justifiable whereas active euthanasia is not? What is Foot's view? What do you think?

The Survival Lottery

JOHN HARRIS

John Harris is the Sir David Alliance Professor of Bioethics at the University of Manchester, England. He is the author or editor of 14 books and over 150 papers. His books include *Violence and Responsibility* (1980), *The Value of Life* (1985),

Source: John Harris, "The Survival Lottery," from *Philosophy, The Journal of the Royal Institute of Philosophy,* 50 (1975): 87–95. Copyright © The Royal Institute of Philosophy 1975. Reprinted with permission of Cambridge University Press.

Wonderwoman and Superman (1992), and *Clones, Genes, and Immortality* (1998).

Harris proposes a lottery to decide who lives and who dies. Whenever there are two or more patients who can be saved by organ transplants, a lottery drawing randomly picks out a person to be sacrificed; this person is required to donate organs so that others can live. Such a scheme seems to conflict with our moral intuition that it is wrong to kill an innocent person, even to save the lives of others. But Harris argues that such a lottery scheme can be defended against objections such as the claim that it is playing God, that killing is wrong but letting die is not wrong, that it violates the right of self-defense, and that it has bad side effects.

LET US SUPPOSE that organ transplant procedures have been perfected; in such circumstances if two dying patients could be saved by organ transplants then, if surgeons have the requisite organs in stock and no other needy patients, but nevertheless allow their patients to die, we would be inclined to say, and be justified in saying, that the patients died because the doctors refused to save them. But if there are no spare organs in stock and none otherwise available, the doctors have no choice, they cannot save their patients and so must let them die. In this case we would be disinclined to say that the doctors are in any sense the cause of their patients' deaths. But let us further suppose that the two dying patients, Y and Z, are not happy about being left to die. They might argue that it is not strictly true that there are no organs which could be used to save them. Y needs a new heart and Z new lungs. They point out that if just one healthy person were to be killed his organs could be removed and both of them be saved. We and the doctors would probably be alike in thinking that such a step, while technically possible, would be out of the question. We would not say that the doctors were killing their patients if they refused to prey upon the healthy to save the sick. And because this sort of surgical Robin Hoodery is out of the question we can tell Y and Z that they cannot be saved, and that when they die they will have died of natural causes and not of the neglect of their doctors. Y and Z do not agree, however, they insist that if the doctors fail to kill a healthy man and use his organs to save

them, then the doctors will be responsible for their deaths.

Many philosophers have for various reasons believed that we must not kill even if by doing so we could save life. They believe that there is a moral difference between killing and letting die. On this view, to kill A so that Y and Z might live is ruled out because we have a strict obligation not to kill but a duty of some lesser kind to save life. A. H. Clough's dictum "Thou shalt not kill but need'st not strive officiously to keep alive" expresses bluntly this point of view. The dying Y and Z may be excused for not being much impressed by Clough's dictum. They agree that it is wrong to kill the innocent and are prepared to agree to an absolute prohibition against so doing. They do not agree, however, that A is more innocent than they are. Y and Z might go on to point out that the currently acknowledged right of the innocent not to be killed, even where their deaths might give life to others, is just a decision to prefer the lives of the fortunate to those of the unfortunate. A is innocent in the sense that he has done nothing to deserve death, but Y and Z are also innocent in this sense. Why should they be the ones to die simply because they are so unlucky as to have diseased organs? Why, they might argue, should their living or dying be left to chance when in so many other areas of human life we believe that we have an obligation to ensure the survival of the maximum number of lives possible?

Y and Z argue that if a doctor refuses to treat a patient, with the result that the patient dies, he has killed that patient as sure as shooting, and that, in exactly the same way, if the doctors refuse Y and Z the transplants that they need, then their refusal will kill Y and Z, again as sure as shooting. The doctors, and indeed the society which supports their inaction, cannot defend themselves by arguing that they are neither expected, nor required by law or convention, to kill so that lives may be saved (indeed, quite the reverse) since this is just an appeal to custom or authority. A man who does his own moral thinking must decide whether, in these circumstances, he ought to save two lives at the cost of one, or one life at the cost of two. The fact that so-called "third parties" have never before been brought into such calculations, have never before been thought of as being involved, is not an argument against their now becoming so. There are, of course, good arguments against allowing doctors simply to haul passers-by off the streets whenever they have a couple of patients in need of new organs. And the harmful side-effects of such a practice in terms of terror and distress to the victims, the witnesses and society generally, would give us further reasons for dismissing the idea. Y and Z realize this and have a proposal, which they will shortly produce, which would largely meet objections to placing such power in the hands of doctors and eliminate at least some of the harmful side-effects.

In the unlikely event of their feeling obliged to reply to the reproaches of Y and Z, the doctors might offer the following argument: they might maintain that a man is only responsible for the death of someone whose life he might have saved, if, in all the circumstances of the case, he ought to have saved the man by the means available. This is why a doctor might be a murderer if he simply refused or neglected to treat a patient who would die without treatment, but not if he could only save the patient by doing something he ought in no circumstances to do—kill the innocent. Y and Z readily agree that a man ought not to do what he ought not to do, but they point out that if the doctors, and for that matter society at large, ought on

balance to kill one man if two can thereby be saved, then failure to do so will involve responsibility for the consequent deaths. The fact that Y's and Z's proposal involves killing the innocent cannot be a reason for refusing to consider their proposal, for this would just be a refusal to face the question at issue and so avoid having to make a decision as to what ought to be done in circumstances like these. It is Y's and Z's claim that failure to adopt their plan will also involve killing the innocent, rather more of the innocent than the proposed alternative.

To back up this last point, to remove the arbitrariness of permitting doctors to select their donors from among the chance passers-by outside hospitals, and the tremendous power this would place in doctors' hands, to mitigate worries about side-effects and lastly to appease those who wonder why poor old A should be singled out for sacrifice, Y and Z put forward the following scheme: they propose that everyone be given a sort of lottery number. Whenever doctors have two or more dying patients who could be saved by transplants, and no suitable organs have come to hand through "natural" deaths, they can ask a central computer to supply a suitable donor. The computer will then pick the number of a suitable donor at random and he will be killed so that the lives of two or more others may be saved. No doubt if the scheme were ever to be implemented a suitable euphemism for "killed" would be employed. Perhaps we would begin to talk about citizens being called upon to "give life" to others. With the refinement of transplant procedures such a scheme could offer the chance of saving large numbers of lives that are now lost. Indeed, even taking into account the loss of the lives of donors, the numbers of untimely deaths each year might be dramatically reduced, so much so that everyone's chance of living to a ripe old age might be increased. If this were to be the consequence of the adoption of such a scheme, and it might well be, it could not be dismissed lightly. It might of course be objected that it is likely that more old people will need transplants to prolong their lives than will the young, and so the scheme would inevitably lead to a society dominated by the old. But if such a society is thought objectionable, there is no reason to suppose that a program could not be designed for the computer that would ensure the maintenance of whatever is considered to be an optimum age distribution throughout the population.

Suppose that inter-planetary travel revealed a world of people like ourselves, but who organized their society according to this scheme. No one was considered to have an absolute right to life or freedom from interference, but everything was always done to ensure that as many people as possible would enjoy long and happy lives. In such a world a man who attempted to escape when his number was up or who resisted on the grounds that no one had a right to take his life, might well be regarded as a murderer. We might or might not prefer to live in such a world, but the morality of its inhabitants would surely be one that we could respect. It would not be obviously more barbaric or cruel or immoral than our own.

Y and Z are willing to concede one exception to the universal application of their scheme. They realize that it would be unfair to allow people who have brought their misfortune on themselves to benefit from the lottery. There would clearly be something unjust about killing the abstemious B so that W (whose heavy smoking has given him lung cancer) and X (whose drinking has destroyed his liver) should be preserved to over-indulge again.

What objections could be made to the lottery scheme? A first straw to clutch at would be the desire for security. Under such a scheme we would never know when we would hear *them* knocking at the door. Every post might bring a sentence of death, every sound in the night might be the sound of boots on the stairs. But, as we have seen, the chances of actually being called upon to make the ultimate sacrifice might be slimmer than is the present risk of being killed on the roads, and most of us do not lie trembling abed, appalled at the prospect of

being dispatched on the morrow. The truth is that lives might well be more secure under such a scheme.

If we respect individuality and see every human being as unique in his own way, we might want to reject a society in which it appeared that individuals were seen merely as interchangeable units in a structure, the value of which lies in its having as many healthy units as possible. But of course Y and Z would want to know why A's individuality was more worthy of respect than theirs.

Another plausible objection is the natural reluctance to play God with men's lives, the feeling that it is wrong to make any attempt to re-allot the life opportunities that fate has determined, that the deaths of Y and Z would be "natural," whereas the death of anyone killed to save them would have been perpetrated by men. But if we are able to change things, then to elect not to do so is also to determine what will happen in the world.

Neither does the alleged moral difference between killing and letting die afford a respectable way of rejecting the claims of Y and Z. For if we really want to counter proponents of the lottery, if we really want to answer Y and Z and not just put them off, we cannot do so by saying that the lottery involves killing and object to it for that reason, because to do so would, as we have seen, just beg the question as to whether the failure to save as many people as possible might not also amount to killing.

To opt for the society which Y and Z propose would be then to adopt a society in which saintliness would be mandatory. Each of us would have to recognize a binding obligation to give up his own life for others when called upon to do so. In such a society anyone who reneged upon this duty would be a murderer. The most promising objection to such a society, and indeed to any principle which required us to kill A in order to save Y and Z, is, I suspect, that we are committed to the right of self-defense. If I can kill A to save Y and Z then he can kill me to save P and Q, and it is only if I am prepared to agree to this that I will opt for the lottery or be prepared to agree to a man's being killed if doing so would save the lives of more than one other man. Of course, there is something paradoxical about basing objections to the lottery scheme on the right of self-defense since, *ex hypothesi,* each person would have a better chance of living to a ripe old age if the lottery scheme were to be implemented. None the less, the feeling that no man should be required to lay down his life for others makes many people shy away from such a scheme, even though it might be rational to accept it on prudential grounds, and perhaps even mandatory on utilitarian grounds. Again, Y and Z would reply that the right of self-defense must extend to them as much as to anyone else, and while it is true that they can only live if another man is killed, they would claim that it is also true that if they are left to die, then someone who lives on does so over their dead bodies.

It might be argued that the institution of the survival lottery has not gone far to mitigate the harmful side-effects in terms of terror and distress to victims, witnesses, and society generally, that would be occasioned by doctors simply snatching passers-by off the streets and disorganizing them for the benefit of the unfortunate. Donors would after all still have to be procured, and this process, however it was carried out, would still be likely to prove distressing to all concerned. The lottery scheme would eliminate the arbitrariness of leaving the life and death decisions to the doctors, and remove the possibility of such terrible power falling into the hands of any individuals, but the terror and distress would remain. The effect of having to apprehend presumably unwilling victims would give us pause. Perhaps only a long period of education or propaganda could remove our abhorrence. What this abhorrence reveals about the rights and wrongs of the situation is, however, more difficult to assess. We might be inclined to say that only monsters could ignore the promptings of conscience so far as to operate the lottery scheme. But the promptings of conscience are

not necessarily the most reliable guide. In the present case Y and Z would argue that such promptings are mere squeamishness, an overnice self-indulgence that costs lives. Death, Y and Z would remind us, is a distressing experience whenever and to whomever it occurs, so the less it occurs the better. Fewer victims and witnesses will be distressed as part of the side-effects of the lottery scheme than would suffer as part of the side-effects of not instituting it.

Lastly, a more limited objection might be made, not to the idea of killing to save lives, but to the involvement of "third parties." Why, so the objection goes, should we not give X's heart to Y or Y's lungs to X, the same number of lives being thereby preserved and no one else's life set at risk? Y's and Z's reply to this objection differs from their previous line of argument. To amend their plan so that the involvement of so called "third parties" is ruled out would, Y and Z claim, violate their right to equal concern and respect with the rest of society. They argue that such a proposal would amount to treating the unfortunate who need new organs as a class within society whose lives are considered to be of less value than those of its more fortunate members. What possible justification could there be for singling out one group of people whom we would be justified in using as donors but not another? The idea in the mind of those who would propose such a step must be something like the following: since Y and Z cannot survive, since they are going to die in any event, there is no harm in putting their names into the lottery, for the chances of their dying cannot thereby be increased and will in fact almost certainly be reduced. But this is just to ignore everything that Y and Z have been saying. For if their lottery scheme is adopted they are not going to die anyway—their chances of dying are no greater and no less than those of any other participant in the lottery whose number may come up. This ground for confining selection of donors to the unfortunate therefore disappears. Any other ground must discriminate against Y and Z as members of a class whose lives are less worthy of respect than those of the rest of society.

It might more plausibly be argued that the dying who cannot themselves be saved by transplants, or by any other means at all, should be the priority selection group for the computer program. But how far off must death be for a man to be classified as "dying"? Those so classified might argue that their last few days or weeks of life are as valuable to them (if not more valuable) than the possibly longer span remaining to others. The problem of narrowing down the class of possible donors without discriminating unfairly against some sub-class of society is, I suspect, insoluble.

Such is the case for the survival lottery. Utilitarians ought to be in favor of it, and absolutists cannot object to it on the ground that it involves killing the innocent, for it is Y's and Z's case that any alternative must also involve killing the innocent. If the absolutist wishes to maintain his objection he must point to some morally relevant difference between positive and negative killing. This challenge opens the door to a large topic with a whole library of literature, but Y and Z are dying and do not have time to explore it exhaustively. In their own case the most likely candidate for some feature which might make this moral difference is the malevolent intent of Y and Z themselves. An absolutist might well argue that while no one intends the deaths of Y and Z, no one necessarily wishes them dead, or aims at their demise for any reason, they do mean to kill A (or have him killed). But Y and Z can reply that the death of A is no part of their plan, they merely wish to use a couple of his organs, and if he cannot live without them . . . *tant pis!* None would be more delighted than Y and Z if artificial organs would do as well, and so render the lottery scheme otiose.

One form of absolutist argument perhaps remains. This involves taking an Orwellian stand on some principle of common decency. The argument would then be that even to enter into the sort of "macabre" calculations that Y and Z propose displays a blunted sensibility, a corrupted and vitiated mind. Forms of this argument have recently been advanced by Noam Chomsky (*American Power and the New Mandarins*) and Stuart Hampshire (*Morality and Pessimism*). The indefatigable Y and Z would of course deny that their calculations are in any sense "macabre," and would present them as the most humane course available in the circumstances. Moreover they would claim that the Orwellian stand on decency is the product of a closed mind, and not susceptible to rational argument. Any reasoned defense of such a principle must appeal to notions like respect for human life, as Hampshire's argument in fact does, and these Y and Z could make conformable to their own position.

Can Y and Z be answered? Perhaps only by relying on moral intuition, on the insistence that we do feel there is something wrong with the survival lottery and our confidence that this feeling is prompted by some morally relevant difference between our bringing about the death of A and our bringing about the deaths of Y and Z. Whether we could retain this confidence in our intuitions if we were to be confronted by a society in which the survival lottery operated, was accepted by all, and was seen to save many lives that would otherwise have been lost, it would be interesting to know.

There would of course be great practical difficulties in the way of implementing the lottery. In so many cases it would be agonizingly difficult to decide whether or not a person had brought his misfortune on himself. There are numerous ways in which a person may contribute to his predicament, and the task of deciding how far, or how decisively, a person is himself responsible for his fate would be formidable. And in those cases where we can be confident that a person is innocent of responsibility for his predicament, can we acquire this confidence in time to save him? The lottery scheme would be a powerful weapon in the hands of someone willing and able to misuse it. Could we ever feel certain that the lottery was safe from unscrupulous computer programmers? Perhaps we should be thankful that such practical difficulties make the lottery an unlikely consequence of the perfection of transplants. Or perhaps we should be appalled.

It may be that we would want to tell Y and Z that the difficulties and dangers of their scheme would be too great a price to pay for its benefits. It is as well to be clear, however, that there is also a high, perhaps an even higher, price to be paid for the rejection of the scheme. That price is the lives of Y and Z and many like them, and we delude ourselves if we suppose that the reason why we reject their plan is that we accept the sixth commandment.

ACKNOWLEDGMENT

Thanks are due to Ronald Dworkin, Jonathan Glover, M. J. Inwood, and Anne Seller for helpful comments.

Review Questions

1. Explain the lottery scheme proposed by Harris. What are its advantages supposed to be?
2. How does Harris reply to the objection that the lottery is "playing God"?
3. What is his answer to those who appeal to the distinction between killing and letting die?
4. What about the right of self-defense? Why doesn't it provide a good objection to the lottery, according to Harris?
5. How does Harris deal with the objection that the lottery would have harmful side effects?

Discussion Questions

1. Harris excludes heavy smokers and drinkers from the lottery scheme. Do you agree that they do not deserve to be saved? Why or why not?
2. Harris challenges us to point out some morally relevant difference between positive and negative killing (as he calls it). Is there such a difference? What is it?
3. Is the lottery scheme immoral or not? Explain your answer.

Justifying Voluntary Euthanasia

PETER SINGER

Peter Singer is the Ira W. DeCamp Professor of Bioethics at the University Center for Human Values, Princeton University. He has written many books, articles, letters, and reviews. A complete list can be found on his home page, www.petersingerlinks. com. Perhaps his most famous book is *Animal Liberation,* first published in 1975, which started the animal liberation movement. His *Practical Ethics* (2e 1993) is

Source: Peter Singer, "Justifying Voluntary Euthanasia," from *Practical Ethics*, 2nd ed. (Cambridge: Cambridge University Press, 1993), pp. 176–178, 193–200. Copyright © Cambridge University Press 1993. Reprinted with the permission of Cambridge University Press.

widely used in applied ethics classes. His most recent book, *The President of Good and Evil* (2004), is an extended attack on the ethics of President George W. Bush.

Singer argues that voluntary euthanasia and assisted suicide are morally justified in cases where a patient is suffering from an incurable and painful or very distressing condition. In such cases, utilitarianism, the theory of rights, and respect for autonomy all provide reasons for allowing voluntary euthanasia or assisted suicide.

VOLUNTARY EUTHANASIA

MOST OF THE GROUPS currently campaigning for changes in the law to allow euthanasia are campaigning for voluntary euthanasia—that is, euthanasia carried out at the request of the person killed.

Sometimes voluntary euthanasia is scarcely distinguishable from assisted suicide. In *Jean's Way,* Derek Humphry has told how his wife Jean, when dying of cancer, asked him to provide her with the means to end her life swiftly and without pain. They had seen the situation coming and discussed it beforehand. Derek obtained some tablets and gave them to Jean, who took them and died soon afterwards.

Dr. Jack Kevorkian, a Michigan pathologist, went one step further when he built a "suicide machine" to help terminally ill people commit suicide. His machine consisted of a metal pole with three different bottles attached to a tube of the kind used to provide an intravenous drip. The doctor inserts the tube in the patient's vein, but at this stage only a harmless saline solution can pass through it. The patient may then flip a switch, which will allow a coma-inducing drug to come through the tube; this is automatically followed by a lethal drug contained in the third bottle. Dr. Kevorkian announced that he was prepared to make the machine available to any terminally ill patient who wished to use it. (Assisting suicide is not against the law in Michigan.) In June 1990, Janet Adkins, who was suffering from Alzheimer's disease, but still competent to make the decision to end her life, contacted Dr. Kevorkian and told him of her wish to die, rather than go through the slow and progressive deterioration that the disease involves. Dr. Kevorkian was in attendance while she made use of his machine, and then reported Janet Adkin's death to the police. He was subsequently charged with murder, but the judge refused to allow the charge to proceed to trial, on the grounds that Janet Adkins had caused her own death. The following year Dr. Kevorkian made his device available to two other people, who used it in order to end their lives.[1]

In other cases, people wanting to die may be unable to kill themselves. In 1973 George Zygmaniak was injured in a motorcycle accident near his home in New Jersey. He was taken to hospital, where he was found to be totally paralysed from the neck down. He was also in considerable pain. He told his doctor and his brother, Lester, that he did not want to live in this condition. He begged them both to kill him. Lester questioned the doctor and the hospital staff about George's prospects of recovery: he was told that they were nil. He then smuggled a gun into the hospital, and said to his brother: "I am here to end your pain, George. Is it all right with you?" George, who was not able to speak because of an operation to assist his breathing, nodded affirmatively. Lester shot him through the temple.

The Zygmaniak case appears to be a clear instance of voluntary euthanasia, although without some of the procedural safeguards that

---

1 Dr. Kevorkian was again charged with murder, and with providing a prohibited substance, in connection with the latter two cases, but once more discharged.

advocates of the legalisation of voluntary euthanasia propose. For instance, medical opinions about the patient's prospects of recovery were obtained only in an informal manner. Nor was there a careful attempt to establish, before independent witnesses, that George's desire for death was of a fixed and rational kind, based on the best available information about his situation. The killing was not carried out by a doctor. An injection would have been less distressing to others than shooting. But these choices were not open to Lester Zygmaniak, for the law in New Jersey, as in most other places, regards mercy killing as murder, and if he had made his plans known, he would not have been able to carry them out.

Euthanasia can be voluntary even if a person is not able, as Jean Humphry, Janet Adkins, and George Zygmaniak were able, to indicate the wish to die right up to the moment the tablets are swallowed, the switch thrown, or the trigger pulled. A person may, while in good health, make a written request for euthanasia if, through accident or illness, she should come to be incapable of making or expressing a decision to die, in pain, or without the use of her mental faculties, and there is no reasonable hope of recovery. In killing a person who has made such a request, who has re-affirmed it from time to time, and who is now in one of the states described, one could truly claim to be acting with her consent.

There is now one country in which doctors can openly help their patients to die in a peaceful and dignified way. In the Netherlands, a series of court cases during the 1980s upheld a doctor's right to assist a patient to die, even if that assistance amounted to giving the patient a lethal injection. Doctors in the Netherlands who comply with certain guidelines (which will be described later in this chapter) can now quite openly carry out euthanasia and can report this on the death certificate without fear of prosecution. It has been estimated that about 2,300 deaths each year result from euthanasia carried out in this way. . . .

JUSTIFYING VOLUNTARY EUTHANASIA

Under existing laws in most countries, people suffering unrelievable pain or distress from an incurable illness who beg their doctors to end their lives are asking their doctors to risk a murder charge. Although juries are extremely reluctant to convict in cases of this kind the law is clear that neither the request, nor the degree of suffering, nor the incurable condition of the person killed, is a defence to a charge of murder. Advocates of voluntary euthanasia propose that this law be changed so that a doctor could legally act on a patient's desire to die without further suffering. Doctors have been able to do this quite openly in the Netherlands, as a result of a series of court decisions during the 1980s, as long as they comply with certain conditions. In Germany, doctors may provide a patient with the means to end her life, but they may not administer the substance to her.

The case for voluntary euthanasia has some common ground with the case for non-voluntary euthanasia, in that death is a benefit for the one killed. The two kinds of euthanasia differ, however, in that voluntary euthanasia involves the killing of a person, a rational and self-conscious being and not a merely conscious being. (To be strictly accurate it must be said that this is not always so, because although only rational and self-conscious beings can consent to their own deaths, they may not be rational and self-conscious at the time euthanasia is contemplated—the doctor may, for instance, be acting on a prior written request for euthanasia if, through accident or illness, one's rational faculties should be irretrievably lost. For simplicity we shall, henceforth, disregard this complication.)

We have seen that it is possible to justify ending the life of a human being who lacks the capacity to consent. We must now ask in what way the ethical issues are different when the being is capable of consenting, and does in fact consent.

Let us return to the general principles about killing. . . . I [have] argued . . . that killing a self-conscious being is a more serious matter than killing a merely conscious being. I gave four distinct grounds on which this could be argued:

1. The classical utilitarian claim that since self-conscious beings are capable of fearing their own death, killing them has worse effects on others.

2. The preference utilitarian calculation that counts the thwarting of the victim's desire to go on living as an important reason against killing.

3. A theory of rights according to which to have a right one must have the ability to desire that to which one has a right, so that to have a right to life one must be able to desire one's own continued existence.

4. Respect for the autonomous decisions of rational agents.

Now suppose we have a situation in which a person suffering from a painful and incurable disease wishes to die. If the individual were not a person—not rational or self-conscious—euthanasia would, as I have said, be justifiable. Do any of the four grounds for holding that it is normally worse to kill a person provide reasons against killing when the individual is a person who wants to die?

The classical utilitarian objection does not apply to killing that takes place only with the genuine consent of the person killed. That people are killed under these conditions would have no tendency to spread fear or insecurity, since we have no cause to be fearful of being killed with our own genuine consent. If we do not wish to be killed, we simply do not consent. In fact, the argument from fear points in favour of voluntary euthanasia, for if voluntary euthanasia is not permitted we may, with good cause, be fearful that our deaths will be unnecessarily drawn out and distressing. In the Netherlands, a nationwide study commissioned by the government found that "Many patients want an assurance that their doctor will assist them to die should suffering become unbearable." Often, having received this assurance, no persistent request for euthanasia eventuated. The availability of euthanasia brought comfort without euthanasia having to be provided.

Preference utilitarianism also points in favour of, not against, voluntary euthanasia. Just as preference utilitarianism must count a desire to go on living as a reason against killing, so it must count a desire to die as a reason for killing.

Next, according to the theory of rights we have considered, it is an essential feature of a right that one can waive one's rights if one so chooses. I may have a right to privacy; but I can, if I wish, film every detail of my daily life and invite the neighbours to my home movies. Neighbours sufficiently intrigued to accept my invitation could do so without violating my right to privacy, since the right has on this occasion been waived. Similarly, to say that I have a right to life is not to say that it would be wrong for my doctor to end my life, if she does so at my request. In making this request I waive my right to life.

Lastly, the principle of respect for autonomy tells us to allow rational agents to live their own lives according to their own autonomous decisions, free from coercion or interference; but if rational agents should autonomously choose to die, then respect for autonomy will lead us to assist them to do as they choose.

So, although there are reasons for thinking that killing a self-conscious being is normally worse than killing any other kind of being, in the special case of voluntary euthanasia most of these reasons count for euthanasia rather than against. Surprising as this result might at first seem, it really does no more than reflect the fact that what is special about self-conscious beings is that they can know that they exist over time and will, unless they die, continue to exist. Normally this continued existence is fervently desired; when the foreseeable continued existence is dreaded rather than desired however, the desire to die may take the place of the normal desire to live, reversing the reasons against killing based on the desire to live. Thus the case for voluntary euthanasia is arguably much stronger than the case for non-voluntary euthanasia.

Some opponents of the legalisation of voluntary euthanasia might concede that all this follows, if we have a genuinely free and rational decision to die: but, they add, we can never be sure that a request to be killed is the result of a free and rational decision. Will not the sick and elderly be pressured by their relatives to end their lives quickly? Will it not be possible to commit outright murder by pretending that a person has requested euthanasia? And even if there is no pressure of falsification, can anyone who is ill, suffering pain, and very probably in a drugged and confused state of mind, make a rational decision about whether to live or die?

These questions raise technical difficulties for the legalisation of voluntary euthanasia, rather than objections to the underlying ethical principles; but they are serious difficulties nonetheless. The guidelines developed by the courts in the Netherlands have sought to meet them by proposing that euthanasia is acceptable only if

- It is carried out by a physician.
- The patient has explicitly requested euthanasia in a manner that leaves no doubt of the patient's desire to die.
- The patient's decision is well-informed, free, and durable.
- The patient has an irreversible condition causing protracted physical or mental suffering that the patient finds unbearable.
- There is no reasonable alternative (reasonable from the patient's point of view) to alleviate the patient's suffering.
- The doctor has consulted another independent professional who agrees with his or her judgment.

Euthanasia in these circumstances is strongly supported by the Royal Dutch Medical Association, and by the general public in the Netherlands. The guidelines make murder in the guise of euthanasia rather far-fetched, and there is no evidence of an increase in the murder rate in the Netherlands.

It is often said, in debates about euthanasia, that doctors can be mistaken. In rare instances patients diagnosed by two competent doctors as suffering from an incurable condition have survived and enjoyed years of good health. Possibly the legalisation of voluntary euthanasia would, over the years, mean the deaths of a few people who would otherwise have recovered from their immediate illness and lived for some extra years. This is not, however, the knockdown argument against euthanasia that some imagine it to be. Against a very small number of unnecessary deaths that might occur if euthanasia is legalised we must place the very large amount of pain and distress that will be suffered if euthanasia is not legalised, by patients who really are terminally ill. Longer life is not such a supreme good that it outweighs all other considerations. (If it were, there would be many more effective ways of saving life—such as a ban on smoking, or a reduction of speed limits to 40 kilometres per hour—than prohibiting voluntary euthanasia.) The possibility that two doctors may make a mistake means that the person who opts for euthanasia is deciding on the balance of probabilities and giving up a very slight chance of survival in order to avoid suffering that will almost certainly end in death. This may be a perfectly rational choice. Probability is the guide of life, and of death, too. Against this, some will reply that improved care for the terminally ill has eliminated pain and made voluntary euthanasia unnecessary. Elisabeth Kübler-Ross, whose *On Death and Dying* is perhaps the best-known book on care for the dying, has claimed that none of her patients request euthanasia. Given personal attention and the right medication, she says, people come to accept their deaths and die peacefully without pain.

Kübler-Ross may be right. It may be possible, now, to eliminate pain. In almost all cases, it may even be possible to do it in a way that leaves patients in possession of their rational faculties and free from vomiting, nausea, or other distressing side-effects. Unfortunately only a minority of dying patients now receive this kind of care. Nor is physical pain the only problem. There can also be other distressing conditions, like bones so fragile they fracture at sudden movements, uncontrollable nausea and vomiting, slow starvation due to a cancerous growth, inability to control one's bowels or bladder, difficulty in breathing, and so on.

Dr. Timothy Quill, a doctor from Rochester, New York, has described how he prescribed barbiturate sleeping pills for "Diane," a patient with a severe form of leukaemia, knowing that she wanted the tablets in order to be able to end her life. Dr. Quill had known Diane for many years, and admired her courage in dealing with previous serious illnesses. In an article in the *New England Journal of Medicine,* Dr. Quill wrote:

> It was extraordinarily important to Diane to maintain control of herself and her own dignity during the time remaining to her. When this was no longer possible, she clearly wanted to die. As a former director of a hospice program, I know how to use pain medicines to keep patients comfortable and lessen suffering. I explained the philosophy of comfort care, which I strongly believe in. Although Diane understood and appreciated this, she had known of people lingering in what was called relative comfort, and she wanted no part of it. When the time came, she wanted to take her life in the least painful way possible. Knowing of her desire for independence and her decision to stay in control, I thought this request made perfect sense. . . . In our discussion it became clear that preoccupation with her fear of a lingering death would interfere with Diane's getting the most out of the time she had left until she found a safe way to ensure her death.

Not all dying patients who wish to die are fortunate enough to have a doctor like Timothy Quill. Betty Rollin has described, in her moving book *Last Wish,* how her mother developed ovarian cancer that spread to other parts of her body. One morning her mother said to her:

> I've had a wonderful life, but now it's over, or it should be. I'm not afraid to die, but I am afraid of this illness, what it's doing to me. . . . There's never any relief from it now. Nothing but nausea and this pain. . . . There won't be any more chemotherapy. There's no treatment anymore. So what happens to me now? I know what happens. I'll die slowly. . . . I don't want that. . . . Who does it benefit if I die slowly? If it benefits my children I'd be willing. But it's not going to do you any good. . . . There's no point in a slow death, none. I've never liked doing things with no point. I've got to end this.

Betty Rollin found it very difficult to help her mother to carry out her desire: "Physician after physician turned down our pleas for help (How many pills? What kind?)." After her book about her mother's death was published, she received hundreds of letters, many from people, or close relatives of people, who had tried to die, failed, and suffered even more. Many of these people were denied help from doctors, because although suicide is legal in most jurisdictions, assisted suicide is not.

Perhaps one day it will be possible to treat all terminally ill and incurable patients in such a way that no one requests euthanasia and the subject becomes a non-issue; but this is now just a utopian ideal, and no reason at all to deny euthanasia to those who must live and die in far less comfortable conditions. It is, in any case, highly paternalistic to tell dying patients that they are now so well looked after that they need not be offered the option of euthanasia. It would be more in keeping with respect for individual freedom and autonomy to legalise euthanasia and let patients decide whether their situation is bearable.

Do these arguments for voluntary euthanasia perhaps give too much weight to individual freedom and autonomy? After all, we do not allow people free choices on matters like, for instance, the taking of heroin. This is a restriction of freedom but, in the view of many, one that can be justified on paternalistic grounds. If preventing people from becoming heroin addicts is justifiable paternalism, why isn't preventing people from having themselves killed?

The question is a reasonable one, because respect for individual freedom can be carried too far. John Stuart Mill thought that the state should never interfere with the individual except to prevent harm to others. The individual's own good, Mill thought, is not a proper reason for state intervention. But Mill may have had too high an opinion of the rationality of a human being. It may occasionally be right to prevent people from making choices that are obviously not rationally based and that we can be sure they will later regret. The prohibition of voluntary euthanasia cannot be justified on paternalistic grounds, however, for voluntary euthanasia is an act for which good reasons exist. Voluntary euthanasia occurs only when, to the best of medical knowledge, a person is suffering from an incurable and painful or extremely distressing condition. In these circumstances one cannot say that to choose to die quickly is obviously irrational. The strength of the case for voluntary euthanasia lies in this combination of respect for the preferences, or autonomy, of those who decide for euthanasia; and the clear rational basis of the decision itself. . . .

Review Questions

1. Distinguish between the cases of Janet Adkins and George Zygmaniak.
2. What are the four grounds for holding that killing a person is wrong? According to Singer, how do these grounds support voluntary euthanasia and assisted suicide?
3. What difficulties does Singer discuss? How does he reply?

Discussion Questions

1. Singer accepts the guidelines for voluntary euthanasia developed by the courts in the Netherlands. Are these acceptable? Why or why not?
2. Did Janet Adkins do anything wrong? How about Lester Zygmaniak?
3. Should the law be changed to allow voluntary euthanasia or assisted suicide for terminally ill patients?

Is There a Duty to Die?

JOHN HARDWIG

John Hardwig is professor of philosophy and head of the department at the University of Tennessee, Knoxville. He is the author of *Is There a Duty to Die? and Other Essays in Bioethics* (1999), which is mainly articles previously published. For more publications see his personal website at http://web.utk.edu/~philosop/hardwig.html.

Source: John Hardwig, "Is There a Duty to Die?" *Hasting Center Report* 27, no. 2 (1997): 34–42. Reprinted by permission of the publisher.

Hardwig argues that there is a duty to die that goes beyond refusing life-prolonging treatment. In some cases this duty may require one to end one's life, even in the absence of any terminal illness, and even if one would prefer to live. These are cases in which the burdens of providing care become too great, such that they outweigh the obligation to provide care. In reply to objections, Hardwig denies that there are higher duties such as a duty to God, that the duty to die is inconsistent with human dignity, and that the sacrifice of life is always greater than the burden of caring. He does not specify exactly who has this duty to die, but he lists a number of considerations such as age, illness, lifestyle, and having had a rich and full life. He does not believe that the incompetent have any such duty, and he notes that social policies such as providing long-term care would dramatically reduce the incidence of the duty. Finally, he argues that the duty to die gives meaning to death because it affirms moral agency and family connections.

WHEN RICHARD LAMM MADE THE statement that old people have a duty to die, it was generally shouted down or ridiculed. The whole idea is just too preposterous to entertain. Or too threatening. In fact, a fairly common argument against legalizing physician-assisted suicide is that if it were legal, some people might somehow get the idea that they have a duty to die. These people could only be the victims of twisted moral reasoning or vicious social pressure. It goes without saying that there is no duty to die.

But for me the question is real and very important. I feel strongly that I may very well some day have a duty to die. I do not believe that I am idiosyncratic, morbid, mentally ill, or morally perverse in thinking this. I think many of us will eventually face precisely this duty. But I am first of all concerned with my own duty. I write partly to clarify my own convictions and to prepare myself. Ending my life might be a very difficult thing for me to do.

This notion of a duty to die raises all sorts of interesting theoretical and metaethical questions. I intend to try to avoid most of them because I hope my argument will be persuasive to those holding a wide variety of ethical views. Also, although the claim that there is a duty to die would ultimately require theoretical underpinning, the discussion needs to begin on the normative level. As is appropriate to my attempt to steer clear of theoretical commitments, I will use "duty," "obligation," and "responsibility" interchangeably, in a pretheoretical or pre-analytic sense.[1]

CIRCUMSTANCES AND A DUTY TO DIE

Do many of us really believe that no one ever has a duty to die? I suspect not. I think most of us probably believe that there is such a duty, but it is very uncommon. Consider Captain Oates, a member of Admiral Scott's expedition to the South Pole. Oates became too ill to continue. If the rest of the team stayed with him, they would all perish. After this had become clear, Oates left his tent one night, walked out into a raging blizzard, and was never seen again.[2] That may have been a heroic thing to do, but we might be able to agree that it was also no more than his duty.

---

1 Given the importance of relationships in my thinking, "responsibility"—rooted as it is in "respond"—would perhaps be the most appropriate word. Nevertheless, I often use "duty" despite its legalistic overtones, because Lamm's famous statement has given the expression "duty to die" a certain familiarity. But I intend no implication that there is a law that grounds this duty, nor that someone has a right corresponding to it.

2 For a discussion of the Oates case, see Tom L. Beauchamp, "What Is Suicide?" in *Ethical Issues in Death and Dying,* ed. Tom L. Beauchamp and Seymour Perlin (Englewood Cliffs, N.J.: Prentice-Hall, 1978).

It would have been wrong for him to urge—or even to allow—the rest to stay and care for him.

This is a very unusual circumstance—a "lifeboat case"—and lifeboat cases make for bad ethics. But I expect that most of us would also agree that there have been cultures in which what we would call a duty to die has been fairly common. These are relatively poor, technologically simple, and especially nomadic cultures. In such societies, everyone knows that if you manage to live long enough, you will eventually become old and debilitated. Then you will need to take steps to end your life. The old people in these societies regularly did precisely that. Their cultures prepared and supported them in doing so.

Those cultures could be dismissed as irrelevant to contemporary bioethics; their circumstances are so different from ours. But if that is our response, it is instructive. It suggests that we assume a duty to die is irrelevant to us because our wealth and technological sophistication have purchased exemption for us . . . except under very unusual circumstances like Captain Oates's.

But have wealth and technology really exempted us? Or are they, on the contrary, about to make a duty to die common again? We like to think of modern medicine as all triumph with no dark side. Our medicine saves many lives and enables most of us to live longer. That is wonderful, indeed. We are all glad to have access to this medicine. But our medicine also delivers most of us over to chronic illnesses and it enables many of us to survive longer than we can take care of ourselves, longer than we know what to do with ourselves, longer than we even are ourselves.

The costs—and these are not merely monetary—of prolonging our lives when we are no longer able to care for ourselves are often staggering. If further medical advances wipe out many of today's "killer diseases"—cancers, heart attacks, strokes, ALS, AIDS, and the rest—then one day most of us will survive long enough to become demented or debilitated. These developments could generate a fairly widespread duty to die. A fairly common duty to die might turn out to be only the dark side of our life-prolonging medicine and the uses we choose to make of it.

Let me be clear. I certainly believe that there is a duty to refuse life-prolonging medical treatment and also a duty to complete advance directives refusing life-prolonging treatment. But a duty to die can go well beyond that. There can be a duty to die before one's illnesses would cause death, even if treated only with palliative measures. In fact, there may be a fairly common responsibility to end one's life in the absence of any terminal illness at all. Finally, there can be a duty to die when one would prefer to live. Granted, many of the conditions that can generate a duty to die also seriously undermine the quality of life. Some prefer not to live under such conditions. But even those who want to live can face a duty to die. These will clearly be the most controversial and troubling cases; I will, accordingly, focus my reflections on them.

THE INDIVIDUALISTIC FANTASY

Because a duty to die seems such a real possibility to me, I wonder why contemporary bioethics has dismissed it without serious consideration. I believe that most bioethics still shares in one of our deeply embedded American dreams: the individualistic fantasy. This fantasy leads us to imagine that lives are separate and unconnected, or that they could be so if we chose. If lives were unconnected, things that happened in my life would not or need not affect others. And if others were not (much) affected by my life, I would have no duty to consider the impact of my decisions on others. I would then be free morally to live my life however I please, choosing whatever life and death I prefer for myself. The way I live would be nobody's business but my own. I certainly would have no duty to die if I preferred to live.

Within a health care context, the individualistic fantasy leads us to assume that the patient is the only one affected by decisions about her medical treatment. If only the patient were affected, the relevant questions when making treatment decisions would be precisely those we ask: What will benefit the patient? Who can best decide that? The pivotal issue would always be simply whether the patient wants to live like this and whether she would consider herself better off dead.[3] "Whose life is it, anyway?" we ask rhetorically.

But this is morally obtuse. We are not a race of hermits. Illness and death do not come only to those who are all alone. Nor is it much better to think in terms of the bald dichotomy between "the interests of the patient" and "the interests of society" (or a third-party payer), as if we were isolated individuals connected only to "society" in the abstract or to the other, faceless members of our health maintenance organization.

Most of us are affiliated with particular others and most deeply, with family and loved ones. Families and loved ones are bound together by ties of care and affection, by legal relations and obligations, by inhabiting shared spaces and living units, by interlocking finances and economic prospects, by common projects and also commitments to support the different life projects of other family members, by shared histories, by ties of loyalty. This life together of family and loved ones is what defines and sustains us; it is what gives meaning to most of our lives. We would not have it any other way. We would not want to be all alone, especially when we are seriously ill, as we age, and when we are dying.

But the fact of deeply interwoven lives debars us from making exclusively self-regarding decisions, as the decisions of one member of a family may dramatically affect the lives of all the rest.

The impact of my decisions upon my family and loved ones is the source of many of my strongest obligations and also the most plausible and likeliest basis of a duty to die. "Society," after all, is only very marginally affected by how I live, or by whether I live or die.

A BURDEN TO MY LOVED ONES

Many older people report that their one remaining goal in life is not to be a burden to their loved ones. Young people feel this, too: when I ask my undergraduate students to think about whether their death could come too late, one of their very first responses always is, "Yes, when I become a burden to my family or loved ones." Tragically, there are situations in which my loved ones would be much better off—all things considered, the loss of a loved one notwithstanding—if I were dead.

The lives of our loved ones can be seriously compromised by caring for us. The burdens of providing care or even just supervision twenty-four hours a day, seven days a week are often overwhelming.[4] When this kind of caregiving goes on for years, it leaves the caregiver exhausted, with no time for herself or life of her own. Ultimately, even her health is often destroyed. But it can also be emotionally devastating simply to live with a spouse who is increasingly distant, uncommunicative, unresponsive, foreign, and unreachable. Other family members' needs often go unmet as the caring capacity of the family is exceeded. Social life and friendships evaporate, as there is no opportunity to go out to see friends and the home is no longer a place suitable for having friends in.

---

3 Most bioethicists advocate a "patient-centered ethics"—an ethics which claims only the patient's interests should be considered in making medical treatment decisions. Most health care professionals have been trained to accept this ethic and to see themselves as patient advocates. For arguments that a patient-centered ethics should be replaced by a family-centered ethics see John Hardwig, "What About the Family?" *Hastings Center Report* 20, no. 2 (1990): 5–10; Hilde L. Nelson and James L. Nelson, *The Patient in the Family* (New York: Routledge, 1995).

4 A good account of the burdens of caregiving can be found in Elaine Brody, *Women in the Middle: Their Parent-Care Years* (New York: Springer Publishing Co., 1990). Perhaps the best article-length account of these burdens is Daniel Callahan, "Families as Caregivers; the Limits of Morality" in *Aging and Ethics: Philosophical Problems in Gerontology*, ed. Nancy Jecker (Totowa N.J.: Humana Press, 1991).

We must also acknowledge that the lives of our loved ones can be devastated just by having to pay for health care for us. One part of the recent SUPPORT study documented the financial aspects of caring for a dying member of a family. Only those who had illnesses severe enough to give them less than a 50 percent chance to live six more months were included in this study. When these patients survived their initial hospitalization and were discharged about one-third required considerable caregiving from their families; in 20 percent of cases a family member had to quit work or make some other major lifestyle change; almost one-third of these families lost all of their savings; and just under 30 percent lost a major source of income.[5]

If talking about money sounds venal or trivial, remember that much more than money is normally at stake here. When someone has to quit work, she may well lose her career. Savings decimated late in life cannot be recouped in the few remaining years of employability, so the loss compromises the quality of the rest of the caregiver's life. For a young person, the chance to go to college may be lost to the attempt to pay debts due to an illness in the family, and this decisively shapes an entire life.

A serious illness in a family is a misfortune. It is usually nobody's fault; no one is responsible for it. But we face choices about how we will respond to this misfortune. That's where the responsibility comes in and fault can arise. Those of us with families and loved ones always have a duty not to make selfish or self-centered decisions about our lives. We have a responsibility to try to protect the lives of loved ones from serious threats or greatly impoverished quality, certainly an obligation not to make choices that will jeopardize or seriously compromise their futures. Often, it would be wrong to do just what we want or just what is best for ourselves; we should choose in light of what is best for all

5 Kenneth E. Covinsky et al., "The Impact of Serious Illness on Patients' Families," *JAMA 272* (1994): 1839–44.

concerned. That is our duty in sickness as well as in health. It is out of these responsibilities that a duty to die can develop.

I am not advocating a crass, quasi-economic conception of burdens and benefits, nor a shallow, hedonistic view of life. Given a suitably rich understanding of benefits, family members sometimes do benefit from suffering through the long illness of a loved one. Caring for the sick or aged can foster growth, even as it makes daily life immeasurably harder and the prospects for the future much bleaker. Chronic illness or a drawn-out death can also pull a family together, making the care for each other stronger and more evident. If my loved ones are truly benefiting from coping with my illness or debility, I have no duty to die based on burdens to them.

But it would be irresponsible to blithely assume that this always happens, that it will happen in my family, or that it will be the fault of my family if they cannot manage to turn my illness into a positive experience. Perhaps the opposite is more common: A hospital chaplain once told me that he could not think of a single case in which a family was strengthened or brought together by what happened at the hospital.

Our families and loved ones also have obligations, of course—they have the responsibility to stand by us and to support us through debilitating illness and death. They must be prepared to make significant sacrifices to respond to an illness in the family. I am far from denying that. Most of us are aware of this responsibility and most families meet it rather well. In fact, families deliver more than 80 percent of the long-term care in this country, almost always at great personal cost. Most of us who are a part of a family can expect to be sustained in our time of need by family members and those who love us.

But most discussions of an illness in the family sound as if responsibility were a one-way street. It is not, of course. When we become seriously ill or debilitated, we too may have to make sacrifices. To think that my loved ones must bear whatever burdens my illness, debility, or dying process might impose upon them is to reduce them to means to my well-being. And that would be immoral. Family solidarity, altruism, bearing the burden of a loved one's misfortune, and loyalty are all important virtues of families, as well. But they are all also two-way streets.

OBJECTIONS TO A DUTY TO DIE

To my mind, the most serious objections to the idea of a duty to die lie in the effects on my loved ones of ending my life. But to most others, the important objections have little or nothing to do with family and loved ones. Perhaps the most common objections are: (1) there is a higher duty that always takes precedence over a duty to die; (2) a duty to end one's own life would be incompatible with a recognition of human dignity or the intrinsic value of a person; and (3) seriously ill, debilitated, or dying people are already bearing the harshest burdens and so it would be wrong to ask them to bear the additional burden of ending their own lives.

These are all important objections; all deserve a thorough discussion. Here I will only be able to suggest some moral counterweights—ideas that might provide the basis for an argument that these objections do not always preclude a duty to die.

An example of the first line of argument would be the claim that a duty to God, the giver of life, forbids that anyone take her own life. It could be argued that this duty always supersedes whatever obligations we might have to our families. But what convinces us that we always have such a religious duty in the first place? And what guarantees that it always supersedes our obligations to try to protect our loved ones?

Certainly, the view that death is the ultimate evil cannot be squared with Christian theology. It does not reflect the actions of Jesus or those of his early followers. Nor is it clear that the belief that life is sacred requires that we never take it. There

are other theological possibilities.[6] In any case, most of us—bioethicists, physicians, and patients alike—do not subscribe to the view that we have an obligation to preserve human life as long as possible. But if not, surely we ought to agree that I may legitimately end my life for other-regarding reasons, not just for self-regarding reasons.

Secondly, religious considerations aside, the claim could be made that an obligation to end one's own life would be incompatible with human dignity or would embody a failure to recognize the intrinsic value of a person. But I do not see that in thinking I had a duty to die I would necessarily be failing to respect myself or to appreciate my dignity or worth. Nor would I necessarily be failing to respect you in thinking that you had a similar duty. There is surely also a sense in which we fail to respect ourselves if in the face of illness or death, we stoop to choosing just what is best for ourselves. Indeed, Kant held that the very core of human dignity is the ability to act on a self-imposed moral law, regardless of whether it is in our interest to do so.[7] We shall return to the notion of human dignity.

A third objection appeals to the relative weight of burdens and thus, ultimately, to considerations of fairness or justice. The burdens that an illness creates for the family could not possibly be great enough to justify an obligation to end one's life—the sacrifice of life itself would be a far greater burden than any involved in caring for a chronically ill family member.

---

6 Larry Churchill, for example, believes that Christian ethics takes us far beyond my present position: "Christian doctrines of stewardship prohibit the extension of one's own life at a great cost to the neighbor . . . And such a gesture should not appear to us a sacrifice, but as the ordinary virtue entailed by a just, social conscience." Larry Churchill, *Rationing Health Care in America* (South Bend, Ind.: Notre Dame University Press, 1988), p. 112.

7 Kant, as is well known, was opposed to suicide. But he was arguing against taking your life out of self-interested motives. It is not clear that Kant would or we should consider taking your life out of a sense of duty to be wrong. See Hilde L. Nelson, "Death with Kantian Dignity," *Journal of Clinical Ethics* 7 (1996): 215–21.

But is this true? Consider the following case:

An 87-year-old woman was dying of congestive heart failure. Her APACHE score predicted that she had less than a 50 percent chance to live for another six months. She was lucid, assertive, and terrified of death. She very much wanted to live and kept opting for rehospitalization and the most aggressive life-prolonging treatment possible. That treatment successfully prolonged her life (though with increasing debility) for nearly two years. Her 55-year-old daughter was her only remaining family, her caregiver, and the main source of her financial support. The daughter duly cared for her mother. But before her mother died, her illness had cost the daughter all of her savings, her home, her job, and her career.

This is by no means an uncommon sort of case. Thousands of similar cases occur each year. Now, ask yourself which is the greater burden:

a) To lose a 50 percent chance of six more months of life at age 87?

b) To lose all your savings, your home, and your career at age 55?

Which burden would you prefer to bear? Do we really believe the former is the greater burden? Would even the dying mother say that (a) is the greater burden? Or has she been encouraged to believe that the burdens of (b) are somehow morally irrelevant to her choices?

I think most of us would quickly agree that (b) is a greater burden. That is the evil we would more hope to avoid in our lives. If we are tempted to say that the mother's disease and impending death are the greater evil, I believe it is because we are taking a "slice of time" perspective rather than a "lifetime perspective."[8] But surely the lifetime perspective is the appropriate perspective when weighing burdens. If (b) is the greater burden, then we must admit

that we have been promulgating an ethics that advocates imposing greater burdens on some people in order to provide smaller benefits for others just because they are ill and thus gain our professional attention and advocacy.

A whole range of cases like this one could easily be generated. In some, the answer about which burden is greater will not be clear. But in many it is. Death—or ending your own life—is simply not the greatest evil or the greatest burden.

This point does not depend on a utilitarian calculus. Even if death were the greatest burden (thus disposing of any simple utilitarian argument), serious questions would remain about the moral justifiability of choosing to impose crushing burdens on loved ones in order to avoid having to bear this burden oneself. The fact that I suffer greater burdens than others in my family does not license me simply to choose what I want for myself, nor does it necessarily release me from a responsibility to try to protect the quality of their lives.

I can readily imagine that, through cowardice, rationalization, or failure of resolve, I will fail in this obligation to protect my loved ones. If so, I think I would need to be excused or forgiven for what I did. But I cannot imaging it would be morally permissible for me to ruin the rest of my partner's life to sustain mine or to cut off my sons' careers, impoverish them, or compromise the quality of their children's lives simply because I wish to live a little longer. This is what leads me to believe in a duty to die.

WHO HAS A DUTY TO DIE?

Suppose, then, that there can be a duty to die. Who has a duty to die? And when? To my mind, these are the right questions, the questions we should be asking. Many of us may one day badly need answers to just these questions.

But I cannot supply answers here, for two reasons. In the first place, answers will have to be very particular and contextual. Our concrete duties are often situated, defined in part by the myriad details of our circumstances, histories,

---

8 Obviously, I owe this distinction to Norman Daniels. Norman Daniels, *Am I My Parents' Keeper? An Essay on Justice Between the Young and the Old* (New York: Oxford University Press, 1988). Just as obviously, Daniels is not committed to my use of it here.

and relationships. Though there may be principles that apply to a wide range of cases and some cases that yield pretty straightforward answers, there will also be many situations in which it is very difficult to discern whether one has a duty to die. If nothing else, it will often be very difficult to predict how one's family will bear up under the weight of the burdens that a protracted illness would impose on them. Momentous decisions will often have to be made under conditions of great uncertainty.

Second and perhaps even more importantly, I believe that those of us with family and loved ones should not define our duties unilaterally, especially not a decision about a duty to die. It would be isolating and distancing for me to decide without consulting them what is too much of a burden for my loved ones to bear. That way of deciding about my moral duties is not only atomistic, it also treats my family and loved ones paternalistically. They must be allowed to speak for themselves about the burdens my life imposes on them and how they feel about bearing those burdens.

Some may object that it would be wrong to put a loved one in a position of having to say, in effect, "You should end your life because caring for you is too hard on me and the rest of the family." Not only will it be almost impossible to say something like that to someone you love, it will carry with it a heavy load of guilt. On this view, you should decide by yourself whether you have a duty to die and approach your loved ones only after you have made up your mind to say good-bye to them. Your family could then try to change your mind, but the tremendous weight of moral decision would be lifted from their shoulders.

Perhaps so. But I believe in family decisions. Important decisions for those whose lives are interwoven should be made together, in a family discussion. Granted, a conversation about whether I have a duty to die would be a tremendously difficult conversation. The temptations to be dishonest could be enormous. Nevertheless, if I am contemplating a duty to die, my family and I

should, if possible, have just such an agonizing discussion. It will act as a check on the information, perceptions, and reasoning of all of us. But even more importantly, it affirms our connectedness at a critical juncture in our lives and our life together. Honest talk about difficult matters almost always strengthens relationships.

However, many families seem unable to talk about death at all, much less a duty to die. Certainly most families could not have this discussion all at once, in one sitting. It might well take a number of discussions to be able to approach this topic. But even if talking about death is impossible, there are always behavioral clues—about your caregiver's tiredness, physical condition, health, prevailing mood, anxiety, financial concerns, outlook, overall well-being, and so on. And families unable to talk about death can often talk about how the caregiver is feeling, about finances, about tensions within the family resulting from the illness, about concerns for the future. Deciding whether you have a duty to die based on these behavioral clues and conversation about them honors your relationships better than deciding on your own about how burdensome you and your care must be.

I cannot say when someone has a duty to die. Still, I can suggest a few features of one's illness, history, and circumstances that make it more likely that one has a duty to die. I present them here without much elaboration or explanation.

1) A duty to die is more likely when continuing to live will impose significant burdens—emotional burdens, extensive caregiving, destruction of life plans, and, yes, financial hardship—on your family and loved ones. This is the fundamental insight underlying a duty to die.

2) A duty to die becomes greater as you grow older. As we age, we will be giving up less by giving up our lives, if only because we will sacrifice fewer remaining years of life and a smaller portion of our life plans. After all, it's not as if we would be immortal and live forever if we could just manage to avoid a duty to die. To have reached the age of, say, seventy-five or eighty years without being ready to die is itself a

moral failing, the sign of a life out of touch with life's basic realities.[9]

3) A duty to die is more likely when you have already lived a full and rich life. You have already had a full share of the good things life offers.

4) There is greater duty to die if your loved ones' lives have already been difficult or impoverished, if they have had only a small share of the good things that life has to offer (especially if through no fault of their own).

5) A duty to die is more likely when your loved ones have already made great contributions—perhaps even sacrifices—to make your life a good one. Especially if you have not made similar sacrifices for their well-being or for the well-being of other members of your family.

6) To the extent that you can make a good adjustment to your illness or handicapping condition, there is less likely to be a duty to die. A good adjustment means that smaller sacrifices will be required of loved ones and there is more compensating interaction for them. Still, we must also recognize that some diseases—Alzheimer or Huntington chorea—will eventually take their toll on your loved ones no matter how courageously, resolutely, even cheerfully you manage to face that illness.

7) There is less likely to be a duty to die if you can still make significant contributions to the lives of others, especially your family. The burdens to family members are not only or even primarily financial, neither are the contributions to them. However, the old and those who have terminal illnesses must also bear in mind that the loss their family members will feel when they die cannot be avoided, only postponed.

8) A duty to die is more likely when the part of you that is loved will soon be gone or seriously compromised. Or when you soon will no longer be capable of giving love. Part of the horror of dementing disease is that it destroys the capacity to nurture and sustain relationships, taking away a person's agency and the emotions that bind her to others.

9) There is a greater duty to die to the extent that you have lived a relatively lavish lifestyle instead of saving for illness or old age. Like most upper middle-class Americans, I could easily have saved more. It is a greater wrong to come to your family for assistance if your need is the result of having chosen leisure or a spendthrift lifestyle. I may eventually have to face the moral consequences of decisions I am now making.

These, then, are some of the considerations that give shape and definition to the duty to die. If we can agree that these considerations are all relevant, we can see that the correct course of action will often be difficult to discern. A decision about when I should end my life will sometimes prove to be every bit as difficult as the decision about whether I want treatment for myself.

CAN THE INCOMPETENT HAVE A DUTY TO DIE?

Severe mental deterioration springs readily to mind as one of the situations in which I believe I could have a duty to die. But can incompetent people have duties at all? We can have moral duties we do not recognize or acknowledge, including duties that we never recognized. But can we have duties we are unable to recognize? Duties when we are unable to understand the concept of morality at all? If so, do others have a moral obligation to help us carry out this duty? These are extremely difficult theoretical questions. The reach of moral agency is severely strained by mental incompetence.

I am tempted to simply bypass the entire question by saying that I am talking only about competent persons. But the idea of a duty to die clearly raises the specter of one person claiming that another—who cannot speak for herself—has such a duty. So I need to say that I can make no sense of the claim that someone has a duty to die if the person has never been

9 Daniel Callahan, *The Troubled Dream of Life* (New York: Simon & Schuster, 1993).

able to understand moral obligation at all. To my mind, only those who were formerly capable of making moral decisions could have such a duty.

But the case of formerly competent persons is almost as troubling. Perhaps we should simply stipulate that no incompetent person can have a duty to die, not even if she affirmed belief in such a duty in an advance directive. If we take the view that formerly competent people may have such a duty, we should surely exercise extreme caution when claiming a formerly competent person would have acknowledged a duty to die or that any formerly competent person has an unacknowledged duty to die. Moral dangers loom regardless of which way we decide to resolve such issues.

But for me personally, very urgent practical matters turn on their resolution. If a formerly competent person can no longer have a duty to die (or if other people are not likely to help her carry out this duty), I believe that my obligation may be to die while I am still competent, before I become unable to make and carry out that decision for myself. Surely it would be irresponsible to evade my moral duties by temporizing until I escape into incompetence. And so I must die sooner than I otherwise would have to. On the other hand, if I could count on others to end my life after I become incompetent, I might be able to fulfill my responsibilities while also living out all my competent or semi-competent days. Given our society's reluctance to permit physicians, let alone family members, to perform aid-in-dying, I believe I may well have a duty to end my life when I can see mental incapacity on the horizon.

There is also the very real problem of sudden incompetence—due to a serious stroke or automobile accident, for example. For me, that is the real nightmare. If I suddenly become incompetent, I will fall into the hands of a medical-legal system that will conscientiously disregard my moral beliefs and do what is best for me, regardless of the consequences for my loved ones. And that is not at all what I would have wanted!

SOCIAL POLICIES AND A DUTY TO DIE

The claim that there is a duty to die will seem to some a misplaced response to social negligence. If our society were providing for the debilitated, the chronically ill, and the elderly as it should be, there would be only very rare cases of a duty to die. On this view, I am asking the sick and debilitated to step in and accept responsibility because society is derelict in its responsibility to provide for the incapacitated.

This much is surely true: There are a number of social policies we could pursue that would dramatically reduce the incidence of such a duty. Most obviously, we could decide to pay for facilities that provided excellent long-term care (not just health care!) for all chronically ill, debilitated, mentally ill, or demented people in this country. We probably could still afford to do this. If we did, sick, debilitated, and dying people might still be morally required to make sacrifices for their families. I might, for example, have a duty to forgo personal care by a family member who knows me and really does care for me. But these sacrifices would only rarely include the sacrifice of life itself. The duty to die would then be virtually eliminated.

I cannot claim to know whether in some abstract sense a society like ours should provide care for all who are chronically ill or debilitated. But the fact is that we Americans seem to be unwilling to pay for this kind of long-term care, except for ourselves and our own. In fact, we are moving in precisely the opposite direction—we are trying to shift the burdens of caring for the seriously and chronically ill onto families in order to save costs for our health care system. As we shift the burdens of care onto families, we also dramatically increase the number of Americans who will have a duty to die.

I must not, then, live my life and make my plans on the assumption that social institutions will protect my family from my infirmity and debility. To do so would be irresponsible. More likely, it will be up to me to protect my loved ones.

A DUTY TO DIE AND THE MEANING OF LIFE

A duty to die seems very harsh, and often it would be. It is one of the tragedies of our lives that someone who wants very much to live can nevertheless have a duty to die. It is both tragic and ironic that it is precisely the very real good of family and loved ones that gives rise to this duty. Indeed, the genuine love, closeness, and support-iveness of family members is a major source of this duty: we could not be such a burden if they did not care for us. Finally, there is deep irony in the fact that the very successes of our life-prolonging medicine help to create a widespread duty to die. We do not live in such a happy world that we can avoid such tragedies and ironies. We ought not to close our eyes to this reality or pre-tend that it just doesn't exist. We ought not to minimize the tragedy in any way.

And yet, a duty to die will not always be as harsh as we might assume. If I love my family, I will want to protect them and their lives. I will want not to make choices that compromise their futures. Indeed, I can easily imagine that I might want to avoid compromising their lives more than I would want anything else. I must also admit that I am not necessarily giving up so much in giving up my life: the conditions that give rise to a duty to die would usually already have compromised the quality of the life I am required to end. In any case, I personally must confess that at age fifty-six, I have already lived a very good life, albeit not yet nearly as long a life as I would like to have.

We fear death too much. Our fear of death has lead to a massive assault on it. We still crave after virtually any life-prolonging technology that we might conceivably be able to produce. We still too often feel morally impelled to pro-long life—virtually any form of life—as long as possible. As if the best death is the one that can be put off longest.

We do not even ask about meaning in death, so busy are we with trying to postpone it. But we will not conquer death by one day developing a technology so magnificent that no one will have to die. Nor can we conquer death by postponing it ever longer. We can conquer death only by finding meaning in it.

Although the existence of a duty to die does not hinge on this, recognizing such a duty would go some way toward recovering meaning in death. Paradoxically, it would restore dignity to those who are seriously ill or dying. It would also reaffirm the connections required to give life (and death) meaning. I close now with a few words about both of these points.

First, recognizing a duty to die affirms my agency and also my moral agency. I can still do things that make an important difference in the lives of my loved ones. Moreover, the fact that I still have responsibilities keeps me within the community of moral agents. My illness or debil-ity has not reduced me to a mere moral patient (to use the language of the philosophers). Though it may not be the whole story, surely Kant was onto something important when he claimed that human dignity rests on the capacity for moral agency within a community of those who respect the demands of morality.

By contrasts, surely there is something deeply insulting in a medicine and an ethic that would ask only what I want (or would have wanted) when I become ill. To treat me as if I had no moral responsibilities when I am ill or debili-tated implies that my condition has rendered me morally incompetent. Only small children, the demented or insane, and those totally lacking in the capacity to act are free from moral duties. There is dignity, then, and a kind of meaning in moral agency, even as it forces extremely diffi-cult decisions upon us.

Second, recovering meaning in death requires an affirmation of connections. If I end my life to spare the futures of my loved ones, I testify in my death that I am connected to them. It is because I love and care for precisely these people (and I know they care for me) that I wish not to be such a burden to them. By contrast, a life in which I am free to choose whatever I want for myself is a life unconnected to others. A bioethics that would treat me as if I had no serious moral responsibilities does what it can to marginalize, weaken, or even destroy my connections with others.

But life without connection is meaningless. The individualistic fantasy, though occasionally liberating, is deeply destructive. When life is good and vitality seems unending, life itself and life lived for yourself may seem quite sufficient. But if not life, certainly death without connection is meaningless. If you are only for yourself, all you have to care about as your life draws to a close is yourself and your life. Everything you care about will then perish in your death. And that—the end of everything you care about—is precisely the total collapse of meaning. We can, then, find meaning in death only through a sense of connection with something that will survive our death.

This need not be connections with other people. Some people are deeply tied to land (for example, the family farm), to nature, or to a transcendent reality. But for most of us, the connections that sustain us are to other people. In the full bloom of life, we are connected to others in many ways—through work, profession, neighborhood, country, shared faith and worship, common leisure pursuits, friendship. Even the guru meditating in isolation on his mountain top is connected to a long tradition of people united by the same religious quest.

But as we age or when we become chronically ill, connections with other people usually become much more restricted. Often, only ties with family and close friends remain and remain important to us. Moreover, for many of us, other connections just don't go deep enough. As Paul Tsongas has reminded us, "When it comes time to die, no one says, 'I wish I had spent more time at the office.'"

If I am correct, death is so difficult for us partly because our sense of community is so weak. Death seems to wipe out everything when we can't fit it into the lives of those who live on. A death motivated by the desire to spare the futures of my loved ones might well be a better death for me than the one I would get as a result of opting to continue my life as long as there is any pleasure in it for me. Pleasure is nice, but it is meaning that matters.

. . .

I don't know about others, but these reflections have helped me. I am now more at peace about facing a duty to die. Ending my life if my duty required might still be difficult. But for me, a far greater horror would be dying all alone or stealing the futures of my loved ones in order to buy a little more time for myself. I hope that if the time comes when I have a duty to die, I will recognize it, encourage my loved ones to recognize it too, and carry it out bravely.

ACKNOWLEDGMENTS

I wish to thank Mary English, Hilde Nelson, Jim Bennett, Tom Townsend, the members of the Philosophy Department at East Tennessee State University, and anonymous reviewers of the *Report* for many helpful comments on earlier versions of this paper. In this paper, I draw on material in John Hardwig, "Dying at the Right Time; Reflections on (Un)Assisted Suicide" in *Practical Ethics,* ed. H. LaFollette (London: Blackwell, 1996), with permission.

Review Questions

1. Hardwig begins with the case of Captain Oates. What is this case supposed to prove?
2. What are the requirements of the duty to die in Hardwig's view?
3. What is the "individualistic fantasy," as Hardwig calls it? What is wrong with this fantasy?
4. What is Hardwig's position on the burdens of providing care to the ill?
5. According to Hardwig, what is the most serious objection to the idea of a duty to die?
6. What are the most common objections? How does Hardwig reply to these objections?

7. Hardwig lists nine considerations relevant to the duty to die. What are they?
8. What is Hardwig's view of the incompetent? Do they have any duty to die?
9. What social policies would dramatically reduce the incidence of the duty to die according to Hardwig?

Discussion Questions

1. Is there any duty to die? If so, does it require one to actively end one's life? Why or why not?
2. How much of a burden would you accept to care for a family member? Would you be willing to provide full-time care? Would you give up a career?
3. Does Hardwig have a good reply to the objection that there is a higher duty to God? Explain your view.
4. Do you agree with Hardwig that excellent long-term care should be provided for all chronically ill, debilitated, mentally ill, or demented people in this country? If so, how should this be financed?
5. Does the duty to die give meaning to death as Hardwig says? Why or why not?

Problem Cases

1. Terri Schiavo

(For more information see the Terri Schiavo Foundation, www.terrisfight.org.) Terri Schiavo, forty, has been in a persistent vegetative state since 1990 when her heart stopped temporarily and she suffered brain damage. The cause was diagnosed by doctors as potassium deficiency. She was twenty-six at the time and had not signed a living will. Since then she has been kept alive with a feeding tube that supplies nutrition and hydration.

According to the National Institute for Neurological Disorders and Stroke (www.ninds.nin.gov), people in a persistent vegetative state (PVS) have lost their thinking abilities and awareness of surroundings. They retain noncognitive function, normal sleep patterns, breathing and circulation. They may be able to cry or laugh, and may appear somewhat normal. But they do not speak or respond to commands.

Ms. Schiavo has been in this state for thirteen years. It is generally agreed that the prognosis is poor for PVS patients who do not become responsive in six months. Also, Ms. Schiavo suffered severe brain damage because oxygen was cut off to her brain for fourteen minutes when her heart stopped. This makes a full recovery unlikely.

Michael Schiavo, the husband and legal guardian of Ms. Schiavo, has sought to have the feeding tube removed since 1998, testifying that his wife told him that she would never want to be kept alive artificially. Her parents, Robert and Mary Schindler, have fought Mr. Schiavo every step of the way. They have made videos of their daughter smiling, grunting and moaning in response to her mother's voice, and following a balloon with her eyes. They believe their daughter may recover some day.

On October 21, 2003, the Florida Legislature and House passed a bill known as Terri's bill which allowed Jeb Bush, Florida's governor, to issue an executive order that Ms. Schiavo be kept alive with a feeding tube. Mr. Bush, the brother of President George W. Bush, is a Roman Catholic who believes passionately in the sanctity of life. The hastily passed law overrode years of court rulings and came six days after Ms Schiavo's feeding tube had been removed.

Mr. Schiavo immediately sued, arguing that the law was unconstitutional. On May 6, 2004, Judge Douglas Baird of the Sixth Circuit Court struck down Terri's law as unconstitutional. He wrote that the law authorizes the governor to summarily deprive Florida citizens of their constitutional right to privacy. The ruling voided the law and allowed Ms. Schiavo's feeding tube to be disconnected. But lawyers for both sides said that the tube would remain in place while Mr. Bush appealed.

Should Ms. Schiavo be kept alive with a feeding tube or not? Why or why not?

Who has the right to make a life-or-death decision in this case? Does Governor Bush have this right? Does the husband and legal guardian have the right to decide? What about the parents? Should they get to decide?

Suppose Ms. Schiavo had signed a living will specifically saying that she did not want to be kept alive with a feeding tube. Should her instructions be followed? Why or why not?

2. *Tracy Lynn Latimer*

Tracy suffered from a severe form of cerebral palsy, but she was not terminally ill. At the age of twelve, she was quadriplegic and bedridden most of the time, although she was able to get about in a wheelchair. Her condition was permanent, having been caused by neurological damage at the time of her birth. She was said to have the mental capacity of a four-month-old baby, and could communicate only by means of facial expressions such as laughing or crying. According to Laura Latimer, her mother, Tracy enjoyed music, bonfires, and being with her family and the circus. She liked to play music on the radio attached to her wheelchair, which she could control with a special button. She was completely dependent on others for her care. She had five to six seizures daily, despite taking anti-epileptic medication. Like many quadriplegic children with cerebral palsy, Tracy developed scoliosis, an abnormal curvature and rotation in the back. She underwent numerous surgeries in her short life, including operations to implant metal rods that supported her back. Tracy was thought to be in a great deal of pain, and the pain could not be reduced by medication because the pain medication conflicted with her anti-seizure medication, and she had difficulty swallowing. Before her death she had developed further problems in her right hip, which had become dislocated and caused considerable pain.

Tracy's doctors anticipated that she would have to undergo repeated surgeries. She could have been fed with a feeding tube into her stomach. This treatment would have improved her nutrition and health, and might have allowed more effective pain medication to be administered. This option was rejected by the parents as being intrusive and as representing the first step on a path of preserving Tracy's life artificially.

Tracy was scheduled to undergo further surgery on November 19, 1993. This was to correct the dislocated hip. The procedure involved removing her upper thigh bone, which would leave her lower leg loose without any connecting bone. It would be held in place by muscle and tissue. The expected recovery time for this surgery was one year. The Latimers were told that this operation would be very painful, and the doctors said that further surgery would be required to relieve pain in various joints in Tracy's body. According to Laura Latimer, these further surgeries were perceived as mutilations. Robert Latimer, the father, decided that Tracy's life was not worth living, and decided to take her life.

On October 24, 1993, while his wife and Tracy's siblings were at church, Robert carried Tracy to his pickup truck parked in a shed. He put her in the cab of the truck, and inserted a hose from the truck's exhaust pipe into the cab. Tracy died from carbon monoxide poisoning.

Robert was initially charged with first degree murder and convicted by a jury of second degree murder. The Court of Appeal for Saskatchewan upheld this conviction and a life sentence with no eligibility for parole for ten years. The case was appealed, and in a second trial, Robert was again convicted of second degree murder. A third appeal was made and rejected by the Court on June 13, 2001.

There is no doubt that Robert killed Tracy. He confessed to the crime and re-enacted his actions on videotape. But how should he be punished? The community where the Latimers lived, in North Battleford, Saskatchewan, reacted to the crime with sympathy rather than anger. By all accounts, Robert was a caring and involved parent who was well-liked by the community. Some jury members who found him guilty were upset by the life sentence. Did he deserve this sentence? In his defense, Robert said the killing was an act of mercy to save his daughter from long-term pain and suffering. Do you agree? If so, was his act morally wrong or not? Why or why not?

3. Cruzan v. Director, Missouri Department of Health (U. S. Supreme Court. 110 S. Ct. 2841 [1990])

In this case, the U.S. Supreme Court ruled on a petition to terminate the artificial nutrition and hydration of Nancy Cruzan, a twenty-five-year-old woman existing in a persistent vegetative state following an automobile accident.

On the night of January 11, 1983, Cruzan rolled her car over while driving down Elm Road in Jasper County, Missouri. She was found lying in a ditch. She was not breathing, and her heart was not beating. Paramedics were able to restore her breathing and heartbeat, but she remained unconscious. She remained in a coma for about three weeks. To keep her alive, surgeons implanted a gastrostomy feeding and hydration tube; she remained in a persistent vegetative state—a condition in which a person exhibits motor reflexes but no sign of consciousness or cognitive function.

After it became clear that Cruzan had practically no chance of recovery, her parents asked the doctors to terminate the artificial feeding and hydration. The doctors and the parents agreed that this would cause Cruzan's death. The doctors refused to do this without a court order. The parents petitioned a court and received authorization to terminate treatment. But the Supreme Court of Missouri reversed the decision of the trial court and ruled that treatment could not be terminated without "clear and convincing evidence" that termination is what Cruzan would have wanted.

The case went to the U.S. Supreme Court, and it upheld the judgment of the Missouri Supreme Court that termination of treatment was unconstitutional in this case. The decision was 5 to 4, and the majority opinion was written by Justice William H. Rehnquist. In his opinion, Rehnquist granted that a competent person has a right to refuse lifesaving nutrition and hydration. But he ruled that in the case of an incompetent person such as Nancy Cruzan, it is constitutional for Missouri to require that feeding and hydration be terminated only if there is clear and convincing evidence that this is what Cruzan would have wanted. Because such evidence was not provided, the decision to deny the request for termination was upheld.

In later developments, the parents presented new evidence to show that Cruzan would have chosen termination of treatment, and the feeding and hydration were stopped. Nancy Cruzan finally died in December of 1990, seven years after the accident.

This case raises several troubling questions:

1. What would be the AMA position in this case? Are artificial feeding and hydration ordinary or extraordinary means of prolonging life? If they are ordinary means, then is cessation of treatment not allowed? If they are extraordinary means, then is cessation of treatment allowed? Is the AMA position defensible in this case?

2. Is termination of treatment in this case active or passive euthanasia? Is it an act that causes Cruzan's death, or does it just allow her to die from natural causes? Does it cause death or permit death?

3. Suppose that there were no "clear and convincing evidence" that termination of treatment is what Cruzan would have wanted. Does this mean that termination is wrong in this case? On the other hand, suppose that there were such evidence. Does this mean that termination is not wrong?

4. The Case of Baby Jane Doe

In October 1983, Baby Jane Doe (as the infant was called by the court to protect her anonymity) was born with spina bifida and a host of other congenital defects. According to the doctors consulted by the parents, the child would be severely mentally retarded, be bedridden, and suffer considerable pain. After consultations with doctors and religious counselors, Mr. and Mrs. A (as the parents were called in the court documents) decided not to consent to lifesaving surgery.

At this point, a right-to-life activist lawyer tried to legally force lifesaving surgery in the Baby Doe case, but two New York appeals courts and a state children's agency decided not to override the parents' right to make a decision in the case. Then the U.S. Justice Department intervened in the case. It sued to obtain records from the University Hospital in Stony Brook, New York, to determine if the hospital had violated a federal law that forbids discrimination against the handicapped. Dr. C. Everett Koop, the U.S. surgeon general, appeared on television to express the view that the government has the moral obligation to intercede on behalf of such infants in order to protect their right to life.

Two weeks later, Federal District Judge Leonard Wexler threw out the Justice Department's unusual suit. Wexler found no discrimination. The hospital had been willing to do the surgery but had failed to do so because the parents refused to consent to the surgery. Wexler found the parents' decision to be a reasonable one in view of the circumstances.

The day after the ruling, the Justice Department appealed. On January 9, 1984, federal regulations were issued preventing federally funded hospitals from withholding treatment in such cases.

Do parents have a right to make life-or-death decisions for their defective children? Why or why not?

Do you agree with Dr. Koop that the government has a moral obligation to save the lives of such infants, even when their parents do not wish it? Explain your position.

If the government forces us to save the lives of defective infants like Baby Doe, then should it assume the responsibility for the cost of surgery, intensive care, and so on? If so, then how much money should be spent on this program? If not, then who is going to pay the bills?

5. Carolyn Heibrun

(Reported by Katha Pollitt in *The New York Times Magazine,* December 28, 2003. Also see Heibrun's book *The Last Gift of Time* (1997).) Heibrun was a famous professor of modern British literature at Columbia University. She was the first woman to be given tenure at Columbia. She taught there for thirty-three years, resigning in 1992 to protest the fact that her male colleagues refused to promote a woman.

She committed suicide at the age of seventy-seven by overdosing with pills, and putting a plastic bag over her head so that she would be found without muss or fuss by a friend. She had long intended to kill herself at age seventy. In her book, *The Last Gift of Time,* she said, "Quit while you're ahead was, and is, my motto." "Having supposed the sixties would be downhill all the way, I had long held a determination to commit suicide at seventy." When she killed herself (in 2003), she was not sick and her son said that she was not depressed. She had turned in an essay on Henry James the week before she died, and the December 2003 issue of *The Women's Review of Books* had her essay on Patricia Highsmith.

In her review of Heibrun's life in *The New York Times Magazine,* Katha Pollitt characterizes Heibrun's suicide as rational, that is, it was done to avoid something worse. Committing suicide to avoid execution or humiliation was practiced in Rome—consider Brutus, Cleopatra, or Seneca; also it was traditional in medieval Japan. But is it rational to commit suicide to avoid the difficulties of old age? Does concern about being a burden to your family justify suicide in old age, even if you are still in good health? What is your view?

6. How Much Is Human Life Worth?

(Reported by Jim Holt in *The New York Times,* March 28, 2004). Discussions of suicide and euthanasia often mention the high cost of keeping the old and the ill alive. If human life is infinitely valuable, as some would say, then the cost of prolonging life doesn't matter. We should spend whatever is necessary to keep people alive. On the other hand, most people think that human life has only a finite value. People die all the time from disease, but few claim that we should spend as much keeping old and/or ill people alive as we spend on more important matters such as war and sports. So how much should we spend keeping a person alive? What is a human life worth? It is interesting to see that in 2000 the U.S. government put a price on human life—$6.1 million. At least that is the figure the Environmental Protection Agency came up with when it was considering removing arsenic from drinking water. Arsenic causes diseases like cancer, and it will predictably kill a certain number of people. But reducing the arsenic in water is expensive, and gets more expensive as the poison levels approach zero. So how much should the government spend to save one statistical life? First the E.P.A said $6.1 million per life saved. But later, in 2002, the E.P.A. revised the price of human life downward to $3.7 million, or $2.3 million if you are older than 70.

Following this line of thinking, as you get older your life is worth less and less. Does the value of your life reduce as you get older? Are the old worth less than the young? Are the lives of sick or disabled people worth less than the healthy and able-bodied? How much is your life worth to you? Can you come with a price tag?

Suggested Readings

1. For more information on euthanasia and suicide see the International Task Force on Euthanasia and Assisted Suicide website (http://www.iaetf.org). For a website opposing euthanasia see Euthanasia.com (http://www.euthanasia.com). A website sympathetic to euthanasia, having the slogan "Good Life, Good Death," is the Euthanasia World Directory (http://www.finalexit.org).
2. Stephen G. Potts, "Looking for the Exit Door: Killing and Caring in Modern Medicine," *Houston Law Review* 25 (1988): 504–11, is a physician who argues that the legalized practice of voluntary euthanasia will have many bad effects. Also, he denies that patients have any right to be killed.
3. Susan M. Wolf, "Gender, Feminism, and Death: Physician-Assisted Suicide," in Susan M. Wolf, ed., *Feminism and Bioethics: Beyond Reproduction* (Oxford University Press, 1996), argues that if physician-assisted suicide and euthanasia are legalized in the United States, more women than men will die.
4. John Hardwig, *Is There a Duty to Die?* (London: Routledge, 2000), has several essays by Hardwig, critical commentaries by Nat Hentoff, Daniel Callahan, and others, and a response by Hardwig on dying responsibly.
5. Felicia Ackerman, "'For Now Have I My Death': The 'Duty to Die' versus the Duty to Help the Ill Stay Alive," Midwest Studies in Philosophy, XXIV (2000), pp. 172–185, relies to Hardwig.
6. James M. Humber and Robert F. Almeder, eds., *Is There a Duty to Die?* (Totowa, New Jersey: Humana Press, 2000), is a collection of articles by twelve philosophers critically responding to John Hardwig on the duty to die.
7. John D. Moreno, ed., *Arguing Euthanasia: The Controversy Over Mercy Killing, Assisted Suicide, and the "Right to Die"* (New York: Simon & Schuster, 1995), is a collection of articles on the Death with Dignity movement, including papers by Ronald Dworkin, Sidney Hook, and Daniel Callahan.

8. Gerald Dworkin, R.G. Frey, and Sissela Bok, *Euthanasia and Physician-Assisted Suicide: For and Against* (Cambridge: Cambridge University Press, 1998). Dworkin and Frey argue that physician-assisted suicide is morally permissible and ought to be legal, while Bok is against legalizing physician-assisted suicide and active voluntary euthanasia.

9. Margaret P. Battin, Rosamond Rhoades, and Anita Silvers, eds., *Physician Assisted Suicide: Expanding the Debate* (London: Routledge, 1998), is a collection of essays on the legalization of physician-assisted suicide, with some for it and others against it.

10. Daniel Callahan, "Killing and Allowing to Die," *Hastings Center Report,* 19 (January/ February 1989): 5–6, defends the distinction between killing and allowing to die attacked by Rachels.

11. *Derek Humphry's Final Exit* (Hemlock Society, 1991) is a controversial book that tells you how to commit suicide or get assistance from a doctor. Critics of the book charge that there has been a 31 percent increase in plastic-bag suicides, the method recommended in the book.

12. St. Thomas Aquinas, *Summa Theologica* 2 (New York: Benziger Brothers, 1925), part 2, question 64, argues that suicide is unnatural and immoral.

13. Richard B. Brandt, "On the Morality and Rationality of Suicide," in *A Handbook for the Study of Suicide,* ed. Seymour Perlin (Oxford: Oxford University Press, 1975), pp. 61–76, maintains that it is not wrong, blameworthy, or irrational for a person suffering from a painful terminal illness to commit suicide. Brandt argues that it is morally right to actively terminate defective newborns in "Defective Newborns and the Morality of Termination," in *Infanticide and the Value of Life,* ed. Marvin Kohl (Amherst, NY: Prometheus Books, 1978), pp. 46–57.

14. Arthur J. Dyck, "An Alternative to the Ethic of Euthanasia," in *To Live and to Let Die,* ed. R. H. Williams (New York: Springer-Verlag, 1973), pp. 98–112, attacks the ethic of euthanasia and defends an ethic of benemortasia, which forbids suicide but allows a person to refuse medical interventions that prolong dying.

15. J. Gay-Williams, "The Wrongfulness of Euthanasia," in *Intervention and Reflection: Basic Issues in Medical Ethics,* 5th ed., ed. Ronald Munson (Belmont, CA: Wadsworth, 1996), pp. 168–71, argues that euthanasia is inherently wrong because it is unnatural, is contrary to self-interest, and has bad effects.

16. Philippa Foot, "The Problem of Abortion and the Doctrine of Double Effect," *Oxford Review,* 5 (1967): 5–15, presents a classic discussion of the Doctrine of Double Effect. She discusses euthanasia in "Euthanasia," *Philosophy and Public Affairs* 6 (Winter 1977): 85–112.

17. Jonathan Glover, *Causing Death and Saving Lives* (Harmondsworth, U.K.: Penguin, 1977), applies utilitarianism to the problem of euthanasia and to other problems of killing, such as abortion and capital punishment.

18. *Infanticide and the Value of Life,* ed. Marvin Kohl (New York: Prometheus Books, 1978), is an anthology that concentrates on the morality of euthanasia for severely defective newborns.

19. *Killing and Letting Die,* ed. Bonnie Steinbock (Englewood Cliffs, NJ: Prentice-Hall, 1980), is a collection of readings that focus on the controversial distinction between killing and letting die.

20. Tom L. Beauchamp, "A Reply to Rachels on Active and Passive Euthanasia," in *Ethical Issues in Death and Dying,* ed. Tom L. Beauchamp and Seymour Perlin (Englewood Cliffs, NJ: Prentice-Hall, 1978), pp. 246–58, defends the moral significance of the distinction between active and passive euthanasia.

21. Thomas D. Sullivan, "Active and Passive Euthanasia: An Impertinent Distinction?" *Human Life Review* 3 (Summer 1977): 40–46, argues that Rachels's distinction between

active and passive euthanasia is impertinent and irrelevant. Rachels's reply to Sullivan is titled "More Impertinent Distinctions," in *Biomedical Ethics,* ed. T. A. Mappes and J. S. Zembaty (New York: McGraw-Hill, 1981), pp. 355–59.

22. John Ladd, "Positive and Negative Euthanasia," in *Ethical Issues Relating to Life and Death,* ed. John Ladd (Oxford: Oxford University Press, 1979), pp. 164–86, argues that no clear distinction can be made between killing and letting die but that they are not morally equivalent, either. His own position is that the distinction always depends on the context.

23. James Rachels, "Euthanasia," in *Matters of Life and Death,* 3rd ed., ed. Tom Regan (New York: Random House, 1993), pp. 30–68, relates the history of euthanasia, discusses the arguments for and against active euthanasia, and concludes with a proposal of how to legalize active euthanasia.

24. James Rachels, *The End of Life: Euthanasia and Morality* (Oxford: Oxford University Press, 1986), develops his view of euthanasia and defends it from criticism.

25. Robert Young, "Voluntary and Nonvoluntary Euthanasia," *The Monist* 59 (April 1976): 264–82, reviews a number of arguments used to show that voluntary active euthanasia is not justified and concludes that none of them is successful.

26. John A. Robertson, "Involuntary Euthanasia of Defective Newborns," *Stanford Law Review* 27 (January 1975): 213–61, argues that the utilitarian defense of euthanasia for defective newborns does not succeed in showing that it is justified.

27. Robert F. Weir, *Selective Nontreatment of Handicapped Newborns: Moral Dilemmas in Neonatal Medicine* (Oxford: Oxford University Press, 1984), discusses moral issues relating to the care and treatment of defective or handicapped newborns.

28. "Cruzan: Clear and Convincing?" *Hastings Center Report* 20 (Sept./Oct. 1990): 5–11, has six articles discussing the Cruzan case.

Chapter 4

Capital Punishment

Introduction

Factual Background

Since 1976 there have been 909 executions in the United States. The number of people put to death each year is increasing. In 2003 there were 65 executions, compared with 45 in 1996 and 31 in 1994. There were 98 executions in 1999. There were only 11 executions in the years 1976 to 1983. Very few women have been executed; the case of one of them, a 38-year-old born-again Christian named Karla Faye Tucker, received worldwide attention. (See the third Problem Case.) As for minorities, an almost equal number of whites and blacks have been executed since 1930, even though blacks constituted only about a tenth of the U.S. population during this period. A recent statistical study in Philadelphia found that for similar crimes, blacks received the death penalty at a 38 percent higher rate than all others.

As of April 2004, there were a total of 3,503 prisoners on death row awaiting capital punishment in the 38 states having this punishment. Of these, 1,473 were black, 353 were Hispanic, 1,596 white, and 81 classified as other. There were 49 women, including one who used to be a man.

In the past 20 years, at least 96 innocent men have been sentenced to death, and a number of men now on death row claim they are innocent. Since 1973, over 100 prisoners have been released from death row with evidence of their innocence. These innocent inmates spent about 9 years in prison before being released. In 2003, Governor George Ryan of Illinois commuted all of Illinois's death sentences. As one of his reasons for eliminating the death sentences, he cited the fact that 17 men had been wrongly convicted, including one who was unjustly imprisoned for 15 years. (See the last Problem Case.)

The death penalty is expensive. California spends $90 million a year on capital punishment. In Florida, the average total cost per executed prisoner is $3.2 million. In Texas, the cost per case is $2.3 million, but this is still three times the cost of keeping a criminal in maximum security for forty years. In 2003, the State of Kansas issued a report saying that capital cases are 70 percent more expensive than comparable noncapital cases, including incarceration. Various studies in North Carolina, Texas, Florida, and other states showed that the total costs of the death penalty exceeded the costs of life without parole sentences by about 38 percent.

The most common method of execution is lethal injection; thirty-seven states use this method. Electrocution is used in eight states, and the gas chamber in five states. Hanging is used in two states, and the firing squad is used in three states. Lethal injection is offered as an alternative method in every state having executions except Nebraska, which uses only electrocution.

The Eighth Amendment to the Constitution of the United States prohibits cruel and unusual punishment. For example, the medieval punishment of cutting off the hands of thieves seems to be cruel and unusual punishment. Is the death penalty another example of cruel and unusual punishment, and thus unconstitutional? The U.S. Supreme Court has given contradictory answers, saying it is unconstitutional in the cases of *Furman* (1972) and *Woodson* (1976), and then reversing itself and affirming that it is constitutional in *Gregg v. Georgia* (1976).

To be more specific, in the case of *Furman v. Georgia* (1972), the U. S. Supreme Court ruled (by a mere 5-to-4 majority) that the death penalty was unconstitutional because it was being administered in an arbitrary and capricious manner. Juries were allowed to impose the death sentence without any explicit guidelines or standards, and the result was that blacks were much more likely to receive the death penalty than whites.

After the *Furman* decision, states wishing to retain the death penalty reacted in two ways. One was to correct the arbitrary discretion of juries by making the death penalty mandatory for certain crimes. But in *Woodson v. North Carolina* (1976), the Court ruled (again by a 5-to-4 majority) that mandatory death sentences were unconstitutional.

The second attempt to counter the objection raised in *Furman* was to provide standards for juries. Georgia specified in its law ten statutory aggravating circumstances, one of which the jury had to find beyond reasonable doubt in order to render a death sentence. This second approach proved to be successful, for in *Gregg v. Georgia* (1976) the majority ruled, with Justices Marshall and Brennan dissenting, that the death penalty is not unconstitutional for the crime of murder, provided there are safeguards against any arbitrary or capricious imposition by juries.

In the case of *Atkins v. Virginia* (2002), the Supreme Court ruled that the execution of those with mental retardation is cruel and unusual punishment that is banned by the Eighth Amendment. Prior to the decision, eighteen states and the federal government prohibited such executions.

The Readings

The first reading is taken from *Gregg v. Georgia* (1976), the landmark decision legalizing the death penalty. In their majority opinion, Justices Steward, Powell, and Stevens try to explain why the death penalty is not cruel and unusual, and thus not in violation of the Eighth Amendment. They begin with an explanation of the concept of cruel and unusual. In their view, a punishment is cruel and unusual if it either fails to accord with evolving standards of decency or fails to accord with the dignity of humans that is the basic concept underlying the Eighth Amendment. This second stipulation rules out excessive punishment that involves unnecessary pain or is disproportionate to the crime. They argue that the death penalty does not satisfy either of these stipulations. It is acceptable to the majority of people. (A Gallup Poll in 2003 found that 64 percent supported the death penalty and 32 percent opposed it.) In 1976 thirty-five states had the death penalty, and in 2004 there were thirty-eight capital-punishment states. Furthermore, they argue, the death penalty is not excessive because it achieves two important social purposes, retribution and deterrence.

To fully understand the appeal to retribution, it is necessary to examine the theory on which it is based, namely, retributivism. The classical formulation of this theory is given by Immanuel Kant in the readings. According to Kant, the only justification for punishing a person is guilt. If a person is guilty of a crime, then justice requires that he or she be punished; if a person is not guilty, then no punishment is justified. In other words, guilt is both a necessary and a sufficient condition for justified punishment. Furthermore, Kant's view is that the punishment must fit the crime (or be proportionate to the crime) according to the biblical principle of retaliation (*lex talionis*) that says "eye for eye, tooth for tooth, life for life." Now what punishment fits the crime of murder using this principle? Kant insists that death, and only death, is the proper punishment for murder; no other punishment will satisfy the requirements of legal justice.

The other purpose of punishment that the justices appeal to in the majority opinion in *Gregg* is deterrence. The justices admit that the statistical evidence for deterrence seems inconclusive. Nevertheless, the justices still believe that the death penalty is a deterrent for carefully contemplated murders, such as murder for hire and murder by a person already in prison.

Critics present various objections to capital punishment. It is intentionally killing a person, and as such it is wrong unless proven otherwise. Thus the burden of proof is on those who want to defend it. It results in the execution of innocent people, and this injustice cannot be corrected. It is unfairly applied to minorities and the poor. Contrary to what the Supreme Court justices say, critics claim there is substantial evidence that capital punishment is not a better deterrent than life imprisonment, and in fact there is evidence that it acts as a counterdeterrent—that is, that it motivates suicidal people to commit murder. The 2002 FBI *Uniform Crime Report* says that the South accounts for over 80 percent of executions but also has the highest murder rate. By contrast, the Northeast, which has less than 1 percent of all executions in the country, has the lowest murder rate.

Ernest van den Haag replies to some of the objections raised by critics. The fact that the death penalty is applied in a discriminatory or capricious fashion is irrelevant to its justice or morality according to van den Haag. All that matters is whether or not the person to be executed deserves the punishment. If it is morally justified, then its distribution is irrelevant. Furthermore, the application of capital punishment is no more or less unjust than any other punishment. As for the fact that innocent people are executed, van den Haag points out that many human activities such as trucking cost the lives of innocent bystanders, and we do not give up these activities just because innocent people die. He agrees with the Supreme Court justices that there is no conclusive statistical evidence that the death penalty is a better deterrent than alternative punishments. But like the justices, he believes that death is feared more than imprisonment, and for this reason it deters some murderers who are not deterred by imprisonment. He adds, using a version of the best-bet argument (as I shall call it), that it is better to save the lives of a few prospective victims by deterring their murderers than to preserve the lives of convicted murderers because of the possibility that executing them will not deter others. The victim's lives are valuable and the lives of murderers are not. Instead of risking innocent lives by not executing, we should end the worthless lives of murderers, and bet that this will save some innocent lives. Van den Haag goes on to assert that the costs of the death penalty are not as important as doing justice, that the penalty is not inhuman or degrading or inconsistent with human dignity. It is the only fitting retribution for heinous crimes like murder.

Jeffrey H. Reiman raises difficulties for both Kant and van den Haag. Even if we accept Kant's retributivist law of *lex talionis*, it does not follow that we ought to do to criminals exactly what they did to their victims. Such an exact application of the *lex talionis* would require us to rape rapists and torture torturers, and such punishments are rejected by Reiman as horrible and uncivilized. Certainly torture seems to be a cruel and unusual punishment that is banned by the Eighth Amendment. As for van den Haag's commonsense argument that the death penalty will deter murderers who fear death more than imprisonment, Reiman replies that criminals committing crimes already face a substantial risk of death, and that doesn't deter them. In response to van den Haag's best-bet argument, Reiman points out that there might be a deterrent effect produced by *not* executing. If so, we will save more innocent lives by not executing than by executing. (In support of this, there is the statistic noted previously that the murder rate is higher in the South where most of the executions occur, and lower in the Northeast where only a few are executed.)

Philosophical Issues

How do we justify punishment? This is the basic issue at the heart of the debate about capital punishment. There seem to be two main theories about this, utilitarianism and retributivism.

Utilitarians justify punishment by appealing to good consequences, such as rehabilitation, protection of society, and deterrence of crime. Of course, capital punishment does not rehabilitate the person killed, and imprisonment would do the job of protecting society from criminals. Capital punishment is not necessary for protection of society. It seems, then, that deterrence of crime is the only possible justification of the death penalty for utilitarians, and indeed there has been much debate about the deterrence value of the death penalty.

Three main arguments have been used to demonstrate that execution deters criminals. First, there is the appeal to statistics. Even though the Supreme Court justices in the *Gregg* decision and van den Haag think that the statistics are inconclusive, critics do not agree. They claim that there is evidence that refutes the claim that capital punishment is a better deterrent than life imprisonment. According to a survey of the former and present presidents of the country's top academic criminological societies, 84 percent of these experts rejected the claim that the death penalty acts as a deterrent to murder. Ernest van den Haag admits this in "End the Death Penalty: Use Life Without Parole"—see the Suggested Readings.

Second, there are intuitive or commonsense arguments used by both the Supreme Court justices and van den Haag. The justices think that those who calculate their crimes will be deterred, and van den Haag believes that those who fear death will be motivated to avoid it. Against this, critics claim that instead of being deterred, suicidal people will be motivated to commit capital crimes. As we have seen, Reiman thinks the argument is based on unwarranted assumptions.

Third, there is van den Haag's best-bet argument, the argument that given uncertainties about whether execution deters, the best bet is to execute, for this involves gambling with guilty lives rather than innocent ones. The bet, of course, is that the executions will deter and thus save innocent lives. Critics deny the uncertainty; they claim that we have substantial evidence that execution does not deter better than life imprisonment. Reiman accepts the brutalization hypothesis that murders increase following executions rather than decrease. So if we want to save innocent lives, the best bet is to not execute murderers.

The other theory that is the focus of debate is retributivism. There are at least two different retributive principles, *lex talionis* and the principle of proportionality. The principle of proportionality says that the punishment should fit the crime or be proportional to the crime, so that a serious crime should receive a harsh punishment. No doubt murder is a serious crime, but is death the only punishment that fits this crime, as Kant says? Why isn't life imprisonment without parole a punishment that fits this crime, too? The trouble with the principle of proportionality is that it doesn't tell us which punishments fit which crimes. Not only is this a problem for the crime of murder, it is also a problem for crimes such as rape and torture and treason. Perhaps these crimes should be punished by execution, too. Or maybe death is not harsh enough; perhaps those crimes should be punished by solitary confinement or castration or even torture.

The biblical principle of *lex talionis* requires us to do to the criminal what he or she has done, "an eye for an eye." This principle is attacked by critics. They claim that this principle does not justify capital punishment because of the simple fact that most murderers are sent to prison, not executed. Clearly, we think that many crimes of murder do not deserve the death penalty; for example, we do not have the death sentence for homicides that are unpremeditated or accidental. Another objection is that we do have the death sentence for nonhomicidal crimes such as treason. This shows that the death sentence can be justified for crimes other than murder.

Gregg v. Georgia (1976)

THE U.S. SUPREME COURT

Potter Stewart (1915–1985) and Lewis F. Powell, Jr. (1908–1998) served as associate justices of the U.S. Supreme Court. John Paul Stevens continues to serve as an associate justice. Thurgood Marshall (1908–1993) retired from the Court in 1991; he was the first African American ever to be appointed.

The main issue before the Court in the case of *Gregg v. Georgia* (1976) was whether or not the death penalty violates the Eighth Amendment prohibition of

---

Source: Supreme Court, *Gregg v. Georgia* (1976).

cruel and unusual punishment. The majority of the Court, with Justice Marshall and Justice Brennan dissenting, held that the death penalty does not violate the Eighth Amendment because it is in accord with contemporary standards of decency. It serves both a deterrent and a retributive purpose, and in the case of the Georgia law being reviewed it is no longer arbitrarily applied.

In his dissenting opinion, Justice Marshall objects that the death sentence is excessive because a less severe penalty—life imprisonment—would accomplish the legitimate purposes of punishment. In reply to the claim that the death sentence is necessary for deterrence, Marshall asserts that the available evidence shows that this is not the case. As for the appeal to retribution, Marshall argues that the justification for the death penalty is not consistent with human dignity.

THE ISSUE IN THIS CASE is whether the imposition of the sentence of death for the crime of murder under the law of Georgia violates the Eighth and Fourteenth Amendments.

I

The petitioner, Troy Gregg, was charged with committing armed robbery and murder. In accordance with Georgia procedure in capital cases, the trial was in two stages, a guilt stage and a sentencing stage. . . .

. . . The jury found the petitioner guilty of two counts of murder.

At the penalty stage, which took place before the same jury . . . the trial judge instructed the jury that it could recommend either a death sentence or a life prison sentence on each count. . . . The jury returned verdicts of death on each count.

The Supreme Court of Georgia affirmed the convictions and the imposition of the death sentences for murder. . . . The death sentences imposed for armed robbery, however, were vacated on the grounds that the death penalty had rarely been imposed in Georgia for that offense. . . .

II

. . . The Georgia statute, as amended after our decision in Furman v. Georgia (1972), retains the death penalty for six categories of crime:

murder, kidnapping for ransom or where the victim is harmed, armed robbery, rape, treason, and aircraft hijacking. . . .

III

We address initially the basic contention that the punishment of death for the crime of murder is, under all circumstances, "cruel and unusual" in violation of the Eighth and Fourteenth Amendments of the Constitution. In Part IV of this opinion, we will consider the sentence of death imposed under the Georgia statutes at issue in this case.

The Court on a number of occasions has both assumed and asserted the constitutionality of capital punishment. In several cases that assumption provided a necessary foundation for the decision, as the Court was asked to decide whether a particular method of carrying out a capital sentence would be allowed to stand under the Eighth Amendment. But until *Furman v. Georgia* (1972), the Court never confronted squarely the fundamental claim that the punishment of death always, regardless of the enormity of the offense or the procedure followed in imposing the sentence, is cruel and unusual punishment in violation of the Constitution. Although this issue was presented and addressed in *Furman,* it was not resolved by the Court. Four justices would have held that capital punishment is not unconstitutional *per se;* two justices would have reached the opposite conclusion; and three justices, while agreeing that the statutes then before the Court were invalid as applied, left open the question whether such punishment may ever be imposed. We now hold that the punishment of death does not invariably violate the Constitution.

A

The history of the prohibition of "cruel and unusual" punishment already has been reviewed at length. The phrase first appeared in the English Bill of Rights of 1689, which was drafted by Parliament at the accession of William and Mary. The English version appears to have been directed against punishments unauthorized by statute and beyond the jurisdiction of the sentencing court, as well as those disproportionate to the offense involved. The American draftsmen, who adopted the English phrasing in drafting the Eighth Amendment, were primarily concerned, however, with proscribing "tortures" and other "barbarous" methods of punishment.

In the earliest cases raising Eighth Amendment claims, the Court focused on particular methods of execution to determine whether they were too cruel to pass constitutional muster. The constitutionality of the sentence of death itself was not at issue, and the criterion used to evaluate the mode of execution was its similarity to "torture" and other "barbarous" methods. . . .

But the Court has not confined the prohibition embodied in the Eighth Amendment to "barbarous" methods that were generally outlawed in the 18th century. Instead, the Amendment has been interpreted in a flexible and dynamic manner. The Court early recognized that "a principle to be vital must be capable of wider application than the mischief which gave it birth." Thus the clause forbidding "cruel and unusual" punishments "is not fastened to the obsolete but may acquire meaning as public opinion becomes enlightened by a humane justice." . . .

It is clear from the foregoing precedents that the Eighth Amendment has not been regarded as a static concept. As Mr. Chief Justice Warren said, in an oft quoted phrase, "[t]he Amendment must draw its meaning from the evolving standards of decency that mark the progress of a maturing society." Thus, an assessment of contemporary values concerning the infliction of a challenged sanction is relevant to the application of the Eighth Amendment. As we develop below more fully, this assessment does not call for a subjective judgment. It requires, rather, that we look to objective indicia that reflect the public attitude toward a given sanction.

But our cases also make clear that public perceptions of standards of decency with respect to criminal sanctions are not conclusive. A penalty also must accord with "the dignity of man," which is the "basic concept underlying the Eighth Amendment." This means, at least, that the punishment not be "excessive." When a form of punishment in the abstract (in this case, whether capital punishment may ever be imposed as a sanction for murder) rather than in the particular (the propriety of death as a penalty to be applied to a specific defendant for a specific crime) is under consideration, the inquiry into "excessiveness" has two aspects. First, the punishment must not involve the unnecessary and wanton infliction of pain. Second, the punishment must not be grossly out of proportion to the severity of the crime.

B

Of course, the requirements of the Eighth Amendment must be applied with an awareness of the limited role to be played by the courts. This does not mean that judges have no role to play, for the Eighth Amendment is a restraint upon the exercise of legislative power. . . .

But, while we have an obligation to ensure that constitutional bounds are not over-reached, we may not act as judges as we might as legislators. . . .

Therefore, in assessing a punishment selected by a democratically elected legislature against the constitutional measure, we presume its validity. We may not require the legislature to select the least severe penalty possible so long as the penalty selected is not cruelly inhumane or disproportionate to the crime involved. And a heavy burden rests on those who would attack the judgment of the representatives of the people.

This is true in part because the constitutional test is intertwined with an assessment of contemporary standards and the legislative judgment weighs heavily in ascertaining such standards. [I]n a democratic society legislatures, not courts, are constituted to respond to the will and consequently the moral values of the people."

The deference we owe to the decisions of the state legislatures under our federal system is enhanced where the specification of punishments is concerned, for "these are peculiarly questions of legislative policy." Caution is necessary lest this Court become, "under the aegis of the Cruel and Unusual Punishment Clause, the ultimate arbiter of the standards of criminal responsibility . . . throughout the country." A decision that a given punishment is impermissible under the Eighth Amendment cannot be reversed short of a constitutional amendment. The ability of the people to express their preference through the normal democratic processes, as well as through ballot referenda, is shut off. Revisions cannot be made in the light of further experience.

C

In the discussion to this point we have sought to identify the principles and considerations that guide a court in addressing an Eighth Amendment claim. We now consider specifically whether the sentence of death for the crime of murder is a *per se* violation of the Eighth and Fourteenth Amendments to the Constitution. We note first that history and precedent strongly support a negative answer to this question.

The imposition of the death penalty for the crime of murder has a long history of acceptance both in the United States and in England. . . .

It is apparent from the text of the Constitution itself that the existence of capital punishment was accepted by the Framers. At the time the Eighth Amendment was ratified, capital punishment was a common sanction in every State. Indeed, the First Congress of the United States enacted legislation providing death as the penalty for specified crimes. . . .

For nearly two centuries, this Court, repeatedly and often expressly, has recognized that capital punishment is not invalid *per se*. . . .

Four years ago, the petitioners in *Furman* and its companion cases predicated their argument primarily upon the asserted proposition that standards of decency had evolved to the point where capital punishment no longer could be tolerated. The petitioners in those cases said, in effect, that the evolutionary process had come to an end, and that standards of decency required that the Eighth Amendment be construed finally as prohibiting capital punishment for any crime regardless of its depravity and impact on society. This view was accepted by two Justices. Three other Justices were unwilling to go so far; focusing on the procedures by which convicted defendants were selected for the death penalty rather than on the actual punishment inflicted, they joined in the conclusion that the statutes before the Court were constitutionally invalid.

The petitioners in the capital cases before the Court today renew the "standards of decency" argument, but developments during the four years since *Furman* have undercut substantially the assumptions upon which their argument rested. Despite the continuing debate, dating back to the nineteenth century, over the morality and utility of capital punishment, it is now evident that a large proportion of American society continues to regard it as an appropriate and necessary criminal sanction.

The most marked indication of society's endorsement of the death penalty for murder is the legislative response to *Furman*. The legislatures of at least thirty-five States have enacted new statutes that provide for the death penalty for at least some crimes that result in the death of another person. And the Congress of the United States, in 1974, enacted a statute providing the death penalty for aircraft piracy that results in death. These recently adopted statutes have attempted to address the concerns expressed by the Court in *Furman* primarily (i) by specifying the factors to be weighed and the procedures to be followed in deciding when to impose a capital sentence, or (ii) by making the death penalty mandatory for specified crimes. But all of the post-*Furman* statutes make clear that capital punishment itself has not been rejected by the elected representatives of the people. . . .

The jury also is a significant and reliable objective index of contemporary values because it is so directly involved. The Court has said that "one of the most important functions any jury can perform in making . . . a selection [between life imprisonment and death for a defendant convicted in a capital case] is to maintain a link between contemporary community values and the penal system." It may be true that evolving standards have influenced juries in recent decades to be more discriminating in imposing the sentence of death. But the relative infrequency of jury verdicts imposing death sentence does not indicate rejection of capital punishment *per se*. Rather, the reluctance of juries in many cases to impose the sentence may well reflect the humane feeling that this most irrevocable of sanctions should be reserved for a small number of extreme cases. Indeed, the actions of juries in many states since *Furman* are fully compatible with the legislative judgments, reflected in the new statutes, as to the continued utility and necessity of capital punishment in appropriate cases. At the close of 1974 at least 254 persons had been sentenced to death since *Furman,* and by the end of March 1976, more than 460 persons were subject to death sentences.

As we have seen, however, the Eighth Amendment demands more than that a challenged punishment be acceptable to contemporary society. The Court also must ask whether it comports with the basic concept of human dignity at the core of the amendment. Although we cannot "invalidate a category of penalties because we deem less severe penalties adequate to serve the ends of penology," the sanction imposed cannot be so totally without penological justification that it results in the gratuitous infliction of suffering.

The death penalty is said to serve two principal social purposes: retribution and deterrence of capital crimes by prospective offenders.[1]

In part, capital punishment is an expression of society's moral outrage at particularly offensive conduct. This function may be unappealing to many, but it is essential in an ordered society that asks its citizens to rely on legal processes rather than self-help to vindicate their wrongs.

> The instinct for retribution is part of the nature of man, and channeling that instinct in the administration of criminal justice serves an important purpose in promoting the stability of a society governed by law. When people begin to believe that organized society is unwilling or unable to impose upon criminal offenders the punishment they "deserve," then there are sown the seeds of anarchy—of self-help, vigilante justice, and lynch law. *Furman v. Georgia* (Stewart, J., concurring).

Retribution is no longer the dominant objective of the criminal law, but neither is it a forbidden objective nor one inconsistent with our respect for the dignity of men. Indeed, the decision that capital punishment may be the appropriate sanction in extreme cases is an expression of the community's belief that certain crimes are themselves so grievous an affront to humanity that the only adequate response may be the penalty of death.

Statistical attempts to evaluate the worth of the death penalty as a deterrent to crimes of potential offenders have occasioned a great deal of debate. The results simply have been inconclusive. . . .

Although some of the studies suggest that the death penalty may not function as a significantly greater deterrent than lesser penalties, there is no

---

1 Another purpose that has been discussed is the incapacitation of dangerous criminals and the consequent prevention of crimes that they may otherwise commit in the future.

convincing empirical evidence either supporting or refuting this view. We may nevertheless assume safely that there are murderers, such as those who act in passion, for whom the threat of death has little or no deterrent effect. But for many others, the death penalty undoubtedly is a significant deterrent. There are carefully contemplated murders, such as murder for hire, where the possible penalty of death may well enter into the cold calculus that precedes the decision to act. And there are some categories of murder, such as murder by a life prisoner, where other sanctions may not be adequate.

The value of capital punishment as a deterrent of crime is a complex factual issue the resolution of which properly rests with the legislatures, which can evaluate the results of statistical studies in terms of their own local conditions and with a flexibility of approach that is not available to the courts. Indeed, many of the post-*Furman* statutes reflect just such a responsible effort to define those crimes and those criminals for which capital punishment is most probably an effective deterrent.

In sum, we cannot say that the judgment of the Georgia Legislature that capital punishment may be necessary in some cases is clearly wrong. Considerations of federalism, as well as respect for the ability of a legislature to evaluate, in terms of its particular State, the moral consensus concerning the death penalty and its social utility as a sanction, require us to conclude, in the absence of more convincing evidence, that the infliction of death as a punishment for murder is not without justification and thus is not constitutionally severe.

Finally, we must consider whether the punishment of death is disproportionate in relation to the crime for which it is imposed. There is no question that death as a punishment is unique in its severity and irrevocability. When a defendant's life is at stake, the Court has been particularly sensitive to insure that every safeguard is observed. But we are concerned here only with the imposition of capital punishment for the crime of murder, and when a life has been taken deliberately by the offender,[2] we cannot say that the punishment is invariably disproportionate to the crime. It is an extreme sanction, suitable to the most extreme of crimes.

We hold that the death penalty is not a form of punishment that may never be imposed, regardless of the circumstances of the offense, regardless of the character of the offender, and regardless of the procedure followed in reaching the decision to impose it.

IV

We now consider whether Georgia may impose the death penalty on the petitioner in this case.

A

While *Furman* did not hold that the infliction of the death penalty *per se* violates the Constitution's ban on cruel and unusual punishments, it did recognize that the penalty of death is different in kind from any other punishment imposed under our system of criminal justice. Because of the uniqueness of the death penalty, *Furman* held that it could not be imposed under sentencing procedures that created a substantial risk that it would be inflicted in an arbitrary and capricious manner. . . .

Furman mandates that where discretion is afforded a sentencing body on a matter so grave as the determination of whether a human life should be taken or spared, that discretion must be suitably directed and limited so as to minimize the risk of wholly arbitrary and capricious action.

It is certainly not a novel proposition that discretion in the area of sentencing be exercised in an informed manner. We have long recognized that "[f]or the determination of sentences, justice generally requires . . . that there be taken into account the circumstances of the offense

2 We do not address here the question whether the taking of the criminal's life is a proportionate sanction where no victim has been deprived of life—for example, when capital punishment is imposed for rape, kidnapping, or armed robbery that does not result in the death of any human being.

together with the character and propensities of the offender." . . .

Jury sentencing has been considered desirable in capital cases in order "to maintain a link between contemporary community values and the penal system—a link without which the determination of punishment could hardly reflect 'the evolving standards of decency that mark the progress of a maturing society.'" But it creates special problems. Much of the information that is relevant to the sentencing decision may have no relevance to the question of guilt, or may even be extremely prejudicial to a fair determination of that question. This problem, however, is scarcely insurmountable. Those who have studied the question suggest that a bifurcated procedure—one in which the question of sentence is not considered until the determination of guilt has been made—is the best answer. . . . When a human life is at stake and when the jury must have information prejudicial to the question of guilt but relevant to the question of penalty in order to impose a rational sentence, a bifurcated system is more likely to ensure elimination of the constitutional deficiencies identified in *Furman*.

But the provision of relevant information under fair procedural rules is not alone sufficient to guarantee that the information will be properly used in the imposition of punishment, especially if sentencing is performed by a jury. Since the members of a jury will have had little, if any, previous experience in sentencing, they are unlikely to be skilled in dealing with the information they are given. To the extent that this problem is inherent in jury sentencing, it may not be totally correctable. It seems clear, however, that the problem will be alleviated if the jury is given guidance regarding the factors about the crime and the defendant that the State, representing organized society, deems particularly relevant to the sentencing decision. . . .

While some have suggested that standards to guide a capital jury's sentencing deliberations are impossible to formulate, the fact is that such standards have been developed. When the

drafters of the Model Penal Code faced this problem, they concluded "that it is within the realm of possibility to point to the main circumstances of aggravation and of mitigation that should be weighed *and weighed against each other* when they are presented in a concrete case."[3] While such standards are by necessity

[3] The Model Penal Code proposes the following standards:

(3) Aggravating Circumstances.

(a) The murder was committed by a convict under sentence of imprisonment.

(b) The defendant was previously convicted of another murder or of a felony involving the use or threat of violence to the person.

(c) At the time the murder was committed the defendant also committed another murder.

(d) The defendant knowingly created a great risk of death to many persons.

(e) The murder was committed while the defendant was engaged or was an accomplice in the commission of, or an attempt to commit, or flight after committing or attempting to commit robbery, rape or deviate sexual intercourse by force or threat of force, arson, burglary or kidnapping.

(f) The murder was committed for the purpose of avoiding or preventing a lawful arrest or effecting an escape from lawful custody.

(g) The murder was committed for pecuniary gain.

(h) The murder was especially heinous, atrocious or cruel, manifesting exceptional depravity.

(4) Mitigating Circumstances.

(a) The defendant has no significant history of prior criminal activity.

(b) The murder was committed while the defendant was under the influence of extreme mental or emotional disturbance.

(c) The victim was a participant in the defendant's homicide conduct or consented to the homicidal act.

(d) The murder was committed under circumstances which the defendant believed to provide a moral justification or extenuation for his conduct.

(e) The defendant was an accomplice in a murder committed by another person and his participation in the homicide act was relatively minor.

(f) The defendant acted under duress or under the domination of another person.

(g) At the time of the murder, the capacity of the defendant to appreciate the criminality (wrongfulness) of his conduct or to conform his conduct to the requirements of law was impaired as a result of mental disease or defect or intoxication.

(h) The youth of the defendant at the time of the crime. (ALI Model Penal Code §210.6, Proposed Official Draft 1962).

somewhat general, they do provide guidance to the sentencing authority and thereby reduce the likelihood that it will impose a sentence that fairly can be called capricious or arbitrary. Where the sentencing authority is required to specify the factors it relied upon in reaching its decision, the further safeguard of meaningful appellate review is available to ensure that death sentences are not imposed capriciously or in a freakish manner.

In summary, the concerns expressed in *Furman* that the penalty of death not be imposed in an arbitrary or capricious manner can be met by a carefully drafted statute that ensures that the sentencing authority is given adequate information and guidance. As a general proposition these concerns are best met by a system that provides for a bifurcated proceeding at which the sentencing authority is apprised of the information relevant to the imposition of sentence and provided with standards to guide its use of the information.

We do not intend to suggest that only the above-described procedures would be permissible under *Furman* or that any sentencing system constructed along these general lines would inevitably satisfy the concerns of *Furman,* for each distinct system must be examined on an individual basis. Rather, we have embarked upon this general exposition to make clear that it is possible to construct capital-sentencing systems capable of meeting *Furman's* constitutional concerns.

B

We now turn to consideration of the constitutionality of Georgia's capital-sentencing procedures. In the wake of *Furman,* Georgia amended its capital punishment statute, but chose not to narrow the scope of its murder provisions. Thus, now as before *Furman,* in Georgia "[a] person commits murder when he unlawfully and with malice aforethought, either express or implied, causes the death of another human being." All persons convicted of murder "shall be punished by death or by imprisonment for life."

Georgia did act, however, to narrow the class of murderers subject to capital punishment by specifying ten statutory aggravating circumstances, one of which must be found by the jury to exist beyond a reasonable doubt before a death sentence can ever be imposed. In addition, the jury is authorized to consider any other appropriate aggravating or mitigating circumstances. The jury is not required to find any mitigating circumstance in order to make a recommendation of mercy that is binding on the trial court, but it must find a *statutory* aggravating circumstance before recommending a sentence of death.

These procedures require the jury to consider the circumstances of the crime and the criminal before it recommends sentence. No longer can a Georgia jury do as Furman's jury did: reach a finding of the defendant's guilt and then, without guidance or direction, decide whether he should live or die. Instead, the jury's attention is directed to the specific circumstances of the crime: Was it committed in the course of another capital felony? Was it committed for money? Was it committed on a peace officer or judicial officer? Was it committed in a particularly heinous way or in a manner that endangered the lives of many persons? In addition, the jury's attention is focused on the characteristics of the person who committed the crime: Does he have a record of prior convictions for capital offenses? Are there any special facts about this defendant that mitigate against imposing capital punishment (e.g., his youth, the extent of his cooperation with the police, his emotional state at the time of the crime)? As a result, while some jury discretion still exists, "the discretion to be exercised is controlled by clear and objective standards so as to produce nondiscriminatory application."

As an important additional safeguard against arbitrariness and caprice, the Georgia statutory scheme provides for automatic appeal of all death sentences to the State's Supreme Court. That court is required by statute to review each sentence of death and determine whether it was imposed under the influence of passion or prejudice, whether the evidence supports the jury's finding of statutory aggravating circumstance, and whether the sentence is disproportionate compared to those sentences imposed in similar cases.

In short, Georgia's new sentencing procedures require as a prerequisite to the imposition of the death penalty, specific jury findings as to the circumstances of the crime or the character of the defendant. Moreover, to guard further against a situation comparable to that presented in *Furman,* the Supreme Court of Georgia compares each death sentence with the sentences imposed on similarly situated defendants to ensure that the sentence of death in a particular case is not disproportionate. On their face these procedures seem to satisfy the concerns of *Furman.* No longer should there be "no meaningful basis for distinguishing the few cases in which [the death penalty] is imposed from the many cases in which it is not.". . .

V

The basic concern of *Furman* centered on those defendants who were being condemned to death capriciously and arbitrarily. Under the procedures before the Court in that case, sentencing authorities were not directed to give attention to the nature or circumstances of the crime committed or to the character or record of the defendant. Left unguided, juries imposed the death sentence in a way that could only be called freakish. The new Georgia sentencing procedures, by contrast, focus the jury's attention on the particularized nature of the crime and the particularized characteristics of the individual defendant. While the jury is permitted to consider any aggravating or mitigating circumstances, it must find and identify at least one statutory aggravating factor before it may impose a penalty of death. In this way the jury's discretion is channeled. No longer can a jury wantonly and freakishly impose the death sentence; it is always circumscribed by the legislative guidelines. In addition, the review function of the Supreme Court of Georgia affords additional assurance that the concerns that prompted our decision in *Furman* are not present to any significant degree in the Georgia procedure applied here.

For the reasons expressed in this opinion, we hold that the statutory system under which Gregg was sentenced to death does not violate the Constitution. Accordingly, the judgment of the Georgia Supreme Court is affirmed.

DISSENTING OPINION

In *Furman v. Georgia* (1972) (concurring opinion), I set forth at some length my views on the basic issue presented to the Court in [this case]. The death penalty, I concluded, is a cruel and unusual punishment prohibited by the Eighth and Fourteenth Amendments. That continues to be my view.

I have no intention of retracing the "long and tedious journey" that led to my conclusion in *Furman.* My sole purposes here are to consider the suggestion that my conclusion in *Furman* has been undercut by developments since then, and briefly to evaluate the basis for my Brethren's holding that the extinction of life is a permissible form of punishment under the Cruel and Unusual Punishments Clause.

In *Furman,* I concluded that the death penalty is constitutionally invalid for two reasons. First, the death penalty is excessive. And second, the American people, fully informed as to the purposes of the death penalty and its liabilities, would in my view reject it as morally unacceptable.

Since the decision in *Furman,* the legislatures of thirty-five States have enacted new statutes authorizing the imposition of the death sentence for certain crimes, and Congress has enacted a law providing the death penalty for air piracy resulting in death. I would be less than candid if I did not acknowledge that these developments have a significant bearing on a realistic assessment of the moral acceptability of the death penalty to the American people. But if the constitutionality of the death penalty turns, as I have urged, on the opinion of an *informed* citizenry, then even the enactment of new death statutes cannot be viewed as conclusive. In *Furman,* I observed that the American people are largely unaware of the information critical to a judgment on the morality of the death penalty, and concluded that if they were better informed they would consider it shocking, unjust, and unacceptable. A recent study, conducted after the enactment of the post-*Furman* statutes, has confirmed that the American people know little about the death penalty, and that the opinions of an informed public would differ significantly from those of a public unaware of the consequences and effects of the death penalty.

Even assuming, however, that the post-*Furman* enactment of statutes authorizing the death penalty renders the prediction of the views of an informed citizenry an uncertain basis for a constitutional decision, the enactment of those statutes has no bearing whatsoever on the conclusion that the death penalty is unconstitutional because it is excessive. An excessive penalty is invalid under the Cruel and Unusual Punishments Clause "even though popular sentiment may favor" it. The inquiry here, then, is simply whether the death penalty is necessary to accomplish the legitimate legislative purposes in punishment, or whether a less severe penalty—life imprisonment—would do as well.

The two purposes that sustain the death penalty as nonexcessive in the Court's view are general deterrence and retribution. In *Furman,* I canvassed the relevant data on the deterrent effect of capital punishment. The state of knowledge at that point, after literally centuries of debate, was summarized as follows by a United Nations Committee:

> It is generally agreed between the retentionists and abolitionists, whatever their opinions about the validity of comparative studies of deterrence, that the data which now exist show no correlation between the existence of capital punishment and lower rates of capital crime.

The available evidence, I concluded in *Furman,* was convincing that "capital punishment is not necessary as a deterrent to crime in our society.". . .

The evidence I reviewed in *Furman* remains convincing, in my view, that "capital punishment is not necessary as a deterrent to crime in our society." The justification for the death penalty must be found elsewhere.

The other principal purpose said to be served by the death penalty is retribution. The notion that retribution can serve as a moral justification for the sanction of death finds credence in the opinion of my Brothers Stewart, Powell, and Stevens. . . . It is this notion that I find to be the most disturbing aspect of today's unfortunate [decision].

The concept of retribution is a multifaceted one, and any discussion of its role in the criminal law must be undertaken with caution. On one level, it can be said that the notion of retribution or reprobation is the basis of our insistence that only those who have broken the law be punished, and in this sense the notion is quite obviously central to a just system of criminal sanctions. But our recognition that retribution plays a crucial role in determining who may be punished by no means requires approval of retribution as a general justification for punishment. It is the question whether retribution can provide a moral justification for punishment—in particular, capital punishment—that we must consider.

My Brothers Stewart, Powell, and Stevens offer the following explanation of the retributive justification for capital punishments:

> The instinct for retribution is part of the nature of man, and channeling that instinct in the administration of criminal justice serves an important purpose in promoting the stability of a society governed by law. When people begin to believe that organized society is unwilling or unable to impose upon criminal offenders the punishment they "deserve," then there are sown the seeds of anarchy—of self-help, vigilante justice, and lynch law.

This statement is wholly inadequate to justify the death penalty. As my Brother Brennan stated in *Furman,* "[t]here is no evidence whatever that utilization of imprisonment rather than death encourages private blood feuds and other disorders." It simply defies belief to suggest that the death penalty is necessary to prevent the American people from taking the law into their own hands.

In a related vein, it may be suggested that the expression of moral outrage through the imposition of the death penalty serves to reinforce basic moral values—that it marks some crimes as particularly offensive and therefore to be avoided. The argument is akin to a deterrence argument, but differs in that it contemplates the individual's shrinking from antisocial conduct, not because he fears punishment, but because he has been told in the strongest possible way that the conduct is wrong. This contention, like the previous one, provides no support for the death penalty. It is inconceivable that any individual concerned about conforming his conduct to what society says is "right" would fail to realize that murder is "wrong" if the penalty were simply life imprisonment.

The foregoing contentions—that society's expression of moral outrage through the imposition of the death penalty preempts the citizenry from taking the law into its own hands and reinforces moral values—are not retributive in the purest sense. They are essentially utilitarian in that they portray the death penalty as valuable because of its beneficial results. These justifications for the death penalty are inadequate because the penalty is, quite clearly I think, not necessary to the accomplishment of those results.

There remains for consideration, however, what might be termed the purely retributive justification for the death penalty—that the death penalty is appropriate, not because of its beneficial effect on society, but because the taking of the murderer's life is itself morally good. Some of the language of the opinion of my Brothers Stewart, Powell, and Stevens . . . appears positively to embrace this notion of retribution for

its own sake as a justification for capital punishment. They state:

> [T]he decision that capital punishment may be the appropriate sanction in extreme cases is an expression of the community's belief that certain crimes are themselves so grievous an affront to humanity that the only adequate response may be the penalty of death.

They then quote with approval from Lord Justice Denning's remarks before the British Commission on Capital Punishment:

> The truth is that some crimes are so outrageous that society insists on adequate punishment, because the wrong-doer deserves it, irrespective of whether it is a deterrent or not.

Of course, it may be that these statements are intended as no more than observations as to the popular demands that it is thought must be responded to in order to prevent anarchy. But the implication of the statements appears to me to be quite different—namely, that society's judgment that the murderer "deserves" death must be respected not simply because the preservation of order requires it, but because it is appropriate that society make the judgment and carry it out. It is the latter notion, in particular, that I consider to be fundamentally at odds with the Eighth Amendment. The mere fact that the community demands the murderer's life in return for the evil he has done cannot sustain the death penalty, for as Justices Stewart, Powell, and Stevens remind us, "the Eighth Amendment demands more than that a challenged punishment be acceptable to contemporary society." To be sustained under the Eighth Amendment, the death penalty must "compor[t] with the basic concept of human dignity at the core of the Amendment"; the objective in imposing it must be "[consistent] with our respect for the dignity of [other] men." Under these standards, the taking of life "because the wrongdoer deserves it" surely must fail, for such a punishment has as its very basis the total denial of the wrongdoer's dignity and worth.

The death penalty, unnecessary to promote the goal of deterrence or to further any legitimate notion of retribution, is an excessive penalty forbidden by the Eighth and Fourteenth Amendments. I respectfully dissent from the Court's judgment upholding the [sentence] of death imposed upon the [petitioner in this case].

Review Questions

1. How did the justices rule in *Furman v. Georgia* (1972), and by contrast, how do they rule in this case?
2. According to the justices, what is the basic concept underlying the Eighth Amendment?
3. According to the justices, in what two ways may a punishment be excessive?
4. According to the justices, why doesn't the death penalty violate contemporary standards of decency?
5. The justices say that the death penalty serves two principal social purposes. What are they, and how are they supposed to work?
6. What safeguards against the arbitrary and capricious application of the death sentence are suggested by the justices?
7. Explain Justice Marshall's objections and his criticisms of the majority opinion.

Discussion Questions

1. The Georgia statute retains the death penalty for six crimes, including rape, armed robbery, and treason. Do you agree that persons guilty of these crimes should receive the death sentence? Explain your view.
2. Try to give a precise definition of the phrase "cruel and unusual." Can you do it?
3. How could it be conclusively proven that the death penalty deters potential criminals better than life imprisonment?
4. Should the instinct for retribution be satisfied? Defend your answer.

The Retributive Theory of Punishment

IMMANUEL KANT

For biographical information on Kant, see his reading in Chapter 1.

In Kant's retributive theory of punishment, punishment is justified not by any good results but simply by the criminal's guilt. Criminals must pay for their crimes; otherwise an injustice has occurred. Furthermore, the punishment must fit the crime. Kant asserts that the only punishment that is appropriate for the crime of murder is the death of the murderer. As he puts it, "Whoever has committed a murder must *die*."

Source: Immanuel Kant, "The Retributive Theory of Punishment" from *The Philosophy of Law*, Part II, trans. W. Hastie (1887).

JUDICIAL OR JURIDICAL punishment (*poena forensis*) is to be distinguished from natural punishment (*poena naturalis*), in which crime as vice punishes itself, and does not as such come within the cognizance of the legislator. Juridical punishment can never be administered merely as a means for promoting another good, either with regard to the criminal himself or to civil society, but must in all cases be imposed only because the individual on whom it is inflicted *has committed a crime.* For one man ought never to be dealt with merely as a means subservient to the purpose of another, nor be mixed up with the subjects of real right. Against such treatment his inborn personality has a right to protect him, even although he may be condemned to lose his civil personality. He must first be found guilty and *punishable,* before there can be any thought of drawing from his punishment any benefit for himself or his fellow-citizens. The penal law is a categorical imperative; and woe to him who creeps through the serpent-windings of utilitarianism to discover some advantage that may discharge him from the justice of punishment, or even from the due measure of it, according to the pharisaic maxim: "It is better that *one* man should die than that the whole people should perish." For if justice and righteousness perish, human life would no longer have any value in the world. What, then, is to be said of such a proposal as to keep a criminal alive who has been condemned to death, on his being given to understand that if he agreed to certain dangerous experiments being performed upon him, he would be allowed to survive if he came happily through them? It is argued that physicians might thus obtain new information that would be of value to the commonweal. But a court of justice would repudiate with scorn any proposal of this kind if made to it by the medical faculty; for justice would cease to be justice, if it were bartered away for any consideration whatever.

But what is the mode and measure of punishment which public justice takes as its principle and standard? It is just the principle of equality, by which the pointer of the scale of justice is made to incline no more to the one side than the other. It may be rendered by saying that the undeserved evil which any one commits on another, is to be regarded as perpetrated on himself. Hence it may be said: "If you slander another, you slander yourself; if you steal from another, you steal from yourself; if you strike another, you strike yourself; if you kill another, you kill yourself." This is the right of retaliation (*jus talionis*); and properly understood, it is the only principle which in regulating a public court, as distinguished from mere private judgment, can definitely assign both the quality and the quantity of a just penalty. All other standards are wavering and uncertain; and on account of other considerations involved in them, they contain no principle comfortable to the sentence of pure and strict justice. It may appear, however, that difference of social status would not admit the application of the principle of retaliation, which is that of "like with like." But although the application may not in all cases be possible according to the letter, yet as regards the effect it may always be attained in practice, by due regard being given to the disposition and sentiment of the parties in the higher social sphere. Thus a pecuniary penalty on account of a verbal injury, may have no direct proportion to the injustice of slander; for one who is wealthy may be able to indulge himself in this offense for his own gratification. Yet the attack committed on the honor of the party aggrieved may have its equivalent in the pain inflicted upon the pride of the aggressor, especially if he is condemned by the judgment of the court, not only to retract and apologize, but to submit to some meaner ordeal, as kissing the hand of the injured person. In like manner, if a man of the highest rank has violently assaulted an innocent citizen of the lower orders, he may be condemned not only to apologize but to undergo a solitary and painful imprisonment, whereby, in addition to the discomfort endured, the vanity of the offender would be painfully affected, and the very shame of his position would constitute an adequate retaliation after the principle of like with like. But how then would we render the statement:

"If you *steal* from another, you steal from yourself"? In this way, that whoever steals anything makes the property of all insecure; he therefore robs himself of all security in property, according to the right of retaliation. Such a one has nothing, and can acquire nothing, but he has the will to live; and this is only possible by others supporting him. But as the state should not do this gratuitously, he must for this purpose yield his powers to the state to be used in penal labour; and thus he falls for a time, or it may be for life, into a condition of slavery. But whoever has committed murder, must *die*. There is, in this case, no juridical substitute or surrogate, that can be given or taken for the satisfaction of justice. There is no *likeness* or proportion between life, however painful, and death; and therefore there is no equality between the crime of murder and the retaliation of it but what is judicially accomplished by the execution of the criminal. His death, however, must be kept free from all maltreatment that would make the humanity suffering in his person loathsome or abominable. Even if a civil society resolved to dissolve itself with the consent of all its members—as might be supposed in the case of a people inhabiting an island resolving to separate and scatter themselves throughout the whole world—the last murderer lying in the prison ought to be executed before the resolution was carried out. This ought to be done in order that everyone may realize the desert of his deeds, and that bloodguiltiness may not remain upon the people; for otherwise they might all be regarded as participators in the murder as a public violation of justice.

The equalization of punishment with crime, is therefore only possible by the cognition of the judge extending even to the penalty of death, according to the right of retaliation.

Review Questions

1. According to Kant, who deserves judicial punishment?
2. Why does Kant reject the maxim "It is better that *one* man should die than that the whole people should perish"?
3. How does Kant explain the principle of retaliation?

Discussion Questions

1. Does Kant have any good reason to reject the "serpent-windings of utilitarianism"?
2. Is death always a just punishment for murder? Can you think of any exceptions?

The Ultimate Punishment: A Defense of Capital Punishment

ERNEST VAN DEN HAAG

Ernest van den Haag (1915–2002) was John M. Olin Professor of Jurisprudence and Public Policy at Fordham University. For many years he had a private practice in psychoanalytical counseling, and for forty-five years he was a consultant and contributor to the *National Review*. His books include *The Fabric of Society* (1957),

Political Violence and Civil Disobedience (1973), and *Punishing Criminals: Concerning a Very Old and Painful Question* (1975).

Van den Haag replies to various objections to capital punishment. The fact that capital punishment is applied in a discriminatory manner is irrelevant to its morality. Nor does it matter if innocents die, because many activities such as trucking and construction cost the lives of innocent bystanders. The cost is not as important as doing justice. It is not excessive punishment for heinous crimes, and it is not inconsistent with human dignity. Van den Haag agrees that there is no conclusive evidence showing that the death penalty is a more effective deterrent than other punishments. But he thinks that deterrence is not decisive for either those opposed or those in favor of the death penalty. Still he believes that the death penalty is feared more than imprisonment, and for that reason deters some potential murderers. He goes on to use a subtle argument, sometimes called the "best-bet argument," to conclude that we should still use the death penalty because it might save innocents whose lives are more valuable than guilty murderers who are executed. In effect, the death penalty is a better bet than other punishments because it involves gambling with guilty lives rather than innocent lives.

IN AN AVERAGE YEAR ABOUT 20,000 homicides occur in the United States. Fewer than 300 convicted murderers are sentenced to death. But because no more than 30 murderers have been executed in any recent year, most convicts sentenced to death are likely to die of old age.[1] Nonetheless, the death penalty looms large in discussions: It raises important moral questions independent of the number of executions.[2]

The death penalty is our harshest punishment.[3] It is irrevocable: it ends the existence of those punished, instead of temporarily imprisoning them. Further, although not intended to cause physical pain, execution is the only corporal punishment still applied to adults.[4] These singular characteristics contribute to the perennial, impassioned controversy about capital punishment.

I. DISTRIBUTION

Consideration of the justice, morality, or usefulness of capital punishment is often conflated with objections to its alleged discriminatory or capricious distribution among the guilty. Wrongly so. If capital punishment is immoral *in se,* no distribution cannot affect the quality of what is distributed, be it punishments or rewards. Discriminatory or capricious distribution thus could not justify abolition of the death penalty. Further, maldistribution inheres no more in capital punishment than in any other punishment.

Maldistribution between the guilty and the innocent is, by definition, unjust. But the injustice does not lie in the nature of the punishment.

---

1 Death row as a semipermanent residence is cruel, because convicts are denied the normal amenities of prison life. Thus, unless death row residents are integrated into the prison population, the continuing accumulation of convicts on death row should lead us to accelerate either the rate of executions or the rate of commutations. I find little objection to integration.

2 The debate about the insanity defense is important for analogous reasons.

3 Some writers, for example, Cesare Bonesana, Marchese di Beccaria, have thought that life imprisonment is more severe. *See* C. Beccaria, *DeiDelitti e Delle Pene* (1764) pp. 62–70. More recently, Jacques Barzun has expressed this view. *See* Barzun, *In Favor of Capital Punishment,* in *The Death Penalty in America,* ed. H. Bedau (1964), p. 154. However, the overwhelming majority of both abolitionists and of convicts under death sentence prefer life imprisonment to execution.

4 For a discussion of the sources of opposition to corporal punishment, see E. van den Haag, *Punishing Criminals* (1975) pp. 196–206.

Because of the finality of the death penalty, the most grievous maldistribution occurs when it is imposed on the innocent. However, the frequent allegations of discrimination and capriciousness refer to maldistribution among the guilty and not to the punishment of the innocent.[5]

Maldistribution of any punishment among those who deserve it is irrelevant to its justice or morality. Even if poor or black convicts guilty of capital offenses suffer capital punishment, and other convicts equally guilty of the same crimes do not, a more equal distribution, however desirable, would merely be more equal. It would not be more just to the convicts under sentence of death.

Punishments are imposed on persons, not on racial or economic groups. Guilt is personal. The only relevant question is, does the person to be executed deserve the punishment? Whether or not others who deserved the same punishment, whatever their economic or racial group, have avoided execution is irrelevant. If they have, the guilt if the executed convicts would not be diminished, nor would their punishment be less deserved. To put the issue starkly, if the death penalty were imposed on guilty blacks, but not on guilty whites, or, if it were imposed by a lottery among the guilty, this irrationally discriminatory or capricious distribution would neither make the penalty unjust, nor cause anyone to be unjustly punished, despite the undue impunity bestowed on others.[6]

Equality, in short, seems morally less important than justice. And justice is independent of distributional inequalities. The ideal of equal justice demands that justice be equally distributed, not that it be replaced by equality. Justice requires that as many of the guilty as possible be punished, regardless of whether others have avoided punishment. To let these others escape the deserved punishment does not do justice to them, or to society. But it is not unjust to those who could not escape.

These moral considerations are not meant to deny that irrational discrimination, or capriciousness, would be inconsistent with constitutional requirements. But I am satisfied that the Supreme Court has in fact provided for adherence to the constitutional requirement of equality as much as is possible. Some inequality is indeed unavoidable as a practical matter in any system.[7] But, *ultra posse nemo obligatur* (nobody is bound beyond ability).[8]

Recent data reveal little direct racial discrimination in the sentencing of those arrested and convicted of murder.[9] The abrogation of the death penalty for rape has eliminated a major source of racial discrimination. Concededly, some discrimination based on the race of murder victims may exist; yet, this discrimination affects criminal murder victimizers in an unexpected way. Murderers of whites are thought more likely to be executed than murderers of blacks.

---

5 *See infra* pp. 1664–65.

6 Justice Douglas, concurring in *Furman v. Georgia*, 408 U.S. 238 (1972), wrote that "a law which . . . reaches that [discriminatory] result in practice has no more sanctity that a law which in terms provides the same." *Id.* at 256 (Douglas, J., concurring). Indeed, a law legislating this result "in terms" would be inconsistent with the "equal protection of the laws" provided the result could be changed by changing the distributional practice. Thus, Justice Douglas notwithstanding, a discriminatory result does not make the death penalty unconstitutional, unless the penalty ineluctable must produce that result to an unconstitutional degree.

7 The ideal of equality, unlike the ideal retributive justice (which can be approximated separately in each instance), is clearly unattainable unless all guilty persons are apprehended, and thereafter tried, convicted, and sentenced by the same court, at the same time. Unequal justice is the best we can do; it is still better than the injustice, equal or unequal, that occurs if, for the sake of equality, we deliberately allow some who could be punished to escape.

8 Equality, even without justice, may remain a strong psychological, and therefore political, demand. Yet Charles Black, by proving the *inevitability* of "caprice" (inequality), undermines his own constitutional argument, because it seems unlikely that the Constitution's fifth and fourteenth amendments were meant to authorize the death penalty only under unattainable conditions. See Black, *Capital Punishment: The Inevitability of Caprice and Mistake* (1974).

9 See Bureau of Justice Statistics, U.S. Dept of Justice, Bulletin No. NCJ-98,399, Capital Punishment, 1984, at 9 (1985); Johnson, *The Executioner's Bias, Nat'l Rev.* (Nov. 15, 1985) 44.

Black victims, then, are less fully vindicated than white ones. However, because most black murderers kill blacks, black murderers are spared the death penalty more often than are white murderers. They fare better than most white murderers.[10] The motivation behind unequal distribution of the death penalty may well have been to discriminate against blacks, but the result has favored them. Maldistribution is thus a straw man for empirical as well as analytical reasons.

II. MISCARRIAGES OF JUSTICE

In a recent survey Professors Hugo Adam Bedau and Michael Radelet found that 7,000 persons were executed in the United States between 1900 and 1985 and that 35 were innocent of capital crimes.[11] Among the innocents they list Sacco and Vanzetti as well as Ethel and Julius Rosenberg. Although their data may be questionable, I do not doubt that, over a long enough period, miscarriages of justice will occur even in capital cases.

Despite precautions, nearly all human activities, such as trucking, lighting, or construction, cost the lives of some innocent bystanders. We do not give up these activities, because the advantages, moral or material, outweigh the unintended losses.[12] Analogously, for those who think the death penalty just, miscarriages of justice are offset by the moral benefits and the usefulness of doing justice. For those who think the death penalty unjust even when it does not miscarry, miscarriages can hardly be decisive.

III. DETERRENCE

Despite much recent work, there has been no conclusive statistical demonstration that the death penalty is a better deterrent than are alternative punishments.[13] However, deterrence is less than decisive for either side. Most abolitionists acknowledge that they would continue to favor abolition even if the death penalty were shown to deter more murders than alternatives could deter.[14] Abolitionists appear to value the life of a convicted murderer or, at least, his nonexecution, more highly than they value the lives of the innocent victims who might be spared by deterring prospective murderers.

Deterrence is not altogether decisive for me either. I would favor retention of the death penalty as retribution even if it were shown that the threat of execution could not deter prospective murderers not already deterred by the threat of imprisonment.[15] Still, I believe the death penalty,

---

10 It barely need be said that any discrimination *against* (for example, black murderers of whites) must also be discrimination *for* (for example, black murderers of blacks).

11 Bedau and Radelet, *Miscarriages of Justice in Potentially Capital Cases* (1st draft, Oct. 1985) (on file at Harvard Law School Library).

12 An excessive number of trucking accidents or of miscarriages of justice could offset the benefits gained by trucking or the practice of doing justice. We are, however, far from this situation.

13 For a sample of conflicting views on the subject, see Baldus and Cole, "A Comparison of the Work of Thorsten Sellin and Isaac Ehrlich on the Deterrent Effect of Capital Punishment," 85 *Yale L.J.* 170 (1975); Bowers and Pierce, "Deterrence or Brutalization: What Is the Effect of Executions?" 26 *Crime & Delinq.* 453 (1980); Bowers and Pierce "The Illusion of Deterrence in Isaac Ehrlich's Research on Capital Punishment," 85 *Yale L.J.* 187 (1975); Ehrlich, "Fear of Deterrence: A Critical Evaluation of the 'Report of the Panel on Research on Deterrent and Incapacitate Effects'," 6 *J Legal Stud.* 293 (1977); Ehrlich, "The Deterrent Effect of Capital Punishment: A Question of Life and Death," 65 *Am. Econ. Rev.* 397 (1975): 415–16; Ehrlich and Gibbons, "On the Measurement of the Deterrent Effect of Capital Punishment and the Theory of Deterrence," 6 *J. Legal Stud.* 35 (1977).

14 For most abolitionists, the discrimination argument, *see supra* pp. 1662–64, is similarly nondecisive: they would favor abolition even if there could be no racial discrimination.

15 If executions were shown to increase the murder rate in the long run, I would favor abolition. Sparing the innocent victims who would be spared, *ex hypothesi*, by the nonexecution of murderes would be more important to me than the execution, however just, of murderers. But although there is a lively discussion of the subject, no serious evidence exists to support the hypothesis that executions produce a higher murder rate. *Cf.* Phllips, "*The deterrent Effect of Capital Punishment: New Evidence on an Old Controversy,*" 86 *Am. J. Soc.* 139 (1980) (arguing that murder rates drop immediately after executions of criminals).

because of its finality, is more feared than imprisonment, and deters some prospective murderers not deterred by the thought of imprisonment. Sparing the lives of even a few prospective victims by deterring their murderers is more important than preserving the lives of convicted murderers because of the possibility, or even the probability, that executing them would not deter others. Whereas the lives of the victims who might be saved are valuable, that of the murderer has only negative value, because of his crime. Surely the criminal law is meant to protect the lives of potential victims in preference to those of actual murderers.

Murder rates are determined by many factors; Neither the severity nor the probability of the threatened sanction is always decisive. However, for the long run, I share the view of Sir James Fitzjames Stephen: "Some men, probably, abstain from murder because they fear that if they committed murder they would be hanged. Hundreds of thousands abstain from it because they regard it with horror. One great reason why they regard it with horror is that murderers are hanged."[16] Penal sanctions are useful in the long run for the formation of the internal restraints so necessary to control crime. The severity and finality of the death penalty is appropriate to the seriousness and the finality of murder.[17]

IV. INCIDENTAL ISSUES: COST, RELATIVE SUFFERING, BRUTALIZATION

Many nondecisive issues are associated with capital punishment. Some believe that the monetary cost of appealing a capital sentence is excessive.[18] Yet most comparisons of the cost of life imprisonment with the cost of execution, apart from their dubious relevance, are flawed at least by the implied assumption that life prisoners will generate no judicial costs during their imprisonment. At any rate, the actual monetary costs are trumped by the importance of doing justice.

Others insist that a person sentenced to death suffers more than his victim suffered, and that this (excess) suffering is undue according to the *lex talionis* (rule of retaliation).[19] We cannot know whether the murderer on death row suffers more than his victim suffered; however, unlike the murderer, the victim deserved none of the suffering inflicted. Further, the limitations of the *lex talionis* were meant to restrain private vengeance, not the social retribution that has taken its place. Punishment—regardless of the motivation—is not intended to revenge, offset, or compensate for the victim's suffering, or to be measured by it. Punishment is to vindicate the law and the social order undermined by the crime. This is why a kidnapper's penal confinement is not limited to the period for which he imprisoned his victim; nor is a burglar's confinement meant merely to offset the suffering or the harm he caused his victim; nor is it meant only to offset the advantage he gained.[20]

Another argument heard at least since Beccaria[21] is that, by killing a murderer, we encourage, endorse, or legitimize unlawful killing Yet, although all punishments are meant to be unpleasant, it is seldom argued that they legitimize the unlawful imposition of identical unpleasantness. Imprisonment is not thought to legitimize

---

16 H. Gross, *A Theory of Criminal Justice* 489 (1979) (attributing this passage to Sir James Fitzjames Stephen).

17 *Weems v. United States*, 217 U.S. 349 (1910) suggests that penalties be proportionate to the seriousness of the crime—a common theme in criminal law. Murder, therefore, demands more than life imprisonment. In modern times, our sensibility requires that the range of punishments be narrower than the range of crime—but not so narrow as to exclude the death penalty.

18 *Cf.* Kaplan "Administering Capital Punishment," 36 *U. Fla. L. Rev.* 177, 178 (1984): 190–91 (noting the high cost of appealing a capital sentence).

19 For an example of this view, see A. Camus, *Reflections on the Guillotine* (1959), pp. 24–30. On the limitations allegedly imposed by the *lex talionis*, see Reiman "*Justice, Civilization and the Death Penalty: Answering van den Haag*," 14 *Phil. & Pub. Aff.* 115, (1985) 119–34.

20 Thus restitution (a civil liability) cannot satisfy the punitive purpose of penal sanctions, whether the purpose be retributive or deterrent.

21 *See supra* note 3.

kidnapping; neither are fines thought to legitimize robbery. The difference between murder and execution, or between kidnapping and imprisonment, is that the first is unlawful and undeserved, the second a lawful and deserved punishment for an unlawful act. The physical similarities of the punishment to the crime are irrelevant. The relevant difference is not physical, but social.[22]

V. JUSTICE, EXCESS, DEGRADATION

We threaten punishments in order to deter crime. We impose them not only to make the threats credible but also as retribution (justice) for the crimes that were not deterred. Threats and punishments are necessary to deter and deterrence is a sufficient practical justification for them. Retribution is an independent moral justification.[23] Although penalties can be unwise, repulsive, or inappropriate, and those punished can be pitiable, in a sense the infliction of legal punishment on a guilty person cannot be unjust. By committing the crime, the criminal volunteered to assume the risk of receiving a legal punishment that he could have avoided by not committing the crime. The punishment he suffers is the punishment he voluntarily risked suffering and, therefore, it is no more unjust to him than any other event for which one knowingly volunteers to assume the risk. Thus, the death penalty cannot be unjust to the guilty criminal.[24]

There remain, however, two moral objections. The penalty may be regarded as always excessive as retribution and always morally degrading. To regard the death penalty as always excessive, one must believe that no crime—no matter how heinous—could possibly justify capital punishment. Such a belief can be neither corroborated nor refuted; it is an article of faith.

Alternatively, or concurrently, one may believe that everybody, the murderer no less than the victim, has an imprescriptible (natural?) right to life. The law therefore should not deprive anyone of life. I share Jeremy Bentham's view that any such "natural and imprescriptible rights" are "nonsense upon stilts."[25]

Justice Brennan has insisted that the death penalty is "uncivilized" "inhuman," inconsistent with "human dignity" and with "the sanctity of

---

22 Some abolitionists challenge: If the death penalty is just and severs as a deterrent, why not televise executions? The answer is simple. The death, even of a murderer, however will-deserved, should not serve as public entertainment. It so served in earlier centuries. But in this respect our sensibility has changed for the better, I believe. Further, television unavoidably would trivialize executions, wedged in, as they would be, between game shows, situation comedies, and the like. Finally, because televised executions would focus on the physical aspects of the punishment, rather than the nature of the crime and the suffering of the victim, a televised execution would present the executed as the victim of the state. Far from communicating the moral significance of the execution, television would shift that focus to the pitiable fear of the murderer. We no longer place in cases those sentenced to imprisonment to expose them to public view. Why should we so expose those sentenced to execution?

23 See van den Haag, "Punishment as a Device for Controlling the Crime Rate," 33 Rutgers L. Rev. (1981) 706, 719 (explaining why the desire for retribution, although independent, would have to be satisfied even if deterrence were the only purpose of punishment).

24 An explicit threat of punitive action is necessary to the justification of any legal punishment: nulla poena sine lege (no punishment without [preexisting] law). To be sufficiently justified, the threat must in turn have a rational and legitimate purpose. "Your money or your life" does not qualify; nor does the threat of an unjust law; nor, finally, does a threat that is altogether disproportionate to the importance of its purpose. In short, preannouncement legitimizes the threatened punishment only if the threat is warranted. But this leaves a very wide range of justified threats. Furthermore, the punished person is aware of the penalty for his actions and thus volunteers to take the risk even of an unjust punishment. His victim, however doesn't act illegally and thus doesn't volunteer to risk anything The question whether any self-inflicted injury—such as legal punishment—ever can be unjust to a person who knowingly risked it is a matter that requires more analysis than possible here.

25 The Works of Jeremy Bentham, ed. J. Bowring (1973), p. 105. However, I would be more polite about prescriptible natural rights, which Bentham described as "simple nonsense." Id. (It does not matter whether natural rights are called "moral" or "human" rights as they currently are by most writers.)

life,"[26] that it "treats members of the human race as nonhumans, as objects to be toyed with and discarded,"[27] that it is "uniquely degrading to human dignity"[28] and "by its very nature, [involves] a denial of the executed person's humanity."[29] Justice Brennan does not say why he thinks execution "uncivilized." Hitherto most civilizations have had the death penalty, although it has been discarded in Western Europe, where it is currently unfashionable probably because of its abuse by totalitarian regimes.

By "degrading," Justice Brennan seems to mean that execution degrades the executed convicts. Yet philosophers, such as Immanuel Kant and G.F.W. Hegel, have insisted that, when deserved, execution, far from degrading the executed convict, affirms his humanity by affirming his rationality and his responsibility for his actions. They thought that execution, when

26 *The Death Penalty in America*, 3rd ed., ed. H. Bedau (1982), pp. 256–63 (quoting *Furman v. Georgia*, 408 U.S. 238, 286, 305 (1972) (Brennan, J., concurring).

27 *Id.* at 272–73; *see also Gregg v. Georgia*, 428 U.S. 153 230 (1976) (Brennan, J., dissenting).

28 *Furman v. Georgia*, 408 U.S. 238, 291 (1972) (Brennan, J., concurring).

29 *Id.* at 290.

deserved, is required for the sake of the convict's dignity. (Does not life imprisonment violate human dignity more than execution, by keeping alive a prisoner deprived of all autonomy?[30])

Common sense indicates that it cannot be death—our common fate—that is inhuman. Therefore, Justice Brennan must mean that death degrades when it comes not as a natural or accidental event, but as a deliberate social imposition. The murderer learns through his punishment that his fellow men have found him unworthy of living; that because he has murdered, he is being expelled from the community of the living. This degradation is self-inflicted. By murdering, the murderer has so dehumanized himself that he cannot remain among the living. The social recognition of his self-degradation is the punitive essence of execution. To believe, as Justice Brennan appears to, that the degradation is inflicted by the execution reverses the direction of casuality.

Execution of those who have committed heinous murders may deter only one murder per year. If it does, it seems quite warranted. It is also the only fitting retribution for murder I can think of.

30 *See* Barzun, *supra* note 3, *passim*.

Review Questions

1. How does van den Haag reply to the objection that capital punishment is discriminatory?
2. What is his response to the claim that innocent people are mistakenly executed?
3. According to van den Haag, why does the possibility or probability of deterrence support the use of the death penalty?
4. How does he reply to the objections about cost, excessive suffering, legitimizing killing, the right to life, and human dignity?

Discussion Questions

1. Do you agree that the death penalty is the harshest punishment? Can you think of worse punishments?
2. Are you willing to accept the execution of innocent people as van den Haag does? Why or why not?
3. Are you convinced by van den Haag's arguments about deterrence? (You may want to read Reiman's objections in the next reading.)

Justice, Civilization, and the Death Penalty

JEFFREY H. REIMAN

Jeffrey H. Reiman is William Fraser McDowell Professor of Philosophy at The American University in Washington, D.C. He is the author of *In Defense of Political Philosophy* (1972), *The Rich Get Richer and the Poor Get Prison* (1997), and *Abortion and the Ways We Value Life* (1999).

Reiman begins with a careful discussion of retributivism. He distinguishes between two versions of the doctrine, *lex talionis* and proportional retributivism, and between two different retributive approaches to punishment, a Hegelian and a Kantian approach. Then he argues that it does not follow from the retributivist principle that we ought to impose the death penalty even for crimes of murder because, like torture, it is too horrible to be used by civilized people. He concludes with a reply to van den Haag's arguments. He rejects van den Haag's commonsense argument that execution deters more than life imprisonment, and he is not convinced by van den Haag's argument (sometimes called the best-bet argument) that we should execute murderers rather than risk the lives of innocent people whose murders might have been deterred. According to Reiman, the problem is that *not* killing murderers may also have a deterrent effect, so innocent lives are risked no matter whether we execute or not.

ON THE ISSUE OF CAPITAL PUNISHMENT, there is as clear a clash of moral intuitions as we are likely to see. Some (now a majority of Americans) feel deeply that justice requires payment in kind and thus that murderers should die; and others (once, but no longer, nearly a majority of Americans) feel deeply that the state ought not be in the business of putting people to death.[1]

Source: Jeffrey H. Reiman, "Justice, Civilization, and the Death Penalty: Answering van den Haag," from *Philosophy & Public Affairs*, Vol. 14 (Spring 1985), pp. 141–147. Copyright © 1985 by Blackwell Publishers. Reprinted by permission of Blackwell Publishers.

1 Asked in a 1981 Gallup Poll, "Are you in favor of the death penalty for persons convicted of murder?" 66.25% were in favor, 25% were opposed, and 8.75% had no opinion. Asked the same question in 1966, 47.5% were opposed, 41.25% were in favor, and 11.25% had no opinion (Timothy J. Flanagan, David J. van Alstyne, and Michael R. Gottfredson, eds., *Sourcebook of Criminal Justice Statistics—1981,* U.S. Department of Justice, Bureau of Justice Statistics [Washington, D.C.: U.S. Government Printing Office, 1982], p. 209).

Arguments for either side that do not do justice to the intuitions of the other are unlikely to persuade anyone not already convinced. And, since, as I shall suggest, there is truth on both sides, arguments are easily refutable, leaving us with nothing but conflicting intuitions and no guidance from reason in distinguishing the better from the worse. In this context, I shall try to make an argument for the abolition of the death penalty that does justice to the intuitions on both sides. I shall sketch out a conception of retributive justice that accounts for the justice of executing murderers, and then I shall argue that *though the death penalty is a just punishment for murder,* abolition of the death penalty is a part of the civilizing mission of modern states. . . .

I. JUST DESERTS AND JUST PUNISHMENTS

In my view, the death penalty is a just punishment for murder because the *lex talionis,* an eye for an eye, and so on, is just, although, as I shall suggest at the end of this section, it can only be rightly applied when its implied preconditions are satisfied. The *lex talionis* is a version of retributivism. Retributivism—as the word itself suggests—is the doctrine that the offender should be *paid back* with suffering the deserves because of the evil he has done, and the *lex talionis* asserts that injury equivalent to that he imposed is what the offender deserves. But the *lex talionis* is not the only version of retributivism. Another, which I shall call "proportional retributivism," holds that what retribution requires is not equality of injury between crimes and punishments, but "fit" or proportionality, such that the worst crime is punished with the society's worst penalty, and so on, though the society's worst punishment need not duplicate the injury of the worst crime.[2] Later, I shall try to show how a form of proportional retributivism is compatible with acknowledging the justice of the *lex talionis*. Indeed, since I shall defend the justice of the *lex talionis,* I take such compatibility as a necessary condition of the validity of any form of retributivism.

There is nothing self-evident about the justice of the *lex talionis* nor, for that matter, or retributivism.[3] The standard problem confronting those who would justify retributivism is that of overcoming the suspicion that it does no more than sanctify the victim's desire to hurt the offender back. Since serving that desire amounts to hurting the offender simply for the satisfaction that the victim derives from seeing the offender suffer, and since deriving satisfaction from the suffering of others seems primitive, the policy of imposing suffering on the offender for no other purpose than giving satisfaction to his victim seems primitive as well. Consequently, defending retributivism requires showing that the suffering imposed on the wrongdoer has some worthy point beyond the satisfaction of victims. In what follows, I shall try to identify a proposition— which I call the *retributivist principle*—that I take to be the nerve of retributivism. I think this principle accounts for the justice of the *lex talionis* and indicates the point of the suffering demanded by retributivism. Not to do too much of the work of the death penalty advocate, I shall make no extended argument for this principle beyond suggesting the considerations that make it plausible. I shall identify these considerations by drawing, with considerable license, on Hegel and Kant.

I think that we can see the justice of the *lex talionis* by focusing on the striking affinity between it and the *golden rule*. The *golden rule* mandates "Do unto others as you would have others do unto you," while the *lex talionis* counsels "Do unto others as they have done unto you." It would not be too far-fetched to say that the *lex talionis* is the law enforcement arm of the golden rule, at least in the sense that if people were actually treated as they treated others, then everyone would necessarily follow the golden rule because then people could only willingly act toward others as they were willing to have others act toward them. This is not to suggest that the *lex talionis* follows from the golden rule, but rather that the two share a common moral inspiration: the equality of persons. Treating others as you *would* have them treat you means treating others as equal to you, because adopting the golden rule as one's guiding principle implies that one counts the suffering of others to be as great a calamity as one's own suffering, that one counts one's right to impose suffering on others

---

2 "The most extreme form of retributivism is the law of retaliation: 'an eye for an eye'" (Stanley I. Benn, "Punishment," *The Encyclopedia of Philosophy 7.* ed. Paul Edwards [New York: Macmillan. 1967, p. 32]. Hugo Bedau writes: "retributive justice need not be thought to consist of *lex talionis.* One may reject that principle as too crude and still embrace the retributive principle that the severity of punishments should be graded according to the gravity of the offense" (Hugo Bedan, "Capital Punishment," in *Matters of Life and Death,* ed. Tom Regan [New York: Random House, 1980], p. 177). See also, Andrew von Hirsch, "Doing Justice: The Principle of Commensurate Deserts," and Hyman Gross, "Proportional Punishment and Justifiable Sentences," in *Sentencing,* eds. H. Gross and A. von Hirsch (New York: Oxford University Press, 1981), pp. 243–56 and 272–83, respectively.

3 Stanley Benn writes: "to say 'it is fitting' or 'justice demands' that the guilty should suffer is only to affirm that punishment is right, not to give grounds for thinking so" (Benn, "Punishment," p. 30).

as no greater than their right to impose suffering on one, and so on. This leads to the *lex talionis* by two approaches that start from different points and converge.

I call the first approach "Hegelian" because Hegel held (roughly) that crime upsets the quality between persons and retributive punishment restores that equality by "annulling" the crime. As we have seen, acting according to the golden rule implies treating others as your equals. Conversely, violating the golden rule implies the reverse: Doing to another what you would *not* have that person do to you violates the equality of persons by asserting a right toward the other that the other does not possess toward you. Doing back to you what you did "annuls" your violation by reasserting that the other has the same right toward you that you assert toward him. Punishment according to the *lex talionis* cannot heal the injury that the other has suffered at your hands, rather it rectifies the indignity he has suffered, by restoring him to equality with you.

"Equality of persons" here does not mean equality of concern for their happiness, as it might for a utilitarian. On such a (roughly) utilitarian understanding of equality, imposing suffering on the wrongdoer equivalent to the suffering he has imposed would have little point. Rather, equality of concern for people's happiness would lead us to impose as little suffering on the wrongdoer as was compatible with maintaining the happiness of others. This is enough to show that retributivism (at least in this "Hegelian" form) reflects a conception of morality quite different from that envisioned by utilitarianism. Instead of seeing morality as administering does of happiness to individual recipients, the retributivist envisions morality as maintaining the relations appropriate to equally sovereign individuals. A crime, rather than representing a unit of suffering added to the already considerable suffering in the world, is an assault on the sovereignty of an individual that temporarily places one person (the criminal) in a position of illegitimate sovereignty over another (the victim). The victim (or his representative, the state) then has the right to rectify this loss of standing relative to the criminal by meting out a punishment that reduces the criminal's sovereignty in the degree to which he vaunted it above his victim's. It might be thought that this is a duty, not just a right, but that is surely too much. The victim has the right to forgive the violator without punishment, which suggests that it is by virtue of having the right to punish the violator (rather than the duty) that the victim's quality with the violator is restored.

I call the second approach "Kantian" since Kant held (roughly) that, since reason (like justice) is no respecter of the sheer difference between individuals, when a rational being decides to act in a certain way toward his fellows, he implicitly authorizes similar action by his fellows toward him. A version of the golden rule, then, is a requirement of reason: Acting rationally, one always acts as he would have others act toward him. Consequently, to act toward a person as he has acted toward others is to treat him as a rational being, that is, as if his act were the product of a rational decision. From this, it may be concluded that we have a duty to do to offenders what they have done, since this amounts to according them the respect due rational beings. Here too, however, the assertion of a duty to punish seems excessive, since, if this duty arises because doing to people what they have done to others is necessary to accord them the respect due rational beings, then we would have a duty to do to all rational persons *everything*—good, bad, or indifferent—that they do to others. The point rather is that, by his acts, a rational being *authorizes* others to do the same to him, he doesn't *compel* them to. Here too, then, the argument leads to a right, rather than a duty, to exact the *lex talionis*. And this is supported by the fact that we can conclude from Kant's argument that a rational being cannot validly complain of being treated in the way he has treated others, and where there is no valid complaint, there is no injustice, and where there is no injustice, others have acted within their rights.

It should be clear that the Kantian argument also rests on the equality of persons, because a rational agent only implicitly authorizes having done to him action similar to what he has done to another, if he and the other are similar in the relevant ways.

The "Hegelian" and "Kantian" approaches arrive at the same destination from opposite sides. The "Hegelian" approach starts from the victim's equality with the criminal, and infers from it the victim's right to do to the criminal what the criminal has done to the victim. The "Kantian" approach starts from the criminal's rationality, and infers from it the criminal's authorization of the victim's right to do to the criminal what the criminal has done to the victim. Taken together, these approaches support the following proposition: The equality and rationality of persons implies that an offender deserves and his victim has the right to impose suffering on the offender equal to that which he imposed on the victim. This is the proposition I call the *retributivist principle,* and I shall assume henceforth that it is true. This principle provides that the *lex talionis* is the criminal's just desert and the victim's (or as his representative, the state's) right. Moreover, the principle also indicates the point of retributive punishment, namely, it affirms the equality and rationality of persons, victims and offenders alike.[4] And the point of this affirmation is, like any moral affirmation, to make a statement, to the criminal, to impress upon him his equality with his victim (which earns him a like fate) and his rationality (by which his actions are held to authorize his fate), and to the society, so that recognition of the equality and rationality of persons becomes a visible part of our shared moral environment that none can ignore in justifying their actions to one another. . . .

The truth of the retributivist principle establishes the justice of the *lex talionis,* but, since it establishes this as a right of the victim rather than a duty, it does not settle the question of whether or to what extent the victim or the state should exercise this right and exact the *lex talionis.* This is a separate moral question because strict adherence to the *lex talionis* amounts to allowing criminals, even the most barbaric of them, to dictate our punishing behavior. It seems certain that there are at least some crimes, such as rape or torture, that we ought not try to match. And this is not merely a matter of imposing an alternative punishment that produces an equivalent amount of suffering, as, say, some number of years in prison that might "add up" to the harm caused by a rapist or a torturer. Even if no amount of time in prison would add up to the harm caused by a torturer, it still seems that we ought not torture him even if this were the only way of making him suffer as much as he has made his victim suffer. Or, consider someone who has committed several murders in cold blood. On the *lex talionis,* it would seem that such a criminal might justly be brought to within an inch of death and then revived (or to within a moment of execution and then reprieved) as many times as he has killed (minus one), and then finally executed. But surely this is a degree of cruelty that would be monstrous.[5] . . .

I suspect that it will be widely agreed that the state ought not administer punishments of the sort described above even if required by the letter of the *lex talionis,* and thus, even granting the justice of *lex talionis,* there are occasions on

4 Herbert Morris defends retributivism on parallel grounds. See his "Persons and Punishment," *The Monist* 52, no. 4 (October 1968): 475–501. Isn't what Morris calls "the right to be treated as a person" essentially the right of a rational being to be treated only as he has authorized, implicitly or explicitly, by his own free choices?

5 Bedau writes: "Where criminals set the limits of just methods of punishment, as they will do if we attempt to give exact and literal implementation to *lex talionis,* society will find itself descending to the cruelties and savagery that criminals employ. But society would be deliberately authorizing such acts, in the cool light of reason, and not (as is often true of vicious criminals) impulsively or in hatred and anger or with an insane or unbalanced mind. Moral restraints, in short, prohibit us from trying to make executions perfectly retributive" (Bedau, "Capital Punishment," p. 176).

which it is morally appropriate to diverge from its requirements. . . .

This way of understanding just punishment enables us to formulate proportional retributivism so that it is compatible with acknowledging the justice of the *lex talionis:* If we take the *lex talionis* as spelling out the offender's just deserts, and if other moral considerations require us to refrain from matching the injury caused by the offender while still allowing us to punish justly, then surely we impose just punishment if we impose the closest morally acceptable approximation to the *lex talionis.* Proportional retributivism, then, in requiring that the worst crime be punished by the society's worst punishment and so on, could be understood as translating the offender's just desert into its nearest equivalent in the society's table of morally acceptable punishments. Then the two versions of retributivism (*lex talionis* and proportional) are related in that the first states what just punishment would be if nothing but the offender's just desert mattered, and the second locates just punishment at the meeting point of the offender's just deserts and the society's moral scruples. And since this second version only modifies the requirements of the *lex talionis* in light of other moral considerations, it is compatible with believing that the *lex talionis* spells out the offender's just deserts, much in the way that modifying the obligations of promisers in light of other moral considerations is compatible with believing in the binding nature of promises. . . .

II. CIVILIZATION, PAIN, AND JUSTICE

As I have already suggested, from the fact that something is justly deserved, it does not automatically follow that it should be done, since there may be other moral reasons for not doing it such that, all told, the weight of moral reasons swings the balance against proceeding. The same argument that I have given for the justice of the death penalty for murderers proves the justice of beating assaulters, raping rapists, and torturing torturers. Nonetheless, I believe, and suspect that most would agree, that it would not be right for us to beat assaulters, rape rapists, or torture torturers, *even though it were their just deserts*—and even if this were the only way to make them suffer as much as they had made their victims suffer. Calling for the abolition of the death penalty, though it be just, then, amounts to urging that as a society we place execution in the same category of sanction as beating, raping, and torturing, and treat it as something it would not be right for us to do to offenders, *even if it were their just deserts.* . . .

Progress in civilization is characterized by a lower tolerance for one's own pain and that suffered by others. And this is appropriate, since, via growth in knowledge, civilization brings increased power to prevent or reduce pain and, via growth in the ability to communicate and interact with more and more people, civilization extends the circle of people with whom we empathize.[6] If civilization is characterized by lower tolerance for our own pain and that of others, then publicly refusing to do horrible things to our fellows both signals the level of our civilization *and, by our example, continues the work of civilizing.* And this gesture is all the more powerful if we refuse to do horrible things to those who deserve them. I contend then that the more things we are able to include in this category, the more civilized we are and the more civilizing. Thus we gain from including torture in this category, and if execution is especially horrible, we gain still more by including it. . . .

6 Van den Haag writes that our ancestors "were not as repulsed by physical pain as we are. The change has to do not with our greater smartness or moral superiority but with a new outlook pioneered by the French and American revolutions [namely, that assertion of human equality and with it 'universal identification'], and by such mundane things as the invention of anesthetics, which make pain much less of an everyday experience" ([Ernest van den Haag and John P. Conrad, *The Death Penalty: A Debate* (New York: Plenum Press, 1983)]. p. 215: cf. van den Haag's *Punishing Criminals* [New York: Basic Books, 1975], pp. 196–206).

What can be said of reducing the horrible things that we do to our fellows even when deserved? First of all, given our vulnerability to pain, it seems clearly a gain. Is it however an unmitigated gain? That is, would such a reduction ever amount to a loss? It seems to me that there are two conditions under which it would be a loss, namely, if the reduction made our lives more dangerous, or if not doing what is justly deserved were a loss in itself. Let us leave aside the former, since, as I have already suggested and as I will soon indicate in greater detail, I accept that if some horrible punishment is necessary to deter equally or more horrible acts, then we may have to impose the punishment. Thus my claim is that reduction in the horrible things we do to our fellows is an advance in civilization *as long as our lives are not thereby made more dangerous,* and that it is only then that we are called upon to extend that reduction as part of the work of civilization. Assuming then, for the moment, that we suffer no increased danger by refraining from doing horrible things to our fellows when they justly deserve them, does such refraining to do what is justly deserved amount to a loss?

It seems to me that the answer to this must be that refraining to do what is justly deserved is only a loss where it amounts to doing an injustice. But such refraining to do what is just is not doing what is unjust, unless what we do instead falls below the bottom end of the range of just punishments. Otherwise, it would be unjust to refrain from torturing torturers, raping rapists, or beating assaulters. In short, I take it that if there is no injustice in refraining from torturing torturers, then there is no injustice in refraining to do horrible things to our fellows generally, when they deserve them, as long as what we do instead is compatible with believing that they do deserve them. And thus that if such refraining does not make our lives more dangerous, then it is no loss, and given our vulnerability to pain, it is a gain. Consequently, reduction in the horrible things we do to our fellows, when not necessary to our protection, is an advance in civilization that we are called upon to continue once we consciously take upon ourselves the work of civilization.

To complete the argument, however, I must show that execution is horrible enough to warrant its inclusion alongside torture. Against this it will be said that execution is not especially horrible since it only hastens a fate that is inevitable for us.[7] I think that this view overlooks important differences in the manner in which people reach their inevitable ends. I contend that execution is especially horrible, and it is so in a way similar to (though not identical with) the way in which torture is especially horrible. I believe we view torture as especially awful because of two of its features, which also characterize execution: intense pain and the spectacle of one human being completely subject to the

7 Van den Haag seems to waffle on the question of the unique awfulness of execution. For instance, he takes it not to be revolting in the way that earcropping is, because "We all must die. But we must not have our ears cropped" (p. 190), and here he cites John Stuart Mill's parliamentary defense of the death penalty in which Mill maintains that execution only *hastens* death. Mill's point was to defend the claim that "There is not . . . any human infliction which makes an impression on the imagination so entirely out of proportion to its real severity as the punishment of death" (Mill, "Parliamentary Debate," p. 273). And van den Haag seems to agree since he maintains that, since "we cannot imagine our own nonexistence . . . , [t]he fear of the death penalty is in part the fear of the unknown. It . . . rests on a confusion" (pp. 258–59). On the other hand, he writes that "Execution sharpens our separation anxiety because death becomes clearly foreseen. . . . Further, and perhaps most important, when one is executed he does not just die, he is put to death, forcibly expelled from life. He is told that he is too depraved, unworthy of living with other humans" (p. 258). I think, incidentally, that it is an overstatement to say that we cannot imagine our own nonexistence. If we can imagine any counterfactual experience, for example, how we might feel if we didn't know something that we do in fact know, then it doesn't seem impossible to imagine what it would "feel like" not to live. I think I can arrive at a pretty good approximation of this by trying to imagine how things "felt" to me in the eighteenth century. And, in fact, the sense of the awful difference between being alive and not that enters my experience when I do this makes the fear of death—not as a state, but as the absence of life—seem hardly to rest on a confusion.

power of another. This latter is separate from the issue of pain since it is something that offends us about unpainful things, such as slavery (even voluntarily entered) and prostitution (even voluntarily chosen as an occupation).[8] Execution shares this separate feature, since killing a bound and defenseless human being enacts the total subjugation of that person to his fellows. I think, incidentally, that this accounts for the general uneasiness with which execution by lethal injection has been greeted. Rather than humanizing the event, it seems only to have purchased a possible reduction in physical pain at the price of increasing the spectacle of subjugation—with no net gain in the attractiveness of the death penalty. Indeed, its net effect may have been the reverse.

In addition to the spectacle of subjugation, execution, even by physically painless means, is also characterized by a special and intense psychological pain that distinguishes it from the loss of life that awaits us all. Interesting in this regard is the fact that although we are not terribly squeamish about the loss of life itself, allowing it in war, self-defense, as a necessary cost of progress, and so on, we are, as the extraordinary hesitance of our courts testifies, quite reluctant to execute. I think this is because execution involves the most psychologically painful features of deaths. We normally regard death from human causes as worse than death from natural causes, since a humanly caused shortening of life lacks the consolation of unavoidability. And we normally regard death whose coming is foreseen by its victim as worse than sudden death, because a foreseen death adds to the loss of life the terrible consciousness of that impending loss.[9] As a humanly caused death whose advent is foreseen by its victim, an execution combines the worst of both.

Thus far, by analogy with torture, I have argued that execution should be avoided because of how horrible it is to the one executed. But there are reasons of another sort that follow from the analogy with torture. Torture is to be avoided not only because of what it says about *what* we are willing to do to our fellows, but also because of what it says about *us* who are willing to do it. To torture someone is an awful spectacle not only because of the intensity of pain imposed, but because of what is required to be able to impose such pain on one's fellows. The tortured body cringes, using its full exertion to escape the pain imposed upon it—it literally begs for relief with its muscles as it does with its cries. To torture someone is to demonstrate a capacity to resist this begging, and that in turn demonstrates a kind of hardheartedness that a society ought not parade.

And this is true not only of torture, but of all severe corporal punishment. Indeed, I think this constitutes part of the answer to the puzzling question of why we refrain from punishments like whipping, even when the alternative (some months in jail versus some lashes) seems more costly to the offender. Imprisonment is painful to be sure, but it is a reflective pain, one that comes with comparing what is to what might have been, and that can be temporarily ignored by thinking about other things. But physical pain has an urgency that holds body and mind in a fierce grip. Of physical pain, as Orwell's Winston Smith recognized, "you could only

---

8 I am not here endorsing this view of voluntarily entered slavery or prostitution. I mean only to suggest that it is *the belief* that these relations involve the extreme subjugation of one person to the power of another that is at the basis of their offensiveness. What I am saying is quite compatible with finding that this belief is false with respect to voluntarily entered slavery or prostitution.

9 This is no doubt partly due to modern skepticism about an afterlife. Earlier peoples regarded a foreseen death as a blessing allowing time to make one's peace with God. Writing of an early Middle Ages, Phillippe Aries says, "In this world that was so familiar with death, sudden death was a vile and ugly death; it was frightening; it seemed a strange and monstrous thing nobody dared talk about" (Phillippe Aries, *The Hour of Our Death* [New York: Vintage, 1982], p. 11).

wish one thing: that it should stop."[10] Refraining from torture in particular and corporal punishment in general, we both refuse to put a fellow human being in this grip *and* refuse to show our ability to resist this wish. The death penalty is the last corporal punishment used officially in the modern world. And it is corporal not only because administered via the body, but because the pain of foreseen, humanly administered death strikes us with the urgency that characterizes intense physical pain, causing grown men to cry, faint, and lose control of their bodily functions. There is something to be gained by refusing to endorse the hardness of heart necessary to impose such a fate.

By placing execution alongside torture in the category of things we will not do to our fellow human beings even when they deserve them, we broadcast the message that totally subjugating a person to the power of others *and* confronting him with the advent of his own humanly administered demise is too horrible to be done by civilized human beings to their fellows even when they have earned it: too horrible to do, and too horrible to be capable of doing. And I contend that broadcasting this message loud and clear would in the long run contribute to the general detestation of murder and be, to the extent to which it worked itself into the hearts and minds of the populace, a deterrent. In short, refusing to execute murderers though they deserve it both reflects and continues the taming of the human species that we call civilization. Thus, I take it that the abolition of the death penalty, though it is just punishment for murder, is part of the civilizing mission of modern states.

III. CIVILIZATION, SAFETY, AND DETERRENCE

Earlier I said that judging a practice too horrible to do even to those who deserve it does not exclude the possibility that it could be justified if necessary to avoid even worse consequences. Thus, were the death penalty clearly proven a better deterrent to the murder of innocent people than life in prison, we might have to admit that we had not yet reached a level of civilization at which we could protect ourselves without imposing this horrible fate on murderers, and thus we might have to grant the necessity of instituting the death penalty.[11] But this is far from proven. The available research by no means clearly indicates that the death penalty reduces the incidence of homicide more than life imprisonment does. Even the econometric studies of Isaac Ehrlich, which purport to show that each execution saves seven or eight potential murder victims, have not changed this fact, as is testified to by the controversy and objections from equally respected statisticians that Ehrlich's work has provoked.[12]

---

10 George Orwell, *1984* (New York: New American Library, 1983; originally published in 1949), p. 197.

11 I say "might" here to avoid the sticky question of just how effective a deterrent the death penalty would have to be to justify overcoming our scruples about executing. It is here that the other considerations often urged against capital punishment—discrimination, irrevocability, the possibility of mistake, and so on—would play a role. Omitting such qualifications, however, my position might crudely be stated as follows: *Just desert limits what a civilized society may do to deter crime, and deterrence limits what a civilized society may do to give criminals their just deserts.*

12 Isaac Ehrlich. "The Deterrent Effect of Capital Punishment: A Question of Life or Death," *American Economic Review* 65 (June 1975): 397–417. For reactions to Ehrlich's work, see Alfred Blumstein, Jacqueline Cohen, and Daniel Nagin, eds., *Deterrence and Incapacitation: Estimating the Effects of Criminal Sanctions on Crime Rates* (Washington, D.C.: National Academy of Sciences, 1978), esp. pp. 59–63 and 336–60; Brian E. Forst, "The Deterrent Effect on Capital Punishment: A Cross-State Analysis," *Minnesota Law Review* 61 (May 1977): 743–67, Deryck Beyleveld, "Ehrlich's Analysis of Deterrence," *British Journal of Criminology* 22 (April 1982): 101–23, and Isaac Ehrlich, "On Positive Methodology, Ethics and Polemics in Deterrence Research," *British Journal of Criminology* 22 (April 1982): 124–39. Much of the criticism of Ehrlich's work focuses on the fact that he found a deterrence impact of executions in the period from 1993–1969, which includes the period 1963–1969, a time when hardly any executions were carried

Conceding that it has not been proven that the death penalty deters more murders than life imprisonment, van den Haag has argued that neither has it been proven that the death penalty does not deter more murders,[13] and thus we must follow common sense which teaches that the higher the cost of something, the fewer people will choose it, and therefore at least some potential murderers who would not be deterred by life imprisonment will be deterred by the death penalty. Van den Haag writes:

> . . . our experience shows that the greater the penalty, the more it deters.
> . . . Life in prison is still life, however unpleasant. In contrast, the death penalty does not just threaten to make life unpleasant—it threatens to take life altogether. This difference is perceived by those affected. We find that when they have the choice between life in prison and execution, 99% of all prisoners under sentence of death prefer life in prison. . . .
> From this unquestioned fact a reasonable conclusion can be drawn in favor of the superior deterrent effect of the death penalty. Those who have the choice in practice . . . fear death more than they fear life in prison. . . . If they do, it follows that the threat of the death penalty, all other things equal, is likely to deter more than the threat of life in prison. One is most deterred by what one fears most. From which it follows that whatever statistics fail, or do not fail, to show, the death penalty is likely to be more deterrent than any other. [pp. 68–69]

Those of us who recognize how commonsensical it was, and still is, to believe that the sun moves around the earth, will be less willing than Professor van den Haag to follow common sense here, especially when it comes to doing something awful to our fellows. Moreover, there are good reasons for doubting common sense on this matter. Here are four:

1. From the fact that one penalty is more feared than another, it does not follow that the more feared penalty will deter more than the less feared, unless we know that the less feared penalty is not fearful enough to deter everyone who can be deterred—and this is just what we don't know with regard to the death penalty Though I fear the death penalty more than life in prison, I can't think of any act that the death penalty would deter me from that an equal likelihood of spending my life in prison wouldn't deter me from as well. Since it seems to me that whoever would be deterred by a given likelihood of death would be deterred by an *equal* likelihood of life behind bars, I suspect that the common-sense argument only seems plausible because we evaluate it unconsciously assuming that potential criminals will face larger likelihoods of death sentences than of life sentences. If the likelihoods were equal, it seems to me that where life imprisonment was improbable enough to make it too distant a possibility to worry much about, a similar low probability of death would have the same effect. After all, we are undeterred by small likelihoods of death every time we walk the streets. And if life imprisonment were sufficiently probable to pose a real deterrent threat, it would pose as much of a deterrent threat as death. And this is just what most of the research we have on the comparative deterrent impact of execution versus life imprisonment suggests.

---

out and crime rates rose for reasons that are arguably independent of the existence or nonexistence of capital punishment. When the 1963–1969 period is excluded, no significant deterrent effect shows. Prior to Ehrlich's work, research on the comparative deterrent impact of the death penalty versus life imprisonment indicated no increase in the incidence of homicide in states that abolished the death penalty and no greater incidence of homicide in states without the death penalty compared to similar states with the death penalty. See Thorsten Sellin, *The Death Penalty* (Philadelphia: American Law Institute, 1959).

13 Van den Haag writes: "Other studies published since Ehrlich's contend that his results are due to the techniques and periods he selected, and that different techniques and periods yield different results. Despite a great deal of research on all sides, one cannot say that the statistical evidence is conclusive. Nobody has claimed to have *disproved* that the death penalty may deter more than life imprisonment. But one cannot claim, either, that it has been proved statistically in a conclusive manner that the death penalty does deter more than alternative penalties. This lack of proof does not amount to disproof" (p. 65).

2. In light of the fact that roughly 500 to 700 suspected felons are killed by the police in the line of duty every year, and the fact that the number of privately owned guns in America is substantially larger than the number of households in America, it must be granted that anyone contemplating committing a crime *already* faces a substantial risk of ending up dead as a result.[14] It's hard to see why anyone *who is not already deterred by this* would be deterred by the addition of the more distant risk of death after apprehension, conviction, and appeal. Indeed, this suggests that people consider risks in a much crueler way than van den Haag's appeal to common sense suggests—which should be evident to anyone who contemplates how few people use seatbelts (14% of drivers, on some estimates), when it is widely known that wearing them can spell the difference between life (outside prison) and death.[15]

3. Van den Haag has maintained that deterrence doesn't work only by means of cost-benefit calculations made by potential criminals. It works also by the lesson about the wrongfulness of murder that is slowly learned in a society that subjects murderers to the ultimate punishment (p. 63). But if I am correct in claiming that the refusal to execute even those who deserve it has a civilizing effect, then the refusal to execute also teaches a lesson about the wrongfulness of murder. My claim here is admittedly speculative, but no more so than van den Haag's to the contrary. And my view has the added virtue of accounting for the failure of research to show an increased deterrent effect from executions *without having to deny the plausibility of van den Haag's common-sense argument that at least some additional potential murderers will be deterred by the prospect of the death penalty*. If there is a deterrent effect from *not executing,* then it is understandable that while executions will deter some murderers, this effect will be balanced out by the weakening of the deterrent effect of not executing, such that no net reduction in murders will result.[16] And this, by the way, also disposes of van den Haag's argument that, in the absence of knowledge one way or the other on the deterrent effect of executions, we should execute murderers rather than risk the lives of innocent people whose murders might have been deterred if we had. If there is a deterrent effect of not executing, it follows that we risk innocent lives either way. And if this is so, it seems that the only reasonable course of action is to refrain from imposing what we know is a horrible fate.[17]

---

14 On the number of people killed by the police, see Lawrence W. Sherman and Robert H. Langworthy, "Measuring Homicide by Police Officers," *Journal of Criminal Law and Criminology 70,* no. 4 (Winter 1979): 546–60; on the number of privately owned guns, see Franklin Zimring, *Firearms and Violence in American Life* (Washington, D.C.: U.S. Government Printing Office, 1968), pp. 6–7.

15 *AAA World* (Potomac ed.) 4, no. 3 (May-June 1984). pp. 18c and 18i.

16 A related claim has been made by those who defend the so-called brutalization hypothesis by presenting evidence to show that murders *increase* following an execution. See, for example, William J. Bowers and Glenn L. Pierce, "Deterrence or Brutalization: What Is the Effect of Executions?" *Crime & Delinquency* 26, no. 4 (October 1980): 453–84. They conclude that each execution gives rise to two additional homicides in the month following and that these are real additions, not just a change in timing of the homicides (ibid. p. 481). My claim, it should be noted, is not identical to this, since, as I indicate in the text, what I call "the deterrence effect of not executing" is not something whose impact is to be seen immediately following executions but over the long haul, and, further, my claim is compatible with finding no net increase in murders due to executions. Nonetheless, should the brutalization hypothesis be borne out by further studies, it would certainly lend support to the notion that there is a deterrent effect of not executing.

17 Van den Haag writes: "If we were quite ignorant about the marginal deterrent effects of execution, we would have to choose—like it or not—between the certainty of the convicted murderer's death by execution and the likelihood of the survival of future victims of other murderers on the one hand, and on the other his certain survival and the likelihood of the death of new victims. I'd rather execute a man convicted of having murdered others than put the lives of innocents at risk. I find it hard to understand the opposite choice" (p. 69). Conway was able to counter this argument earlier by pointing out that the research on the marginal deterrent effects of execution was not *inconclusive* in the sense

4. Those who still think that van den Haag's common-sense argument for executing murderers is valid will find that the argument proves more than they bargained for. Van den Haag maintains that, in the absence of conclusive evidence on the relative deterrent impact of the death penalty versus life imprisonment, we must follow common sense and assume that if one punishment is more fearful than another, it will deter some potential criminals not deterred by the less fearful punishment. Since people sentenced to death will almost universally try to get their sentences changed to life in prison, it follows that death is more fearful than life imprisonment,

and thus that it will deter some additional murderers. Consequently, we should institute the death penalty to save the lives these additional murderers would have taken. But, since people sentenced to be tortured to death would surely try to get their sentences changed to simple execution, the same argument proves that death-by-torture will deter still more potential murderers. Consequently, we should institute death-by-torture to save the lives these additional murderers would have taken. Anyone who accepts van den Haag's argument is then confronted with a dilemma: Until we have conclusive evidence that capital punishment is a greater deterrent to murder than life imprisonment, we must grant *either* that we should not follow common sense and not impose the death penalty; *or* we should follow common sense and torture murderers to death. In short, either we must abolish the electric chair or reinstitute the rack. Surely, this is the *reductio ad absurdum* of van den Haag's common-sense argument.

of *tending to point both ways,* but rather in the sense of *giving us no reason to believe that capital punishment saves more lives than life imprisonment.* He could then answer van den Haag by saying that the choice is not between risking the lives of murderers and risking the lives of innocents, but between killing a murderer with no reason to believe lives will be saved and sparing a murderer with no reason to believe lives will be lost (Conway, "Capital Punishment and Deterrence." [*Philosophy & Public Affairs* 3, no. 4], pp. 442–43). This, of course, makes the choice to spare the murderer more understandable than van den Haag allows. Events, however, have overtaken Conway's argument. The advent of Ehrlich's research, contested though it may be, leaves us in fact with research that tends to point both ways.

CONCLUSION

I believe that, taken together, these arguments prove that we should abolish the death penalty though it is a just punishment for murder.

Review Questions

1. What is Reiman's distinction between *lex talionis* and proportional retributivism?
2. Explain the affinity that Reiman sees between *lex talionis* and the golden rule.
3. What is the Hegelian approach to crime and punishment, as distinguished from the utilitarian view?
4. What is the Kantian view as Reiman explains it?
5. What is the retributivist principle? Why doesn't it settle the question about the application of *lex talionis* according to Reiman?
6. Why does Reiman reject the claim that we should rape rapists and torture torturers?
7. On Reiman's view, why is execution similar to torture?
8. How does Reiman reply to van den Haag?

Discussion Questions

1. What is the appropriate punishment for the crimes of rape and torture?
2. Is execution really similar to torture, as Reiman says? Why or why not?
3. How could van den Haag reply to Reiman's arguments?

Problem Cases

1. Gary Graham

(This case was widely reported in the media, including coverage in Europe where opposition to the death penalty is unanimous.) Gary Graham, a black man also known as Shaka Shankofa, was convicted in 1981 of killing Bobby Lambert (53) during a robbery attempt at a Houston supermarket. Mr. Lambert was shot to death at night in the parking lot of a Safeway supermarket. There was no physical evidence linking Graham to the crime. Mr. Graham was arrested with a .22 caliber pistol a week after the murder, but the police firearms examiner determined that Mr. Graham's weapon could not have fired the fatal bullet. Mr. Graham claimed that he was miles away from the Safeway when the crime occurred. Four witnesses who passed polygraph tests stated that Mr. Graham was with them the night of the murder.

The jury convicted Mr. Graham based on the testimony of one witness, Bernadine Skillern, who insisted she saw him through the windshield of her car that night. She testified that she saw the assailant's face for two or three seconds, from a distance of thirty to forty feet. She said, "I saw that young man walk up and shoot that man." Mr. Graham was seventeen at the time, a minor.

There were other eyewitnesses in the store. One of them was standing next to the killer in the supermarket checkout line. She had the best look at the killer, and she emphatically said that Mr. Graham was the wrong man. At the trial she was not asked if Mr. Graham was the suspect. Of the six living crime scene witnesses other than Ms. Skillern, all described the assailant as shorter than Mr. Lambert, who was 5'6" tall. Mr. Graham was 5'9" tall.

Mr. Graham had a court-appointed lawyer, Ron Mock, who failed to investigate the case. Mr. Mock later admitted that he believed Graham was guilty and therefore he did nothing to find proof of innocence. None of the other witnesses were called to testify at the trial, and no investigation was done about the lack of physical evidence.

Mr. Graham received the death sentence, but his execution was delayed five times on appeal. The appeal for a new trial was denied, based on a Texas rule that bars court review on any evidence of innocence brought forward more that thirty days after the trial conviction.

Mr. Graham was executed in June 2000 after the Texas Board of Pardons and Paroles denied a final clemency petition, and Texas Governor George W. Bush refused to grant a stay of execution. During Bush's five years as governor, the state of Texas carried out 134 executions, the most in the nation.

In general, should juveniles (under eighteen at the time of crime) be executed? (Nineteen states plus the federal government have an age minimum of at least eighteen for capital punishment.)

Based on the evidence given, did Gary Graham deserve to die? Suppose, for the sake of discussion, that Mr. Mock was right and Mr. Graham was indeed guilty as charged. Should he still be executed?

In 2004 Texas had 458 inmates on death row, more than any state except California, which had 634. Should they all be promptly executed with no more appeals? Why or why not?

2. Napoleon Beazley

(Reported by Jim Yardley in *The New York Times,* August 10, 2001). On April 19, 1994, Napoleon Beazley and two friends ambushed John Luttig on his driveway in Tyler, Texas. It was supposed to be a carjacking, but in a panic Mr. Beazley shot Mr. Luttig twice in the head, killing him as his wife crawled under the car.

When he committed this crime, Mr. Beazley was seventeen years old. Only six countries in the world execute juvenile offenders, and only thirteen of the thirty-eight states having the death penalty provide the death penalty for juveniles. Texas is one of those states. Mr. Beazley was found guilty and received the death sentence after the two codefendants agreed to a plea bargain, and testified against him. The two codefendants escaped capital prosecution.

Mr. Beazley was black, and Mr. Luttig was white. Mr. Luttig also happened to be the father of a very prominent federal judge, Michael Luttig of the Court of Appeals for the Fourth Circuit in Virginia. Judge Luttig closely observed and participated in the case against Mr. Beazley. As a result, the prosecution was able to dismiss a prospective African-American juror and seated an all-white jury, including Maxine Herbst, who was president of the local branch of the Daughters of the Confederacy and displayed the Confederate flag from her home.

On August 13, 2001, the U.S. Supreme Court turned down a request for a stay of execution for Mr. Beazley. Three justices, Antonin Scalia, David Souter, and Clarence Thomas, disqualified themselves because of their close ties with Judge Luttig. Because a majority is needed for a stay of execution, the Court's 3–3 decision was a defeat for Mr. Beazley.

This case raises some important questions. Is it fair to have an all-white jury for a black defendant? How can we provide a fair trial when the rich and powerful are involved?

3. Karla Fay Tucker

(Reported by Daniel Pedersen in *Newsweek,* February 2, 1998.) On June 13, 1983, a few hours before dawn, Tucker used a pickax to kill two people who had annoyed her. The male victim, Jerry Lynn Dean, had once dripped motor oil on her living-room carpet and had cut up some photographs of Tucker's mother. The female victim, Deborah Thorton, just happened to be asleep beside Dean in his Houston apartment; Tucker didn't even know her. Tucker and her boyfriend hacked away at both victims until they were dead and then left a two-foot blade imbedded seven inches into Thorton's chest. On a tape played at her trial, Tucker boasted that she had felt a surge of sexual pleasure with every swing of the pickax.

Tucker was found guilty and was sentenced to death by lethal injection. But fourteen years later, shortly before she was to be executed, Tucker launched an impressive last-minute campaign to have her sentence commuted to life imprisonment. Her appeal attracted worldwide media attention. One reason for all the publicity was Tucker's gender. Texas has had more executions than any other state, and the death penalty is popular in Texas, but a woman had not been executed there since the middle of the Civil War.

Tucker's appeal was not based on her gender, however. She claimed that when she committed the crime, she was a drug-addicted prostitute, but now she was a born-again Christian who was sincerely repentant and reformed. She was married to a prison minister. She was an active evangelist, writing essays and making antidrug videotapes. She appeared on Pat Robertson's Christian cable TV show, The 700 Club. She managed to muster the support of a wide variety of character witnesses and sympathizers, including Pope John Paul II, Bianca Jagger, the European Parliament, prison guards, former prosecutors, the detective who arrested her, one of the jurors in her case, and even the brother of the woman she murdered.

Tucker's appeal was unsuccessful. The Texas parole board voted 16 to 0 against commuting her sentence. Texas Governor George W. Bush refused to grant a thirty-day reprieve, and the Supreme Court rejected Tucker's final appeal less than an hour before she was put to death.

At 6:45 P.M. on February 3, 1998, Tucker was pronounced dead, eight minutes after the injection of lethal drugs. In Europe, opinion writers called it a "barbaric act." In the United States, some feminists voiced approval that women had achieved equal rights in capital litigation; not like Russia, where the death penalty is used for men but not women.

Was the execution of Tucker justified or not? Why or why not?

If there is a death penalty, should it be applied equally to men and women? What is your view?

4. The Sacco-Vanzetti Case

On April 15, 1920, a paymaster for a shoe company in South Braintree, Massachusetts, and his guard were shot and killed by two men who escaped with more than $15,000. Witnesses thought the two men were Italians, and Nicola Sacco and Bartolomeo Vanzetti were arrested. Both men were anarchists and had evaded the army draft. Upon their arrest, they made false statements. Both carried firearms; but neither had a criminal record, nor was there any evidence that they had the money. In July 1921, they were found guilty and sentenced to death. The conduct of the trial by Judge Webster Thayer was criticized, and indeed much of the evidence against them was later discredited. The court denied their appeal for a new trial, and Governor Alvan T. Fuller, after postponing the execution, allowed them to be executed on August 22, 1927. Many regarded the two as innocent, prompting worldwide sympathy demonstrations. The case has been the subject of many books, most of which agree that Vanzetti was innocent but that Sacco may have been guilty. The gun found on Sacco was tested with modern ballistics equipment in 1961, and these tests seem to show that the gun had been used to kill the guard.

Was it morally right to execute these two men? Why or why not?

5. Governor George Ryan of Illinois

(See George Ryan, "I Must Act," in Hugo Bedau and Paul Cassell, eds., *Debating the Death Penalty* (Oxford: Oxford University Press, 2004), pp. 218–34). George Ryan was the thirty-ninth governor of Illinois. On January 11, 2003, he announced the commutation of all of Illinois's death sentences. In a speech delivered at Northwestern University College of Law, Governor Ryan explained his reasons for ending the death sentence in Illinois. To begin with, seventeen men had been wrongly convicted. One of these men, Aaron Patterson, was unjustly imprisoned for fifteen years. Another one of the condemned, LeRoy Orange, lost seventeen of the best years of his life on death row. Most of the major allies of the U.S.—Europe, Canada, Mexico, and most of South and Central American—do not have the death penalty. Even Russia has called a moratorium on the punishment. The death penalty has been abolished in twelve states and in none of these states has the homicide rate increased. In Illinois one is five times more likely to get the death sentence for first-degree murder in rural areas than in Cook County. Nearly half of the three hundred or so capital cases in Illinois had been reversed for a new trial or resentencing. Thirty-three of the death row inmates were represented at trial by an attorney who had later been disbarred or suspended from practicing law. Thirty-five of the black defendants had been convicted or condemned by all-white juries. More than two-thirds of the inmates on death row were black. Forty-six inmates were convicted on the basis of testimony from jailhouse informants. Illinois had the dubious distinction of having exonerated more men than it had executed: thirteen men found innocent, twelve executed. The overwhelming majority of those executed were psychotic, alcoholic, drug addicted, or mentally ill. They were poor; few people with money or prestige are convicted of capital crimes, and even fewer are executed. All these considerations led Governor Ryan to conclude that the Illinois death penalty system is arbitrary and capricious, and therefore immoral.

Do you agree with Governor Ryan or not? Why or why not?

Suggested Readings

1. For facts about the death penalty see the Death Penalty Information Center (http://www.deathpenalty.org). For current information see the American Civil Liberties (http://www.aclu.org). The death penalty is defended on Pro-Death Penalty.Com (http://www.prodeathpenalty.com). For objections to the death penalty see the Campaign to End the Death Penalty (http://www.nodeathpenalty.ort/index.html). Death Penalty Focus (http://www.deathpenalty.org) and the National Coalition to Abolish the Death Penalty (http://www.ncadp.org) provide more information online about the death penalty.
2. Hugo Adam Bedau, "The Case Against the Death Penalty," on the ACLU archives (http://archive.aclu.org/library/case against death.html), presents eight objections to the death penalty. The ACLU is opposed to the death penalty.
3. Hugo Bedau and Paul Cassell, eds., *Debating the Death Penalty* (Oxford: Oxford University Press, 2004), contains essays for and against the death penalty. Bedau presents a history of the death penalty in the United States Louis P. Pojman and Paul Cassell defend it.
4. Louis P. Pojman and Jeffrey Reiman, *The Death Penalty: For and Against* (Lanham, MD: Rowman and Littlefeld Publishers, 1988). Pojman defends the utilitarian argument that capital punishment is justified because it deters potential murderers, and Reiman replies with objections.

5. Ernest van den Haag, "End the Death Penalty; Use Life without Parole," *USA Today,* April 8, 1994, changes his mind and says that the evidence for abolition of capital punishment is "beyond dispute." He says, "The death penalty is a failure as a tool of law, justice or public safety."

6. Jonathan Glover, *Causing Death and Saving Lives* (Harmondsworth, U.K.: Pelican Books, 1977), pp. 228–45, attacks Kant's retributive theory and argues for the abolition of the death penalty from a utilitarian point of view.

7. Hugo Adam Bedau, "How to Argue About the Death Penalty," *Israel Law Review* 25, 2–4 (Summer/Autumn 1991): 466–80, argues that a preponderance of reasons favors the abolition of the death penalty.

8. Hugo Adam Bedau, "Capital Punishment," in *Matters of Life and Death,* 3rd ed., ed. Tom Regan (New York: Random House, 1993), pp. 160–94, argues that neither the appeal to retribution nor the appeal to deterrence justifies the death penalty as opposed to the alternative punishment of life imprisonment.

9. Hugo Adam Bedau, ed., *The Death Penalty in America,* 3rd ed. (Oxford: Oxford University Press, 1982), provides a number of useful articles on factual data relevant to the death penalty, and articles both for and against it.

10. Mark Costanzo, *Just Revenge: Costs and Consequences of the Death Penalty* (New York: St. Martin's Press, 1997), covers various aspects of the death penalty and concludes that it should be abolished.

11. Robert M. Baird and Stuart E. Rosenbaum, eds., *Punishment and the Death Penalty: The Current Debate* (Amherst, NY: Prometheus Books, 1995), is an anthology with readings on the justification of punishment and the death penalty.

12. Tom Sorell, *Moral Theory and Capital Punishment* (Oxford: Blackwell, 1988) defends the death penalty.

13. Tom Sorell, "Aggravated Murder and Capital Punishment," *Journal of Applied Philosophy,* 10 (1993): 201–13, argues in favor of the death penalty for the most serious murders.

14. Charles L. Black, Jr., *Capital Punishment: The Inevitability of Caprice and Mistake* (New York: W. W. Norton, 1981), maintains that mistakes cannot be eliminated from the imposition of the death penalty, and for that reason it ought to be abolished.

15. Walter Berns, *For Capital Punishment* (New York: Basic Books, 1979), defends a retributivist justification of capital punishment.

16. Robert S. Gerstein, "Capital Punishment–'Cruel and Unusual?' A Retributivist Response," *Ethics* 85 (January 1975): 75–79, defends retributivism against the complaint that it is mere vengeance.

17. Steven Goldberg, "On Capital Punishment," *Ethics* 85 (October 1974): 67–74, examines the factual issue of whether or not the death penalty is a uniquely effective deterrent. A revised version titled "Does Capital Punishment Deter?" appears in *Today's Moral Problems,* 2nd ed., ed. Richard A. Wasserstrom (New York: Macmillan, 1979), pp. 538–51.

18. Sidney Hook, "The Death Sentence," in *The Death Penalty in America,* ed. Hugo Adam Bedau (Garden City, NY: Doubleday, 1967), supports the retention of the death penalty in two cases: (1) defendants convicted of murder who choose death rather than life imprisonment, and (2) those who have been sentenced to prison for murder and then murder again while in prison.

19. Bruce N. Waller, "From Hemlock to Lethal Injection: The Case for Self-Execution," *International Journal of Applied Philosophy* 4 (Fall 1989): 53–58, argues that prisoners condemned to death should be offered the chance to kill themselves.

20. Robert Johnson, "This Man Has Expired. Witness to an Execution," *Commonweal* (January 13, 1989): 9–13, gives a detailed and graphic description of an electric-chair execution.

21. Stephen Nathanson, *An Eye for an Eye? The Morality of Punishing Death* (Lanham, MD: Roman & Littlefield, 1987), discusses issues surrounding the death penalty and develops a case for abolishing it.

22. Welsh S. White, *The Death Penalty in the Nineties* (Ann Arbor: University of Michigan Press, 1991), examines the way the death penalty has been administered in the nineties.

Chapter 5

Sexuality and Marriage

Introduction

Factual Background

There are numerous studies of human sexuality, containing a wealth of information. I will confine myself to a few basic facts. People are not either homosexual or heterosexual; another sexual orientation is bisexuality—that is, being sexually attracted to people of both sexes. The percentage of both sexes who are bisexual is believed to be about the same as those who are homosexual, though there is debate. At one extreme, the Kinsey studies in 1948 and 1953 reported that 37 percent of men in the United States had achieved orgasm through contact with another male after adolescence, and that about 10 percent of white American males were exclusively homosexual for at least three years of their lives. Only 4 percent of the men were exclusively homosexual throughout their lives; that is, most of the men counted as homosexual were bisexual. Only 2 to 3 percent of women reported being exclusively lesbian. At the other extreme, Tom Smith's National Opinion Research Center research (http://www.norc.uchicago.edu/online/sex) reported that after age 18 less than 1 percent of sexually active males are gay and 4 percent bisexual.

It is generally agreed that masturbation is common. One study found that 92 percent of males and 73 percent of females had masturbated by age 20. Oral sex is also common. According to the American Psychological Association, approximately 90 percent of all heterosexual married couples have engaged in oral sex. As recently as 1960, every state in the country had an antisodomy law banning oral or anal sex. In 37 states these laws have been repealed or blocked by state courts. Of the 13 states retaining sodomy laws, 4 states (Texas, Kansas, Oklahoma, and Missouri) prohibit oral and anal sex between same-sex couples. The other nine states ban consensual sodomy for everyone.

In the *Bowers* case (see the Problem Cases), the Supreme Court ruled that Georgia's antisodomy law did not violate the U.S. Constitution. But in June 2003 the Court reversed itself in the case of *Lawrence and Garner v. Texas*. The Court ruled that a Texas state law banning private consensual sex between adults of the same sex was unconstitutional. The ruling established a broad constitutional right to sexual privacy. In the majority opinion Justice Anthony Kennedy said, "The petitioners are entitled to respect for their private lives. The state cannot demean their existence or control their destiny by making their private sexual conduct a crime." This ruling apparently invalidates the antisodomy laws in the thirteen states having them.

According to U.S. Census figures, there are around half a million gay couples in the United States. Nearly 40 percent of these pairs reside in California, Florida, New York, and Texas. Although many of these pairs wish to be legally married, same-sex marriage is illegal in 38 states. In the case of *Baker v. Vermont* (1999), the Supreme Court of Vermont ruled that the common benefits clause of the Vermont

constitution requires that same-sex couples not be deprived of the benefits and protections extended to opposite-sex couples. In April 2000, the Vermont legislature
approved a bill allowing same-sex civil unions. As defined by the Vermont law, civil
unions are not quite the same as full-fledged marriages but they come close. They
don't apply to federal benefits such as Social Security and their validity in other
states has not been tested (but no doubt will be), but in Vermont they will function
like marriages—that is, they confer marital-style benefits such as tax breaks and
inheritance rights. So far, hundreds of couples, many of them from out of state,
have received Vermont civil union certificates.

The objection to civil unions is that they do not have all the benefits of marriage.
In February 2004 the Massachusetts Supreme Court ruled that only full marriage
rights for same-sex couples conforms to the state's constitution. The court rejected
using civil unions as a remedy because civil unions relegate same-sex couples to a
different status than heterosexual couples, and this unequal treatment is unconstitutional. In response to the Massachusetts ruling, President George W. Bush
announced that he would endorse an amendment to the U.S. Constitution called
the Federal Marriage Amendment. The proposed amendment says, "Marriage in the
United States shall consist only of the union of a man and a woman." Defenders of
the amendment say it is a compromise that will not stop state legislatures from
allowing civil unions. It remains to be seen if this amendment will be passed.
Amending the Constitution requires a two-thirds majority in both the House and
Senate, and ratification by 38 of the 50 states.

The Readings

The Judeo-Christian tradition holds that the main purpose of sex is the procreation
of children within the context of marriage. Nonmarital sex—adultery, premarital sex,
fornication, prostitution, masturbation, and homosexuality—is morally wrong. In
the first reading, the Vatican Declaration on Sexual Ethics presents an influential
statement of this traditional Christian view of sex.

To understand this traditional view of sex, we need to review the natural law theory used to support it. (For more on natural law theory see the Aquinas reading in
the first chapter.) In natural law theory, human action is naturally directed toward
certain goals and purposes, such as life and procreation. These natural goals and
purposes are good, and to interfere with them is morally wrong. Accordingly, if the
natural goal or purpose of sexual activity is reproduction within the context of marriage, then interfering with this natural goal is morally wrong.

The Vatican Declaration espouses this natural law theory. According to the Declaration, homosexuality is seriously disordered because it contradicts its finality; that
is, it opposes the natural end of sex, which is procreation. Masturbation is also a serious disorder for the same reason. Premarital sexual relations are condemned because
they often exclude the prospect of children, and even if children are produced, they
will be deprived of a proper and stable environment.

Alan Goldman (see the Suggested Readings) presents a different view of sex. He
rejects the "means–end analysis" of sex that sees sex as merely a means to some end
such as reproduction. Instead, Goldman proposes the idea of "plain sex"—that is,

sex that is not a means to some further end such as reproduction, communication, or the expression of love, but is simply the satisfaction of sexual desire. As Goldman defines it, sexual desire is simply the desire for contact with another person's body and for the pleasure such contact produces, and not the desire to reproduce, to communicate, or to express love. Given this account of sex, masturbation is not really sex at all; rather it is just an imaginary substitute for sex. But nongenital activities such as kissing, embracing, or massaging can be sexual in Goldman's view if they satisfy sexual desire as he defines it. As for homosexuality, Goldman agrees that it is a sexual perversion, but for him this just means that it is statistically abnormal, and not that it is morally wrong. In general, Goldman thinks that sexuality has no intrinsic morality; sexual behavior, like any other behavior, has to be morally evaluated in terms of moral principles, such as Kant's principle of reciprocity.

John Corvino agrees that homosexual sex is not wrong just because it is abnormal. He goes on to argue that it is not wrong just because it is or is not practiced by other animals, or because it does not proceed from innate desires, or because it is disgusting or offensive, or because it violates an organ's principle purpose. On the last point, he points out that sexual organs can have other purposes besides procreation; they can be used to express love or to give and receive pleasure. He finds nothing wrong with using the sexual organs for these other purposes.

Bradshaw does not agree with Corvino. He discusses two reasons for saying that homosexual acts are morally wrong. First, they are condemned in the Bible. The passage most often quoted (by both Bradshaw and Corvino) is Leviticus 18:22: "You shall not lie with a male as with a woman; it is an abomination." Another passage that is quoted is Roman 1:26–27 where St. Paul attacks the shameless and unnatural intercourse of men with other men. Bradshaw interprets these condemnations of homosexuality as universally applicable to all people at all times. Corvino gives a different interpretation. He claims that biblical sayings should be put in historical context. Some of them may have been appropriate in biblical times, but they don't apply now. Biblical attacks on homosexuality are in the same category as injunctions against charging interest or endorsements of slavery. According to Corvino, these sayings are not taken seriously now.

Bradshaw has a second and main reason for holding that homosexual acts are morally wrong. They involve a misuse of the body, a violation of the body's "moral space." The idea is that heterosexual sex somehow "fits" the body's moral space while homosexual sex does not. Presumably Corvino would reply that there is no one proper sexual "fit," and that there are other "fits" besides the heterosexual one. Furthermore, it is doubtful that rape or prostitution "fits" the body's moral space even if it is heterosexual and reproductive.

Bradshaw implies that homosexuality is inferior to heterosexuality; it is a perversion and a mere counterfeit of heterosexual love. Martha Nussbaum finds a different view in the writings of Plato and Aristotle. According to Nussbaum, Plato's dialogues such as the Symposium and Phaedrus depict male–male love to be, on the whole, superior to male–female love because of its potential for spirituality and friendship. Aristotle also finds male–male relationships to have the potential for the highest form of friendship, a potential not found in male–female relationships.

Sam Schulman and Jonathan Rauch debate the morality of same-sex or gay marriage. Schulman says he is passionately and instinctively opposed to homosexual marriage. He agrees with those who predict that gay marriage will produce measurable harm to the family and children, but he does not think that this objection gets to the heart of the matter. In his view the essence of marriage does not involve romantic love or sexual attraction, since it is a truism, he claims, that most married people feel little sexual or romantic attraction to each other. Rather the essence of marriage is to sanction the connection which alone creates new life. Marriage is an institution that is built around female procreativity, and as such it is an institution based on women. To say that two men are married, then, is in Schulman's view conceptually absurd or impossible. It like being a father to a pebble or a brother to a puppy.

Rauch agrees that love is not what defines marriage although it is certainly a desirable element. He grants that society should care about marriage because it protects children, but he points out that gay couples may have children, either through adoption or if they are lesbians, by using artificial insemination. He doubts that allowing gay marriage will produce measurable harm to heterosexual marriages or children, because we are talking about only 3 to 5 percent of the population. Greater changes have been produced by making it easier to get a divorce, with the result that half of today's new marriages will end in divorce. What needs to be done is to strengthen the institution of marriage by making divorce harder to get, and encouraging more people to get married, including gay couples. The benefit of gay marriage in Rauch's view is that it has a taming effect on young males and it provides caretaking for old homosexuals. It provides two of the main social purposes of marriage. The third purpose, having and raising children, is not always satisfied, but then childless heterosexual couples do not satisfy this purpose of marriage either.

Philosophical Issues

What counts as sex? This is a basic issue raised by the readings. The Vatican Declaration seems to assume that only genital sex counts; it speaks about "genital acts" and ignores nongenital acts, such as kissing or embracing. Goldman thinks that nongenital acts can satisfy a sexual desire as he defines it; indeed, he believes that the baby's desire to be cuddled is a sexual desire. But oddly enough, it seems that reproductive sex that is done solely because of the desire to procreate, and not because of any desire for contact with another person's body or any desire for the pleasure produced, would not be sexual, in Goldman's view.

What counts as sexual perversion? This is a related issue that comes up in the readings. The view of the Vatican Declaration is that nonreproductive sex such as masturbation is a perversion, and the fact that masturbation is statistically normal is irrelevant. Does this mean that kissing is a perversion because it is nonreproductive? What about sex between married couples who are infertile? In Goldman's view, what is sexually perverse is what is statistically abnormal. It seems to follow that masturbation is not perverse; it is normal. But reproductive sex in an unusual position would be perverse because it is statistically abnormal.

Are sexual perversions morally wrong? Goldman does not think so, because in his view the concept of sexual perversion is merely statistical, not evaluative. What is sexually perverse is what is statistically abnormal, but this does not mean that it is immoral. The Vatican Declaration has a different view; perversion involves unnaturalness, and what is unnatural is wrong. Homosexuality and masturbation are unnatural in that they contradict the finality or natural purpose of sex, which is reproduction, and for that reason they are not just wrong but also serious disorders.

But is reproduction the natural purpose of sex? Goldman agrees that this may be "nature's purpose," but he denies that it is always or usually our purpose. He mentions the analogy with eating. The natural purpose of eating may be nourishment, but that is not always our purpose in eating; we eat for enjoyment too. Similarly, the natural purpose of sex may be reproduction, but that is not always our goal; we usually have sex for enjoyment. Indeed, in Goldman's analysis sexual desire is the desire for contact with another person's body and for the pleasure produced; it is different from the desire for reproduction. Sexual activity satisfies sexual desire, a desire that is different from the desire to reproduce.

What is the purpose of marriage? This is another interesting question discussed in the readings. The Vatican Declaration, Bradshaw, and Schulman seem to agree that having and raising children is the main purpose of marriage. But as Rauch notes in the reading, this makes it hard to understand why sterile heterosexual couples should be married. Another answer is that love is the essential purpose of marriage. But even though love is a desirable element of marriage, Rauch does not think it is either necessary or sufficient for marriage. One may love another without being married, and people may marry for reasons other than love. Schulman claims it is a truism that married people feel little romantic attraction to each other, and adds that in the past most people married for reasons other than love. Schulman thinks the essence of marriage has to do with having children and female productivity. Rauch believes that there are two main social purposes of marriage besides having and raising children: the taming or civilizing of young males and the care that married couples provide for each other.

Declaration on Sexual Ethics

THE VATICAN

The Declaration on Sexual Ethics was issued in Rome by the Sacred Congregation for the Doctrine of the Faith on December 29, 1975.

The authors defend the Christian doctrine that "every genital act must be within the framework of marriage." Premarital sex, masturbation, and homosexuality are specifically condemned, and chastity is recommended as a virtue.

Source: The Vatican, "Declaration on Sexual Ethics."

1. ACCORDING TO CONTEMPORARY scientific research, the human person is so profoundly affected by sexuality that it must be considered as one of the factors which give to each individual's life the principal traits that distinguish it. In fact it is from sex that the human person receives the characteristics which, on the biological, psychological and spiritual levels, make that person a man or a woman, and thereby largely condition his or her progress towards maturity and insertion into society. Hence sexual matters, as is obvious to everyone, today constitute a theme frequently and openly dealt with in books, reviews, magazines, and other means of social communication.

In the present period, the corruption of morals has increased, and one of the most serious indications of this corruption is the unbridled exaltation of sex. Moreover, through the means of social communication and through public entertainment this corruption has reached the point of invading the field of education and of infecting the general mentality.

In this context certain educators, teachers, and moralists have been able to contribute to a better understanding and integration into life of the values proper to each of the sexes; on the other hand there are those who have put forward concepts and modes of behavior which are contrary to the true moral exigencies of the human person. Some members of the latter group have even gone so far as to favor a licentious hedonism.

As a result, in the course of a few years, teachings, moral criteria, and modes of living hitherto faithfully preserved have been very much unsettled, even among Christians. There are many people today who, being confronted with so many widespread opinions opposed to the teachings which they received from the Church, have come to wonder what they must still hold as true.

2. The Church cannot remain indifferent to this confusion of minds and relaxation of morals. It is a question, in fact, of a matter which is of the utmost importance both for the personal lives of Christians and for the social life of our time.[1]

The Bishops are daily led to note the growing difficulties experienced by the faithful in obtaining knowledge of wholesome moral teaching, especially in sexual matters, and of the growing difficulties experienced by pastors in expounding this teaching effectively. The Bishops know that by their pastoral charge they are called upon to meet the needs of their faithful in this very serious matter, and important documents dealing with it have already been published by some of them or by Episcopal Conferences. Nevertheless, since the erroneous opinions and resulting deviations are continuing to spread everywhere, the Sacred Congregation for the Doctrine of the Faith, by virtue of its function in the universal Church[2] and by a mandate of the Supreme Pontiff, has judged it necessary to publish the present Declaration.

3. The people of our time are more and more convinced that the human person's dignity and vocation demand that they should discover, by the light of their own intelligence, the values innate in their nature, that they should ceaselessly develop these values and realize them in their lives, in order to achieve an ever greater development.

In moral matters man cannot make value judgments according to his personal whim: "In the depths of his conscience, man detects a law which he does not impose on himself, but which holds him to obedience. . . . For man has in his heart a law written by God. To obey it is the very dignity of man; according to it he will be judged."[3]

Moreover, through his revelation God has made known to us Christians his plan of salvation,

---

1 See Vatican II, *Pastoral Constitution on the Church in the World of Today,* no. 47: *Acta Apostolicae Sedis* 58 (1966) 1067 [*The Pope Speaks* XI, 289–290].

2 See the Apostolic Constitution *Regimini Ecclesiae Universae* (August 15, 1967), no. 29: *AAS* 59 (1967) 897 [*TPS* XII, 401–402].

3 *Pastoral Constitution on the Church in the World of Today,* no. 16: *AAS* 58 (1966) 1037 [*TPS* XI, 268].

and he has held up to us Christ, the Saviour and Sanctifier, in his teaching and example, as the supreme and immutable law of life: "I am the light of the world; anyone who follows me will not be walking in the dark, he will have the light of life."[4]

Therefore there can be no true promotion of man's dignity unless the essential order of his nature is respected. Of course, in the history of civilization many of the concrete conditions and needs of human life have changed and will continue to change. But all evolution of morals and every type of life must be kept within the limits imposed by the immutable principles based upon every human person's constitutive elements and essential relations—elements and relations which transcend historical contingency.

These fundamental principles, which can be grasped by reason, are contained in "the divine law—eternal, objective, and universal—whereby God orders, directs, and governs the entire universe and all the ways of the human community, by a plan conceived in wisdom and love. Man has been made by God to participate in this law, with the result that, under the gentle disposition of divine Providence, he can come to perceive ever increasingly the unchanging truth."[5] This divine law is accessible to our minds.

4. Hence, those many people are in error who today assert that one can find neither in human nature nor in the revealed law any absolute and immutable norm to serve for particular actions other than the one which expresses itself in the general law of charity and respect for human dignity. As a proof of their assertion they put forward the view that so-called norms of the natural law or precepts of Sacred Scripture are to be regarded only as given expressions of a form of particular culture at a certain moment of history.

But in fact, divine Revelation and, in its own proper order, philosophical wisdom, emphasize the authentic exigencies of human nature. They thereby necessarily manifest the existence of immutable laws inscribed in the constitutive elements of human nature and which are revealed to be identical in all beings endowed with reason.

Furthermore, Christ instituted his Church as "the pillar and bulwark of truth."[6] With the Holy Spirit's assistance, she ceaselessly preserves and transmits without error the truths of the moral order, and she authentically interprets not only the revealed positive law but "also . . . those principles of the moral order which have their origin in human nature itself"[7] and which concern man's full development and sanctification. Now in fact the Church throughout her history has always considered a certain number of precepts of the natural law as having an absolute and immutable value, and in their transgression she has seen a contradiction of the teaching and spirit of the Gospel.

5. Since sexual ethics concern certain fundamental values of human and Christian life, this general teaching equally applies to sexual ethics. In this domain there exist principles and norms which the Church has always unhesitatingly transmitted as part of her teaching, however much the opinions and morals of the world may have been opposed to them. These principles and norms in no way owe their origin to a certain type of culture, but rather to knowledge of the divine law and of human nature. They therefore cannot be considered as having become out of date or doubtful under the pretext that a new cultural situation has arisen.

---

4 *Jn* 8, 12.

5 *Declaration on Religious Freedom*, no. 3: *AAS* 58 (1966) 931 [*TPS* XI, 86].

6 1 *Tm* 3, 15.

7 *Declaration on Religious Freedom*, no. 14: *AAS* 58 (1966) 940 [*TPS* XI, 93]. See also Pius XI, Encyclical *Casti Connubii* (December 31, 1930): *AAS* 22 (1930) 579–580; Pius XII, Address of November 2, 1954 *AAS* 46 (1954) 671–672 [*TPS* 1 380–381]; John XXIII, Encyclical *Mater et Magistra* (May 25, 1961), no. 239: *AAS* 53 (1961) 457 [*TPS* VII, 388]; Paul VI, Encyclical *Humanae Vitae* (July 25, 1968), no. 4: *AAS* 60 (1968) 483 [*TPS* XIII, 331–332].

It is these principles which inspired the exhortations and directives given by the Second Vatican Council for an education and an organization of social life taking account of the equal dignity of man and woman while respecting their difference.[8]

Speaking of "the sexual nature of man and the human faculty of procreation," the Council noted that they "wonderfully exceed the dispositions of lower forms of life."[9] It then took particular care to expound the principles and criteria which concern human sexuality in marriage, and which are based upon the finality of the specific function of sexuality.

In this regard the Council declares that the moral goodness of the acts proper to conjugal life, acts which are ordered according to true human dignity, "does not depend solely on sincere intentions or on an evaluation of motives. It must be determined by objective standards. These, based on the nature of the human person and his acts, preserve the full sense of mutual self-giving and human procreation in the context of true love."[10]

These final words briefly sum up the Council's teaching—more fully expounded in an earlier part of the same Constitution[11]—on the finality of the sexual act and on the principal criterion of its morality: it is respect for its finality that ensures the moral goodness of this act.

This same principle, which the Church holds from divine Revelation and from her authentic interpretation of the natural law, is also the basis of her traditional doctrine, which states that the use of the sexual function has its true meaning and moral rectitude only in true marriage."[12]

6. It is not the purpose of the present declaration to deal with all the abuses of the sexual faculty, nor with all the elements involved in the practice of chastity. Its object is rather to repeat the Church's doctrine on certain particular points, in view of the urgent need to oppose serious errors and widespread aberrant modes of behavior.

7. Today there are many who vindicate the right to sexual union before marriage, at least in those cases where a firm intention to marry and an affection which is already in some way conjugal in the psychology of the subjects require this completion, which they judge to be connatural. This is especially the case when the celebration of the marriage is impeded by circumstances or when this intimate relationship seems necessary in order for love to be preserved.

This opinion is contrary to Christian doctrine, which states that every genital act must be within the framework of marriage. However firm the intention of those who practice such premature sexual relations may be, the fact remains that these relations cannot ensure, in sincerity and fidelity, the interpersonal relationship between a man and a woman, nor especially can they protect this relationship from whims and caprices. Now it is a stable union that Jesus willed, and he restored its original requirement, beginning with the sexual difference. "Have you not read that the creator from the beginning made them male and female and that he said: This is why a man must leave father and mother, and cling to his wife, and the two become one body? They are no longer two, therefore, but one body. So then, what God has united, man must not divide."[13] Saint Paul will be even more explicit when he shows that if unmarried people

---

8 See Vatican II, *Declaration on Christian Education,* nos. 1 and 8: *AAS* 58 (1966) 729–730, 734–736 [*TPS* XI, 201–202, 206–207]; *Pastoral Constitution on the Church in the World of Today,* nos. 29, 60, 67: *AAS* 58 (1966) 1048–1049, 1080–181, 1088–1089 [*TPS* XI, 276–277, 299–300, 304–305].

9 *Pastoral Constitution on the Church in the World of Today,* no. 51: *AAS* 58 (1966) 1072 [*TPS* XI, 293].

10 *Loc. cit.;* see also no. 49: *AAS* 58 (1966) 1069–1070 [*TPS* XI, 291–292].

11 See *Pastoral Constitution on the Church in the World of Today,* nos. 49–50: *AAS* 58 (1966) 1069–1072 [*TPS* XI, 291–293].

12 The present Declaration does not review all the moral norms for the use of sex, since they have already been set forth in the encyclicals *Casti Connubii* and *Humanae Vitae.*
13 *Mt 19,* 4–6.

or widows cannot live chastely they have no other alternative than the stable union of marriage: ". . . it is better to marry than to be aflame with passion."[14] Through marriage, in fact, the love of married people is taken up into that love which Christ irrevocably has for the Church,[15] while dissolute sexual union[16] defiles the temple of the Holy Spirit which the Christian has become. Sexual union therefore is only legitimate if a definitive community of life has been established between the man and the woman.

This is what the Church has always understood and taught,[17] and she finds a profound agreement with her doctrine in men's reflection and in the lessons of history.

Experience teaches us that love must find its safeguard in the stability of marriage, if sexual intercourse is truly to respond to the requirements of its own finality and to those of human dignity. These requirements call for a conjugal contract sanctioned and guaranteed by society— a contract which establishes a state of life of capital importance both for the exclusive union of the man and the woman and for the good of their family and of the human community. Most often, in fact, premarital relations exclude the possibility of children. What is represented to be conjugal love is not able, as it absolutely should be, to develop into paternal and maternal love. Or, if it does happen to do so, this will be to the detriment of the children, who will be deprived of the stable environment in which they ought to develop in order to find in it the way and the means of their insertion into society as a whole.

14 1 *Cor* 7, 9.
15 See *Eph* 5, 25–32.
16 Extramarital intercourse is expressly condemned in 1 *Cor* 5, 1; 6, 9; 7, 2; 10, 8; *Eph* 5, 5–7; 1 *Tm* 1, 10; *Heb* 13, 4; there are explicit arguments given in 1 *Cor* 6, 12–20.
17 See Innocent IV, Letter *Sub Catholicae professione* (March 6, 1254) (*DS* 835); Pius II, Letter *Cum sicut accepimus* (November 14, 1459) (*DS* 1367); Decrees of the Holy Office on September 24, 1665 (*DS* 2045) and March 2, 1679 (*DS* 2148); Pius XI, Encyclical *Casti Conubii* (December 31, 1930): *AAS* 22 (1930) 538–539.

The consent given by people who wish to be united in marriage must therefore be manifested externally and in a manner which makes it valid in the eyes of society. As far as the faithful are concerned, their consent to the setting up of a community of conjugal life must be expressed according to the laws of the Church. It is a consent which makes their marriage a Sacrament of Christ.

8. At the present time there are those who, basing themselves on observations in the psychological order, have begun to judge indulgently, and even to excuse completely, homosexual relations between certain people. This they do in opposition to the constant teaching of the Magisterium and to the moral sense of the Christian people.

A distinction is drawn, and it seems with some reason, between homosexuals whose tendency comes from a false education, from a lack of normal sexual development, from habit, from bad example, or from other similar causes, and is transitory or at least not incurable; and homosexuals who are definitively such because of some kind of innate instinct or a pathological constitution judged to be incurable.

In regard to this second category of subjects, some people conclude that their tendency is so natural that it justifies in their case homosexual relations within a sincere communion of life and love analogous to marriage insofar as such homosexuals feel incapable of enduring a solitary life.

In the pastoral field, these homosexuals must certainly be treated with understanding and sustained in the hope of overcoming their personal difficulties and their inability to fit into society. Their culpability will be judged with prudence. But no pastoral method can be employed which would give moral justification to these acts on the grounds that they would be consonant with the condition of such people. For according to the objective moral order, homosexual relations are acts which lack an essential and indispensable finality. In Sacred Scripture they are condemned as a serious depravity and even presented as the sad consequence of rejecting

God.[18] This judgment of Scripture does not of course permit us to conclude that all those who suffer from this anomaly are personally responsible for it, but it does attest to the fact that homosexual acts are intrinsically disordered and can in no case be approved.

9. The traditional Catholic doctrine that masturbation constitutes a grave moral disorder is often called into doubt or expressly denied today. It is said that psychology and sociology show that it is a normal phenomenon of sexual development, especially among the young. It is stated that there is real and serious fault only in the measure that the subject deliberately indulges in solitary pleasure closed in on self ("ipsation"), because in this case the act would indeed be radically opposed to the loving communion between persons of different sex which some hold is what is principally sought in the use of the sexual faculty.

This opinion is contradictory to the teaching and pastoral practice of the Catholic Church. Whatever the force of certain arguments of a biological and philosophical nature, which have sometimes been used by theologians, in fact both the Magisterium of the Church—in the course of a constant tradition—and the moral sense of the faithful have declared without hesitation that masturbation is an intrinsically and seriously disordered act."[19] The main reason is that, whatever the motive for acting in this way, the deliberate use of the sexual faculty outside normal conjugal relations essentially contradicts the finality of the faculty. For it lacks the sexual relationship called for by the moral order, namely the relationship which realizes "the full sense of mutual self-giving and human procreation in the context of true love."[20] All deliberate exercise of sexuality must be reserved to this regular relationship. Even if it cannot be proved that Scripture condemns this sin by name, the tradition of the Church has rightly understood it to be condemned in the New Testament when the latter speaks of "impurity," "unchasteness," and other vices contrary to chastity and continence.

Sociological surveys are able to show the frequency of this disorder according to the places, populations, or circumstances studied. In this way facts are discovered, but facts do not constitute a criterion for judging the moral value of human acts.[21] The frequency of the phenomenon in question is certainly to be linked with man's innate weakness following original sin; but it is also to be linked with the loss of a sense of God, with the corruption of morals engendered by the commercialization of vice, with the unrestrained licentiousness of so many public entertainments and publications, as well as with the neglect of modesty, which is the guardian of chastity.

On the subject of masturbation modern psychology provides much valid and useful information for formulating a more equitable judgment on moral responsibility and for orienting pastoral action. Psychology helps one to see how the immaturity of adolescence (which can sometimes persist

---

18 *Rom* 1:24–27: "in consequence, God delivered them up in their lusts to unclean practices; they engaged in the mutual degradation of their bodies, these men who exchanged the truth of God for a lie and worshipped and served the creature rather than the Creator—blessed be he forever, amen! God therefore delivered them to disgraceful passions. Their women exchanged natural intercourse for unnatural, and the men gave up natural intercourse with women and burned with lust for one another. Men did shameful things with men, and thus received in their own persons the penalty for their perversity." See also what St. Paul says of sodomy in 1 *Cor* 6, 9; 1 *Tm* 1, 10.

19 See Leo IX, Letter *Ad splendidum nitentes* (1054) (*DS* 687–688); Decree of the Holy Office on March 2, 1679 (*DS* 2149); Pius XII, Addresses of October 8, 1953: *AAS* 45 (1953) 677–678, and May 19, 1956: *AAS* 48 (1956) 472–473.

20 *Pastoral Constitution on the Church in the World of Today*, no. 51: *AAS* 58 (1966) 1072 [*TPS* XI, 2931.]

21 See Paul VI, Apostolic Exhortation *Quinque iam anni* (December 8, 1970): *AAS* 63 (1971) 102 [*TPS* XV, 329]: "If sociological surveys are useful for better discovering the thought patterns of the people of a particular place, the anxieties and needs of those to whom we proclaim the word of God, and also the oppositions made to it by modern reasoning through the widespread notion that outside science there exists no legitimate form of knowledge, still the conclusions drawn from such surveys could not of themselves constitute a determining criterion of truth."

after that age), psychological imbalance, or habit can influence behavior, diminishing the deliberate character of the act and bringing about a situation whereby subjectively there may not always be serious fault. But in general, the absence of serious responsibility must not be presumed; this would be to misunderstand people's moral capacity.

In the pastoral ministry, in order to form an adequate judgment in concrete cases, the habitual behavior of people will be considered in its totality, not only with regard to the individual's practice of charity and of justice but also with regard to the individual's care in observing the particular precepts of chastity. In particular, one will have to examine whether the individual is using the necessary means, both natural and supernatural, which Christian asceticism from its long experience recommends for overcoming passions and progressing in virtue. . . .

Review Questions

1. What is the traditional Christian doctrine about sex, according to the declaration?
2. Why does the declaration find premarital sexual relations to be immoral?
3. What is the declaration's objection to homosexuality?
4. What is wrong with masturbation, according to the declaration?

Discussion Questions

1. Is celibacy a violation of natural law? Explain your view.
2. Is contraception wrong too? Defend your answer.
3. Is procreation the only natural purpose of sex? Defend your position

Why Shouldn't Tommy and Jim Have Sex?
A Defense of Homosexuality

JOHN CORVINO

John Corvino is assistant professor of philosophy at Wayne State University in Detroit, Michigan. He is the editor of *Same Sex: Debating the Ethics, Science, and Culture of Homosexuality* (1997). Our reading is taken from this anthology.

Source: John Corvino, ed., *Same Sex: Debating the Ethics, Science, and Culture of Homosexuality* (Rowman and Littlefield Publishers, 1997), pp. 3–16. Reprinted with permission.

This essay grew out of a lecture, "What's (Morally) Wrong with Homosexuality?" which I first delivered at the University of Texas in 1992 and have since delivered at numerous other universities around the country. I am grateful to countless audience members, students, colleagues, and friends for helpful dialogue over the years. I would especially like to thank the following individuals for detailed comments on recent drafts of the paper: Edwin B. Allaire, Jonathan M. Bell, Daniel Bonevac, David Bradshaw, David Cleaves, Mary Beth Mader, Richard D. Mohr, Jonathan Rauch, Robert Schuessler, James Sterba, Alan Soble, and Thomas Williams. I dedicate this article to Carlos Casillas.

Corvino identifies five meanings of *unnatural* and argues that none of these meanings provides any reason for concluding that homosexuality is morally wrong. He claims that the biblical injunctions against homosexuality no longer apply today; they are like the injunctions against lending money for interest. Besides, there are many religions, and we can hardly avoid violating some religious belief. But in Corvino's view the fact that we do so is no basis for moral censure. Corvino concludes that homosexual sex is not morally evil but is morally good, at least when it is practiced by people like Tommy and Jim.

TOMMY AND JIM are a homosexual couple I know. Tommy is an accountant; Jim is a botany professor. They are in their forties and have been together fourteen years, the last five of which they've lived in a Victorian house that they've lovingly restored. Although their relationship has had its challenges, each has made sacrifices for the sake of the other's happiness and the relationship's long-term success.

I assume that Tommy and Jim have sex with each other (although I've never bothered to ask). Furthermore, I contend that they probably *should* have sex with each other. For one thing, sex is pleasurable. But it is also much more than that: a sexual relationship can unite two people in a way that virtually nothing else can. It can be an avenue of growth, of communication, and of lasting interpersonal fulfillment. These are reasons why most heterosexual couples have sex even if they don't want children, don't want children yet, or don't want additional children. And if these reasons are good enough for most heterosexual couples, then they should be good enough for Tommy and Jim.

Of course, having a reason to do something does not preclude there being an even better reason for not doing it. Tommy might have a good reason for drinking orange juice (it's tasty and nutritious) but an even better reason for not doing so (he's allergic). The point is that one would need a pretty good reason for denying a sexual relationship to Tommy and Jim, given the intense benefits widely associated with such relationships. The question I shall consider in this paper is thus quite simple: Why shouldn't Tommy and Jim have sex?[1]

HOMOSEXUAL SEX IS "UNNATURAL"

Many contend that homosexual sex is "unnatural." But what does that mean? Many things that people value—clothing, houses, medicine, and government, for example—are unnatural in some sense. On the other hand, many things that people detest—disease, suffering, and death, for example—are "natural" in the sense that they occur "in nature." If the unnaturalness charge is to be more than empty rhetorical flourish, those who levy it must specify what they mean. Borrowing from Burton Leiser, I will examine several possible meanings of "unnatural."[2]

1 Although my central example in the essay is a gay male couple, much of what I say will apply mutatis mutandis to lesbians as well, since many of the same arguments are used against them. This is not to say gay male sexuality and lesbian sexuality are largely similar or that discussions of the former will cover all that needs to be said about the latter. Furthermore, the fact that I focus on a long-term, committed relationship should not be taken to imply any judgment about homosexual activity outside of such unions. If the argument of this essay is successful, then the evaluation of homosexual activity outside of committed unions should be largely (if not entirely) similar to the evaluation of *hetero*-sexual activity outside of committed unions.

2 Burton M. Leiser, *Liberty, Justice, and Morals: Contemporary Value Conflicts* (New York: Macmillan, 1986), 51–57.

What Is Unusual or Abnormal Is Unnatural

One meaning of "unnatural" refers to that which deviates from the norm, that is, from what most people do. Obviously, most people engage in heterosexual relationships. But does it follow that it is wrong to engage in homosexual relationships? Relatively few people read Sanskrit, pilot ships, play the mandolin, breed goats, or write with both hands, yet none of these activities is immoral simply because it is unusual. As the Ramsey Colloquium, a group of Jewish and Christian scholars who oppose homosexuality, writes, "The statistical frequency of an act does not determine its moral status."[3] So while homosexuality might be unnatural in the sense of being unusual, that fact is morally irrelevant.

What Is Not Practiced by Other Animals Is Unnatural

Some people argue, "Even animals know better than to behave homosexually; homosexuality must be wrong." This argument is doubly flawed. First it rests on a false premise. Numerous studies—including Anne Perkins's study of "gay" sheep and George and Molly Hunt's study of "lesbian" seagulls—have shown that some animals do form homosexual pair-bonds.[4] Second, even if animals did not behave homosexually, that fact would not prove that homosexuality is immoral. After all, animals don't cook their food, brush their teeth, participate in religious worship, or attend college; human beings do all of these without moral censure. Indeed, the idea that animals could provide us with our standards—especially our sexual standards—is simply amusing.

What Does Not Proceed from Innate Desires Is Unnatural

Recent studies suggesting a biological basis for homosexuality have resulted in two popular

positions. One side proposes that homosexual people are "born that way" and that it is therefore natural (and thus good) for them to form homosexual relationships. The other side maintains that homosexuality is a lifestyle choice, which is therefore unnatural (and thus wrong). Both sides assume a connection between the origin of homosexual orientation, on the one hand, and the moral value of homosexual activity, on the other. And insofar as they share that assumption, both sides are wrong.

Consider first the pro-homosexual side: "They are born that way; therefore it's natural and good." This inference assumes that all innate desires are good ones (i.e., that they should be acted upon). Bur that assumption is clearly false. Research suggests that some people are born with a predisposition toward violence, but such people have no more right to strangle their neighbors than anyone else. So while people like Tommy and Jim may be born with homosexual tendencies, it doesn't follow that they ought to act on them. Nor does it follow that they ought *not* to act on them, even if the tendencies are not innate. I probably do not have any innate tendency to write with my left hand (since I, like everyone else in my family, have always been right-handed), but it doesn't follow that it would be immoral for me to do so. So simply asserting that homosexuality is a lifestyle choice will not show that it is an immoral lifestyle choice.

Do people "choose" to be homosexual? People certainly don't seem to choose their sexual *feelings,* at least not in any direct or obvious way. (Do you? Think about it.) Rather, they find certain people attractive and certain activities arousing, whether they "decide" to or not. Indeed, most people at some point in their lives wish that they could control their feelings more—for example, in situations of unrequited love—and find it frustrating that they cannot. What they *can* control to a considerable degree is how and when they act upon those feelings. In that sense, both homosexuality and heterosexuality involve lifestyle choices. But in either case, determining the origin of the feelings will not determine whether it is moral to act on them.

3 The Ramsey Colloquium, "The Homosexual Movement," *First Things* (March 1994), 15–20.
4 For an overview of some of these studies, see Simon LeVay, *Queer Science* (Boston: MIT Press, 1996), chap. 10.

What Violates an Organ's Principal Purpose Is Unnatural

Perhaps when people claim that homosexual sex is unnatural they mean that it cannot result in procreation. The idea behind the argument is that human organs have various natural purposes: eyes are for seeing, ears are for hearing, genitals are for procreating. According to this argument, it is immoral to use an organ in a way that violates its particular purpose.

Many of our organs, however, have multiple purposes. Tommy can use his mouth for talking, eating, breathing, licking stamps, chewing gum, kissing women, or kissing Jim; and it seems rather arbitrary to claim that all but the last use are "natural."[5] (And if we say that some of the other uses are "unnatural, but not immoral," we have failed to specify a morally relevant sense of the term "natural.")

Just because people can and do use their sexual organs to procreate, it does not follow that they should not use them for other purposes. Sexual organs seem very well suited for expressing love, for giving and receiving pleasure, and for celebrating, replenishing, and enhancing a relationship—even when procreation is not a factor. Unless opponents of homosexuality are prepared to condemn heterosexual couples who use contraception or individuals who masturbate, they must abandon this version of the unnaturalness argument. Indeed, even the Roman Catholic Church, which forbids contraception and masturbation, approves of sex for sterile couples and of sex during pregnancy, neither of which can lead to procreation. The Church concedes here that intimacy and pleasure are morally legitimate purposes for sex, even in cases where procreation is impossible. But since homosexual sex can achieve these purposes as well, it is inconsistent for the Church to condemn it on the grounds that it is not procreative.

One might object that sterile heterosexual couples do not *intentionally* turn away from procreation, whereas homosexual couples do. But this distinction doesn't hold. It is no more possible for Tommy to procreate with a woman whose uterus has been removed than it is for him to procreate with Jim.[6] By having sex with either one, he is intentionally engaging in a non-procreative sexual act.

Yet one might press the objection further and insist that Tommy and the woman *could* produce children if the woman were fertile: whereas homosexual relationships are essentially infertile, heterosexual relationships are only incidentally so. But what does that prove? Granted, it might require less of a miracle for a woman without a uterus to become pregnant than for Jim to become pregnant, but it would require a miracle nonetheless. Thus it seems that the real difference here is not that one couple is fertile and the other not, nor that one couple "could" be fertile (with the help of a miracle) and the other not, but rather that one couple is male-female and the other male-male. In other words, sex between Tommy and Jim is wrong because it's male-male—i.e., because it's homosexual. But that, of course, is no argument at all.[7]

What Is Disgusting or Offensive Is Unnatural

It often seems that when people call homosexuality "unnatural" they really just mean that

5 I have borrowed some items in this list from Richard Mohr's pioneering work *Gays/Justice* (New York: Columbia University Press, 1988), 36.

6 I am indebted to Andrew Koppelman and Stephen Macedo for helpful discussions on this point. See Andrew Koppelman's argument in chapter 4 of *Same Sex: Debating the Ethics, Science, and Culture of Homosexuality* (Rowman & Littlefield Publishers, 1997), and Stephen Macedo's article "Homosexuality and the Conservative Mind," *Georgetown Law Journal* 84, no. 2 (1995), 261, 276.

7 For a fuller explication of this type of natural law argument, see John Finnis, "Law, Morality and 'Sexual Orientation,'" *Notre Dame Law Review* 69, no. 5 (1994), 1049–76; revised, shortened, and reprinted in chapter 3 of *Same Sex: Debating the Ethics, Science, and Culture of Homosexuality* (Rowman & Littlefield Publishers, 1997). For a cogent and well-developed response, see chapter 4, *Same Sex: Debating the Ethics, Science, and Culture of Homosexuality* (Rowman & Littlefield Publishers, 1997), and Stephen Macedo, "Homosexuality and the Conservative Mind, *Georgetown Law Journal* 84, no. 2 (1995), 261–300.

it's disgusting. But plenty of morally neutral activities—handling snakes, eating snails, performing autopsies, cleaning toilets, and so on—disgust people. Indeed, for centuries, most people found interracial relationships disgusting, yet that feeling—which has by no means disappeared—hardly proves that such relationships are wrong. In sum, the charge that homosexuality is unnatural, at least in its most common forms, is longer on rhetorical flourish than on philosophical cogency. At best it expresses an aesthetic judgment, not a moral judgment.

HOMOSEXUAL SEX IS HARMFUL

One might instead argue that homosexuality is harmful. The Ramsey Colloquium, for instance, argues that homosexuality leads to the breakdown of the family and, ultimately, of human society, and it points to the "alarming rates of sexual promiscuity, depression, and suicide and the ominous presence of AIDS within the homosexual subculture."[8] Thomas Schmidt marshals copious statistics to show that homosexual activity undermines physical and psychological health.[9] Such charges, if correct, would seem to provide strong evidence against homosexuality. But are the charges correct? And do they prove what they purport to prove?

One obvious (and obviously problematic) way to answer the first question is to ask people like Tommy and Jim. It would appear that no one is in a better position to judge the homosexual lifestyle than those who know it firsthand. Yet it is unlikely that critics would trust their testimony. Indeed, the more homosexual people try to explain their lives, the more critics accuse them of deceitfully promoting an agenda. (It's like trying to prove that you're not crazy. The more you object, the more people think, "That's exactly what a crazy person would say.")

One might instead turn to statistics. An obvious problem with this tack is that both sides of the debate bring forth extensive statistics and "expert" testimony, leaving the average observer confused. There is a more subtle problem as well. Because of widespread antigay sentiment, many homosexual people won't acknowledge their romantic feelings to themselves, much less to researchers.[10] I have known a number of gay men who did not "come out" until their forties and fifties, and no amount of professional competence on the part of interviewers would have been likely to open their closets sooner. Such problems compound the usual difficulties of finding representative population samples for statistical study.

Yet even if the statistical claims of gay rights opponents were true, they would not prove what they purport to prove, for several reasons. First, as any good statistician realizes, correlation does not equal cause. Even if homosexual people were more likely to commit suicide, be promiscuous, or contract AIDS than the general population, it would not follow that their homosexuality causes them to do these things. An alternative—and very plausible—explanation is that these phenomena, like the disproportionately high crime rates among African Americans, are at least partly a function of society's treatment of the group in question. Suppose you were told from a very early age that the romantic feelings that you experienced were sick, unnatural, and disgusting. Suppose further that expressing these feelings put you at risk of social ostracism or, worse yet, physical violence. Is it not plausible that you would, for instance, be more inclined to depression than you would be without such obstacles? And that

8 The Ramsey Colloquium, "Homosexual Movement," 19.
9 Thomas Schmidt, "The Price of Love" in *Straight and Narrow? Compassion and Clarity in the Homosexuality Debate* (Downers Grove, IL: InterVarsity Press, 1995), chap. 6

10 Both the American Psychological Association and the American Public Health Association have conceded this point: "Reliable data on the incidence of homosexual orientation are difficult to obtain due to the criminal penalties and social stigma attached to homosexual behavior and the consequent difficulty of obtaining representative samples of people to study" (*Amici Curiae* Brief in *Bowers v. Hardwick*, Supreme Court No. 85–140 [October Term 1985]).

such depression could, in its extreme forms, lead to suicide or other self-destructive behaviors? (It is indeed remarkable that couples like Tommy and Jim continue to flourish in the face of such obstacles.)

A similar explanation can be given for the alleged promiscuity of homosexuals.[11] The denial of legal marriage, the pressure to remain in the closet, and the overt hostility toward homosexual relationship are all more conducive to transient, clandestine encounters than they are to long-term unions. As a result, that which is challenging enough for heterosexual couples— settling down and building a life together— becomes far more challenging for homosexual couples.

Indeed, there is an interesting tension in the critics' position here. Opponents of homosexuality commonly claim that "marriage and the family . . . are fragile institutions in need of careful and continuing support."[12] And they point to the increasing prevalence of divorce and premarital sex among heterosexuals as evidence that such support is declining. Yet they refuse to concede that the complete absence of similar support for homosexual relationships might explain many of the alleged problems of homosexuals. The critics can't have it both ways: if heterosexual marriages are in trouble despite the various social, economic, and legal incentives for

keeping them together, society should be little surprised that homosexual relationships—which not only lack such supports, but face overt hostility—are difficult to maintain.

One might object that if social ostracism were the main cause of homosexual people's problems, then homosexual people in more "tolerant" cities like New York and San Francisco should exhibit fewer such problems than their small-town counterparts; yet statistics do not seem to bear this out. This objection underestimates the extent of antigay sentiment in our society. By the time many gay and lesbian people move to urban centers, they have already been exposed to (and may have internalized) considerable hostility toward homosexuality. Moreover, the visibility of homosexuality in urban centers makes gay and lesbian people there more vulnerable to attack (and thus more likely to exhibit certain difficulties). Finally, note that urbanites *in general* (not just homosexual urbanites) tend to exhibit higher rates of promiscuity, depression, and sexually transmitted disease than the rest of the population.

But what about AIDS? Opponents of homosexuality sometimes claim that even if homosexual sex is not, strictly speaking, immoral, it is still a bad idea, since it puts people at risk for AIDS and other sexually transmitted diseases. But that claim is misleading: it is infinitely more risky for Tommy to have sex with a woman who is HIV-positive than with Jim, who is HIV-negative. Obviously, it's not homosexuality that's harmful, it's the virus; and the virus may be carried by both heterosexual and homosexual people.

Now it may be true (in the United States, at least) that homosexual males are statistically more likely to carry the virus than heterosexual females and thus that homosexual sex is *statistically* more risky than heterosexual sex (in cases where the partner's HIV status is unknown). But opponents of homosexuality need something stronger than this statistical claim. For if it is wrong for men to have sex with men because their doing so puts them at a higher AIDS risk than heterosexual sex, then it is also wrong for

11 It is worth noting that allegations of promiscuity are probably exaggerated. The study most commonly cited to prove homosexual male promiscuity, the Bell and Weinberg study, took place in 1978, in an urban center (San Francisco), at the height of the sexual revolution—hardly a broad sample. See Alan P. Bell and Martin S. Weinberg, *Homosexualities* (New York: Simon & Schuster, 1978). The far more recent and extensive University of Chicago study agreed that homosexual and bisexual people "have higher average numbers of partners than the rest of the sexually active people in the study," but it concluded that the differences in the mean number of partners "do not appear very large." See Edward O. Laumann et al., *The Social Organization of Sexuality: Sexual Practices in the United States* (Chicago: University of Chicago Press, 1994), 314, 316. I am grateful to Andrew Koppelman for drawing my attention to the Chicago study.
12 The Ramsey Colloquium, "Homosexual Movement," 19.

women to have sex with men because their doing so puts them at a higher AIDS risk than homosexual sex (lesbians as a group have the lowest incidence of AIDS). Purely from the standpoint of AIDS risk, women ought to prefer lesbian sex.

If this response seems silly, it is because there is obviously more to choosing a romantic or sexual partner than determining AIDS risk. And a major part of the decision, one that opponents of homosexuality consistently overlook, is considering whether one can have a mutually fulfilling relationship with the partner. For many people like Tommy and Jim, such fulfillment—which most heterosexuals recognize to be an important component of human flourishing—is only possible with members of the same sex.

Of course, the foregoing argument hinges on the claim that homosexual sex can only cause harm indirectly. Some would object that there are certain activities—anal sex, for instance—that for anatomical reasons are intrinsically harmful. But an argument against anal intercourse is by no means tantamount to an argument against homosexuality: neither all nor only homosexuals engage in anal sex. There are plenty of other things for both gay men and lesbians to do in bed. Indeed, for women, it appears that the most common forms of homosexual activity may be *less* risky than penile-vaginal intercourse, since the latter has been linked to cervical cancer.[13]

In sum, there is nothing *inherently* risky about sex between persons of the same gender. It is only risky under certain conditions: for instance, if they exchange diseased bodily fluids or if they engage in certain "rough" forms of sex that could cause tearing of delicate tissue. Heterosexual sex is equally risky under such conditions. Thus, even if statistical claims like those of Schmidt and the Ramsey Colloquium were true, they would not prove that homosexuality is immoral. At best, they would prove that homosexual people—like everyone else—ought to take great care when deciding to become sexually active.

Of course, there's more to a flourishing life than avoiding harm. One might argue that even if Tommy and Jim are not harming each other by their relationship, they are still failing to achieve the higher level of fulfillment possible in a heterosexual relationship, which is rooted in the complementarity of male and female. But this argument just ignores the facts: Tommy and Jim are homosexual *precisely because* they find relationships with men (and, in particular, with each other) more fulfilling than relationships with women. Even evangelicals (who have long advocated "faith healing" for homosexuals) are beginning to acknowledge that the choice for most homosexual people is not between homosexual relationships and heterosexual relationships, but rather between homosexual relationships and celibacy.[14] What the critics need to show, therefore, is that no matter how loving, committed, mutual, generous, and fulfilling the relationship may be, Tommy and Jim would flourish more if they were celibate. Given the evidence of their lives (and of others like them), this is a formidable task indeed.

Thus far I have focused on the allegation that homosexuality harms those who engage in it. But what about the allegation that homosexuality harms other, nonconsenting parties? Here I will briefly consider two claims: that homosexuality threatens children and that it threatens society.

Those who argue that homosexuality threatens children may mean one of two things. First, they may mean that homosexual people are child molesters. Statistically, the vast majority of reported cases of child sexual abuse involve

13 See S. R. Johnson, E. M. Smith, and S. M. Guenther, "Comparison of Gynecological Health Care Problems between Lesbian and Bisexual Women," *Journal of Reproductive Medicine* 32 (1987), 805–811.

14 See, for example, Stanton L. Jones, "the Loving Opposition," *Christianity Today* 37 no. 8 (July 19, 1993).

young girls and their fathers, stepfathers, or other familiar (and presumably heterosexual) adult males.[15] But opponents of homosexuality argue that when one adjusts for relative percentage in the population, homosexual males appear more likely than heterosexual males to be child molesters. As I argued above, the problems with obtaining reliable statistics on homosexuality render such calculations difficult. Fortunately, they are also unnecessary.

Child abuse is a terrible thing. But when a heterosexual male molests a child (or rapes a woman or commits assault), the act does not reflect upon all heterosexuals. Similarly, when a homosexual male molests a child, there is no reason why that act should reflect upon all homosexuals. Sex with adults of the same sex is one thing; sex with *children* of the same sex is quite another. Conflating the two not only slanders innocent people, it also misdirects resources intended to protect children. Furthermore, many men convicted of molesting young boys are sexually attracted to adult women and report no attraction to adult men.[16] To call such men "homosexual," or even "bisexual," is probably to stretch such terms too far.[17]

Alternatively, those who charge that homosexuality threatens children might mean that the increasing visibility of homosexual relationships makes children more likely to become homosexual. The argument for this view is patently circular. One cannot prove that doing *X* is bad by arguing that it causes other people to do *X*, which is bad. One must first establish independently that *X* is bad. That said, there is not a shred of evidence to demonstrate that exposure to homosexuality leads children to become homosexual.

But doesn't homosexuality threaten society? A Roman Catholic priest once put the argument to me as follows: "Of course homosexuality is bad for society. If everyone were homosexual, there would be no society." Perhaps it is true that if everyone were homosexual, there would be no society. But if everyone were a celibate priest, society would collapse just as surely, and my friend the priest didn't seem to think that he was doing anything wrong simply by failing to procreate. Jeremy Bentham made the point somewhat more acerbically roughly 200 years ago: "If then merely out of regard to population it were right that [homosexuals] should be burnt alive, monks ought to be roasted alive by a slow fire."[18]

From the fact that the continuation of society requires procreation, it does not follow that *everyone* must procreate. Moreover, even if such an obligation existed, it would not preclude homosexuality. At best, it would preclude *exclusive* homosexuality: homosexual people who occasionally have heterosexual sex can procreate just fine. And given artificial insemination, even those who are exclusively homosexual can procreate. In short, the priest's claim—if everyone were homosexual, there would be no society—is false; and even if it were true, it would not establish that homosexuality is immoral.

---

15 See Danya Glaser and Stephen Frosh, *Child Sexual Abuse,* 2nd ed. (Houndmills, England: Macmillan, 1993), 13–17; and Kathleen Goulbourn Faller, *Understanding Child Sexual Maltreatment* (Newbury Park, CA: Sage, 1990), 16–20.

16 See Frank G. Bolton Jr., Larry A. Morris, and Ann E. MacEachron, *Males at Risk: The Other Side of Child Sexual Abuse* (Newbury Park, CA: Sage, 1989), 61.

17 Part of the problem here arises from the grossly simplistic categorization of people into two (or, at best, three) sexual orientations: Heterosexual, homosexual, and bisexual. Clearly, there is great variety within (and beyond) these categories. See Frederick Suppe, "Explaining Homosexuality: Philosophical Issues, and Who Cares Anyhow?" in Timothy F. Murphy, ed., *Gay Ethics: Controversies in Outing, Civil Rights, and Sexual Science* (New York: Harrington Park Press, 1994), esp. 223–268, published simultaneously in the *Journal of Homosexuality* 27, nos. 3–4: 223–268.

18 "An Essay on 'Paederasty,'" in Robert Baker and Frederick Elliston, eds., *The Philosophy of Sex* (Buffalo, NY: Prometheus, 1984), 360–361. Bentham uses the word "paederast" where we would use the term "homosexual"; the latter term was not coined until 1869, and the term "heterosexual" was coined a few years after that. Today, "pederasty" refers to sex between men and boys—a different phenomenon from the one Bentham was addressing.

The Ramsey Colloquium commits a similar fallacy.[19] Noting (correctly) that heterosexual marriage promotes the continuation of human life, it then infers that homosexuality is immoral because it fails to accomplish the same.[20] But from the fact that procreation is good, it does not follow that childlessness is bad—a point that the members of the colloquium, several of whom are Roman Catholic priests, should readily concede.

I have argued that Tommy and Jim's sexual relationship harms neither them nor society. On the contrary, it benefits both. It benefits them because it makes them happier—not merely in a short-term, hedonistic sense, but in a long-term, "big picture" sort of way. And, in turn, it benefits society, since it makes Tommy and Jim more stable, more productive, and more generous than they would otherwise be. In short, their relationship—including its sexual component—provides the same kinds of benefits that infertile heterosexual relationships provide (and perhaps other benefits as well). Nor should we fear that accepting their relationship and others like it will cause people to flee in droves from the institution of heterosexual marriage. After all, as Thomas Williams points out, the usual response to a gay person is not "How come *he* gets to be gay and I don't?"[21]

HOMOSEXUALITY VIOLATES BIBLICAL TEACHING

At this point in the discussion, many people turn to religion. "If the secular arguments fail to prove that homosexuality is wrong," they say,

"so much the worse for secular ethics. This failure only proves that we need God for morality." Since people often justify their moral beliefs by appeal to religion, I will briefly consider the biblical position.

At first glance, the Bible's condemnation of homosexual activity seems unequivocal. Consider, for example, the following two passages, one from the "Old" Testament and one from the "New":[22]

> You shall not lie with a male as with a woman; it is an abomination. (Lev. 18:22)

> For this reason God gave them up to degrading passions. Their women exchanged natural intercourse for unnatural, and in the same way also the men, giving up natural intercourse with women, were consumed with passion for one another. Men committed shameless acts with men and received in their own persons the due penalty for their error. (Rom. 1:26–27)

Note, however, that these passages are surrounded by other passages that relatively few people consider binding. For example, Leviticus also declares,

> The pig . . . is unclean for you. Of their flesh you shall not eat, and their carcasses you shall not touch; they are unclean for you. (11:7–8)

Taken literally, this passage not only prohibits eating pork, but also playing football, since footballs are made of pigskin. (Can you believe that the University of Notre Dame so flagrantly violates Levitical teaching?)

Similarly, St. Paul, author of the Romans passage, also writes, "Slaves, obey your earthly masters with fear and trembling, in singleness of heart, as you obey Christ" (Eph. 6:5)—morally problematic advice if there ever were any. Should we interpret this passage (as Southern plantation owners once did) as implying that it is immoral for slaves to escape? After all, God himself says in Leviticus,

> [Y]ou may acquire male and female slaves . . . from among the aliens residing with you, and

19 The Ramsey Colloquium, "Homosexual Movement," 17–18.

20 The argument is a classic example of the fallacy of denying the antecedent: if X promotes procreation, then X is good; X does not promote procreation, therefore X is not good. Compare: if X is president, then X lives in the White House; Chelsea Clinton is not president, therefore Chelsea Clinton does not live in the White House.

21 Actually, Williams makes the point with regard to celibacy, while making an analogy between celibacy and homosexuality. See chapter 6 of this volume.

22 All biblical quotations are from the New Revised Standard Version.

from their families that are with you, who have been born in your land; and they may be your property. You may keep them as a possession for your children after you, for them to inherit as property. (25:44–46)

How can people maintain the inerrancy of the Bible in light of such passages? The answer, I think, is that they learn to interpret the passages *in their historical context.*

Consider the Bible's position on usury, the lending of money for interest (for *any* interest, not just excessive interest). The Bible condemns this practice in no uncertain terms. In Exodus God says that "if you lend money to my people, to the poor among you you shall not exact interest from them" (22:25). Psalm 15 says that those who lend at interest may not abide in the Lord's tent or dwell on his holy hill (1–5). Ezekiel calls usury "abominable"; compares it to adultery, robbery, idolatry, and bribery; and states that anyone who "takes advanced or accrued interest . . . shall surely die; his blood shall be upon himself" (18:13).[23]

Should believers therefore close their savings accounts? Not necessarily. According to orthodox Christian teaching, the biblical prohibition against usury no longer applies. The reason is that economic conditions have changed substantially since biblical times, such that usury no longer has the same negative consequences it had when the prohibitions were issued. Thus, the practice that was condemned by the Bible differs from contemporary interest banking in morally relevant ways.[24]

Yet are we not in a similar position regarding homosexuality? Virtually all scholars agree that homosexual relations during biblical times were vastly different from relationships like Tommy and Jim's. Often such relations were integral to pagan practices. In Greek society, they typically involved older men and younger boys. If those are the kinds of features that the biblical authors had in mind when they issued their condemnations, and such features are no longer typical, then the biblical condemnations no longer apply. As with usury, substantial changes in cultural context have altered the meaning and consequences—and thus the moral value—of the practice in question. Put another way, using the Bible's condemnations of homosexuality against contemporary homosexuality is like using its condemnations of usury against contemporary banking.

Let me be clear about what I am *not* claiming here. First, I am not claiming that the Bible has been wrong before and therefore may be wrong this time. The Bible may indeed by wrong on some matters, but for the purpose of this argument I am assuming its infallibility. Nor am I claiming that the Bible's age renders it entirely inapplicable to today's issues. Rather, I am claiming that when we do apply it, *we must pay attention to morally relevant cultural differences between biblical times and today.* Such attention will help us distinguish between specific time-bound prohibitions (for example, laws against usury or homosexual relations) and the enduring moral values they represent (for example, generosity or respect for persons). And as the above argument shows, my claim is not very controversial. Indeed, to deny it is to commit oneself to some rather strange views on slavery, usury, women's roles, astronomy, evolution, and the like.

Here, one might also make an appeal to religious pluralism. Given the wide variety of religious beliefs (e.g., the Muslim belief that women should cover their faces, the Orthodox Jewish belief against working on Saturday, the Hindu belief that cows are sacred and should not be eaten), each of us inevitably violates the religious beliefs of others. But we normally don't view such violations as occasions for moral censure, since we distinguish between beliefs that depend on particular revelations and beliefs that can be justified independently (e.g., that stealing is wrong). Without an independent justification

---

23 See also Deut. 23:19, Lev. 25:35–37, Neh. 5:7–10, Jer. 15:10, Ezek. 22:12, and Luke 6:35. For a fuller explication of the analogy between homosexuality and usury, see John Corvino, "The Bible Condemned Usurers, Too," *Harvard Gay and Lesbian Review* 3, no. 4 (Fall 1996): 11–12.

24 See Richard P. McBrien, *Catholicism,* study ed. (San Francisco: Harper & Row, 1981), 1020.

for condemning homosexuality, the best one can say is, "My religion says so." But in a society that cherishes religious freedom, that reason alone does not normally provide grounds for moral or legal sanctions. That people still fall back on that reason in discussions of homosexuality suggests that they may not have much of a case otherwise.

CONCLUSION

As a last resort, opponents of homosexuality typically change the subject: "But what about incest, polygamy, and bestiality? If we accept Tommy and Jim's sexual relationship, why shouldn't we accept those as well?" Opponents of interracial marriage used a similar slippery-slope argument in the 1960s when the Supreme Court struck down antimiscegenation laws.[25] It was a bad argument then, and it is a bad argument now.

Just because there are no good reasons to oppose interracial or homosexual relationships, it does not follow that there are no good reasons to oppose incestuous, polygamous, or bestial relationships. One might argue, for instance, that incestuous relationships threaten delicate familial bonds, or that polygamous relationships result in unhealthy jealousies (and sexism), or that bestial relationships—do I need to say it?—aren't really "relationships" at all, at least not in the sense we've been discussing.[26] Perhaps even better arguments could be offered (given much

more space than I have here). The point is that there is no logical connection between homosexuality, on the one hand, and incest, polygamy, and bestiality, on the other.

Why, then, do critics continue to push this objection? Perhaps it's because accepting homosexuality requires them to give up one of their favorite arguments: "It's wrong because we've always been taught that it's wrong." This argument—call it the argument from tradition—has an obvious appeal: people reasonably favor tried-and-true ideas over unfamiliar ones, and they recognize the foolishness of trying to invent morality from scratch. But the argument from tradition is also a dangerous argument, as any honest look at history will reveal.

I conclude that Tommy and Jim's relationship, far from being a moral abomination, is exactly what it appears to be to those who know them: a morally positive influence on their lives and on others. Accepting this conclusion takes courage, since it entails that our moral traditions are fallible. But when these traditions interfere with people's happiness for no sound reason, they defeat what is arguably the very point of morality: promoting individual and communal well-being. To put the argument simply, Tommy and Jim's relationship makes them better people. And that's not just good for Tommy and Jim: that's good for everyone.

---

25 *Loving v. Virginia*, 388 U.S. 1967.
26 One might object here that I am equivocating on the term "relationship," since throughout the essay I have been discussing acts, not relationships. But I maintain that Tommy and Jim's sexual act is *relational* in a way that

Tommy and Fido's simply could not be. Even apart from their love for each other, Tommy and Jim have capacities for mutual communication and respect that Tommy and Fido simply do not have. Thus, one can approve of Tommy and Jim's sexual act without implying anything about Tommy and Fido's (possible) sexual acts; the two are fundamentally different.

Review Questions

1. Corvino distinguishes between five meanings of *unnatural*. What are they?
2. Why doesn't Corvino accept any of these meanings of *unnatural* as a reason for concluding that homosexual sex is morally wrong?
3. Is homosexual sex harmful to those who engage in it? What is Corvino's view?

4. How does Corvino reply to the charge that homosexual sex is harmful to children and a threat to society?
5. Why doesn't Corvino accept biblical injunctions against homosexuality?
6. What is the slippery slope argument against homosexuality? Why does Corvino reject it?

Discussion Questions

1. Is homosexual sex in some sense unnatural? If so, does it follow that it is immoral? Explain your answers.
2. Do the biblical injunctions against homosexuality apply today? Why or why not?
3. Does homosexuality harm the institution of marriage? Why or why not?

A Reply to Corvino

DAVID BRADSHAW

David Bradshaw is assistant professor of philosophy at the University of Kentucky.

Bradshaw replies to Corvino. He claims that Corvino is confused because he fails to distinguish between three levels of opposition to homosexuality. There is opposition to the gay rights movement, opposition to the homosexual lifestyle, and opposition to homosexual practice. Bradshaw is mainly concerned with the third sort of opposition. He argues that homosexual practice is morally wrong because it is prohibited in the Bible and because it violates the body's moral space.

AFTER READING JOHN CORVINO'S ESSAY "Why Shouldn't Tommy and Jim Have Sex? A Defense of Homosexuality," one is left with the impression that the conservative position on homosexuality is nothing but a tissue of confusions. Surely it is a marvel that so many otherwise reasonable people have for so long persisted in such an erroneous view. Perhaps, as Corvino suggests, the explanation is mere prejudice. Or perhaps it is not. I believe that much of the confusion

that Corvino finds is of his own making, caused by his insistence on treating arguments that really have quite distinct purposes as if they were all trying to show the same thing: that homosexual intercourse is always wrong. Now this is certainly a position that many conservatives (myself included) do hold, but it does not follow that every conservative argument is aimed at defending it. Many have more modest aims, and to treat them all as if they were intended to show that homosexuality *in every case* is immoral can only lead to confusion. (I will use the term "homosexuality" throughout to indicate the practice of same-sex intercourse and not merely homosexual orientation.)

Source: David Bradshaw, "A Reply to Corvino" from *Same Sex: Debating the Ethics, Science, and Culture of Homosexuality,* pp. 17–30, (Roman and Littlefield, 1997). Reprinted by permission.

In what follows, I will first attempt to clarify how the various elements of the conservative position fit together. I will distinguish three levels of opposition to homosexuality, only the third of which is concerned to maintain that homosexual intercourse is always wrong. Although I will not attempt to defend every conservative argument in detail, placing the arguments within their proper context will make it apparent that most of Corvino's objections are misguided. Following this preliminary survey, the bulk of the essay will be devoted to elaborating the single argument which I think best illuminates the deeper issues involved.

A TAXONOMY OF CONSERVATISM

Most public debate over homosexuality tends to focus, not on the morality of homosexual intercourse as such, but on the various changes to public policy advocated by the gay rights movement. It is important to recognize that one need not hold a moral belief against homosexuality in order to oppose the gay rights movement. Consider the analogy of smoking. Many Americans would deny that it is immoral to smoke, but would also resist any concerted effort to increase public acceptance of smoking. (Imagine, for example, an attempt by the tobacco companies to infiltrate pro-smoking material into the public schools.) Such a position is perfectly consistent, for not every decision about public policy need be based on strictly moral considerations. Other factors that rightly carry weight include public health and safety, demands on the public treasury, the well-being of institutions that are essential to society, and respect for established custom and the wishes of the majority, even when one personally believes those wishes to be ill-founded.

Much of the opposition to the gay rights movement is grounded on considerations such as these. We must therefore distinguish the first level of opposition from one that goes further. The second level lodges a specifically moral objection to homosexuality. It is limited, however,

in that it objects to what may be called the "homosexual lifestyle"—that is, to the persistent practice of homosexuality as that practice *typically* exists in our society. As Corvino rightly observes, many of the points most frequently made in this connection really apply only to the practices of male homosexuals: they include that sex among male homosexuals is wildly promiscuous, that it spreads disease, and that it is highly correlated with other evils both sexual (sadism, masochism, child molestation) and non-sexual (suicide, alcoholism, drug abuse). What makes all of this a bit confusing is that an argument based on such premises may belong to either of the two levels. The distinction is one of purpose. If the aim is to show that, as a matter of public policy, homosexuality ought not to be conceded the same legitimacy as heterosexuality, then the argument belongs to the first level; if the aim is to show that it is wrong for an individual to follow a homosexual lifestyle, then the argument belongs to the second.

There is another type of objection to the homosexual lifestyle, one that applies equally to males and females. This one deserves special mention because only a garbled version of it appears in Corvino's essay. Properly stated, the argument is that the mutual attraction of male and female is so important to the foundations of society that to adopt a way of life that publicly and persistently repudiates it is a moral evil. Note that religious celibates do not repudiate the heterosexual norm in the relevant way; they confirm it, for their celibacy is recognized by both themselves and others as a sacrifice made in pursuit of a higher good. Nor is there any repudiation in the attitude of those who, for whatever reason, simply do not feel or act upon an attraction to the opposite sex. The source of offense is the proffering of homosexuality as an *alternative* to heterosexuality—an "alternative lifestyle," one capable of providing the same sort of companionship and sexual pleasure as heterosexual marriage. This is felt by opponents to be a sort of counterfeiting of a basic human good. Like any counterfeit, it is bogus, but it is also sufficiently plausible to have the potential for doing serious harm.

Just as with the arguments directed against male homosexuality, an argument against the public acceptance of homosexuality as an equal alternative to heterosexual marriage can work at two levels. The first level argues that to give homosexuality the same sort of legitimacy as heterosexuality tends to destroy the delicate web of sanctions and incentives through which society channels the sexual impulse in a constructive direction. The second level argues that anyone who lives publicly as a homosexual by that very action endorses and helps propagate a sort of counterfeit good, a false alternative to the heterosexual norm.

All of these arguments are interesting and important. In the interests of space, however, I will not pursue them further here.[1] There is yet a third level of opposition to homosexuality, and it is the one that goes deepest. In describing the second level, I emphasized the word "typically," for of course there are many varieties of homosexual practice. Let us imagine a homosexual act performed in such a way that it does not damage bodily tissues (as does anal sex, for example), does not spread disease, is not part of a promiscuous lifestyle, has no harmful public repercussions, and, in general, shares none of the characteristics that have so far been mentioned as objectionable. Is such an act wrong? Is it wrong *simply in virtue of being a sexual act between two persons of the same sex,* without regard to its further characteristics? That is the question that is at the heart of the moral issues surrounding homosexuality, and it is the one on which I wish to focus.

At least two sorts of arguments can be brought to bear at this point.[2] One is based on religious authority. Although in this essay my main interest does not lie in that direction, I must say a word about such arguments because of what seems to me the misleading treatment of them by Corvino. Like Corvino, I will take the biblical injunctions as representative. It should be noted, however, that opposition to homosexuality is the dominant tradition in most of the world's major religions, including not only Judaism and Christianity, but also Hinduism and Islam.[3]

Corvino writes that "[v]irtually all scholars agree that homosexual relations during biblical times were vastly different from relationships like Tommy and Jim's." This is true as far as it goes; monogamous and committed homosexuality did not exist in antiquity, particularly among males. But why should that affect the meaning of the biblical commandments? They are not stated in a way that would restrict them to acts occurring in a particular context. The passages in Leviticus refer simply to a man lying with a man as with a woman (18:22, 20:13). Even more to the point, St. Paul explicitly bases his position on the deviation of same-sex intercourse from "natural" intercourse—that between man and woman (Rom. 1:26–27). This makes it clear that his objection is to same-sex intercourse as such, and not solely to its associations in the culture of his time.[4]

---

1 See Jeffrey Satinover, *Homosexuality and the Politics of Truth* (Grand Rapids, MI: Baker books, 1995). Much of this work could be read as a point-by-point rebuttal of the section of Corvino's essay dealing with harm. To take only a single example, Corvino cites the University of Chicago study as evidence that promiscuity among homosexuals is not as great as widely believed (note 11). But, as Satinover observes, this study was meant to be a representative sampling of the entire population and therefore included only a relatively small number of homosexuals. Other studies involving larger numbers of homosexuals have continued to show high rates of promiscuity.

2 I ignore an argument popular in antiquity to the effect that homosexual acts both manifest and intensify a sort of character defect. See chapter 3 by John Finnis in this volume; cf. Ramsay MacMullen, "Greek Attitudes to Roman Love," *Historia* 27 (1982): 484–502.

3 See A. Swidler, ed., *Homosexuality and World Religions* (Valley Forge, PA: Trinity Press, 1993).

4 See the exchange between Daniel A. Helminiak and Thomas E. Schmidt in chapters 7 and 8 of *Same Sex: Debating the Ethics, Science, and Culture of Homosexuality* (Rowman & Littlefield Publishers, 1997).

Corvino also appeals to religious pluralism. He claims that, whatever one thinks of the biblical teachings, they do not "provide grounds for moral or legal sanctions." The question of what are the appropriate grounds for *legal* sanctions is a large one that raises tricky issues of constitutional interpretation. Since Corvino does not address those issues, he can scarcely be said to have argued for his view, and I shall simply register my disagreement without pursuing the issue further. The main point at issue between us is that of the appropriate grounds for *moral* judgment. Here, Corvino's examples blur an important distinction. Many biblical commandments, such as the dietary laws and prohibition of working on Saturday, are clearly intended as binding only on Jews; others, like the commandment against murder given to Noah (Gen. 9:6), are clearly meant to be universally applicable. The reason they are conceived as universally applicable is that they purport to make explicit a standard that, in some sense, is already given in the nature of things; thus Cain, for example, was at fault for his murder of Abel, although there was at that time no explicit commandment against murder.

To which of these two classes do the commandments against homosexuality belong? One important clue is the fact that the people of Sodom and Gomorrah were held accountable for their homosexual acts, despite the fact that they were non-Jews and lived long before the time of Leviticus.[5] More generally, a strong case can be made—although I will not attempt to make it here—that the commandments against homosexuality are simply one aspect of a broader sexual ethic rooted in the creation account in Genesis.[6] As such, they are binding upon the entire human race.

What all this means is that, *if* one takes the Bible as authoritative, one is bound to regard homosexuality as wrong. That may seem an elementary point, but it is so widely denied (or ignored) today that it bears emphasizing. Of course, we can hardly stop with this conclusion. Many people do not accept the authority of the Bible, and even those who accept it recognize that there is a need to do more than simply repeat the traditional teaching. In the remainder of this essay, I will provide an argument against same-sex intercourse that does not rely on religious authority. . . .

Homosexuality is one of a number of sexual practices that traditionally have been regarded as perversions. Others include bestiality, necrophilia, coprophilia, fetishism, and pederasty. To classify all of these as perversions does not mean that they are all wrong to the same degree or for the same reasons, but it does suggest that they share a certain inner kinship. I wish to explore that traditional view by examining bestiality and homosexuality in parallel with each other. I will argue that, despite their manifest differences, both practices involve a similar violation of the body's moral space.

Although there is an enormous variety of sexual mores and customs, virtually all societies regard at least one kind of sex as morally unproblematic: that of a married man and woman who engage in intercourse with the willingness (and often the positive hope) that their union will be blessed with children. Since a union of this sort directly contributes to the perpetuation of society, it is not surprising that it should escape moral censure. The first point I wish to argue is that there is also a deeper reason at work—namely, that this sort of intercourse "fits" the body's moral space uniquely well. I do not wish to argue (here, at any rate) that only such intercourse is morally acceptable. My claim is, rather, that it provides a paradigmatic case through which we can begin to understand the relationship between sexual intercourse and the body's moral space.

What is it about intercourse of this particular type that makes it morally appealing? Part of the answer is surely that in such a case the sexual act is the consummation of a joint commitment of

5 I am aware, of course, that revisionists claim that the sin of the Sodomites was inhospitality. See Thomas Schmidt, *Straight and Narrow? Compassion and Clarity in the Homosexuality Debate* (Downers Grove, IL: InterVarsity Press, 1995), 86–89 for a decisive refutation.

6 See Schmidt, *Straight and Narrow?*, chapter 3.

the persons involved to share their lives together and to enter together the great enterprise of bearing and rearing children. The word "consummation" is worth pausing to weigh carefully. It comes from *consummare,* "to sum up, complete, finish." Implicit in the word is the assumption that the commitment is incomplete and unfinished without the corresponding physical act. The act expresses and realizes the commitment, making it tangibly present and giving it a place in the bodily order. When it does so, the act attains special significance, for it manifests in the body the decision made by the two persons to entrust to each other their past achievements and future hopes. They grant to their union a certain causal autonomy; they pledge with their bodies, as it were, that they are willing to accept whatever consequences their union produces, up to and including the possibility of new life.

This is not yet the whole answer. It is also important that in such cases the sexual act typically evinces (and is partly motivated by) a delight in the *kind* of being that the other is. "O brave new world that has such people in't!"—that is what Miranda in *The Tempest* exclaims upon encountering men.[7] Much though we may smile at her naiveté, she speaks for the whole human race. Every lover knows that love is more than simply a delight in the other qua individual; man also delights in the femininity of woman, and woman delights in the masculinity of man. Part of what makes erotic love such a powerful experience is the surprise and gratitude one feels in finding that what one has admired from afar even in strangers is now available as a kind of gift in the beloved. What had seemed foreign and unapproachable becomes as close as one's own flesh.

Now it is precisely the masculinity or femininity of the beloved, in its physical dimension, that is engaged in the sexual act. This means that there is possible in the type of intercourse that I have described a certain integration among the physical act, the attitude of commitment it

consummates, and the larger dimensions of human society. The act is a reenactment at a personal level of the drama of the mutual need, attraction, and union of man and woman that has been repeated in countless times and countless ways throughout human history. As such, it is a way of personally participating in one of the deepest roots of human society. I do not mean to suggest that an explicit awareness of this dimension is always present. What is present is the participation itself, the fact that this private and particular act recapitulates in a small way the universal bonding of man and woman.

Here, then, are at least two important reasons why intercourse in a committed, monogamous, heterosexual relationship, with an openness to the possibility of children, is a paradigmatic case of a "fit" between the sexual act and the body's moral space. First, such an act consummates the mutual commitment of the two persons involved. It unites body and spirit in a single harmonious endeavor; it raises the body to the level of the spirit and focuses the spirit within the body. Second, the act engages the body in a profoundly human way. It integrates the body within a drama that is and always has been the primary means by which the two halves of the human race come to value one another.

Let us now see whether this discussion can shed any light on bestiality. I shall simply assume that the reader shares with me the intuition that bestiality is wrong. Discussing sexual morality with one who does not share such a basic intuition would be a bit like discussing music with one who is tone-deaf. Perhaps something could be said to get through in the end, but the discussion would have to begin much further back than is possible here.

The question I would ask is not whether bestiality is wrong, but *why* it is wrong. Corvino remarks that a bestial relationship is not a "relationship" at all. That is true as far as it goes, but it scarcely scratches the surface of the problem. Why, after all, should we require that sex must take place within a "relationship"? What is so special about that? Furthermore, merely to remark that a man

7 William Shakespeare, *The Tempest,* v.I.183.

and an animal cannot share a "relationship" seems far too weak. Bestiality is not only wrong, but abhorrent and perverse—more like, say, cannibalism or wanton cruelty to small animals than like fraud or drunken driving. Nothing in the requirement that sex take place within a "relationship" seems to answer to the deep-seated feeling of disgust that bestiality arouses within us.

I submit that the reason why bestiality is wrong is that it is an abuse of the body. It is a paradigmatic case of a sexual violation of the body's moral space. And, if we ask why that is so, we have only to compare it to the opposite paradigm, that of intercourse within a heterosexual, monogamous relationship. Intercourse with an animal allows the possibility neither of commitment nor of procreation. It consummates nothing. It also fails to engage the body in a uniquely human way, a way that would resonate with the larger dimensions of human existence. For these reasons, there is an important sense in which it disengages the body both from the individual psyche and from society at large. The net result is a sort of fragmentation of the person. The body is left isolated from the other dimensions of personhood, having no other role than that of providing a coarse kind of pleasure.

Consider now a somewhat different case. Suppose that the act were with a talking animal, one as fully rational as a human being and fully engaged in human society. In such a case, an attitude of commitment could be present. But how much else could not! First, because of the biological mismatch of the two bodies, there could be no procreation. This means that the attitude of commitment would remain permanently unfulfilled; there could be no consummation, no "drawing down" of the commitment to the level of physical and tangible reality. Second, the sexual act would not resonate with the larger dimensions of human existence; it would remain isolated from the mutual fascination of man and woman, together with all the structures of society to which that fascination has given shape. Indeed, it would actually be a repudiation of that fascination, for it would be an attempt to find the solaces that

men and women traditionally have found in one another in an entirely different source.

For these reasons, regardless of how tenderly or affectionately such an act might be performed, it would fail to achieve anything like the integration among body, soul, and society that is present in the paradigmatic case. Like "normal" bestiality, though to a lesser degree, it would contribute to the fragmentation, rather than the integration, of the person. And for that reason, like "normal" bestiality, though to a lesser degree, it would be a violation of the body's moral space.[8]

This case seems to me identical in its morally relevant characteristics to same-sex intercourse among human beings. In saying this, I do not wish to invoke whatever feelings of disgust may attach to the thought of intercourse with even an intelligent animal. Readers who have such feelings are asked to lay them aside for the moment. The morally relevant characteristics I have in mind are the two that I have emphasized: the inability of the sexual act, due to the permanent structure of the bodies involved, to serve as a *consummation* in the sense that I have described; and its inability, for the same reason, to connect in any significant way with the larger dimensions of human existence.

I conclude that same-sex intercourse is a violation of the body's moral space, in the same way and for the same reasons as would be intercourse with an intelligent animal. Again, in saying this, I do not wish to transfer to homosexuality precisely the same feelings of disgust that (rightly) attach to bestiality. I readily concede that intercourse with an animal is worse than that with a human being of the same sex. The only likeness I wish to assert between same-sex intercourse and bestiality is that both are perversions, in that both involve a very fundamental abuse of the body.

Before closing, I should attempt to head off an important objection. There are various reasons

8 For a brilliant fictional exploration of the fragmentation of the person through the abuse of sex, see Walker Percy's novel *Love in the Ruins* (New York: Farrar, Straus & Giroux, 1971). See also John Wauck, "Fables of Alienation," *Human Life Review* (Spring 1991): 73–91.

that may result in even a heterosexual couple being permanently unable to bear children. Does my argument imply that sex would be illegitimate in their case as well? Not at all. One important difference is that, even in such a case, the second of the characteristics I have mentioned—the participation of the act within the larger human drama—is fully present. In addition, there is a fundamental difference between the bar that prevents such a couple from bearing children and that which similarly prevents two persons of the same sex from doing so. In the heterosexual case, the inability is due to some special circumstance, such as sterility or dismemberment, whereas in the homosexual case, it is due to the given form of the body. If our aim is to respect the moral space created by the body, then it is entirely reasonable that the latter sort of bar should have important moral consequences, whereas the former should and does not.

CONCLUSION

The argument that I have presented regarding the body's moral space does not rely on those discussed in the first section of this chapter. However, once this argument is grasped the others gain considerably in force and coherence. We can now understand why homosexuality is so widely viewed as a kind of counterfeit of married, heterosexual love. We can also understand why so many religions forbid same-sex intercourse and why the Jewish and Christian Scriptures, in particular, treat it as a serious offense before God. Finally—though I think too much can be made of this point—it becomes a bit more intelligible why homosexuality is regularly correlated with promiscuity and a variety of other unseemly and reckless kinds of behavior. Lacking the capacity of heterosexuality to integrate body, spirit, and society, it leaves those who partake in it isolated both from society at large and from their own bodily existence. This is not the fault of prejudice against homosexuals; it is an intrinsic limitation of the act itself.

There is a cliché—a wholly true cliché—that one must hate the sin and love the sinner. I would add that part of loving the sinner *is* to hate the sin. Only when the sin is seen as what it is, as wrong and destructive, can the truly important work of repentance and healing begin.

Review Questions

1. Why does Bradshaw think that Corvino is confused?
2. According to Bradshaw, what is the first level of opposition to homosexuality. How is it analogous to opposition to smoking?
3. What is the second level of opposition, according to Bradshaw? What arguments are used to support it?
4. Explain Bradshaw's third level of opposition to homosexuality.
5. How does Bradshaw defend the biblical injunctions against homosexuality?
6. Explain Bradshaw's notion of moral space. What examples does he use to illustrate this notion?
7. According to Bradshaw, what is the relation between sexual intercourse and the body's moral space? Why does same-sex intercourse violate the body's moral space?

Discussion Questions

1. Is oral sex morally wrong if done in private by consenting adults? Is it still wrong when performed by heterosexual married couples?
2. Does masturbation violate the body's moral space? What about heterosexual rape?
3. Is homosexual sex analogous to bestiality? Explain your answer.

Plato and Aristotle on Love

MARTHA NUSSBAUM

Martha Nussbaum is the Ernst Freund Distinguished Service Professor of Law and Ethics, appointed in the Philosophy Department, Law School and Divinity School at the University of Chicago. Her recent books include *Upheavals of Thought* (2003), *Women and Human Development* (2001), and *Sex and Social Justice* (2000). For her picture and more information on her many books and articles see her website, www.law.uchicago.edu/faculty/nussbaum.

Nussbaum discusses the view of male–male love found in the writings of Plato and Aristotle. In Plato's dialogues *Symposium* and *Phaedrus,* male–male love is praised as providing spiritual communication and friendship. It is a primary source of insight into the nature of the good and the beautiful. Aristotle also finds male–male love to have the potential for the highest form of friendship, which is based on mutual well-wishing and mutual awareness of good character. This potential is not found in male–female relationships, because Aristotle thought females incapable of good character. Both Plato and Aristotle are critical of relationships based only on bodily pleasure.

PLATO'S DIALOGUES CONTAIN several extremely moving celebrations of male–male love, and judge this form of love to be, on the whole, superior to male–female love because of its potential for spirituality and friendship. The *Symposium* contains a series of speeches, each expressing conventional views about this subject that Plato depicts in an appealing light. The speech by Phaedrus points to the military advantages derived by including homosexual couples in a fighting force: Because of their intense love, each will fight better, wishing to show himself in the best light before his lover. The speech of Pausanias criticizes males who seek physical pleasure alone in their homosexual relationships, and praises those who seek in sex deeper spiritual communication. Pausanias mentions that tyrants will sometimes promulgate the view that same-sex relations are shameful in order to discourage the

kind of community of dedication to political liberty that such relations foster. The speech of Aristophanes holds that all human beings are divided halves of formerly whole beings, and that sexual desire is the pursuit of one's lost other half; he points out that the superior people in any society are those whose lost "other half" is of the same sex—especially the male–male pairs—since these are likely to be the strongest and most warlike and civically minded people. Finally, Socrates's speech recounts a process of religious-mystical education in which male–male love plays a central guiding role and is a primary source of insight and inspiration into the nature of the good and beautiful.

Plato's *Phaedrus* contains a closely related praise of the intellectual, political, and spiritual benefits of a life centered around male–male love. Plato says that the highest form of human life is one in which a male pursues "the love of a young man along with philosophy," and is transported by passionate desire. He describes the experience of falling in love with another male

Source: Martha Nussbaum, "Reply to Finnis." Reprinted from the legal depositions from the trial in Colorado on the constitutionality of Amendment 2.

in moving terms, and defends relationships that are mutual and reciprocal over relationships that are one-sided. He depicts his pairs of lovers as spending their life together in the pursuit of intellectual and spiritual activities, combined with political participation. (Although no marriages for these lovers are mentioned, it was the view of the time that this form of life does not prevent its participants from having a wife at home, whom they saw only rarely and for procreative purposes.)

Aristotle speaks far less about sexual love than does Plato, but it is evident that he too finds in male–male relationships the potential for the highest form of friendship, a friendship based on mutual well-wishing and mutual awareness of good character and good aims. He does not find this potential in male–female relationships, since he holds that females are incapable of good character. Like Pausanias in Plato's *Symposium,* Aristotle is critical of relationships that are superficial and concerned only with bodily pleasure; but he finds in male–male relationships—including many that begin in this way—the potential for much richer developments.

The ideal city of the Greek Stoics was built around the idea of pairs of male lovers whose bonds gave the city rich sources of motivation for virtue. Although the Stoics wished their "wise man" to eliminate most passions from his life, they encouraged him to foster a type of erotic love that they defined as "the attempt to form a friendship inspired by the perceived beauty of young men in their prime." They held that this love, unlike other passions, was supportive of virtue and philosophical activity.

Review Questions

1. According to Nussbaum, how do Plato's dialogues describe male–male love? What is the highest form of human life? How does marriage fit in the picture?
2. How does Aristotle view male–male love according to Nussbaum? Why is it superior to male–female love?

Discussion Questions

1. What is the highest or best form of love? Does it involve friendship? Does it require bodily pleasure? Does it have a spiritual aspect? Explain your view.

Gay Marriage—and Marriage

SAM SCHULMAN

Sam Schulman is a New York writer whose work has appeared in the *New York Press,* the *Jewish World Review,* the *Spectator* (London), and elsewhere. Formerly he was professor of English at Boston University.

Schulman is passionately and instinctively opposed to gay marriage, but he is disappointed by the arguments advanced against it. He begins with a discussion of the standard arguments for it, namely the civil–rights argument and the utilitarian argument, which he calls the Bawer/Sullivan line. Then he turns to the case against gay marriage: the argument that it will harm families and children, Kurtz's slippery slope argument that gay marriage will lead to legalized polygamy or even the abolition of marriage, and Gallagher's view that the purpose of marriage is to create stable families. In Schulman's view, however, the heart of the matter is the simple truth that the essence of marriage is to sanction the connection of opposites that creates new human life. Given this essence, to say that a man is married to another man is like saying that he is a father to a pebble or a brother to a puppy. Such a "marriage" is not just unnatural, it is impossible.

THE FEELING SEEMS TO BE growing that gay marriage is inevitably coming our way in the U.S., perhaps through a combination of judicial fiat and legislation in individual states. Growing, too, is the sense of a shift in the climate of opinion. The American public seems to be in the process of changing its mind—not actually in favor of gay marriage, but toward a position of slightly revolted tolerance for the idea. Survey results suggest that people have forgotten why they were so opposed to the notion even as recently as a few years ago.

It is curious that this has happened so quickly. With honorable exceptions, most of those who are passionately on the side of the traditional understanding of marriage appear to be at a loss for words to justify their passion; as for the rest, many seem to wish gay marriage had never been proposed in the first place, but also to have resigned themselves to whatever happens. In this respect, the gay-marriage debate is very different from the abortion debate, in which few with an opinion on either side have been so disengaged.

I think I understand why this is the case: as someone passionately and instinctively opposed to the idea of homosexual marriage, I have found myself disappointed by the arguments I have seen advanced against it. The strongest of these arguments predict measurable harm to the family and to our arrangements for the upbringing and well-being of children. I do not doubt the accuracy of those arguments.* But they do not seem to get at the heart of the matter.

To me, what is at stake in this debate is not only the potential unhappiness of children, grave as that is; it is our ability to maintain the most basic components of our humanity. I believe, in fact, that we are at an "Antigone moment." Some of our fellow citizens wish to impose a radically new understanding upon laws and institutions that are both very old and fundamental to our organization as individuals and as a society. As Antigone said to Creon, we are being asked to tamper with "unwritten and unfailing laws, not of now, nor of yesterday; they always live, and no one knows their origin in time." I suspect, moreover, that everyone knows this is the case, and that, paradoxically, this very awareness of just how much is at stake is what may have induced, in defenders of those same "unwritten and unfailing laws," a kind of paralysis.

Admittedly, it is very difficult to defend that which is both ancient and "unwritten"—the arguments do not resolve themselves into a neat parade of documentary evidence, research

*For a summary of the scant research on children raised in homes with same-sex parents as of six or seven years ago, see James Q. Wilson, "Against Homosexual Marriage," in COMMENTARY, March 1996.

results, or citations from the legal literature. Admittedly, too, proponents of this radical new understanding have been uncommonly effective in presenting their program as something that is not radical at all but as requiring merely a slight and painless adjustment in our customary arrangements. Finally, we have all learned to practice a certain deference to the pleas of minorities with a grievance, and in recent years no group has benefited more from this society-wide dispensation than homosexuals. Nevertheless, in the somewhat fragmentary notes that follow, I hope to re-articulate what I am persuaded everyone knows to be the case about marriage, and perhaps thereby encourage others with stronger arguments than mine to help break the general paralysis.

Let us begin by admiring the case *for* gay marriage. Unlike the case for completely unrestricted abortion, which has come to be something of an embarrassment even to those who advance it, the case for gay marriage enjoys the decided advantage of appealing to our better moral natures as well as to our reason. It deploys two arguments. The first centers on principles of justice and fairness and may be thought of as the civil-rights argument. The second is at once more personal and more utilitarian, emphasizing the degradation and unhappiness attendant upon the denial of gay marriage and, conversely, the human and social happiness that will flow from its legal establishment.

Both arguments have been set forth most persuasively by two gifted writers, Bruce Bawer and Andrew Sullivan, each of whom describes himself as a social conservative. In their separate ways, they have been campaigning for gay marriage for over a decade. Bawer's take on the subject is succinctly summarized in his 1993 book, *A Place at the Table;* Sullivan has held forth on the desirability of legalizing gay marriage in numerous articles, on his website (andrewsullivan.com), and in an influential book, *Virtually Normal* (1995).

The civil-rights argument goes like this. Marriage is a legal state conferring real, tangible benefits on those who participate in it: specifically, tax breaks as well as other advantages when it comes to inheritance, property ownership, and employment benefits. But family law, since it limits marriage to heterosexual couples over the age of consent, clearly discriminates against a segment of the population. It is thus a matter of simple justice that, in Sullivan's words, "all public (as opposed to private) discrimination against homosexuals be ended and that every right and responsibility that heterosexuals enjoy as public citizens be extended to those who grow up and find themselves emotionally different." Not to grant such rights, Sullivan maintains, is to impose on homosexuals a civil deprivation akin to that suffered by black Americans under Jim Crow.

The utilitarian argument is more subtle; just as the rights argument seems aimed mainly at liberals, this one seems mostly to have in mind the concerns of conservatives. In light of the disruptive, anarchic, violence-prone behavior of many homosexuals (the argument runs), why should we *not* encourage the formation of stable, long-term, monogamous relationships that will redound to the health of society as a whole? In the apt words of a letter-writer in COMMENTARY in 1996:

> [H]omosexual marriage . . . preserves and promotes a set of moral values that are essential to civilized society. Like heterosexual marriage, it sanctions loyalty, unselfishness, and sexual fidelity; it rejects the promiscuous, the self-serving, the transitory relationship. Given the choice between building family units and preventing them, any conservative should favor the former.

Bawer, for his part, has come close to saying that the inability of many male homosexuals to remain faithful in long-term relationships is a *consequence* of the lack of marriage rights—a burning sign of the more general stigma under which gays labor in our society and which can be redressed by changes in law. As it happens, though, this particular line of argument is already somewhat out of date and is gradually

being phased out of the discussion. The tolera-
tion of gay styles of life has come about on its
own in American society, without the help of
legal sanctions, and protecting gay couples from
the contempt of bigots is not the emergency
Bawer has depicted. Quite the contrary: with
increasing numbers of gay partners committing
themselves to each other for life, in full and
approving view of their families and friends,
advocates of gay marriage need no longer call
upon the law to light (or force) the way; they
need only ask it to ratify a trend.

In brief, legalizing gay marriage would, in
Andrew Sullivan's summary formulation,

> offer homosexuals the same deal society now of-
> fers heterosexuals: general social approval and
> specific legal advantages in exchange for a deeper
> and harder-to-extract-yourself-from commitment
> to another human being. Like straight marriage,
> it would foster social cohesion, emotional secu-
> rity, and economic prudence.

The case is elegant, and it is compelling. But it
is not unanswerable. And answers have indeed
been forthcoming, even if, as I indicated at the
outset, many of them have tended to be couched
somewhat defensively. Thus, rather than repudi-
ating the very idea of an abstract "right" to
marry, many upholders of the traditional definition of marriage tacitly concede such a right, only
going on to suggest that denying it to a minority
amounts to a lesser hurt than conferring it would
impose on the majority, and especially on children, the weakest members of our society.

Others, to be sure, have attacked the Bawer/
Sullivan line more forthrightly. In a September
2000 article in COMMENTARY, "What Is Wrong
with Gay Marriage," Stanley Kurtz challenged
the central contention that marriage would do
for gay men what it does for straights—i.e.,
"domesticate" their natural male impulse to
promiscuity. Citing a number of academic "queer
theorists" and radical gays, Kurtz wrote:

> In contrast to moderates and "conservatives"
> like Andrew Sullivan, who consistently play down

[the] difference [between gays and straights]
in order to promote their vision of gays as
monogamists-in-the-making, radical gays have
argued—more knowledgeably, more powerfully,
and more vocally than any opponent of same-sex
marriage would dare to do—that homosexuality,
and particularly male homosexuality, is by its
very nature incompatible with the norms of traditional monogamous marriage.

True, Kurtz went on, such radical gays nevertheless support same-sex marriage. But what motivates them is the hope of "eventually undoing
the institution [of marriage] altogether," by dele-
gitimizing age-old understandings of the family
and thus (in the words of one such radical)
"striking at the heart of the organization of
Western culture and societies."

Nor are radical gays the only ones to entertain such destructive ambitions. Queuing up
behind them, Kurtz warned, are the proponents of polygamy, polyandry, and polyamor-
ism, all ready to argue that their threesomes,
foursomes, and other "nontraditional" arrangements are entitled to the same rights as everyone else's. In a recent piece in the *Weekly
Standard*, Kurtz has written that the "bottom"
of this particular slippery slope is "visible from
where we stand":

> Advocacy of legalized polygamy is growing. A
> network of grass-roots organizations seeking
> legal recognition for group marriage already
> exists. The cause of legalized group marriage is
> championed by a powerful faction of family-law
> specialists. Influential legal bodies in both the
> United States and Canada have presented radi-
> cal programs of marital reform, . . . [even] the
> abolition of marriage. The ideas behind this
> movement have already achieved surprising in-
> fluence with a prominent American politician
> [Al Gore].

Like other critics of same-sex marriage, Kurtz
has himself been vigorously criticized, especially
by Sullivan. But he is almost certainly correct as
to political and legal realities. If we grant rights
to one group because they have demanded it—
which is, practically, how legalized gay marriage

will come to pass—we will find it exceedingly awkward to deny similar rights to others ready with their own dossiers of "victimization." In time, restricting marriage rights to couples, whether straight or gay, can be made to seem no less arbitrary than the practice of restricting marriage rights to one man and one woman. Ultimately, the same must go for incestuous relationships between consenting adults—a theme to which I will return.

A different defense of heterosexual marriage has proceeded by circling the wagons around the institution itself. According to this school of thought, ably represented by the columnist Maggie Gallagher, the essential purpose of that institution is to create stable families:

> Most men and women are powerfully drawn to perform a sexual act that can and does generate life. Marriage is our attempt to reconcile and harmonize the erotic, social, sexual, and financial needs of men and women with the needs of their partner and their children.

Even childless marriages protect this purpose, writes Gallagher, by ensuring that, as long as the marriage exists, neither the childless husband nor the childless wife is likely to father or mother children outside of wedlock.

Gallagher is especially strong on the larger, social meaning of heterosexual marriage, which she calls "inherently normative":

> The laws of marriage do not create marriage, but in societies ruled by law they help trace the boundaries and sustain the public meanings of marriage. . . . Without this shared, public aspect, perpetuated generation after generation, marriage becomes what its critics say it is: a mere contract, a vessel with no particular content, one of a menu of sexual lifestyles, of no fundamental importance to anyone outside a given relationship.

Human relationships are by nature difficult enough, Gallagher reminds us, which is why communities must do all they can to strengthen and not to weaken those institutions that keep us up to a mark we may not be able to achieve through our own efforts. The consequences of not doing so will be an intensification of all the other woes of which we have so far had only a taste in our society and which are reflected in the galloping statistics of illegitimacy, cohabitation, divorce, and fatherlessness. For Gallagher, the modest request of gay-marriage advocates for "a place at the table" is thus profoundly selfish as well as utterly destructive—for gay marriage "would require society at large to gut marriage of its central presumptions about family in order to accommodate a few adults' desires."

James Q. Wilson, Maggie Gallagher, Stanley Kurtz, and others—including William J. Bennett in *The Broken Hearth* (2001)—are right to point to the deleterious private and public consequences of instituting gay marriage. Why, then, do their arguments fail to satisfy completely? Partly, no doubt, it is because the damage they describe is largely prospective and to that degree hypothetical; partly, as I remarked early on, the defensive tone that invariably enters into these polemics may rob them of the force they would otherwise have. I hardly mean to deprecate that tone: anyone with homosexual friends or relatives, especially those participating in long-standing romantic relationships, must feel abashed to find himself saying, in effect, "You gentlemen, you ladies, are at one and the same time a fine example of fidelity and mutual attachment—and the thin edge of the wedge." Nevertheless, in demanding the right to marry, that is exactly what they are.

To grasp what is at the other edge of that wedge—that is, what stands to be undone by gay marriage—we have to distinguish marriage itself from a variety of other goods and values with which it is regularly associated by its defenders and its aspirants alike. Those values—love and monogamous sex and establishing a home, fidelity, childbearing and childrearing, stability, inheritance, tax breaks, and all the rest—are not the same as marriage. True, a good marriage generally contains them, a bad marriage is generally deficient in them, and in law, religion, and custom, even under the strictest of moral regimes, their absence can be grounds for ending the union. But the *essence* of marriage resides elsewhere, and those who seek to arrange a kind of marriage for the inherently unmarriageable are looking for those things in the wrong place.

The largest fallacy of all arises from the emphasis on romantic love. In a book published last year, Tipper and Al Gore defined a family as those who are "joined at the heart"— "getting beyond words, legal formalities, and even blood ties." The distinction the Gores draw in this sentimental and offhand way is crucial, but they utterly misconstrue it. Hearts can indeed love, and stop loving. But what exactly does this have to do with marriage, which can follow, precede, or remain wholly independent of that condition?

It is a truism that many married people feel little sexual or romantic attraction to each other—perhaps because they have been married too long, or perhaps, as some men have always claimed, because the death of sexual desire is coincident with the wedding ceremony. ("All comedies are ended by a marriage," Byron wittily and sadly remarked.) Many people—in ages past, certainly most people—have married for reasons other than sexual or romantic attraction. So what? I could marry a woman I did not love, a woman I did not feel sexually attracted to or want to sleep with, and our marriage would still be a marriage, not just legally but in its *essence*.

The truth is banal, circular, but finally unavoidable: by definition, the essence of marriage is to sanction and solemnize that connection of opposites which alone creates new life. (Whether or not a given married couple does in fact create new life is immaterial.) Men and women *can* marry only because they belong to different, opposite, sexes. In marriage, they surrender those separate and different sexual allegiances, coming together to form a new entity. Their union is not a formalizing of romantic love but represents a certain idea—a construction, an abstract thought—about how best to formalize the human condition. This thought, embodied in a promise or a contract, is what holds marriage together, and the creation of this idea of marriage marks a key moment in the history of human development, a triumph over the alternative idea, which is concubinage.

Let me try to be more precise. Marriage can only concern my connection to a woman (and not to a man) because, as my reference to concubinage suggests, marriage is an institution that is built around female sexuality and female procreativity. (The very word "marriage" comes from the Latin word for mother, *mater*.) It exists for the gathering-in of a woman's sexuality under the protective net of the human or divine order, or both. This was so in the past and it is so even now, in our supposedly liberated times, when a woman who is in a sexual relationship without being married is, and is perceived to be, in a different state of being (not just a different legal state) from a woman who is married.

Circumstances have, admittedly, changed. Thanks to contraception, the decision to marry no longer precedes sexual intercourse as commonly as it did 50 years ago, when, for most people, a fully sexual relationship could begin only with marriage (and, when, as my mother constantly reminds me, one married *for* sex). Now the decision can come later; but come it almost certainly must. Even with contraception, even with feminism and women's liberation, the feeling would appear to be nearly as strong as ever that, for a woman, a sexual relationship must either end in marriage, or end.

This is surely understandable, for marriage *benefits* women, again not just in law but essentially. A woman can control who is the father of her children only insofar as there is a civil and private order that protects her from rape; marriage is the bulwark of that order. The 1960s feminists had the right idea: the essential thing for a woman is to control her own body. But they were wrong that this is what abortion is for; it is, rather, what marriage is for. It is humanity's way of enabling a woman to control her own body and to know (if she cares to) who is the father of her children.

Yes, marriage tends to regulate or channel the sexual appetite of men, and this is undoubtedly a good thing for women. But it is not the ultimate good. A husband, no matter how unfaithful, cannot introduce a child who is not his wife's own into a marriage without her knowledge; she alone has the power to do such a thing. For a woman, the fundamental advantage of marriage is thus not to regulate her husband but to empower herself—to regulate who has access to her person, and to marshal the resources of her husband and of the wider community to help her raise her children.

Every human relationship can be described as an enslavement, but for women the alternative to marriage is a much worse enslavement—which is why marriage, for women, is often associated as much with sexual freedom as with sexual constraint. In the traditional Roman Catholic cultures of the Mediterranean and South America, where virginity is fiercely protected and adolescent girls are hardly permitted to "date," marriage gives a woman the double luxury of controlling her sexuality and, if she wishes, extending it.

For men, by contrast, the same phenomenon—needing to be married in order to feel safe and free in a sexual relationship—simply does not exist. Men may wish to marry, but for more particular reasons: because they want to have children, or because they want to make a woman they love happy, or because they fear they will otherwise lose the woman they love. But it is rare for a man to feel essentially incomplete, or unprotected, in a sexual relationship that has not been solemnized by marriage. In fact, a man desperate to marry is often considered to have something wrong with him—to be unusually controlling or needy.

Because marriage is an arrangement built around female sexuality, because the institution has to do with women far more than it has to do with men, women will be the victims of its destruction. Those analysts who have focused on how children will suffer from the legalization of gay marriage are undoubtedly correct—but this will not be the first time that social developments perceived as advances for one group or another have harmed children. After all, the two most important (if effortless) achievements of the women's movement of the late 1960s were the right to abort and the right—in some social classes, the commandment—to join the professional workforce, both manifestly harmful to the interests of children.

But with the success of the gay-liberation movement, it is women themselves, all women, who will be hurt. The reason is that gay marriage takes something that belongs essentially to women, is crucial to their very freedom, and empties it of meaning.

Why should I not be able to marry a man? The question addresses a class of human phenomena that can be described in sentences but nonetheless cannot be. However much I might wish to, I cannot be a father to a pebble—I cannot be a brother to a puppy—I cannot make my horse my consul. Just so, I cannot, and should not be able to, marry a man. If I want to be a brother to a puppy, are you abridging my rights by not permitting it? I may say that I please; saying it does not mean that it can be.

In a gay marriage, one of two men must play the woman, or one of two women must play the man. "Play" here means travesty—burlesque. Not that their love is a travesty; but their participation in a ceremony that apes the marriage bond, with all that goes into it, is a travesty. Their taking-over of the form of this crucial and fragile connection of opposites is a travesty of marriage's purpose of protecting, actually and symbolically, the woman who enters into marriage with a man. To burlesque that purpose weakens those protections, and is essentially and profoundly anti-female.

Radical feminists were right, to an extent, in insisting that men's and women's sexuality is so different as to be inimical. Catharine MacKinnon has proclaimed that in a "patriarchal" society, all sexual intercourse is rape. Repellent as her view is, it is formed around a kernel of truth. There is something inherently violative about sexual intercourse—and there is something dangerous about being a woman in a sexual relationship with a man to whom she is not yet married. Among the now-aging feminists of my generation, no less than among their mothers, such a woman is commonly thought to be a *victim*.

Marriage is a sign that the ever-so-slight violation that is involved in a heterosexual relationship has been sanctioned by some recognized authority. That sanction is also what makes divorce a scandal—for divorce cannot truly undo the sanction of sexual intercourse, which is to say the sanction to create life, with one's original partner. Even in the Jewish tradition, which regards marriage (but not love) in a completely unsacralized way, divorce, though perfectly legal, does not erase the ontological status of the earlier marriage. (The Talmud records that God weeps when a man puts aside his first wife.) This sanction does not exist for homosexual couples. They are not opposites; they are the same. They live in a world of innocence, and neither their union nor their disunion partakes of the act of creation.

This brings us back to the incest ban, with which marriage is intimately and intricately connected. Indeed, marriage exists for the same reason that incest must not: because in our darker, inhuman moments we are driven toward that which *is* the same as ourselves and away from that which is fundamentally different from ourselves. Therefore we are enjoined from committing incest, negatively, and commanded to join with our opposite, positively—so that humanity may endure.

Homosexuals are, of course, free to avoid the latter commandment—and those who choose to do so are assuredly capable of leading rich and satisfying lives. The same goes for all those non-homosexuals who have decided or been advised not to marry in certain circumstances—for example, if they wish to be members of celibate religious communities, or ascetic soldiers in a cause, or geniuses (as Cyril Connolly warned,

"there is no more somber enemy of good art than the pram in the hall"). Men and women alike now spend more time as sexually mature adults outside of marriage than ever before, and some number of them live together in unreal or mock marriages of one kind or another. The social status of homosexuals is no better and no worse than that of anyone else who lives in an unmarried condition.

What of simple compassion? What do we owe to our fellow-beings who wish, as they might put it, to achieve a happiness they see we are entitled to but which we deny to them? From those of us who oppose gay marriage, Andrew Sullivan demands *some* "reference to gay people's lives or relationships or needs." But the truth is that many people have many needs that are not provided for by law, by government, or by society at large—and for good reason.

Insofar as I care for my homosexual friend *as* a friend, I am required to say to him that, if a lifelong monogamous relationship is what you want, I wish you that felicity, just as I hope you would wish me the same. But insofar as our lives as citizens are concerned, or even as human beings, your monogamy and the durability of your relationship are, to be blunt about it, matters of complete indifference. They are of as little concern to our collective life as if you were to smoke cigars or build model railroads in your basement or hang-glide, and of less concern to society than the safety of your property when you leave your house or your right not to be overcharged by the phone company.

That is not because you are gay. It is because, in choosing to conduct your life as you have every right to do, you have stepped out of the area of shared social concern—in the same sense as has anyone, of whatever sexuality, who chooses not to marry. There are millions of lonely people, of whom it is safe to say that the majority are in heterosexual marriages. But marriage, though it may help meet the needs of the lonely, does not exist because it is an answer to those needs; it is an arrangement that has to do with empowering women to avoid even greater unhappiness, and with sustaining the future history of the species.

Marriage, to say it for the last time, is what connects us with our nature and with our animal origins, with how all of us, heterosexual and homosexual alike, came to be. It exists not because of custom, or because of a conspiracy (whether patriarchal or matriarchal), but because, through marriage, the *world* exists. Marriage is how we are connected backward in time, through the generations, to our Creator (or, if you insist, to the primal soup), and forward to the future beyond the scope of our own lifespan. It is, to say the least, bigger than two hearts beating as one.

Severing this connection by defining it out of existence—cutting it down to size, transforming it into a mere contract between chums—sunders the natural laws that prevent concubinage and incest. Unless we resist, we will find ourselves entering on the path to the abolition of the human. The gods move very fast when they bring ruin on misguided men.

Review Questions

1. According to Schulman, what is the strongest argument against gay marriage? Why isn't he satisfied with it?
2. Why does Schulman think we are at an "Antigone moment?"
3. State and explain the civil-rights argument for gay marriage. How do critics reply?
4. What is the utilitarian argument for gay marriage? How does Stanley Kurtz reply?
5. Explain Maggie Gallagher's view of marriage.
6. According to Schulman, what is the essence of marriage? Why is marriage built around female sexuality?
7. Why does Schulman think that he should not be able to marry a man? What exactly is his argument?
8. Why does Schulman believe that divorce is a scandal?
9. What is the connection between the incest ban and marriage according to Schulman?

Discussion Questions

1. Does gay marriage harm families and children? If so, then how does it do this? Is this harm comparable to the harm caused by divorce and poverty?
2. Kurtz argues that if we allow gay marriage, then we will have to allow polygamy, and even the abolition of marriage. Is there a good reply to this slippery slope argument? Explain your answer.
3. Schulman claims it is a fallacy to think romantic love and sexual attraction are the essence of marriage. Do you agree? Why or why not?
4. If the purpose of marriage is to have and raise children, then why do we allow childless marriages? What does Gallagher say about this? What do you think?
5. Is gay marriage analogous to being a father to a pebble or a brother to a puppy? Why or why not?
6. Schulman says that in a gay marriage one of two men must play the woman, or one of two women must play the man. Is this true? Why can't married men still be men, or married women still be women? For that matter, why do married people have to play traditional gender roles at all?

Who Needs Marriage?

JONATHAN RAUCH

Jonathan Rauch writes a biweekly column for *National Journal* and is writer in residence at the Brookings Institution in Washington, D.C. He is the author of *Kindly Inquisitors* (1993), *Demosclerosis* (1994), and *Government's End: Why Washington Stopped Working* (1999).

Rauch replies to the Hayekian argument (as he calls it) that reforming marriage by allowing gays to marry will produce chaos in our society or destroy the institution of marriage. He doubts that extending marriage to a mere 3 to 5 percent of the population will have as much an effect on marriage as other changes, such as no-fault divorce. (He is in favor of strengthening the institution of marriage by making divorce harder to get.) Furthermore, even if a social change (like allowing contraception) has bad effects, it may still be right. And social changes can have good effects, too. As for the purpose of marriage, Rauch denies that love is essential for marriage. He grants that having and raising children is one of the main purposes of marriage, but it is not the only purpose. He suggests that marriage has two other social purposes—it tames and civilizes young males and it provides the married person with a reliable caregiver. He argues that gay marriage accomplishes these two additional social purposes, and so it should be allowed and even encouraged for gay people.

WHATEVER ELSE MARRIAGE may or may not be, it is certainly falling apart. Half of today's new marriages will end in divorce, and far more costly still (from a social point of view) are the marriages that never happen at all, leaving mothers poor, children fatherless, and neighborhoods chaotic. With a sense of timing worthy of Neville Chamberlain, at just this moment, homosexuals are pressing to be able to marry, and Hawaii's courts are moving toward letting them do so. I'll believe in gay marriage in America when I see it, but if it gets as far as being even temporarily legalized in Hawaii, then the uproar about this final insult to a besieged institution will be deafening.

Whether gay marriage makes sense—and, for that matter, whether straight marriages makes sense—depends on what marriage is actually for. Oddly enough, at the moment, secular thinking on this question is shockingly sketchy. Gay activists say: marriage is for love, and we love each other, therefore we should be able to marry. Traditionalists say: marriage is for children, and homosexuals do not (or should not) have children, therefore you should not be able to marry. That, unfortunately, pretty well covers the spectrum. I say "unfortunately" because both views are wrong. They misunderstand and impoverish the social meaning of marriage.

I admit to being an interested party: I am a homosexual, and I want the right to marry. In fact, I want more than the right; I want the actual marriage (when Mr. Wonderful comes along, God willing). Nevertheless, I do not want to destroy the most basic of all social institutions,

Source: "Who Needs Marriage" from *Beyond Queer: Challenging Gay Left Orthodoxy,* edited by Bruce Bawer (Free Press, 1996), pp. 296–313. Reprinted by permission.

backbone of the family, and bedrock of civilization. It is not enough for gay marriage to make sense for gay people; if they ask society to recognize and bless it, it should also make sense from society's broader point of view.

So what is marriage for?

AGAINST LOVE

In its religious dress, marriage has a straightforward justification. It is as it is because that is how God wants it. Depending on the religion, God has various things to say about who may marry and what should go on within a marriage. Modern marriage is, of course, based upon traditions that religion helped to codify and enforce. But religious doctrine has no special standing in the world of secular law and policy, with all due apologies to the "Christian nation" crowd. If we want to know what and whom marriage is for in modern America, we need a sensible secular doctrine.

At one point, marriage in secular society was largely a matter of business: cementing family ties, providing social status for men and economic support for women, conferring dowries, and so on. Marriages were typically arranged, and "love" in the modern sense was no prerequisite. In Japan today, there are remnants of this system, and it works surprisingly well. Couples stay together because they view their marriage as a partnership: an investment in social stability for themselves and their children. Because Japanese couples don't expect as much emotional fulfillment as Americans do, they are less inclined to break up. They also take a somewhat more relaxed attitude toward adultery. What's a little extracurricular love, provided that each partner is fulfilling his or her many other marital duties?

In the West, of course, love is a defining element. The notion of lifelong love is charming, if ambitious, and certainly love is a desirable element of marriage. It cannot, however, be the defining element in society's eyes. You may or may not love your husband, but the two of you are just as married either way. You may love your mistress, but that certainly does not make her your spouse. Love helps make sense of marriage from an emotional point of view, but it is not terribly important, I think, in making sense of marriage from the point of view of social policy.

If blessing love does not define the purpose of secular marriage, what does? Neither the law nor secular thinking provides a very clear answer to this question. Today, marriage is almost entirely a voluntary arrangement whose contents are up to the people making the deal. There are few if any behaviors that automatically end a marriage. If a man beats his wife—which is about the worst thing he can do to her—he may be convicted of assault, but his marriage is not automatically dissolved. Couples can be adulterous (or "open") yet still be married, so long as that is what they choose to be. They can be celibate, too; consummation is not required. All in all, it is an impressive and also rather astonishing victory for modern individualism that so important an institution should be so bereft of formal social instruction as to what should go on inside of it.

Secular society tells us only a few things about marriage. Among them are the following. First, marriage happens only with the consent of the parties. Second, the parties are not children. Third, a number of parties is two. Fourth, one is a man and the other is a woman. Within those rules, a marriage is whatever anyone says it is. So the standard rules say almost nothing about what marriage is for.

AGAINST TRADITION

Perhaps it doesn't matter what marriage is for. Perhaps it is enough simply to say that marriage is as it is and should not be tampered with. This sounds like a crudely reactionary position. In fact, however, of all the arguments against reforming marriage, it is probably the most powerful.

I'll call it a Hayekian argument, after the great libertarian economist F. A. Hayek, who developed this line of thinking in his book *The Fatal Conceit*. In a market system, the prices generated by impersonal forces may not make sense from any one person's point of view, but they encode far more information than even the cleverest person could ever gather. In a similar fashion, human societies evolve rich and complicated webs of nonlegal rules in the forms of customs, traditions, and institutions. Like prices, the customs generated by societies may often seem irrational or arbitrary. But the very fact that they are the customs that have evolved implies that there is a kind of practical logic embedded in them that may not be apparent from even a sophisticated analysis. And the web of custom cannot be torn apart and reordered at will, because once its internal logic is violated, it falls apart. Intellectuals, like Marxists or feminists, who seek to deconstruct and rationally rebuild social traditions will produce not better order, but merely chaos. Thus hallowed social tradition should not be tampered with except in the very last extremity.

For secular intellectuals who are unhappy with the evolved framework for marriage and who are excluded from it—in other words, for people like me—this Hayekian argument is very troubling. It is also very powerful. Age-old stigmas on illegitimacy and out-of-wedlock pregnancy were crude and unfair to women and children. On the male side, shotgun marriages were, in an informal way, coercive and intrusive. But when modern societies began playing around with the age-old stigmas on illegitimacy and divorce and all the rest, whole portions of the social structure just caved in.

So the Hayekian view argues strongly against gay marriage. It says that the current rules for marriage may not be the best ones, and they may even be unfair. But they are all we have, and once you say that marriage need not be male-female, soon marriage will stop being anything at all. You can't mess with the formula without causing unforeseen consequences, possibly including the implosion of the institution of marriage itself.

But I demur. There are problems with the Hayekian position. The biggest is that it is untenable in its extreme form and unhelpful in its milder version. In its extreme form, it implies that no social reforms should ever be undertaken.

Indeed, no social laws should be passed, because they will interfere with the natural evolution of social mores. One would thus have to say that because in the past slavery was customary in almost all human societies, it should not have been forcibly abolished. Obviously, neither Hayek nor his sympathizers would actually say this. They would point out that slavery violated fundamental moral principles and was scaldingly inhumane. But in doing so, they do what must be done if we are to be human: they establish a moral platform from which to judge social rules. They thus acknowledge that abstracting social debate from moral concerns is not possible.

If the ban on gay marriage were only mildly unfair and if the social costs of changing it were certain to be enormous, then the ban could stand on Hayekian grounds. However, if there is any social policy today that has a fair claim to being scaldingly inhumane, it is the ban on gay marriage. As conservatives tirelessly and rightly point out, marriage is the most fundamental institution of society. To bar any class of people from marrying as they choose is an extraordinary deprivation. When, not so long ago, it was illegal in parts of America for blacks to marry whites, no one could claim this was a trivial disenfranchisement. Granted, gay marriage raises issues that interracial marriage does not; but no one can argue that the deprivation itself is a minor one.

To outweigh such a serious claim and rule out homosexual marriage purely on Hayekian grounds, saying that bad things might happen is not enough. Bad things might always happen. Bad things happened as a result of legalizing contraception, but that did not make it the wrong thing to do, and in any case, good things happened also. It is not at all clear, on the merits, that heterosexual marriage would be eroded by legalizing homosexual marriage. On the contrary, marriage might be strengthened if it were held out as the norm for everybody, including homosexuals.

Besides, it seems doubtful that extending marriage to, say, another 3 or 5 percent of the population would have anything like the effects that no-fault divorce has had, to say nothing of contraception and the sexual revolution. By now, the "traditional" understanding of marriage has been tampered with by practically everybody in all kinds of ways. It is hard to think of a bigger affront to tradition, for instance, than allowing married women to own property independently of their husbands or allowing them to charge their husbands with rape. Surely it is a bit unfair to say that marriage may be reformed for the sake of anyone and everyone except homosexuals, who must respect the dictates of tradition.

Faced with these problems, the milder version of the Hayekian argument says, not that social traditions shouldn't be tampered with at all, but that they shouldn't be tampered with lightly. Fine, and thank you. In this case, no one is talking about casual messing around or about some lobby's desire to score political points; the issue is about allowing people to live as grown-ups and full citizens. One could write pages on this point, but I won't. I'll set human rights claims to one side and in return ask the Hayekians to recognize that appeals to blind tradition and to the risks inherent in social change do not, a priori, settle anything in this instance. They merely warn against frivolous change. If the issue at hand is whether gay marriage is good or bad for society as well as for gay people, there is no avoiding a discussion about the *purpose* of marriage.

AGAINST CHILDREN

So we turn to what has become the standard view of marriage's purpose. Its proponents would probably like to call it a child-centered view, but a more accurate description would call it an antigay view, as will become clear. Whatever you call it, it is certainly the view that is heard most often, and in the context of the debate over gay marriage, it is heard almost exclusively. In its most straightforward form, it goes as follows (I quote from James Q. Wilson's fine book *The Moral Sense*):

> A family is not an association of independent people; it is a human commitment designed to make possible the rearing of moral and healthy

children. Governments care—or ought to care—about families for this reason, and scarcely for any other.

Wilson speaks about "family" rather than "marriage" as such, but one may, I think, read him as speaking of marriage without doing any injustice to his meaning. The resulting proposition—government ought to care about marriage almost entirely because of children and scarcely for any other reason—seems reasonable. It certainly accords with our commonsense feeling that marriage and children go together. But there are problems. The first, obviously, is that gay couples may have children, either through adoption or (for lesbians) by using artificial insemination. I will leave for some other essay the contentious issue of gay adoption. For now, the obvious point is that if the mere presence of children is the test, then homosexual relationships can certainly pass it.

You might note, correctly, that heterosexual marriages are more likely to wind up with children in the mix than homosexual ones. When granting marriage licenses to heterosexuals, however, we do not ask how likely the couple is to have children. We assume that they are entitled to get married whether they end up with children or not. Understanding this, conservatives often then make an interesting further move. In seeking to justify the state's interest in marriage, they shift from the actual presence of children to the anatomical possibility of making them. Hadley Arkes, a law professor and prominent opponent of homosexual marriage, makes the case this way:

> The traditional understanding of marriage is grounded in the "natural teleology of the body"—in the inescapable fact that only a man and a woman, and only two people, not three, can generate a child. Once marriage is detached from that natural teleology of the body, what ground of principle would thereafter confine marriage to two people rather than some larger grouping? That is, on what ground of principle would the law reject the claim of a gay couple that their love is not confined to a coupling of two, but that they are woven into a larger ensemble with yet another person or two?

What he seems to be saying is that where the possibility of natural children is nil, the meaning of marriage is nil. If marriage is allowed between members of the same sex, then the concept of marriage has been emptied of content except to ask whether the parties love each other. Then anything goes, including polygamy. This reasoning presumably is what antigay activists have in mind when they claim that once gay marriage is legal, marriage to pets will follow close behind.

Arkes and his sympathizers have here made two mistakes, both of them instructive. To see them, break down the Arkes-type claim into two components:

1. Two-person marriage derives its special status from the anatomical possibility that the partners can create natural children.

2. Apart from 1, two-person marriage has no purpose sufficiently strong to justify its special status. That is, absent justification 1, anything goes.

The first proposition is peculiar, because it is wholly at odds with the way society actually views marriage. Leave aside the insistence that natural, as opposed to adoptive, children define the importance of marriage. The deeper problem, apparent right away, is the issue of sterile heterosexual couples. Here the "anatomical possibility" crowd has a problem, for a homosexual union is, anatomically speaking, nothing but one variety of sterile union and no different even in principle: a woman without a uterus has no more potential for giving birth than a man without a vagina.

It may sound like carping to stress the case of barren heterosexual marriage; the vast majority of newlywed heterosexual couples, after all, can have children and probably will. But the point here is fundamental. There are far more sterile heterosexual unions in America than homosexual ones. The "anatomical possibility" crowd cannot have it both ways. If the possibility of children is what gives meaning to marriage, then a postmenopausal woman who tries to take out a marriage license should be turned away at the courthouse door. What's more, she should be hooted at and condemned for stretching the meaning of marriage beyond its natural basis and so reducing the institution to frivolity. People at the Family Research Council or Concerned Women for America should point at her and say, "If she can marry, why not polygamy? Why not marriage to pets?"

Obviously, the "anatomical" conservatives do not say this, because they are sane. They instead flail around, saying that sterile men and women were at least born with the right-shaped parts for making children, and so on. As they struggle to include sterile heterosexual marriages while excluding homosexual ones, their position is soon revealed to be a nonposition. It says that the "natural children" rationale defines marriage when homosexuals are involved but not when heterosexuals are involved. When the parties to union are sterile heterosexuals, the justification for marriage must be something else. But what?

Now arises the oddest part of the "anatomical" argument. Look at proposition 2 above. It says that, absent the anatomical justification for marriage, anything goes. In other words, it dismisses the idea that there might be some other compelling reasons for society to sanctify marriage above other kinds of relationships. Why would anybody want to make this move? I'll just hazard a guess: to exclude homosexuals. Any rationale that justifies sterile heterosexual marriages can also apply to homosexual ones. For instance, marriage makes women more financially secure. Very nice, say the conservatives. But that rationale could be applied to lesbians, so it's definitely out.

The end result of this stratagem is perverse to the point of being funny. The attempt to ground marriage in children (or the anatomical possibility thereof) falls flat. But having lost that reason for marriage, the antigay people can offer no other. In their fixation on excluding homosexuals, they leave themselves no consistent justification for the privileged status of *heterosexual* marriage. They thus tear away any coherent foundation that secular marriage might have, which is precisely the opposite of what they claim they want to do. If they have to undercut marriage to save it from homosexuals, so be it!

If you feel my argument here has a slightly Thomist ring, the reason, of course, is that the "child-centered" people themselves do not really believe that natural children are the only, or even the overriding, reason society blesses marriage. In the real world, it's obvious that sterile people have every right to get married and that society benefits by allowing and, indeed, encouraging them to do so. No one seriously imagines that denying marriage to a sterile heterosexual couple would strengthen the institution of marriage, or that barring sterile marriages would even be a decent thing to do. The "natural children" people know this perfectly well, and they admit it implicitly when they cheerfully bless sterile unions. In truth, their real posture has nothing at all to do with children, or even with the "anatomical possibility" of children. It is merely antigay. All it really says is this: the defining purpose of marriage is to exclude homosexuals.

This is not an answer to the question of what marriage is for. Rather, it makes of marriage, as Richard Mohr aptly puts it, "nothing but an empty space, delimited only by what it excludes—gay couples." By putting a nonrationale at the center of modern marriage, these conservatives leave the institution worse off than if they had never opened their mouths. This is not at all helpful.

If one is to set hypocrisy aside, one must admit that there are compelling reasons for marriage other than children—reasons that may or may not apply to homosexual unions. What might those reasons be?

ROGUE MALES
AND AILING MATES

For the record, I would be the last to deny that children are one central reason for the privileged status of marriage. Rather, I gladly proclaim it. When men and women get together, children

are a likely outcome; and, as we are learning in ever more unpleasant ways, when children appear without two parents, all kinds of trouble ensues. Without belaboring the point, I hope I won't be accused of saying that children are a trivial reason for marriage. They just cannot be the only reason.

And what are the others? I can think of several possibilities, such as the point cited above about economic security for women (or men). There is a lot of intellectual work to be done trying to sort out which are the essential reasons and which incidental. It seems to me that the two strongest candidates are these: settling males and providing reliable caregivers. Both purposes are critical to the functioning of a humane and stable society, and both are much better served by marriage—that is, by one-to-one lifelong commitment—than by any other institution.

Wilson writes, in *The Moral Sense,* of the human male's need to hunt, defend, and attack. "Much of the history of civilization can be thought of as an effort to adapt these male dispositions to contemporary needs by restricting aggression or channeling it into appropriate channels," he says. I think it is probably fair to say that civilizing young males is one of any society's two or three biggest problems. Wherever unattached males gather in packs, you see no end of trouble: wildings in Central Park, gangs in Los Angeles, football hooligans in Britain, skinheads in Germany, fraternity hazings in universities, grope lines in the military, and (in a different but ultimately no less tragic way) the bathhouses and wanton sex of gay San Francisco or New York in the 1970s.

For taming males, marriage is unmatched. "Of all the institutions through which men may pass—schools, factories, the military—marriage has the largest effect," Wilson writes. A token of the casualness of current thinking about marriage is that the man who wrote those words could, later in the very same book, say that government should care about fostering families for "scarcely any other" reason than children. If marriage—that is, the binding of men into couples—did nothing else, its power to settle men, to keep them at home and out of trouble, would be ample justification for its special status.

Of course, women and older men don't generally travel in marauding or orgiastic packs. But in their case, the second rationale comes strongly into play. A second enormous problem for society is what to do when someone is beset by some sort of burdensome contingency. It could be cancer, a broken back, unemployment, or depression; it could be exhaustion from work or stress under pressure. If marriage has any meaning at all, it is that when you collapse from a stroke, there will be at least one other person whose "job" is to drop everything and come to your aid; or that when you come home after being fired by the postal service, there will be someone to persuade you not to commit a massacre.

All by itself, marriage is society's first and, often, second and third line of support for the troubled individual. Absent a spouse, the burdens of contingency fall immediately and sometimes crushingly upon people who have more immediate problems of their own (relatives, friends, neighbors), then upon charities and welfare programs that are expensive and often not very good. From the broader society's point of view, the unattached person is an accident waiting to happen. Married people are happier, healthier, and live longer; married men have lower rates of homicide, suicide, accidents, and mental illness. In large part, the reason is simply that married people have someone to look after them, and know it.

Obviously, both of these rationales—the need to settle males, the need to have people looked after—apply to sterile people as well as to fertile ones, and apply to childless couples as well as to ones with children. The first explains why everybody feels relieved when the town delinquent gets married, and the second explains why everybody feels happy when an aging widow takes a second husband. From a social point of view, it seems to me, both rationales are far more compelling as justification of marriage's special status than, say, love. And both of them apply to homosexuals as well as to heterosexuals.

Take the matter of settling men. It is probably true that women and children, more than just the fact of marriage, help civilize men. But that hardly means that the settling effect of marriage on homosexual men is negligible. To the contrary, being tied into a committed relationship plainly helps stabilize gay men. Even without marriage, coupled gay men have steady sex partners and relationships that they value, so they tend to be less wanton. Add marriage, and you bring to bear a further array of stabilizing influences. One of the main benefits of publicly recognized marriage is that it binds couples together not only in their own eyes, but also in the eyes of society at large. Around the partners is weaved a web of expectations that they will spend nights together, go to parties together, take out mortgages together, buy furniture at Ikea together, and so on—all of which helps tie them together and keep them off the streets and at home. ("It's 1:00 A.M.; do you know where your husband is?" Chances are you do.) Surely that is a very good thing, especially as compared to the closet-gay culture of furtive sex with innumerable partners in parks and bathhouses.

The other benefit of marriage—caretaking—clearly applies to homosexuals, with no reservations at all. One of the first things many people worry about when coming to terms with their homosexuality is, "Who will take care of me when I'm old?" Society needs to care about this, too, as the AIDS crisis has made horribly clear. If that crisis showed anything, it is that homosexuals can and will take care of each other, sometimes with breathtaking devotion—and that no institution can begin to match the care of a devoted partner. Legally speaking, marriage creates kin. Surely, society's interest in kin creation is strongest of all for people who are unlikely to be supported by children in old age and who may well be rejected by their own parents in youth.

Gay marriage, then, is far from being a mere exercise in political point making or rights mongering. On the contrary, it serves two of the three social purposes that make marriage so indispensable and irreplaceable for heterosexuals. Two out of three may not be the whole ball of wax, but it is more than enough to give society a compelling interest in marrying off homosexuals.

Moreover, marriage is the *only* institution that adequately serves these purposes. People who are uncomfortable with gay marriage—including some gay people—argue that the benefits can just as well be had through private legal arrangements and domestic-partnership laws. But only the fiduciary and statutory benefits of marriage can be arranged that way, and therein lies a world of difference. The promise of one-to-one lifetime commitment is very hard to keep. The magic of marriage is that it wraps a dense ribbon of social approval around each partnership, then reinforces commitment with a hundred informal mechanisms from everyday greetings ("How's the wife?") to gossipy sneers ("Why does she put up with that cheating bastard Bill?"). The power of marriage is not just legal, but social. It seals its promise with the smiles and tears of family, friends, and neighbors. It shrewdly exploits ceremony (big, public weddings) and money (expensive gifts, dowries) to deter casual commitment and to make bailing out embarrassing. Stag parties and bridal showers signal that what is beginning is not just a legal arrangement, but a whole new stage of life. "Domestic-partner" laws do none of these things. Me, I can't quite imagine my mother sobbing with relief as she says, "Thank heaven, Jonathan has finally found a domestic partner."

I'll go further: far from being a substitute for the real thing, "lite" marriage more likely undermines it. Marriage is a deal between a couple and society, not just between two people: society recognizes the sanctity and autonomy of the pair-bond, and in exchange, each spouse commits to being the other's caregiver, social worker, and police officer of first resort. Each marriage is its own little society within society. Any step that weakens this deal by granting the legal benefits of marriage without also requiring the public commitment is begging for trouble.

From gay couples' point of view, pseudo-marriage is second best to the real thing; but from society's point of view, it may be the worst policy of all. From both points of view, gay marriage—real social recognition, real personal commitment, real social pressure to shore up personal commitment—makes the most sense. That is why government should be wary of offering "alternatives" to marriage. And, one might add, that is also why the full social benefits of gay marriage will come only when churches as well as governments customarily bless it: when women marry women in big church weddings as mothers weep and priests, solemnly smiling, intone the vows.

AGAINST GAY DIVORCE

So gay marriage makes sense for several of the same reasons that straight marriage makes sense; fine. That would seem a natural place to stop. But the logic of the argument compels one to go a twist further. If I am right, then there are implications for heterosexuals and homosexuals alike—not entirely comfortable ones.

If society has a strong interest in seeing people married off, then it must also have some interest in seeing them stay together. For many years, that interest was assumed and embodied in laws and informal stigmas that made divorce a painful experience. My guess is that this was often bad for adults but quite good for children, though you could argue that point all day. In any event, things have radically changed. Today, more and more people believe that a divorce should be at least a bit harder to get.

I'm not going to wade into the debate about toughening the divorce laws. Anyway, in a liberal society, there is not much you can do to keep people together without trampling their rights. The point that's relevant here is that, if I'm right, the standard way of thinking about this issue is incomplete, even misleading. The usual argument is that divorce is bad for children, which is why we should worry about it. I wouldn't deny this for a moment. Some people advocate special counseling or cooling-off periods for divorcing couples with children. That may well be a good idea. But it should not be assumed that society has no interest in helping childless couples stay together, also—for just the reason I've outlined.

Childless couples, of course, include gay couples. In my opinion, if one wants to shore up the institution of marriage, then one had better complicate divorce (if that's what you're going to do) for all couples, including gay ones and childless heterosexual ones. Otherwise, you send the message that marriage can be a casual affair if you don't happen to have children. Gay spouses should understand that once they are together, they are *really* together. The upshot is that gay divorce should be every bit as hard to get as straight divorce—and both should probably be harder to get than is now the case.

Another implication follows, too. If it is good for society to have people attached, then it is not enough just to make marriage available. Marriage should also be *expected*. This, too, is just as true for homosexuals as for heterosexuals. So if homosexuals are justified in expecting access to marriage, society is equally justified in expecting them to use it. I'm not saying that out-of-wedlock sex should be scandalous or that people should be coerced into marriage or anything like that. The mechanisms of expectation are more subtle. When Grandma cluck-clucks over a still-unmarried young man, or when Mom says she wishes her little girl would settle down, she is expressing a strong and well-justified preference—one that is quietly echoed in a thousand ways throughout society and that produces subtle but important pressure to form and sustain unions. This is a good and necessary thing, and it will be as necessary for homosexuals as for heterosexuals. If gay marriage is recognized, single gay people over a certain age should not be surprised when they are subtly disapproved of or pitied. That is a vital part of what makes marriage work.

Moreover, if marriage is to work, it cannot be merely a "lifestyle option." It must be privileged. That is, it must be understood to be better, on average, than other ways of living. Not mandatory, not good where everything else is bad, but better: a general norm, rather than a personal taste. The biggest worry about gay marriage, I think, is that homosexuals might get it but then mostly not use it. Unlike a conservative friend of mine, I don't think that gay neglect of marriage would greatly erode what remains of the bonding power of heterosexual marriage (remember, homosexuals are only a tiny fraction of the population). But it would certainly not help, and in any case, it would denude the benefits and cheapen the meaning of homosexual marriage. And heterosexual society would rightly feel betrayed if, after legalization, homosexuals treated marriage as a minority taste rather than as a core institution of life. It is not enough, I think, for gay people to say we want the right to marry. If we do not use it, shame on us.

Review Questions

1. Why does Rauch reject a religious account of marriage?
2. Why isn't love the defining element of marriage, according to Rauch?
3. What is the Hayekian argument? Why doesn't Rauch accept it?
4. What is the antigay view of marriage, as Rauch calls it? Why does Rauch reject this view?
5. What are the main social purposes of marriage, in Rauch's view?
6. Why is Rauch in favor of making divorce harder to get?

Discussion Questions

1. What do you think is the primary purpose of marriage? Defend your answer.
2. Do you agree that divorce should be harder to get? Explain your answer.
3. Has Rauch given a satisfactory reply to Schulman? Why or why not?

Problem Cases

1. Goodridge vs. Department of Public Health (2003)

(For the text of the decision see www.FindLaw.com). In this case, the Massachusetts Supreme Court ruled (4–3) that a state law banning same-sex marriage violated the Massachusetts constitution, and ordered a stay of entry of the judgment for 180 days to "permit the Legislature to take such action as it may deem appropriate in light of this opinion."

In the majority opinion, Chief Justice Margaret H. Marshall said that marriage is a vital social institution that brings stability to society and provides love and mutual support to those who are married. It provides many legal, financial, and social bene-fits. The question before the court was "whether, consistent with the Massachusetts Constitution, the Commonwealth could deny those protections, benefits, and obli-gations to two individuals of the same sex who wish to marry." In ruling that the Commonwealth could not do so, the majority opinion said that the Massachusetts Constitution "affirms the dignity and equality of all individuals" and "forbids the creation of second-class citizens."

Furthermore, the court argued that the marriage ban for same-sex couples "works a deep and scarring hardship" on same-sex families "for no rational reason." It prevents children of same-sex couples from enjoying the advantages that flow from a "stable family structure in which children will be reared, educated, and socialized." "It cannot be rational under our laws," the court held, "to penalize chil-dren by depriving them of State benefits" because of their parents' sexual orientation.

The court denied that the primary purpose of marriage is procreation. Rather the purpose of marriage "is the exclusive and permanent commitment of marriage partners to one another, not the begetting of children, that is the sine qua non of marriage."

The majority opinion changed the common-law definition of civil marriage to mean "the voluntary union of two persons as spouses, to the exclusion of all others." The court noted that civil marriage was a civil right, and concluded that "the right to marry means little if it does not include the right to marry the person of one's choice."

There were three dissenting opinions. Justice Cordy argued that the marriage statute defining marriage as the union of one man and one woman did not violate the Massachusetts Constitution because "it furthers the legitimate State purpose of ensuring, promoting, and supporting an optimal social structure for the bearing and raising of children."

Justice Spina stated that what was at stake in the case was not the unequal treat-ment of individuals, but rather "the power of the Legislature to effectuate social change without interference from the courts." He said that the "power to regulate marriage lies with the Legislature, not with the judiciary."

Justice Sosman held that the issue was whether changing the definition of mar-riage "can be made at this time without damaging the institution of marriage." She asserted that "it is rational for the Legislature to postpone any redefinition of mar-riage that would include same-sex couples until such time as it is certain that redefi-nition will not have unintended and undesirable social consequences."

Do you agree with the majority opinion or with one or more of the dissenting opinions? Explain your position.

In May 2004, the state of Massachusetts issued thousands of marriage licenses to same-sex couples. Did this produce any harm to heterosexual marriages or to the institution of marriage? If so, explain the nature of this harm.

2. Dan Conlin and Bob Elsen

Dan Conlin and Bob Elsen are gay partners living in San Francisco, California. Conlin is 42, and Elsen is 41. Conlin is a physician with a prosperous gastroenterology practice. Elsen is also a doctor. They met during their residences at New England Deaconess Hospital in Boston. They have a magnificent home in family-friendly Ashbury Heights and a stable, loving relationship. They both come from big, supportive families.

There are very few gay men with adopted children in the Bay Area. The norm for same-sex parents is lesbian couples whose children have been fathered by sperm donors. Yet Conlin and Elsen were highly motivated to adopt and raise children. After advertising, they found a pregnant woman in Florida who did not want her child. They witnessed the birth of the child, Michael, and became his legal guardians. (Same-sex couples cannot legally adopt children in Florida, but they can in California.) The formal legal adoption of Michael by Conlin and Elsen occurred in California. They also adopted another newborn boy, Matthew, who was born in Reno, Nevada. Again the legal adoption was performed in California.

Both adoptions are open. That is to say, Colin and Elsen know the identity and location of the biological mothers, and vice versa. But the relationships between the children and mothers is distant. The men give the mothers birthday pictures, and Michael's mother calls occasionally, but other than that there is no contact.

Michael refers to his adoptive parents as "Daddy Dan" and "Daddy Bob" and does not seem to miss his mother. The children do not lack contact with women. They have a full-time female nanny, Coco, nurses at the doctor's office, and various women in the circle of friends. Other children seem to have no problem with the fact that the children have two dads and no mom around.

Is there any reason why gay men such as Conlin and Elsen should or should not be allowed to adopt children? If so, what is it? Or if not, why not?

3. Timothy R. McVeigh

Senior Chief Petty Officer McVeigh was a sailor stationed in Honolulu. (He is no relation to the convicted Oklahoma City bomber.) The Navy tried to discharge him, saying that he had violated the "Don't Ask, Don't Tell" policy on homosexuals by posting a profile page on America Online listing his first name, his residence in Honolulu, his birthdate, and his marital status as "gay."

In January 1998 (see the story in *The New York Times,* May 9, 1998), U.S. District Judge Stanley Sporkin ruled that the Navy went too far in investigating McVeigh. The judge said that the Navy violated the 1986 Electronic Communications Privacy Act by obtaining confidential information about McVeigh from AOL without a warrant or a court order. In March, Sporkin told the Navy to comply with his order reinstating McVeigh and giving him the right to continue managing nuclear attack submarines. McVeigh had been assigned to clerical work instead of his management work.

The "Don't Ask, Don't Tell" policy was put in place after President Bill Clinton ordered the Pentagon to review its long-time policy of banning homosexuals. But the official policy of the Pentagon still is to prohibit homosexuals and lesbians from serving in the military. The Pentagon stated its rationale for banning gays in the military in a policy statement issued in 1982. The statement claims that men or women who engage in homosexual conduct undermine "discipline, good order, and morale." The military has maintained this policy despite evidence that a large number of gays and lesbians now serve in the military.

Is the "Don't Ask, Don't Tell" policy a good one? Why or why not?

Is it true that gays or lesbians undermine "discipline, good order, and morale"? Explain your answer.

4. Bowers v. Hardwick (1986) (For the full text of the Supreme Court decision, see www.sodomylaws.org/ bowers/bowers_v_hardwick.htm.)

In August 1982, Michael Hardwick was drinking beer in a bar when police, in an attempt to harass gays, arrested him for displaying an open beer bottle. Hardwick paid the fine. But apparently the police did not know this, or ignored it, and a police officer went to Hardwick's house, supposedly to collect the fine. One of Hardwick's friends let the officer in, and the officer observed Hardwick in the bedroom engaged in sex with another man. The officer arrested Hardwick (but not the other male) and charged him with violating the sodomy law.

In 1986 the Georgia law stated that "a person commits the offense of sodomy when he performs or submits to any sexual act involving the sex organ of one person and the mouth or anus of another." The punishment for this crime was "imprisonment for not less than one nor more than 20 years."

Hardwick brought suit in federal district court challenging the constitutionality of the Georgia statute. He argued that the sodomy law was unconstitutional because it violated the Fourteenth Amendment. A federal appeals court agreed that the Fourteenth Amendment protected privacy, including sexual behavior. The court did not require that the Georgia statute be overturned, however; it just required Georgia to demonstrate that the law served a compelling state interest. It was the decision that Georgia be required to defend the sodomy law that was reviewed by the Supreme Court.

In a 5-to-4 decision, the Supreme Court ruled for Georgia, represented by Attorney General Michael Bowers. The majority opinion was written by associate justice Byron R. White. White argued that the Constitution does not confer a fundamental right to engage in sodomy. White noted that prior cases, such as *Roe,* had recognized a right of privacy in cases of abortion, contraception, procreation, and marriage, but he denied that this right of privacy extended to consensual acts of sodomy, even if such acts occur in the privacy of the home. Furthermore, White maintained that the majority sentiments about the immorality of sodomy are an adequate basis for the law.

In his opinion White speaks only of homosexual sodomy, but the Georgia law made no distinction between homosexual and heterosexual sodomy; it applied to heterosexual sodomy as well. Should heterosexual sodomy be illegal? Is it immoral? If not, then why not say the same about homosexual sodomy?

Is it a good idea to have restrictive laws regulating the private sexual behavior of consenting adults? If so, how should they be enforced?

Is majority opinion an adequate basis for laws? What would be the consequences if our laws were based entirely on public sentiments?

5. Sexual Abstinence

Sexual abstinence is usually defined as voluntarily refraining from sexual intercourse before marriage. But what counts as sexual intercourse? Is oral sex included or not? Surveys of sexual behavior indicate an increase in the popularity of oral sex among teenagers, which is not perceived as being real sexual intercourse. That was the view taken by President Bill Clinton in the Monica Lewinsky affair. Groups promoting sexual abstinence such as True Love Waits, www.truelovewaits.com, however, define sexual abstinence as "sexual purity," which means saying no to genital intercourse, oral sex, or even sexual touching. Also, it means not looking at pornography or dwelling on thoughts of sex.

Some groups promote sexual abstinence as a spiritual practice commanded by God. Others consider it necessary for a good marriage. The argument given by conservative groups such as The Heritage Foundation, www.heritage.org, is that sexual abstinence has good effects; it reduces the incidence of unwanted pregnancy, abortion, sexually transmitted disease, depression, suicide, and poverty. Consider the following facts and figures:

Twenty percent of adolescent girls have had sexual intercourse before age 15, and of these 1 in 7 becomes pregnant. Nearly 30 percent of girls who started sexual activity at ages 13 or 14 have had an abortion. By contrast, about 12 percent of girls who began sexual activity in their early 20s have had an abortion. Nearly 40 percent of girls who commence sexual activity at ages 13 or 14 will give birth outside of wedlock. By contrast, 9 percent of women who begin sexual activity at ages 21 or 22 will give birth outside of marriage.

Because single mothers are more likely to be poor, early sexual activity is linked to higher levels of child and maternal poverty.

Every day, 8,000 teenagers in the United States become infected with a sexually transmitted disease. In 2003, nearly 3 million teenagers became infected. Overall, about one fourth of the nation's sexually active teenagers have been infected.

Sexually active girls are more than three times more likely to be depressed than are girls who are not sexually active. Boys who are sexually active are more than twice as likely to be depressed as are those who are not sexually active. Sexually active girls are nearly three times more likely to attempt suicide than are girls who are not sexually active. Sexually active teenage boys are eight times more likely to attempt suicide than are boys who are not sexually active.

How would you define sexual abstinence? Does it include not masturbating? Does it mean not touching, and not thinking about sex?

The facts seem to support the view that teenagers, that is, those under age 21, should practice sexual abstinence. Do you agree? Why or why not? What about adults, those over age 21? Should they abstain from sex until they are married? How about old folks, people over age 50? If they are divorced or never married should they abstain from sex?

Roman Catholicism requires priests and nuns to practice celibacy or sexual abstinence. Is this a good idea?

Some married Catholics practice celibacy so that they will not have children. (The Church forbids the use of contraceptives, and the so-called rhythm method is unreliable.) Is married celibacy compatible with the purpose of marriage? What do you think?

Is "safe sex" a viable alternative to sexual abstinence? Why or why not?

6. Polygamy. (For more information see www.polygamy.com)

Polygamy is usually defined as the practice of a man having more than one wife at the same time, where we are talking about consenting adults and not children or those who do not agree to such an arrangement. Also, we are not concerned with serial polygamy, that is, when a man marries one woman, divorces her, then marries another woman, and so on, so that he has more than one wife over time.

Consensual polygamy is not quite the same as bigamy. Legally bigamy is defined as legally marrying one person when already legally married to another, usually keeping the second marriage a secret. All 50 states have statutues making bigamy a crime. In most states, bigamy is a felony.

It is estimated that there are over 100,000 consensual polygamists in the United States. They avoid presecution for bigamy by not registering their plural marriages with the state. Then they are guilty of cohabitation or fornication or adultery, but even though these are crimes in many states, they are not usually prosecuted.

Defenders of polygamy appeal to religious texts that condone it or command it. The Old Testament has several such passages. Exodus 21:10 says, "If he take him another wife; her food, her raiment, and her duty of marriage, shall he not diminish." Deuteronomy 25:7–10 says that if a man dies without children, then his brother is obliged to marry the widow. Deuteronomy 21:15–17 addresses the inheritance rights of children of two different wives. David had at least seven wives, apart from Bathsheba. King Solomon had many wives and concubines as well. Jacob limited himself to four wives.

Islam specifically recommends polygamy, but limits the number of wives to four. The Koran 4:3 says, "Marry women of your choice, two or three or four; but if you fear that you shall not be able to deal justly with them, then only one or one that your right hands possess. That will be more suitable, to prevent you from doing injustice." The Prophet Muhammad argued that if wars cause the number of women to greatly exceed the number of men, then men should marry the extra women to care for them.

In the United States, the majority of those practicing polygamy are Mormon Fundamentalists who believe they are following God's law as set forth in Section 132 of The Doctrine and Covenants. The revered prophet Joseph Smith describes plural marriage as part of "the most holy and important doctrine ever revealed to man on earth" and he taught that a man needs at least three wives to attain the fullness of exaltation in the afterlife. (Quoted by Jon Krakauer in *Under The Banner of Heaven* (Doubleday, 2003), p. 6) According to Krakauer, there are more than thirty thousand Mormon Fundamentalist polygamists living in Canada, Mexico, and throughout the American West.

Polygamy seems to be a practice that is at the heart of Islam and Mormon Fundamentalism. Does religious tolerance require us to allow polygamy when it is practiced for religious reasons? Why or why not?

Should polygamy be illegal? If so, how would the law be enforced?

Is polygamy immoral? If you think so, then explain your reasons for believing this.

Polyandry—a woman having more than one husband at the same time—is condemned in the Koran, the Bible, and in Mormon Fundamendalism. But why? Isn't this just a bias against women? If polygamy is allowable, then why not allow polyandry? For that matter, why not allow polyamory, which is any combination of more than one partner?

Suggested Readings

1. The Electronic Journal of Human Sexuality (http://www.ejhs.org) has scholarly book reviews and articles on human sexuality. The Kinsey Institute, http://www.indiana.edu/^Kinsey, does research on human sexuality and reproduction. For information on same-sex marriage and links to other websites see Gayscape, www.jwpunishing.com/gayscape. The Family Research Council, www.frc.org, and Focus on the Family, www.family.org, promote a traditional view of marriage and oppose same-sex marriage.
2. Alan Goldman, "Plain Sex," Philosophy & Public Affairs 6 (Spring 1977), pp. 267–287, attacks the means-end analysis of sex that requires sex to a means to some end such as reproduction. Plain sex is sex that fulfills sexual desire without he used to satisfy some other goal and as such it is not intrinsically immoral.
3. Alfred C. Kinsey et al., *Sexual Behavior in the Human Male* (Philadelphia: W. B. Saunders, 1948). This is the classic study that remains authoritative despite attacks on Kinsey's own sexual behavior and his methods.
4. Alfred C. Kinsey et al., *Sexual Behavior in the Human Female* (Philadelphia: W. B. Saunders, 1953).
5. June M. Reinisch, *The Kinsey Institute New Report on Sex* (New York: St. Martin's Press, 1991), claims to give accurate answers to the questions people ask most about sex, based on a new national survey.
6. James Howard Jones and Alfred C. Kinsey, *A Public/Private Life* (New York: Norton, 1997), tells all about Kinsey, including his masochism, voyeurism, bisexuality, and active sex life. Jones argues that Kinsey's findings were not as objective as claimed but were biased in various ways.
7. Bruce M. King, *Human Sexuality Today,* 2nd ed. (Englewood Cliffs, NJ: Prentice-Hall, 1996), is a recent textbook that covers all aspects of human sexuality from anatomy to paraphilias.
8. Robert T. Michael et al., *Sex in America: A Definitive Survey* (New York: Warner, 1995) is a detailed report of a national survey of adult sexual behavior. An expanded version for professionals is *The Social Organization of Sexuality* (Chicago: University of Chicago Press, 1994).

9. Paul Cameron, "A Case against Homosexuality," *Human Life Review* 4 (Summer 1978): 17–49, contends that homosexuality should be discriminated against as an undesirable lifestyle because it produces undesirable personality traits, a self-centered orientation, irresponsibility, and a tendency toward suicide and homicide.

10. Richard D. Mohr, *The Little Book of Gay Rights* (Boston: Beacon Press, 1994), attacks those, including Christians, who want to discriminate against homosexuals, and defends gay rights.

11. Robert Baird and Katherine Baird, eds., *Homosexuality: Debating the Issues* (Amherst, NY: Prometheus Books, 1995), is an anthology dealing with the morality of homosexuality.

12. William Dudley, ed., *Homosexuality–Opposing Viewpoints* (San Deigo: Greenhaven Press, 1993), is an anthology presenting arguments for and against allowing homosexuality.

13. Peter A. Bertocci, *Sex, Love, and the Person* (Ashland, OH: Sheed & Ward, 1967), defends conventional morality.

14. Vincent C. Punzo, *Reflective Naturalism* (New York: Macmillan, 1969), argues against premarital sex. In his view, marriage is constituted by mutual and total commitment; absent commitment, sexual unions are morally deficient.

15. Andrea Dworkin, *Intercourse* (New York: The Free Press, 1987), presents the radical feminist view that heterosexual intercourse is a patriarchal institution that degrades and enslaves women.

16. Burton Leiser, *Liberty, Justice and Morals,* 2nd ed. (New York: Macmillan, 1979). In chapter 2, Leiser attacks arguments that homosexuality is immoral.

17. Michael Ruse, *Homosexuality: A Philosophical Inquiry* (Oxford: Basil Blackwell, 1990), gives a careful and detailed discussion of various issues related to homosexuality. He argues that it is not unnatural, not immoral, and not a sexual perversion.

18. Michael Levin, "Why Homosexuality Is Abnormal," *The Monist* 67, 2 (1984): 260–76, argues that homosexuality is inherently abnormal and immoral because it is a misuse of body parts.

19. Richard Taylor, *Having Love Affairs* (Amherst, NY: Prometheus Books, 1982), claims that people have a right to love affairs even if they are married. He also thinks there is nothing wrong with people living together without being legally married.

20. Jeffner Allen, ed., *Lesbian Philosophies* (Buffalo: State University of New York Press, 1990). This is a collection of articles on lesbianism by lesbians. It includes a candid account of lesbian sex by Marilyn Frye; one of the important features is the lack of phallocentricity (to use her term).

21. John Arthur, *The Unfinished Constitution* (Belmont, CA: Wadsworth, 1989), reviews and attacks the Supreme Court decision in *Bowers v. Hardwick* (1986).

22. Onora O'Neill, "Between Consenting Adults," *Philosophy and Public Affairs* 14, 3 (Summer 1985): 252–77, examines sexual relations from a Kantian perspective that focuses on respect for persons.

23. Morris B. Kaplan, "Intimacy and Equality: The Question of Lesbian and Gay Marriage," *The Philosophical Forum* 25 (Summer 1994): 333–60, argues that gays and lesbians should be granted the same rights as heterosexuals to marry or to form domestic partnerships.

24. Robin West, "The Harms of Consensual Sex," *APA Newsletter* 94 (Spring 1995): 52–55 holds that some noncoercive, noncriminal heterosexual transactions are harmful to women.

Chapter 6

Liberty and Drugs

Introduction

In a speech given in November 2003, President George W. Bush said, "I believe every person has the ability and the right to be free." He said, "Freedom is worth fighting for, dying for, and standing for." Clearly, President Bush considers freedom or liberty to be extremely important, more important that life itself. But what does it mean to be free? What restrictions on liberty are justified? What is included or excluded in the right to be free? These general questions are addressed in the first three readings. The other readings take up a more specific question about liberty, namely, should people be free to take any drug they choose?

The focus in the last three readings is on so-called recreational drugs such as alcohol, nicotine, marijuana, and cocaine. Alcohol is the most popular recreational drug in the United States. It is estimated that about 180 million people have consumed alcohol. According to the National Institute on Alcohol Abuse and Alcoholism (www.niaaa.gov), in 2001 alcohol was implicated in 37,795 traffic crashes and 42,116 fatalities. Thousands more died of liver cirrhosis.

The second leading drug is tobacco or, more accurately, the nicotine contained in the tobacco. As the cigarette company memo puts it, cigarettes are a "nicotine delivery system." About 160 million Americans have smoked. According to the National Centers for Chronic Disease Prevention and Health Promotion (www.cdc.gov), smoking tobacco is the leading cause of death in the United States, causing one of every five deaths, or more than 440,000 deaths each year. This estimate includes 35,000 deaths from secondhand smoke exposure. Cigarette smoking kills an estimated 264,000 men and 178,000 women in the United States each year. More deaths are caused each year by tobacco use than by all deaths from HIV, illegal drug use, alcohol use, motor vehicle injuries, suicides, and murders combined. Smoking dramatically increases the risk for mouth, throat, and lung cancer. If you smoke, you are twice as likely to die from a heart attack and twice as likely to get a stomach ulcer. According to the 2004 report by Surgeon General Richard H. Carmona, smoking also causes cancers of the cervix, kidney, pancreas, and stomach, as well as abdominal aortic aneurysms, acute leukemia, cataracts, and pneumonia. In short, Dr. Carmona reports that "smoking causes disease in nearly every organ of the body at every stage of life."

According to government figures, marijuana is the third most popular recreational drug in the United States. Despite 64 years of criminal prohibition, 75 million U.S. citizens have smoked marijuana. Prolonged use of marijuana has been associated with apathy and loss of motivation. In large doses it may cause panicky states or illusions. In rare cases, large doses may cause psychosis or loss of contact with reality. Marijuana also has medical uses. It has been used to treat glaucoma, multiple sclerosis, and nausea and pain in cancer patients. (For more about marijuana see the fourth Problem Case.)

The next most popular recreational drug in the United States is cocaine, with an estimated 25 million people having used it. By comparison, only 3 million people have used heroin. There is great risk associated with cocaine use, whether it is ingested by snorting, injecting, or smoking. Excessive doses may lead to seizures and death from respiratory failure, stroke, cerebral hemorrhage, or heart failure. Chronic heroin use can lead to collapsed veins, liver disease, pneumonia, and risk for contacting HIV, hepatitis B and C, and other viruses.

Although it does not produce nearly as much death and disease as alcohol and nicotine and has medical uses, marijuana is an illegal drug, first federally prohibited in 1937. The criminalization of marijuana has been expensive. It is estimated that the war on marijuana costs taxpayers more than $9 billion a year. (By comparison, treating the diseases caused by smoking costs about $75 billion a year, according to government figures.) There have been more than 12 million marijuana arrests in the United States since 1970, including a record 704,812 arrests in 1999. About 88 percent of all marijuana arrests are for possession rather than manufacture or distribution. Currently, over 60,000 marijuana offenders are in prison.

The Readings

John Stuart Mill presents what is often called the harm principle. This is the principle that the only justification for interfering with liberty is self-protection or harm to others. Self-harm does not justify limiting liberty. As Mill explains it, this principle applies to adults, not children, and it includes liberty of thought and feeling, "absolute freedom of opinion and sentiment on all subjects," liberty of tastes and pursuits, and the freedom to unite with others for any purpose. Mill gives a utilitarian defense of this principle. A society in which these liberties are respected is better than one in which they are restricted. As he puts it, "Mankind are greater gainers by suffering each other to live as seems good to themselves, than by compelling each to live as seems good to the rest."

Gerald Dworkin responds to Mill. As he interprets it, Mill's harm principle involves at least two principles. The first says that self-protection or prevention of harm to others is sometimes a sufficient warrant to limit a person's freedom. He thinks that almost everyone will accept this principle. His focus is on a second principle he finds in Mill, the negative principle that the individual's own good is never a sufficient reason for restricting the individual's freedom. Against this, Dworkin defends paternalism, which is the view that interference with a person's freedom can be justified in some cases where this is for the person's good. An obvious example of this is when parents restrict their children's freedom. But when is a society justified in interfering with an adult's freedom? One case is when the person wants his or her freedom restricted. A classical example of this is when Odysseus commands his men to tie him to the mast so that the Sirens will not enchant him. A modern example is when people agree to pay higher taxes. Another case is when people are irrational. If not wearing a seat belt while driving is irrational, and Dworkin is inclined to think it is, then a good case can be made for requiring people to wear seat belts. Another set of cases involves decisions made under extreme psychological or sociological pressure. He thinks, for example, that dueling should be illegal, and that a waiting period should be enforced on people who want to commit suicide. Finally there are cases where people don't seem to understand the danger of some activity. For example, people who want to smoke should be required to learn about the dangers of smoking.

John Hospers explains and defends a right to liberty. As he puts it, "Each human being has the right to live his life as he chooses, compatibly with the equal right of all other beings to live their lives as they choose." In other words, this right allows you act as you choose unless your action interferes with the equal liberty of others. Notice that Hospers's account of this right is very similar to Rawls's first principle of justice, the principle that each person is to have an equal right to the most extensive basic liberty compatible with a similar liberty for others. Hospers does recognize other rights, such as a right to life and a right to property, but these rights do not impose any obligation to act positively. The right to life does not require you to give people food, clothing, housing, or medical care. It only protects human beings from the use of force by others, for example, by law forbidding killing and all kinds of physical violence. Hospers claims that the right to property is the most misunderstood and underappreciated of human rights. The property in question includes anything you own including your money. This means that when the government takes your money away by taxing you for something other than defense of your rights, it is violating your rights.

Szasz applies Mill's principle to drugs. He quotes the principle at the end of his article, including the passage where Mill says "over himself, over his own body and mind, the individual is sovereign." As Szasz interprets it, Mill's principle gives each individual the right to take a drug, any drug, just because he or she wants to take it, and not to cure an illness. Szasz admits that taking drugs may harm the individual taking them, but on Mill's harm principle self-harm does not justify limiting liberty. Szasz does put limits on the right to use drugs. He does not believe that children have this right, and holds that acts that harm others, such as drug-intoxicated driving, should be punished strictly and severely.

Wilson also applies Mill's harm principle to drugs, but he comes to a different conclusion than Szasz. He claims that the use of highly addictive and dangerous drugs such as heroin and cocaine harms others and this justifies making them illegal. Specifically, he claims that drug users harm their children by neglecting them, harm their spouses by abusing them, and harm their employers by being careless and lazy. Furthermore, Wilson argues that the use of drugs such as cocaine is immoral, and this is another reason why these drugs should be illegal.

Shapiro replies to Wilson. According to Shapiro, Wilson and others who think that legalization of drugs such as cocaine and heroin will produce an explosion of addiction have a false view of addiction. This false view, which Shapiro calls the standard view, says that illegal drugs are inherently addictive because of their pharmacology—their chemical composition and its effects on the brain. But this fails to explain the fact that few users of these drugs become addicts. For example, Shapiro cites the statistic that fewer than 5 percent of powder cocaine users use it daily. Furthermore, Shapiro argues that cravings, tolerance, and withdrawal symptoms cannot explain addiction. The alternative view proposed by Shapiro is that addiction is the result of the individual's mindset, personality, values, and expectations as well as the social or cultural setting. The fact that only half of the people who smoke succeed in quitting supports the alternative view. Shapiro concludes that his argument undercuts the worry that legalizing cocaine and heroin will produce an explosion of addiction.

Philosophical Issues

Is Mill's harm principle acceptable? This is perhaps the most important philosophical issue raised in the readings. Dworkin says that only extreme pacifists or anarchists would deny that self-protection or harm to others justifies the exercise of compulsion by society or individuals. But he raises doubts about the negative thesis that self-harm never justifies limiting a person's freedom. He argues that Mill's utilitarian argument does not show that paternalistic restrictions on an adult's freedom are absolutely prohibited, but only that there is a presumption against them. He seems to accept Mill's view that freedom of thought and choice have a value independent of consequences, but he argues that there are still several types of cases where paternal interferences with freedom are justified.

Hospers does not agree. He believes that the government or individuals should never interfere with a person's right to liberty, even if this produces harm to the individual. He specifically rejects all laws protecting individuals from themselves, such as laws against fornication and other sexual behavior, alcohol, and drugs.

Szasz agrees with Hospers. He regards human freedom as a fundamental right, and this includes the right to injure yourself or even kill yourself. On his view, the right of freedom includes the right to self-medicate and it does not matter that the drugs being used are dangerous and addictive.

In contrast to Szasz, Wilson seems to accept paternalism, since he argues that drugs such as heroin and cocaine should be illegal just because they are bad for you. This is a good reason for making them illegal independent from any harm caused to others. Wilson also says that drug treatment should be legally compulsory for drug-dependent people because they have short time horizons and a weak capacity for commitment. In other words, drug-dependent people are like children who cannot take care of themselves.

The other important question raised in the readings is whether drugs such as heroin, cocaine, and marijuana should be illegal. Consistent with his libertarian position, Hospers holds that there should be no laws against drugs as long as the taking of the drugs poses no threat to anyone else. He accepts the prohibition of the sale of drugs to minors. He claims that drug addiction is a psychological problem that has no solution, but this is not a good reason for making drugs illegal. Lots of things are addictive and not illegal. In fact, Hospers argues that it would be better to make drugs such as heroin legal. He points out that this would stop the enormous traffic in illegal sales and reduce crime. He claims that drug addicts commit 75 percent of the burglaries in New York City, and these crimes would stop if drugs were legalized.

Although Dworkin does not accept Hospers's libertarianism, he does seem to agree with Hospers about the drug laws. Near the end of the reading, he says that the history of drug legislation in the United States is a good example of the "ignorance, ill-will, and stupidity" of lawmakers.

Wilson does not agree. He thinks that drugs such as heroin should be illegal just because they harm the drug users. He supports his position by arguing that these drugs also produce harm to others, namely the children, spouses, and employers of the drug addicts. He adds a moral argument that using drugs such as heroin or cocaine is immoral because it debases one's life.

Szasz rejects the argument that drugs such as marijuana, heroin, methadone, or morphine should be illegal because they are dangerous and addictive. Alcohol, tobacco, and coffee are all addictive but not illegal. Dynamite and guns are much more dangerous than drugs, and they are not illegal. Many more people die from guns and cigarettes than from using marijuana. As for the argument that drugs should be illegal because they are harmful, Szasz points out that nicotine is more harmful to health than marijuana, and yet nicotine is legal. The only reason for keeping nicotine legal and marijuana illegal is precedent, not evidence.

Shapiro raises questions about the effects of legalizing drugs such as cocaine and heroin. Unlike Wilson, he does not think that legalizing these drugs will produce a dramatic increase in drug addiction. If making these drugs legal disrupts people's lives, this would tend to reduce the use of these drugs.

On Liberty

JOHN STUART MILL

For biographical information on Mill, see his reading in Chapter 1.

Mill begins with his principle of liberty, that the only justification for interfering with liberty is to prevent harm to others. Harming yourself never justifies restricting your liberty. Mill distinguishes between liberty of consciousness, liberty of tastes and pursuits, and liberty in meeting others. He argues on utilitarian grounds that freedom of expression on any opinion should be allowed.

THE OBJECT OF THIS ESSAY is to assert one very simple principle, as entitled to govern absolutely the dealings of society with the individual in the way of compulsion and control, whether the means used be physical force in the form of legal penalties, or the moral coercion of public opinion. That principle is, that the sole end for which mankind are warranted, individually or collectively, in interfering with the liberty of action of any of their number, is self-protection. That the only purpose for which power can be rightfully exercised over any member of a civilized community, against his will, is to prevent harm to others. His own good, either physical or moral, is not a sufficient warrant. He cannot rightfully be compelled to do or forbear because it will be better for him to do so, because it will make him happier, because, in the opinions of others, to do so would be wise, or even right.

Source: John Stuart Mill,"On Liberty" from *Utilitarianism* (London, 1859).

These are good reasons for remonstrating with him, or reasoning with him, or persuading him, or entreating him, but not for compelling him, or visiting him with any evil in case he do otherwise. To justify that, the conduct from which it is desired to deter him, must be calculated to produce evil to some one else. The only part of the conduct of any one, for which he is amenable to society, is that which concerns others. In the part which merely concerns himself, his independence is, of right, absolute. Over himself, over his own body and mind, the individual is sovereign.

It is, perhaps, hardly necessary to say that this doctrine is meant to apply only to human beings in the maturity of their faculties. We are not speaking of children, or of young persons below the age which the law may fix as that of manhood or womanhood. Those who are still in a state to require being taken care of by others, must be protected against their own actions as well as against external injury. . . .

But there is a sphere of action in which society, as distinguished from the individual, has, if any, only an indirect interest; comprehending all that portion of a person's life and conduct which affects only himself, or if it also affects others, only with their free, voluntary, and undeceived consent and participation. When I say only himself, I mean directly, and in the first instance: for whatever affects himself, may affect others through himself; and the objection which may be grounded on this contingency will receive consideration in the sequel. This, then, is the appropriate region of human liberty. It comprises, first, the inward domain of consciousness; demanding liberty of conscience, in the most comprehensive sense; liberty of thought and feeling; absolute freedom of opinion and sentiment on all subjects, practical or speculative, scientific, moral or theological. The liberty of expressing and publishing opinions may seem to fall under a different principle, since it belongs to that part of the conduct of an individual which concerns other people; but, being almost of as much importance as the liberty of thought itself, and resting in great part on the same reasons, is practically inseparable from it. Secondly, the principle requires liberty of tastes and pursuits; of framing the plan of our life to suit our own character; of doing as we like, subject to such consequences as may follow: without impediment from our fellow creatures, so long as what we do does not harm them, even though they should think our conduct foolish, perverse, or wrong. Thirdly, from this liberty of each individual, follows the liberty, within the same limits, of combination among individuals; freedom to unite, for any purpose not involving harm to others: the persons combining being supposed to be of full age, and not forced or deceived.

No society in which these liberties are not, on the whole, respected, is free, whatever may be its form of government; and none is completely free in which they do not exist absolute and unqualified. The only freedom which deserves the name, is that of pursuing our own good in our own way, so long as we do not attempt to deprive others of theirs, or impede their efforts to obtain it. Each is the proper guardian of his own health, whether bodily, or mental and spiritual. Mankind are greater gainers by suffering each other to live as seems good to themselves, than by compelling each to live as seems good to the rest. . . .

ON THE LIBERTY OF THOUGHT AND DISCUSSION

. . . If all mankind minus one, were of one opinion, and only one person were of the contrary opinion, mankind would be no more justified in silencing that one person, than he, if he had the power, would be justified in silencing mankind. Were an opinion a personal possession of no value except to the owner; if to be obstructed in the enjoyment of it were simply a private injury, it would make some difference whether the injury was inflicted only on a few persons or on many. But the peculiar evil of silencing the expression of an opinion is, that it is robbing the human race; posterity as well as the existing generation; those who dissent from the opinion, still more than those who hold it. If the opinion is right, they are deprived of the opportunity of exchanging error for truth: if wrong, they lose, what is almost as great a benefit, the clearer perception and livelier impression of truth, produced by its collision with error.

It is necessary to consider separately these two hypotheses, each of which has a distinct branch of the argument corresponding to it. We can never be sure that the opinion we are endeavouring to stifle is a false opinion; and if we were sure, stifling it would be an evil still.

First: the opinion which it is attempted to suppress by authority may possibly be true. Those who desire to suppress it, of course deny its truth; but they are not infallible. They have no authority to decide the question for all mankind, and exclude every other person from the means of judging. To refuse a hearing to an opinion, because they are sure that it is false, is to assume that *their* certainty is the same thing as *absolute* certainty. All silencing of discussion is an assumption of infallibility. Its condemnation may be allowed to rest on this common argument, not the worse for being common.

Unfortunately for the good sense of mankind, the fact of their fallibility is far from carrying the weight in their practical judgement, which is always allowed to it in theory; for while every one well knows himself to be fallible, few think it necessary to take any precautions against their own fallibility, or admit the supposition that any opinion, of which they feel very certain, may be one of the examples of the error to which they acknowledge themselves to be liable. . . .

Let us now pass to the second division of the argument, and dismissing the supposition that any of the received opinions may be false, let us assume them to be true, and examine into the worth of the manner in which they are likely to be held, when their truth is not freely and openly canvassed. However unwillingly a person who has a strong opinion may admit the possibility that his opinion may be false, he ought to be moved by the consideration that however true it may be, if it is not fully, frequently, and

fearlessly discussed, it will be held as a dead dogma, not a living truth.

There is a class of persons (happily not quite so numerous as formerly) who think it enough if a person assents undoubtingly to what they think true, though he has no knowledge whatever of the grounds of the opinion, and could not make a tenable defence of it against the most superficial objections. Such persons, if they can once get their creed taught from authority, naturally think that no good, and some harm, comes of it being allowed to be questioned. Where their influence prevails, they make it nearly impossible for the received opinion to be rejected wisely and considerately, though it may still be rejected rashly and ignorantly; for to shut out discussion entirely is seldom possible, and when it once gets in, beliefs not grounded on conviction are apt to give way before the slightest semblance of an argument. Waiving, however, this possibility—assuming that the true opinion abides in the mind, but abides as a prejudice, a belief independent of, and proof against, argument—this is not the way in which truth ought to be held by a rational being. This is not knowing the truth. Truth, thus held, is but one superstition the more, accidentally clinging to the words which enunciate a truth.

If the intellect and judgement of mankind ought to be cultivated, a thing which Protestants at least do not deny, on what can these faculties be more appropriately exercised by any one, than on the things which concern him so much that it is considered necessary for him to hold opinions on them? If the cultivation of the understanding consists in one thing more than in another, it is surely in learning the grounds of one's own opinions. Whatever people believe, on subjects on which it is of the first importance to believe rightly, they ought to be able to defend against at least the common objections. But, some one may say, "Let them be *taught* the grounds of their opinions. It does not follow that opinions must be merely parroted because they are never heard controverted. Persons who learn geometry do not simply commit the theorems to memory, but understand and learn likewise the demonstrations; and it would be absurd to say that they remain ignorant of the grounds of geometrical truths, because they never hear any one deny, and attempt to disprove them." Undoubtedly: and such teaching suffices on a subject like mathematics, where there is nothing at all to be said on the wrong side of the question. The peculiarity of the evidence of mathematical truths is, that all the argument is on one side. There are no objections, and no answers to objections. But on every subject on which difference of opinion is possible, the truth depends on a balance to be struck between two sets of conflicting reasons. . . . He who knows only his own side of the case, knows little of that. His reasons may be good, and no one may have been able to refute them. But if he is equally unable to refute the reasons on the opposite side; if he does not so much as know what they are, he has no ground for preferring either opinion. The rational position for him would be suspension of judgement, and unless he contents himself with that, he is either led by authority, or adopts, like the generality of the world, the side to which he feels most inclination. Nor is it enough that he should hear the arguments of adversaries from his own teachers, presented as they state them, and accompanied by what they offer as refutations. That is not the way to do justice to the arguments, or bring them into real contact with his own mind. He must be able to hear them from persons who actually believe them; who defend them in earnest, and do their very utmost for them. He must know them in their most plausible and persuasive form; he must feel the whole force of the difficulty which the true view of the subject has to encounter and dispose of; else he will never really possess himself of the portion of truth which meets and removes that difficulty. . . .

. . . The fact, however, is, that not only the grounds of the opinion are forgotten in the absence of discussion, but too often the meaning of the opinion itself. The words which convey it, cease to suggest ideas, or suggest only a small portion of those they were originally employed to communicate. Instead of a vivid conception and a living belief, there remain only a few phrases retained by rote; or, if any part, the shell and husk only of the meaning is retained, the finer essence being lost. The great chapter in human history which this fact occupies and fills, cannot be too earnestly studied and meditated on.

It is illustrated in the experience of almost all ethical doctrines and religious creeds. They are all full of meaning and vitality to those who originate them, and to the direct disciples of the originators. Their meaning continues to be felt in undiminished strength, and is perhaps brought out into even fuller consciousness, so long as the struggle lasts to give the doctrine or creed an ascendancy over other creeds. At last it either prevails, and becomes the general opinion, or its progress stops; it keeps possession of the ground it has gained, but ceases to spread further. When either of these results has become apparent, controversy on the subject flags, and gradually dies away. . . .

It still remains to speak of one of the principal causes which make diversity of opinion advantageous, and will continue to do so until mankind shall have entered a stage of intellectual advancement which at present seems at an incalculable distance. We have hitherto considered only two possibilities: that the received opinion may be false, and some other opinion, consequently, true; or that, the received opinion being true, a conflict with the opposite error is essential to a clear apprehension and deep feeling of its truth. But there is a commoner case than either of these; when the conflicting doctrines, instead of being one true and the other false, share the truth between them; and the nonconforming opinion is needed to supply the remainder of the truth, of which the received doctrine embodies only a part. Popular opinions, on subjects not palpable to sense, are often true, but seldom or never the whole truth. They are a part of the truth; sometimes a greater, sometimes a smaller part, but exaggerated, distorted, and disjoined from the truths by which they ought to be accompanied and limited. Heretical opinions, on the other hand, are generally some of these suppressed and neglected truths, bursting the bonds which kept them down, and either seeking reconciliation with the truth contained in the common opinion, or fronting it as enemies, and setting themselves up, with similar exclusiveness, as the whole truth. The latter case is hitherto the most frequent, as, in the human mind, one-sidedness has always been the rule, and many-sidedness the exception. Hence, even in revolutions of opinion, one part of the truth usually sets while another rises. Even progress, which ought to superadd, for the most part only substitutes, one partial and incomplete truth for another; improvement consisting chiefly in this, that the new fragment of truth is more wanted, more adapted to the needs of the time, than that which it displaces. Such being the partial character of prevailing opinions, even when resting on a true foundation, every opinion which embodies somewhat of the portion of truth which the common opinion omits, ought to be considered precious, with whatever amount of error and confusion that truth may be blended. No sober judge of human affairs will feel bound to be indignant because those who force on our notice truths which we should otherwise have overlooked, overlook some of those which we see. Rather, he will think that so long as popular truth is one-sided, it is more desirable than otherwise that unpopular truth should have one-sided asserters too; such being usually the most energetic, and the most likely to compel reluctant attention to the fragment of wisdom which they proclaim as if it were the whole. . . .

We have now recognized the necessity to the mental well-being of mankind (on which all their other well-being depends) of freedom of opinion, and freedom of the expression of opinion, on four distinct grounds; which we will now briefly recapitulate.

First, if any opinion is compelled to silence, that opinion may, for aught we can certainly know, be true. To deny this is to assume our own infallibility.

Secondly, though the silenced opinion be an error, it may, and very commonly does, contain a portion of truth; and since the general or prevailing opinion on any subject is rarely or never the whole truth, it is only by the collision of adverse opinions that the remainder of the truth has any chance of being supplied.

Thirdly, even if the received opinion be not only true, but the whole truth; unless it is suffered to be, and actually is, vigorously and earnestly contested, it will, by most of those who receive it, be held in the manner of a prejudice, with little comprehension or feeling of its rational grounds. And not only this, but, fourthly, the meaning of the doctrine itself will be in danger of being lost, or enfeebled, and deprived of its vital effect on the character and conduct: the dogma becoming a mere formal profession, inefficacious for good, but cumbering the ground, and preventing the growth of any real and heartfelt conviction, from reason or personal experience. . . .

Review Questions

1. State and explain Mill's principle of liberty.
2. What are the three domains of liberty, according to Mill?
3. Why does Mill think that silencing the expression of opinion is evil?

Discussion Questions

1. Are there any opinions that should be censored? What are they?
2. Is Mill's principle of liberty compatible with his utilitarianism? Why or why not?

What Libertarianism Is

JOHN HOSPERS

John Hospers is emeritus professor of philosophy at the University of Southern California. He has written over 100 articles and several books, including *Libertarianism* (1971), *Understanding the Arts* (1982), and *Human Conduct* 3e (1996).

Hospers begins with several different statements of the libertarian doctrine, which says that every person is the owner of his or her life. This basic thesis entails a right to liberty that is interpreted as a right to act as you choose unless your action infringes on the equal liberty of others to act as they choose. Hospers also recognizes a right to property and a right to life. These rights are interpreted negatively; that is, they imply only that no one, not even the government, has a right to interfere with your life or property. These rights to not imply any positive duty to help others by giving them food, clothing, medical care, or housing. But since these rights are violated by an initial use of force, the government does have one and only one proper role, and that is to prevent this initial use of force and to retaliate against those who initiate the use of force. All other possible roles of the government, including protecting people from self-injurious behavior such as the use of heroin, or requiring people to help each other, are emphatically rejected by Hospers.

THE POLITICAL PHILOSOPHY THAT is called libertarianism (from the Latin *libertas,* liberty) is the doctrine that every person is the owner of his own life, and that no one is the owner of anyone else's life; and that consequently every human being has the right to act in accordance with his own choices, unless those actions infringe on the equal liberty of other human beings to act in accordance with their choices.

There are several other ways of stating the same libertarian thesis:

1. *No one is anyone else's master, and no one is anyone else's slave.* Since I am the one to decide how my life is to be conducted just as you decide about yours, I have no right (even if I had the power) to make you my slave and be your master, nor have you the right to become the master by enslaving me. Slavery is *forced* servitude, and since no one owns the life of anyone else, no one has the right to enslave another. Political theories past and present have traditionally been concerned with who should be the master (usually the king, the dictator, or government bureaucracy) and who should be the slaves, and what the extent of the slavery should be. Libertarianism holds that no one has the right to use force to enslave the life of another, or any portion or aspect of that life.

2. *Other men's lives are not yours to dispose of.* I enjoy seeing operas; but operas are expensive to produce. Opera-lovers often say, "The state (or the city, etc.) should subsidize opera, so that we can all see it.

Source: John Hospers, "What Libertarianism Is," in *Liberty for the 21st Century,* edited by Tibor R. Machan and Douglas B. Rasmussen (Lanham, MD: Rowman & Littlefield, 1995. Reprinted by permission.

Also it would be for people's betterment, cultural benefit, etc." But what they are advocating is nothing more or less than legalized plunder. They can't pay for the productions themselves, and yet they want to see opera, which involves a large number of people and their labor; so what they are saying in effect is, "Get the money through legalized force. Take a little bit more out of every worker's paycheck every week to pay for the operas we want to see." But I have no right to take by force from the workers' pockets to pay for what I want.

Perhaps it would be better if he *did* go to see opera—then I should try to convince him to go voluntarily. But to take the money from him forcibly, because in my opinion it would be good for *him,* is still seizure of his earnings, which is plunder.

Besides, if I have the right to force him to help pay for my pet projects, hasn't he equally the right to force me to help pay for his? Perhaps he in turn wants the government to subsidize rock-and-roll, or his new car, or a house in the country? If I have the right to milk him, why hasn't he the right to milk me? If I can be a moral cannibal, why can't he too?

We should beware of the inventors of utopias. They would remake the world according to their vision—with the lives and fruits of the labor of *other* human beings. Is it someone's utopian vision that others should build pyramids to beautify the landscape? Very well, then other men should provide the labor; and if he is in a position of political power, and he can't get men to do it voluntarily, then he must *compel* them to "cooperate"—i.e. he must enslave them.

A hundred men might gain great pleasure from beating up or killing just one insignificant human being; but other men's lives are not theirs to dispose of. "In order to achieve the worthy goals of the next five-year-plan, we must forcibly collectivize the peasants . . ."; but other men's lives are not theirs to dispose of. Do you want to occupy, rent-free, the mansion that another man has worked for twenty years to buy? But other men's lives are not yours to dispose of. Do you want operas so badly that everyone is forced to work harder to pay for their subsidization through taxes? But other men's lives are not yours to dispose of. Do you want to have free medical care at the expense of other people, whether they wish to provide it or not? But this would require them to work longer for you whether they want to or not, and other men's lives are not yours to dispose of. . . .

3. *No human being should be a nonvoluntary mortgage on the life of another.* I cannot claim your life, your work, or the products of your effort as mine. The fruit of one man's labor should not be fair game for every freeloader who comes along and demands it as his own. The orchard that has been carefully grown, nurtured, and harvested by its owner should not be ripe for the plucking for any bypasser who has a yen for the ripe fruit. The wealth that some men have produced should not be fair game for looting by government, to be used for whatever purposes its representatives determine, no matter what their motives in so doing may be. The theft of your money by a robber is not justified by the fact that he used it to help his injured mother.

It will already be evident that libertarian doctrine is embedded in a view of the rights of man. Each human being has the right to live his life as he chooses, compatibly with the equal right of all other human beings to live their lives as they choose.

All man's rights are implicit in the above statement. Each man has the right to life: any attempt by others to take it away from him, or even to injure him, violates this right, through the use of coercion against him. Each man has the right to liberty: to conduct his life in accordance with the alternatives open to him without coercive action by others, And every man has the right to property: to work to sustain his life (and the lives of whichever others he chooses to sustain, such as his family) and to retain the fruits of his labor.

People often defend the rights of life and liberty but denigrate property rights, and yet the right to property is as basic as the other two: indeed, without property rights no other rights are possible. Depriving you of property is depriving you of the means by which you live. . . .

I have no right to decide how *you* should spend your time or your money. I can make that decision for myself, but not for you, my neighbor. I may deplore your choice of lifestyle, and I may talk with you about it provided you are willing to listen to me. But I have no right to use force to change it. Nor have I the right to decide how you should spend the money you have earned. I may appeal to you to give it to the Red Cross, and you may prefer to go to prize-fights. But that is your decision, and however much I may chafe about it I do not have the right to interfere forcibly with it, for example by robbing you in order to use the money in accordance with *my* choices. (If I have the right to rob you, have you also the right to rob me?)

When I claim a right, I carve out a niche, as it were, in my life, saying in effect, "This activity I must be able to perform without interference from others. For you and everyone else, this is off limits." And so I put up a "no trespassing" sign, which marks off the area of my right. Each individual's right is his "no trespassing" sign in relation to me and others. I may not encroach upon his domain any more than he upon mine, without my consent. Every right entails a duty, true—but the duty is only that of *forbearance*— that is, of *refraining* from violating the other person's right. If you have a right to life, I have no right to take your life; if you have a right to the products of your labor (property), I have no right to take it from you without your consent. The nonviolation of these rights will not guarantee you protection against natural catastrophes such as floods and earthquakes, but it will protect you against the aggressive activities *of*

other men. And rights, after all, have to do with one's relations to other human beings, not with one's relations to physical nature.

Nor were these rights created by government; governments—some governments, obviously not all—*recognize* and *protect* the rights that individuals already have. Governments regularly forbid homicide and theft; and, at a more advanced stage, protect individuals against such things as libel and breach of contract. . . .

The *right to property* is the most misunderstood and unappreciated of human rights, and it is one most constantly violated by governments. "Property" of course does not mean only real estate; it includes anything you can call your own—your clothing, your car, your jewelry, your books and papers.

The right of property is not the right to just *take* it from others, for this would interfere with *their* property rights. It is rather the right to work for it, to obtain non-coercively, the money or services which you can present in voluntary exchange.

The right to property is consistently underplayed by intellectuals today, sometimes even frowned upon, as if we should feel guilty for upholding such a right in view of all the poverty in the world. But the right to property is absolutely basic. It is your hedge against the future. It is your assurance that what you have worked to earn will still be there and be yours, when you wish or need to use it, especially when you are too old to work any longer.

Government has always been the chief enemy of the right to property. The officials of government, wishing to increase their power, and finding an increase of wealth an effective way to bring this about seize some or all of what a person has earned—and since government has a monopoly of physical force within the geographical area of the nation, it has the power (but not the right) to do this. When this happens, of course, every citizen of that country is insecure: he knows that no matter how hard he works the government can swoop down on him at any time and confiscate his earnings and possessions. A person sees his life savings wiped out in a moment when the tax-collectors descend to deprive him of the fruits of his work; or, an industry which has been fifty years in the making and cost millions of dollars and millions of hours of time and planning, is nationalized overnight. Or the government, via inflation, cheapens the currency, so that hard-won dollars aren't worth anything any more. The effect of such actions, of course, is that people lose hope and incentive: if no matter how hard they work the government agents can take it all away, why bother to work at all, for more than today's needs? Depriving people of property is *depriving them of the means by which they live*—the freedom of the individual citizen to do what he wishes with his own life and to plan for the future. Indeed only if property rights are respected is there any point to planning for the future and working to achieve one's goals. *Property rights are what makes long-range planning possible*—the kind of planning which is a distinctively human endeavor, as opposed to the day-by-day activity of the lion who hunts, who depends on the supply of game tomorrow but has no real insurance against starvation in a day or a week. Without the right to property, the right to life itself amounts to little: how can you sustain your life if you cannot plan ahead? and how can you plan ahead if the fruits of your labor can at any moment be confiscated by government? . . .

Indeed, the right to property may well be considered second only to the right to life. Even the freedom of speech is limited by considerations of property. If a person visiting in your home behaves in a way undesired by you, you have every right to evict him; he can scream or agitate elsewhere if he wishes, but not in your home without your consent. Does a person have a right to shout obscenities in a cathedral? No, for the owners of the cathedral (presumably the Church) have not allowed others on their property for that purpose; one may go there to worship or to visit, but not just for any purpose one wishes. Their property right is prior to your or my wish to scream or expectorate or write graffiti on their building. Or, to take the stock

example, does a person have a right to shout "Fire!" falsely in a crowded theater? No, for the theater owner has permitted others to enter and use his property only for a specific purpose, that of seeing a film or watching a stage show. If a person heckles or otherwise disturbs other members of the audience, he can be thrown out. (In fact, he can be removed for any reason the owner chooses, provided his admission money is returned). And if he shouts "Fire!" when there is no fire, he may be endangering other lives by causing a panic or stampede. The right to free speech doesn't give one the right to say anything anywhere; it is circumscribed by property rights.

Again, some people seem to assume that the right to free speech (including written speech) means that they can go to a newspaper publisher and demand that he print in his newspaper some propaganda or policy statement for their political party (or other group). But of course they have no right to the use of his newspaper. Ownership of the newspaper is the product of his labor, and he has a right to put into his newspaper whatever he wants, for whatever reason. If he excludes material which many readers would like to have in, perhaps they can find it in another newspaper or persuade him to print it himself (if there are enough of them, they will usually do just that). Perhaps they can even cause his newspaper to fail. But as long as he owns it, he has the right to put in it what he wishes; what would a property right be if he could not do this? They have no right to place their material in his newspaper without his consent—not for free, nor even for a fee. Perhaps other newspapers will include it, or perhaps they can start their own newspaper (in which case they have a right to put in it what they like). If not, an option open to them would be to mimeograph and distribute some handbills.

In exactly the same way, no one has a right to "free television time" unless the owner of the television station consents to give it; it is his station, he has the property rights over it, and it is for him to decide how to dispose of his time.

He may not decide wisely, but it is his right to decide as he wishes. If he makes enough unwise decisions, and courts enough unpopularity with the viewing public or the sponsors, he may have to go out of business; but as he is free to make his own decisions, so is he free to face their consequences. (If the government owns the television station, then government officials will make the decisions, and there is no guarantee of *their* superior wisdom. The difference is that when "the government" owns the station, you are forced to help pay for its upkeep through your taxes, whether the bureaucrat in charge decides to give you television time or not.)

"But why have *individual* property rights? Why not have lands and houses owned by everybody together?" Yes, this involves no violation of individual rights, as long as everybody consents to this arrangement and no one is forced to join it. The parties to it may enjoy the communal living enough (at least for a time) to overcome certain inevitable problems: that some will work and some not, that some will achieve more in an hour than others can do in a day, and still they will all get the same income. The few who do the most will in the end consider themselves "workhorses" who do the work of two or three or twelve, while the others will be "freeloaders" on the efforts of these few. But as long as they can get out of the arrangement if they no longer like it, no violation of rights is involved. They got in voluntarily, and they can get out voluntarily; no one has used force.

"But why not say that everybody owns everything? That we *all* own everything there is?"

To some this may have a pleasant ring—but let us try to analyze what it means. If everybody owns everything, then everyone has an equal right to go everywhere, do what he pleases, take what he likes, destroy if he wishes, grow crops or burn them, trample them under, and so on. Consider what it would be like in practice. Suppose you have saved money to buy a house for yourself and your family. Now suppose that the principle, "everybody owns everything," becomes adopted. Well then, why shouldn't every itinerant hippie just come in and take over, sleeping in your beds and eating in your kitchen and not bothering to replace the food supply or clean up the mess? After all, it belongs to all of us, doesn't it? So we have just as much right to it as you, the buyer, have. What happens if we *all* want to sleep in the bedroom and there's not room for all of us? Is it the strongest who wins?

What would be the result? Since no one would be responsible for anything, the property would soon be destroyed, the food used up, the facilities nonfunctional. Beginning as a house that *one* family could use, it would end up as a house that *no one* could use. And if the principle continued to be adopted, no one would build houses any more—or anything else. What for? They would only be occupied and used by others, without remuneration.

Suppose two men are cast ashore on an island, and they agree that each will cultivate half of it. The first man is industrious and grows crops and builds a shelter, making the most of the situation with which he is confronted. The second man, perhaps thinking that the warm days will last forever, lies in the sun, picks coconuts while they last, and does a minimum of work to sustain himself. At the time of harvest, the second man has nothing to harvest, nor does he assist the first man in his labors. But later when there is a dearth of food on the island, the second man comes to the first man and demands half of the harvest as his right. But of course he has no right to the product of the first man's labors. The first man may freely choose to give part of his harvest to the second out of charity rather than see him starve; but that is just what it is—charity, not the second man's right.

How can any of man's rights be violated? Ultimately, only by the use of force. I can make suggestions to you, I can reason with you, entreat you (if you are willing to listen), but I cannot *force* you without violating your rights; only by forcing you do I cut the cord between your free decisions and your actions. Voluntary relations between individuals involve no deprivation of rights, but murder, assault, and rape do, because in doing these things I make you the unwilling victim of my actions. A man's beating his wife involves no violation of rights if she *wanted* to be beaten. *Force is behavior that requires the unwilling involvement of other persons.*

Thus the use of force need not involve the use of physical violence. If I trespass on your property or dump garbage on it, I am violating your property rights, as indeed I am when I steal your watch; although this is not force in the sense of violence, it *is* a case of your being an unwilling victim of my action. Similarly, if you shout at me so that I cannot be heard when I try to speak, or blow a siren in my ear, or start a factory next door which pollutes my land, you are again violating my rights (to free speech, to property); I am, again, an unwilling victim of your actions. Similarly, if you steal a manuscript of mine and publish it as your own, you are confiscating a piece of my property and thus violating my right to keep what is the product of my labor. Of course, if I give you the manuscript with permission to sign your name to it and keep the proceeds, no violation of rights is involved—any more than if I give you permission to dump garbage on my yard.

According to libertarianism, the role of government should be limited to the retaliatory use of force against those who have initiated its use. It should not enter into any other areas, such as religion, social organization, and economics.

GOVERNMENT

Government is the most dangerous institution known to man. Throughout history it has violated the rights of men more than any individual or group of individuals could do: it has killed people, enslaved them, sent them to forced labor and concentration camps, and regularly robbed and pillaged them of the fruits of their expended labor. Unlike individual criminals, government has the power to arrest and try; unlike individual criminals, it can surround and encompass a person totally, dominating every aspect of one's life,

so that one has no recourse from it but to leave the country (and in totalitarian nations even that is prohibited). Government throughout history has a much sorrier record than any individual, even that of a ruthless mass murderer. The signs we see on bumper stickers are chillingly accurate: "Beware: the Government Is Armed and Dangerous."

The only proper role of government, according to libertarians, is that of the protector of the citizen against aggression by other individuals. The government, of course, should never initiate aggression; its proper role is as the embodiment of the *retaliatory* use of force against anyone who initiates its use.

If each individual had constantly to defend himself against possible aggressors, he would have to spend a considerable portion of his life in target practice, karate exercises, and other means of self-defenses, and even so he would probably be helpless against groups of individuals who might try to kill, maim, or rob him. He would have little time for cultivating those qualities which are essential to civilized life, nor would improvements in science, medicine, and the arts be likely to occur. The function of government is to take this responsibility off his shoulders: the government undertakes to defend him against aggressors and to punish them if they attack him. When the government is effective in doing this, it enables the citizen to go about his business unmolested and without constant fear for his life. To do this, of course, government must have physical power—the police, to protect the citizen from aggression within its borders, and the armed forces, to protect him from aggressors outside. Beyond that, the government should not intrude upon his life, either to run his business, or adjust his daily activities, or prescribe his personal moral code.

Government, then, undertakes to be the individual's protector; but historically governments have gone far beyond this function. Since they already have the physical power, they have not hesitated to use it for purposes far beyond that which was entrusted to them in the first place. Undertaking initially to protect its citizens against aggression, it has often itself become an aggressor—a far greater aggressor, indeed, than the criminals against whom it was supposed to protect its citizens. Governments have done what no private citizen can do: arrest and imprison individuals without a trial and send them to slave labor camps. Government must have power in order to be effective—and yet the very means by which alone it can be effective make it vulnerable to the abuse of power, leading to managing the lives of individuals and even inflicting terror upon them.

What then should be the function of government? In a word, the *protection of human rights*.

1. *The right to life:* libertarians support all such legislation as will protect human beings against the use of force by others, for example, laws against killing, attempted killing, maiming, beating, and all kinds of physical violence.

2. *The right to liberty:* there should be no laws compromising in any way freedom of speech, of the press, and of peaceable assembly. There should be no censorship of ideas, books, films, or of anything else by government.

3. *The right to property:* libertarians support legislation that protects the property rights of individuals against confiscation, nationalization, eminent domain, robbery, trespass, fraud and misrepresentation, patent and copyright, libel and slander.

Someone has violently assaulted you. Should he be legally liable? Of course. He has violated one of your rights. He has knowingly injured you, and since he has initiated aggression against you he should be made to expiate.

Someone has negligently left his bicycle on the sidewalk where you trip over it in the dark and injure yourself. He didn't do it intentionally; he didn't mean you any harm. Should he be legally liable? Of course; he has, however

unwittingly, injured you, and since the injury is caused by him and you are the victim, he should pay.

Someone across the street is unemployed. Should you be taxed extra to pay for his expenses? Not at all. You have not injured him, you are not responsible for the fact that he is unemployed (unless you are a senator or bureaucrat who agitated for further curtailing of business, which legislation passed, with the result that your neighbor was laid off by the curtailed business). You may voluntarily wish to help him out, or better still, try to get him a job to put him on his feet again; but since you have initiated no aggressive act against him, and neither purposely nor accidentally injured him in any way, you should not be legally penalized for the fact of his unemployment. (Actually, it is just such penalties that increase unemployment.)

One man, A, works hard for years and finally earns a high salary as a professional man. A second man, B, prefers not to work at all, and to spend wastefully what money he has (through inheritance), so that after a year or two he has nothing left. At the end of this time he has a long siege of illness and lots of medical bills to pay. He demands that the bills be paid by the government—that is, by the taxpayers of the land, including Mr. A.

But of course B has no such right. He chose to lead his life in a certain way—that was his voluntary decision. One consequence of that choice is that he must depend on charity in case of later need. Mr. A chose not to live that way. (And if everyone lived like Mr. B, on whom would he depend in case of later need?) Each has a right to live in the way he pleases, but each must live with the consequences of his own decision (which, as always, fall primarily on himself). He cannot, in time of need, claim A's beneficence as his right. . . .

Laws may be classified into three types: (1) laws protecting individuals against themselves, such as laws against fornication and other sexual behavior, alcohol, and drugs; (2) laws protecting individuals against aggressions by other individuals, such as laws against murder, robbery, and fraud; (3) laws requiring people to help one another; for example, all laws which rob Peter to pay Paul, such as welfare.

Libertarians reject the first class of laws totally. Behavior which harms no one else is strictly the individual's own affair. Thus, there should be no laws against becoming intoxicated, since whether or not to become intoxicated is the individual's own decision; but there should be laws against driving while intoxicated, since the drunken driver is a threat to every other motorist on the highway (drunken driving falls into type 2). Similarly, there should be no laws against drugs (except the prohibition of sale of drugs to minors) as long as the taking of these drugs poses no threat to anyone else. Drug addiction is a psychological problem to which no present solution exists. Most of the social harm caused by addicts, other than to themselves, is the result of thefts which they perform in order to continue their habit—and then the *legal* crime is the theft, not the addiction. The actual cost of heroin is about ten cents a shot; if it were legalized, the enormous traffic in illegal sale and purchase of it would stop, as well as the accompanying proselytization to get new addicts (to make more money for the pusher) and the thefts performed by addicts who often require eighty dollars a day just to keep up the habit. Addiction would not stop, but the crimes would: it is estimated that 75 percent of the burglaries in New York City today are performed by addicts, and all these crimes could be wiped out at one stroke through the legalization of drugs. (Only when the taking of drugs could be shown to constitute a threat to *others,* should it be prohibited by law. It is only laws protecting people against *themselves* that libertarians oppose.)

Laws should be limited to the second class only: aggression by individuals against other individuals. These are laws whose function is to protect human beings against encroachment by others; and this, as we have seen, is (according to libertarianism) the sole function of government.

Libertarians also reject the third class of laws totally: no one should be forced by law to help others, not even to tell them the time of day if requested, and certainly not to give them a portion of one's weekly paycheck. Governments, in the guise of humanitarianism, have given to some by taking from others (charging a "handling fee" in the process, which, because of the government's waste and inefficiency, sometimes is several hundred percent). And in so doing they have decreased incentive, violated the rights of individuals, and lowered the standard of living of almost everyone.

All such laws constitute what libertarians call *moral cannibalism.* A cannibal in the physical sense is a person who lives off the flesh of other human beings. A *moral* cannibal is one who believes he has a right to live off the "spirit" of other human beings—who believes that he has a moral claim on the productive capacity, time, and effort expended by others.

It has become fashionable to claim virtually everything that one needs or desires as one's *right.* Thus, many people claim that they have a right to a job, the right to free medical care, to free food and clothing, to a decent home, and so on. Now if one asks, apart from any specific context, whether it would be desirable if everyone had these things, one might well say yes. But there is a gimmick attached to each of them: *At whose expense?* Jobs, medical care, education, and so on, don't grow on trees. These are goods and services *produced only by men.* Who, then, is to provide them, and under what conditions?

If you have a right to a job, who is to supply it? Must an employer supply it even if he doesn't want to hire you? What if you are unemployable, or incurably lazy? (If you say "the government must supply it," does that mean that a job must be created for you which no employer needs done, and that you must be kept in it regardless of how much or little you work?) If the employer is forced to supply it at his expense even if he doesn't need you, then isn't *he* being enslaved to that extent? What ever happened to *his* right to conduct his life and his affairs in accordance with his choices?

If you have a right to free medical care, then, since medical care doesn't exist in nature as wild apples do, some people will have to supply it to you for free: that is, they will have to spend their time and money and energy taking care of you whether they want to or not. What ever happened to *their* right to conduct their lives as they see fit? Or do you have a right to violate theirs? Can there be a right to violate rights?

All those who demand this or that as a "free service" are consciously or unconsciously evading the fact that there is in reality no such thing as free services. All manmade goods and services are the result of human expenditure of time and effort. There is no such thing as "something for nothing" in this world. If you demand something free, you are demanding that other men give their time and effort to you without compensation. If they voluntarily choose to do this, there is no problem; but if you demand that they be *forced* to do it, you are interfering with their right not to do it if they so choose. "Swimming in this pool ought to be free!" says the indignant passerby. What he means is that others should build a pool, others should provide the materials, and still others should run it and keep it in functioning order, so that *he* can use it without fee. But what right has he to the expenditure of *their* time and effort? To expect something "for free" is to expect it *to be paid for by others* whether they choose to or not.

Many questions, particularly about economic matters, will be generated by the libertarian account of human rights and the role of government. Should government have no role in assisting the needy, in providing social security, in legislating minimum wages, in fixing prices and putting a ceiling on rents, in curbing monopolies, in erecting tariffs, in guaranteeing jobs, in managing the money supply? To these and all similar questions the libertarian answers with an unequivocal no.

"But then you'd let people go hungry!" comes the rejoinder. This, the libertarian insists, is precisely what would not happen; with the restrictions removed, the economy would flourish as never before. With the controls taken off business, existing enterprises would expand and new ones would spring into existence satisfying more and more consumer needs; millions more people would be gainfully employed instead of subsisting on welfare, and all kinds of research and production, released from the stranglehold of government, would proliferate, fulfilling man's needs and desires as never before. It has always been so whenever government has permitted men to be free traders on a free market. But *why* this is so, and how the free market is the best solution to all problems relating to the material aspect of man's life, is another and far longer story. . . .

Review Questions

1. How does Hospers explain libertarianism?
2. What are the three most basic human rights according to Hospers?
3. According to Hospers, why is the government "the chief enemy of the right to property?"
4. In Hospers' view, what is wrong with holding that everybody owns everything?
5. Hospers claims that human rights can be violated in only one way. How?
6. What is the only proper role of government according to libertarians?
7. How does Hospers propose to deal the problem of unemployment?
8. Which type of laws do libertarians accept? Which laws do they reject?
9. Why does Hospers think that people will not be hungry if libertarianism is followed?

Discussion Questions

1. Hospers thinks that the right to property is just as important as the right to life. Do you agree? Why or why not?
2. Hospers says, "I may deplore your choice of life-style, . . . but I have no right to use force to change it." Can you think of any exceptions to this? What are they?
3. Hospers claims that human rights can be violated only by the use of force. Is this true? Explain your answer.
4. "A man's beating his wife involves no violation of rights if she *wanted* to be beaten." What is your view of voluntary wife-beating? Is this an acceptable practice?
5. Hospers says, "Libertarians support all such legislation as will protect human beings against the use of force by others." How would he apply this to abortion, euthanasia, and capital punishment?
6. Hospers rejects all laws which protect individuals from themselves, for example, laws prohibiting prostitution and drugs. Do you agree that all such laws should be abolished? Explain your view of these paternalistic laws.
7. Hospers is totally opposed to any welfare laws. Should all such laws be eliminated? What is your view?
8. Hospers denies that you have a right to a job, medical care, food, or anything free. Do you agree? Do you have any positive rights at all, as distinguished from the negative rights of noninterference?

Paternalism

GERALD DWORKIN

Gerald Dworkin is chair and professor of philosophy at the University of California, Davis. He is the author of *The Theory and Practice of Autonomy* (1988).

Dworkin defines paternalism, roughly, as interference with a person's liberty for his or her own good. For example, there are laws forbidding the use of certain drugs, which may harm the user but do not lead to antisocial behavior. He wants to defend paternalism by replying to Mill's attack in the previous reading. He argues that Mill's utilitarian argument only establishes a presumption against paternalism, not an absolute prohibition. Mill's second and stronger argument is that freedom of choice has an absolute value independent of consequences. But Dworkin contends that this still allows for restricting the freedom of adults in certain circumstances. These are cases where the person chooses the restriction or is irrational or lacks willpower or is under extreme psychological or sociological pressure or doesn't understand the danger of the choice. He adds that the burden of proof is on those who want to impose restrictions, and that if there is some alternative way of accomplishing the desired end that doesn't restrict liberty, then society must adopt it.

Source: From *Morality and the Law* 1st edition by Wasserstrom. © 1971. Reprinted with permission of Wadsworth, a division of Thomson Learning: www.thomsonrights.com. Fax 800 730-2215.

Neither one person, nor any number of persons, is warranted in saying to another human creature of ripe years, that he shall not do with his life for his own benefit what he chooses to do with it. [Mill]

I do not want to go along with a volunteer basis. I think a fellow should be compelled to become better and not let him use his discretion whether he wants to get smarter, more healthy or more honest. [General Hershey]

I TAKE AS MY STARTING point the "one very simple principle" proclaimed by Mill in *On Liberty* . . . "That principle is, that the sole end for which mankind are warranted, individually or collectively, in interfering with the liberty of action of any of their number, is self-protection. That the only purpose for which power can be rightfully exercised over any member of a civilized community, against his will, is to prevent harm to others. He cannot rightfully be compelled to do or forbear because it will be better for him to do so, because it will make him happier, because, in the opinion of others, to do so would be wise, or even right."

This principle is neither "one" nor "very simple." It is at least two principles; one asserting that self-protection or the prevention of harm to others is sometimes a sufficient warrant and the other claiming that the individual's own good is *never* a sufficient warrant for the exercise of compulsion either by the society as a whole or by its individual members. I assume that no one, with the possible exception of extreme pacifists or anarchists, questions the correctness of the first half of the principle. This essay is an examination of the negative claim embodied in Mill's principle—the objection to paternalistic interferences with a man's liberty.

I

By paternalism I shall understand roughly the interference with a person's liberty of action justified by reasons referring exclusively to the welfare, good, happiness, needs, interests or values of the person being coerced. One is always well-advised to illustrate one's definitions by examples but it is not easy to find "pure" examples of paternalistic interferences. For almost any piece of legislation is justified by several different kinds of reasons and even if historically a piece of legislation can be shown to have been introduced for purely paternalistic motives, it may be that advocates of the legislation with an anti-paternalistic outlook can find sufficient reasons justifying the legislation without appealing to the reasons which were originally adduced to support it. Thus, for example, it may be that the original legislation requiring motorcyclists to wear safety helmets was introduced for purely paternalistic reasons. But the Rhode Island Supreme Court recently upheld such legislation on the grounds that it was "not persuaded that the legislature is powerless to prohibit individuals from pursuing a course of conduct which could conceivably result in their becoming public charges," thus clearly introducing reasons of a quite different kind. Now I regard this decision as being based on reasoning of a very dubious nature but it illustrates the kind of problem one has in finding examples. The following is a list of the kinds of interferences I have in mind as being paternalistic.

II

1. Laws requiring motorcyclists to wear safety helmets when operating their machines.
2. Laws forbidding persons from swimming at a public beach when lifeguards are not on duty.
3. Laws making suicide a criminal offense.
4. Laws making it illegal for women and children to work at certain types of jobs.
5. Law regulating certain kinds of sexual conduct, e.g. homosexuality among consenting adults in private.
6. Laws regulating the use of certain drugs which may have harmful consequences to the user but do not lead to anti-social conduct.

7. Laws requiring a license to engage in certain professions with those not receiving a license subject to fine or jail sentence if they do engage in the practice.

8. Laws compelling people to spend a specified fraction of their income on the purchase of retirement annuities (Social Security).

9. Laws forbidding various forms of gambling (often justified on the grounds that the poor are more likely to throw away their money on such activities than the rich who can afford to).

10. Laws regulating the maximum rates of interest for loans.

11. Laws against duelling.

In addition to laws which attach criminal or civil penalties to certain kinds of action there are laws, rules, regulations, decrees which make it either difficult or impossible for people to carry out their plans and which are also justified on paternalistic grounds. Examples of this are:

1. Laws regulating the types of contracts which will be upheld as valid by the courts, e.g. (an example of Mill's to which I shall return) no man may make a valid contract for perpetual involuntary servitude.

2. Not allowing assumption of risk as a defense to an action based on the violation of a safety statute.

3. Not allowing as a defense to a charge of murder or assault the consent of the victim.

4. Requiring members of certain religious sects to have compulsory blood transfusions. This is made possible by not allowing the patient to have recourse to civil suits for assault and battery and by means of injunctions.

5. Civil commitment procedures when these are specifically justified on the basis of preventing the person being committed from harming himself. The D.C.

Hospitalization of the Mentally Ill Act provides for involuntary hospitalization of a person who "is mentally ill, and because of that illness, is likely to injure himself or others if allowed to remain at liberty," The term injure in this context applies to unintentional as well as intentional injuries.

All of my examples are of existing restrictions on the liberty of individuals. Obviously one can think of interferences which have not yet been imposed. Thus one might ban the sale of cigarettes, or require that people wear safety-belts in automobiles (as opposed to merely having them installed), enforcing this by not allowing motorists to sue for injuries even when caused by other drivers if the motorist was not wearing a seat-belt at the time of the accident.

I shall not be concerned with activities which though defended on paternalistic grounds are not interferences with the liberty of persons, e.g. the giving of subsidies in kind rather than in cash on the grounds that the recipients would not spend the money on the goods which they really need, or not including a $1,000 deductible provision in a basic protection automobile insurance plan on the ground that the people who would elect it could least afford it. Nor shall I be concerned with measures such as "truth-in-advertising" acts and Pure Food and Drug legislation which are often attacked as paternalistic but which should not be considered so. In these cases that is provided—it is true by the use of compulsion—is information which it is presumed that rational persons are interested in having in order to make wise decisions. There is no interference with the liberty of the consumer unless one wants to stretch a point beyond good sense and say that his liberty to apply for a loan without knowing the true rate of interest is diminished. It is true that sometimes there is sentiment for going further than providing information, for example when laws against usurious interest are passed preventing those who might wish to contract loans at high rates of interest from doing so, and these measures may correctly be considered paternalistic.

III

Bearing these examples in mind, let me return to a characterization of paternalism. I said earlier that I meant by the term, roughly, interference with a person's liberty for his own good. But, as some of the examples show, the class of persons whose good is involved is not always identical with the class of persons whose freedom is restricted. Thus, in the case of professional licensing it is the practitioner who is directly interfered with but it is the would-be patient whose interests are presumably being served. Not allowing the consent of the victim to be a defense to certain types of crime primarily affects the would-be aggressor but it is the interests of the willing victim that we are trying to protect. Sometimes a person may fall into both classes as would be the case if we banned the manufacture and sale of cigarettes and a given manufacturer happened to be a smoker as well.

Thus we may first divide paternalistic interferences into "pure" and "impure" cases. In "pure" paternalism the class of persons whose freedom is restricted is identical with the class of persons whose benefit is intended to be promoted by such restrictions. Examples: the making of suicide a crime, requiring passengers in automobiles to wear seat-belts, requiring a Christian Scientist to receive a blood transfusion. In the case of "impure" paternalism in trying to protect the welfare of a class of persons we find that the only way to do so will involve restricting the freedom of other persons besides those who are benefited. Now it might be thought that there are no cases of "impure" paternalism since any such case could always be justified on nonpaternalistic grounds, i.e. in terms of preventing harm to others. Thus we might ban cigarette manufacturers from continuing to manufacture their product on the grounds that we are preventing them from causing illness to others in the same way that we prevent other manufacturers from releasing pollutants into the atmosphere, thereby causing danger to the members of the community. The difference is, however, that in the former but not the latter case the harm is of such a nature that it could be avoided by those individuals affected if they so chose. The incurring of the harm requires, so to speak, the active cooperation of the victim. It would be mistaken theoretically and hypocritical in practice to assert that our interference in such cases is just like our interference in standard cases of protecting others from harm. At the very least someone interfered with in this way can reply that no one is complaining about his activities. It may be that impure paternalism requires arguments or reasons of a stronger kind in order to be justified, since there are persons who are losing a portion of their liberty and they do not even have the solace of having it be done "in their own interest." Of course in some sense, if paternalistic justifications are ever correct, then we are protecting others, we are preventing some from injuring others, but it is important to see the differences between this and the standard case.

Paternalism then will always involve limitations on the liberty of some individuals in their own interest but it may also extend to interferences with the liberty of parties whose interests are not in question.

IV

Finally, by way of some more preliminary analysis, I want to distinguish paternalistic interference with liberty from a related type with which it is often confused. Consider, for example, legislation which forbids employees to work more than, say, 40 hours per week. It is sometimes argued that such legislation is paternalistic for if employees desired such a restriction on their hours of work they could agree among themselves to impose it voluntarily. But because they do not the society imposes its own conception of their best interests upon them by the use of coercion. Hence this is paternalism.

Now it may be that some legislation of this nature is, in fact, paternalistically motivated. I am not denying that. All I want to point out is that there is another possible way of justifying such measures which is not paternalistic in nature. It is not paternalistic because, as Mill puts it in a similar context, such measures are "required not to overrule the judgment of individuals respecting their own interest, but to give effect to that judgment: they being unable to give effect to it except by concert, which concert again cannot be effectual unless it receives validity and sanction from the law." (*Principles of Political Economy*).

The line of reasoning here is a familiar one first found in Hobbes and developed with great sophistication by contemporary economists in the last decade or so. There are restrictions which are in the interests of a class of persons taken collectively but are such that the immediate interest of each individual is furthered by his violating the rule when others adhere to it. In such cases the individuals involved may need the use of compulsion to give effect to their collective judgment of their own interest by guaranteeing each individual compliance by the others. In these cases compulsion is not used to achieve some benefit which is not recognized to be a benefit by those concerned, but rather because it is the only feasible means of achieving some benefit which *is* recognized as such by all concerned. This way of viewing matters provides us with another characterization of paternalism in general. Paternalism might be thought of as the use of coercion to achieve a good which is not recognized as such by those persons for whom the good is intended. Again while this formulation captures the heart of the matter—it is surely what Mill is objecting to in *On Liberty*—the matter is not always quite like that. For example, when we force motorcyclists to wear helmets we are trying to promote a good—the protection of the person from injury—which is surely recognized by most of the individuals concerned. It is not that a cyclist doesn't value his bodily integrity; rather, as a supporter of such legislation would put it, he either places, perhaps irrationally, another value or good (freedom from wearing a helmet) above that of physical well-being or, perhaps, while recognizing the danger in the

abstract, he either does not fully appreciate it or he underestimates the likelihood of its occurring. But now we are approaching the question of possible justifications of paternalistic measures and the rest of this essay will be devoted to that question.

V

I shall begin for dialectical purposes by discussing Mill's objections to paternalism and then go on to discuss more positive proposals.

An initial feature that strikes one is the absolute nature of Mill's prohibitions against paternalism. It is so unlike the carefully qualified admonitions of Mill and his fellow Utilitarians on other moral issues. He speaks of self-protection as the *sole* end warranting coercion, of the individual's own goals as *never* being a sufficient warrant. Contrast this with his discussion of the prohibition against lying in *Utilitarianism:*

> Yet that even this rule, sacred as it is, admits of possible exception, is acknowledged by all moralists, the chief of which is where the withholding of some fact . . . would save an individual . . . from great and unmerited evil.

The same tentativeness is present when he deals with justice:

> It is confessedly unjust to break faith with any one: to violate an engagement, either express or implied, or disappoint expectations raised by our own conduct, at least if we have raised these expectations knowingly and voluntarily. Like all the other obligations of justice already spoken of, this one is not regarded as absolute, but as capable of being overruled by a stronger obligation of justice on the other side.

This anomaly calls for some explanation. The structure of Mill's argument is as follows:

1. Since restraint is an evil the burden of proof is on those who propose such restraint.

2. Since the conduct which is being considered is purely self-regarding, the normal

appeal to the protection of the interests of others is not available.

3. Therefore we have to consider whether reasons involving reference to the individual's own good, happiness, welfare, or interests are sufficient to overcome the burden of justification.

4. We either cannot advance the interests of the individual by compulsion, or the attempt to do so involves evils which outweigh the good done.

5. Hence the promotion of the individual's own interests does not provide a sufficient warrant for the use of compulsion.

Clearly the operative premise here is (4), and it is bolstered by claims about the status of the individual as judge and appraiser of his welfare, interests, needs, etc.:

With respect to his own feelings and circumstances, the most ordinary man or woman has means of knowledge immeasurably surpassing those that can be possessed by any one else.

He is the man most interested in his own well-being: the interest which any other person, except in cases of strong personal attachment, can have in it is trifling, compared to that which he himself has.

These claims are used to support the following generalizations concerning the utility of compulsion for paternalistic purposes.

The interferences of society to overrule his judgment and purposes in what only regards himself must be grounded on general presumptions; which may be altogether wrong, and even if right, are as likely as not to be misapplied to individual cases.

But the strongest of all the arguments against the interference of the public with purely personal conduct is that when it does interfere, the odds are that it interferes wrongly and in the wrong place.

All errors which the individual is likely to commit against advice and warning are far outweighed by the evil of allowing others to constrain him to what they deem his good.

Performing the utilitarian calculation by balancing the advantages and disadvantages we find that: "Mankind are greater gainers by suffering each other to live as seems good to themselves, than by compelling each other to live as seems good to the rest." Ergo, (4).

This classical case of a utilitarian argument with all the premises spelled out is not the only line of reasoning present in Mill's discussion. There are asides, and more than asides, which look quite different and I shall deal with them later. But this is clearly the main channel of Mill's thought and it is one which has been subjected to vigorous attack from the moment it appeared—most often by fellow Utilitarians. The link that they have usually seized on is, as Fitzjames Stephen put it in *Liberty, Equality, Fraternity,* the absence of proof that the "mass of adults are so well acquainted with their own interests and so much disposed to pursue them that no compulsion or restraint put upon them by any others for the purpose of promoting their interest can really promote them." Even so sympathetic a critic as H. L. A. Hart is forced to the conclusion that:

In Chapter 5 of his essay [On Liberty] Mill carried his protests against paternalism to lengths that may now appear to us as fantastic . . . No doubt if we no longer sympathise with this criticism this is due, in part, to a general decline in the belief that individuals know their own interest best.

Mill endows the average individual with "too much of the psychology of a middle-aged man whose desires are relatively fixed, not liable to be artificially stimulated by external influences; who knows what he wants and what gives him satisfaction or happiness; and who pursues these things when he can."

Now it is interesting to note that Mill himself was aware of some of the limitations on the doctrine that the individual is the best judge of his own interests. In his discussion of government intervention in general (even where the intervention does not interfere with liberty but provides alternative institutions to those of the market) after making claims which are parallel to those just discussed, e.g. "People understand their own business and their own interests better, and care for them more, than the government does, or can be expected to do." He goes on to an intelligent discussion of the "very large and conspicuous exceptions" to the maxim that:

> Most persons take a juster and more intelligent view of their own interest, and of the means of promoting it than can either be prescribed to them by a general enactment of the legislature, or pointed out in the particular case by a public functionary.

Thus there are things

> of which the utility does not consist in ministering to inclinations, nor in serving the daily uses of life, and the want of which is least felt where the need is greatest. This is peculiarly true of those things which are chiefly useful as tending to raise the character of human beings. The uncultivated cannot be competent judges of cultivation. Those who most need to be made wiser and better, usually desire it least, and, if they desired it, would be incapable of finding the way to it by their own lights.
> . . . A second exception to the doctrine that individuals are the best judges of their own interest, is when an individual attempts to decide irrevocably now what will be best for his interest at some future and distant time. The presumption in favor of individual judgment is only legitimate, where the judgment is grounded on actual, and especially on present, personal experience; not where it is formed antecedently to experience, and not suffered to be reversed even after experience has condemned it.

The upshot of these exceptions is that Mill does not declare that there should never be government interference with the economy but rather that

> . . . in every instance, the burden of making out a strong case should be thrown not on those who resist but on those who recommend government interference. Letting alone, in short,

should be the general practice: every departure from it, unless required by some great good, is a certain evil.

In short, we get a presumption, not an absolute prohibition. The question is why doesn't the argument against paternalism go the same way?

I suggest that the answer lies in seeing that in addition to a purely utilitarian argument Mill uses another as well. As a Utilitarian, Mill has to show, in Fitzjames Stephen's words, that: "Self-protection apart, no good object can be attained by any compulsion which is not in itself a greater evil than the absence of the object which the compulsion obtains." To show this is impossible; one reason being that it isn't true. Preventing a man from selling himself into slavery (a paternalistic measure which Mill himself accepts as legitimate), or from taking heroin, or from driving a car without wearing seat-belts may constitute a lesser evil than allowing him to do any of these things. A consistent Utilitarian can only argue against paternalism on the grounds that it (as a matter of fact) does not maximize the good. It is always a contingent question that may be refuted by the evidence. But there is also a non-contingent argument which runs through *On Liberty*. When Mill states that "there is a part of the life of every person who has come to years of discretion, within which the individuality of that person ought to reign uncontrolled either by any other person or by the public collectively," he is saying something about what it means to be a person, an autonomous agent. It is because coercing a person for his own good denies this status as an independent entity that Mill objects to it so strongly and in such absolute terms. To be able to choose is a good that is independent of the wisdom of what is chosen. A man's "mode of laying out his existence is the best, not because it is the best in itself, but because it is his own mode." It is the privilege and proper condition of a human being, arrived at the maturity of his faculties, to use and interpret experience in his own way.

As further evidence of this line of reasoning in Mill, consider the one exception to his prohibition against paternalism.

In this and most civilised countries, for example, an engagement by which a person should sell himself, or allow himself to be sold, as a slave, would be null and void; neither enforced by law nor by opinion. The ground for thus limiting his power of voluntarily disposing of his own lot in life, is apparent, and is very clearly seen in this extreme case. The reason for not interfering, unless for the sake of others, with a person's voluntary acts, is consideration for his liberty. His voluntary choice is evidence that what he so chooses is desirable, or at least endurable, to him, and his good is on the whole best provided for by allowing him to take his own means of pursuing it. But by selling himself for a slave, he abdicates his liberty; he foregoes any future use of it beyond that single act. He therefore defeats, in his own case, the very purpose which is the justification of allowing him to dispose of himself. He is no longer free; but is thenceforth in a position which has no longer the presumption in its favour, that would be afforded by his voluntarily remaining in it. The principle of freedom cannot require that he should be free not to be free. It is not freedom to be allowed to alienate his freedom.

Now leaving aside the fudging on the meaning of freedom in the last line it is clear that part of this argument is incorrect. While it is true that *future* choices of the slave are not reasons for thinking that what he chooses then is desirable for him, what is at issue is limiting his immediate choice; and since this choice is made freely, the individual may be correct in thinking that his interests are best provided for by entering such a contract. But the main consideration for not allowing such a contract is the need to preserve the liberty of the person to make future choices. This gives us a principle—a very narrow one—by which to justify some paternalistic interferences. Paternalism is justified only to preserve a wider range of freedom for the individual in question. How far this principle could be

extended, whether it can justify all the cases in which we are inclined upon reflection to think paternalistic measures justified, remains to be discussed. What I have tried to show so far is that there are two strains of argument in Mill—one a straight-forward Utilitarian mode of reasoning and one which relies not on the goods which free choice leads to but on the absolute value of the choice itself. The first cannot establish any absolute prohibition but at most a presumption and indeed a fairly weak one given some fairly plausible assumptions about human psychology; the second, while a stronger line of argument, seems to me to allow on its own grounds a wider range of paternalism than might be suspected. I turn now to a consideration of these matters.

VI

We might begin looking for principles governing the acceptable use of paternalistic power in cases where it is generally agreed that it is legitimate. Even Mill intends his principles to be applicable only to mature individuals, not those in what he calls "non-age." What is it that justifies us in interfering with children? The fact that they lack some of the emotional and cognitive capacities required in order to make fully rational decisions. It is an empirical question to just what extent children have an adequate conception of their own present and future interests but there is not much doubt that there are many deficiencies. For example, it is very difficult for a child to defer gratification for any considerable period of time. Given these deficiencies and given the very real and permanent dangers that may befall the child it becomes not only permissible but even a duty of the parent to restrict the child's freedom in various ways. There is however an important moral limitation on the exercise of such parental power which is provided by the notion of the child eventually coming to see the correctness of his parent's interventions. Parental paternalism may be thought of as a wager by the parent on the child's subsequent recognition of the wisdom of the restrictions. There is an emphasis on what could be called future-oriented consent—on what the child will come to welcome, rather than on what he does welcome.

The essence of this idea has been incorporated by idealist philosophers into various types of "real-will" theory as applied to fully adult persons. Extensions of paternalism are argued for by claiming that in various respects, chronologically mature individuals share the same deficiencies in knowledge, capacity to think rationally, and the ability to carry out decisions that children possess. Hence in interfering with such people we are in effect doing what they would do if they were fully rational. Hence we are not really opposing their will, hence we are not really interfering with their freedom. The dangers of this move have been sufficiently exposed by Berlin in his *Two Concepts of Freedom*. I see no gain in theoretical clarity nor in practical advantage in trying to pass over the real nature of the interferences with liberty that we impose on others. Still the basic notion of consent is important and seems to me the only acceptable way of trying to delimit an area of justified paternalism.

Let me start by considering a case where the consent is not hypothetical in nature. Under certain conditions it is rational for an individual to agree that others should force him to act in ways which, at the time of action, the individual may not see as desirable. If, for example, a man knows that he is subject to breaking his resolves when temptation is present, he may ask a friend to refuse to entertain his requests at some later stage.

A classical example is given in the Odyssey when Odysseus commands his men to tie him to the mast and refuse all future orders to be set free, because he knows the power of the Sirens to enchant men with their songs. Here we are on relatively sound ground in later refusing Odysseus' request to be set free. He may even claim to have changed his mind but since it is *just* such changes that he wished to guard against we are entitled to ignore them.

A process analogous to this may take place on a social rather than individual basis. An electorate may mandate its representatives to pass legislation which when it comes time to "pay the price" may be unpalatable. I may believe that a tax increase is necessary to halt inflation though I may resent the lower pay check each month. However in both this case and that of Odysseus the measure to be enforced is specifically requested by the party involved and at some point in time there is genuine consent and agreement on the part of those persons whose liberty is infringed. Such is not the case for the paternalistic measures we have been speaking about. What must be involved here is not consent to specific measures but rather consent to a system of government, run by elected representatives, with an understanding that they may act to safe-guard our interests in certain limited ways.

I suggest that since we are all aware of our irrational propensities, deficiencies in cognitive and emotional capacities, and avoidable and unavoidable ignorance it is rational and prudent for us to in effect take out "social insurance policies." We may argue for and against proposed paternalistic measures in terms of what fully rational individuals would accept as forms of protection. Now clearly, since the initial agreement is not about specific measures we are dealing with a more-or-less blank check and therefore there have to be carefully defined limits. What I am looking for are certain kinds of conditions which make it plausible to suppose that rational men could reach agreement to limit their liberty even when other men's interests are not affected.

Of course as in any kind of agreement schema there are great difficulties in deciding what rational individuals would or would not accept. Particularly in sensitive areas of personal liberty, there is always a danger of the dispute over agreement and rationality being a disguised version of evaluative and normative disagreement.

Let me suggest types of situations in which it seems plausible to suppose that fully rational individuals would agree to having paternalistic restrictions imposed upon them. It is reasonable to suppose that there are "goods" such as health which any person would want to have in order to pursue his own good—no matter how that good is conceived. This is an argument used in connection with compulsory education for children but it seems to me that it can be extended to other goods which have this character. Then one could agree that the attainment of such goods should be promoted even when not recognized to be such, at the moment by the individuals concerned.

An immediate difficulty arises from the fact that men are always faced with competing goods and that there may be reasons why even a value such as health—or indeed life—may be over-ridden by competing values. Thus the problem with the Christian Scientist and blood transfusions. It may be more important for him to reject "impure substances" than to go on living. The difficult problem that must be faced is whether one can give sense to the notion of a person irrationally attaching weights to competing values.

Consider a person who knows the statistical data on the probability of being injured when not wearing seat-belts in an automobile and knows the types and gravity of the various injuries. He also insists that the inconvenience attached to fastening the belt every time he gets in and out of the car out of the car out-weighs for him the possible risks to himself. I am inclined in this case to think that such a weighing is irrational. Given his life-plans, which we are assuming are those of the average person, his interests and commitments already undertaken, I think it is safe to predict that we can find inconsistencies in his calculations at some point. I am assuming that this is not a man who for some conscious or unconscious reasons is trying to injure himself nor is he a man who just likes to "live dangerously." I am assuming that he is like us in all the relevant respects but just puts an enormously high negative value on inconvenience—one which does not seem comprehensible or reasonable.

It is always possible, of course, to assimilate this person to creatures like myself. I, also, neglect to fasten my seat-belt and I concede such behavior is not rational but not because I weigh the inconvenience differently from those who fasten the belts. It is just that having made (roughly) the same calculation as everybody else I ignore it in my actions. [Note: a much better case of weakness of the will than those usually given in ethics texts.] A plausible explanation for this deplorable habit is that although I know in some intellectual sense what the probabilities and risks are I do not fully appreciate them in an emotionally genuine manner.

We have two distinct types of situation in which a man acts in a nonrational fashion. In one case he attaches incorrect weights to some of his values; in the other he neglects to act in accordance with his actual preferences and desires. Clearly there is a stronger and more persuasive argument for paternalism in the latter situation. Here we are really not—by assumption—imposing a good on another person. But why may we not extend our interference to what we might call evaluative delusions? After all, in the case of cognitive delusions we are prepared, often, to act against the expressed will of the person involved. If a man believes that when he jumps out the window he will float upwards—Robert Nozick's example—would not we detain him, forcibly if necessary? The reply will be that this man doesn't wish to be injured and if we could convince him that he is mistaken as to the consequences of his action he would not wish to perform the action. But part of what is involved in claiming that the man who doesn't fasten his seat-belts is attaching an incorrect weight to the inconvenience of fastening them is that if he were to be involved in an accident and severely injured he would look back and admit that the inconvenience wasn't as bad as all that. So there is a sense in which if I could convince him of the consequences of his action he also would not wish to continue his present course of action. Now the notion of consequences being used here is covering a lot of ground. In one case it's being used to indicate what will or can happen as a result of a course of action and in the other it's making a prediction about the future evaluation of the consequences—in the first sense—of a course of action. And whatever the difference between facts and values—whether it be hard and fast or soft and slow—we are genuinely more reluctant to consent to interferences where evaluative differences are the issue. Let me now consider another factor which comes into play in some of these situations which may make an important difference in our willingness to consent to paternalistic restrictions.

Some of the decisions we make are of such a character that they produce changes which are in one or another way irreversible. Situations are created in which it is difficult or impossible to return to anything like the initial stage at which the decision was made. In particular, some of these changes will make it impossible to continue to make reasoned choices in the future. I am thinking specifically of decisions which involve taking drugs that are physically or psychologically addictive and those which are destructive of one's mental and physical capacities.

I suggest we think of the imposition of paternalistic interferences in situations of this kind as being a kind of insurance policy which we take out against making decisions which are far-reaching, potentially dangerous and irreversible. Each of these factors is important. Clearly there are many decisions we make that are relatively irreversible. In deciding to learn to play chess I could predict in view of my general interest in games that some portion of my free time was going to be preempted and that it would not be easy to give up the game once I acquired a certain competence. But my whole life-style was not going to be jeopardized in an extreme manner. Further it might be argued that even with addictive drugs such as heroin one's normal life plans would not be seriously interfered with if an inexpensive and adequate supply were readily available. So this type of argument might have a much narrower scope than appears to be the case at first.

A second class of cases concerns decisions which are made under extreme psychological and sociological pressures. I am not thinking here of the making of the decision as being something one is pressured into—e.g. a good reason for making duelling illegal is that unless this is done many people might have to manifest their courage and integrity in ways in which they would rather not do so—but rather of decisions, such as that to commit suicide, which are usually made at a point where the individual is not thinking clearly and calmly about the nature of his decision. In addition, of course, this comes under the previous heading of all-too-irrevocable decisions. Now there are practical steps which a society could take if it wanted to decrease the possibility of suicide—for example not paying social security benefits to the survivors or, as religious institutions do, not allowing persons to be buried with the same status as natural deaths. I think we may count these as interferences with the liberty of persons to attempt suicide and the question is whether they are justifiable.

Using my argument schema the question is whether rational individuals would consent to such limitations. I see no reason for them to consent to an absolute prohibition but I do think it is reasonable for them to agree to some kind of enforced waiting period. Since we are all aware of the possibility of temporary states, such as great fear or depression, that are inimical to the making of well-informed and rational decisions, it would be prudent for all of us if there were some kind of institutional arrangement whereby we were restrained from making a decision which is so irreversible. What this would be like in practice is difficult to envisage and it may be that if no practical arrangements were feasible we would have to conclude that there should be no restriction at all on this kind of action. But we might have a "cooling off" period, in much the same way that we now require couples who file for divorce to go through a waiting period. Or, more far-fetched, we might imagine a Suicide Board composed of a psychologist and another member picked by the applicant. The Board would be required to meet and talk with the person proposing to take his life, though its approval would not be required.

A third class of decisions—these classes are not supposed to be disjoint—involves dangers which are either not sufficiently understood or appreciated correctly by the persons involved. Let me illustrate, using the example of cigarette smoking, a number of possible cases.

1. A man may not know the facts—e.g. smoking between 1 and 2 packs a day shortens life expectancy 6.2 years, the costs and pain of the illness caused by smoking, etc.

2. A man may know the facts, wish to stop smoking, but not have the requisite will-power.

3. A man may know the facts but not have them play the correct role in his calculation because, say, he discounts the danger psychologically since it is remote in time and/or inflates the attractiveness of other consequences of his decision which he regards as beneficial.

In case 1 what is called for is education, the posting of warnings, etc. In case 2 there is no theoretical problem. We are not imposing a good on someone who rejects it. We are simply using coercion to enable people to carry out their own goals. (Note: There obviously is a difficulty in that only a subclass of the individuals affected wish to be prevented from doing what they are doing.) In case 3 there is a sense in which we are imposing a good on someone in that given his current appraisal of the facts he doesn't wish to be restricted. But in another sense we are not imposing a good since what is being claimed—and what must be shown or at least argued for—is that an accurate accounting on his part would lead him to reject his current

course of action. Now we all know that such cases exist, that we are prone to disregarding dangers that are only possibilities, that immediate pleasures are often magnified and distorted.

If in addition the dangers are severe and far-reaching, we could agree to allow the state a certain degree of power to intervene in such situations. The difficulty is in specifying in advance, even vaguely, the class of cases in which intervention will be legitimate.

A related difficulty is that of drawing a line so that it is not the case that all ultra-hazardous activities are ruled out, e.g. mountain-climbing, bull-fighting, sports-car racing, etc. There are some risks—even very great ones—which a person is entitled to take with his life.

A good deal depends on the nature of the deprivation—e.g. does it prevent the person from engaging in the activity completely or merely limit his participation—and how important to the nature of the activity is the absence of restriction when this is weighed against the role that the activity plays in the life of the person. In the case of automobile seat-belts, for example, the restriction is trivial in nature, interferes not at all with the use or enjoyment of the activity, and does, I am assuming, considerably reduce a high risk of serious injury. Whereas, for example, making mountain-climbing illegal completely prevents a person from engaging in an activity which may play an important role in his life and his conception of the person he is.

In general, the easiest cases to handle are those which can be argued about in the terms which Mill thought to be so important—a concern not just for the happiness or welfare, in some broad sense, of the individual but rather a concern for the autonomy and freedom of the person. I suggest that we would be most likely to consent to paternalism in those instances in which it preserves and enhances for the individual his ability to rationally consider and carry out his own decisions.

I have suggested in this essay a number of types of situations in which it seems plausible that rational men would agree to granting the legislative powers of a society the right to impose restrictions on what Mill calls "self-regarding" conduct. However, rational men knowing something about the resources of ignorance, ill-will and stupidity available to the law-makers of a society—a good case in point is the history of drug legislation in the United States—will be concerned to limit such intervention to a minimum. I suggest in closing two principles designed to achieve this end.

In all cases of paternalistic legislation there must be a heavy and clear burden of proof placed on the authorities to demonstrate the exact nature of the harmful effects (or beneficial consequences) to be avoided (or achieved) and the probability of their occurrence. The burden of proof here is twofold—what lawyers distinguish as the burden of going forward and the burden of persuasion. That the authorities have the burden of going forward means that it is up to them to raise the question and bring forward evidence of the evils to be avoided. Unlike the case of new drugs where the manufacturer must produce some evidence that the drug has been tested and found not harmful, no citizen has to show with respect to self-regarding conduct that it is not harmful or promotes his best interests. In addition the nature and cogency of the evidence for the harmfulness of the course of action must be set at a high level. To paraphrase a formulation of the burden of proof for criminal proceedings—better 10 men ruin themselves than one man be unjustly deprived of liberty.

Finally, I suggest a principle of the least restrictive alternative. If there is an alternative way of accomplishing the desired end without restricting liberty although it may involve great expense, inconvenience, etc., the society must adopt it.

Review Questions

1. How does Dworkin define paternalism? Give examples.
2. Distinguish between pure and impure paternalism.
3. According to Dworkin, why isn't legislation preventing employees from working more than forty hours a week an example of paternalism?
4. Explain Mill's utilitarian argument against paternalism. How does Dworkin reply? What is Mill's second argument?
5. Why does Dworkin think that paternal parentalism is justified? What are the limits on this kind of paternalism?
6. Dworkin argues that rational people will accept restrictions on their liberty in certain situations. What are these situations?
7. Dworkin proposes two principles to limit paternalistic restrictions. What are they?

Discussion Questions

1. Jehova's Witnesses refuse blood transfusions because eating blood is prohibited in the Bible. (See Leviticus 3:17 and 17:10. Leviticus 7:26 says, "Moreover ye shall eat no manner of blood.") Should people who choose to obey the Biblical prohibitions be forced to have blood transfusions for medical reasons? Why or why not?
3. Should automobile drivers be required to wear seat beats? What about those who ride motorcycles? Should they be forced to wear helmets when they ride? Explain your view.
4. Should suicide be illegal? What is Dworkin's view? What do you think?
5. There is overwhelming evidence that smoking cigarettes is harmful to the smoker. Is that a good reason for making cigarettes illegal? If not, then why is smoking marijuana illegal?

The Ethics of Addiction

THOMAS SZASZ

Thomas Szasz is professor of psychiatry emeritus at the State University of New York Health Sciences Center in Syracuse, New York, and adjunct scholar at the Cato Institute in Washington, D.C. He is the author of many books, including *Our Right to Drugs* (1996), *Insanity* (1997), *Cruel Compassion* (1998), *Fatal Freedom* (1999), and *Pharmacracy* (2001). For a bibliography of all his writings and more information see The Thomas S. Szasz Cybercenter for Liberty and Responsibility, www.szasz.com.

Szasz attacks the World Health Organization definition of drug addiction and propaganda used to justify the prohibition of drugs. He offers an account of drug addiction that is different from the disease model, and argues that adults have a constitutional and moral right to use drugs.

AN ARGUMENT IN FAVOR OF LETTING AMERICANS TAKE ANY DRUGS THEY WANT TO TAKE

To avoid clichés about "drug abuse," let us analyze its official definition. According to the World Health Organization, "Drug addiction is a state of periodic or chronic intoxication detrimental to the individual and to society, produced by the repeated consumption of a drug (natural or synthetic). Its characteristics include: (1) an overpowering desire to need (compulsion) to continue taking the drug and to obtain it by any means, (2) a tendency to increase the dosage, and (3) a psychic (psychological) and sometimes physical dependence on the effects of the drug."

Since this definition hinges on the harm done to both the individual and society, it is clearly an ethical one. Moreover, by not specifying what is "detrimental," it consigns the problem

of addiction to psychiatrists who define the patient's "dangerousness to himself and others."

Next, we come to the effort to obtain the addictive substance "by any means." This suggests that the substance must be prohibited, or is very expensive, and is hence difficult for the ordinary person to obtain (rather than that the person who wants it has an inordinate craving for it). If there were an abundant and inexpensive supply of what the "addict" wants, there would be no reason for him to go to "any means" to obtain it. Thus by the WHO's definition, one can be addicted only to a substance that is illegal or otherwise difficult to obtain. This surely removes the problem of addiction from the realm of medicine or psychiatry, and puts it squarely into that of morals and laws.

In short, drug addiction or drug abuse cannot be defined without specifying the proper or improper uses of certain pharmacologically active agents. The regular administration of morphine by a physician to a patient dying of cancer is the paradigm of the proper use of a narcotic; whereas even its occasional self-administration by a physically healthy person for the purpose of "pharmacological pleasure" is the paradigm of drug abuse.

I submit that these judgments have nothing whatever to do with medicine, pharmacology, or psychiatry. They are moral judgments. Indeed, our present views on addiction are astonishingly similar to some of our former views on sex. Until recently, masturbation—or self-abuse, as it was called—was professionally declared, and popularly accepted, as both the cause and the symptom of a variety of illnesses. Even today, homosexuality—called a "sexual perversion"—is regarded as a disease by medical and psychiatric experts as well as by "well-informed" laymen.

To be sure, it is now virtually impossible to cite a contemporary medical authority to support the concept of self-abuse. Medical opinion holds that whether a person masturbates or not is medically irrelevant; and it is a matter of personal morals or life-style. On the other hand, it is virtually impossible to cite a contemporary medical authority to oppose the concept of drug abuse. Medical opinion holds that drug abuse is a major medical, psychiatric, and public health problem; that drug addiction is a disease similar to diabetes, requiring prolonged (or life-long) and careful, medically supervised treatment; and that taking or not taking drugs is primarily, if not solely, a matter of medical responsibility.

Thus the man on the street can only believe what he hears from all sides—that drug addiction is a disease, "like any other," which has now reached "epidemic proportions," and whose "medical" containment justifies the limitless expenditure of tax monies and the corresponding aggrandizement and enrichment of noble medical warriors against this "plague."

PROPAGANDA TO JUSTIFY PROHIBITION

Like any social policy, our drug laws may be examined from two entirely different points of view: technical and moral. Our present inclination is either to ignore the moral perspective or to mistake the technical for the moral.

Since most of the propagandists against drug use seek to justify certain repressive policies because of the alleged dangerousness of various drugs, they often falsify the facts about the pharmacological properties of the drugs they seek to prohibit. They do so for two reasons: first, because many substances in daily use are just as harmful as the substances they want to prohibit; second, because they realize that dangerousness alone is never a sufficiently persuasive argument to justify prohibition of any drug, substance, or artifact. Accordingly, the more they ignore the moral dimensions of the problem, the more they must escalate their fraudulent claims about the dangers of drugs.

To be sure, some drugs are more dangerous than others. It is easier to kill someone with heroin than with aspirin. But is also easier to kill oneself by jumping off a high building than a low one. In the case of drugs, we regard their potentiality for self-injury as justification for their prohibition; in the case of buildings, we do not.

Furthermore, we systematically blur and confuse the two quite different ways in which narcotics may cause death: by a deliberate act of suicide or by accidental overdose.

Every individual is capable of injuring or killing himself. This potentiality is a fundamental expression of human freedom. Self-destructive behavior may be regarded as sinful and penalized by means of informal sanctions. But it should not be regarded as a crime or (mental) disease, justifying or warranting the use of the police powers of the state for its control.

Therefore, it is absurd to deprive an adult of a drug (or of anything else) because he might use it to kill himself. To do so is to treat everyone the way institutional psychiatrists treat the so-called suicidal mental patient: they not only imprison such a person but take everything away from him—shoelaces, belts, razor blades, eating utensils, and so forth—until the "patient" lies naked on a mattress in a padded cell—lest he kill himself. The result is degrading tyrannization.

Death by accidental overdose is an altogether different matter. But can anyone doubt that this danger now looms so large precisely because the sale of narcotics and many other drugs is illegal? Those who buy illicit drugs cannot be sure what drug they are getting or how much of it. Free trade in drugs, with governmental action limited to safeguarding the purity of the product and the veracity of the labeling, would reduce the risk of accidental overdose with "dangerous drugs" to the same levels that prevail, and that we find acceptable, with respect to other chemical agents and physical artifacts that abound in our complex technological society.

This essay is not intended as an exposition on the pharmacological properties of narcotics and other mind-affecting drugs. However, I want to make it clear that in my view, *regardless* of their danger, all drugs should be "legalized" (a misleading term I employ reluctantly as a concession to common usage). Although I recognize that some drugs—notably heroin, the amphetamines, and LSD, among those now in vogue—may have undesirable or dangerous consequences, I favor free trade in drugs for the same reason the Founding Fathers favored free trade in ideas. In an open society, it is none of the government's business what idea a man puts into his mind; likewise, it should be none of the government's business what drug he puts into his body.

WITHDRAWAL PAINS
FROM TRADITION

It is a fundamental characteristic of human beings that they get used to things: one becomes habituated, or "addicted," not only to narcotics, but to cigarettes, cocktails before dinner, orange juice for breakfast, comic strips, and so forth. It is similarly a fundamental characteristic of living organisms that they acquire increasing tolerance to various chemical agents and physical stimuli: the first cigarette may cause nothing but nausea and headache; a year later, smoking three packs a day may be pure joy. Both alcohol and opiates

are "addictive" in the sense that the more regularly they are used, the more the user craves them and the greater his tolerance for them becomes. Yet none of this involves any mysterious process of "getting hooked." It is simply an aspect of the universal biological propensity for *learning,* which is especially well developed in man. The opiate habit, like the cigarette habit or food habit, can be broken—and without any medical assistance—provided the person wants to break it. Often he doesn't. And why, indeed, should he, if he has nothing better to do with his life? Or, as happens to be the case with morphine, if he can live an essentially normal life under its influence?

Actually, opium is much less toxic than alcohol. Just as it is possible to be an "alcoholic" and work and be productive, so it is (or, rather, it used to be) possible to be an opium addict and work and be productive. . . .

I am not citing this evidence to recommend the opium habit. The point is that we must, in plain honesty, distinguish between pharmacological effects and personal inclinations. Some people take drugs to help them function and conform to social expectations; others take them for the very opposite reason, to ritualize their refusal to function and conform to social expectations. Much of the "drug abuse" we now witness—perhaps nearly all of it—is of the second type. But instead of acknowledging that "addicts" are unfit or unwilling to work and be "normal," we prefer to believe that they act as they do because certain drugs—especially heroin, LSD, and the amphetamines—make them "sick." If only we could get them "well," so runs this comforting view, they could become "productive" and "useful" citizens. To believe this is like believing that if an illiterate cigarette smoker would only stop smoking, he would become an Einstein. With a falsehood like this, one can go far. No wonder that politicians and psychiatrists love it.

The concept of free trade in drugs runs counter to our cherished notion that everyone must work and idleness is acceptable only under special conditions. In general, the obligation to work is greatest for healthy, adult, white men. We tolerate idleness on the part of children, women, Negroes, the aged, and the sick, and even accept the responsibility to support them. But the new wave of drug abuse affects mainly young adults, often white males, who are, in principle at least, capable of working and supporting themselves. But they refuse: they "drop out"; and in doing so, they challenge the most basic values of our society.

The fear that free trade in narcotics would result in vast masses of our population spending their days and nights smoking opium or mainlining heroin, rather than working and taking care of their responsibilities, is a bugaboo that does not deserve to be taken seriously. Habits of work and idleness are deep-seated cultural patterns. Free trade in abortions has not made an industrious people like the Japanese give up work for fornication. Nor would free trade in drugs convert such a people from hustlers to hippies. Indeed, I think the opposite might be the case: it is questionable whether, or for how long, a responsible people can tolerate being treated as totally irresponsible with respect to drugs and drug-taking. In other words, how long can we live with the inconsistency of being expected to be responsible for operating cars and computers, but not for operating our own bodies?

Although my argument about drug-taking is moral and political, and does not depend upon showing that free trade in drugs would also have fiscal advantages over our present policies, let me indicate briefly some of its economic implications.

The war on addiction is not only astronomically expensive; it is also counterproductive. On April 1, 1967, New York State's narcotics addiction control program, hailed as "the most massive ever tried in the nation," went into effect. "The program, which may cost up to $400 million in three years," reported the *New York Times,* "was hailed by Governor Rockefeller as 'the start of an unending war.'" . . . In short, the detection and rehabilitation of addicts is good

business. We now know that the spread of witchcraft in the late Middle Ages was due more to the work of witchmongers than to the lure of witchcraft. Is it not possible that the spread of addiction in our day is due more to the work of addictmongers than to the lure of narcotics?

Let us see how far some of the monies spent on the war on addiction could go in supporting people who prefer to drop out of society and drug themselves. Their "habit" itself would cost next to nothing; free trade would bring the price of narcotics down to a negligible amount. . . . free trade in narcotics would be more economical for those of us who work, even if we had to support legions of addicts, than is our present program of trying to "cure" them. Moreover, I have not even made use, in my economic estimates, of the incalculable sums we would save by reducing crimes now engendered by the illegal traffic in drugs.

THE RIGHT OF SELF-MEDICATION

Clearly, the argument that marijuana—or heroin, methadone, or morphine—is prohibited because it is addictive or dangerous cannot be supported by facts. For one thing, there are many drugs, from insulin to penicillin, that are neither addictive nor dangerous but are nevertheless also prohibited; they can be obtained only through a physician's prescription. For another, there are many things, from dynamite to guns, that are much more dangerous than narcotics (especially to others) but are not prohibited. As everyone knows, it is still possible in the United States to walk into a store and walk out with a shotgun. We enjoy this right not because we believe that guns are safe but because we believe even more strongly that civil liberties are precious. At the same time, it is not possible in the United States to walk into a store and walk out with a bottle of barbiturates, codeine, or other drugs.

I believe that just as we regard freedom of speech and religion as fundamental rights, so we should also regard freedom of self-medication as a fundamental right. Like most rights, the right of self-medication should apply only to adults; and it should not be an unqualified right. Since these are important qualifications, it is necessary to specify their precise range.

John Stuart Mill said (approximately) that a person's right to swing his arm ends where his neighbor's nose begins. And Oliver Wendell Holmes said that no one has a right to shout "Fire!" in a crowded theater. Similarly, the limiting condition with respect to self-medication should be the inflicting of actual (as against symbolic) harm on others.

Our present practices with respect to alcohol embody and reflect this individualistic ethic. We have the right to buy, possess, and consume alcoholic beverages. Regardless of how offensive drunkenness might be to a person, he cannot interfere with another person's "right" to become inebriated so long as that person drinks in the privacy of his own home or at some other appropriate location, and so long as he conducts himself in an otherwise law-abiding manner. In short, we have a right to be intoxicated—in private. Public intoxication is considered an offense to others and is therefore a violation of the criminal law. It makes sense that what is a "right" in one place may become, by virtue of its disruptive or disturbing effect on others, an offense somewhere else.

The right to self-medication should be hedged in by similar limits. Public intoxication, not only with alcohol but with any drug, should be an offense punishable by the criminal law. Furthermore, acts that may injure others—such as driving a car—should, when carried out in a drug-intoxicated state, be punished especially strictly and severely. The right to self-medication must thus entail unqualified responsibility for the effects of one's drug-intoxicated behavior on others. For unless we are willing to hold ourselves responsible for our own behavior, and hold others responsible for theirs, the liberty to use drugs (or to engage in other acts) degenerates into a license to hurt others.

Such, then, would be the situation of adults, if we regarded the freedom to take drugs as a fundamental right similar to the freedom to read

and worship. What would be the situation of children? Since many people who are now said to be drug addicts or drug abusers are minors, it is especially important that we think clearly about this aspect of the problem.

I do not believe, and I do not advocate, that children should have a right to ingest, inject, or otherwise use any drug or substance they want. Children do not have the right to drive, drink, vote, marry, or make binding contracts. They acquire these rights at various ages, coming into their full possession at maturity, usually between the ages of eighteen and twenty-one. The right to self-medication should similarly be withheld until maturity.

In short, I suggest that "dangerous" drugs be treated, more or less, as alcohol is treated now. Neither the use of narcotics, nor their possession, should be prohibited, but only their sale to minors. Of course, this would result in the ready availability of all kinds of drugs among minors—though perhaps their availability would be no greater than it is now, but would only be more visible and hence more easily subject to proper controls. This arrangement would place responsibility for the use of all drugs by children where it belongs: on parents and their children. This is where the major responsibility rests for the use of alcohol. It is a tragic symptom of our refusal to take personal liberty and responsibility seriously that there appears to be no public desire to assume a similar stance toward other "dangerous" drugs.

Consider what would happen should a child bring a bottle of gin to school and get drunk there. Would the school authorities blame the local liquor stores as pushers? Or would they blame the parents and the child himself? There is liquor in practically every home in America and yet children rarely bring liquor to school. Whereas marijuana, Dexedrine, and heroin—substances children usually do not find at home and whose very possession is a criminal offense—frequently find their way into the school.

Our attitude toward sexual activity provides another model for our attitude toward drugs.

Although we generally discourage children below a certain age from engaging in sexual activity with others, we do not prohibit such activities by law. What we do prohibit by law is the sexual seduction of children by adults. The "pharmacological seduction" of children by adults should be similarly punishable. In other words, adults who give or sell drugs to children should be regarded as offenders. Such a specific and limited prohibition—as against the kinds of generalized prohibitions that we had under the Volstead Act or have now with respect to countless drugs—would be relatively easy to enforce. Moreover, it would probably be rarely violated, for there would be little psychological interest and no economic profit in doing so.

THE TRUE FAITH: SCIENTIFIC MEDICINE

What I am suggesting is that while addiction is ostensibly a medical and pharmacological problem, actually it is a moral and political problem. We ought to know that there is no necessary connection between facts and values, between what is and what ought to be. Thus, objectively quite harmful acts, objects, or persons may be accepted and tolerated—by minimizing their dangerousness. Conversely, objectively quite harmless acts, objects, or persons may be prohibited and persecuted—by exaggerating their dangerousness. It is always necessary to distinguish—and especially so when dealing with social policy—between description and prescription, fact and rhetoric, truth and falsehood.

In our society, there are two principal methods of legitimizing policy: social tradition and scientific judgment. More than anything else, time is the supreme ethical arbiter. Whatever a social practice might be, if people engage in it, generation after generation, that practice becomes acceptable.

Many opponents of illegal drugs admit that nicotine may be more harmful to health than marijuana; nevertheless, they urge that smoking cigarettes should be legal but smoking marijuana should not be, because the former habit is socially accepted while the latter is not. This is a perfectly reasonable argument. But let us understand it for what it is—a plea for legitimizing old and accepted practices, and for illegitimizing novel and unaccepted ones. It is a justification that rests on precedent, not evidence.

The other method of legitimizing policy, ever more important in the modern world, is through the authority of science. In matters of health, a vast and increasingly elastic category, physicians play important roles as legitimizers and illegitimizers. This, in short, is why we regard being medicated by a doctor as drug use, and self-medication (especially with certain classes of drugs) as drug abuse.

This, too is a perfectly reasonable arrangement. But we must understand that it is a plea for legitimizing what doctors do, because they do it with "good therapeutic" intent; and for illegitimatizing what laymen do, because they do it with bad self-abusive ("masturbatory" or mind-altering) intent. This justification rests on the principle of professionalism, not of pharmacology. Hence we applaud the systematic medical use of methadone and call it "treatment for heroin addiction," but decry the occasional nonmedical use of marijuana and call it "dangerous drug abuse."

Our present concept of drug abuse articulates and symbolizes a fundamental policy of scientific medicine—namely, that a layman should not medicate his own body but should place its medical care under the supervision of a duly accredited physician. Before the Reformation, the practice of True Christianity rested on a similar policy—namely, that a layman should not himself commune with God but should place his spiritual care under the supervision of a duly accredited priest. The self-interests of the church and of medicine in such policies are obvious enough. What might be less obvious is the interest of the laity: by delegating responsibility for the spiritual and medical welfare of the people to a class of authoritatively accredited specialists, these policies—and the practices they ensure—relieve individuals from assuming the burdens of responsibility for themselves. As I see it, our present problems with drug use and drug abuse are just one of the consequences of our pervasive ambivalence about personal autonomy and responsibility.

I propose a medical reformation analogous to the Protestant Reformation: specifically, a "protest" against the systematic mystification of man's relationship to his body and his professionalized separation from it. The immediate aim of this reform would be to remove the physician as intermediary between man and his body and to give the layman direct access to the language and contents of the pharmacopoeia. If man had unencumbered access to his own body and the means of chemically altering it, it would spell the end of medicine, at least as we now know it. This is why, with faith in scientific medicine so strong, there is little interest in this kind of medical reform. Physicians fear the loss of their privileges; laymen, the loss of their protections. . . .

LIFE, LIBERTY, AND THE PURSUIT OF HIGHS

Sooner or later we shall have to confront the basic moral dilemma underlying this problem: does a person have the right to take a drug, any drug—not because he needs it to cure an illness, but because he wants to take it?

The Declaration of Independence speaks of our inalienable right to "life, liberty, and the pursuit of happiness." How are we to interpret this? By asserting that we ought to be free to pursue happiness by playing golf or watching television, but not by drinking alcohol, or smoking marijuana, or ingesting pep pills?

The Constitution and the Bill of Rights are silent on the subject of drugs. This would seem to imply that the adult citizen has, or ought to have, the right to medicate his own body as he sees fit. Were this not the case, why should there have been a need for a Constitutional Amendment to outlaw drinking? But if ingesting alcohol was, and is now again, a Constitutional

right, is ingesting opium, or heroin, or barbiturates, or anything else, not also such a right? If it is, then the Harrison Narcotic Act is not only a bad law but is unconstitutional as well, because it prescribes in a legislative act what ought to be promulgated in a Constitutional Amendment.

The questions remain: as American citizens, should we have the right to take narcotics or other drugs? If we take drugs and conduct ourselves as responsible and law-abiding citizens, should we have a right to remain unmolested by the government? Lastly, if we take drugs and break the law, should we have a right to be treated as persons accused of crime, rather than as patients accused of mental illness?

These are fundamental questions that are conspicuous by their absence from all contemporary discussions of problems of drug addiction and drug abuse. The result is that instead of debating the use of drugs in moral and political terms, we define our task as the ostensibly narrow technical problem of protecting people from poisoning themselves with substances for whose use they cannot possibly assume responsibility. This, I think, best explains the frightening national consensus against personal responsibility for taking drugs and for one's conduct while under their influence. . . .

To me, unanimity on an issue as basic and complex as this means a complete evasion of the actual problem and an attempt to master it by attacking and overpowering a scapegoat— "dangerous drugs" and "drug abusers." There is an ominous resemblance between the unanimity with which all "reasonable' men—and especially politicians, physicians, and priests— formerly supported the protective measures of society against witches and Jews, and that with which they now support them against drug addicts and drug abusers.

After all is said and done, the issue comes down to whether we accept or reject the ethical principle John Stuart Mill so clearly enunciated: "The only purpose [he wrote in *On Liberty*] for which power can be rightfully exercised over any member of a civilized community, against his will, is to prevent harm to others. His own good, either physical or moral, is not a sufficient warrant. He cannot rightfully be compelled to do or forbear because it will make him happier, because in the opinions of others, to do so would be wise, or even right. . . . In the part [of his conduct] which merely concerns himself, his independence is, of right, absolute. Over himself, over his own body and mind, the individual is sovereign."

By recognizing the problem of drug abuse for what it is—a moral and political question rather than a medical or therapeutic one—we can choose to maximize the sphere of action of the state at the expense of the individual, or of the individual at the expense of the state. In other words, we could commit ourselves to the view that the state, the representative of many, is more important than the individual; that it therefore has the right, indeed the duty, to regulate the life of the individual in the best interests of the group. Or we could commit ourselves to the view that individual dignity and liberty are the supreme values of life, and that the foremost duty of the state is to protect and promote these values.

In short, we must choose between the ethic of collectivism and individualism, and pay the price of either—or of both.

Review Questions

1. What is the World Health Organization's definition of drug addiction? Why does Szasz think it involves moral judgments rather than medical ones?
2. According to Szasz, what is the propaganda used to justify the prohibition of drugs?
3. Explain Szasz's own view of drug addiction. How is it different from the disease model?
4. Why does Szasz think that the war on drugs is counterproductive? What would be the advantages of free trade in drugs?
5. According to Szasz, why should the freedom to self-medicate be a fundamental right? What are the limits of this right?
6. What are the two principle methods of legitimizing policy? Why doesn't Szasz accept these methods?
7. Explain Szasz's proposal for medical reformation.
8. How do Mill's principle and the Declaration of Independence support Szasz's position?

Discussion Questions

1. Szasz does not offer an explicit definition of drug addiction. How would he define it? Is there such a thing, in his view?
2. What would be the effects of legalizing drugs such as cocaine and heroin? Would there be more bad effects than good effects?
3. If drugs should be prohibited for teenagers, as Szasz says, then why shouldn't they be prohibited for adults?
4. Szasz claims that his proposal for medical reformation is analogous to the Protestant Reformation. Is this a good analogy? Why or why not?

Against Legalization of Drugs

JAMES Q. WILSON

James Q. Wilson is professor emeritus of management and public policy at the University of California, Los Angeles. He was the chairman of the National Advisory Council for Drug Abuse and Prevention in 1972–1973. He is the author or coauthor of 12 books, including *Thinking About Crime* (1985), *Moral Judgment* (1998), *The Moral Sense* (1997), and *The Marriage Problem* (2003).

Wilson replies to those who want to legalize drugs. He makes a case for keeping heroin and cocaine illegal. His main argument is that legalizing these addictive and dangerous drugs will have bad effects in our society, and these bad effects outweigh the costs of keeping them illegal. The bad effects of heroin and cocaine use that justify their illegality include high death rates for users and harm to children, spouses, employers, and others. In addition to his utilitarian argument, Wilson endorses a moral argument for making drugs such as cocaine illegal. Unlike nicotine, he says, cocaine use is immoral—it debases one's life and alters one's soul, and that is why it should be illegal.

IN 1972, THE PRESIDENT appointed me chairman of the National Advisory Council for Drug Abuse Prevention. Created by Congress, the Council was charged with providing guidance on how best to coordinate the national war on drugs. (Yes, we called it a war then, too.) In those days, the drug we were chiefly concerned with was heroin. When I took office, heroin use had been increasing dramatically. Everybody was worried that this increase would continue. Such phrases as "heroin epidemic" were commonplace.

That same year, the eminent economist Milton Friedman published an essay in *Newsweek* in which he called for legalizing heroin. His argument was on two grounds: as a matter of ethics, the government has no right to tell people not to use heroin (or to drink or to commit suicide); as a matter of economics, the prohibition of drug use imposes costs on society that far exceed

the benefits. Others, such as the psychoanalyst Thomas Szasz, made the same argument. . . .

That was 1972. Today, we have the same number of heroin addicts that we had then—half a million, give or take a few thousand. Having that many heroin addicts is no trivial matter; these people deserve our attention. But not having had an increase in that number for over fifteen years is also something that deserves our attention. What happened to the "heroin epidemic" that many people once thought would overwhelm us?

The facts are clear: a more or less stable pool of heroin addicts has been getting older, with relatively few new recruits. In 1976 the average age of heroin users who appeared in hospital emergency rooms was about twenty-seven; ten years later it was thirty-two. More than two-thirds of all heroin uses appearing in emergency rooms are now over the age of thirty. Back in the early 1970s, when heroin got onto the national political agenda, the typical heroin addict was much younger, often a teenager. . . .

Why did heroin lose its appeal for young people? When the young blacks in Harlem were asked why they stopped, more than half mentioned "trouble with the law" or "high cost" (and high cost is, of course, directly the result of law enforcement). Two-thirds said heroin hurt their health; nearly all said they had had a bad experience with it. We need not rely, however, simply on what they said. In New York City in 1973–75, the street price of heroin rose dramatically and its purity sharply declined, probably as a result of the heroin shortage caused by the success of the Turkish government in reducing the supply of opium base and of the French government in closing down heroin-producing laboratories located in and around Marseilles. These were short-lived gains for, just as Friedman predicted, alternative sources of supply—mostly in Mexico—quickly emerged. But the three-year heroin shortage interrupted the easy recruitment of new users.

Health and related problems were no doubt part of the reason for the reduced flow of recruits. Over the preceding years, Harlem youth had watched as more and more heroin users died of overdoses, were poisoned by adulterated doses, or acquired hepatitis from dirty needles. The word got around: heroin can kill you. By 1974 new hepatitis cases and drug-overdose deaths had dropped to a fraction of what they had been in 1970.

Alas, treatment did not seem to explain much of the cessation in drug use. Treatment programs can and do help heroin addicts, but treatment did not explain the drop in the number of *new* users (who by definition had never been in treatment) nor even much of the reduction in the number of experienced users.

No one knows how much of the decline to attribute to personal observation as opposed to high prices or reduced supply. But other evidence suggests strongly that price and supply played a large role. In 1972 the National Advisory Council was especially worried by the prospect that U.S. servicemen returning to this country from Vietnam would bring their heroin habits with them. Fortunately, a brilliant study by Lee Robins of Washington University in St. Louis put that

fear to rest. She measured drug use of Vietnam veterans shortly after they returned home. Though many had used heroin regularly while in Southeast Asia, most gave up the habit when back in the United States. The reason: here, heroin was less available and sanctions on its use were much more pronounced. . . .

RELIVING THE PAST

Suppose we had taken Friedman's advice in 1972. What would have happened? We cannot be entirely certain, but at a minimum we would have placed the young heroin addicts (and, above all, the prospective addicts) in a very different position from the one in which they actually found themselves. Heroin would have been legal. Its price would have been reduced by 95 percent (minus whatever we chose to recover in taxes.) Now that it could be sold by the same people who make aspirin, its quality would have been assured—no poisons, no adulterants. Sterile hypodermic needles would have been readily available at the neighborhood drugstore, probably at the same counter where heroin was sold. No need to travel to big cities or unfamiliar neighborhoods—heroin could have been purchased anywhere, perhaps by mail order.

There would no longer have been any financial or medical reason to avoid heroin use. Anybody could have afforded it. We might have tried to prevent children from buying it, but as we have learned from our efforts to prevent minors from buying alcohol and tobacco, young people have a way of penetrating markets theoretically reserved for adults. Returning Vietnam veterans would have discovered that Omaha and Raleigh had been converted into the pharmaceutical equivalent of Saigon.

Under these circumstances, can we doubt for a moment that heroin use would have grown exponentially? Or that a vastly larger supply of new users would have been recruited? . . .

But we need not rely on speculation, however plausible, that lowered prices and more abundant supplies would have increased heroin usage. Great Britain once followed such a policy and with almost exactly those results. Until the mid-1960s, British physicians were allowed to prescribe heroin to certain classes of addicts. (Possessing these drugs without a doctor's prescription remained a criminal offense.) For many years this policy worked well enough because the addict patients were typically middle-class people who had become dependent on opiate painkillers while undergoing hospital treatment. There was no drug culture. The British system worked for many years, not because it prevented drug abuse, but because there was no problem of drug abuse that would test the system.

All that changed in the 1960s. A few unscrupulous doctors began passing out heroin in wholesale amounts. One doctor prescribed almost 600,000 heroin tablets—that is, over thirteen pounds—in just one year. A youthful drug culture emerged with a demand for drugs far different from that of the older addicts. As a result, the British government required doctors to refer users to government-run clinics to receive their heroin.

But the shift to clinics did not curtail the growth in heroin use. Throughout the 1960s the number of addicts increased—the late John Kaplan of Stanford estimated by fivefold—in part as a result of the diversion of heroin from clinic patients to new users on the streets. An addict would bargain with the clinic doctor over how big a dose he would receive. The patient wanted as much as he could get, the doctor wanted to give as little as was needed. The patient had an advantage in this conflict because the doctor could not be certain how much was really needed. Many patients would use some of their "maintenance" dose and sell the remaining part to friends, thereby recruiting new addicts. As the clinics learned of this, they began to shift their treatment away from heroin and toward methadone, an addictive drug that, when taken orally, does not produce a "high" but will block the withdrawal pains associated with heroin abstinence.

Whether what happened in England in the 1960s was a mini-epidemic or an epidemic depends on whether one looks at numbers or at rates of change. Compared to the United States, the numbers were small. In 1960 there were 68 heroin addicts known to the British government; by 1968 there were 2,000 in treatment and many more who refused treatment. (They would refuse in part because they did not want to get methadone at a clinic if they could get heroin on the street.) Richard Hartnoll estimates that the actual number of addicts in England is five times the number officially registered. At a minimum, the number of British addicts increased by thirtyfold in ten years; the actual increase may have been much larger.

In the early 1980s the numbers began to rise again, and this time nobody doubted that a real epidemic was at hand. The increase was estimated to be 40 percent a year. By 1982 there were thought to be 20,000 heroin users in London alone. Geoffrey Pearson reports that many cities—Glasgow, Liverpool, Manchester, and Sheffield among them—were now experiencing a drug problem that once had been largely confined to London. The problem, again, was supply. The country was being flooded with cheap, high-quality heroin, first from Iran and then from Southeast Asia.

The United States began the 1960s with a much larger number of heroin addicts and probably a bigger at-risk population than was the case in Great Britain. Even though it would be foolhardy to suppose that the British system, if installed here, would have worked the same way or with the same results, it would be equally foolhardy to suppose that a combination of heroin available from leaky clinics and from street dealers who faced only minimal law-enforcement risks would not have produced a much greater increase in heroin use than we actually experienced. My guess is that if we had allowed either doctors or clinics to prescribe heroin, we would have had far worse results than were produced in Britain, if for no other reason than the vastly larger number of addicts with which we began. We would have had to find some way to police thousands (not scores) of physicians and hundreds (not dozens) of clinics. If the British civil service found it difficult to keep heroin in the hands of addicts and out of the hands of recruits when it was dealing with a few hundred people, how well would the American civil service have accomplished the same tasks when dealing with tens of thousands of people?

BACK TO THE FUTURE

Now cocaine, especially in its potent form, crack, is the focus of attention. Now as in 1972 the government is trying to reduce its use. Now as then some people are advocating legalization. Is there any more reason to yield to those arguments today than there was almost two decades ago?*

I think not. If we had yielded in 1972 we almost certainly would have had today a permanent population of several million, not several hundred thousand, heroin addicts. If we yield now we will have a far more serious problem with cocaine.

Crack is worse than heroin by almost any measure. Heroin produces a pleasant drowsiness and, if hygienically administered, has only the physical side effects of constipation and sexual impotence. Regular heroin use incapacitates many users, especially poor ones, for any productive work or social responsibility. They will sit nodding on a street corner, helpless but at least harmless. By contrast, regular cocaine use leaves the user neither helpless nor harmless. When smoked (as with crack) or injected, cocaine produces instant, intense, and short-lived euphoria. The experience generates a powerful desire to repeat it. If the drug is readily available, repeat use will occur. Those people who progress to "bingeing" on cocaine become devoted to the drug and its effects to the exclusion of almost all other considerations—job, family, children, sleep,

---

* I do not take up the question of marijuana. For a variety of reasons—its widespread use and its lesser tendency to addict—it presents a different problem from cocaine or heroin.

food, even sex. Dr. Frank Gawin at Yale and Dr. Everett Ellinwood at Duke report that a substantial percentage of all high-dose, binge users become uninhibited, impulsive, hypersexual, compulsive, irritable, and hyperactive. Their moods vacillate dramatically, leading at times to violence and homicide.

Women are much more likely to use crack than heroin, and if they are pregnant, the effects on their babies are tragic. Douglas Besharov, who has been following the effects of drugs on infants for twenty years, writes that nothing he learned about heroin prepared him for the devastation of cocaine. Cocaine harms the fetus and can lead to physical deformities or neurological damage. Some crack babies have for all practical purposes suffered a disabling stroke while still in the womb. The long-term consequences of this brain damage are lowered cognitive ability and the onset of mood disorders. Besharov estimates that about 30,000 to 50,000 such babies are born every year, about 7,000 in New York City alone. There may be ways to treat such infants, but from everything we now know treatment will be long, difficult, and expensive. Worse, the mothers who are most likely to produce crack babies are precisely the ones who, because of poverty or temperament, are least able and willing to obtain such treatment. In fact, anecdotal evidence suggest that crack mothers are likely to abuse their infants.

The notion that abusing drugs such as cocaine is a "victimless crime" is not only absurd but dangerous. Even ignoring the fetal drug syndrome, crack-dependent people are, like heroin addicts, individuals who regularly victimize their children by neglect, their spouses by improvidence, their employers by lethargy, and their coworkers by carelessness. Society is not and could never be a collection of autonomous individuals. We all have a stake in ensuring that each of us displays a minimal level of dignity, responsibility, and empathy. We cannot, of course, coerce people into goodness, but we can and should insist that some standards must be met if society itself—on which the very existence of the human personality depends—is to persist. Drawing the line that defines those standards is difficult and contentious, but if crack and heroin use do not fall below it, what does? . . .

It is possible that some people will not become heavy users even when the drug is readily available in its most potent form. So far there are no scientific grounds for predicting who will and who will not become dependent. Neither socio-economic background nor personality traits differentiate between casual and intensive users. Thus, the only way to settle the question of who is correct about the effect of easy availability of drug use, Nadelmann or Gawin and Ellinwood, is to try it and see. But that social experiment is so risky as to be no experiment at all, for if cocaine is legalized and if the rate of its abusive use increases dramatically, there is no way to put the genie back in the bottle, and it is not a kindly genie.

HAVE WE LOST?

Many people who agree that there are risks in legalizing cocaine or heroin still favor it because, they think, we have lost the war on drugs. "Nothing we have done has worked" and the current federal policy is just "more of the same." Whatever the costs of greater drug use, surely they would be less than the costs of our present, failed efforts.

That is exactly what I was told in 1972—and heroin is not quite as bad a drug as cocaine. We did not surrender and we did not lose. We did not win, either. What the nation accomplished then was what most efforts to save people from themselves can accomplish: the problem was contained and the number of victims minimized, all at a considerable cost in law enforcement and increased crime. Was the cost worth it? I think so, but many others may disagree. What are the lives of would-be addicts worth? I recall some people saying to me then, "Let them kill themselves." I was appalled. Happily, such views did not prevail.

Have we lost today? Not at all. High-rate cocaine use is not commonplace. The National Institute of Drug Abuse (NIDA) reports that less than 5 percent of high-school seniors used cocaine within the last thirty days. Of course this survey misses young people who have dropped out of school and miscounts those who lie on the questionnaire, but even if we inflate the NIDA estimate by some plausible percentage, it is still not much above 5 percent. Medical examiners reported in 1987 that about 1,500 died from cocaine use; hospital emergency rooms reported about 30,000 admissions related to cocaine abuse.

These are not small numbers, but neither are they evidence of a nationwide plague that threatens to engulf us all. Moreover, cities vary greatly in the proportion of people who are involved with cocaine. To get city-level data we need to turn to drug tests carried out on arrested persons, who obviously are more likely to be drug users than the average citizen. The National Institute of Justice, through its Drug Use Forecasting (DUF) project, collects urinalysis data on arrestees in 22 cities. As we have already seen, opiate (chiefly heroin) use has been flat or declining in most of these cities over the last decade. Cocaine use has gone up sharply, but with great variation among cities. New York, Philadelphia, and Washington, D.C., all report that two-thirds or more of their arrestees tested positive for cocaine, but in Portland, San Antonio, and Indianapolis the percentage was one-third less.

In some neighborhoods, of course, matters have reached crisis proportions. Gangs control the streets, shootings terrorize residents, and drug-dealing occurs in plain view. The police seem barely able to contain matters. But in these neighborhoods—unlike at Palo Alto cocktail parties—the people are not calling for legalization, they are calling for help. And often not much help has come. Many cities are willing to do almost anything about the drug problem except spend more money on it. The federal government cannot change that; only local voters and politicians can. It is not clear that they will.

It took ten years to contain heroin. We have had experience with crack for only about three or four years. Each year we spend perhaps

$11 billion on law enforcement (and some of that goes to deal with marijuana) and perhaps $2 billion on treatment. Large sums, but not sums that should lead anyone to say, "We just can't afford this any more."

The illegality of drugs increases crime, partly because some users turn to crime to pay for their habits, partly because some users are stimulated by certain drugs (such as crack or PCP) to act more violently or ruthlessly than they otherwise would, and partly because criminal organizations seeking to control drug supplies use force to manage their markets. These also are serious costs, but no one knows how much they would be reduced if drugs were legalized. Addicts would no longer steal to pay black-market prices for drugs, a real gain. But some, perhaps a great deal, of that gain would be offset by the great increase in the number of addicts. These people, nodding on heroin or living in the delusion-ridden high of cocaine, would hardly be ideal employees. Many would steal simply to support themselves, since snatch- and-grab, opportunistic crime can be managed even by people unable to hold a regular job or plan an elaborate crime. Those British addicts who get their supplies from government clinics are not models of law-abiding decency. Most are in crime, and though their per-capita rate of criminality may be lower thanks to the cheapness of their drugs, the total volume of crime they produce may be quite large. Of course, society could decide to support all unemployable addicts on welfare, but that would mean that gains from lowered rates of crime would have to be offset by large increases in welfare budgets.

Proponents of legalization claim that the costs of having more addicts around would be largely if not entirely offset by having more money available with which to treat and care for them. The money would come from the taxes levied on the sale of heroin and cocaine.

To obtain this fiscal dividend, however, legalization's supporters must first solve an economic dilemma. If they want to raise a lot of money to pay for welfare and treatment, the tax rate on the drugs will have to be quite high. Even if they themselves do not want a high tax rate, the politicians' love of "sin taxes" would probably guarantee that it would be high anyway. But the higher the tax, the higher the price of the drug, and the higher the price the greater the likelihood that addicts will turn to crime to find the money for it and that criminal organizations will be formed to sell tax-free drugs at below-market rates. If we managed to keep taxes (and thus prices) low, we would get that much less money to pay for welfare and treatment and more people could afford to become addicts. There may be an optimal tax rate for drugs that maximizes revenue while minimizing crime, bootlegging, and the recruitment of new addicts, but our experience with alcohol does not suggest that we know how to find it.

THE BENEFITS OF ILLEGALITY

The advocates of legalization find nothing to be said in favor of the current system except, possibly, that it keeps the number of addicts smaller than it would otherwise be. In fact, the benefits are more substantial than that.

First, treatment. All the talk about providing "treatment on demand" implies that there is a demand for treatment. That is not quite right. There are some drug-dependent people who genuinely want treatment and will remain in it if offered; they should receive it. But there are far more who want only short-term help after a bad crash; once stabilized and bathed, they are back on the street again, hustling. And even many of the addicts who enroll in a program honestly wanting help drop out after a short while when they discover that help takes time and commitment. Drug-dependent people have very short time horizons and a weak capacity for commitment. These two groups—those looking for a quick fix and those unable to stick with a longterm fix—are not easily helped. Even if we increase the number of treatment slots—as we should—we would have to do something to make treatment more effective.

One thing that can often make it more effective is compulsion. Douglas Anglin of UCLA, in common with many other researchers, has found that the longer one stays in a treatment program, the better the chances of a reduction in drug dependency. But he, again like most other researchers, has found that drop-out rates are high. He has also found, however, that patients who enter treatment under legal compulsion stay in the program longer than those not subject to such pressure. His research on the California civil-commitment program, for example, found that heroin users involved with its required drug-testing program had over the long term a lower rate of heroin use than similar addicts who were free from such constraints. If for many addicts compulsion is a useful component of treatment, it is not clear how compulsion could be achieved in a society where purchasing, possessing, and using the drug were legal. It could be managed, I suppose, but I would not want to have to answer the challenge from the American Civil Liberties Union that it is wrong to compel a person to undergo treatment for consuming a legal commodity.

Next, education. We are now investing substantially in drug-education programs in the schools. Though we do not yet know for certain what will work, there are some promising leads. But I wonder how credible such programs would be if they were aimed at dissuading children from doing something perfectly legal. We could, of course, treat drug education like smoking education: inhaling crack and inhaling tobacco are both legal, but you should not do it because it is bad for you. That tobacco is bad for you is easily shown; the Surgeon General has seen to that. But what do we say about crack? It is pleasurable, but devoting yourself to so much pleasure is not a good idea (though perfectly legal)? Unlike tobacco, cocaine will not give you cancer or emphysema, but it will lead you to neglect your duties to family, job, and neighborhood? Everybody is doing cocaine, but you should not?

Again, it might be possible under a legalized regime to have effective drug-prevention programs, but their effectiveness would depend heavily, I think, on first having decided that cocaine use, like tobacco use, is purely a matter of practical consequences; no fundamental moral significance attaches to either. But if we believe—as I do—that dependency on certain mind-altering drugs *is* a moral issue and their illegality rests in part on their immorality, then legalizing them undercuts, if it does not eliminate altogether, the moral message.

That message is at the root of the distinction we now make between nicotine and cocaine. Both are highly addictive; both have harmful physical effects. But we treat the two drugs differently, not simply because nicotine is so widely used as to be beyond the reach of effective prohibition, but because it does not destroy the user's essential humanity. Tobacco shortens one's life, cocaine debases it. Nicotine alters one's habits, cocaine alters one's soul. The heavy use of crack, unlike the heavy use of tobacco, corrodes those natural sentiments of sympathy and duty that constitute our human nature and make possible our social life. To say, as does Nadelmann, that distinguishing morally between tobacco and cocaine is "little more than a transient prejudice" is close to saying that morality itself is but a prejudice.

THE ALCOHOL PROBLEM

Now we have arrived where many arguments about legalizing drugs begin: is there any reason to treat heroin and cocaine differently from the way we treat alcohol?

There is no easy answer to that question because, as with so many human problems, one cannot decide simply on the basis either of moral principles or of individual consequences; one has to temper any policy by a common-sense judgment of what is possible. Alcohol, like heroin, cocaine, PCP, and marijuana, is a drug—that is, a mood-altering substance—and consumed to excess it certainly has harmful consequences: auto accidents, barroom fights, bedroom shootings. It is also, for some people, addictive. We cannot confidently compare the addictive powers of these drugs, but the best evidence suggests that crack and heroin are much more addictive than alcohol.

Many people, Nadelmann included, argue that since the health and financial costs of alcohol abuse are so much higher than those of cocaine and heroin abuse, it is hypocritical folly to devote our efforts to preventing cocaine and drug use. But as Mark Kleiman of Harvard has pointed out, this comparison is quite misleading. What Nadelmann is doing is showing that a *legalized* drug (alcohol) produces greater social harm than *illegal* ones (cocaine and heroin). But of course. Suppose that in the 1920s we had made heroin and cocaine legal and alcohol illegal. Can anyone doubt that Nadelmann would now be writing that it is folly to continue our ban on alcohol because cocaine and heroin are so much more harmful?

And let there be no doubt about it—widespread heroin and cocaine use are associated with all manner of ills. Thomas Bewley found that the mortality rate of British heroin addicts in 1968 was 28 times as high as the death rate of the same age group of non-addicts, even though in England at the time an addict could obtain free or low-cost heroin and clean needles from British clinics. Perform the following mental experiment: suppose we legalize heroin and cocaine in this country. In what proportion of auto fatalities would the state police report that the driver was nodding off on heroin or recklessly driving on a coke high? In what proportion of spouse-assault and child-abuse cases would the local police report that crack was involved? In what proportion of industrial accidents would safety investigators report that the forklift or drillpress operator was in a drug-induced stupor or frenzy? We do not know exactly what the proportion would be, but anyone who asserts that it would not be much higher than it is now would have to believe that these drugs have little appeal except when they are illegal. And that is nonsense.

An advocate of legalization might concede that social harm—perhaps harm equivalent to

that already produced by alcohol—would follow from making cocaine and heroin generally available. But at least, he might add, we would have the problem "out in the open" where it could be treated as a matter of "public health." That is well and good, *if* we knew how to treat—that is, cure—heroin and cocaine abuse. But we do not know how to do it for all the people who would need such help. We are having only limited success in coping with chronic alcoholics. Addictive behavior is immensely difficult to change, and the best methods for changing it—living in drug-free therapeutic communities, becoming faithful members of Alcoholics Anonymous or Narcotics Anonymous—require great personal commitment, a quality that is, alas, in short supply among the very persons—young people, disadvantaged people—who are often most at risk for addiction.

Suppose that today we had, not 15 million alcohol abusers, but half a million. Suppose that we already knew that we have learned from our long experience with the widespread use of alcohol. Would we make whiskey legal? I do not know, but I suspect there would a lively debate. The Surgeon General would remind us of the risks alcohol poses to pregnant women. The National Highway Traffic Safety Administration would point out the likelihood of more highway fatalities caused by drunk drivers. The Food and Drug Administration might find that there is a nontrivial increase in cancer associated with alcohol consumption. At the same time the police would report great difficulties in keeping illegal whiskey out of our cities, officers being corrupted by bootleggers, and alcohol addicts often resorting to crime to feed their habits. Libertarians, for their part, would argue that every citizen has the right to drink anything he wishes and that drinking is, in any event, a "victimless crime."

However the debate might turn out, the central fact would be that the problem was still, at that point, a small one. The government cannot legislate away the addictive tendencies in all of us, nor can it remove completely even the most dangerous addictive substances. But it can cope with harms when the harms are still manageable.

SCIENCE AND ADDICTION

One advantage of containing a problem while it is still containable is that it buys time for science to learn more about it and perhaps discover a cure. Almost unnoticed in the current debate over legalizing drugs is that basic science has made rapid strides in identifying the underlying neurological processes involved in some forms of addiction. Stimulants such as cocaine and amphetamines alter the way certain brain cells communicate with one another. That alteration is complex and not entirely understood, but in simplified form it involves modifying the way in which a neurotransmitter called dopamine sends signals from one cell to another.

When dopamine crosses the synapse between two cells, it is in effect carrying a message from the first cell to activate the second one. In certain parts of the brain that message is experienced as pleasure. After the message is delivered, the dopamine returns to the first cell. Cocaine apparently blocks this return, or "reuptake," so that the excited cell and others nearby continue to send pleasure messages. When the exaggerated high produced by cocaine-influenced dopamine finally ends, the brain cells may (in ways that are still a matter of dispute) suffer from an extreme lack of dopamine, thereby making the individual unable to experience any pleasure at all. This would explain why cocaine users often feel so depressed after enjoying the drug. Stimulants may also affect the way in which other neurotransmitters, such as serotonin and noradrenaline, operate.

Whatever the exact mechanism may be, once it is identified it becomes possible to use drugs to block either the effect of cocaine or its tendency to produce dependency. There have already been experiments using desipramine, imipramine, bromocriptine, carbamazepine, and other chemicals. There are some promising results.

Tragically, we spend very little on such research, and the agencies funding it have not in the past occupied very influential or visible posts in the federal bureaucracy. If there is one aspect of the "war on drugs" metaphor that I dislike, it is the tendency to focus attention almost exclusively on the troops in the trenches, whether engaged in enforcement or treatment, and away from the research-and-development efforts back on the home front where the war may ultimately be decided.

I believe that the prospects of scientists in controlling addiction will be strongly influenced by the size and character of the problem they face. If the problem is a few hundred thousand chronic high-dose users of an illegal product, the chances of making a difference at a reasonable cost will be much greater than if the problem is a few million chronic users of legal substances. Once a drug is legal, not only will its use increase but many of those who then use it will prefer the drug to the treatment: they will want the pleasure, whatever the cost to themselves or their families, and they will resist—probably successfully—any efforts to wean them away from experiencing the high that comes from inhaling a legal substance.

Review Questions

1. What are Milton Friedman's arguments for legalizing heroin?
2. According to Wilson, why did the number of new users of heroin decrease from 1970 to 1974?
3. If heroin had been legalized in 1972, what would have happened, in Wilson's view?
4. Why does Wilson think that crack cocaine is worse than heroin?
5. What is Wilson's view of the war on drugs?
6. According to Wilson, why should drug treatment be compulsory?

7. Explain Wilson's distinction between nicotine and cocaine.
8. What is Nadelmann's argument about alcohol abuse? How does Wilson reply?

Discussion Questions

1. Wilson does not discuss marijuana, but do his arguments show that it should be illegal, too? Why or why not?
2. Wilson notes that making drugs illegal increases crime and costs $11 billion a year for law enforcement. Do the costs of making drugs illegal outweigh the benefits? Explain your position.
3. Wilson argues that drug use should be illegal because it is immoral. Is this a good argument? Why or why not?

Addiction and Drug Policy

DANIEL SHAPIRO

Daniel Shapiro is associate professor of philosophy at West Virginia University. He has published more than 22 articles. His home page is at www.as.wvu.edu/phil/dshapiro_long.html.

Shapiro attacks the standard view that drugs such as cocaine and heroin are addictive because of their pharmacology, that is, because of their chemical composition and the effects they have on the brain. The standard view fails to explain why most illegal drug users do not become addicts. Furthermore, the standard view's explanation of addiction in terms of cravings, tolerance, and withdrawal symptoms is defective. Shapiro proposes an alternative view, which explains drug addiction in terms of the individual's mindset and social or cultural setting rather than pharmacology. He argues that the fact that cigarette smokers have a hard time quitting supports his alternative view. He concludes that his argument undercuts the worry of Wilson and others that legalizing cocaine and heroin would produce an explosion of addiction. In an Addendum, Shapiro argues that even if the legalization of cocaine and heroin made addiction to these drugs as common as cigarette addiction, this would only be a new health problem. It would not ruin people's lives.

MOST PEOPLE THINK that illegal drugs, such as cocaine and heroin, are highly addictive. Usually, their addictiveness is explained by pharma-

Source: Daniel Shapiro, "Addiction and Drug Policy" in John Arthur, ed., *Morality and Moral Controversies*, 7th ed, Prentice-Hall, 2004. By permission of the author. Copyright 1998.

cology: their chemical composition and its effects on the brain are such that, after a while, it's hard to stop using them. This view of drug addiction—I call it the standard view—underlies most opposition to legalizing cocaine and heroin. James Q. Wilson's (1990) arguments are typical: Legalization increases access, and increased access to addictive drugs increases addiction. The standard view also underlies the increasingly popular opinion, given a philosophical defense by Robert Goodin (1989), that cigarette smokers are addicts in the grip of a powerful drug.

However, the standard view is false: Pharmacology, I shall argue, does not by itself do much to explain drug addiction. I will offer a different explanation of drug addiction, and discuss its implications for the debate about drug legalization.

PROBLEMS WITH
THE STANDARD VIEW

We label someone as a drug addict because of his behavior. A drug addict uses drugs repeatedly, compulsively, wants to stop or cut back on his use but finds it's difficult to do so; at its worst, drug addiction dominates or crowds out other activities and concerns. The standard view attempts to explain this compulsive behavior by the drug's effects on the brain. Repeated use of an addictive drug induces cravings, and the user comes to need a substantial amount to get the effect she wants, i.e., develops tolerance. If the user tries to stop, she then suffers very disagreeable effects, called withdrawal symptoms. (For more details on the standard view, see *American Psychiatric Association,* 1994: 176–81.)

Cravings, tolerance, and withdrawal symptoms: Do these explain drug addiction? A craving or strong desire to do something doesn't *make* one do something: One can act on a desire *or* ignore it *or* attempt to extinguish it. Tolerance explains why the user increases her intake to get the effect she wants, but that doesn't explain why she would find it difficult to *stop wanting* this effect. Thus the key idea in the standard view is really withdrawal symptoms, because that is needed to explain the difficulty in extinguishing the desire to take the drug or to stop wanting the effects the drug produces. However, for this explanation to work, these symptoms have to be really bad, for if they aren't, why not just put up with them as a small price to pay for getting free of the drug? However, with-

drawal symptoms aren't *that* bad. Heroin is considered terribly addictive, yet pharmacologists describe its withdrawal symptoms as like having a bad flu for about a week: Typical withdrawal symptoms include fever, diarrhea, sneezing, muscle cramps, and vomiting (Kaplan 1983: 15, 19, 35). While a bad flu is quite unpleasant, it's not so bad that one has little choice but to take heroin rather than experience it. Indeed, most withdrawal symptoms for any drug cease within a few weeks, yet most heavy users who relapse do so after that period and few drug addicts report withdrawal symptoms as the reason for their relapse (Peele 1985: 19–20, 67, Schacter 1982: 436–44, Waldorf 1991:241).

Thus cravings, tolerance, and withdrawal symptoms cannot explain addiction. An additional problem for the standard view is that most drug users, whether they use legal or illegal drugs, do not become addicts, and few addicts remain so permanently. (Cigarette smokers are a partial exception, which I discuss later.) Anonymous surveys of drug users by the Substance Abuse and Mental Health Services Administration indicate that less than 10 percent of those who have tried powder cocaine use it monthly (National Household Survey of Drug Abuse 2001: tables H1 and H2). Furthermore, most monthly users are not addicts; a survey of young adults, for example, (Johnston, for the National Institute on Drug Abuse, 1996: 84–85) found that less than 10 percent of monthly cocaine users used it daily. (Even a daily user need not be an addict; someone who drinks daily is not thereby an alcoholic.) The figures are not appreciably different for crack cocaine (Erickson 1994: 167–74, 231–32, Morgan and Zimmer, 1997: 142–44) and only slightly higher for heroin (Husak 1992: 125, Sullum 2003: 228). These surveys have been confirmed by longitudinal studies—studies of a set of users over time—which indicate that moderate and/or controlled use of these drugs is the norm, not the exception, and that even heavy users do not inevitably march to addiction, let alone remain permanent addicts (Waldorf 1991, Erickson 1994,

Zinberg 1984: 111–34, 152–71). The standard view has to explain the preeminence of controlled use by arguing that drug laws reduce access to illegal drugs. However, I argue below that even with easy access to drugs most people use them responsibly, and so something other than the law and pharmacology must explain patterns of drug use.

AN ALTERNATIVE VIEW

I will defend a view of addiction summed up by Norman Zinberg's book, *Drug, Set, and Setting* (1984) "Drug" means pharmacology, "set" means the individual's mindset, his personality, values, and expectations, and "setting" means the cultural or social surroundings of drug use. This should sound like common sense. Humans are interpretive animals and so what results from drug use depends not just on the experience or effects produced by the drug but *also* on the interpretation of that experience or effects. And how one interprets or understands the experience depends on one's individuality and the cultural or social setting.

I begin with setting. Hospital patients that get continuous and massive doses of narcotics rarely get addicted or crave the drugs after release from the hospital (Peele 1985: 17, Falk 1996: 9). The quantity and duration of their drug use pales in significance compared with the setting of their drug consumption: subsequent ill effects from the drug are rarely interpreted in terms of addiction. A study of Vietnam veterans, the largest study of untreated heroin users ever conducted, provides more dramatic evidence of the role of setting. Three-quarters of Vietnam vets who used heroin in Vietnam became addicted, but after coming home, only half of heroin users in Vietnam continued to use and of those only 12 percent were addicts (Robins, 1980). Wilson also mentions this study, and says that the change was because heroin is illegal in the United States (1990: 22), and while this undoubtedly played a role, so did the difference in social setting: Vietnam, with its absence of

work and family, as well as loneliness and fear of death, helped to promote acceptance of heavy drug use.

Along the same lines, consider the effects of alcohol in different cultures. In Finland, for example, violence and alcohol are linked, for sometimes heavy drinkers end up in fights; in Greece, Italy, and other Mediterranean countries, however, where almost all drinking is moderate and controlled, there is no violence–alcohol link (Peele, 1985: 25). Why the differences? Humans are social or cultural animals, not just products of their biochemistry, and this means, in part, that social norms or rules play a significant role in influencing behavior. In cultures where potentially intoxicating drugs such as alcohol are viewed as supplements or accompaniments to life, moderate and controlled use will be the norm—hence even though Mediterranean cultures typically consume large amounts of alcohol, there is little alcoholism— while in cultures where alcohol is also viewed as a way of escaping one's problems, alcoholism will be more prevalent, which may explain the problem in Finland, and some other Scandinavian cultures. In addition to cultural influences, most people learn to use alcohol responsibly by observing their parents. They see their parents drink at a ballgame or to celebrate special occasions, or with food at a meal, but rarely on an empty stomach; they learn it's wrong to be drunk at work, to drink and drive; they learn that uncontrolled behavior with alcohol is generally frowned upon; they absorb certain norms and values such as "know your limit," "don't drink alone", "don't drink in the morning" and so forth. They learn about rituals that reinforce moderation, such as the phrase "let's have a drink." These informal rules and rituals teach most people how to use alcohol responsibly (Zinberg 1987: 258–62).

While social controls are harder to develop with illicit drugs—accurate information is pretty scarce, and parents feel uncomfortable teaching their children about controlled use—even here sanctions and rituals promoting moderate use exist. For example, in a study of an 11-year follow-up of an informal network of middle-class cocaine users largely connected through ties of friendship, and most of whom were moderate users, the authors concluded that:

> Rather than cocaine overpowering user concerns with family, health, and career, we found that the high value most of our users placed upon family, health, and career achievement . . . mitigated against abuse and addiction. Such group norms and the informal social controls that seemed to stem from them (e.g., expressions of concern, warning about risks, the use of pejorative names like 'coke hog', refusal to share with abusers) mediated the force of pharmacological, physiological, and psychological factors which can lead to addiction. (Murphy 1989: 435).

Even many heavy cocaine users are able to prevent their use from becoming out of control (or out of control for significant periods of time) by regulating the time and circumstances of use (not during work, never too late at night, limit use on weekdays), using with friends rather than alone, employing fixed rules (paying bills before spending money on cocaine), etc. (Waldorf 1991).

Unsurprisingly, these studies of controlled cocaine use generally focus on middle-class users: Their income and the psychological support of friends and family put them at less of a risk of ruining their lives by drug use than those with little income or hope (Peele, 1991: 159–60).

I now examine the effects of set on drug use, that is the effect of expectations, personality, and values. Expectations are important because drug use occurs in a pattern of ongoing activity, and one's interpretation of the drug's effects depends upon expectations of how those effects will fit into or alter those activities. Expectations explain the well-known placebo effect: If people consume something they mistakenly believe will stop or alleviate their pain it often does. Along the same lines, in experiments with American college-age men, aggression and sexual arousal increased when these men were told they were drinking liquor, even though they were drinking

zero percent proof, while when drinking liquor and told they are not, they acted normally (Peele 1985: 17). The role of expectations also explains why many users of heroin, cocaine, and other psychoactive drugs do not like or even recognize the effects when they first take it, and have to be taught to or learn how to appreciate the effects (Peele 1985: 13–14, Waldorf, 1991: 264, Zinberg 1984: 117). The importance of expectations means that those users who view the drug as overpowering them will tend to find their lives dominated by the drug, while those who view it as an enhancement or a complement to certain experiences or activities will tend not to let drugs dominate or overpower their other interests (Peele 1991: 156–58, 169–70).

As for the individual's personality and values, the predictions of common sense are pretty much accurate. Psychologically healthy people are likely to engage in controlled, moderate drug use, or if they find themselves progressing to uncontrolled use, they tend to cut back. On the other hand, drug addicts of all kinds tend to have more psychological problems before they started using illicit drugs (Peele, 1991: 153–54, 157, Zinberg 1984: 74–76.) People who are motivated to control their own lives will tend to make drug use an accompaniment or an ingredient in their lives, not the dominant factor. Those who place a high value on responsibility, work, family, productivity, etc., will tend to fit drug use into their lives, rather than letting it run their lives (Waldorf: 1991: 267, Peele 1991: 160–66). That's why drug use of all kinds, licit or illicit, tends to taper off with age: Keeping a job, raising a family, and so forth leave limited time or motivation for uncontrolled or near-continuous drug use (Peele, 1985: 15). And it's why it's not uncommon for addicts to explain their addiction by saying that they drifted into the addict's life; with little to compete with their drug use, or lacking motivation to substitute other activities or interests, drug use comes to dominate their lives (DeGrandpre 1996: 44–46). Those with richer lives, or who are motivated on an individual and/or cultural level to get richer lives, are less likely to succumb to addiction.

To summarize: Even with easy access to intoxicating drugs, most drug users don't become addicts, or if they do, don't remain addicts for that long, because most people have and are motivated to find better things to do with their lives. These better things result from their individual personality and values and their social or cultural setting.

CIGARETTE SMOKING AND THE ROLE OF PHARMACOLOGY

I've discussed how set and setting influence drug use, but where does pharmacology fit in? Its role is revealed by examining why it is much harder to stop smoking cigarettes—only half of smokers that try to stop smoking succeed in quitting—than to stop using other substances. (For more detail in what follows, see Shapiro 1994, and the references cited therein).

Smokers smoke to relax, to concentrate, to handle anxiety, stress and difficult interpersonal situations, as a way of taking a break during the day, as a social lubricant, as a means of oral gratification—and this is a partial list. Since smoking is a means to or part of so many activities, situations, and moods, stopping smoking is a major life change and major life changes do not come easily. Part of the reason smoking is so integrated into people's lives is pharmacological. Nicotine's effects on the brain are mild and subtle: it doesn't disrupt your life. While addicts or heavy users of other drugs such as cocaine, heroin, or alcohol *also* use their drugs as a means to or part of a variety of activities, situations, and moods, most users of these drugs are not lifelong addicts or heavy users, because these drugs are not so mild, and heavy use has a stronger tendency over time to disrupt people's lives.

The pharmacology of smoking, however, cannot be separated from its social setting. Smoking doesn't disrupt people's lives in part because it is legal. Even with increasing regulations, smokers still can smoke in a variety of sit-uations (driving, walking on public streets, etc.) where one cannot use illegal drugs except in a furtive and secretive manner. Furthermore, the mild effects of nicotine are due to its mild potency—smokers can carefully control their nicotine intake, getting small doses throughout the day—and its mild potency is due partly to smoking being legal. Legal drugs tend to have milder potencies than illegal ones for two reasons. First, illegal markets create incentives for stronger potencies, as sellers will favor concentrated forms of a drug that can be easily concealed and give a big bang for the buck. Second, in legal markets different potencies of the same drug openly compete, and over time the weaker ones come to be preferred—consider the popularity of low tar/nicotine cigarettes and wine and beer over hard liquor.

Thus pharmacology and setting interact: Smoking is well-integrated into people's lives because the nicotine in cigarettes has mild pharmacological effects and because smoking is legal, and nicotine has those mild effects in part because smoking is legal. Pharmacology also interacts with what I've been calling set. The harms of smoking are slow to occur, are cumulative, and largely affect one's health, not one's ability to perform normal activities (at least prior to getting seriously ill). Furthermore, to eliminate these harms requires complete smoking cessation; cutting back rarely suffices (even light smokers increase their chances of getting lung cancer, emphysema, and heart disease). Thus, quitting smoking requires strong motivation, since its bad effects are not immediate, and it does not disrupt one's life. Add to this what I noted earlier, that stopping smoking means changing one's life, and it's unsurprising that many find it difficult to stop.

Thus, it is a mistake to argue, as Goodin did, that the difficulty in quitting is mainly explicable by the effects of nicotine. Smokers are addicted to smoking, an *activity,* and their being addicted to it is not reducible to their being addicted to a *drug.* If my explanation of the relative difficulty of quitting smoking is correct, then the standard view of an addictive drug is quite suspect. That view suggests that knowledge of a drug's pharmacology provides a basis for making reasonable predictions about a drug's addictiveness. However, understanding nicotine's effects upon the brain (which is what Goodin stressed in his explanation of smokers' addiction) does not tell us that it's hard to stop smoking; we only know that once we add information about set and setting. Generalizing from the case of smoking, all we can say is:

> The milder the effects upon the brain, the easier for adults to purchase, the more easily integrated into one's life, and the more the bad effects are cumulative, slow-acting and only reversible upon complete cessation, the more addictive the drug.

Besides, however, being a mouthful, this understanding of drug addiction requires introducing the *interaction* of set and setting with pharmacology to explain the addictiveness potential of various drugs. It is simpler and less misleading to say that people tend to *addict themselves* to various substances (and activities), this tendency varying with various cultural and individual influences.

CONCLUSION

My argument undercuts the worry that legalizing cocaine and heroin will produce an explosion of addiction because people will have access to inherently and powerfully addictive drugs. The standard view that cocaine and heroin are inherently addictive is false, because no drug is *inherently* addictive. The desire of most people to lead responsible and productive lives, in a social setting that rewards such desires, is what controls and limits most drug use. Ironically, if cocaine and heroin in a legal market would be as disruptive as many drug prohibitionists fear, then that is an excellent reason why addiction would not explode under legalization—drug use that tends to thrive is drug use that is woven into, rather than disrupts, responsible people's lives.

ADDENDUM

After I wrote this article, some of my students raised the following objection. I argue that drug addiction that disrupts people's lives would not thrive under legalization, because most people's desire and ability to lead responsible lives would break or prevent such addiction. However, suppose that legalization of cocaine and heroin makes the use of those drugs similar to the use of cigarettes—small, mild doses throughout the day, which are well integrated into people's lives. If legalization brings it about that those who addict themselves to these drugs are like those who addict themselves to smoking—their addiction does not disrupt their lives, but is integrated into it—wouldn't that mean that addiction to these drugs would become as prevalent as cigarette addiction?

It is possible that legalizing heroin and cocaine would make its use similar to the current use of cigarettes. However, if this happened, the main worry about heroin and cocaine addiction would be gone. We would not have a problem of a large increase in the number of people throwing away or messing up their lives. At worst, if legalizing cocaine and heroin produced as bad health effects as cigarette smoking does (which is dubious—see Carwath and Smith 2002: 137–39, and Morgan and Zimmer, 1997: 131, 136, 141), then we would have a new heath problem. Of course, someone might argue that one should not legalize a drug which could worsen the health of a significant percentage of its users, even if that use does not mess up most of its users' lives. It is beyond the scope of this paper to evaluate such arguments (however, see Shapiro, 1994), but notice that the implications of my paper cut against the claim that these health risks were not voluntarily incurred. Since one's drug use partly depends on one's values and personality, then to the extent one can be said to be responsible for the choices influenced by one's values and personality, then to that extent those who addict themselves to a certain drug can be said to have voluntarily incurred the risks involved in that drug use.

References

American Psychiatric Association. (1994) *Diagnostic and Statistical Manual of Mental Disorders.* (4th ed)., Washington, D.C.: Author.

Carnwath, T. and I. Smith. (2002) *Heroin Century.* London: Routledge.

DeGrandpre R. and E. White. (1996). "Drugs: In Care of the Self," *Common Knowledge,* 3:27–48.

Erickson, P., E. Edward, R. Smart, and G. Murray. (1994) *The Steel Drug: Crack and Cocaine in Perspective.* (2nd ed.). New York: MacMillan.

Falk, J. (1996). "Environmental Factors in the Instigation and Maintenance of Drug Abuse," in *Drug Policy and Human Nature,* ed. W. Bickel and R. DeGrandpre. New York: Plenum Press.

Goodin, R. (1989). "The Ethics of Smoking," *Ethics* 99:574–624.

Husak, D. (1992). *Drugs and Rights.* New York: Cambridge University Press.

Johnston, L. D., P. M. O'Malley, and J. G. Bachman. (1996). *Monitoring the Future Study, 1975–1994: National Survey Results on Drug Use. Volume II: College Students and Young Adults.* Rockville, MD: National Institute on Drug Abuse.

Kaplan, J. (1983). *The Hardest Drug: Heroin and Public Policy.* Chicago: University of Chicago Press.

Morgan, J. and L. Zimmerman. (1997). "The Social Pharmacology of Smokeable Cocaine: Not All It's Cracked Up to Be," in *Crack in America: Demon Drugs and Social Justice.* ed. C. Reinarman and H. Levine. Berkeley: California University Press.

Murphy, S., C. Reinarman, and D. Waldorf. (1989). "An 11 Year Follow-Up of a Network of Cocaine Users," *British Journal of Addiction* 84:427–36.

Peele, S. (1985). *The Meaning of Addiction: Compulsive Experience and Its Interpretation.* Lexington, MA: D.C. Heath and Company.

Peele, S. (1991). *The Diseasing of America: Addiction Treatment Out of Control.* Boston: Houghton Mifflin Company.

Robins, L., J. Helzer, M. Hesselbrock, and E. Wish. (1980). "Vietnam Veterans Three Years After Vietnam: How Our Study Changed Our View of Heroin," in *The Yearbook of Substance Use and Abuse.* (Vol. 2), ed. L. Brill and C. Winick. New York: Human Sciences Press.

Schacter, S. (1982). "Recidivism and Self-Cure of Smoking and Obesity," *American Psychologist* 37: 436–44.

Shapiro, D. (1994). "Smoking Tobacco: Irrationality, Addiction and Paternalism," *Public Affairs Quarterly* 8:187–203.

Substance Abuse and Mental Health Services Administration. (2002). *Tables From The 2001 National Household Survey on Drug Abuse.* Department of Health and Human Services, http://www.samhsa.gov/oas/NHSDA/2k1NHSDA/vol2/appendixh_1.htm

Sullum, J. (2003). *Saying Yes: In Defense of Drug Use.* Tarcher/Putnam, New York.

Waldorf, D., C. Reinarman, and S. Murphy. (1991). *Cocaine Changes: The Experience of Using and Quitting.* Philadelphia: Temple University Press.

Wilson, J. (1990). "Against the Legalization of Drugs," *Commentary.* 89:21–28.

Zinberg, N. (1984) *Drug, Set, and Setting.* Yale University Press, New Haven.

Zinberg, N. (1987) "The Use and Misuse of Intoxicants," in *Dealing With Drugs.* ed. R. Hamowy, Lexington: D.C. Health and Company.

Review Questions

1. What is the standard view of drug addiction, as Shapiro calls it?
2. According to Shapiro, what are the problems with the standard view?
3. Explain Shapiro's alternative account of drug addiction, including the concepts of drug, set, and setting.

4. What causes addiction, in Shapiro's view?
5. Shapiro notes that only half of smokers who try to stop succeed in quitting. Why does he think that this fact supports his view of addiction?
6. How does Shapiro reply to the objection that legalizing cocaine and heroin would increase the number of people addicted to these drugs?

Discussion Questions

1. How would Wilson reply to Shapiro? Can the standard view be defended?
2. Suppose that Shaprio's account of addiction is true. Does it follow that cocaine and heroin should be legalized? Why or why not?
3. Should drugs like nicotine and alcohol that produce health problems be legal? Explain your position.

Problem Cases

1. Motorcycle Helmets

According to the National Highway Traffic Safety Administration (NHTSA), www.nhtsa.dot.gov, 27 states allow adults to ride on a motorcycle with no helmet. Many of these states require persons under age 18 to wear helmets. Three states have no helmet laws at all. Currently 19 states, the District of Columbia, and Puerto Rico require all motorcycle operators and passengers to use helmets. The state law requiring helmet use is being challenged in Pennsylvania, which is among at least 12 states considering letting adults decide whether to wear a helmet. This trend started in 1995 when the U.S. Congress repealed a federal law linking highway funds to laws requiring motorcycle helmets.

Not using a helmet when riding a motorcycle is dangerous. According to the American College of Emergency Physicians, www.acep.org., in 2001 3,181 motorcyclists were killed and nearly 60,000 were injured in highway crashes in the United States. Head injury is the leading cause of death in motorcycle crashes, and helmets provide the best protection from head injury. Motorcycle helmets are 67 percent effective in preventing brain injuries. Unhelmeted motorcyclists are more than 3 times more likely to suffer brain injuries in crashes than those using helmets. From 1984 to 2000, the NHTSA estimates that helmets saved the lives of 10,156 motorcyclists. If all motorcycle operators and passengers had worn helmets during that period, it is estimated that 8,463 additional lives would have been saved. In addition to saving lives, the NHTSA estimates that $13.2 billion was saved between 1984 and 1999 because of motorcycle helmet use, and another $11.1 billion could be saved if all used helmets.

Some states have re-enacted laws requiring motorcycle helmet use. These states report reductions in motorcycle deaths following the re-enactment of helmet laws. Oregon reported a 33 percent reduction, Nebraska a 32 percent reduction, and California a 37 percent reduction.

Other states have seen an increase in motorcycle fatalities after repealing their helmet laws. Texas reported a 31 percent increase, and Arkansas reported a 21 percent increase the year after its helmet law was repealed.

Should all motorcyclists be required to use helmets when riding? Why or why not?

2. Smoking in Bars and Restaurants

Some states and cities have recently passed laws prohibiting smoking in bars and restaurants. So far five states—New York, Connecticut, Delaware, Maine, and California—have such laws. Florida has an anti-smoking law that is slightly less restrictive than the laws in the other states. It bans smoking in all enclosed workplaces, and in bars and restaurants where food sales make up at least 10 percent of their business. In addition to these states, various, cities in the United States also have smoking bans for bars and restaurants. In Arizona, Tempe and Gaudalupe ban smoking in restaurants, bars, and bowling alleys. In 2004 Fayetteville, Arkansas, banned smoking in restaurants and bars. In Minnesota, Duluth has smoke-free bars and restaurants, and in May 2004, St. Paul was considering a similar law.

Ireland and Norway went smoke-free in 2004, and Sweden voted to ban smoking in bars and restaurants on June 1, 2005.

Why have these states, cities, and countries banned smoking? It is well-known that smoking is unhealthy for the smoker. There are also risks for those inhaling the secondhand smoke. Public health experts have warned for years that secondhand smoke can increase the risk of lung cancer, heart diseases, and other conditions. But it is only recently that these warnings have been taken seriously. Now the National Center for Chronic Disease Prevention and Health Promotion (CDC) (www.cdc.gov) warns that people at risk for heart disease should avoid buildings and other places that allow indoor smoking. The CDC says that as little as 30 minutes exposure can have a serious and lethal effect. The CDC estimates that 35,000 people die each year from the effects of secondhand smoke. Studies have shown that those who work in restaurants and bars allowing smoking have a substantial exposure to secondhand smoke, and that they are at considerable risk for lung cancer, heart disease, and other conditions.

One objection to the anti-smoking laws is that they hurt business. Ciaran Staunton, the owner of O'Neill's in Manhattan, says that his business is off 20 percent as former patrons head to New Jersy, where they can still smoke in a bar. But Tom Frieden, New York City's health commissioner, says that the data shows that anti-smoking measures have not hurt business in New York City. He notes that four out of five New Yorkers do not smoke.

Another objection is that nonsmokers can go someplace else if they do not like the atmosphere in a bar or restaurant. Why should the smokers have to go somewhere else to smoke? Some smokers insist that they have a right to smoke, and these anti-smoking laws are interfering with this right.

Do you agree that smokers have a right to smoke in bars and restaurants? Why or why not? What about the people who work in the bar or restaurant? Do they have a right to a smoke-free workplace?

Are the anti-smoking laws a good idea or not? Explain your position.

3. Health Insurance

(For detailed information see The Kaiser Commission on Medicaid and the Uninsured, www. Kff.org.)

Between 2001 and 2002, the number of U.S. citizens under age 65 without health insurance increased by 2.4 million, bringing the total to 43.3 million nonelderly uninsured. This growth was the largest increase in the number of uninsured since 1987. The number of uninsured has increased by nearly 10 percent since 2000. Now about 20 percent of the nonelderly lack health insurance.

People in low-income families are the most likely to be uninsured. The U.S. Department of Health and Human Services (http://aspe.gov.) puts the poverty level for a family of four at $18,850. For an individual the figure is $9,310. Over a third of those with low incomes have no health insurance, with adults more likely to be uninsured than children. Public coverage is designed primarily to help low-income children rather than adults. About 20 percent of nonelderly adults have no health insurance compared to 12 percent of children.

Some 56 percent of the uninsured adults worked full time in 2002. There were 26 million full-time workers without health insurance, representing 18 percent of the workforce. Blue-collar workers, who make up 63 percent of the workforce in America, comprise 81 percent of uninsured workers.

Some workers get health insurance provided by their employer. Should all employers be required to provide health insurance for their workers? Why or why not?

Another alternative is universal health care. President Clinton proposed a government program of universal health care for all U.S. citizens, similar to the system in Canada and other industrialized countries. Is this a good idea or not?

Some people who can afford health insurance refuse to get it even though they could not pay for a serious injury or illness. Is it rational for them to not get health insurance? If not, then why not require those with high incomes (400 percent of the poverty level) to have health insurance? Explain your answer.

4. Marijuana

In the summer of 2001, the Canadian Supreme Court ruled that any patient suffering from a terminal or painful illness should be allowed to use marijuana. With a doctor's permission, patients may either grow marijuana for their own use or even get it free from the government, which is paying a company to grow it in an abandoned copper mine in Flin Flon, Manitoba.

Marijuana has a long medical history. Queen Victoria took it for menstrual cramps. It was used widely in the West for pain and sleep until aspirin and sleeping pills came along. Today thousands of patients testify to pot's value. A recent survey in a British medical journal reported that marijuana was better than other available drugs for nausea, but no better for severe pain. But the study was done with marijuana-based medication, not smoked marijuana. Smoked marijuana has an effect that is beneficial to patients in pain—namely, what medical researchers call euphoria. It is hard to see how euphoria could be bad for a person who is in severe pain or is terminally ill.

California has passed Proposition 215, the Compassionate Use Act of 1996. This measure allows seriously ill Californians to obtain and use marijuana for medical purposes such as the treatment of cancer, anorexia, AIDS, chronic pain, spasticity, glaucoma, arthritis, and migraine. Yet in May 2001, the U.S. Supreme Court ruled 8–0 that a federal drug law prohibits the use of marijuana even for medical purposes. The effect of the ruling was to shut down a California organization that was distributing marijuana for medical use.

Is the medical use of marijuana morally wrong? Why or why not? Should it be illegal? Explain and defend your answers.

Most people smoke marijuana for fun, not for medical reasons. It is by far the most popular and widely used illegal drug in the United States. Now that indoor growing is common, marijuana is likely the largest cash crop in the country. About 734,000 people in the United States were arrested for violating marijuana laws during 2001—many more than were arrested for heroin or cocaine. Almost 90 percent of the marijuana arrests were for simple possession, a crime usually classified as a misdemeanor. Possession of more than an ounce, about the same amount as a pack of cigarettes, is in many states a felony. Different states have different punishments for felony possession. In 1992 in Oklahoma, Larry Jackson was charged with felony possession, convicted, and given a life sentence. Police had found 0.16 of a gram, which is 0.005644 of an ounce, in his apartment. In Oklahoma City, Leland James Dodd was given two life sentences, plus ten years, for buying 50 pounds of marijuana from two undercover officers. Despite harsh sentences such as these, most experts agree that the war on marijuana is a failure. (See the Suggested Readings or take a look at the NORML website.)

The Netherlands decriminalized marijuana more than twenty-five years ago. It is sold at government-regulated coffee houses. The Dutch Office for Medical Cannabis supports legislation that will provide marijuana for medical use free through the national health service. Portugal, Spain, Italy, Belgium, and Switzerland have all decriminalized the possession of marijuana for personal use. Should the United States do this too? Why or why not?

5. Ecstasy

MDMA (methylenedioxymethamphetamine), popularly known as ecstasy, has a chemical structure similar to that of the stimulant methamphetamine and the hallucinogen mescaline. It can produce both stimulant and hallucinatory effects. MDMA has been available as a street drug since the 1980s, but its use increased dramatically in the 1990s, particularly among those going to all-night dance parties called raves. It is most often taken orally in tablet form, but it is also available as a powder and is sometimes snorted or smoked.

According to the National Institute of Drug Abuse, over 3 percent of high school students used the drug in 1998, and over 2 percent of college students used the drug in 1997. In 1991, only 0.9 percent of college students used the drug. A network of researchers from twenty-one major U.S. metropolitan areas report an increased use of ecstasy by young adults and adolescents in recent years.

Ecstasy stimulates the release of the neurotransmitter serotonin in the brain, producing a high that lasts from several minutes to an hour. It produces an enhanced sense of pleasure and self-confidence and increased energy. Users say they experience a feeling of closeness with others and a desire to touch them.

Ecstasy users encounter problems similar to those experienced by amphetamine and cocaine users. These problems include confusion, depression, sleep problems, anxiety, and paranoia during, and sometimes weeks after, taking the drug. Physical effects include muscle tension, teeth clenching, nausea, blurred vision, faintness, and chills or sweating. Recent research indicates that heavy ecstasy use causes persistent memory problems and brain damage. Ecstasy-related fatalities at raves have been reported.

Should ecstasy be illegal? Is it immoral to take this drug? Explain your answers.

Suggested Readings

1. The Standford Encylopedia of Philosophy, http://plato.standford.edu, has a short and clear discussion of paternalism by Gerald Dworkin. This website also contains an excellent article on libertarianism by Peter Vallentyne, and a long article on John Stuart Mill by Fred Wilson.
2. A website promoting libertarianism is www.libertarianism.org.
3. The National Organization for the Reform of Marijuana Laws, www.norml.org, promotes the legalization of marijuana. Drug War Chroncle, http://stopthedrugwar.org., promotes the reform of the U.S. drug laws. The U.S. Drug Enforcement Administration (DEA), www.dea.gov., has detailed information on the drug laws, seizures, arrests, and so on. In 2003 the DEA had 9,629 employees and a budget of $1,897,000,000.
4. Patrick Devlin, *The Enforcement of Morals* (Oxford: Oxford University Press, 1987), argues that society has the right to legislate moral behavior, for example, by making drug use or homosexuality illegal.
5. Joel Feinberg, *Harm to Self* (Oxford: Oxford University Press, 1989). This the third volume of Feinberg's *The Moral Limits of the Criminal Law* (in four volumes). In this book, Feinberg covers topics such as paternalism, personal sovereignty, assumption of risk, and consent.
6. Robert Nozick, *Anarchy, State, and Utopia* (New York: Basic Books, 1974), argues that only a minimal state is justified. A more expansive state interferes with essential liberties. Michael Otsuka, *Libertarianism Without Inequality* (Clarendon Press, 2003), critically responds to Nozick.
7. John Kleinig, *Paternalism* (Totowa, NJ: Rowman and Allanheld, 1984), argues that paternalism covers any restriction of thought and expression, and even impositions on those who want to be left alone.
8. Rolf Satorius, ed., *Paternalism* (Minneapolis: University of Minnesota Press, 1983) is a collection that includes Gerald Dworkin, "Paternalism: Some Second Thoughts."
9. Eric Schlosser, *Reefer Madness* (New York: Houghton Mifflin Company, 2003), contains an expose of the war on marijuana—the harsh sentences, the large number imprisoned, the billions spent, the inconsistencies, and so on.
10. Jeffrey A. Miron and Jeffrey Zwiebel, "The Economic Case against Drug Prohibition," *Journal of Economic Perspectives* 9, 4(Fall 1995): 175–92, argue that a free market in drugs is likely to be a far superior policy to the current policies of drug prohibition.
11. Ethan A. Nadelmann, "The Case for Legalization," The Public Interest, 92 (Summer 1988): 3–14, discusses the high cost of drug prohibition, and criticizes our inconsistent moral attitudes toward alcohol and tobacco, on one hand and marijuana and cocaine on the other.
12. Robert E. Goodin, "The Ethics of Smoking," *Ethics* 99 (April 1989): 574–624, defends paternalistic laws that prevent or discourage adult smoking.

13. Daniel Shapiro, "Smoking Tobacco: Irrationality, Addiction, and Paternalism," *Public Affairs Quarterly* 8 (April 1994): 187–203, criticizes Goodin's irrationality and addiction arguments for paternalistic laws designed to prevent or discourage adult smoking.

14. Daniel Shapiro, "Addiction and Drug Policy," in John Arthur, ed., *Morality and Moral Controversies* (Upper Saddle River, NJ: Prentice-Hall, 1999), pp. 353–57, maintains that cocaine and heroin are not addictive because of pharmacological effects on the brain, but because of the individual's personality, values, expectations, and the cultural or social setting.

15. Steven R. Belenko, ed., *Drugs and Drug Policy in America* (Westport, CT: Greenwood Press, 2000), presents a documentary history of American drug policy.

16. *Reefer Madness: The History of Marijuana in America* (New York: St. Martin's Press, 1998), covers the social history of marijuana use in America, from hemp-farming George Washington to Louis Armstrong (who smoked pot every day).

17. Lynn Zimmer and John P. Morgan, *Marijuana Myths Marijuana Facts* (New York: The Lindesmith Center, 1997), reviews scientific research on marijuana and refutes common myths, such as the claim that marijuana is a gateway drug leading to more dangerous drugs such as heroin.

18. Douglas Husak, *Drugs and Rights* (Cambridge: Cambridge University Press, 1992), defends the moral rights of adults to use recreational drugs.

19. Steven B. Duke, "Drug Prohibition: An Unnatural Disaster," *Connecticut Law Review* 27, (Winter 1995): 571–612, argues that drug prohibition is a costly and catastrophic social program.

20. Gregory A. Loken, "The Importance of Being More than Earnest: Why the Case for Drug Legalization Remains Unproven," *Connecticut Law Review* 27 (Winter 1995): 660–91, argues that drug prohibition has reduced crime and that legalization would harm children.

21. William Bennett, "Should Drugs Be Legalized?" in Jeffrey A. Schaler, ed., *Should We Legalize, Decriminalize or Regulate?* (Buffalo, NY: Prometheus Books, 1998), argues against drug legalization.

Chapter 7

The Moral Status of Animals

Introduction

Factual Background

Humans cause a great deal of animal suffering. According to Peter Singer, the use and abuse of animals raised for food in factory farms far exceeds, in numbers, any other kind of mistreatment. In his book *Animal Liberation,* first published in 1975, Singer said that hundreds of millions of cattle, pigs, and sheep were raised and killed in the United States each year. But now Singer says it is over ten *billion* birds and mammals that are raised and killed for food in the United States annually, with tens of millions of animals used in animal experiments. Most of these factory-farmed animals spend their lives confined indoors with no fresh air, sun, or grass until they are slaughtered. But do they suffer? Consider the way they are killed. Gail Eisnitz's book *Slaughterhouse* (see the Suggested Readings) gives graphic descriptions of the way these animals are treated in major American slaughterhouses. There are shocking accounts of animals being skinned and dismembered while still alive and conscious. Or consider the treatment of veal calves. To make their flesh pale and tender, these calves are given special treatment. They are put in narrow stalls and tethered with a chain so that they cannot turn around, lie down comfortably, or groom themselves. They are fed a totally liquid diet to promote rapid weight gain. This diet is deficient in iron; as a result, the calves lick the sides of the stall, which are impregnated with urine containing iron. They are given no water because thirsty animals eat more than ones that drink water. This system of keeping calves has been illegal in Britain for many years, and will become illegal throughout the European Union by 2007. Even Spain, which is criticized for having bull-fighting, has better treatment for its animals raised for food. For example, by 2012, Spain and other European egg producers will be required to give their hens access to a perch and a nesting box to lay their eggs in, and to allow at least 120 square inches per bird. These changes will improve the living situation of over two hundred million birds. By contrast, United States egg producers give their nesting hens only 48 square inches per bird, about half the size of a sheet of letter paper.

Another cause of animal suffering is experimentation. Singer gives a graphic example of this. At the Lovelace Foundation in New Mexico, experimenters forced sixty-four beagles to inhale radioactive strontium 90. Twenty-five of the dogs died; initially, most of them were feverish and anemic, suffering from hemorrhages and bloody diarrhea. One of the deaths occurred during an epileptic seizure, and another resulted from a brain hemorrhage. In a similar experiment, beagles were injected with enough strontium 90 to produce early death in 50 percent of the group.

These dogs were the subject of what is called the LD50 Test. According to PETA Factsheet 6 (see the People for the Ethical Treatment of Animals website, http://www.petaonline.org/), this is a test that measures the amount of a toxic substance that will kill, in a single dose, 50 percent of the animals in a test group. It is a common test, used each year on about 5 million dogs, rabbits, rats, monkeys, and other animals in the United States. It is used to test cosmetics and household products such as weed killers, oven cleaners, insecticides, and food additives to satisfy the FDA (Food and Drug Administration) requirement that a product be "adequately substantiated for safety." But the LD50 Test is not actually required by the FDA. In the administration of the test, no painkillers are used. The experimental substance is forced into the animals' throats or is pumped into their stomachs by a tube, sometimes causing death by stomach rupture or from the sheer bulk of the chemical dose. Substances also are injected under the skin, into a vein, or into the lining of the stomach. They are also often applied to the eyes, rectum, and vagina or are forcibly inhaled through a gas mask.

The Readings

We begin with a classic statement of the view that animals should be treated differently from humans. Kant assumes that humans are self-conscious and rational, whereas animals are not. In Kant's view, this difference implies that we have no direct duties to animals; we have direct duties only to humans who are self-conscious and rational. Our duties to animals are indirect duties to humans. In other words, the moral treatment of animals is only a means of cultivating moral treatment of humans. We should not mistreat animals because this produces mistreatment of humans.

Kant's view is a clear example of what Singer calls speciesism. As Singer defines it, speciesism is "a prejudice or attitude of bias toward the interests of members of one's own species and against those of members of other species." Singer goes on to argue that speciesism is analogous to racism and sexism. It is unjust to discriminate against blacks because of their skin color or against women because of their gender. Their interests—for example, their interest in voting—have to be considered equally with those of whites and men. Similarly, it is unjust to discriminate against nonhuman animals because of their species. Their interests, and particularly their interest in not suffering, have to be considered too.

But how do we go about reducing animal suffering? Does this mean that we should become vegetarians and eat no meat? Singer thinks so, but of course this is very controversial in our meat-eating society. In Singer's view, we should stop eating meat to eliminate factory farming or at least to protest against it; we should not treat animals as means to our end (to use Kant's phrase).

Tom Regan takes a different position on the moral status of nonhuman animals. He agrees with Singer that our treatment of animals is wrong and that speciesism is unjust, but to show this he does not want to appeal to any form of utilitarianism. Utilitarianism is not an acceptable moral theory, he argues, because it treats persons and animals as worthless receptacles for valuable pleasure and because it allows immoral actions if they happen to bring about the best balance of total satisfaction for all those affected by the action. Instead of utilitarianism, Regan defends a rights view. On this view, animals have rights based on their inherent value as experiencing subjects of life, and our treatment of animals is wrong because it violates their rights.

But what exactly is inherent value? Mary Anne Warren argues that inherent value is a mysterious nonnatural property that Regan does not adequately explain. As a result the concept fails to make any clear distinction between those who have rights and those who don't. Warren's own view is that animals have rights, but they are weaker than human rights. These weak animal rights require us to not make animals suffer or to kill them without a good reason. But why don't human infants and the mentally incompetent have weak rights too? Why aren't they in the same moral category as animals? Warren's answer is that infancy and mental incompetence are conditions that we have all experienced or are likely to experience, and this gives us a powerful and practical reason for protecting infants and the mentally incompetent, a reason that is absent in the case of animals. We care about infants and mentally incompetent relatives in a way that we don't care about animals, except for much-loved pets, which are like members of the family.

Roger Scruton defends a position very much like Kant's. In his view, animals are not members of the moral community because they are not rational and not self-conscious. Because they are not moral persons, animals do not have rights or duties. He thinks it is absurd to punish the fox for killing the chicken or to beat a dog for a breach of etiquette. But what about humans who are neither rational nor self-conscious? If animals do not have rights because they are not moral persons, then why not say that marginal humans (as Scruton calls them) do not have rights either? In reply to this important objection, Scruton distinguishes among three types of humans who are not persons: infants, mentally impaired people, and senile and brain-damaged people, who are called "human vegetables." Scruton claims that human vegetables are no longer members of the moral community, and so killing them is understandable, even excusable. Infants are potential members of the moral community and as such they have rights, although not the same rights as adults. Mentally impaired people such as imbeciles and idiots, to use Scruton's examples, also have rights, not because they will ever be members of the moral community, but simply because they are human, and it is a virtue to acknowledge human life as sacrosanct.

Philosophical Issues

What is the criterion of moral standing? Who deserves moral consideration? These are basic issues raised by the readings. Kant says that self-consciousness gives a person moral standing; to use Kant's terminology, a self-conscious being is an end in itself and not just a means. On this criterion, human beings have moral standing as ends, but animals do not; they are mere means to fulfilling human purposes. Or so Kant believed. To be consistent, Kant would have to agree that nonhumans that are self-conscious (for example, chimpanzees) have moral standing, and human beings who are not self-conscious (for example, fetuses) do not have any moral standing.

Scruton has a position similar to Kant's. Humans have rights and duties because they are moral beings endowed with rationality and self-consciousness, and animals do not have rights and duties because they do not have these features. Scruton avoids the problem of nonhuman animals that are rational and self-conscious by simply defining "animals" as "those animals that lack the distinguishing features of the moral being—rationality, self-consciousness, personality, and so on." He complicates his position by adding a principle of the sanctity of human life in order to give mentally impaired humans a moral status, and a potentiality principle in order to give rights to infants.

The utilitarian criterion of moral standing accepted by Singer is sentience or consciousness. Animals are conscious, they are capable of feeling pain or pleasure, so they have moral standing. At least, we have the moral duty to not cause them to suffer without a good reason. But this view is attacked by environmentalists as still another kind of bias—namely, sentientism, the belief that only conscious or sentient beings can have rights or deserve moral consideration. The animal liberation movement has escaped one prejudice, speciesism, only to embrace another one, sentientism. Why not say that nonsentient things, such as forests, have rights too?

Even if animals do have moral standing, is it equal to that of humans? Warren's view is that animals have a lower moral status than humans. Animals have rights, but they are weaker than human rights. This suggests that it is easier to justify killing or harming an animal than a human. We are morally permitted to treat animals in ways that we cannot treat humans. For example, it would be wrong to kill an annoying homeless person, but it would not be wrong to exterminate an annoying rat or a bat that has invaded the house. It would be wrong to perform experiments on an innocent child, but it would not be wrong to experiment on rabbits if this resulted in a new treatment for cancer.

Our Duties to Animals

IMMANUEL KANT

For biographical information on Kant, see his reading in Chapter 1.

Kant maintains that we have no direct duties to animals because they are not self-conscious. Our duties to animals are merely indirect duties to human beings; that is, the duty to animals is a means of cultivating a corresponding duty to humans. For example, we should not be cruel to animals because this tends to produce cruelty to humans.

BAUMGARTEN SPEAKS OF DUTIES towards beings which are beneath us and beings which are above us. But so far as animals are concerned,

Source: Immanuel Kant, "Our Duties to Animals" from *Lectures on Ethics,* trans. Louis Infield (Harper & Row, 1963), pp. 239–241. Reprinted with permission of Routledge Publishing.

we have no direct duties. Animals are not self-conscious and are there merely as a means to an end. That end is man. We can ask, 'Why do animals exist?' But to ask, 'Why does man exist?' is a meaningless question. Our duties towards animals are merely indirect duties towards humanity. Animal nature has analogies to human nature, and by doing our duties to animals in respect of manifestations which correspond to manifestations of human nature, we indirectly do our duty towards humanity. Thus, if a dog has served his master long and faithfully, his service, on the analogy of human service, deserves reward, and when the dog has grown too old to serve, his master ought to keep him until he dies. Such action helps to support us in our duties towards human beings, where they are bounden duties. If then any acts of animals are analogous to human acts and spring from the same principles, we have duties towards the animals because thus we cultivate the corresponding duties towards human beings. If a man shoots his dog because the animal is no longer capable of service, he does not fail in his duty to the dog, for the dog cannot judge, but his act is inhuman and damages in himself that humanity which it is his duty to show towards mankind. If he is not to stifle his human feelings, he must practise kindness towards animals, for he who is cruel to animals becomes hard also in his dealings with men. We can judge the heart of a man by his treatment of animals. Hogarth[1] depicts this in his engravings. He shows how cruelty grows and develops. He shows the child's cruelty to animals, pinching the tail of a dog or a cat; he then depicts the grown man in his cart

1 Hogarth's four engravings, 'The Stages of Cruelty', 1751.

running over a child; and lastly, the culmination of cruelty in murder. He thus brings home to us in a terrible fashion the rewards of cruelty, and this should be an impressive lesson to children. The more we come in contact with animals and observe their behaviour, the more we love them, for we see how great is their care for their young. It is then difficult for us to be cruel in thought even to a wolf. Leibnitz used a tiny worm for purposes of observation, and then carefully replaced it with its leaf on the tree so that it should not come to harm through any act of his. He would have been sorry—a natural feeling for a humane man—to destroy such a creature for no reason. Tender feelings towards dumb animals develop humane feelings towards mankind. In England butchers and doctors do not sit on a jury because they are accustomed to the sight of death and hardened. Vivisectionists who use living animals for their experiments, certainly act cruelly, although their aim is praiseworthy, and they can justify their cruelty, since animals must be regarded as man's instruments; but any such cruelty for sport cannot be justified. A master who turns out his ass or his dog because the animal can no longer earn its keep manifests a small mind. The Greeks' ideas in this respect were high-minded, as can be seen from the fable of the ass and the bell of ingratitude. Our duties towards animals, then, are indirect duties towards mankind.

Review Questions

1. According to Kant, why don't we have direct duties to animals? What is the difference between animals and humans, in Kant's view?
2. What does Kant mean when he says that our duty to animals is only an indirect duty to humans?

Discussion Questions

1. Comatose people and newborn infants do not seem to be self-conscious. Does this mean we have no direct duties to them? What would Kant say? What is your view?
2. People who hunt and kill deer don't usually do the same to humans. Is this a problem for Kant's view? Why or why not?

All Animals Are Equal

PETER SINGER

For biographical information on Singer, see his reading in Chapter 3.

Singer defines speciesism as a prejudice toward the interests of members of one's own species and against those of members of other species. He argues that speciesism is analogous to racism and sexism. If it is unjust to discriminate against women and blacks by not considering their interests, it is also unfair to ignore the interests of animals, particularly their interest in not suffering.

"ANIMAL LIBERATION" may sound more like a parody of other liberation movements than a serious objective. The idea of "The Rights of Animals" actually was once used to parody the case for women's rights. When Mary Wollstonecraft, a forerunner of today's feminists, published her *Vindication of the Rights of Women* in 1792, her views were widely regarded as absurd, and before long an anonymous publication appeared entitled *A Vindication of the Rights of Brutes.* The author of this satirical work (now known to have been Thomas Taylor, a distinguished Cambridge philosopher) tried to refute Mary Wollstonecraft's arguments by showing that they could be carried one stage further. If the argument for equality was sound when applied to women, why should it not be applied to dogs, cats, and horses? The reasoning seemed to hold for these "brutes" too, yet to hold that brutes had rights was manifestly absurd; therefore the reasoning by which this conclusion had been reached must be unsound, and if unsound when applied to brutes, it must also be unsound when applied to women, since the very same arguments had been used in each case.

In order to explain the basis of the case for the equality of animals, it will be helpful to start with an examination of the case for the equality

Source: Peter Singer, "All Animals Are Equal" from *Animal Liberation* (New York: New York Review of Books, 1975), pp. 1–22. Used by permission of the author.

of women. Let us assume that we wish to defend the case for women's rights against the attack by Thomas Taylor. How should we reply?

One way in which we might reply is by saying that the case for equality between men and women cannot validly be extended to nonhuman animals. Women have a right to vote, for instance, because they are just as capable of making rational decisions about the future as men are; dogs, on the other hand, are incapable of understanding the significance of voting, so they cannot have the right to vote. There are many other obvious ways in which men and women resemble each other closely, while humans and animals differ greatly. So, it might be said, men and women are similar beings and should have similar rights, while humans and nonhumans are different and should not have equal rights.

The reasoning behind this reply to Taylor's analogy is correct up to a point, but it does not go far enough. There *are* important differences between humans and other animals, and these differences must give rise to *some* differences in the rights that each have. Recognizing this obvious fact, however, is no barrier to the case for extending the basic principle of equality to nonhuman animals. The differences that exist between men and women are equally undeniable, and the supporters of Women's Liberation are aware that these differences may give rise to different rights. Many feminists hold that women have the right to an abortion on request. It does not follow that since these same feminists are campaigning for equality between men and women they must support the right of men to have abortions too. Since a man cannot have an abortion, it is meaningless to talk of his right to have one. Since a dog can't vote, it is meaningless to talk of its right to vote. There is no reason why either Women's Liberation or Animal Liberation should get involved in such nonsense. The extension of the basic principle of equality from one group to another does not imply that we must treat both groups in exactly the same way, or grant exactly the same rights to both groups. Whether we should do so will depend on the nature of the members of the two groups. The basic principle of equality does not require equal or identical *treatment;* it requires equal *consideration*. Equal consideration for different beings may lead to different treatment and different rights.

So there is a different way of replying to Taylor's attempt to parody the case for women's rights, a way that does not deny the obvious differences between humans and nonhumans but goes more deeply into the question of equality and concludes by finding nothing absurd in the idea that the basic principle of equality applies to so-called brutes. At this point such a conclusion may appear odd; but if we examine more deeply the basis on which our opposition to discrimination on grounds of race or sex ultimately rests, we will see that we would be on shaky ground if we were to demand equality for blacks, women, and other groups of oppressed humans while denying equal consideration to nonhumans. To make this clear we need to see first, exactly why racism and sexism are wrong.

When we say that all human beings, whatever their race, creed, or sex, are equal, what is it that we are asserting? Those who wish to defend hierarchical, inegalitarian societies have often pointed out that by whatever test we choose it simply is not true that all humans are equal. Like it or not we must face the fact that humans come in different shapes and sizes; they come with different moral capacities, different intellectual abilities, different amounts of benevolent feeling and sensitivity to the needs of others, different

abilities to communicate effectively, and different capacities to experience pleasure and pain. In short, if the demand for equality were based on the actual equality of all human beings, we would have to stop demanding equality.

Still, one might cling to the view that the demand for equality among human beings is based on the actual equality of the different races and sexes. Although, it may be said, humans differ as individuals there are no differences between the races and sexes *as such*. From the mere fact that a person is black or a woman we cannot infer anything about that person's intellectual or moral capacities. This, it may be said, is why racism and sexism are wrong. The white racist claims that whites are superior to blacks, but this is false—although there are differences among individuals, some blacks are superior to some whites in all of the capacities and abilities that could conceivably be relevant. The opponent of sexism would say the same: a person's sex is no guide to his or her abilities, and this is why it is unjustifiable to discriminate on the basis of sex.

The existence of individual variations that cut across the lines of race or sex, however, provides us with no defense at all against a more sophisticated opponent of equality, one who proposes that, say, the interests of all those with IQ scores below 100 be given less consideration than the interests of those with ratings over 100. Perhaps those scoring below the mark, would, in this society, be made the slaves of those scoring higher. Would a hierarchical society of this sort really be so much better than one based on race or sex? I think not. But if we tie the moral principle of equality to the factual equality of the different races or sexes, taken as a whole, our opposition to racism and sexism does not provide us with any basis for objecting to this kind of inegalitarianism.

There is a second important reason why we ought not to base our opposition to racism and sexism on any kind of actual equality, even the limited kind that asserts that variations in capacities and abilities are spread evenly between the different races and sexes: we can have no absolute guarantee that these capacities and abilities really are distributed evenly, without regard to race or sex, among human beings. So far as actual abilities are concerned there do seem to be certain measurable differences between both races and sexes. These differences do not, of course, appear in each case, but only when averages are taken. More important still, we do not yet know how much of these differences is really due to the different genetic endowments of the different races and sexes, and how much is due to poor schools, poor housing, and other factors that are the result of past and continuing discrimination. Perhaps all of the important differences will eventually prove to be environmental rather than genetic. Anyone opposed to racism and sexism will certainly hope that this will be so, for it will make the task of ending discrimination a lot easier; nevertheless it would be dangerous to rest the case against racism and sexism on the belief that all significant differences are environmental in origin. The opponent of, say, racism who takes this line will be unable to avoid conceding that *if* differences in ability do after all prove to have some genetic connection with race, racism would in some way be defensible.

Fortunately there is no need to pin the case for equality to one particular outcome of a scientific investigation. The appropriate response to those who claim to have found evidence of genetically based differences in ability between the races or sexes is not to stick to the belief that the genetic explanation must be wrong, whatever evidence to the contrary may turn up: instead we should make it quite clear that the claim to equality does not depend on intelligence, moral capacity, physical strength, or similar matters of fact. Equality is a moral idea, not an assertion of fact. There is no logicially compelling reason for assuming that a factual difference in ability between two people justifies any difference in the amount of consideration we give to their needs and interests. *The principle of the equality of human beings is not a description of an alleged actual equality among humans; it is a prescription of how we should treat humans.*

Jeremy Bentham, the founder of the reforming utilitarian school of moral philosophy, incorporated the essential basis of moral equality into his system of ethics by means of the formula: "Each to count for one and none for more than one." In other words, the interests of every being affected by an action are to be taken into account and given the same weight as the like interests of any other being. A later utilitarian, Henry Sidgwick, put the point in this way: "The good of any one individual is of no more importance, from the point of view (if I may say so) of the Universe, than the good of any other." More recently the leading figures in contemporary moral philosophy have shown a great deal of agreement in specifying as a fundamental presupposition of their moral theories some similar requirement that operates so as to give everyone's interests equal consideration—although these writers generally cannot agree on how this requirement is best formulated.[1]

It is an implication of this principle of equality that our concern for others and our readiness to consider their interests ought not to depend on what they are like or on what abilities they may possess. Precisely what this concern or consideration requires us to do may vary according to the characteristics of those affected by what we do: concern for the well-being of a child growing up in America would require that we teach him to read; concern for the well-being of a pig may require no more than that we leave him alone with other pigs in a place where there is adequate food and room to run freely. But the basic element—the taking into account of the interests of the being, whatever those interests may be— must, according to the principle of equality, be extended to all beings, black or white, masculine or feminine, human or nonhuman.

1 For Bentham's moral philosophy, see his *Introduction to the Principles of Morals and Legislation,* and for Sidgwick's see *The Methods of Ethics* (the passage quoted is form the seventh edition, p. 382). As examples of leading contemporary moral philosophers who incorporate a requirement of equal consideration of interests, see R. M. Hare, *Freedom and Reason* (New York, Oxford University Press, 1963) and John Rawls, *A Theory of Justice* (Cambridge: Harvard University Press, Belknap Press, 1972). For a brief account of the essential agreement on this issue between these and other positions, see R. M. Hare, "Rules of War and Moral Reasoning," *Philosophy and Public Affairs* 1 (1972).

Thomas Jefferson, who was responsible for writing the principle of the equality of men into the American Declaration of Independence, saw this point. It led him to oppose slavery even though he was unable to free himself fully from his slaveholding background. He wrote in a letter to the author of a book that emphasized the notable intellectual achievements of Negroes in order to refute the then common view that they had limited intellectual capacities:

> Be assured that no person living wishes more sincerely than I do, to see a complete refutation of the doubts I have myself entertained and expressed on the grade of understanding allotted to them by nature, and to find that they are on a par with ourselves . . . but whatever be their degree of talent it is no measure of their rights. Because Sir Isaac Newton was superior to others in understanding, he was not therefore lord of the property or person of others.[2]

Similarly when in the 1850s the call for women's rights was raised in the United States a remarkable black feminist named Sojourner Truth made the same point in more robust terms at a feminist convention:

> . . . they talk about this thing in the head; what do they call it? ["Intellect," whispered someone near by.] That's it. What's that got to do with women's rights or Negroes' rights? If my cup won't hold but a pint and yours holds a quart, wouldn't you be mean not to let me have my little half-measure full?[3]

It is on this basis that the case against racism and the case against sexism must both ultimately rest; and it is in accordance with this principle that the attitude that we may call "speciesism," by analogy with racism, must also be condemned. Speciesism—the word is not an attractive one, but I can think of no better term—is a prejudice or attitude of bias toward the interests of members of one's own species and against those

members of other species. It should be obvious that the fundamental objections to racism and sexism made by Thomas Jefferson and Sojourner Truth apply equally to speciesism. If possessing a higher degree of intelligence does not entitle one human to use another for his own ends, how can it entitle humans to exploit nonhumans for the same purpose?[4]

Many philosophers and other writers have proposed the principle of equal consideration of interests, in some form or other, as a basic moral principle, but not many of them have recognized that this principle applies to members of other species as well as to our own. Jeremy Bentham was one of the few who did realize this. In a forward-looking passage written at a time when black slaves had been freed by the French but the British dominions were still being treated in the way we now treat animals, Bentham wrote:

> The day may come when the rest of the animal creation may acquire those rights which never could have been withholden from them but by the hand of tyranny. The French have already discovered that the blackness of the skin is no reason why a human being should be abandoned without redress to the caprice of a tormentor. It may one day come to be recognized that the number of the legs, the villosity of the skin, or the termination of the *os sacrum* are reasons equally insufficient for abandoning a sensitive being to the same fate. What else is it that should trace the insuperable line? Is it the faculty of reason, or perhaps the faculty of discourse? But a full-grown horse or dog is beyond comparison a more rational, as well as a more conversable animal, than an infant of a day or a week or even a month old. But suppose they were otherwise, what would it avail? The question is not, Can they reason? nor Can they talk? but, Can they suffer?[5]

In this passage Bentham points to the capacity for suffering as the vital characteristic that gives a being the right to equal consideration. The capacity for suffering—or more strictly, for

---

2 Letter to Henri Gregoire, February 25, 1809.
3 Reminiscences by Francis D. Gage, from Susan B. Anthony, *The History of Woman Suffrage,* vol. 1; the passage is to be found in the extract in Leslie Tanner, ed., *Voices from Women's Liberation* (New York: Signet, 1970).

4 I owe the term "speciesism" to Richard Ryder.
5 *Introduction to the Principles of Morals and Legislation,* chapter 17.

suffering and/or enjoyment or happiness—is not just another characteristic like the capacity for language or higher mathematics. Bentham is not saying that those who try to mark "the insuperable line" that determines whether the interests of a being should be considered happen to have chosen the wrong characteristic. By saying that we must consider the interests of all beings with the capacity for suffering or enjoyment Bentham does not arbitrarily exclude from consideration any interests at all—as those who draw the line with reference to the possession of reason or language do. The capacity for suffering and enjoyment is *a prerequisite for having interests at all,* a condition that must be satisfied before we can speak of interests in a meaningful way. It would be nonsense to say that it was not in the interests of a stone to be kicked along the road by a schoolboy. A stone does not have interests because it cannot suffer. Nothing that we can do to it could possibly make any difference to its welfare. A mouse, on the other hand, does have an interest in not being kicked along the road, because it will suffer if it is.

If a being suffers there can be no moral justification for refusing to take that suffering into consideration. No matter what the nature of the being, the principle of equality requires that its suffering be counted equally with the like suffering—in so far as rough comparisons can be made—of any other being. If a being is not capable of suffering, or of experiencing enjoyment or happiness, there is nothing to be taken into account. So the limit of sentience (using the term as a convenient if not strictly accurate shorthand for the capacity to suffer and/or experience enjoyment) is the only defensible boundary of concern for the interests of others. To mark this boundary by some other characteristic like intelligence or rationality would be to mark it in an arbitrary manner. Why not choose some other characteristic, like skin color?

The racist violates the principle of equality by giving greater weight to the interests of members of his own race when there is a clash between their interests and the interests of those of another race. The sexist violates the principle of equality by favoring the interests of his own sex. Similarly the speciesist allows the interests of his own species to override the greater interests of members of other species. The pattern is identical in each case.

Most human beings are speciesists. Ordinary human beings—not a few exceptionally cruel or heartless humans, but the overwhelming majority of humans—take an active part in, acquiesce in, and allow their taxes to pay for practices that require the sacrifice of the most important interests of members of other species in order to promote the most trivial interests of our own species. . . .

Animals can feel pain. As we saw earlier, there can be no moral justification for regarding the pain (or pleasure) that animals feel as less important than the same amount of pain (or pleasure) felt by humans. But what exactly does this mean, in practical terms? To prevent misunderstanding I shall spell out what I mean a little more fully.

If I give a horse a hard slap across its rump with my open hand, the horse may start, but it presumably feels little pain. Its skin is thick enough to protect it against a mere slap. If I slap a baby in the same way, however, the baby will cry and presumably does feel pain, for its skin is more sensitive. So it is worse to slap a baby than a horse, if both slaps are administered with equal force. But there must be some kind of blow—I don't know exactly what it would be, but perhaps a blow with a heavy stick—that would cause the horse as much pain as we cause a baby by slapping it with our hand. That is what I mean by "the same amount of pain" and if we consider it wrong to inflict that much pain on a baby for no good reason then we must, unless we are speciesists, consider it equally wrong to inflict the same amount of pain on a horse for no good reason.

There are other differences between humans and animals that cause other complications. Normal adult human beings have mental capacities which will, in certain circumstances, lead them to suffer more than animals would in the same circumstances. If, for instance, we decided to perform extremely painful or lethal scientific experiments on normal adult humans, kidnapped at random from public parks for this purpose, every adult who entered a park would become fearful that he would be kidnapped. The resultant terror would be a form of suffering additional to the pain of the experiment. The same experiments performed on nonhuman animals would cause less suffering since the animals would not have the anticipatory dread of being kidnapped and experimented upon. This does not mean, of course, that it would be right to perform the experiment on animals, but only that there is a reason, which is *not* speciesist, for preferring to use animals rather than normal adult humans, if the experiment is to be done at all. It should be noted, however, that this same argument gives us a reason for preferring to use human infants—orphans perhaps—or retarded humans for experiments, rather than adults, since infants and retarded humans would also have no idea of what was going to happen to them. So far as this argument is concerned nonhuman animals and infants and retarded humans are in the same category; and if we use this argument to justify experiments on nonhuman animals we have to ask ourselves whether we are also prepared to allow experiments on humans, on what basis can we do it, other than a barefaced—and morally indefensible—preference for members of our own species?

There are many areas in which the superior mental powers of normal adult humans make a difference: anticipation, more detailed memory, greater knowledge of what is happening, and so on. Yet these differences do not all point to greater suffering on the part of the normal human being. Sometimes an animal may suffer more because of his more limited understanding. If, for instance, we are taking prisoners in wartime we can explain to them that while they must submit to capture, search, and confinement they will not otherwise be harmed and will be set free at the conclusion of hostilities. If we capture a wild animal, however, we cannot explain that we are not threatening its life. A wild animal cannot distinguish an attempt to overpower and confine from an attempt to kill; the one causes as much terror as the other.

It may be objected that comparisons of the sufferings of different species are impossible to make, and that for this reason when the interests of animals and humans clash the principle of equality gives no guidance. It is probably true that comparisons of suffering between members of different species cannot be made precisely, but precision is not essential. Even if we were to prevent the infliction of suffering on animals only when it is quite certain that the interests of humans will not be affected to anything like the extent that animals are affected, we would be forced to make radical changes in our treatment of animals that would involve our diet, the farming methods we use, experimental procedures in many fields of science, our approach to wildlife and to hunting, trapping and the wearing of furs, and areas of entertainment like circuses, rodeos, and zoos. As a result, a vast amount of suffering would be avoided.

So far I have said a lot about the infliction of suffering on animals, but nothing about killing them. This omission has been deliberate. The application of the principle of equality to the infliction of suffering is, in theory at least, fairly straightforward. Pain and suffering are bad and should be prevented or minimized, irrespective of the race, sex, or species of the being that suffers. How bad a pain is depends on how intense it is and how long it lasts, but pains of the same intensity and duration are equally bad, whether felt by humans or animals.

The wrongness of killing a being is more complicated. I have kept, and shall continue to keep, the question of killing in the background because in the present state of human tyranny over other species the more simple, straightforward principle of equal consideration of pain or pleasure is a sufficient basis for identifying and protesting against all the major abuses of animals that humans practice. Nevertheless, it is necessary to say something about killing.

Just as most humans are speciesists in their readiness to cause pain to animals when they would not cause a similar pain to humans for the same reason, so most humans are speciesists in their readiness to kill other animals when they would not kill humans. We need to proceed more cautiously here, however, because people hold widely differing views about when it is legitimate to kill humans, as the continuing debates over abortion and euthanasia attest. Nor have moral philosophers been able to agree on exactly what it is that makes it wrong to kill humans, and under what circumstances killing a human being may be justifiable.

Let us consider first the view that it is always wrong to take an innocent human life. We may call this the "sanctity of life" view. People who take this view oppose abortion and euthanasia. They do not usually, however, oppose the killing of nonhumans—so perhaps it would be more accurate to describe this view as the "sanctity of *human* life" view.

The belief that human life, and only human life, is sacrosanct is a form of speciesism. To see this, consider the following example.

Assume that, as sometimes happens, an infant has been born with massive and irreparable brain damage. The damage is so severe that the infant can never be any more than a "human vegetable," unable to talk, recognize other people, act independently of others, or develop a sense of self-awareness. The parents of the infant, realizing that they cannot hope for any improvement in their child's condition and being in any case unwilling to spend, or ask the state to spend, the thousands of dollars that would be needed annually for proper care of the infant, ask the doctor to kill the infant painlessly.

Should the doctor do what the parents ask? Legally, he should not, and in this respect the law reflects the sanctity of life view. The life of every human being is sacred. Yet people who would say this about the infant do not object to the killing of nonhuman animals. How can they justify their different judgments? Adult chimpanzees, dogs, pigs, and many other species far surpass the brain-damaged infant in their ability to relate to others, act independently, be self-aware, and any other capacity that could reasonably be said to give value to life. With the most

intensive care possible, there are retarded infants who can never achieve the intelligence level of a dog. Nor can we appeal to the concern of the infant's parents, since they themselves, in this imaginary example (and in some actual cases) do not want the infant kept alive.

The only thing that distinguishes the infant from the animal, in the eyes of those who claim it has a "right to life," is that it is, biologically, a member of the species Homo sapiens, whereas chimpanzees, dogs, and pigs are not. But to use *this* difference as the basis for granting a right to life to the infant and not to the other animals is, of course, pure speciesism.[6] It is exactly the kind of arbitrary difference that the most crude and overt kind of racist uses in attempting to justify racial discrimination.

This does not mean that to avoid speciesism we must hold that it is as wrong to kill a dog as it is to kill a normal human being. The only position that is irredeemably speciesist is the one that tries to make the boundary of the right to life run exactly parallel to the boundary of our own species. Those who hold the sanctity of life view do this because while distinguishing sharply between humans and other animals they allow no distinctions to be made within our own species, objecting to the killing of the severely retarded and the hopelessly senile as strongly as they object to the killing of normal adults.

To avoid speciesism we must allow that beings which are similar in all relevant respects have a similar right to life—and mere membership in our own biological species cannot be a morally

---

6 I am here putting aside religious views, for example the doctrine that all and only humans have immortal souls, or are made in the image of God. Historically these views have been very important, and no doubt are partly responsible for the idea that human life has a special sanctity. Logically, however, these religious views are unsatisfactory, since a reasoned explanation of why it should be that all humans and no nonhumans have immortal souls is not offered. This belief too, therefore, comes under suspicion as a form of speciesism. In any case, defenders of the "sanctity of life" view are generally reluctant to base their position on purely religious doctrines, since these doctrines are no longer as widely accepted as they once were.

relevant criterion for this right. Within these limits we could still hold that, for instance, it is worse to kill a normal adult human, with a capacity for self-awareness, and the ability to plan for the future and have meaningful relations with others, than it is to kill a mouse, which presumably does not share all of these characteristics; or we might appeal to the close family and other personal ties which humans have but mice do not have to the same degree; or we might think that it is the consequences for other humans, who will be put in fear of their own lives, that makes the crucial difference; or we might think it is some combination of these factors, or other factors altogether.

Whatever criteria we choose, however, we will have to admit that they do not follow precisely the boundary of our own species. We may legitimately hold that there are some features of certain beings which make their lives more valuable than those of other beings; but there will surely be some nonhuman animals whose lives, by any standards, are more valuable than the lives of some humans. A chimpanzee, dog, or pig, for instance, will have a higher degree of self-awareness and a greater capacity for meaningful relations with others than a severely retarded infant or someone in a state of advanced senility. So if we base the right to life on these characteristics we must grant these animals a right to life as good as, or better than, such retarded or senile humans.

Now this argument cuts both ways. It could be taken as showing that chimpanzees, dogs, and pigs, along with some other species, have a right to life and we commit a grave moral offense whenever we kill them, even when they are old and suffering and our intention is to put them out of their misery. Alternatively one could take the argument as showing that the severely retarded and hopelessly senile have no right to life and may be killed for quite trivial reasons, as we now kill animals.

Since the focus here is on ethical questions concerning animals and not on the morality of euthanasia I shall not attempt to settle this issue finally. I think it is reasonably clear, though, that while both of the positions just described avoid speciesism, neither is entirely satisfactory. What we need is some middle position that would avoid speciesism but would not make the lives of the retarded and senile as cheap as the lives of pigs and dogs now are, nor make the lives of pigs and dogs so sacrosanct that we think it wrong to put them out of hopeless misery. What we must do is bring nonhuman animals within our sphere of moral concern and cease to treat their lives as expendable for whatever trivial purposes we may have. At the same time, once we realize that the fact that a being is a member of our own species is not in itself enough to make it always wrong to kill that being, we may come to reconsider our policy of preserving human lives at all costs, even when there is no prospect of a meaningful life or of existence without terrible pain.

I conclude, then, that a rejection of speciesism does not imply that all lives are of equal worth. While self-awareness, intelligence, the capacity for meaningful relations with others, and so on are not relevant to the question of inflicting pain—since pain is pain, whatever other capacities, beyond the capacity to feel pain, the being may have—these capacities may be relevant to the question of taking life. It is not arbitrary to hold that the life of a self-aware being, capable of abstract thought, of planning for the future, of complex acts of communication, and so on, is more valuable than the life of a being without these capacities. To see the difference between the issues of inflicting pain and taking life, consider how we would choose within our own species. If we had to choose to save the life of a normal human or a mentally defective human, we would probably choose to save the life of the normal human; but if we had to choose between preventing pain in the normal human or the mental defective—imagine that both have received painful but superficial injuries, and we only have enough painkiller for one of them—it is not nearly so clear how we ought to choose. The same is true when we consider other species. The evil of pain is, in itself, unaffected by the other characteristics of the being that feels the pain; the value of life is affected by these other characteristics.

Normally this will mean that if we have to choose between the life of a human being and the life of another animal we would choose to save the life of the human, but there may be special cases in which the reverse holds true, because the human being in question does not have the capacities of a normal human being. So this view is not speciesist, although it may appear to be at first glance. The preference, in normal cases, for saving a human life over the life of an animal when a choice *has* to be made is a preference based on the characteristics that normal humans have, and not on the mere fact that they are members of our own species. This is why when we consider members of our own species who lack the characteristics of normal humans we can no longer say that their lives are always to be preferred to those of other animals. In general, the question of when it is wrong to kill (painlessly) an animal is one to which we need give no precise answer. As long as we remember that we should give the same respect to the lives of animals as we give to the lives of those humans at a similar mental level, we shall not go far wrong.

In any case, the conclusions that are argued for here flow from the principle of minimizing suffering alone. The idea that it is also wrong to kill animals painlessly gives some of these conclusions additional support which is welcome, but strictly unnecessary. Interestingly enough, this is true even of the conclusion that we ought to become vegetarians, a conclusion that in the popular mind is generally based on some kind of absolute prohibition on killing.

Review Questions

1. Explain the principle of equality that Singer adopts.
2. How does Singer define speciesism?
3. What is the sanctity of life view? Why does Singer reject this view?

Discussion Questions

1. Is speciesism analogous to racism and sexism? Why or why not?
2. Is there anything wrong with killing animals painlessly? Defend your view.
3. Do human interests outweigh animal interests? Explain your position.

The Case for Animal Rights

TOM REGAN

Tom Regan is professor of philosophy at North Carolina State University. He has written or edited more than 20 books and published numerous articles. His books on the subject of animal rights include *All That Dwell Therein* (1982), *The Case for Animal Rights* (1984), and *Empty Cages* (2004). A website devoted to his career can be found at www.lib.ncsu.edu/archives/exhibits/regan.

Source: Tom Regan, "The Case for Animal Rights," from *In Defence of Animals,* ed. Peter Singer, pp. 13–26. Copyright © 1985 Blackwell Publishers. Reprinted with permission.

Regan defends the view that animals have rights based on their inherent value as experiencing subjects of a life. He attacks other views, including indirect-duty views, the cruelty-kindness view (as he calls it), and even Singer's utilitarianism. Although he agrees with Singer that our treatment of animals is wrong and that speciesism is unjust, he denies that it is wrong because of animal suffering. Instead he thinks that our treatment of animals is wrong because we violate the rights of animals.

I REGARD MYSELF as an advocate of animal rights—as a part of the animal rights movement. That movement, as I conceive it, is committed to a number of goals, including:

> the total abolition of the use of animals in science;
>
> the total dissolution of commercial animal agriculture;
>
> the total elimination of commercial and sport hunting and trapping.

There are, I know, people who profess to believe in animal rights but do not avow these goals. Factory farming, they say, is wrong—it violates animals' rights—but traditional animal agriculture is all right. Toxicity tests of cosmetics on animals violates their rights, but important medical research—cancer research, for example—does not. The clubbing of baby seals is abhorrent, but not the harvesting of adult seals. I used to think I understood this reasoning. Not any more. You don't change unjust institutions by tidying them up.

What's wrong—fundamentally wrong—with the way animals are treated isn't the details that vary from case to case. It's the whole system. The forlornness of the veal calf is pathetic, heart wrenching; the pulsing pain of the chimp with electrodes planted deep in her brain is repulsive; the slow, tortuous death of the raccoon caught in the leg-hold trap is agonizing. But what is wrong isn't the pain, isn't the suffering, isn't the deprivation. These compound what's wrong. Sometimes—often—they make it much, much worse. But they are not the fundamental wrong.

The fundamental wrong is the system that allows us to view animals as *our resources,* here for *us*—to be eaten, or surgically manipulated, or exploited for sport or money. Once we accept this view of animals—as our resources—the rest is as predictable as it is regrettable. Why worry about their loneliness, their pain, their death? Since animals exist for us, to benefit us in one way or another, what harms them really doesn't matter—or matters only if it starts to bother us, makes us feel a trifle uneasy when we eat our veal escalope, for example. So, yes, let us get veal calves out of solitary confinement, give them more space, a little straw, a few companions. But let us keep our veal escalope.

But a little straw, more space and a few companions won't eliminate—won't even touch—the basic wrong that attaches to our viewing and treating these animals as our resources. A veal calf killed to be eaten after living in close confinement is viewed and treated in this way: but so, too, is another who is raised (as they say) "more humanely." To right the wrong of our treatment of farm animals requires more than making rearing methods "more humane"; it requires the total dissolution of commercial animal agriculture.

How do we do this, whether we do it or, as in the case of animals in science, whether and how we abolish their use—these are to a large extent political questions. People must change their beliefs before they change their habits. Enough people, especially those elected to public office, must believe in change—must want it—before we will have laws that protect the rights of animals. This process of change is very complicated, very demanding, very exhausting, calling for the efforts of many hands in education, publicity, political organization and activity, down to the licking of envelopes and stamps.

As a trained and practicing philosopher, the sort of contribution I can make is limited but, I like to think, important. The currency of philosophy is ideas—their meaning and rational foundation—not the nuts and bolts of the legislative process, say, or the mechanics of community organization. That's what I have been exploring over the past ten years or so in my essays and talks and, most recently, in my book, *The Case for Animal Rights*. I believe the major conclusions I reach in the book are true because they are supported by the weight of the best arguments. I believe the idea of animal rights has reason, not just emotion, on its side.

In the space I have at my disposal here I can only sketch, in the barest outline, some of the main features of the book. Its main themes—and we should not be surprised by this—involve asking and answering deep, fundamental moral questions about what morality is, how it should be understood and what is the best moral theory, all considered. I hope I can convey something of the shape I think this theory takes. The attempt to do this will be (to use a word a friendly critic once used to describe my work) cerebral, perhaps too cerebral. But this is misleading. My feelings about how animals are sometimes treated run just as deep and just as strong as those of my more volatile compatriots. Philosophers do—to use the jargon of the day—have a right side to their brains. If it's the left side we contribute (or mainly should), that's because what talents we have reside there.

How to proceed? We begin by asking how the moral status of animals has been understood by thinkers who deny that animals have rights. Then we test the mettle of their ideas by seeing how well they stand up under the heat of fair criticism. If we start our thinking in this way, we soon find that some people believe that we have no duties directly to animals, that we owe nothing to them, that we can do nothing that wrongs them. Rather, we can do wrong acts that involve animals, and so we have duties regarding them, though none to them. Such views may be called indirect duty views. By way of

illustration: suppose your neighbour kicks your dog. Then your neighbour has done something wrong. But not to your dog. The wrong that has been done is a wrong to you. After all, it is wrong to upset people, and your neighbour's kicking your dog upsets you. So you are the one who is wronged, not your dog. Or again: by kicking your dog your neighbour damages your property. And since it is wrong to damage another person's property, your neighbour has done something wrong—to you, of course, not to your dog. Your neighbour no more wrongs your dog than your car would be wronged if the windshield were smashed. Your neighbour's duties involving your dog are indirect duties to you. More generally, all of our duties regarding animals are indirect duties to one another—to humanity.

How could someone try to justify such a view? Someone might say that your dog doesn't feel anything and so isn't hurt by your neighbour's kick, doesn't care about the pain since none is felt, is as unaware of anything as is your windshield. Someone might say this, but no rational person will, since, among other considerations, such a view will commit anyone who holds it to the position that no human being feels pain either—that human beings don't care about what happens to them. A second possibility is that though both humans and your dog are hurt when kicked, it is only human pain that matters. But, again, no rational person can believe this. Pain is pain wherever it occurs. If your neighbour's causing you pain is wrong because of the pain that is caused, we cannot rationally ignore or dismiss the moral relevance of the pain that your dog feels.

Philosophers who hold indirect duty views—and many still do—have come to understand that they must avoid the two defects just noted: that is, both the view that animals don't feel anything as well as the idea that only human pain can be morally relevant. Among such thinkers the sort of view now favoured is one or other form of what is called *contractarianism*.

Here, very crudely, is the root idea: morality consists of a set of rules that individuals voluntarily agree to abide by, as we do when we sign a contract (hence the name contractarianism). Those who understand and accept the terms of the contract are covered directly; they have rights created and recognized by, and protected in, the contract. And these contractors can also have protection spelled out for others who, though they lack the ability to understand morality and so cannot sign the contract themselves, are loved or cherished by those who can. Thus young children, for example, are unable to sign contracts and lack rights. But they are protected by the contract none the less because of the sentimental interests of others, most notably their parents. So we have, then, duties involving these children, duties regarding them, but no duties to them. Our duties in their case are indirect duties to other human beings, usually their parents.

As for animals, since they cannot understand contracts, they obviously cannot sign; and since they cannot sign, they have no rights. Like children, however, some animals are the objects of the sentimental interest of others. You, for example, love your dog or cat. So those animals that enough people care about (companion animals, whales, baby seals, the American bald eagle), though they lack rights themselves, will be protected because of the sentimental interests of people. I have, then, according to contractarianism, no duty directly to your dog or any other animal, not even the duty not to cause them pain or suffering; my duty not to hurt them is a duty I have to those people who care about what happens to them. As for other animals, where no or little sentimental interest is present—in the case of farm animals, for example, or laboratory rats—what duties we have grow weaker and weaker, perphaps to vanishing point. The pain and death they endure, though real, are not wrong if no one cares about them.

When it comes to the moral status of animals, contractartianism could be a hard view to refute if it were an adequate theoretical approach to the moral status of human beings. It is not adequate in this latter respect, however, which makes the question of its adequacy in the former case,

regarding animals, utterly moot. For consider: morality, according to the (crude) contractarian position before us, consists of rules that people agree to abide by. What people? Well, enough to make a difference—enough, that is, *collectively* to have the power to enforce the rules that are drawn up in the contract. That is very well and good for the signatories but not so good for anyone who is not asked to sign. And there is nothing in contractarianism of the sort we are discussing that guarantees or requires that everyone will have a chance to participate equally in framing the rules of morality. The result is that this approach to ethics could sanction the most blatant forms of social, economic, moral and political injustice, ranging from a repressive caste system to systematic racial or sexual discrimination. Might, according to this theory, does make right. Let those who are the victims of injustice suffer as they will. It matters not so long as no one else—no contractor, or too few of them—cares about it. Such a theory takes one's moral breath away . . . as if, for example, there would be nothing wrong with apartheid in South Africa if few white South Africans were upset by it. A theory with so little to recommend it at the level of the ethics of our treatment of our fellow humans cannot have anything more to recommend it when it comes to the ethics of how we treat our fellow animals.

The version of contractarianism just examined is, as I have noted, a crude variety, and in fairness to those of a contractarian persuasion it must be noted that much more refined, subtle and ingenious varieties are possible. For example, John Rawls, in his *A Theory of Justice,* sets forth a version of contractarianism that forces contractors to ignore the accidental features of being a human being—for example, whether one is white or black, male or female, a genius or of modest intellect. Only by ignoring such features, Rawls believes, can we ensure that the principles of justice that contractors would agree upon are not based on bias or prejudice. Despite the improvement a view such as Rawls's represents over the cruder forms of contractarianism, it remains deficient: it systematically denies that we have direct duties to those human beings who do not have a sense of justice—young children, for instance, and many mentally retarded humans. And yet it seems reasonably certain that, were we to torture a young child or a retarded elder, we would be doing something that wronged him or her, not something that would be wrong if (and only if) other humans with a sense of justice were upset. And since this is true in the case of these humans, we cannot rationally deny the same in the case of animals.

Indirect duty views, then, including the best among them, fail to command our rational assent. Whatever ethical theory we should accept rationally, therefore, it must at least recognize that we have some duties directly to animals, just as we have some duties directly to each other. The next two theories I'll sketch attempt to meet this requirement.

The first I call the cruelty-kindness view. Simply stated, this says that we have a direct duty to be kind to animals and a direct duty not to be cruel to them. Despite the familiar, reassuring ring of these ideas, I do not believe that this view offers an adequate theory. To make this clearer, consider kindness. A kind person acts from a certain kind of motive—compassion or concern, for example. And that is a virtue. But there is no guarantee that a kind act is a right act. If I am a generous racist, for example, I will be inclined to act kindly towards members of my own race, favouring their interests above those of others. My kindness would be real and, so far as it goes, good. But I trust it is too obvious to require argument that my kind acts may not be above moral reproach—may, in fact, be positively wrong because rooted in injustice. So kindness, notwithstanding its status as a virtue to be encouraged, simply will not carry the weight of a theory of right action.

Cruelty fares no better. People or their acts are cruel if they display either a lack of sympathy for or, worse, the presence of enjoyment in another's suffering. Cruelty in all its guises is a bad thing, a tragic human failing. But just as a person's being motivated by kindness does not guarantee that he or she does what is right, so the absence of cruelty does not ensure that he or she avoids doing what is wrong. Many people who perform abortions, for example, are not cruel, sadistic people. But that fact alone does not settle the terribly difficult question of the morality of abortion. The case is no different when we examine the ethics of our treatment of animals. So, yes, let us be for kindness and against cruelty. But let us not suppose that being for the one and against the other answers questions about moral right and wrong.

Some people think that the theory we are looking for is utilitarianism. A utilitarian accepts two moral principles. The first is that of equality: everyone's interests count, and similar interests must be counted as having similar weight or importance. White or black, American or Iranian, human or animal—everyone's pain or frustration matter, and matter just as much as the equivalent pain or frustration of anyone else. The second principle a utilitarian accepts is that of utility: do the act that will bring about the best balance between satisfaction and frustration for everyone affected by the outcome.

As a utilitarian, then, here is how I am to approach the task of deciding what I morally ought to do: I must ask who will be affected if I choose to do one thing rather than another, how much each individual will be affected, and where the best results are most likely to lie—which option, in other words, is most likely to bring about the best results, the best balance between satisfaction and frustration. That option, whatever it may be, is the one I ought to choose. That is where my moral duty lies.

The great appeal of utilitarianism rests with its uncompromising *egalitarianism:* everyone's interests count and count as much as the like interests of everyone else. The kind of odious discrimination that some forms of contractarianism can justify—discrimination based on race or sex, for example—seems disallowed in principle by utilitarianism, as is speciesism, systematic discrimination based on species membership.

The equality we find in utilitarianism, however, is not the sort an advocate of animal or human rights should have in mind. Utilitarianism has no room for the equal moral rights of different individuals because it has no room for their equal inherent value or worth. What has value for the utilitarian is the satisfaction of an individual's interests, not the individual whose interests they are. A universe in which you satisfy your desire for water, food and warmth is, other things being equal, better than a universe in which these desires are frustrated. And the same is true in the case of an animal with similar desires. But neither you nor the animal have any value in your own right. Only your feelings do.

Here is an analogy to help make the philosophical point clearer: a cup contains different liquids, sometimes sweet, sometimes bitter, sometimes a mix of the two. What has value are the liquids: the sweeter the better, the bitterer the worse. The cup, the container, has no value. It is what goes into it, not what they go into, that has value. For the utilitarian you and I are like the cup; we have no value as individuals and thus no equal value. What has value is what goes into us, what we serve as receptacles for; our feelings of satisfaction have positive value, our feelings of frustration negative value.

Serious problems arise for utilitarianism when we remind ourselves that it enjoins us to bring about the best consequences. What does this mean? It doesn't mean the best consequences for me alone, or for my family or friends, or any other person taken individually. No, what we must do is, roughly, as follows: we must add up (somehow!) the separate satisfactions and frustrations of everyone likely to be affected by our choice, the satisfactions in one column, the frustrations in the other. We must total each column for each of the options before us. That is what it means to say the theory is aggregative. And then we must choose that option which is most likely to bring about the best balance of totalled satisfactions over totalled frustrations. Whatever act would lead to this outcome is the one we ought morally to perform—it is where our moral duty lies. And that act quite clearly might not be the same one that would bring about the best results for me personally, or for my family or friends, or for a lab animal. The best aggregated consequences for everyone concerned are not necessarily the best for each individual.

That utilitarianism is an aggregative theory—different individuals' satisfactions or frustrations are added, or summed, or totalled—is the key objection to this theory. My Aunt Bea is old, inactive, a cranky, sour person, though not physically ill. She prefers to go on living. She is also rather rich. I could make a fortune if I could get my hands on her money, money she intends to give me in any event, after she dies, but which she refuses to give me now. In order to avoid a huge tax bite, I plan to donate a handsome sum of my profits to a local children's hospital. Many, many children will benefit from my generosity, and much joy will be brought to their parents, relatives and friends. If I don't get the money rather soon, all these ambitions will come to naught. The once-in-a-lifetime opportunity to make a real killing will be gone. Why, then, not kill my Aunt Bea? Oh, of course I *might* get caught. But I'm no fool and, besides, her doctor can be counted on to co-operate (he has an eye for the same investment and I happen to know a good deal about his shady past). The deed can be done . . . professionally, shall we say. There is *very* little chance of getting caught. And as for my conscience being guilt-ridden, I am a resourceful sort of fellow and will take more than sufficient comfort—as I lie on the beach at Acapulco—in contemplating the joy and health I have brought to so many others.

Suppose Aunt Bea is killed and the rest of the story comes out as told. Would I have done anything wrong? Anything immoral? One would have thought that I had. Not according to utilitarianism. Since what I have done has brought about the best balance between totalled satisfaction and frustration for all those affected by the outcome, my action is not wrong. Indeed, in killing Aunt Bea the physician and I did what duty required.

This same kind of argument can be repeated in all sorts of cases, illustrating, time after time, how the utilitarian's position leads to results that impartial people find morally callous. It *is* wrong to kill my Aunt Bea in the name of bringing about the best results for others. A good end does not justify an evil means. Any adequate moral theory will have to explain why this is so. Utilitarianism fails in this respect and so cannot be the theory we seek.

What to do? Where to begin anew? The place to begin, I think, is with the utilitarian's view of the value of the individual—or, rather, lack of value. In its place, suppose we consider that you and I, for example, do have value as individuals—what we'll call *inherent value*. To say we have such value is to say that we are something more than, something different from, mere receptacles. Moreover, to ensure that we do not pave the way for such injustices as slavery or sexual discrimination, we must believe that all who have inherent value have it equally, regardless of their sex, race, religion, birthplace and so on. Similarly to be discarded as irrelevant are one's talents or skills, intelligence and wealth, personality or pathology, whether one is loved and admired or despised and loathed. The genius and the retarded child, the prince and the pauper, the brain surgeon and the fruit vendor, Mother Teresa and the most unscrupulous used-car salesman—all have inherent value, all possess it equally, and all have an equal right to be treated with respect, to be treated in ways that do not reduce them to the status of things, as if they existed as resources for others. My value as an individual is independent of my usefulness to you. Yours is not dependent on your usefulness to me. For either of us to treat the other in ways that fail to show respect for the other's independent value is to act immorally, to violate the individual's rights.

Some of the rational virtues of this view—what I call the rights view—should be evident. Unlike (crude) contractarianism, for example, the rights view *in principle* denies the moral tolerability of any and all forms of racial, sexual and social discrimination; and unlike utilitarianism, this view *in principle* denies that we can justify good results by using evil means that violate an individual's rights—denies, for example, that it could be moral to kill my Aunt Bea to harvest beneficial consequences for others. That would be to sanction the disrespectful treatment of the individual in the name of the social good, something the rights view will not—categorically will not—ever allow.

The rights view, I believe, is rationally the most satisfactory moral theory. It surpasses all other theories in the degree to which it illuminates and explains the foundation of our duties to one another—the domain of human morality. On this score it has the best reasons, the best arguments, on its side. Of course, if it were possible to show that only human beings are included within its scope, then a person like myself, who believes in animal rights, would be obliged to look elsewhere.

But attempts to limit its scope to humans only can be shown to be rationally defective. Animals, it is true, lack many of the abilities humans possess. They can't read, do higher mathematics, build a bookcase or make *baba ghanoush*. Neither can many human beings, however, and yet we don't (and shouldn't) say that they (these humans) therefore have less inherent value, less of a right to be treated with respect, than do others. It is the *similarities* between those human beings who most clearly, most non-controversially have such value (the people reading this, for example), not our differences, that matter most. And the really crucial, the basic similarity is simply this: we are each of us the experiencing subject of a life, a conscious creature having an individual welfare that has importance to us whatever our usefulness to others. We want and prefer things, believe and feel things, recall and expect things. And all these dimensions of our life, including our pleasure and pain, our enjoyment and suffering, our satisfaction and frustration, our continued existence or our untimely death—all make a difference to the quality of our life as lived, as experienced, by us as individuals. As the same is true of those animals that concern us (the ones that are eaten and trapped, for example), they too must be viewed as the experiencing subjects of a life, with inherent value of their own.

Some there are who resist the idea that animals have inherent value. "Only humans have such value," they profess. How might this narrow view be defended? Shall we say that only humans have the requisite intelligence, or autonomy, or reason? But there are many, many humans who fail to meet these standards and yet are reasonably viewed as having value above and beyond their usefulness to others. Shall we claim that only humans belong to the right species, the species *Homo sapiens*? But this is blatant speciesism. Will it be said, then, that all—and only—humans have immortal souls? Then our opponents have their work cut out for them. I am myself not ill-disposed to the proposition that there are immortal souls. Personally, I profoundly hope I have one. But I would not want to rest my position on a controversial ethical issue on the even more controversial question about who or what has an immortal soul. That is to dig one's hole deeper, not to climb out. Rationally, it is better to resolve moral issues without making more controversial assumptions than are needed. The question of who has inherent value is such a question, one that is resolved more rationally without the introduction of the idea of immortal souls than by its use.

Well, perhaps some will say that animals have some inherent value, only less than we have. Once again, however, attempts to defend this view can be shown to lack rational justification. What could be the basis of our having more inherent value than animals? Their lack of reason, or autonomy, or intellect? Only if we are willing to make the same judgment in the case of humans who are similarly deficient. But it is not true that such humans—the retarded child, for example, or the mentally deranged—have less inherent value than you or I. Neither, then, can we rationally sustain the view that animals like them in being the experiencing subjects of a life have less inherent value. *All* who have inherent value have it *equally*, whether they be human animals or not.

Inherent value, then, belongs equally to those who are the experiencing subjects of a life. Whether it belongs to others—to rocks and rivers, trees and glaciers, for example—we do not know and may never know. But neither do we need to know, if we are to make the case for animal rights. We do not need to know, for example, how many people are eligible to vote in the next presidential election before we can know whether I am. Similarly, we do not need to know how many individuals have inherent value before we can know that some do. When it comes to the case for animal rights, then, what we need to know is whether the animals that, in our culture, are routinely eaten, hunted and used in our laboratories, for example, are like us in being subjects of a life. And we do know this. We do know that many—literally, billions and billions—of these animals are the subjects of a life in the sense explained and so have inherent value if we do. And since, in order to arrive at the best theory of our duties to one another, we must recognize our equal inherent value as individuals, reason—not sentiment, not emotion—reason compels us to recognize the equal inherent value of these animals and, with this, their equal right to be treated with respect.

That, *very* roughly, is the shape and feel of the case for animal rights. Most of the details of the supporting argument are missing. They are to be found in the book to which I alluded earlier. Here, the details go begging, and I must, in closing, limit myself to four final points.

The first is how the theory that underlies the case for animal rights shows that the animal rights movement is a part of, not antagonistic to, the human rights movement. The theory that rationally grounds the rights of animals also grounds the rights of humans. Thus those involved in the animal rights movement are partners in the struggle to secure respect for human rights—the rights of women, for example, or minorities, or workers. The animal rights movement is cut from the same moral cloth as these.

Second, having set out the broad outlines of the rights view, I can now say why its implications for farming and science, among other fields, are both clear and uncompromising. In the case of the use of animals in science, the rights view is categorically abolitionist. Lab animals are not our tasters; we are not their kings. Because these animals are treated routinely, systematically as if their value were reducible to their usefulness to others, they are routinely, systematically treated with a lack of respect, and thus are their rights routinely, systematically violated. This is just as true when they are used in trivial, duplicative, unnecessary or unwise research as it is when they are used in studies that hold out real promise of human benefits. We can't justify harming or killing a human being (my Aunt Bea, for example) just for these sorts of reasons. Neither can we do so even in the case of so lowly a creature as a laboratory rat. It is not just refinement or reduction that is called for, not just larger, cleaner cages, not just more generous use of anaesthetic or the elimination of multiple surgery, not just tidying up the system. It is complete replacement. The best we can do when it comes to using animals in science is— not to use them. That is where our duty lies, according to the rights view.

As for commercial animal agriculture, the rights view takes a similar abolitionist position. The fundamental moral wrong here is not that animals are kept in stressful close confinement or in isolation, or that their pain and suffering, their needs and preferences are ignored or discounted. All these *are* wrong, of course, but they are not the fundamental wrong. They are symptoms and effects of the deeper, systematic wrong that allows these animals to be viewed and treated as lacking independent value, as resources for us—as, indeed, a renewable resource. Giving farm animals more space, more natural environments, more companions does not right the fundamental wrong, any more than giving lab animals more anaesthesia or bigger, cleaner cages would right the fundamental wrong in their case. Nothing less than the total dissolution of

commerical animal agriculture will do this, just as, for similar reasons I won't develop at length here, morality requires nothing less than the total elimination of hunting and trapping for commercial and sporting ends. The rights view's implications, then, as I have said, are clear and uncompromising.

My last two points are about philosophy, my profession. It is, most obviously, no substitute for political action. The words I have written here and in other places by themselves don't change a thing. It is what we do with the thoughts that the words express—our acts, our deeds— that changes things. All that philosophy can do, and all I have attempted, is to offer a vision of what our deeds should aim at. And the why. But not the how.

Finally, I am reminded of my thoughtful critic, the one I mentioned earlier, who chastised me for being too cerebral. Well, cerebral I have been: indirect duty views, utilitarianism, contractarianism—hardly the stuff deep passions are made of. I am also reminded, however, of the image another friend once set before me— the image of the ballerina as expressive of disciplined passion. Long hours of sweat and toil, of loneliness and practice, of doubt and fatigue: those are the discipline of her craft. But the passion is there too, the fierce drive to excel, to speak through her body, to do it right, to pierce our minds. That is the image of philosophy I would leave with you, not 'too cerebral' but *disciplined passion*. Of the discipline enough has been seen. As for the passion: there are times, and these not infrequent, when tears come to my eyes when I see, or read, or hear of the wretched plight of animals in the hands of humans. Their pain, their suffering, their loneliness, their innocence, their death. Anger. Rage. Pity. Sorrow. Disgust. The whole creation groans under the weight of the evil we humans visit upon these mute, powerless creatures. It *is* our hearts, not just our heads, that call for an end to it all, that demand of us that we overcome, for them, the habits and forces behind their systematic oppression. All great movements, it is written, go through three stages: ridicule, discussion, adoption. It is the realization of this third stage, adoption, that requires both our passion and our discipline, our hearts and our heads. The fate of animals is in our hands. God grant we are equal to the task.

Review Questions

1. According to Regan, what is the fundamental wrong in our treatment of animals?
2. What are indirect-duty views, and why does Regan reject them?
3. What is the cruelty-kindness view? Why isn't it acceptable, according to Regan?
4. What are Regan's objections to utilitarianism?
5. Explain Regan's rights view.
6. What are the implications of Regan's view for science and commercial animal agriculture?

Discussion Questions

1. How would Singer reply to Regan's criticisms of his utilitarianism?
2. What exactly is inherent value and who has it? Do fish and insects have it? How about comatose humans?

Difficulties with the Strong Animal Rights Position

MARY ANNE WARREN

For biographical information on Warren, see her reading in Chapter 2.

Warren explains and then attacks Regan's strong animal rights position, the view that nonhuman animals have the same basic moral rights as humans. She makes two criticisms of Regan's position: It rests on an obscure concept of inherent value, and it fails to draw a sharp line between living things which have inherent value and moral rights and other living things which don't have such value or rights. Warren concludes with a defense of the weak animal rights position—that animal rights are weaker than human rights because humans are rational and animals are not.

TOM REGAN HAS PRODUCED what is perhaps the definitive defense of the view that the basic moral rights of at least some non-human animals are in no way inferior to our own. In *The Case for Animal Rights*, he argues that all normal mammals over a year of age have the same basic moral rights.[1] Non-human mammals have essentially the same right not to be harmed or

Source: Mary Anne Warren, "Difficulties with the Strong Rights Position," from *Between the Species* 2, No. 4 (Fall 1987), pp. 433–441.

1 Tom Regan, *The Case for Animal Rights* (Berkeley: University of California Press, 1983). All page references are to this edition.

killed as we do. I shall call this "the strong animal rights position," although it is weaker than the claims made by some animal liberationists in that it ascribes rights to only some sentient animals.[2]

I will argue that Regan's case for the strong animal rights position is unpersuasive and that this position entails consequences which a reasonable person cannot accept. I do not deny that some non-human animals have moral rights; indeed, I would extend the scope of the rights claim to include all sentient animals, that is, all those capable of having experiences, including experiences of pleasure or satisfaction and pain, suffering, or frustration.[3] However, I do not think that the moral rights of most non-human animals are identical in strength to those of persons.[4] The rights of most non-human animals may be overridden in circumstances which would not justify overriding the rights of persons. There are, for instance, compelling realities which sometimes require that we kill animals for reasons which could not justify the killing of persons. I will call this view "the weak animal rights" position, even though it ascribes rights to a wider range of animals than does the strong animal rights position.

I will begin by summarizing Regan's case for the strong animal rights position and noting two problems with it. Next, I will explore some consequences of the strong animal rights position which I think are unacceptable. Finally, I will outline the case for the weak animal rights position.

REGAN'S CASE

Regan's argument moves through three stages. First, he argues that normal, mature mammals are not only sentient but have other mental capacities as well. These include the capacities for emotion, memory, belief, desire, the use of general concepts, intentional action, a sense of the future, and some degree of self-awareness. Creatures with such capacities are said to be subjects-of-a-life. They are not only alive in the biological sense but have a psychological identity over time and an existence which can go better or worse for them. Thus, they can be harmed or benefited. These are plausible claims, and well defended. One of the strongest parts of the book is the rebuttal of philosophers, such as R. G. Frey, who object to the application of such mentalistic terms to creatures that do not use a human-style language.[5] The second and third stages of the argument are more problematic.

In the second stage, Regan argues that subjects-of-a-life have inherent value. His concept of inherent value grows out of his opposition to utilitarianism. Utilitarian moral theory, he says, treats individuals as "mere receptacles" for morally significant value, in that harm to one individual may be justified by the production of a greater net benefit to other individuals. In opposition to this, he holds that subjects-of-a-life have a value independent of both the value they may place upon their lives or experiences and the value others may place upon them.

Inherent value, Regan argues, does not come in degrees. To hold that some individuals have more inherent value than others is to adopt a "perfectionist" theory, i.e., one which assigns

2 For instance, Peter Singer, although he does not like to speak of rights, includes all sentient beings under the protection of his basic utilitarian principle of equal respect for like interests. (*Animal Liberation* [New York: Avon Books, 1975], p. 3.)

3 The capacity for sentience, like all of the mental capacities mentioned in what follows, is a disposition. Dispositions do not disappear whenever they are not currently manifested. Thus, sleeping or temporarily unconscious persons or non-human animals are still sentient in the relevant sense (i.e., still capable of sentience), so long as they still have the neurological mechanisms necessary for the occurrence of experiences.

4 It is possible, perhaps probable that some non-human animals—such as cetaceans and anthropoid apes—should be regarded as persons. If so, then the weak animal rights position holds that these animals have the same basic moral rights as human persons.

5 See R. G. Frey, *Interests and Rights: The Case Against Animals* (Oxford: Oxford University Press, 1980).

different moral worth to individuals according to how well they are thought to exemplify some virtue(s), such as intelligence or moral autonomy. Perfectionist theories have been used, at least since the time of Aristotle, to rationalize such injustices as slavery and male domination, as well as the unrestrained exploitation of animals. Regan argues that if we reject these injustices, then we must also reject perfectionism and conclude that all subjects-of-a-life have equal inherent value. Moral agents have no more inherent value than moral patients, i.e., subjects-of-a-life who are not morally responsible for their actions.

In the third phase of the argument, Regan uses the thesis of equal inherent value to derive strong moral rights for all subjects-of-a-life. This thesis underlies the Respect Principle, which forbids us to treat beings who have inherent value as mere receptacles, i.e., mere means to the production of the greatest overall good. This principle, in turn, underlies the Harm Principle, which says that we have a direct *prima facie* duty not to harm beings who have inherent value. Together, these principles give rise to moral rights. Rights are defined as valid claims, claims to certain goods and against certain beings, i.e., moral agents. Moral rights generate duties not only to refrain from inflicting harm upon beings with inherent value but also to come to their aid when they are threatened by other moral agents. Rights are not absolute but may be overridden in certain circumstances. Just what these circumstances are we will consider later. But first, let's look at some difficulties in the theory as thus far presented.

THE MYSTERY
OF INHERENT VALUE

Inherent value is a key concept in Regan's theory. It is the bridge between the plausible claim that all normal, mature mammals—human or otherwise—are subjects-of-a-life and the more debatable claim that they all have basic moral rights of the same strength. But it is a highly obscure concept, and its obscurity makes it ill-suited to play this crucial role.

Inherent value is defined almost entirely in negative terms. It is not dependent upon the value which either the inherently valuable individual or anyone else may place upon that individual's life or experiences. It is not (necessarily) a function of sentience or any other mental capacity, because, Regan says, some entities which are not sentient (e.g., trees, rivers, or rocks) may, nevertheless, have inherent value (p. 246). It cannot attach to anything other than an individual; species, eco-systems, and the like cannot have inherent value.

These are some of the things which inherent value is not. But what is it? Unfortunately, we are not told. Inherent value appears as a mysterious non-natural property which we must take on faith. Regan says that it is a *postulate* that subjects-of-a-life have inherent value, a postulate justified by the fact that it avoids certain absurdities which he thinks follow from a purely utilitarian theory (p. 247). But why is the postulate that *subjects-of-a-life* have inherent value? If the inherent value of a being is completely independent of the value that it or anyone else places upon its experiences, then why does the fact that it has certain sorts of experiences constitute evidence that it has inherent value? If the reason is that subjects-of-a-life have an existence which can go better or worse for them, then why isn't the appropriate conclusion that all sentient beings have inherent value, since they would all seem to meet that condition? Sentient but mentally unsophisticated beings may have a less extensive range of possible satisfactions and frustrations, but why should it follow that they have—or may have—no inherent value at all?

In the absence of a positive account of inherent value, it is also difficult to grasp the connection between being inherently valuable and having moral rights. Intuitively, it seems that value is one thing, and rights are another. It does not seem incoherent to say that some things (e.g., mountains, rivers, redwood trees) are inherently valuable and yet are not the sorts of things which can have moral rights. Nor does it seem incoherent to ascribe inherent value to some things which are not individuals, e.g., plant or animal species, though it may well be incoherent to ascribe moral rights to such things.

In short, the concept of inherent value seems to create at least as many problems as it solves. If inherent value is based on some natural property, then why not try to identify that property and explain its moral significance, without appealing to inherent value? And if it is not based on any natural property, then why should we believe in it? That it may enable us to avoid some of the problems faced by the utilitarian is not a sufficient reason, if it creates other problems which are just as serious.

IS THERE A SHARP LINE?

Perhaps the most serious problems are those that arise when we try to apply the strong animal rights position to animals other than normal, mature mammals. Regan's theory requires us to divide all living things into two categories: those which have the same inherent value and the same basic moral rights that we do, and those which have no inherent value and presumably no moral rights. But wherever we try to draw the line, such a sharp division is implausible.

It would surely be arbitrary to draw such a sharp line between normal, mature mammals and all other living things. Some birds (e.g., crows, magpies, parrots, mynahs) appear to be just as mentally sophisticated as most mammals and thus are equally strong candidates for inclusion under the subject-of-a-life criterion. Regan is not in fact advocating that we draw the line here. His claim is only that normal mature mammals are clear cases, while other cases are less clear. Yet, on his theory, there must be such a sharp line *somewhere,* since there are no degrees of inherent value. But why should we believe that there is a sharp line between creatures that are subjects-of-a-life and creatures that are not? Isn't it more likely that "subjecthood" comes in degrees, that some creatures have only a little self-awareness, and only a little capacity to anticipate the future, while some have a little more, and some a good deal more?

Should we, for instance, regard fish, amphibians, and reptiles as subjects-of-a-life? A simple yes-or-no answer seems inadequate. On the one hand, some of their behavior is difficult to explain without the assumption that they have sensations, beliefs, desires, emotions, and memories; on the other hand, they do not seem to exhibit very much self-awareness or very much conscious anticipation of future events. Do they have enough mental sophistication to count as subjects-of-a-life? Exactly how much is enough?

It is still more unclear what we should say about insects, spiders, octopi, and other invertebrate animals which have brains and sensory organs but whose minds (if they have minds) are even more alien to us than those of fish or reptiles. Such creatures are probably sentient. Some people doubt that they can feel pain, since they lack certain neurological structures which are crucial to the processing of pain impulses in vertebrate animals. But this argument is inconclusive, since their nervous systems might process pain in ways different from ours. When injured, they sometimes act as if they are in pain. On evolutionary grounds, it seems unlikely that highly mobile creatures with complex sensory systems would not have developed a capacity for pain (and pleasure), since such a capacity has obvious survival value. It must, however, be admitted that we do not *know* whether spiders can feel pain (or something very like it), let alone whether they have emotions, memories, beliefs, desires, self-awareness, or a sense of the future.

Even more mysterious are the mental capacities (if any) of mobile microfauna. The brisk and efficient way that paramecia move about in their incessant search for food *might* indicate some kind of sentience, in spite of their lack of eyes, ears, brains, and other organs associated with sentience in more complex organisms. It is conceivable—though not very probable—that they, too, are subjects-of-a-life.

The existence of a few unclear cases need not pose a serious problem for a moral theory, but in this case, the unclear cases constitute most of those with which an adequate theory of animal rights would need to deal. The subject-of-a-life criterion can provide us with little or no moral guidance in our interactions with the vast majority of animals. That might be acceptable if it could be supplemented with additional principles which would provide such guidance. However, the radical dualism of the theory precludes supplementing it in this way. We are forced to say that either a spider has the same right to life as you and I do, or it has no right to life whatever—and that only the gods know which of these alternatives is true.

Regan's suggestion for dealing with such unclear cases is to apply the "benefit of the doubt" principle. That is, when dealing with beings that may or may not be subjects-of-a-life, we should act as if they are.[6] But if we try to apply this principle to the entire range of doubtful cases, we will find ourselves with moral obligations which we cannot possibly fulfill. In many climates, it is virtually impossible to live without swatting mosquitoes and exterminating cockroaches, and not all of us can afford to hire someone to sweep the path before we walk, in order to make sure that we do not step on ants. Thus, we are still faced with the daunting task of drawing a sharp line somewhere on the continuum of life forms—this time, a line demarcating the limits of the benefit of the doubt principle.

The weak animal rights theory provides a more plausible way of dealing with this range of cases, in that it allows the rights of animals of different kinds to vary in strength. . . .

WHY ARE ANIMAL RIGHTS WEAKER THAN HUMAN RIGHTS?

How can we justify regarding the rights of persons as generally stronger than those of sentient beings which are not persons? There are a plethora of bad justifications, based on religious premises or false or unprovable claims about the differences between human and non-human nature.

But there is one difference which has a clear moral relevance: people are at least sometimes capable of being moved to action or inaction by the force of reasoned argument. Rationality rests upon other mental capacities, notably those which Regan cites as criteria for being a subject-of-a-life. We share these capacities with many other animals. But it is not just because we are subjects-of-a-life that we are both able and morally compelled to recognize one another as beings with equal basic moral rights. It is also because we are able to "listen to reason" in order to settle our conflicts and cooperate in shared projects. This capacity, unlike the others, may require something like a human language.

Why is rationality morally relevant? It does not make us "better" than other animals or more "perfect." It does not even automatically make us more intelligent. (Bad reasoning reduces our effective intelligence rather than increasing it.) But it is morally relevant insofar as it provides greater possibilities for cooperation and for the nonviolent resolution of problems. It also makes us more dangerous than non-rational beings can ever be. Because we are potentially more dangerous and less predictable than wolves, we need an articulated system of morality to regulate our conduct. Any human morality, to be workable in the long run, must recognize the equal moral status of all persons, whether through the postulate of equal basic moral rights or in some other way. The recognition of the moral equality of other persons is the price we must each pay for their recognition of our moral equality. Without this mutual recognition of moral equality, human society can exist only in a state of chronic and bitter conflict. The war between the sexes will persist so long as there is sexism and male domination; racial conflict will never be eliminated so long as there are racist laws and practices. But, to the extent that we achieve a mutual recognition of equality, we can hope to live together, perhaps as peacefully as wolves, achieving (in part) through explicit moral principles what they do not seem to need explicit moral principles to achieve.

---

6 See, for instance, p. 319, where Regan appeals to the benefit of the doubt principle when dealing with infanticide and late-term abortion.

Why not extend this recognition of moral equality to other creatures, even though they cannot do the same for us? The answer is that we cannot. Because we cannot reason with most non-human animals, we cannot always solve the problems which they may cause without harming them—although we are always obligated to try. We cannot negotiate a treaty with the feral cats and foxes, requiring them to stop preying on endangered native species in return for suitable concessions on our part.

> if rats invade our houses . . . we cannot reason with them, hoping to persuade them of the injustice they do us. We can only attempt to get rid of them.[7]

Aristotle was not wrong in claiming that the capacity to alter one's behavior on the basis of reasoned argument is relevant to the full moral status which he accorded to free men. Of course, he was wrong in his other premise, that women and slaves by their nature cannot reason well enough to function as autonomous moral agents. Had that premise been true, so would his conclusion that women and slaves are not quite the moral equals of free men. In the case of most non-human animals, the corresponding premise is true. If, on the other hand, there are animals with whom we can (learn to) reason, then we are obligated to do this and to regard them as our moral equals.

Thus, to distinguish between the rights of persons and those of most other animals on the grounds that only people can alter their behavior on the basis of reasoned argument does not commit us to a perfectionist theory of the sort Aristotle endorsed. There is no excuse for refusing to recognize the moral equality of some people on the grounds that we don't regard them as quite as rational as we are, since it is perfectly clear that most people can reason well enough to determine how to act so as to respect the basic

rights of others (if they choose to), and that is enough for moral equality.

But what about people who are clearly not rational? It is often argued that sophisticated mental capacities such as rationality cannot be essential for the possession of equal basic moral rights, since nearly everyone agrees that human infants and mentally incompetent persons have such rights, even though they may lack those sophisticated mental capacities. But this argument is inconclusive, because there are powerful practical and emotional reasons for protecting non-rational human beings, reasons which are absent in the case of most non-human animals. Infancy and mental incompetence are human conditions which all of us either have experienced or are likely to experience at some time. We also protect babies and mentally incompetent people because we care for them. We don't normally care for animals in the same way, and when we do—e.g., in the case of much-loved pets—we may regard them as having special rights by virtue of their relationship to us. We protect them not only for their sake but also for our own, lest we be hurt by harm done to them. Regan holds that such "side-effects" are irrelevant to moral rights, and perhaps they are. But in ordinary usage, there is no sharp line between moral rights and those moral protections which are not rights. The extension of strong moral protections to infants and the mentally impaired in no way proves that non-human animals have the same basic moral rights as people.

WHY SPEAK OF "ANIMAL RIGHTS" AT ALL?

If, as I have argued, reality precludes our treating all animals as our moral equals, then why should we still ascribe rights to them? Everyone agrees that animals are entitled to some protection against human abuse, but why speak of animal *rights* if we are not prepared to accept most animals as our moral equals? The weak animal rights position may seem an unstable compromise between the bold claim that animals have

7 Bonnie Steinbock, "Speciesism and the Idea of Equality," *Philosophy* 53 (1978):253.

the same basic moral rights that we do and the more common view that animals have no rights at all.

It is probably impossible to either prove or disprove the thesis that animals have moral rights by producing an analysis of the concept of a moral right and checking to see if some or all animals satisfy the conditions for having rights. The concept of a moral right is complex, and it is not clear which of its strands are essential. Paradigm rights holders, i.e., mature and mentally competent persons, are *both* rational and morally autonomous beings and sentient subjects-of-a-life. Opponents of animal rights claim that rationality and moral autonomy are essential for the possession of rights, while defenders of animal rights claim that they are not. The ordinary concept of a moral right is probably not precise enough to enable us to determine who is right on purely definitional grounds.

If logical analysis will not answer the question of whether animals have moral rights, practical considerations may, nevertheless, incline us to say that they do. The most plausible alternative to the view that animals have moral rights is that, while they do not have *rights,* we are, nevertheless, obligated not to be cruel to them. Regan argues persuasively that the injunction to avoid being cruel to animals is inadequate to express our obligations towards animals, because it focuses on the mental states of those who cause animal suffering, rather than on the harm done to the animals themselves (p. 158). Cruelty is inflicting pain or suffering and either taking pleasure in that pain or suffering or being more or less indifferent to it. Thus, to express the demand for the decent treatment of animals in terms of the rejection of cruelty is to invite the too easy response that those who subject animals to suffering are not being cruel because they regret the suffering they cause but sincerely believe that what they do is justified. The injunction to avoid cruelty is also inadequate in that it does not preclude the killing of animals—for any reason, however trivial—so long as it is done relatively painlessly.

The inadequacy of the anti-cruelty view provides one practical reason for speaking of animal rights. Another practical reason is that this is an age in which nearly all significant moral claims tend to be expressed in terms of rights. Thus, the denial that animals have rights, however carefully qualified, is likely to be taken to mean that we may do whatever we like to them, provided that we do not violate any human rights. In such a context, speaking of the rights of animals may be the only way to persuade many people to take seriously protests against the abuse of animals.

Why not extend this line of argument and speak of the rights of trees, mountains, oceans, or anything else which we may wish to see protected from destruction? Some environmentalists have not hesitated to speak in this way, and, given the importance of protecting such elements of the natural world, they cannot be blamed for using this rhetorical device. But, I would argue that moral rights can meaningfully be ascribed only to entities which have some capacity for sentience. This is because moral rights are protections designed to protect rights holders from harms or to provide them with benefits which matter *to them.* Only beings capable of sentience can be harmed or benefited in ways which matter to them, for only such beings can like or dislike what happens to them or prefer some conditions to others. Thus, sentient animals, unlike mountains, rivers, or species, are at least logically possible candidates for moral rights. This fact, together with the need to end current abuses of animals—e.g., in scientific research . . . —provides a plausible case for speaking of animal rights.

CONCLUSION

I have argued that Regan's case for ascribing strong moral rights to all normal, mature mammals is unpersuasive because (1) it rests upon the obscure concept of inherent value, which is defined only in negative terms, and (2) it seems to preclude any plausible answer to questions about the moral status of the vast majority of sentient animals. . . .

The weak animal rights theory asserts that (1) any creature whose natural mode of life includes the pursuit of certain satisfactions has the right not to be forced to exist without the opportunity to pursue those satisfactions; (2) that any creature which is capable of pain, suffering, or frustration has the right that such experiences not be deliberately inflicted upon it without some compelling reason; and (3) that no sentient being should be killed without good reason. However, moral rights are not an all-or-nothing affair. The strength of the reasons required to override the rights of a non-human organism varies, depending upon—among other things—the probability that it is sentient and (if it is clearly sentient) its probable degree of mental sophistication. . . .

Review Questions

1. Distinguish between what Warren calls the strong animal rights position and the weak animal rights position.
2. What problems does Warren find in Regan's case for the strong animal rights position?
3. Explain Warren's defense of the weak animal rights position.

Discussion Questions

1. Has Warren refuted Regan's strong animal rights position? Does he have an adequate reply?
2. In Warren's view, rationality is essential for having equal basic moral rights. But infants and mentally incompetent humans are not rational; therefore, they do not have moral rights. Does Warren have an acceptable reply to this argument?

The Moral Status of Animals

ROGER SCRUTON

Roger Scruton has held academic posts at many institutions including Princeton, Stanford, Louvain, Guelph (Ontario), and Birkbeck College (London). He has published more than 20 books and countless articles. Our reading is taken from *Animal Rights and Wrongs* (3e 2000). Another book on animals is *On Hunting* (1998).

Scruton defines animals as creatures lacking the features of moral persons such as rationality, self-consciousness, and personality. As Scruton defines them, animals are not members of the moral community, and as such they have neither rights nor duties. In Scruton's view, to attribute rights or duties to animals is a gross and callous abuse of them. The fact that animals suffer, however, does give moral persons some duties to care for them. Pet dogs, for example, have a special claim on their

Source: Roger Scruton, "The Moral Status of Animals," *Animal Rights and Wrongs,* pp. 51–56, 79–83. Used by permission of the author.

care-givers, similar to the claim of children on their parents. Scruton wants to draw a clear line between humans, who are members of the moral community, and animals that are not. But what about so-called marginal humans such as infants, comatose people, and mentally impaired people? If they are not rational or self-conscious, then why are they still members of the moral community? Why do they have rights? Scruton's strategy is to make some distinctions. Infants are potentially members of the moral community, and as such they have rights, but not the same rights as adults. Mentally impaired people such as congenital idiots will never be moral persons, but they still have rights because they are human and all human life is sacrocanct. That leaves senile people and brain-damaged people, people that Scruton calls "human vegetables." For reasons that are not clear, Scruton says that killing them is understandable, even excusable. Presumably, this is because such people are not conscious, or barely so.

. . . I SHALL USE THE TERM 'animal' to mean those animals that lack the distinguishing features of the moral being—rationality, self-consciousness, personality, and so on. If there are non-human animals who are rational and self-conscious, then they, like us, are persons, and should be described and treated accordingly. If *all* animals are persons, then there is no longer a problem as to how we should treat them. They would be full members of the moral community, with rights and duties like the rest of us. But it is precisely because there are animals who are not persons that the moral problem exists. And to treat these non-personal animals as persons is not to grant to them a privilege nor to raise their chances of contentment. It is to ignore what they essentially are and so to fall out of relation with them altogether.

The concept of the person belongs to the ongoing dialogue which binds the moral community. Creatures who are by nature incapable of entering into this dialogue have neither rights nor duties nor personality. If animals had rights, then we should require their consent before taking them into captivity, training them, domesticating them or in any way putting them to our uses. But there is no conceivable process whereby this consent could be delivered or withheld. Furthermore, a creature with rights is duty-bound to respect the rights of others. The fox would be duty-bound to respect the right to life of the chicken and whole species would be condemned out of hand as criminal by nature. Any law which compelled persons to respect the rights of non-human species would weigh so heavily on the predators as to drive them to extinction in a short while. Any morality which really attributed rights to animals would therefore constitute a gross and callous abuse of them.

Those considerations are obvious, but by no means trivial. For they point to a deep difficulty in the path of any attempt to treat animals as our equals. By ascribing rights to animals, and so promoting them to full membership of the moral community, we tie them in obligations that they can neither fulfil nor comprehend. Not only is this senseless cruelty in itself; it effectively destroys all possibility of cordial and beneficial relations between us and them. Only by refraining from personalising animals do we behave towards them in ways that they can understand. And even the most sentimental animal lovers know this, and confer 'rights' on their favourites in a manner so selective and arbitrary as to show that they are not really dealing with the ordinary moral concept. When a dog savages a sheep no one believes that the dog, rather than its owner, should be sued for damages. Sei Shonagon, in *The Pillow Book,* tells of a dog breaching some rule of court etiquette and being horribly beaten, as the law requires. The scene is most disturbing to the modern reader. Yet surely, if dogs have rights, punishment is what they must expect when they disregard their duties.

But the point does not concern rights only. It concerns the deep and impassable difference between personal relations, founded on dialogue, criticism and the sense of justice, and animal relations, founded on affections and needs. The moral problem of animals arises because they cannot enter into relations of the first kind, while we are so much bound by those relations that they seem to tie us even to creatures who cannot themselves be bound by them.

Defenders of 'animal liberation' have made much of the fact that animals suffer as we do: they feel pain, hunger, cold and fear and therefore, as Singer puts it, have 'interests' which form, or ought to form, part of the moral equation. While this is true, it is only part of the truth. There is more to morality than the avoidance of suffering: to live by no other standard than this one is to avoid life, to forgo risk and adventure, and to sink into a state of cringing morbidity. Moreover, while our sympathies ought to be— and unavoidably will be—extended to the animals, they should not be indiscriminate. Although animals have no rights, we still have duties and responsibilities towards them, or towards some of them. These will cut across the utilitarian equation, distinguishing the animals who are close to us and who have a claim on our protection from those towards whom our duties fall under the broader rule of charity.

This is important for two reasons. Firstly, we relate to animals in three distinct situations, which define three distinct kinds of responsibility: as pets, as domestic animals reared for human purposes and as wild creatures. Secondly, the situation of animals is radically and often irreversibly changed as soon as human beings take an interest in them. Pets and other domestic animals are usually entirely dependent on human care for their survival and well-being; and wild animals, too, are increasingly dependent on human measures to protect their food supplies and habitats.

Some shadow version of the moral law therefore emerges in our dealings with animals. I cannot blithely count the interests of my dog as on a par with the interests of any other dog, wild or domesticated, even though they have an equal capacity for suffering and an equal need for help. My dog has a special claim on me, not wholly dissimilar from the claim of my child. I caused it to be dependent on me precisely by leading it to expect that I would cater for its needs.

The situation is further complicated by the distinction between species. Dogs form life-long attachments and a dog brought up by one person may be incapable of living comfortably with another. A horse may be bought or sold many times, with little or no distress, provided it is properly cared for by each of its owners. Sheep maintained in flocks are every bit as dependent on human care as dogs and horses; but they do not notice it and regard their shepherds and guardians as little more than aspects of the environment, which rise like the sun in the morning and depart like the sun at night. . . .

It will be said that *natura non fecit saltus*— that nature makes no leaps—and therefore that between the moral being and the cognitive animal there ought to be a continuum, with a grey area in which it simply cannot be determined whether rights, duties and so on are to be imputed on the basis of what we observe. The existence of this continuum is precisely what motivates people who advocate animal 'rights' or who recommend at least that we extend to animals the protection offered by the moral law. To behave in any other way is to make an absolute division, where in fact there is only a gradual transition and a difference of degree.

Two points should be made in answer to this argument. First, the distinguishing features of the moral being—including rationality and self-consciousness—belong to another *system* of behaviour from that which characterises the merely cognitive animal. The transition from the one behavioural system to the other is as absolute a transition as that from vegetable to sentient life, or that from sentience to appetite. This is confirmed by all the other concepts which seem to pile in irresistibly behind the ideas of rationality and personhood—concepts which suggest a distinct form of mental life, unknown to the lower animals.

The second point is this. It is true that we arrive at the rational from the merely animal by the route of behaviour, and that there are degrees of complexity both before and after the transition. But we are dealing here, in Hegel's phrase, with a 'transition from quantity to quality'. Something wholly new emerges as a result of a process which merely adapts what is old. An analogy may help to understand the point. An array of dots on a canvas may look like an array of dots and nothing more. But suddenly, with the addition of just one more dot, a face appears. And this face has a character, a meaning and an identity which no array of dots could ever have. In a similar way, at a certain level of complexity, the behaviour of an animal becomes the expression of a self-conscious person. And this transition is well likened to the emergence of a face, a look, a gaze. Another subject now stands before me, seeing me, not as an animal sees me, but I to I. . . .

But this brings me to a vexed question, much emphasised by Regan and Singer, the question of 'marginal humans', as Regan describes them. Even if we grant a distinction between moral beings and other animals, and recognise the importance of rationality, self-consciousness and moral dialogue in defining it, we must admit that many human beings do not lie on the moral side of the dividing line. For example, infants are *not yet* members of the moral community; senile and brain-damaged people are *no longer* members; congenital idiots *never will be* members. Are we to say that they have no rights? Or are we to say that, since they differ in no fundamental respect from animals, that we ought in consistency to treat other animals as we treat these 'marginal' humans? Whichever line we take, the hope of making an absolute moral distinction between human and animal life collapses.

It seems to me that we should clearly distinguish the case of 'pre-moral' infants, from those of the 'post-moral' and 'non-moral' human adults. The former are *potential* moral beings, who will naturally develop, in the conditions of society, into full members of the moral community. Our attitude towards them depends on this fact; and indeed, it is only because we look on them as incipiently rational that we eventually elicit the behaviour that justifies our treatment. Just as an acorn is, by its nature, the seed of an oak tree, so is an infant, by its nature, a potential rational being. And it is only by treating it as such that we enable it to realise this potential and so to become what it essentially is.

The other cases of 'marginal humans' are more problematic. And this is instinctively recognised by all who have to deal with them. Infanticide is an inexcusable crime; but the killing of a human vegetable, however much we shrink from it, may often strike us as understandable, even excusable. Although the law may treat this act as murder, we ourselves, and especially those upon whom the burden falls to protect and nurture this unfortunate creature, will seldom see it in such a light. On the other hand, to imagine that we can simply dispose of mental cripples is to display not only a callousness towards the individual, but also a cold and calculating attitude to the human species and the human form. It is part of human virtue to acknowledge human life as sacrosanct, to recoil from treating other humans, however hopeless their life may seem to us, as merely disposable and to look for the signs of personality wherever the human eye seems able to meet and return our gaze. This is not part of virtue only; it is a sign of piety. And . . . virtue and piety are cornerstones of moral thinking.

There is a further point to be made. Our world makes sense to us because we divide it into kinds, distinguishing animals and plants by species and instantly recognising the individual as an example of the universal. This recognitional expertise is essential to survival and especially to the survival of the hunter-gatherer. And it is essential also to the moral life. I relate to you as a human being and accord to you the privileges attached to the kind. It is in the nature of human beings that, in normal conditions, they become members of a moral community, governed by duty and protected by rights. Abnormality in this respect does not cancel membership. It merely compels us to adjust our response. Infants and imbeciles belong to the same kind as you or me: the kind whose normal instances are also moral beings. It is this that causes us to extend to them the shield that we consciously extend to each other and which is built collectively through our moral dialogue.

It is not just that dogs and bears do not belong to the moral community. They have no potential for membership. They are not *the kind of thing* that can settle disputes, that can exert sovereignty over its life and respect the sovereignty of others, that can respond to the call of duty or take responsibility on a matter of trust. Moreover, it should be noted that we do not accord to infants and imbeciles the same rights as we accord to normal adults: in many of our dealings with them we assume the right to by-pass their consent. Their disabilities have moral consequences. And although infants cause us no difficulties, since we curtail their rights only in order to enhance them, imbeciles cause us real moral problems.

Much more needs to be said about these difficult cases; for our purposes it is enough, however, to recognise that the difficulty arises not because we make no distinction between moral beings and animals, but precisely because we do make such a distinction, and on very good grounds. It is precisely this that lands us with such an intractable problem, when our instinctive reverence for human beings is thwarted by their inability to respond to it. Our difficulties over 'marginal humans' do not cast doubt on the moral distinction between people and animals; on the contrary, they confirm it.

Review Questions

1. How does Scruton use the term "animal?" By contrast, who is a person, that is, a member of the moral community?
2. According to Scruton, why don't animals have rights or duties?
3. Why does Scruton think there is more to morality than the avoidance of suffering?
4. In Scruton's view, what are our duties to animals?
5. Why does Scruton think there is a clear difference between persons and animals?
6. How does he deal with the problem of so-called marginal humans who are not persons? Do they have rights?

Discussion Questions

1. Scruton seems to assume that rights imply duties, that if animals had rights, then they would have duties. Do you agree? Why or why not?
2. Scruton insists that human life is sacrosanct, but he grants that killing a so-called human vegetable is excusable. Is this consistent? Why or why not?
3. Compare Scruton and Warren on marginal humans. Is either view acceptable to you? Why or why not?

Problem Cases

1. Killing Chickens

Suppose a farmer raises happy chickens on this farm. They are well fed, they have plenty of room, they have a comfortable place to sleep; in short, they are well cared for and happy. Each year the farmer kills the oldest chickens, the ones that will die of disease or old age. He kills them quickly and with little or no pain. Then he thanks the chickens for their bodies; he is a religious man and believes that the chickens have eternal souls that blissfully unite with the Great Spirit after death and that killing them does not harm the eternal souls. In fact, liberating the chicken souls from their mortal bodies is a natural and good thing to do. That done, he carefully prepares the chicken meat and eats it with great relish. He replaces the chickens he kills with new chickens each year so that the chicken population remains stable.

Does this farmer do anything that is morally wrong? Explain your position.

2. The Draize Test

The Draize eye test is used by cosmetic companies such as Revlon and Procter & Gamble to test the eye irritancy of their products—cosmetics, hair shampoos, and so on. The substance to be tested is injected into the eyes of rabbits; more specifically, 0.1 milligrams (a large-volume dose) is injected into the conjunctival sac of one eye of each of six rabbits, with the other eye serving as a control. The lids are held together for one second and then the animal is released. The eyes are examined at 24, 48, and 72 hours to see if there is corneal damage. Although the test is very painful, as you can imagine, anesthetics are not used. The eyes are not washed. Very large doses are used (often resulting in permanent eye damage) to provide a large margin of safety in extrapolating for human response.

Should companies continue to test their new products in this way? Why or why not?

3. Eating Whales

(Reported by Andrew Pollack in *The New York Times,* May 3, 1993.) Eating whale meat is popular in Japan. At the crowded restaurant of Kiyoo Tanahahi in Tokyo, customers dine on whale steak, whale bacon, fried whale, smoked whale, raw whale, and whale tongue. Of course, to satisfy the Japanese demand for whale meat, many whales must be hunted and killed. But the International Whaling Commission, the thirty-nine-nation group that regulates whaling, has a moratorium on commercial whaling that has been in effect since 1986. The position of Japan and Norway, the two countries that continue to hunt and kill whales, is that the moratorium is no longer necessary to protect whales. It was originally put in place to protect species of whales endangered by decades of excessive whaling; now, according to Japan and Norway, it is no longer needed for certain types of whales. They estimate that there are more than 760,000 minkes (a relatively small whale) in the Southern Hemisphere. Japan claims that killing 2,000 minkes a year has no effect on the total population.

Those opposed think that all whales, including the minkes, should be protected. They point out that whales are majestic creatures with high intelligence, and they argue it is morally wrong to kill them. Japan replies that the ban on whaling is just a form of discrimination against Japan and the imposition of one nation's morals on another. Why should Western nations be allowed to kill chickens, cows, and pigs, and Japan not be allowed to kill whales?

What do you think? Should there be a ban on whaling? If so, should Western nations stop killing chickens, cows, and pigs?

4. Human Rights for Apes

(Reported by Seth Mydaus in *The New York Times,* August 12, 2001.) Some scientists link the five great apes into one biologically similar group. The five types of apes are chimpanzees, gorillas, orangutans, bonobos, and humans. Humans are just another type of ape. These scientists note that humans and chimpanzees are 99 percent identical genetically, have similar blood groups, and have similar brain structures. Humans and chimpanzees show nearly identical behavior in their first three years of life. All five types of ape have self-awareness and moral awareness, as displayed in their behavior.

One of the rights-for-apes advocates, Richard Wranghan, a chimpanzee expert at Harvard University, describes chimpanzees as follows: "Like humans, they laugh, make up after a quarrel, support each other in times of trouble, medicate themselves with chemical and physical remedies, stop each other from eating poisonous foods, collaborate in the hunt, help each other over physical boundaries, raid neighboring groups, lose their tempers, get excited by dramatic weather, invent ways to show off, have family traditions and group traditions, make tools, devise plans, deceive, play tricks, grieve, and are cruel and are kind."

If chimpanzees and other apes are so like humans, then why not give them basic human rights, a right to live and a right not to suffer from cruel treatment, such as in medical experiments?

Moreover, rights-for-apes advocates want to recognize the other four great apes as persons under law rather than property. As such, they would be provided with guardians to safeguard their rights, like young or impaired humans.

In 1999, New Zealand became the first nation to adopt a law giving rights to apes. They are protected from scientific experimentation not in their interest.

Do great apes deserve basic human rights? Should they be treated as persons under the law? What is your view?

5. Hunting Baby Seals

(Reported by Clifford Krauss in *The New York Times,* April 5, 2004). In the 1970s animal rights advocates succeeded in shutting down the American and European markets for the fur of baby harp seals. But now the market has revived. Seal products are banned in the United States, but new markets have emerged in Russia, Ukraine, and Poland, with a fashion trend for sealskin hats and accessories. The price for top-grade harp sealskin has more than doubled since 2001, to about $42. Canadian officials say that seal hunting is worth about $30 million annually to the

Newfoundland economy, which has suffered from the collapse of cod fishing. There are about 5,000 hunters and 350 workers who process the skins. In 2004, the Canadian government increased the quota of seals killed to 350,000, the largest number hunted in at least a half century. The large increase is possible, officials say, because the seal population was replenished during the long hunting slump. The Canadian harp seal population has tripled in size since 1970, according to the Department of Fisheries and Oceans, to more than five million today.

How are the seals hunted? On the ice fields of the Gulf of St. Lawrence, men with clubs roam in snowmobiles looking for the silvery young pups. The seal pups have not been weaned from their mother's milk and do not know how to swim. They cannot escape and are easy to kill. The men club them over the head, crushing the skull, and sometimes leaving the seals in convulsions. Then the men drag the bodies to waiting ships or skin them on the spot.

In the past, hunters skinned the pups while they were still alive, but new regulations were added in 2004 to stop this. Now the hunters are required to examine the skull of the seal or touch the eyes to guarantee that the seal is brain dead before skinning. The government requires novice seal hunters to obtain an assistant's license and to train for two years before getting a professional license. The killing of whitecoats—the youngest pups up to 12 days old, is now banned. The regulations say that only seals that have shed their white coats are "beaters." The beaters are at least three weeks old, and have a black-spotted silvery fur that is valuable.

Animal rights advocates are revving up a campaign against the hunting of baby harp seals. They are calling for a tourism boycott of Canada. They are flying journalists over the ice fields to photograph the slaughter.

The hunters say they are just trying to make a living. Jason Spence, the 32-year-old captain of Ryan's Pride, a fishing boat hunting seals in the Gulf of St. Lawrence, argues that hunting seals is no worse than "people taking the heads off chickens, butchering cows, and butchering pigs."

What is your view of hunting seals? Is it just like killing chickens, cows, and pigs? Is it morally objectionable? Why or why not?

Suggested Readings

1. Ethics Updates (http://ethics.acusd.edu/animal/html) is a very useful website for research on animal rights, abortion, and other topics. There are links to various home pages relating to animals and animal rights, as well as online articles and bibliographical guides. The People for the Ethical Treatment of Animals website (http://www.peta.org) has action alerts and current information about the treatment of animals around the world.

2. Peter Singer, *Animal Liberation,* 2nd ed. (New York Review/Random House, 1975; revised edition, New York Review/Random House, 1990; reissued with a new preface, Ecco, 2001), presents the now-classic critique of our treatment of animals together with relevant factual material.

3. *The Animal Ethics Reader,* ed. Susan J. Armstrong and Richard G. Botzler (London: Routledge, 2003) is a comprehensive anthology about animals including sections on the

moral status of animals, animals for food, animal experimentation, zoos, rodeos, pets, animal law, and so on.

4. Paola Cavalieri, *The Animal Question: Why Non-Humans Deserve Human Rights,* trans. Catherine Woolland (Oxford: Oxford University Press, 2004), argues that we should extend basic moral and legal rights to nonhuman animals.

5. Gail Eisnitz, *Slaughterhouse: The Shocking Story of Greed, Neglect, and Inhuman Treatment Inside* the U.S. Meat Industry (Buffalo, NY: Prometheus Books, 1997), gives a vivid account of dirty conditions and cruel treatment of animals in slaughterhouses.

6. Eric Schlosser, *Fast Food Nation: The Dark Side of the All-American Meat* (New York: HarperCollins, 2002) is an expose of the fast-food industry revealing how the food is produced and what's really in it.

7. Leslie Pickering Francis and Richard Norman, "Some Animals Are More Equal than Others," *Philosophy* 53 (Oct. 1978): 507–27, agree with Singer that it is wrong to cause animal suffering but deny that this requires us to adopt vegetarianism or abandon animal experimentation.

8. Roger Crisp, "Utilitarianism and Vegetarianism," *International Journal of Applied Philosophy* 4 (1988): 41–49, argues that utilitarianism morally requires us both to abstain from eating the flesh of intensively reared animals and to eat the flesh of certain nonintensively reared animals. He calls this the Compromise Requirement View.

9. Bonnie Steinbock, "Speciesism and the Idea of Equality," *Philosophy* 53, 204 (April 1978): 247–56, presents a defense of speciesism. Although she agrees with Singer that nonhuman suffering deserves some moral consideration, Steinbock denies that this consideration should be equal to that given to humans.

10. R. G. Frey, *Interests and Rights: The Case against Animals* (Oxford: Clarendon Press, 1980), argues that animals have neither interests nor moral rights.

11. Joel Feinberg, "The Rights of Animals and Unborn Generations," in William T. Blackstone, ed., *Philosophy and Environmental Crisis* (Athens, GA: University of Georgia Press, 1974), analyzes the concept of a right and contends that humans and animals have rights but rocks and whole species do not. Future generations have rights but only contingent on their coming into existence.

12. H. J. McCloskey, "Moral Rights and Animals," *Inquiry* 22 (Spring/Summer 1979): 25–54, attacks Feinberg's analysis of the concept of a right and presents his own account. According to McCloskey, a right is an entitlement to something and not a claim against someone. In his view, animals do not have rights.

13. James Rachels, *Created from Animals: The Moral Implications of Darwinism* (Oxford: Oxford University Press, 1990), defends animal rights.

14. Stephen R. L. Clark, *Animals and Their Moral Standing* (New York: Routledge, 1997). This book collects the major writings of Clark on animals. It includes discussions of the rights of wild animals, the problems with speciesism, and the difficulty of calculating costs and benefits.

15. Kerry S. Walters and Lisa Pormess, eds., *Ethical Vegetarianism: From Pythagoras to Peter Singer* (Albany: State University of New York Press, 1999). This anthology covers the two-thousand-year Western tradition of vegetarianism, beginning with Pythagoras, Seneca, and Plutarch.

16. Frances Moore Lappé, *Diet for a Small Planet,* 20th anniversary edition (New York: Ballantine Books, 1992). This is the latest edition of the classic best-selling book that tells you how to be a vegetarian and why you should be one.

17. Daniel A. Dombrowski, *Babies and Beasts: The Argument from Marginal Cases* (Urbana, IL: University of Illinois Press, 1997), discusses an important argument used to defend

animal rights, the argument that there is no morally relevant difference between animals and "marginal humans," such as the severely mentally retarded.

18. Daniel R. Dombrowski, *The Philosophy of Vegetarianism* (Amherst, MA: University of Massachusetts Press, 1984), presents a history of the arguments for vegetarianism, beginning with Porphyry's *On Abstinence.*

19. Mary Midgley, *Animals and Why They Matter* (Athens, GA: University of Georgia Press, 1998), explains why we should have moral concern for animals. Unlike many others, she does not rely on utilitarianism.

20. Josephine Donovan and Carol J. Adams, eds., *Beyond Animal Rights: A Feminist Caring Ethic for the Treatment of Animals* (La Vergne, TN: Continuum Publishers, 1996). This anthology has eight articles that extend the feminist care ethic to the treatment of animals, thus moving beyond the appeal to animal rights.

21. Tom Regan and Peter Singer, eds., *Animal Rights and Human Obligations* (Upper Saddle River, NJ: Prentice-Hall, 1989). This is a collection of articles on animals that includes discussions of animal rights, the treatment of farm animals, and the treatment of animals in science.

22. Carl Cohen, "The Case for the Use of Animals in Biomedical Research," *The New England Journal of Medicine* 315 (Oct. 2, 1986): 865–70, defends speciesism and the use of animals in biomedical research. Cohen attacks both Singer and Regan, arguing that speciesism is not analogous to racism and sexism and that animals have no rights.

23. Barbara F. Orlans, *In the Name of Science: Issues in Responsible Animal Experimentation* (Oxford: Oxford University Press, 1993), gives a detailed and well-informed discussion of the issues raised by animal experimentation.

24. Barbara Orlans and Rebecca Dresser, *The Human Use of Animals: Case Studies in Ethical Choice* (Oxford: Oxford University Press, 1997). This book presents various cases of research using animals, including baboon–human liver transplants, cosmetic safety testing, Washoe and other language-using chimpanzees, and monkeys without mothers.

25. Deborah Blum, *The Monkey Wars* (Oxford: Oxford University Press, 1977), gives detailed information about various animal activists, from the moderate Animal Welfare Institute to the radical Animal Liberation Front (now on the FBI's terrorist list). Among other things, we find out about Washoe and four other chimpanzees who were trained in the use of sign language.

26. Harlan B. Miller and William H. Williams, eds., *Ethics and Animals* (Totowa, NJ: Humana Press, 1983). This is an anthology dealing with topics such as animal rights, hunting, and animal experimentation.

27. Bernard E. Rollin, *The Unheeded Cry: Animal Consciousness, Animal Pain and Science* (Oxford: Oxford University Press, 1989), surveys attitudes toward animal consciousness and pain, beginning with George Romanes in the nineteenth century.

Chapter 8

The Environment and Consumption

Introduction

Factual Background

Environmentalists claim that human beings are rapidly destroying the natural environment. Among other things, they say that the industrial consumer society is causing global warming (see the Problem Cases), ozone depletion, and acid rain. These are complicated phenomena, however, and not everyone agrees about their causes and effects. Let us confine our attention to two clear cases of environmental harm: the destruction of redwood forests and the extinction of plant and animal species.

Coastal redwoods, or *Sequoia sempervirens,* are rare trees found mostly along the California coast and into southern Oregon. Over a long period of time, they grow to a huge size—the tallest such tree alive today is a 370-foot-tall redwood whose location biologists refuse to disclose, to protect its fragile habitat from visitors.

Despite their obvious beauty, only 4 percent of the original redwood forests remain standing today. Lumber companies have cut down almost all of them to make money, and to satisfy the demand for timber. Deforesting is a very profitable business; at today's prices a single redwood can contain wood worth hundreds of thousands of dollars.

According to Dr. Reed F. Noss, codirector of the Conservation Biology Institute (http://www.consbio.org/) and editor of *The Redwood Forest: History, Ecology, and Conservation of the Coastal Redwoods* (see the Suggested Readings), redwoods that have been cut down are gone forever. They cannot be regrown. The reason for this is a phenomenon called fog drip. When fog rolls over a redwood, water suspended in the fog drips down the tree's limbs, needles, and trunk, soaking the ground with an immense amount of water—the equivalent of a drenching rainstorm. If the redwoods are cut down, then the water in the fog passes right by. Deforested areas warm up and dry out quickly, and they do not get enough water to sustain redwood growth. Once sites are clear-cut, they no longer benefit from the fog.

The largest remaining stand of redwoods is about 10,000 acres of ancient forest known as the Headwaters Grove, located more than 225 miles north of San Francisco. Until recently, the forest was owned by Pacific Lumber. The company planned to clear-cut the forest and had marked the trees to be cut with slashes of blue paint, but they were stopped by radical environmental activists, including members of the group Earth First! The activists blocked logging roads and even climbed and occupied trees to keep them from being cut. One of the activists, Julia "Butterfly" Hill, lived on a 2000-foot-tall ancient redwood tree named Luna from December 1997 to December 1999. (For photos of Julia and Luna see www.ottermedia.com/index.html.)

Environmentalists have been fighting with Pacific Lumber for over 12 years about the fate of the redwoods, as well as the company's plans to log another

20,000 acres of forest. In September 1998, however, the environmentalists won a partial victory. The California legislature voted to purchase the Headwaters Grove from Pacific Lumber for $495 million. Under the legislation, the forest will be set aside forever as a nature preserve, with California paying $245 million and the federal government contributing $250 million.

The destruction of forests affects not only humans but other species of animals and plants as well. According to the World Wildlife Fund (http://www.world-wildlife.org/), about 90 percent of the world's species are found in forested areas. For example, the Headwaters Grove is the habitat of several threatened species, including the coho salmon and the marbled murrelet, a winged relative of the penguin, which nests on the wide branches of the old redwoods. But 94 percent of the world's remaining forests are unprotected, and already more than half of them have been lost, along with their plant and animal life. The World Wildlife Fund estimates that if deforestation continues at the present rate, about one-fifth of all plant and animal species on the planet will be lost in the next twenty years. The Global 2000 Report projects a loss of up to 20 percent of the earth's species within a few decades unless present trends are reversed.

Environmentalists argue that the destruction of the environment is the result of consumption of resources by industrial consumer societies like the United States. According to the Worldwatch Institute State of the World 2004 Report (www.worldwatch.org/pubs/sow/2004), forests, wetlands, and other natural places are shrinking rapidly to make way for more and bigger houses, farms, malls, and factories. More than 90 percent of paper still comes from trees despite the existence of alternative sources. An estimated 75 percent of global fish stocks are now fished at or beyond their sustainable limit. Cars and other forms of transportation account for nearly 30 percent of world energy use and 95 percent of global oil consumption. There are more private vehicles in the United States today than there are people licensed to drive them. Many of these vehicles are SUVs like the Hummer H2, which weighs 8,600 pounds and gets an average of 9 miles per gallon, the worst gas mileage of any civilian vehicle. The average size of refrigerators in U.S. households increased by 10 percent between 1972 and 2001, and the average number per home rose as well. New houses were 38 percent bigger in 2000 than in 1975, despite having fewer people in each household on average. With just 4.5 percent of the world's population, the United States releases 25 percent of the global carbon dioxide gas, which contributes to global warming and other climate changes.

The rest of the world is starting to catch up with U.S. consumerism. According to the Worldwatch State of the World 2004 Report, about 1.7 billion people worldwide have entered the consumer class, adopting the diet, transportation systems, and lifestyles that used to be limited to the rich nations of Europe, North America, and Japan. In China alone, 240 million people have joined the ranks of consumers, a number than will soon surpass the United States.

Environmentalists also argue that consumption and waste in industrial countries indirectly produces harm to other people, because the money wasted on consumer items could be used to help others in need. While people in the United States spend over $50,000 to buy a new Hummer H2, children in other countries are dying or suffering from lack of food and medical care. The richest 20 percent of humanity consume 86 percent of all goods and services, while the poorest fifth consume just 1.3 percent of the goods and services. About 2.6 billion people lack basic sanitation and 1.3 billion have no access to clean water. About 900 million people have no access to modern health services of any kind. In April 2003, nearly 13 million people in southern Africa were facing extreme food shortages. This is a persistent problem in Africa, caused by a mixture of poverty, bad weather, poor governance, and economic collapse. In addition, over 30 million people in Africa are suffering from AIDS, and every day 5,000 die. Meanwhile, people in rich nations spend $18 billion on makeup, compared with $12 billion for women's reproductive health care. Americans and Europeans spend $17 billion on pet food, while worldwide elimination of hunger and malnutrition would cost about $19 billion. Global spending on advertising, which is necessary to stimulate more consumption, is now at $435 billion, and is increasing faster than income or population. Speaking of income, consider the fact that in 2003, the average large-company CEO in the United States received compensation totaling over $8 million. Compare this income with the rest of the world, where 2.8 billion people barely survive on $2 a day, and another 1.2 billion live in extreme poverty on less than $1 a day.

The Readings

The readings begin with Aldo Leopold's classic view about environmental preservation, a view he calls the *land ethic*. As Leopold explains it, the land ethic is the result of a natural extension of ethics, an ecological evolution, that begins with a moral concern with individuals (as in the Ten Commandments), moves to relations between the individual and the society (as in the golden rule), and ends up with a moral concern for the land. By "the land" Leopold means not just soils but also waters, plants, and animals, including human beings—all of which form a biotic community. Humans are not the conquerors or owners of this community, but citizens of it. According to Leopold, what is right is what tends to preserve the integrity, stability, and beauty of the land, the biotic community, and whatever does not do this is wrong.

J. Baird Callicott discusses conflicts between Leopold's land ethic and two other views, the view that only human beings have moral standing (which he calls ethical humanism and Singer labels speciesism) and the view that extends moral concern to sentient animals but not to the environment. He refers to this view as humane moralism or the animal liberation movement. (Critics of the animal liberation movement sometimes label it sentientism, since they think it is just another form of bias, like speciesism.) Callicott sees the animal liberation movement as hostile to Leopold's land ethic. For example, consider hunting, killing, and eating animals. Singer and Regan think this is seriously wrong, but Callicott notes that Leopold was an enthusiastic hunter and eater of animal flesh. Why didn't Leopold care about the suffering of animals? Because from the point of view of his land ethic, the killing and eating of individual animals is morally inconsequential. What matters is not the pain and suffering of individuals but the preservation of the land, including whole species. For this to be accomplished, individual animals must be killed; otherwise, there will be overpopulation and the land will be damaged. Another difference between the animal liberation movement and Leopold's land ethic concerns domestic animals. Singer and Regan agree that domestic animals should not be killed and eaten because this causes more suffering. But Leopold was indifferent, and Callicott explains why. Domestic animals are creations of humans that are a ruinous blight on the landscape, as bad as a fleet of four-wheel-drive off-road vehicles. Unlike wild animals, domestic cattle, sheep, or pigs have no natural place in the environment, and so they contribute to the erosion of the integrity, stability, and beauty of the biotic community. Callicott concludes that when all things are considered, the animal liberation movement is hopelessly impractical, whereas, by contrast, the land ethic is very practical, although still hard to implement.

In the 1994 preface to his article, however, Callicott separates his own view from that of Leopold. Unlike Leopold, he now thinks we do have moral responsibilities to domestic animals as members of mixed human–animal communities, and now he thinks that vegetarianism is indicated by the land ethic, since it would be better for the environment if forests were not destroyed to make pasture for cattle. Rather than emphasizing the conflicts between the three views (the land ethic, ethical humanism, and the animal liberation movement), now he thinks that they should unite to oppose activities that are destroying human, mixed, and biotic communities.

Alan Thein Durning presents facts and figures about the overconsumption of natural resources by industrial nations such as the United States. He says that an estimated two-thirds of emissions of carbon dioxide, the principal greenhouse gas, comes from the use of fossil fuels. The richest tenth of Americans pump 11 tons of carbon dioxide into the atmosphere annually, while the poor release only one-tenth of a ton each year. In industrial countries, fuels burned release three-fourths of the sulfur and nitrogen oxides that cause acid rain. Industrial countries generate most of the world's toxic chemical wastes. Furthermore, the fossil fuels that keep the consumer society going in industrial countries are taken from the earth at great cost. Taking coal, oil, and natural gas from the earth disrupts many habitats; refining them produces toxic wastes; and burning them pollutes the air. Durning argues that preserving the natural environment will require us to practice family planning, adopt a nonconsumer lifestyle, and develop new technologies, such as automobiles that go farther on a tank of fuel.

Peter Singer condemns the consumer society, not because it produces damage to the environment, but because it ignores the suffering of other people. When people waste their money on luxury items such as fur coats instead of giving to famine relief, needy people in other countries suffer and die. In his view, luxury items are morally insignificant trivia compared to necessities such as food and medical care. He believes that people should give away enough to the needy to ensure that the consumer society slows down and eventually disappears. His argument is straightforward. It is obvious that suffering from lack of food and other necessities is bad. We ought to prevent something unless we have to sacrifice something morally significant. But luxury items are not morally significant; they are frivolous trivia. So we should give up these luxuries in order to help needy people.

Garrett Hardin (see the Suggested Reading) does not agree. He argues that rich nations have no obligation to help poor nations because doing this leads to environmental disaster. He compares nations to lifeboats. Just as lifeboats have a limited carrying capacity, so nations have limited resources. If you try to put too many people in a lifeboat, the boat will sink and everybody will drown. Similarly, if a nation tries to feed too many people, it will exhaust its resources. As Hardin puts it, the result will be a "tragedy of the commons" where natural resources such as land and air are ruined. In fact, giving food to starving people in poor countries just makes matters worse. The food acts as a ratchet; it results in a population increase, and then there are more starving people, and if you feed them you have even more starving people, and so on, in a vicious cycle.

Philosophical Issues

In this chapter the debate continues about who or what is the proper object of moral concern. Is it just human beings, humans and animals, whole species, or biotic communities, such as forests? As Callicott argues in the reading, Leopold seems to hold that our concern should be with the land and not with animals or even humans, but of course this is opposed by Kant and his followers, who insist that only self-conscious and rational beings are the proper objects of moral concern, and by Mill, Bentham, Singer, and other utilitarians, who think that all sentient beings, including animals, should have moral standing.

In the preface to his article, Callicott suggests an interesting solution to the problem. He asks us to think of ourselves as belonging to three different moral communities, each having its own set of peculiar duties and obligations. There is the human community of family, friends, fellow citizens, and so on; the mixed community of humans and animals; and the biotic community as a whole. Callicott thinks these duties and obligations are often convergent and mutually reinforcing, and indeed this may be so. The problem is that Callicott gives no way of resolving conflicts between the different duties and obligations. For example, what would he say to the employee of the lumber company who works to feed her family? Isn't her obligation to take care of her family stronger than her duty to preserve the forests? In general, this problem of conflicts between human interests and duties and environmental preservation seems to remain unresolved in the chapter.

Another issue is whether it even makes sense to say that we have duties to collections of living things such as species or forests. The standard view held by most philosophers is that we have duties to individuals who have desires, wants, interests, or rights. But a biotic community such as a forest or a collection of animals does not have any desires, wants, interests, or rights, and so it could not be the object of moral duty or obligation. The answer given by Leopold is that we must enlarge the boundary of the moral community to include the land, that is, the soils, waters, plants, and animals. The question is whether it makes sense to do this, particularly when we are talking about nonliving and nonconscious things such as soil and water.

What has intrinsic value? This is a basic question raised by the chapter. A standard view is that nature itself has no intrinsic value; it has no value by itself apart from its use. Nature has only instrumental value as something that produces human satisfaction. Imagine a planet overflowing with plant life but with no humans or sentient beings of any kind. Does this planet have any value at all? The standard view says it does not; yet Leopold's land ethic seems to hold that such a planet does have intrinsic value or inherent value. The problem is to explain how something could have value without an evaluator.

A more practical question is raised by Singer. We live in a consumer society where people constantly acquire, use, and throw away consumer items such as fashionable clothes and shoes. Is this morally defensible? Singer does not think so. He believes people in consumer societies should give money to charity rather than wasting their money on luxury items.

But how do we distinguish between necessities and luxuries? Singer does not give a clear answer, but does say that new clothes that are purchased to look well-dressed rather than warm are not an important need. It would be better to wear old clothes and give to famine relief. This suggests that on his view, needs are limited to what is necessary for survival, namely food, shelter, clothing, and medical care. Perhaps he would include education as well, but maybe not entertainment and sports.

The Land Ethic

ALDO LEOPOLD

Aldo Leopold was an employee of the U.S. Forest Service and a professor of wildlife management at the University of Wisconsin. Our reading is taken from his classic book about the environment, *A Sand County Almanac* (1947).

Leopold proposes to extend our moral concern beyond humans and human society to the land. As he puts it, the land ethic enlarges the moral community to include soils, waters, plants, and animals—all of which are collectively the land. According to the land ethic, humans are not conquerors of the land, but rather biotic citizens of it. What is right is what preserves the integrity, stability, and beauty of the land, and whatever does not do this is wrong.

WHEN GODLIKE ODYSSEUS returned from the wars in Troy, he hanged all on one rope a dozen slave-girls of his household whom he suspected of misbehavior during his absence.

This hanging involved no question of propriety. The girls were property. The disposal of property was then, as now, a matter of expediency, not of right or wrong.

Concepts of right and wrong were not lacking from Odysseus' Greece: witness the fidelity of his wife through the long years before at last his black-prowed galleys clove the wine-dark seas for home. The ethical structure of that day covered wives, but had not yet been extended to human chattels. During the three thousand years which have since elapsed, ethical criteria have been extended to many fields of conduct, with

Source: Aldo Leopold, "The Land Ethic" from *A Sand County Almanac: And Sketches Here and There* by Aldo Leopold. Copyright 1949, 1953, 1966, renewed 1977 by Oxford University Press, Inc. Used by permission of Oxford University Press, Inc.

corresponding shrinkages in those judged by expediency only.

THE ETHICAL SEQUENCE

This extension of ethics, so far studied only by philosophers, is actually a process in ecological evolution. Its sequences may be described in ecological as well as in philosophical terms. An ethic, ecologically, is a limitation on freedom of action in the struggle for existence. An ethic, philosophically, is a differentiation of social from antisocial conduct. These are two definitions of one thing. The thing has its origin in the tendency of interdependent individuals or groups to evolve modes of cooperation. The ecologist calls these symbioses. Politics and economics are advanced symbioses in which the original free-for-all competition has been replaced, in part, by cooperative mechanisms with an ethical content.

The complexity of cooperative mechanisms has increased with population density, and with the efficiency of tools. It was simpler, for example, to define the antisocial uses of sticks and stones in the days of the mastodons than of bullets and billboards in the age of motors.

The first ethics dealt with the relation between individuals; the Mosaic Decalogue is an example. Later accretions dealt with the relation between the individual and society. The Golden Rule tries to integrate the individual to society; democracy to integrate social organization to the individual.

There is as yet no ethic dealing with man's relation to land and to the animals and plants which grow upon it. Land, like Odysseus' slave-girls, is still property. The land-relation is still strictly economic, entailing privileges but not obligations.

The extension of ethics to this third element in human environment is, if I read the evidence correctly, an evolutionary possibility and an ecological necessity. It is the third step in a sequence. The first two have already been taken. Individual thinkers since the days of Ezekiel and Isaiah have asserted that the despoliation of land is not only inexpedient but wrong. Society, however, has not yet affirmed their belief. I regard the present conservation movement as the embryo of such an affirmation.

An ethic may be regarded as a mode of guidance for meeting ecological situations so new or intricate, or involving such deferred reactions, that the path of social expediency is not discernible to the average individual. Animal instincts are modes of guidance for the individual in meeting such situations. Ethics are possibly a kind of community instinct in-the-making.

THE COMMUNITY CONCEPT

All ethics so far evolved rest upon a single premise: that the individual is a member of a community of interdependent parts. His instincts prompt him to compete for his place in the community, but his ethics prompt him also to cooperate (perhaps in order that there may be a place to compete for).

The land ethic simply enlarges the boundaries of the community to include soils, waters, plants, and animals, or collectively: the land.

This sounds simple: do we not already sing our love for and obligation to the land of the free and the home of the brave? Yes, but just what and whom do we love? Certainly not the soil, which we are sending helter-skelter downriver. Certainly not the waters, which we assume have no function except to turn turbines, float barges, and carry off sewage. Certainly not the plants, of which we exterminate whole communities without batting an eye. Certainly not the animals, of which we have already extirpated many of the largest and most beautiful species. A land ethic of course cannot prevent the alteration, management, and use of these "resources" but it does affirm their right to continued existence, and, at least in spots, their continued existence in a natural state.

In short, a land ethic changes the role of *Homo sapiens* from conqueror of the land-community to plain member and citizen of it. It implies respect for his fellow-members, and also respect for the community as such.

In human history, we have learned (I hope) that the conqueror role is eventually self-defeating. Why? Because it is implicit in such a role that the conqueror knows, *ex cathedra,* just what makes the community clock tick, and just what and who is valuable, and what and who is worthless, in community life. It always turns out that he knows neither, and this is why his conquests eventually defeat themselves.

In the biotic community, a parallel situation exists. Abraham knew exactly what the land was for: it was to drip milk and honey into Abraham's mouth. At the present moment, the assurance with which we regard this assumption is inverse to the degree of our education.

The ordinary citizen today assumes that science knows what makes the community clock tick; the scientist is equally sure that he does not. He knows that the biotic mechanism is so complex that its workings may never be fully understood.

That man is, in fact, only a member of a biotic team is shown by an ecological interpretation of history. Many historical events, hitherto explained solely in terms of human enterprise, were actually biotic interactions between people and land. The characteristics of the land determined the facts quite as potently as the characteristics of the men who lived on it.

Consider, for example, the settlement of the Mississippi valley. In the years following the Revolution, three groups were contending for its control: the native Indian, the French and English traders, and the American settlers. Historians wonder what would have happened if the English at Detroit had thrown a little more weight into the Indian side of those tipsy scales which decided the outcome of the colonial migration into the cane-lands of Kentucky. It is time now to ponder the fact that the cane-lands, when subjected to the particular mixture of forces represented by the cow, plow, fire, and axe of the pioneer, became bluegrass. What if the plant succession inherent in this dark and bloody ground had, under the impact of these forces, given us some worthless sedge shrub, or weed? Would Boone and Kenton have held out? Would there have been any overflow into Ohio, Indiana, Illinois, and Missouri? Any Louisiana Purchase? Any transcontinental union of new states? Any Civil War?

Kentucky was one sentence in the drama of history. We are commonly told what the human actors in this drama tried to do, but we are seldom told that their success, or the lack of it, hung in large degree on the reaction of particular soils to the impact of the particular forces exerted by their occupancy. In the case of Kentucky, we do not even know where the bluegrass came from—whether it is a native species, or a stowaway from Europe.

Contrast the cane-lands with what hindsight tells us about the Southwest, where the pioneers were equally brave, resourceful, and persevering. The impact of the occupancy here brought no bluegrass, or other plant fitted to withstand the bumps and buffetings of hard use. This region, when grazed by livestock, reverted through a series of more and more worthless grasses, shrubs, and weeds to a condition of unstable equilibrium. Each recession of plant types bred erosion; each increment to erosion bred a further recession of plants. The result today is a progressive and mutual deterioration, not only of plants and soils, but of the animal community subsisting thereon. The early settlers did not expect this: on the ciénegas of New Mexico some even cut ditches to hasten it. So subtle has been its progress that few residents of the region are aware of it. It is quite invisible to the tourist who finds this wrecked landscape colorful and charming (as indeed it is, but it bears scant resemblance to what it was in 1848).

This same landscape was "developed" once before, but with quite different results. The Pueblo Indians settled the Southwest in pre-Columbian times, but they happened *not* to be equipped with range livestock. Their civilization expired, but not because their land expired.

In India, regions devoid of any sod-forming grass have been settled, apparently without wrecking the land, by the simple expedient of carrying the grass to the cow, rather than vice versa.

(Was this the result of some deep wisdom, or was it just good luck? I do not know.)

In short, the plant succession steered the course of history; the pioneer simply demonstrated, for good or ill, what successions inhered in the land. Is history taught in this spirit? It will be, once the concept of land as a community really penetrates our intellectual life.

THE ECOLOGICAL CONSCIENCE

Conservation is a state of harmony between men and land. Despite nearly a century of propaganda, conservation still proceeds at a snail's pace; progress still consists largely of letterhead pieties and convention oratory. On the back forty we still slip two steps backward for each forward stride.

The usual answer to this dilemma is "more conservation education." No one will debate this, but is it certain that only the *volume* of education needs stepping up? Is something lacking in the *content* as well?

It is difficult to give a fair summary of its content in brief form, but as I understand it, the content is substantially this: obey the law, vote right, join some organizations, and practice what conservation is profitable on your own land; the government will do the rest.

Is not this formula too easy to accomplish anything worthwhile? It defines no right or wrong, assigns no obligation, calls for no sacrifice, implies no change in the current philosophy of values. In respect of land-use, it urges only enlightened self-interest. Just how far will such education take us? An example will perhaps yield a partial answer.

By 1930 it had become clear to all except the ecologically blind that southwestern Wisconsin's topsoil was slipping seaward. In 1933 the farmers were told that if they would adopt certain remedial practices for five years, the public would donate CCC labor to install them, plus the necessary machinery and materials. The offer was widely accepted, but the practices were widely forgotten when the five-year contract period was up. The farmers continued only those practices that yielded an immediate and visible economic gain for themselves.

This led to the idea that maybe farmers would learn more quickly if they themselves wrote the rules. Accordingly the Wisconsin Legislature in 1937 passed the Soil Conservation District Law. This said to farmers, in effect: *We, the public, will furnish you free technical service and loan you specialized machinery, if you will write your own rules for land-use. Each county may write its own rules, and these will have the force of law.* Nearly all the counties promptly organized to accept the proffered help, but after a decade of operation, no *county has yet written a single rule.* There has been visible progress in such practices as strip-cropping, pasture renovation, and soil liming, but none in fencing woodlots against grazing, and none in excluding plow and cow from steep slopes. The farmers, in short, have selected those remedial practices which were profitable anyhow, and ignored those which were profitable to the community, but not clearly profitable to themselves.

When one asks why no rules have been written, one is told that the community is not yet ready to support them; education must precede rules. But the education actually in progress makes no mention of obligations to land over and above those dictated by self-interest. The net result is that we have more education but less soil, fewer healthy woods, and as many floods as in 1937.

The puzzling aspect of such situations is that the existence of obligations over and above self-interest is taken for granted in such rural community enterprise as the betterment of roads, schools, churches, and baseball teams. Their existence is not taken for granted, nor as yet seriously discussed, in bettering the behavior of the water that falls on the land, or in the preserving of the beauty or diversity of the farm landscape. Land-use ethics are still governed wholly by economic self-interest, just as social ethics were a century ago.

To sum up: we asked the farmer to do what he conveniently could to save his soil, and he has done just that, and only that. The farmer who clears the woods off a 75 per cent slope, turns his cows into the clearing, and dumps its rainfall, rocks, and soil into the community creek, is still (if otherwise decent) a respected member of society. If he puts lime on his fields and plants his crops on contour, he is still entitled to all the privileges and emoluments of his Soil Conservation District. The District is a beautiful piece of social machinery, but it is coughing along on two cylinders because we have been too timid, and too anxious for quick success, to tell the farmer the true magnitude of his obligations. Obligations have no meaning without conscience, and the problem we face is the extension of the social conscience from people to land.

No important change in ethics was ever accomplished without an internal change in our intellectual emphasis, loyalties, affections, and convictions. The proof that conservation has not yet touched these foundations of conduct lies in the fact that philosophy and religion have not yet heard of it. In our attempt to make conservation easy, we have made it trivial.

SUBSTITUTES FOR A LAND ETHIC

When the logic of history hunger for bread and we hand out a stone, we are at pains to explain how much the stone resembles bread. I now describe some of the stones which serve in lieu of a land ethic.

One basic weakness in a conservation system based wholly on economic motives is that most members of the land community have no economic value. Wildflowers and songbirds are examples. Of the 22,000 higher plants and animals native to Wisconsin, it is doubtful whether more than 5 percent can be sold, fed, eaten, or otherwise put to economic use. Yet these creatures are members of the biotic community, and if (as I believe) its stability depends on its integrity, they are entitled to continuance.

When one of these non-economic categories is threatened, and if we happen to love it, we invent subterfuges to give it economic importance. At the beginning of the century songbirds were supposed to be disappearing. Ornithologists jumped to the rescue with some distinctly shaky evidence to the effect that insects would eat us up if birds failed to control them. The evidence had to be economic in order to be valid.

It is painful to read these circumlocutions today. We have no land ethic yet, but we have at least drawn nearer the point of admitting that birds should continue as a matter of biotic right, regardless of the presence or absence of economic advantage to us.

A parallel situation exists in respect of predatory mammals, raptorial birds, and fish-eating birds. Time was when biologists somewhat overworked the evidence that these creatures preserve the health of game by killing weaklings, or that they control rodents for the farmer, or that they prey only on "worthless" species. Here again, the evidence had to be economic in order to be valid. It is only in recent years that we hear the more honest argument that predators are members of the community, and that no special interest has the right to exterminate them for the sake of a benefit, real or fancied, to itself. Unfortunately this enlightened view is still in the talk stage. In the field the extermination of predators goes merrily on: witness the impending erasure of the timber wolf by fiat of Congress, the Conservation Bureaus, and many state legislatures.

Some species of trees have been "read out of the party" by economics-minded foresters because they grow too slowly, or have too low a sale value to pay as timber crops: white cedar, tamarack, cypress, beech, and hemlock are examples. In Europe, where forestry is ecologically more advanced, the non-commercial tree species are recognized as members of the native forest community, to be preserved as such, within reason. Moreover some (like beech) have been found to have a valuable function in building up soil fertility. The interdependence of the forest and its constituent tree species, ground flora, and fauna is taken for granted.

Lack of economic value is sometimes a character not only of species or groups, but of entire biotic communities: marshes, bogs, dunes, and "deserts" are examples. Our formula in such cases is to relegate their conservation to government as refuges, monuments, or parks. The difficulty is that these communities are usually interspersed with more valuable private lands; the government cannot possibly own or control such scattered parcels. The net effect is that we have relegated some of them to ultimate extinction over large areas. If the private owner were ecologically minded, he would be proud to be the custodian of a reasonable proportion of such areas, which add diversity and beauty to his farm and to his community.

In some instances, the assumed lack of profit in these "waste" areas has proved to be wrong, but only after most of them had been done away with. The present scramble to reflood muskrat marshes is a case in point.

There is a clear tendency in American conservation to relegate to government all necessary jobs that private landowners fail to perform. Government ownership, operation, subsidy, or regulation is now widely prevalent in forestry, range management, soil and watershed management, park and wilderness conservation, fisheries management, and migratory bird management, with more to come. Most of this growth in governmental conservation is proper and logical, some of it is inevitable. That I imply no disapproval of it is implicit in the fact that I have spent most of my life working for it. Nevertheless the question arises: What is the ultimate magnitude of the enterprise? Will the tax base carry its eventual ramifications? At what point will governmental conservation, like the mastodon, become handicapped by its own dimensions? The answer, if there is any, seems to be in a land ethic, or some other force which assigns more obligation to the private landowner.

Industrial landowners and users, especially lumbermen and stockmen, are inclined to wail long and loudly about the extension of government ownership and regulation to land, but (with notable exceptions) they show little disposition to develop the only visible alternative: the voluntary practice of conservation on their own lands.

When the private landowner is asked to perform some nonprofitable act for the good of the community, he today assents only with outstretched palm. If the act costs him cash this is fair and proper, but when it costs only forethought, open-mindedness, or time, the issue is at least debatable. The overwhelming growth of land-use subsidies in recent years must be ascribed, in large part, to the government's own agencies for conservation education: the land bureaus, the agricultural colleges, and the extension services. As far as I can detect, no ethical obligation toward land is taught in these institutions.

To sum up: a system of conservation based solely on economic self-interest is hopelessly lopsided. It tends to ignore, and thus eventually to eliminate, many elements in the land community that lack commercial value, but that are (as far as we know) essential to its healthy functioning. It assumes, falsely, I think, that the economic parts of the biotic clock will function without the uneconomic parts. It tends to relegate to government many functions eventually too large, too complex, or too widely dispersed to be performed by government.

An ethical obligation on the part of the private owner is the only visible remedy for these situations.

THE LAND PYRAMID

An ethic to supplement and guide the economic relation to land presupposes the existence of some mental image of land as a biotic mechanism. We can be ethical only in relation to something we can see, feel, understand, love, or otherwise have faith in.

The image commonly employed in conservation education is "the balance of nature." For reasons too lengthy to detail here, this figure of speech fails to describe accurately what little we know about the land mechanism. A much truer image is the one employed in ecology: the biotic pyramid. I shall first sketch the pyramid as a symbol of land, and later develop some of its implications in terms of land-use.

Plants absorb energy from the sun. This energy flows through a circuit called the biota, which may be represented by a pyramid consisting of layers. The bottom layer is the soil. A plant layer rests on the soil, an insect layer on the plants, a bird and rodent layer on the insects, and so on up through various animal groups to the apex layer, which consists of the larger carnivores.

The species of a layer are alike not in where they came from, or in what they look like, but rather in what they eat. Each successive layer depends on those below it for food and often for other services, and each in turn furnishes food and services to those above. Proceeding upward, each successive layer decreases in numerical abundance. Thus, for every carnivore there are hundreds of his prey, thousands of their prey, millions of insects, uncountable plants. The pyramidal form of the system reflects this numerical progression from apex to base. Man shares an intermediate layer with the bears, raccoons, and squirrels which eat both meat and vegetables.

The lines of dependency for food and other services are called food chains. Thus soil-oak-deer-Indian is a chain that has now been largely converted to soil-corn-cow-farmer. Each species, including ourselves, is a link in many chains. The deer eats a hundred plants other than oak, and the cow a hundred plants other than corn. Both, then, are links in a hundred chains. The pyramid is a tangle of chains so complex as to seem disorderly, yet the stability of the system proves it to be a highly organized structure. Its functioning depends on the cooperation and competition of its diverse parts.

In the beginning, the pyramid of life was low and squat; the food chains short and simple. Evolution has added layer after layer, link after link. Man is one of thousands of accretions to the height and complexity of the pyramid. Science has given us many doubts, but it has given us at least one certainty: the trend of evolution is to elaborate and diversify the biota.

Land, then, is not merely soil; it is a fountain of energy flowing through a circuit of soils, plants, and animals. Food chains are the living channels which conduct energy upward; death and decay return it to the soil. The circuit is not closed; some energy is dissipated in decay, some is added by absorption from the air, some is stored in soils, peats, and long-lived forests; but it is a sustained circuit, like a slowly augmented revolving fund of life. There is always a net loss by downhill wash, but this is normally small and offset by the decay of rocks. It is deposited in the ocean and, in the course of geological time, raised to form new lands and new pyramids.

The velocity and character of the upward flow of energy depend on the complex structure of the plant and animal community, much as the upward flow of sap in a tree depends on its complex cellular organization. Without this complexity, normal circulation would presumably not occur. Structure means the characteristic numbers, as well as the characteristic kinds and functions, of the component species. This interdependence between the complex structure of the land and its smooth functioning as an energy unit is one of its basic attributes.

When a change occurs in one part of the circuit, many other parts must adjust themselves to it. Change does not necessarily obstruct or divert the flow of energy; evolution is a long series of self-induced changes, the net result of which has been to elaborate the flow mechanism and to lengthen the circuit. Evolutionary changes, however, are usually slow and local. Man's invention of tools has enabled him to make changes of unprecedented violence, rapidity, and scope.

One change is in the composition of floras and faunas. The larger predators are lopped off the apex of the pyramid; food chains, for the first time in history, become shorter rather than longer. Domesticated species from other lands are substituted for wild ones, and wild ones are moved to new habitats. In this worldwide pooling of faunas and floras, some species get out of bounds as pests and diseases, others are extinguished. Such effects are seldom intended or foreseen; they represent unpredicted and often untraceable readjustments in the structure. Agricultural science is largely a race between the emergence of new pests and the emergence of new techniques for their control.

Another change touches the flow of energy through plants and animals and its return to the soil. Fertility is the ability of soil to receive, store, and release energy. Agriculture, by overdrafts on the soil, or by too radical a substitution of domestic for native species in the superstructure, may derange the channels of flow or deplete storage. Soils depleted of their storage, or of the organic matter which anchors it, wash away faster than they form. This is erosion.

Waters, like soil, are part of the energy circuit. Industry, by polluting waters or obstructing them with dams, may exclude the plants and animals necessary to keep energy in circulation.

Transportation brings about another basic change: the plants or animals grown in one region are now consumed and returned to the soil in another. Transportation taps the energy stored in rocks, and in the air, and uses it elsewhere; thus we fertilize the garden with nitrogen gleaned by the guano birds from the fishes of seas on the other side of the Equator. Thus the formerly localized and self-contained circuits are pooled on a worldwide scale.

The process of altering the pyramid for human occupation releases stored energy, and this often gives rise, during the pioneering period, to a deceptive exuberance of plant and animal life, both wild and tame. These releases of biotic capital tend to becloud or postpone the penalties of violence.

This thumbnail sketch of land as an energy circuit conveys three basic ideas:

1. That land is not merely soil.

2. That the native plants and animals kept the energy circuit open; others may or may not.

3. That man-made changes are of a different order than evolutionary changes, and have effects more comprehensive than is intended or foreseen.

These ideas, collectively, raise two basic issues: Can the land adjust itself to the new order? Can the desired alterations be accomplished with less violence?

Biotas seem to differ in their capacity to sustain violent conversion. Western Europe, for example, carries a far different pyramid than Caesar found there. Some large animals are lost; swampy forests have become meadows or plowland; many new plants and animals are introduced, some of which escape as pests; the remaining natives are greatly changed in distribution and abundance. Yet the soil is still there and, with the help of imported nutrients, still fertile; the waters flow normally; the new structure seems to function and to persist. There is no visible stoppage or derangement of the circuit.

Western Europe, then, has a resistant biota. Its inner processes are tough, elastic, resistant to strain. No matter how violent the alterations, the pyramid, so far, has developed some new *modus vivendi* which preserves its habitability for man, and for most of the other natives.

Japan seems to present another instance of radical conversion without disorganization.

Most other civilized regions, and some as yet barely touched by civilization, display various stages of disorganization, varying from initial symptoms to advanced wastage. In Asia Minor and North Africa diagnosis is confused by climatic changes, which may have been either the cause or the effect of advanced wastage. In the United States the degree of disorganization varies locally; it is worst in the Southwest, the Ozarks, and parts of the South, and least in New England and the Northwest. Better land-uses may still arrest it in the less advanced regions. In parts of Mexico, South America, South Africa, and Australia a violent and accelerating wastage is in progress, but I cannot assess the prospects.

This almost world-wide display of disorganization in the land seems to be similar to disease in an animal, except that it never culminates in complete disorganization or death. The land recovers, but at some reduced level of complexity, and with a reduced carrying capacity for people, plants, and animals. Many biotas currently regarded as "lands of opportunity" are in fact already subsisting on exploitative agriculture, i.e., they have already exceeded their sustained carrying capacity. Most of South America is overpopulated in this sense.

In arid regions we attempt to offset the process of wastage by reclamation, but it is only too evident that the prospective longevity of reclamation projects is often short. In our own West, the best of them may not last a century.

The combined evidence of history and ecology seems to support one general deduction: the less violent the man-made changes, the greater the probability of successful readjustment in the pyramid. Violence, in turn, varies with human population density; a dense population requires a more violent conversion. In this respect, North America has a better chance for permanence than Europe, if she can contrive to limit her density.

This deduction runs counter to our current philosophy, which assumes that because a small increase in density enriched human life, that an indefinite increase will enrich it indefinitely. Ecology knows of no density relationship that holds for indefinitely wide limits. All gains from density are subject to a law of diminishing returns.

Whatever may be the equation for men and land, it is improbable that we as yet know all its terms. Recent discoveries in mineral and vitamin nutrition reveal unsuspected dependencies in the up-circuit: incredibly minute quantities of certain substances determine the value of soils to plants, of plants to animals. What of the down-circuit? What of the vanishing species, the preservation of which we now regard as an esthetic luxury? They helped build the soil; in what unsuspected ways may they be essential to its maintenance? Professor Weaver proposes that we use prairie flowers to reflocculate the wasting soils of the dust bowl; who knows for what purpose cranes and condors, otters and grizzlies may some day be used?

LAND HEALTH
AND THE A-B CLEAVAGE

A land ethic, then, reflects the existence of an ecological conscience, and this in turn reflects a conviction of individual responsibility for the health of the land. Health is the capacity of the land for self-renewal. Conservation is our effort to understand and preserve this capacity.

Conservationists are notorious for their dissensions. Superficially these seem to add up to mere confusion, but a more careful scrutiny reveals a single plane of cleavage common to many specialized fields. In each field one group (A) regards the land as soil and its function as commodity-production; another group (B) regards the land as a biota, and its function as something broader. How much broader is admittedly in a state of doubt and confusion.

In my own field, forestry, group A is quite content to grow trees like cabbages, with cellulose as the basic forest commodity. It feels no inhibition against violence; its ideology is agronomic. Group B, on the other hand, sees forestry as fundamentally different from agronomy because it employs natural species, and manages a natural environment rather than creating an artificial one. Group B prefers natural reproduction on principle. It worries on biotic as well as economic grounds about the loss of species like chestnut and the threatened loss of the white pines. It worries about a whole series of secondary forest functions: wildlife, recreation, watersheds, wilderness areas. To my mind, Group B feels the stirrings of an ecological conscience.

In the wildlife field, a parallel cleavage exists. For Group A the basic commodities are sport and meat; the yardsticks of production are ciphers of take in pheasants and trout. Artificial propagation is acceptable as a permanent as well as a temporary recourse—if its unit costs permit. Group B, on the other hand, worries about a whole series of biotic side-issues. What is the cost in predators of producing a game crop? Should we have further recourse to exotics? How can management restore the shrinking species, like prairie grouse, already hopeless as shootable game? How can management restore the threatened rarities, like trumpeter swan and whooping crane? Can management principles be extended to wildflowers? Here again it is clear to me that we have the same A-B cleavage as in forestry.

In the larger field of agriculture I am less competent to speak, but there seem to be somewhat parallel cleavages. Scientific agriculture was actively developing before ecology was born, hence a slower penetration of ecological concepts might be expected. Moreover the farmer, by the very nature of his techniques, must modify the biota more radically than the forester or the wildlife manager. Nevertheless, there are many discontents in agriculture which seem to add up to a new vision of 'biotic farming.'

Perhaps the most important of these is the new evidence that poundage or tonnage is no measure of the food-value of farm crops; the products of fertile soil may be qualitatively as well as quantitatively superior. We can bolster poundage from depleted soils by pouring on imported fertility, but we are not necessarily bolstering food-value. The possible ultimate ramifications of this idea are so immense that I must leave their exposition to abler pens.

The discontent that labels itself "organic farming," while bearing some of the earmarks of a cult, is nevertheless biotic in its direction, particularly in its insistence on the importance of soil flora and fauna.

The ecological fundamentals of agriculture are just as poorly known to the public as in other fields of land-use. For example, few educated people realize that the marvelous advances in technique made during recent decades are improvements in the pump, rather than the well. Acre for acre, they have barely sufficed to offset the sinking level of fertility.

In all of these cleavages, we see repeated the same basic paradoxes: man the conqueror *versus* man the biotic citizen; science the sharpener of his sword *versus* science the searchlight on his universe; land the slave and servant *versus* land the collective organism. Robinson's injunction to Tristram may well be applied, at this juncture, to *Homo sapiens* as a species in geological time:

Whether you will or not
You are a King, Tristram, for you are one
Of the time-tested few that leave the world,
When they are gone, not the same place it was
Mark what you leave.

THE OUTLOOK

It is inconceivable to me that an ethical relation to land can exist without love, respect, and admiration for land, and a high regard for its value. By value, I of course mean something far broader than mere economic value; I mean value in the philosophical sense.

Perhaps the most serious obstacle impeding the evolution of a land ethic is the fact that our educational and economic system is headed away from, rather than toward, an intense consciousness of land. Your true modern is separated from the land by many middlemen, and by innumerable physical gadgets. He has no vital relation to it; to him it is the space between cities on which crops grow. Turn him loose for a day on the land, and if the spot does not happen to be a golf links or a "scenic" area, he is bored stiff. If crops could be raised by hydroponics instead of farming, it would suit him very well. Synthetic substitutes for wood, leather, wool, and other natural land products suit him better than the originals. In short, land is something he has "outgrown."

Almost equally serious as an obstacle to a land ethic is the attitude of the farmer for whom the land is still an adversary, or a taskmaster that keeps him in slavery. Theoretically, the mechanization of farming ought to cut the farmer's chains, but whether it really does is debatable.

One of the requisites for an ecological comprehension of land is an understanding of ecology, and this is by no means co-extensive with "education"; in fact, much higher education seems deliberately to avoid ecological concepts. An understanding of ecology does not necessarily originate in courses bearing ecological labels; it is quite as likely to be labeled geography, botany, agronomy, history, or economics. This is as it should be, but whatever the label, ecological training is scarce.

The case for a land ethic would appear hopeless but for the minority which is in obvious revolt against these "modern" trends.

The "key-log" which must be moved to release the evolutionary process for an ethic is simply this: quit thinking about decent land-use as solely an economic problem. Examine each question in terms of what is ethically and esthetically right, as well as what is economically expedient. A thing is right when it tends to preserve the integrity, stability, and beauty of the biotic community. It is wrong when it tends otherwise.

It of course goes without saying that economic feasibility limits the tether of what can or cannot be done for land. It always has and it always will. The fallacy the economic determinists have tied around our collective neck, and which we now need to cast off, is the belief that economics determines *all* land-use. This is simply not true. An innumerable host of actions and attitudes, comprising perhaps the bulk of all land relations, is determined by the land-users' tastes and predilections, rather than by his purse. The bulk of all land relations hinges on investments of time, forethought, skill, and faith rather than on investments of cash. As a land-user thinketh, so is he.

I have purposely presented the land ethic as a product of social evolution because nothing so important as an ethic is ever "written." Only the most superficial student of history supposes that Moses "wrote" the Decalogue; it evolved in the minds of a thinking community, and Moses wrote a tentative summary of it for a "seminar." I say tentative because evolution never stops.

The evolution of a land ethic is an intellectual as well as emotional process. Conservation is paved with good intentions which prove to be futile, or even dangerous, because they are devoid of critical understanding either of the land, or of economic land-use. I think it is a truism that as the ethical frontier advances from the individual to the community, its intellectual content increases.

The mechanism of operation is the same for any ethic: social approbation for right actions: social disapproval for wrong actions.

By and large, our present problem is one of attitudes and implements. We are remodeling the Alhambra with a steam-shovel, and we are proud of our yardage. We shall hardly relinquish the shovel, which after all has many good points, but we are in need of gentler and more objective criteria for its successful use.

Review Questions

1. How does Leopold explain his proposed extension of ethics?
2. What is the land ethic, according to Leopold? What is the role of humans in this ethic?
3. According to Leopold, what is wrong with a conservation system based on economic motives?
4. Explain Leopold's image of the biotic pyramid. Where are humans located on the pyramid, and how can they affect it?
5. How does Leopold view the health of the land, and what role should humans play?
6. How does Leopold define right and wrong?

Discussion Questions

1. Are Leopold's definitions of right and wrong acceptable to you? Why or why not?
2. Is hunting compatible with the land ethic? Explain your answer.
3. Do the owners of land have the right to use it as they wish? What would Leopold say? What do you think?

Animal Liberation: A Triangular Affair

J. BAIRD CALLICOTT

J. Baird Callicott is professor of philosophy and religion studies in the Institute of Applied Sciences at the University of North Texas. He is the author of *In Defense of the Land Ethic: Essays in Environmental Philosophy* (1989), *Earth's Insights: A Survey of Ecological Ethics from the Mediterranean Basin to the Australian Outback* (1994), *Beyond the Land Ethic: More Essays in Environmental Philosophy* (1999), and *American Indian Environmental Philosophy* (2004). His picture and curriculum vitae can be seen at www.phil.unt.edu/faculty/vjbc.html.

The "triangular affair" Callicott discusses is the conflict between three different positions: (1) ethical humanists, who accord moral standing to humans only; (2) humane moralists, or animal liberationists, who extend moral standing to animals; and (3) Leopold's land ethic, which gives primary moral concern to the land. Callicott is mainly concerned with defending the land ethic from attacks by animal liberationists. In the course of his defense, he explains why hunting, killing, and eating animals is justified, at least in Leopold's land ethic (but not in his own view, as he explains in the preface), and why he thinks animal liberation, in the final analysis, is "utterly unpracticable." By contrast, he finds the land ethic eminently practicable, although he admits that its implementation would be very difficult, requiring enormous economic reform and a revolution in attitudes and lifestyles.

PREFACE (1994)

I WROTE "A Triangular Affair" to sharply distinguish environmental ethics from animal liberation/rights when the former seemed to be overshadowed by the latter. Back in the late 1970s and early 1980s, when the piece was conceived and composed, many people seemed to conflate the two. In my youthful zeal to draw attention to the then unheralded Leopold land ethic, I made a few remarks that in retrospect appear irresponsible.

Most important, I no longer think that the land ethic is misanthropic. "All ethics so far

Source: J. Baird Callicott, "Animal Liberation: A Triangular Affair," from *Environmental Ethics* 2, 4 (Winter 1980). Reprinted with permission. Some footnotes have been renumbered.

evolved," Leopold wrote, "rest upon a single premiss: that the individual is a member of a community of interdependent parts. . . . The land ethic simply enlarges the boundaries of the community to include soils, waters, plants, and animals, or collectively: the land." The biotic community and its correlative land ethic *does not replace* our several human communities and their correlative ethics—our duties and obligations to family and family members, to municipality and fellow-citizens, to country and countrymen, to humanity and human beings. Rather it *supplements* them. Hence the land ethic leaves our traditional human morality quite intact and pre-emptive.

Second in importance, I now think that we do in fact have duties and obligations—implied by the essentially communitarian premises of the land ethic—to domestic animals, as well as to wild fellow-members of the biotic community and to the biotic community as a whole. Farm animals, work animals, and pets have long been members of what Mary Midgley calls the "mixed" community. They have entered into a kind of implicit social contract with us which lately we have abrogated. Think of it this way. Each of us belongs to several hierarchically ordered human communities, each with its peculiar set of duties and obligations; to various mixed human-animal domestic communities, with their peculiar sets of duties and obligations; and to the biotic community, with its peculiar set of duties and obligations (which in sum Leopold called the land ethic). The land ethic no more eclipses our moral responsibilities in regard to domestic animals than it does our moral responsibilities in regard to other people.

Further, I now think that a vegetarian diet is indicated by the land ethic, no less than by the animal welfare ethics. Rainforests are felled to make pasture for cattle. Better for the environment if we ate forest fruits instead of beef. Livestock ruin watercourses and grasslands. And raising field crops for animal feed increases soil erosion and ground-water depletion.

Finally, though certainly I still wish there were far more bears than actually there are, a target ratio of one bear for every two people seems a bit extravagant.

"A Triangular Affair" clearly distinguishes between holistic environmental ethics, on the one hand, and individualistic "moral humanism" and "humane moralism," on the other. And that remains a serviceable distinction. Moralists of every stripe, however, must make common cause against the forces that are often simultaneously destroying human, mixed, and biotic communities. The differences between human, humane, and environmental concerns are real, and sometimes conflictive. But just as often they are convergent and mutually reinforcing. And all our ethical concerns can be theoretically unified, I am convinced, by a communitarian moral philosophy, thus enabling conflicts, when they do arise, to be adjudicated rationally.

ENVIRONMENTAL ETHICS AND ANIMAL LIBERATION

Partly because it is so new to Western philosophy (or at least heretofore only scarcely represented) *environmental ethics* has no precisely fixed conventional definition in glossaries of philosophical terminology. Aldo Leopold, however, is universally recognized as the father or founding genius of recent environmental ethics. His "land ethic" has become a modern classic and may be treated as the standard example, the paradigm case, as it were, of what an environmental ethic is. *Environmental ethics* then can be defined ostensively by using Leopold's land ethic as the exemplary type. I do not mean to suggest that all environmental ethics should necessarily conform to Leopold's paradigm, but the extent to which an ethical system resembles Leopold's land ethic might be used, for want of anything better, as a criterion to measure the extent to which it is or is not of the environmental sort.

It is Leopold's opinion, and certainly an overall review of the prevailing traditions of Western ethics, both popular and philosophical, generally confirms it, that traditional Western systems of ethics have not accorded moral standing to nonhuman beings.[1] Animals and plants, soils and waters, which Leopold includes in his community of ethical beneficiaries, have traditionally enjoyed no moral standing, no rights, no respect, in sharp contrast to human persons whose rights and interests ideally must be fairly and equally considered if our actions are to be considered "ethical" or "moral." One fundamental and novel feature of the Leopold land ethic, therefore, is the extension of *direct* ethical considerability from people to nonhuman natural entities.

At first glance, the recent ethical movement usually labeled "animal liberation" or "animal rights" seems to be squarely and centrally a kind of environmental ethics. The more uncompromising among the animal liberationists have

1 Aldo Leopold, *A Sand County Almanac* (New York: Oxford University Press, 1949), pp. 202–203.

demanded equal moral consideration on behalf of cows, pigs, chickens, and other apparently enslaved and oppressed nonhuman animals. The theoreticians of this new hyperegalitarianism have coined such terms as *speciesism* (on analogy with *racism* and *sexism*) and *human chauvinism* (on analogy with *male chauvinism*), and have made animal liberation seem, perhaps not improperly, the next and most daring development of political liberalism. Aldo Leopold also draws upon metaphors of political liberalism when he tells us that his land ethic "changes the role of *Homo sapiens* from conqueror of the land community to plain member and citizen of it."[2] For animal liberationists it is as if the ideological battles for equal rights and equal consideration for women and for racial minorities have been all but won, and the next and greatest challenge is to purchase equality, first theoretically and then practically, for all (actually only *some*) animals regardless of species. This more rhetorically implied than fully articulated historical progression of moral rights from fewer to greater numbers of "persons" (allowing that animals may also be persons) as advocated by animal liberationists, also parallels Leopold's scenario in "The Land Ethic" of the historical extension of "ethical criteria" to more and more "fields of conduct" and to larger and larger groups of people during the past three thousand or so years.[3] As Leopold develops it, the land ethic is a cultural "evolutionary possibility," the next "step in a sequence."[4] For Leopold, however, the next step is much more sweeping, much more inclusive than the animal liberationists envision, since it "enlarges the boundaries of the [moral] community to include soils, waters, [and] plants . . ." as well as animals.[5] Thus, the animal liberation movement *could* be construed as partitioning Leopold's perhaps undigestable and totally inclusive environmental

ethic into a series of more assimilable stages: today animal rights, tomorrow equal rights for plants, and after that full moral standing for rocks, soil, and other earthy compounds, and perhaps sometime in the still more remote future, liberty and equality for water and other elementary bodies.

Put just this way, however, there is something jarring about such a graduated progression in the exfoliation of a more inclusive environmental ethic, something that seems absurd. A more or less reasonable case might be made for rights for some animals, but when we come to plants, soils, and waters, the frontier between plausibility and absurdity appears to have been crossed. Yet, there is no doubt that Leopold sincerely proposes that *land* (in his inclusive sense) be ethically regarded. The beech and chestnut, for example, have in his view as much "biotic right" to life as the wolf and the deer, and the effects of human actions on mountains and streams for Leopold is an ethical concern as genuine and serious as the comfort and longevity of brood hens.[6] In fact, Leopold to all appearances never considered the treatment of brood hens on a factory farm or steers in a feed lot to be a pressing moral issue. He seems much more concerned about the integrity of the farm *wood lot* and the effects of clear-cutting steep slopes on neighboring *streams*.

Animal liberationists put their ethic into practice (and display their devotion to it) by becoming vegetarians, and the moral complexities of vegetarianism have been thoroughly debated in the recent literature as an adjunct issue to animal rights. (No one however has yet expressed, as among Butler's Erewhonians, qualms about eating plants, though such sentiments might be expected to be latently present, if the rights of plants are next to be defended.) Aldo Leopold, by contrast did not even condemn hunting animals, let alone eating them, nor did he personally abandon hunting, for which he had had an enthusiasm since boyhood, upon becoming convinced that

2 Ibid., p. 204.
3 Ibid., pp. 201–203.
4 Ibid., p. 203.
5 Ibid., p. 204.

6 Ibid., p. 221 (trees); pp. 129–133 (mountains); p. 209 (streams).

his ethical responsibilities extended beyond the human sphere. There are several interpretations for this behavioral peculiarity. One is that Leopold did not see that his land ethic actually ought to prohibit hunting, cruelly killing, and eating animals. A corollary of this interpretation is that Leopold was so unperspicacious as deservedly to be thought stupid—a conclusion hardly comporting with the intellectual subtlety he usually evinces in most other respects. If not stupid, then perhaps Leopold was hypocritical. But if a hypocrite, we should expect him to conceal his proclivity for blood sports and flesh eating and to treat them as shameful vices to be indulged secretively. As it is, bound together between the same covers with "The Land Ethic" are his unabashed reminiscences of killing and consuming *game*. This term (like *stock*) when used of animals, moreover, appears to be morally equivalent to referring to a sexually appealing young woman as a "piece" or to a strong, young black man as a "buck"—if animal rights, that is, are to be considered as on a par with women's rights and the rights of formerly enslaved races. A third interpretation of Leopold's approbation of regulated and disciplined sport hunting (and *a fortiori* meat eating) is that it is a form of human/animal behavior not inconsistent with the land ethic as he conceived it. A corollary of this interpretation is that Leopold's land ethic and the environmental ethic of the animal liberation movement rest upon very different theoretical foundations, and that they are thus two very different forms of environmental ethics.

The urgent concern of animal liberationists for the suffering of *domestic* animals, toward which Leopold manifests an attitude which can only be described as indifference, and the urgent concern of Leopold, on the other hand, for the disappearance of *species* of plants as well as animals and for soil erosion and stream pollution, appear to be symptoms not only of very different ethical perspectives, but profoundly different cosmic visions as well. The neat similarities, noted at the beginning of this discussion, between the environmental ethic of the animal liberation movement and the classical Leopoldian land ethic appear in light of these observations to be rather superficial and to conceal substrata of thought and value which are not at all similar. The theoretical foundations of the animal liberation movement and those of the Leopoldian land ethic may even turn out not to be companionable, complementary, or mutually consistent. The animal liberationists may thus find themselves not only engaged in controversy with the many conservative philosophers upholding *apartheid* between man and "beast," but also faced with an unexpected dissent from another, very different, system of environmental ethics. Animal liberation and animal rights may well prove to be a triangular rather than, as it has so far been represented in the philosophical community, a polar controversy.

ETHICAL HUMANISM AND HUMANE MORALISM

The orthodox response of "ethical humanism" (as this philosophical perspective may be styled) to the suggestion that nonhuman animals should be accorded moral standing is that such animals are not worthy of this high perquisite. Only human beings are rational, or capable of having interests, or possess *self*-awareness, or have linguistic abilities, or can represent the future, it is variously argued. These essential attributes taken singly or in various combinations make people somehow exclusively deserving of moral consideration. The so-called "lower animals," it is insisted, lack the crucial qualification for ethical considerability and so may be treated (albeit humanely, according to some, so as not to brutalize man) as things or means, not as persons or as ends.

The theoreticians of the animal liberation movement ("humane moralists" as they may be called) typically reply as follows. Not all human beings qualify as worthy of moral regard, according to the various criteria specified. Therefore, by parity of reasoning, human persons who do not so qualify as moral patients may be treated, as animals often are, as mere things or means (e.g., used in vivisection experiments, disposed of if their existence is inconvenient, eaten, hunted, etc., etc.). But the ethical humanists would be morally outraged if irrational and inarticulate infants, for example, were used in painful or lethal medical experiments, or if severely retarded people were hunted for pleasure. Thus, the double-dealing, the hypocrisy, of ethical humanism appears to be exposed. Ethical humanism, though claiming to discriminate between worthy and unworthy ethical patients on the basis of objective criteria impartially applied, turns out after all, it seems, to be *speciesism,* a philosophically indefensible prejudice (analogous to racial prejudice) against animals. The tails side of this argument is that some animals, usually the "higher" lower animals (cetaceans, other primates, etc.), as ethological studies seem to indicate, may meet the criteria specified for moral worth, although the ethical humanists, even so, are not prepared to grant them full dignity and the rights of persons. In short, the ethical humanists' various criteria for moral standing do not include all or only human beings, humane moralists argue, although in practice ethical humanism wishes to make the class of morally considerable beings coextensive with the class of human beings.

The humane moralists, for their part, insist upon *sentience* (*sensibility* would have been a more precise word choice) as the only relevant capacity a being need possess to enjoy full moral standing. If animals, they argue, are conscious entities who, though deprived of reason, speech, forethought or even *self*-awareness (however that may be judged), are capable of suffering, then their suffering should be as much a matter of ethical concern as that of our fellow human beings, or strictly speaking, as our very own. What, after all, has rationality or any of the other allegedly uniquely human capacities to do with ethical standing? Why, in other words, should beings who reason or use speech (etc.) qualify for moral status, and those who do not fail to qualify? Isn't this just like saying that only persons with white skin should be free, or that only persons who beget and not those who bear should own property? The criterion seems utterly

unrelated to the benefit for which it selects. On the other hand, the capacity to suffer is, it seems, a more relevant criterion for moral standing because—as Bentham and Mill, notable among modern philosophers, and Epicurus, among the ancients, aver—pain is evil, and its opposite, pleasure and freedom from pain, good. As moral agents (and this seems axiomatic), we have a duty to behave in such a way that the effect of our actions is to promote and procure good, so far as possible, and to reduce and minimize evil. That would amount to an obligation to produce pleasure and reduce pain. Now pain is pain wherever and by whomever it is suffered. As a *moral* agent, I should not consider my pleasure and pain to be of greater consequence in determining a course of action than that of other persons. Thus, by the same token, if animals suffer pain—and among philosophers only strict Cartesians would deny that they do—then we are morally obliged to consider their suffering as much an evil to be minimized by conscientious moral agents as human suffering. Certainly actions of ours which contribute to the suffering of animals, such as hunting them, butchering and eating them, experimenting on them, etc., are on these assumptions morally reprehensible. Hence, a person who regards himself or herself as not aiming in life to live most selfishly, conveniently, or profitably, but rightly and in accord with practical principle, if convinced by these arguments, should, among other things, cease to eat the flesh of animals, to hunt them, to wear fur and leather clothing and bone ornaments and other articles made from the bodies of animals, to eat eggs and drink milk, if the animal producers of these commodities are retained under inhumane circumstances, and to patronize zoos (as sources of psychological if not physical torment of animals). On the other hand, since certain very simple animals are almost certainly insensible to pleasure and pain, they may and indeed should be treated as morally inconsequential. Nor is there any *moral* reason why trees should be respected or rivers or mountains or anything which is, though living or tributary to life processes, unconscious. The humane moralists, like the moral humanists, draw a firm distinction between those beings worthy of moral consideration and those not. They simply insist upon a different but quite definite cut-off point on the spectrum of natural entities, and accompany their criterion with arguments to show that it is more ethically defensible (granting certain assumptions) and more consistently applicable than that of the moral humanists.

THE FIRST PRINCIPLE OF THE LAND ETHIC

The fundamental principle of humane moralism, as we see, is Benthamic. Good is equivalent to pleasure and, more pertinently, evil is equivalent to pain. The presently booming controversy between moral humanists and humane moralists appears, when all the learned dust has settled, to be essentially internecine; at least, the lines of battle are drawn along familiar watersheds of the conceptual terrain.[7] A classical ethical theory, Bentham's, has been refitted and pressed into service to meet relatively new and unprecedented ethically relevant situations—the problems raised especially by factory farming and ever more exotic and frequently ill-conceived scientific research employing animal subjects. Then, those with Thomist, Kantian, Lockean, Moorean (etc.)

ethical affiliation have heard the bugle and have risen to arms. It is no wonder that so many academic philosophers have been drawn into the fray. The issues have an apparent newness about them; moreover, they are socially and politically *avant garde.* But there is no serious challenge to cherished first principles. Hence, without having to undertake any creative ethical reflection or exploration, or any reexamination of historical ethical theory, a fresh debate has been stirred up. The familiar historical positions have simply been retrenched, applied, and exercised.

But what about the third (and certainly minority) party to the animal liberation debate? What sort of reasonable and coherent moral theory would at once urge that animals (and plants and soils and waters) be included in the same class with people as beings to whom ethical consideration is owed and yet not object to some of them being slaughtered (whether painlessly or not) and eaten, others hunted, trapped, and in various other ways seemingly cruelly

---

7 John Rodman, "The Liberation of Nature" (p. 95), comments: "Why do our 'new ethics' seem so old? . . . Because the attempt to produce a 'new ethics' by the process of 'extension' perpetuates the basic assumptions of the conventional modern paradigm, however much it fiddles with the boundaries." When the assumptions remain conventional, the boundaries are, in my view, scalar, but triangular when both positions are considered in opposition to the land ethic. The scalar relation is especially clear when two other positions, not specifically discussed in the text, the reverence-for-life ethic and pan-moralism, are considered. The reverence-for-life ethic (as I am calling it in deference to Albert Schweitzer) seems to be the next step on the scale after the humane ethic. William Frankena considers it so in "Ethics and the Environment," *Ethics and Problems of the 21st Century,* pp. 3–20. W. Murry Hunt ("Are *Mere Things* Morally Considerable?" *Environmental Ethics* 2 (1980): 59–65) has gone a step past Schweitzer, and made the bold

suggestion that *everything* should be accorded moral standing, pan-moralism. Hunt's discussion shows clearly that there is a similar logic ("slippery slope" logic) involved in taking each downward step, and thus a certain commonality of underlying assumptions among all the ethical types to which the land ethic stands in opposition. Hunt is not unaware that his suggestion may be interpreted as a *reductio ad absurdum* of the whole matter, but insists that that is not his intent. The land ethic is not part of this linear series of steps and hence may be represented as a point off the scale. The principal difference . . . is that the land ethic is collective or "holistic" while the others are distributive or "atomistic." Another relevant difference is that moral humanism, humane moralism, reverence-for-life ethics, and the limiting case, pan-moralism, either openly or implicitly espouse a pecking-order model of nature. The land ethic, founded upon an ecological model of nature emphasizing the contributing roles played by various species in the economy of nature, abandons the "higher"/"lower" ontological and axiological schema, in favor of a functional system of value. The land ethic, in other words, is inclined to establish value distinctions not on the basis of higher and lower orders of being, but on the basis of the importance of organisms, minerals, and so on to the biotic community. Some bacteria, for example, may be of greater value to the health or economy of nature than dogs, and thus command more respect.

used? Aldo Leopold provides a concise statement of what might be called the categorical imperative or principal precept of the land ethic: "A thing is right when it tends to preserve the integrity, stability, and beauty of the biotic community. It is wrong when it tends otherwise."[8] What is especially note-worthy, and that to which attention should be directed in this proposition, is the idea that the good of the biotic *community* is the ultimate measure of the moral value, the rightness or wrongness, of actions. Thus, to hunt and kill a white-tailed deer in certain districts may not only be ethically permissible, it might actually be a moral requirement, necessary to protect the local environment, taken as a whole, from the disintegrating effects of a cervid population explosion. On the other hand, rare and endangered animals like the lynx should be especially nurtured and preserved. The lynx, cougar, and other wild feline predators, from the neo-Benthamite perspective (if consistently and evenhandedly applied) should be regarded as merciless, wanton, and incorrigible murderers of their fellow creatures, who not only kill, it should be added, but cruelly toy with their victims, thus increasing the measure of pain in the world. From the perspective of the land ethic, predators generally should be nurtured and preserved as critically important members of the biotic communities to which they are native. Certain plants, similarly, may be overwhelmingly important to the stability, integrity, and beauty of biotic communities, while some animals, such as domestic sheep (allowed perhaps by egalitarian and humane herdspersons to graze freely and to reproduce themselves without being harvested for lamb and mutton) could be a pestilential threat to the natural floral community of a given locale. Thus, the land ethic is logically coherent in demanding at once that moral consideration be given to plants as well as to animals and yet in permitting animals to be killed, trees felled, and so on. In every case the effect upon ecological systems is the decisive

8 Ibid., pp. 224–225.

factor in the determination of the ethical quality of actions. . . .

THE LAND ETHIC AND THE ECOLOGICAL POINT OF VIEW

. . . Since ecology focuses upon the relationships between and among things, it inclines its students toward a more holistic vision of the world. Before the rather recent emergence of ecology as a science the landscape appeared to be, one might say, a collection of objects, some of them alive, some conscious, but all the same, an aggregate, a plurality of separate individuals. With this "atomistic" representation of things it is no wonder that moral issues might be understood as competing and mutually contradictory clashes of the "rights" of separate individuals, each separately pursuing its "interests." Ecology has made it possible to apprehend the same landscape as an articulate unity (without the least hint of mysticism or ineffability). Ordinary organic bodies have articulated and discernible parts (limbs, various organs, myriad cells); yet, because of the character of the network of relations among those parts, they form in a perfectly familiar sense a second-order whole. Ecology makes it possible to see land, similarly, as a unified system of integrally related parts, as, so to speak, a third-order organic whole.

Another analogy that has helped ecologists to convey the particular holism which their science brings to reflective attention is that land is integrated as a human community is integrated. The various parts of the "biotic community" (individual animals and plants) depend upon one another *economically* so that the system as such acquires distinct characteristics of its own. Just as it is possible to characterize and define collectively peasant societies, agrarian communities, industrial complexes, capitalist, communist, and socialist economic systems, and so on, ecology characterizes and defines various biomes as desert, savanna, wetland, tundra, wood land, etc., communities, each with its particular "professions," "roles," or "niches."

Now we may think that among the duties we as moral agents have toward ourselves is the duty of self-preservation, which may be interpreted as a duty to maintain our own organic integrity. It is not uncommon in historical moral theory, further, to find that in addition to those peculiar responsibilities we have in relation both to ourselves and to other persons severally, we also have a duty to behave in ways that do not harm the fabric of society *per se*. The land ethic, in similar fashion, calls our attention to the recently discovered integrity—in other words, the unity—of the biota and posits duties binding upon moral agents in relation to that whole. Whatever the strictly formal logical connections between the concept of a social community and moral responsibility, there appears to be a strong psychological bond between that idea and conscience. Hence, the representation of the natural environment as, in Leopold's terms, "one humming community" (or, less consistently in his discussion, a third-order organic being) brings into play, whether rationally or not, those stirrings of conscience which we feel in relation to delicately complex, functioning social and organic systems.

The neo-Benthamite humane moralists have, to be sure, digested one of the metaphysical implications of modern biology. They insist that human beings must be understood continuously with the rest of organic nature. People are (and are only) animals, and much of the rhetorical energy of the animal liberation movement is spent in fighting a rear guard action for this aspect of Darwinism against those philosophers who still cling to the dream of a special metaphysical status for people in the order of "creation." To this extent the animal liberation movement is biologically enlightened and argues from the taxonomical and evolutionary continuity of man and beast to moral standing for some nonhuman animals. Indeed, pain, in their view the very substance of evil, is something that is conspicuously common to people and other sensitive animals, something that we as people experience not in virtue of our metasimian cerebral capabilities, but because of our participation in a more generally animal, limbic-based consciousness. *If* it is pain and suffering that is the ultimate evil besetting human life, and this not in virtue of our humanity but in virtue of our animality, then it seems only fair to promote freedom from pain for those animals who share with us in this mode of experience and to grant them rights similar to ours as a means to this end.

Recent ethological studies of other primates, cetaceans, and so on, are not infrequently cited to drive the point home, but the biological information of the animal liberation movement seems to extend no further than this—the continuity of human with other animal life forms. The more recent ecological perspective especially seems to be ignored by humane moralists. The holistic outlook of ecology and the associated value premium conferred upon the biotic community, its beauty, integrity, and stability may simply not have penetrated the thinking of the animal liberationists, or it could be that to include it would involve an intolerable contradiction with the Benthamite foundations of their ethical theory. Bentham's view of the "interests of the community" was bluntly reductive. With his characteristic bluster, Bentham wrote, "The community is a fictitious *body* composed of the individual persons who are considered as constituting as it were its *members*. The interest of the community then is, what?—the sum of the interests of the several members who compose it."[9] Bentham's very simile—the community is like a body composed of members—gives the lie to his reduction of its interests to the sum of its parts taken severally. The interests of a person are not those of his or her cells summed up and averaged out. Our organic health and well-being, for example, require vigorous exercise and metabolic stimulation which cause stress and often pain to various parts of the body and a more rapid turnover in the life cycle of our individual cells. For the sake of the person taken as whole, some parts may be,

9 *An Introduction to the Principles of Morals and Legislation* (Oxford: Oxford University Press, 1823), chap. 1, sec. 4.

as it were, unfairly sacrificed. On the level of so-cial organization, the interests of society may not always coincide with the sum of the interests of its parts. Discipline, sacrifice, and individual re-straint are often necessary in the social sphere to maintain social integrity as within the bodily or-ganism. A society, indeed, is particularly vulnera-ble to disintegration when its members become preoccupied totally with their own particular in-terest, and ignore those distinct and independent interests of the community as a whole. One ex-ample, unfortunately, our own society, is alto-gether too close at hand to be examined with strict academic detachment. The United States seems to pursue uncritically a social policy of re-ductive utilitarianism, aimed at promoting the happiness of all its members severally. Each spe-cial interest accordingly clamors more loudly to be satisfied while the community as a whole be-comes noticeably more and more infirm eco-nomically, environmentally, and politically.

The humane moralists, whether or not they are consciously and deliberately follow-ing Bentham on this particular, nevertheless, in point of fact, are committed to the welfare of certain kinds of animals distributively or reduc-tively in applying their moral concern for non-human beings. They lament the treatment of animals, most frequently farm and laboratory animals, and plead the special interests of these beings. We might ask, from the perspective of the land ethic, what the effect upon the natural environment taken as whole would be if domes-tic animals were actually liberated? There is, almost certainly, very little real danger that this might actually happen, but it would be instruc-tive to speculate on the ecological consequences.

ᵀHICAL HOLISM

we take up this question, however, some
ᵗnterest remain to be considered on the
holistic versus a reductive envi-
· To pit the one against the other
ᵛwithout further qualification
A society is constituted by

its members, an organic body by its cells, and the ecosystem by the plants, animals, minerals, fluids, and gases which compose it. One cannot affect a system as a whole without affecting at least some of its components. An environmental ethic which takes as its *summum bonum* the integrity, stability, and beauty of the biotic community is not conferring moral standing on something *else* besides plants, animals, soils, and waters. Rather, the former, the good of the community as a whole, serves as a standard for the assessment of the relative value and rel-ative ordering of its constitutive parts and therefore provides a means of adjudicating the often mutually contradictory demands of the parts considered separately for *equal* consider-ation. If diversity does indeed contribute to stability (a classical "law" of ecology), then *spec-imens* of rare and endangered species, for example, have a *prima facie* claim to preferen-tial consideration from the perspective of the land ethic. Animals of those species, which, like the honey bee, function in ways critically impor-tant to the economy of nature, moreover, would be granted a greater claim to moral attention than psychologically more complex and sensitive ones, say, rabbits and moles, which seem to be plentiful, globally distributed, reproductively efficient, and only routinely integrated into the natural economy. Animals and plants, moun-tains, rivers, seas, the atmosphere are the *imme-diate* practical beneficiaries of the land ethic. The well-being of the biotic community, the biosphere as a whole, cannot be logically sepa-rated from their survival and welfare.

Some suspicion may arise at this point that the land ethic is ultimately grounded in *human* interests, not in those of nonhuman natural en-tities. Just as we might prefer a sound and at-tractive house to one in the opposite condition so the "goodness" of a whole, stable, and beau-tiful environment seems rather to be of the in-strumental, not the autochthonous, variety. The question of ultimate value is a very sticky one for environmental as well as for all ethics and cannot be fully addressed here. It is my view that there can be no value apart from an evaluator, that all value is as it were in the eye of the beholder. The value that is attributed to the ecosystem, therefore, is humanly dependent or (allowing that other living things may take a certain delight in the well-being of the whole of things, or that the gods may) at least dependent upon some variety of morally and aesthetically sensitive consciousness. Granting this, however, there is a further, very crucial distinction to be drawn. It is possible that while things may only have value because we (or someone) values them, they may nonetheless be valued for themselves as well as for the contribution they might make to the realization of our (or someone's) interests. Children are valued for themselves by most parents. Money, on the other hand, has only an instrumental or indirect value. Which sort of value has the health of the biotic community and its members severally for Leopold and the land ethic? It is especially difficult to separate these two general sorts of value, the one of moral significance, the other merely selfish, when something that may be valued in *both ways at once* is the subject of consideration. Are pets, for example, well-treated, like children, for the sake of themselves, or, like mechanical appliances, because of the sort of services they provide their owners? Is a healthy biotic community something we value because we are so utterly and (to the biologically well-informed) so obviously dependent upon it not only for our happiness but for our very survival, or may we also perceive it disinterestedly as having an independent worth? Leopold insists upon a noninstrumental value for the biotic community and *mutatis mutandis* for its constituents. According to Leopold, collective enlightened self-interest on the part of human beings does not go far enough; the land ethic in his opinion (and no doubt this reflects his own moral intuitions) requires "love, respect, and admiration for land, and a high regard for its value." The land ethic, in Leopold's view, creates "obligations over and above self-interest." And "obligations have no meaning without conscience, and the problem we face is the extension of the social conscience from people to land."[10] If, in other words, any genuine ethic is possible, if it is possible to value *people* for the sake of themselves, then it is equally possible to value *land* in the same way.

Some indication of the genuinely biocentric value orientation of ethical environmentalism is indicated in what otherwise might appear to be gratuitous misanthropy. The biospheric perspective does not exempt *Homo sapiens* from moral evaluation in relation to the well-being of the community of nature taken as a whole. The preciousness of individual deer, as of any other specimen, is inversely proportional to the population of the species. Environmentalists, however reluctantly and painfully, do not omit to apply the same logic to their own kind. As omnivores, the population of human beings should, perhaps, be roughly twice that of bears, allowing for differences of size. A global population of more than four billion persons and showing no signs of an orderly decline presents an alarming prospect to humanists, but it is at present a global disaster (the more *per capita* prosperity, indeed, the more disastrous it appears) for the biotic community. If the land ethic were only a means of managing nature for the sake of man, misleadingly phrased in moral terminology, then man would be considered as having an ultimate value essentially different from that of his "resources." The extent of misanthropy in modern environmentalism thus may be taken as a measure of the degree to which it is biocentric. Edward Abbey in his enormously popular *Desert Solitaire* bluntly states that he would sooner shoot a man than a snake.[11] Abbey may not be simply depraved; this is perhaps only his way of dramatically making the point that the human population has become so disproportionate from the biological point of view that if one had to choose between a specimen of *Homo sapiens* and a specimen of a rare even if

10 Leopold, *Sand County Almanac*, pp. 223 and 209.
11 Edward Abbey, *Desert Solitaire* (New York: Ballantine Books, 1968), p. 20.

unattractive species, the choice would be moot. Among academicians, Garret Hardin, a human ecologist by discipline who has written extensively on ethics, environmental and otherwise, has shocked philosophers schooled in the preciousness of human life with his "lifeboat" and "survival" ethics and his "wilderness economics." In context of the latter, Hardin recommends limiting access to wilderness by criteria of hardiness and woodcraft and would permit no emergency roads or airborne rescue vehicles to violate the pristine purity of wilderness areas. If a wilderness adventurer should have a serious accident, Hardin recommends that he or she get out on his or her own or die in the attempt. Danger, from the strictly human-centered, psychological perspective, is part of the wilderness experience, Hardin argues, but in all probability his more important concern is to protect from mechanization the remnants of wild country that remain even if the price paid is the incidental loss of human life which, from the perspective once more of the biologist, is a commodity altogether too common in relation to wildlife and to wild landscapes."[12] . . .

. . . Modern systems of ethics have, it must be admitted, considered the principle of the equality of persons to be inviolable. This is true, for example, of both major schools of modern ethics, the utilitarian school going back to Bentham and Mill, and the deontological, originating with Kant. The land ethic manifestly does not accord equal moral worth to each and every member of the biotic community; the moral worth of individuals (including, n.b., human individuals) is relative, to be assessed in accordance with the particular relation of each to the collective entity which Leopold called "land."

There is, however, a classical Western ethic, with the best philosophical credentials, which

assumes a similar holistic posture (with respect to the social moral sphere). I have in mind Plato's moral and social philosophy. Indeed, two of the same analogies figuring in the conceptual foundations of the Leopold land ethic appear in Plato's value theory. From the ecological perspective, according to Leopold as I have pointed out, land is like an organic body or like a human society. According to Plato, body, soul, and society have similar structures and corresponding virtues. The goodness of each is a function of its structure or organization and the relative value of the parts or constituents of each is calculated according to the contribution made to the integrity, stability, and beauty of each whole. In the *Republic,* Plato, in the very name of virtue and justice, is notorious for, among other things, requiring infanticide for a child whose only offense was being born without the sanction of the state, making presents to the enemy of guardians who allow themselves to be captured alive in combat, and radically restricting the practice of medicine to the dressing of wounds and the curing of seasonal maladies on the principle that the infirm and chronically ill not only lead miserable lives but contribute nothing to the good of the polity. Plato, indeed, seems to regard individual human life and certainly human pain and suffering with complete indifference. On the other hand, he shrinks from nothing so long as it seems to him to be in the interest of the community. Among the apparently inhuman recommendations that he makes to better the community are a program of eugenics involving a phony lottery (so that those whose natural desires are frustrated, while breeding proceeds from the best stock as in a kennel or stable, will blame chance, not the design of the rulers), the destruction of the pair bond and nuclear family (in the interests of greater military and bureaucratic efficiency and group solidarity), and the utter abolition of private property.

When challenged with the complaint that he is ignoring individual human happiness (and the happiness of those belonging to the most

12 Garrett Hardin, "The Economics of Wilderness," *Natural History* 78 [1969]: 173–177. Hardin is blunt: "Making great and spectacular efforts to save the life of an individual makes sense only when there is a shortage of people. I have not lately heard that there is a shortage of people" (p. 176).

privileged class at that), he replies that it is the well-being of the community as a whole, not that of any person or special class at which his legislation aims. This principle is readily accepted, first of all, in our attitude toward the body, he reminds us—the separate interests of the parts of which we acknowledge to be subordinate to the health and well-being of the whole—and secondly, assuming that we accept his faculty psychology, in our attitude toward the soul—whose multitude of desires must be disciplined, restrained, and, in the case of some, altogether repressed in the interest of personal virtue and a well-ordered and morally responsible life.

Given these formal similarities to Plato's moral philosophy, we may conclude that the land ethic—with its holistic good and its assignment of differential values to the several parts of the environment irrespective of their intelligence, sensibility, degree of complexity, or any other characteristic discernible in the parts considered separately—is somewhat foreign to modern systems of ethical philosophy, but perfectly familiar in the broader context of classical Western ethical philosophy. If, therefore, Plato's system of public and private justice is properly an "ethical" system, then so is the land ethic in relation to environmental virtue and excellence.

REAPPRAISING DOMESTICITY

Among the last philosophical remarks penned by Aldo Leopold before his untimely death in 1948 is the following: "Perhaps such a shift of values [as implied by the attempt to weld together the concepts of ethics and ecology] can be achieved by reappraising things unnatural, tame, and confined in terms of things natural, wild, and free."[13] John Muir, in a similar spirit of reappraisal, had noted earlier the difference between the wild mountain sheep of the Sierra and the ubiquitous domestic variety. The latter, which Muir described as "hooved locusts," were only, in his estimation,

"half alive" in comparison with their natural and autonomous counterparts.[14] One of the more distressing aspects of the animal liberation movement is the failure of almost all its exponents to draw a sharp distinction between the very different plights (and rights) of wild and domestic animals. But this distinction lies at the very center of the land ethic. Domestic animals are creations of man. They are living artifacts, but artifacts nevertheless, and they constitute yet another mode of extension of the works of man into the ecosystem. From the perspective of the land ethic a herd of cattle, sheep, or pigs is as much or more a ruinous blight on the landscape as a fleet of four-wheel drive off-road vehicles. There is thus something profoundly incoherent (and insensitive as well) in the complaint of some animal liberationists that the "natural behavior" of chickens and bobby calves is cruelly frustrated on factory farms. It would make almost as much sense to speak of the natural behavior of tables and chairs.

Here a serious disanalogy (which no one to my knowledge has yet pointed out) becomes clearly evident between the liberation of blacks from slavery (and more recently, from civil inequality) and the liberation of animals from a similar sort of subordination and servitude. Black slaves remained, as it were, metaphysically autonomous: they were by nature if not by convention free beings quite capable of living on their own. They could not be enslaved for more than a historical interlude, for the strength of the force of their freedom was too great. They could, in other words, be retained only by a continuous counterforce, and only temporarily. This is equally true of caged wild animals. African cheetahs in American and European zoos are captive, not indentured, beings. But this is not true of cows, pigs, sheep, and chickens. They have been bred to docility, tractability, stupidity, and dependency. It is literally meaningless to

---

13 Leopold, *Sand County Almanac*, p. ix.

14 See John Muir, "The Wild Sheep of California," *Overland Monthly* 12 (1874): 359.

suggest that they be liberated. It is, to speak in hyperbole, a logical impossibility.

Certainly it is a practical impossibility. Imagine what would happen if the people of the world became morally persuaded that domestic animals were to be regarded as oppressed and enslaved persons and accordingly *set free*. In one scenario we might imagine that like former American black slaves they would receive the equivalent of forty acres and a mule and be turned out to survive on their own. Feral cattle and sheep would hang around farm outbuildings waiting forlornly to be sheltered and fed, or would graze aimlessly through their abandoned and deteriorating pastures. Most would starve or freeze as soon as winter settled in. Reproduction which had been assisted over many countless generations by their former owners might be altogether impossible in the feral state for some varieties, and the care of infants would be an art not so much lost as never acquired. And so in a very short time, after much suffering and agony, these species would become abruptly extinct. Or, in another scenario beginning with the same simple emancipation from human association, survivors of the first massive die-off of untended livestock might begin to recover some of their remote wild ancestral genetic traits and become smaller, leaner, heartier, and smarter versions of their former selves. An actual contemporary example is afforded by the feral mustangs ranging over parts of the American West. In time such animals as these would become (just as the mustangs are now) competitors both with their former human masters and (with perhaps more tragic consequences) indigenous wildlife for food and living space.

Foreseeing these and other untoward consequences of immediate and unplanned liberation of livestock, a human population grown morally more perfect than at present might decide that they had a duty, accumulated over thousands of years, to continue to house and feed as before their former animal slaves (whom they had rendered genetically unfit to care for themselves), but not to butcher them or make other ill use of them, including frustrating their "natural" behavior, their right to copulate freely, reproduce, and enjoy the delights of being parents. People, no longer having meat to eat, would require more vegetables, cereals, and other plant foods, but the institutionalized animal incompetents would still consume all the hay and grains (and more since they would no longer be slaughtered) than they did formerly. This would require clearing more land and bringing it into agricultural production with further loss of wildlife habitat and ecological destruction. Another possible scenario might be a decision on the part of people not literally to liberate domestic animals but simply to cease to breed and raise them. When the last livestock have been killed and eaten (or permitted to die "natural" deaths), people would become vegetarians and domestic livestock species would thus be rendered deliberately extinct (just as they had been deliberately created). But there is surely some irony in an outcome in which the beneficiaries of a humane extension of conscience are destroyed in the process of being saved.

The land ethic, it should be emphasized, as Leopold has sketched it, provides for the *rights* of nonhuman natural beings to a share in the life processes of the biotic community. The conceptual foundation of such rights, however, is less conventional than natural, based upon, as one might say, evolutionary and ecological entitlement. Wild animals and native plants have a particular place in nature, according to the land ethic, which domestic animals (because they are products of human art and represent an extended presence of human beings in the natural world) do not have. The land ethic, in sum, is as much opposed, though on different grounds, to commercial traffic in wildlife, zoos, the slaughter of whales and other marine mammals, etc., as is the humane ethic. Concern for animal (and plant) rights and well-being is as fundamental to the land ethic as to the humane ethic, but the difference between naturally evolved and humanly bred species is an essential consideration for the one, though not for the other.

The "shift of values" which results from our "reappraising things unnatural, tame, and confined in terms of things natural, wild, and free" is especially dramatic when we reflect upon the definitions of *good* and *evil* espoused by Bentham and Mill and uncritically accepted by their contemporary followers. Pain and pleasure seem to have nothing at all to do with good and evil if our appraisal is taken from the vantage point of ecological biology. Pain in particular is primarily information. In animals, it informs the central nervous system of stress, irritation, or trauma in outlying regions of the organism. A certain level of pain under optimal organic circumstances is indeed desirable as an indicator of exertion—of the degree of exertion needed to maintain fitness, to stay "in shape," and of a level of exertion beyond which it would be dangerous to go. An arctic wolf in pursuit of a caribou may experience pain in her feet or chest because of the rigors of the chase. There is nothing bad or wrong in that. Or, consider a case of injury. Suppose that a person in the course of a wilderness excursion sprains an ankle. Pain informs him or her of the injury and by its intensity the amount of further stress the ankle may endure in the course of getting to safety. Would it be better if pain were not experienced upon injury or, taking advantage of recent technology, anaesthetized? Pleasure appears to be, for the most part (unfortunately it is not always so) a reward accompanying those activities which contribute to organic maintenance, such as the pleasures associated with eating, drinking, grooming, and so on, or those which contribute to social solidarity like the pleasures of dancing, conversation, teasing, etc., or those which contribute to the continuation of the species, such as the pleasures of sexual activity and of being parents. The doctrine that life is the happier the freer it is from pain and that the happiest life conceivable is one in which there is continuous pleasure uninterrupted by pain is biologically preposterous. A living mammal which experienced no pain would be one which had a lethal dysfunction of the nervous system. The idea that pain is evil and ought to be minimized or eliminated is as primitive a notion as that of a tyrant who puts to death messengers bearing bad news on the supposition that thus his well-being and security is improved.

More seriously still, the value commitments of the humane movement seem at bottom to betray a world-denying or rather a life-loathing philosophy. The natural world as actually constituted is one in which one being lives at the expense of others. Each organism, in Darwin's metaphor, struggles to maintain its own organic integrity. The more complex animals seem to experience (judging from our own case, and reasoning from analogy) appropriate and adaptive psychological accompaniments to organic existence. There is a palpable passion for self-preservation. There are desire, pleasure in the satisfaction of desires, acute agony attending injury, frustration, and chronic dread of death. But these experiences are the psychological substance of living. To live *is* to be anxious about life, to feel pain and pleasure in a fitting mixture, and sooner or later to die. That is the way the system works. If nature as a whole is good, then pain and death are also good. Environmental ethics in general require people to play fair in the natural system. The neo-Benthamites have in a sense taken the uncourageous approach. People have attempted to exempt themselves from the life/death reciprocities of natural processes and from ecological limitations in the name of a prophylactic ethic of maximizing rewards (pleasure) and minimizing unwelcome information (pain). To be fair, the humane moralists seem to suggest that we should attempt to project the same values into the nonhuman animal world and to widen the charmed circle—no matter that it would be biologically unrealistic to do so or biologically ruinous if, per impossible, such an environmental ethic were implemented.

There is another approach. Rather than imposing our alienation from nature and natural processes and cycles of life on other animals, we human beings could reaffirm our participation in nature by accepting life as it is given without a sugar coating. Instead of imposing artificial legalities, rights, and so on on nature, we might take the opposite course and accept and affirm natural biological laws, principles, and limitations in the human personal and social spheres. Such appears to have been the posture toward life of tribal peoples in the past. The chase was relished with its dangers, rigors, and hardships as well as its rewards: animal flesh was respectfully consumed; a tolerance for pain was cultivated; virtue and magnanimity were prized; lithic, floral, and faunal spirits were worshipped; population was routinely optimized by sexual continency, abortion, infanticide, and stylized warfare; and other life forms, although certainly appropriated, were respected as fellow players in a magnificent and awesome, if not altogether idyllic, drama of life. It is impossible today to return to the symbiotic relationship of Stone Age man to the natural environment, but the ethos of this by far the longest era of human existence could be abstracted and integrated with a future human culture seeking a viable and mutually beneficial relationship with nature. Personal, social, and environmental *health* would, accordingly, receive a premium value rather than comfort, self-indulgent pleasure, and anaesthetic insulation from pain. Sickness would be regarded as a worse evil than death. The pursuit of health or wellness at the personal, social, and environmental levels would require self-discipline in the form of simple diet, vigorous exercise, conservation, and social responsibility.

Leopold's prescription for the realization and implementation of the land ethic—the reappraisal of things unnatural, tame, and confined in terms of things natural, wild, and free—does not stop, in other words, with a reappraisal of nonhuman domestic animals in terms of their wild (or willed) counterparts; the human ones should be similarly reappraised. This means, among other things, the reappraisal of the comparatively recent values and concerns of "civilized" *Homo sapiens* in terms of those of our "savage" ancestors. Civilization has insulated and alienated us from the rigors and challenges of the natural environment. The hidden agenda of the humane ethic is the imposition of the anti-natural prophylactic ethos of comfort and soft pleasure on an even wider scale. The land ethic, on the other hand, requires a shrinkage, if at all possible, of the domestic sphere; it rejoices in a recrudescence of wilderness and a renaissance of tribal cultural experience.

The converse of those goods and evils, axiomatic to the humane ethic, may be illustrated and focused by the consideration of a single issue raised by the humane morality: a vegetarian diet. Savage people seem to have had, if the attitudes and values of surviving tribal cultures are representative, something like an intuitive grasp of ecological relationships and certainly a morally charged appreciation of eating. There is nothing more intimate than eating, more symbolic of the connectedness of life, and more mysterious. What we eat and how we eat is by no means an insignificant ethical concern.

From the ecological point of view, for human beings universally to become vegetarians is tantamount to a shift of trophic niche from omnivore with carnivorous preferences to herbivore. The shift is a downward one on the trophic pyramid, which in effect shortens those food chains terminating with man. It represents an increase in the efficiency of the conversion of solar energy from plant to human biomass, and thus, by bypassing animal intermediates, increases available food resources for human beings. The human population would probably, as past trends overwhelmingly suggest, expand in accordance with the potential thus afforded. The net result would be fewer nonhuman beings and more human beings, who, of course, have requirements of life far more elaborate than even those of domestic animals, requirements which would tax other "natural resources" (trees for shelter, minerals mined at the expense of topsoil and its vegetation, etc.) more than under present circumstances. A vegetarian human population is therefore *probably* ecologically catastrophic.

Meat eating as implied by the foregoing remarks may be more *ecologically* responsible than a wholly vegetable diet. Meat, however, purchased at the supermarket, externally packaged and internally laced with petrochemicals, fattened in feed lots, slaughtered impersonally, and, in general, mechanically processed from artificial insemination to microwave roaster, is an affront not only to physical metabolism and bodily health but to conscience as well. From the perspective of the land ethic, the immoral aspect of the factory farm has to do far less with the suffering and killing of non-human animals than with the monstrous transformation of living things from an organic to a mechanical mode of being. Animals, beginning with the Neolithic Revolution, have been debased through selective breeding, but they have nevertheless remained animals. With the Industrial Revolution an even more profound and terrifying transformation has overwhelmed them. They have become, in Ruth Harrison's most apt description, "animal machines." The very presence of animals, so emblematic of delicate, complex organic tissue, surrounded by machines, connected to machines, penetrated by machines in research laboratories or crowded together in space-age "production facilities" is surely the more real and visceral source of our outrage at vivisection and factory farming than the contemplation of the quantity of pain that these unfortunate beings experience. I wish to denounce as loudly as the neo-Benthamites this ghastly abuse of animal life, but also to stress that the pain and suffering of research and agribusiness animals is not greater than that endured by free-living wildlife as a consequence of predation, disease, starvation, and cold—indicating that there is something immoral about vivisection and factory farming which is not an ingredient in the natural lives and deaths of wild beings. That immoral something is the transmogrification of organic to mechanical processes.

Ethical vegetarianism to all appearances insists upon the human consumption of plants (in a paradoxical moral gesture toward those animals whose very existence is dependent upon human carnivorousness), even when the tomatoes are grown hydroponically, the lettuce generously coated with chlorinated hydrocarbons, the potatoes pumped up with chemical fertilizers, and the cereals stored with the help of chemical preservatives. The land ethic takes as much exception to the transmogrification of plants by mechanicochemical means as to that of animals. The important thing, I would think, is not to eat vegetables as opposed to animal flesh, but to resist factory farming in all its manifestations, including especially its liberal application of pesticides, herbicides, and chemical fertilizers to maximize the production of *vegetable* crops.

The land ethic, with its ecological perspective, helps us to recognize and affirm the organic integrity of self and the untenability of a firm distinction between self and environment. On the ethical question of what to eat, it answers, not vegetables instead of animals, but organically as opposed to mechanicochemically produced food. Purists like Leopold prefer, in his expression, to get their "meat from God," i.e., to hunt and consume wildlife and to gather wild plant foods, and thus to live within the parameters of the aboriginal human ecological niche. Second best is eating from one's own orchard, garden, henhouse, pigpen, and barnyard. Third best is buying or bartering organic foods from one's neighbors and friends.

CONCLUSION

Philosophical controversy concerning animal liberation/rights has been most frequently represented as a polar dispute between traditional moral humanists and seemingly *avant garde* humane moralists. Further, animal liberation has been assumed to be closely allied with environmental ethics, possibly because in Leopold's classical formulation moral standing and indeed rights (of some unspecified sort) is accorded nonhuman beings, among them animals. The purpose of this discussion has been to distinguish sharply environmental ethics from the animal liberation/rights movement both in theory and practical application and to suggest, thereupon, that there is an underrepresented, but very important, point of view respecting the problem of the moral status of nonhuman animals. The debate over animal liberation, in short, should be conceived as triangular, not polar, with land ethics or environmental ethics, the third and, in my judgment, the most creative, interesting, and practicable alternative. Indeed, from this third point of view moral humanism and humane moralism appear to have much more in common with one another than either have with environmental or land ethics.

On reflection one might even be led to suspect that the noisy debate between these parties has served to drown out the much deeper challenge to "business as usual" ethical philosophy represented by Leopold and his exponents, and to keep ethical philosophy firmly anchored to familiar modern paradigms.

Moral humanism and humane moralism, to restate succinctly the most salient conclusions of this essay, are *atomistic* or distributive in their theory of moral value, while environmental ethics (again, at least, as set out in Leopold's outline) is *holistic* or collective. Modern ethical theory, in other words, has consistently located moral value in individuals and set out certain metaphysical reasons for including some individuals and excluding others. Humane moralism remains firmly within this modern convention and centers its attention on the competing criteria for moral standing and rights holding, while environmental ethics locates ultimate value in the "biotic community" and assigns differential moral value to the constitutive individuals relatively to that standard. This is perhaps the most fundamental theoretical difference between environmental ethics and the ethics of animal liberation.

Allied to this difference are many others. One of the more conspicuous is that in environmental ethics, plants are included within the parameters of the ethical theory as well as animals. Indeed, inanimate entities such as oceans and lakes, mountains, forests, and wetlands are assigned a greater value than individual animals and in a way quite different from systems which accord them moral considerability through a further multiplication of competing individual loci of value and holders of rights.

There are intractable practical differences between environmental ethics and the animal liberation movement. Very different moral obligations follow in respect, most importantly, to domestic animals, the principal beneficiaries of the humane ethic. Environmental ethics sets a very low priority on domestic animals as they very frequently contribute to the erosion of the integrity, stability, and beauty of the biotic communities into which they have been insinuated. On the other hand, animal liberation, if pursued at the practical as well as rhetorical level, would have ruinous consequences on plants, soils, and waters, consequences which could not be directly reckoned according to humane moral theory. As this last remark suggests, the animal liberation/animal rights movement is in the final analysis utterly unpracticable. An imagined society in which all animals capable of sensibility received equal consideration or held rights to equal consideration would be so ludicrous that it might be more appropriately and effectively treated in satire than in philosophical discussion. The land ethic, by contrast, even though its ethical purview is very much wider, is nevertheless eminently practicable, since, by reference to a single good, competing individual claims may be adjudicated and relative values and priorities assigned to the myriad components of the biotic community. This is not to suggest that the implementation of environmental ethics as social policy would be easy. Implementation of the land ethic would require discipline, sacrifice, retrenchment, and massive economic reform, tantamount to a virtual revolution in prevailing attitudes and life styles. Nevertheless, it provides a unified and coherent practical principle and thus a decision procedure at the practical level which a distributive or atomistic ethic may achieve only artificially and so imprecisely as to be practically indeterminate.

Review Questions

1. Explain the conflict that Callicott sees between the animal liberation movement and Leopold's land ethic.
2. Callicott explores three possible interpretations of Leopold's practice of hunting, killing, and eating animals. What are they?

3. Distinguish between ethical humanism, humane moralism, and the land ethic, as Callicott explains them.
4. According to Callicott, what kind of value does the land ethic place on the land?
5. Explain Callicott's comparison of the land ethic with Plato's moral and social philosophy.
6. Why does Callicott think that the distinction between wild and domestic animals is important? What are the implications of this distinction?
7. How does the land ethic view pain and pleasure, according to Callicott? Why are pain and death good?
8. What is Callicott's view of vegetarianism?
9. Why does he think that the animal liberation movement is, in the final analysis, utterly unpracticable?

Discussion Questions

1. Is the land ethic any more practicable than animal liberation? Explain your answer.
2. How would vegetarians and animal liberationists such as Rachels, Singer, and Regan respond to Callicott? Do they have an adequate response?
3. Callicott quotes Edward Abbey's saying that he would rather shoot a man than a snake, presumably because humans are a threat to the land while snakes are not. Does the land ethic ultimately require the extermination of humans to preserve the land? Why or why not?

The Environmental Costs of Consumption

ALAN THEIN DURNING

Alan Thein Durning is executive director of the Northwest Environment Watch, an organization he founded in 1993. Before that he was senior researcher at the World-watch Institute in Washington DC. He is the author of *This Place on Earth 2001* (2001), *Green-Collar Jobs* (1999), and *How Much is Enough* (1992), from which our reading is taken.

Durning describes the excessive consumption of resources by industrial nations such as the United States and the effect this has on the natural environment. He is particularly concerned about the consumption of fossil fuels (coal, oil, and natural gas). Taking these materials from the earth disrupts countless habitats, and burning them causes a large portion of the world's air pollution. He believes that preserving the natural environment will require a combination of technological change, population stabilization, and a value change from a consumer to a non-consumer lifestyle.

ECONOMISTS USE THE WORD consume to mean "utilize economic goods," but the *Shorter Oxford Dictionary*'s definition is more appropriate to ecologists: "To make away with or destroy; to waste or squander; to use up." The economies that cater to the global consumer society are responsible for the lion's share of the damage that humans have inflicted on common global resources.[1]

The consumer class's use of fossil fuels, for example, causes an estimated two thirds of the emissions of carbon dioxide from this source. (Carbon dioxide is the principal greenhouse gas.) The poor typically are responsible for the release of a tenth of a ton of carbon apiece each year through burning fossil fuels; the middle-income class, half a ton; and the consumers, 3.5 tons. In the extreme case, the richest tenth of Americans pump 11 tons into the atmosphere annually.[2]

Parallel class-by-class evidence for other ecological hazards is hard to come by, but comparing industrial countries, home to most of the consumers, with developing countries, home to most of the middle-income and poor, gives a sense of the orders of magnitude. Industrial countries, with one fourth of the globe's people, consume 40–86 percent of the earth's various natural resources. (See Table 1.)[3]

Table 1
Consumption of Selected Goods, Industrial and Developing Countries, Late Eighties

Good	Industrial Countries' Share of World Consumption (percent)	Consumption Gap Between Industrial and Developing Countries (ratio of per capita consumption rates)
Aluminum	86	19
Chemicals	86	18
Paper	81	14
Iron and steel	80	13
Timber	76	10
Energy	75	10
Meat	61	6
Fertilizers	60	5
Cement	52	3
Fish	49	3
Grain	48	3
Fresh water	42	3

Source: See footnote 3.

1 *Shorter Oxford Dictionary* quoted in Paul Ekins, "The Sustainable Consumer Society: A Contradiction in Terms?" *International Environmental Affairs,* Fall 1991.

2 Carbon emissions exclude the 7–33 percent that originate from forest clearing. Although this somewhat biases the figures against the consumer class—forest clearing emissions are concentrated in rural areas of developing countries, where many of the poor live—emissions of other greenhouse gases, such as chlorofluorocarbons, are more concentrated in the consumer society than fossil-derived carbon dioxide. Thus, fossil-fuel carbon emissions are a relatively good overall indicator of responsibility for global warming. The estimates of emissions by class assume—plausibly—that carbon emissions and world income distribution coincide, and were calculated by combining income distribution data from World Bank, *World Development Report 1991* (New York: Oxford University Press, 1991), with carbon emissions data from Gregg Marland et al., *Estimates of CO, Emissions from Fossil Fuel Burning and Cement Manufacturing, Based on the United*

Nations Energy Statistics and the U.S. Bureau of Mines Cement Manufacturing Data (Oak Ridge, Tenn.: Oak Ridge National Laboratory, 1989), and from Thomas Boden et al, *Trends '91* (Oak Ridge, Tenn.: Oak Ridge National Laboratory, in press), and comparing them with Ronald V. A. Sprout and James H. Weaver, "1988 International Distribution of Income" (unpublished data) provided by Ronald V. A. Sprout, U.N. Economic Commission for Latin America and the Caribbean, Washington Office, Washington, D.C., private communication, January 2, 1992.

3 Table 1 based on U.N. data for 1987–88 reported in Jyoti Parikh and Kirir Parikh, "Role of Unsustainable Consumption Patterns and Population in Global Environmental Stress," *Sustainable Development* (New Delhi), October 1991, with the exceptions of timber (industrial roundwood) from U.N. Food and Agriculture Organization (FAO), *Forestry Statistics Today for Tomorrow, 1961–89, Wood and Wood Products* (Rome: 1991), of fish from FAO, *Fisheries Statistics Commodities Yearbook 1989* (Rome: 1991), of meat from *Production Yearbook 1989* (Rome: 1990), and of water from World Resources Institute, *World Resources 1990–91* (New York: Oxford University Press, 1990).

From the crust of the earth, we take minerals; from the forests, timber; from the farms, grain and meat; from the oceans, fish; and from the rivers, lakes, and aquifers, fresh water. The average resident of an industrial country consumes 3 times as much fresh water, 10 times as much energy, and 19 times as much aluminum as someone in a developing country. The ecological impacts of our consumption even reach into the local environments of the poor. Our appetite for wood and minerals, for example, motivates the road builders who open tropical rain forests to poor settlers, resulting in the slash-and-burn forest clearing that is condemning countless species to extinction.

High consumption translates into huge impacts. In industrial countries, the fuels burned release perhaps three fourths of the sulfur and nitrogen oxides that cause acid rain. Industrial countries' factories generate most of the world's hazardous chemical wastes. Their military facilities have built more than 99 percent of the world's nuclear warheads. Their atomic power plants have generated more than 96 percent of the world's radioactive waste. And their air conditioners, aerosol sprays, and factories release almost 90 percent of the chlorofluorocarbons that destroy the earth's protective ozone layer.[4]

As people climb from the middle-income to the consumer class, their impact on the environment makes a quantum leap—not so much because they consume more of the same things but because they consume different things. For example, South African blacks, most of them in the middle-income class, spend their limited budgets largely on basic food and clothing, things that are produced with relatively little damage to the environment. Meanwhile, South Africa's consumer-class whites spend most of their larger budgets on housing, electricity, fuel, and transportation—all more damaging to the environment.[5]

Jyoti Parikh and his colleagues at the Indira Gandhi Institute for Development Research in Bombay used U.N. data to compare consumption patterns in more than 100 countries. Ranking them by gross national product per person, they noticed that as income rises, consumption of ecologically less damaging products such as grains rises slowly. In contrast, purchases of cars, gasoline, iron, steel, coal, and electricity, all ecologically more damaging to produce, multiply rapidly.[6]

The furnishing of our consumer life-style—things like automobiles, throwaway goods and packaging, a high-fat diet, and air conditioning—can only be provided at great environmental costs. Our way of life depends on enormous and continuous inputs of the very commodities that are most damaging to the earth to produce: energy, chemicals, metals, and paper. In the United States, those four industries are all in the top five of separate industry-by-industry rankings for energy intensity and toxic emissions, and similarly dominate the most-wanted lists for polluting the air with sulfur and nitrogen oxides, particulates, and volatile organic compounds.[7]

In particular, the fossil fuels that power the consumer society are its most ruinous input. Wresting coal, oil, and natural gas from the earth permanently disrupts countless habitats;

4 Acid rain, hazardous chemicals, and chlorofluorocarbons are Worldwatch Institute estimates based on World Resources Institute, *World Resources 1991–91;* nuclear warheads from Swedish International Peace Research Institute, *SIPRI Yearbook 1990: World Armaments and Disarmament* (Oxford: Oxford University Press, 1990); radioactive waste is Worldwatch Institute estimate based on cumulative nuclear-power electricity production from International Atomic Energy Agency, *Nuclear Power Reactors in the World* (Vienna: 1991).

5 Brian Huntley et al., *South African Environments into the 21st Century* (Cape Town, South Africa: Human & Rousseau Tafelberg, 1989).
6 Parikh and Parikh, "Unsustainable Consumption Patterns."
7 Energy intensity and toxics emissions from Michael Renner, *Jobs in a Sustainable Economy,* Worldwatch Paper 104 (Washington, D.C.: Worldwatch Institute, September 1991); air pollution from U.S. Environmental Protection Agency, Office of Air Quality Planning and Standards, *National Air Pollution Estimates 1940–89* (Washington, D.C.: 1991).

Table 2
Per Capita Consumption of Energy, Selected Countries, 1989

Country	Energy (kilograms of coal equivalent)
United States	10,127
Soviet Union	6,546
West Germany	5,377
Japan	4,032
Mexico	1,689
Turkey	958
China	810
Brazil	798
India	307
Indonesia	274
Nigeria	192
Bangladesh	69

Source: See footnote 8.

burning them causes an overwhelming share of the world's air pollution; and refining them generates huge quantities of toxic wastes. Estimating from the rough measure of national averages, the consumer class depends on energy supplies equal to at least 2,000 kilograms per capita of average-grade coal a year. The poor use energy equal to less than 400 kilograms per person, and the middle-income class falls in between. (See Table 2.)[8]

Fortunately, once people join the consumer class, their impact ceases to grow as quickly because their attention tends to switch to high-value, low-resource goods and services. Eric

Larson of Princeton University studies the use of chemicals, energy, metals, and paper in both industrial and developing countries. He has found that per capita consumption of most of these things has been stable in industrial countries since the mid-seventies, after surging upward in preceding decades.[9]

Larson attributes some of the change to higher energy prices, but argues that a more fundamental transition lies behind it. In the places that best exemplify the global consumer society, he believes, markets for bulky products such as automobiles and appliances and for infrastructure-building raw materials such as cement are largely saturated. We consumers are spending our extra earnings on high-tech goods and services, from computers and compact disk players to health insurance and fitness club memberships, all of which are gentler to the environment than were earlier generations of consumer goods.[10]

That per capita resource use in the consumer class reaches a plateau is a hopeful sign, yet the plateau is far too high for all the world's people to attain without devastating the planet. Already, the natural systems that sustain our societies are fraying badly, demonstrating that our global economy is getting too big for the global biosphere. If all the world's people were responsible for carbon dioxide concentrations on a par with the consumer class, global emissions of this

---

8 Table 2 from United Nations, *1989 Energy Statistics Yearbook* (New York: 1991). Per capita consumption figures are easily misread to mean "personal consumption" when in fact they measure "societal consumption." Environmental damage per capita far exceeds environmental damage caused directly by an individual consumer's habits and choices. Household waste, for example, accounts for less than half the weight of all refuse in industrial countries. Per person greenhouse gas emissions exceed personal emissions from home and car by at least a factor of two. See James R. Udall, "Domestic Calculations," *Sierra*, July/August 1989, and

more generally, Allan Schnaiberg, "The Political Economy of Consumption: Ecological Policy Limits," Northwestern University, Evanston, Ill., presented at American Association for the Advancement of Science Annual Meeting, Washington, D.C., February 1991.

9 Eric D. Larson, "Trends in the Consumption of Energy-Intensive Materials in Industrialized Countries and Implications for Developing Regions," paper for International Symposium on Environmentally Sound Energy Technologies and Their Transfer to Developing Countries and European Economies in Transition, Milan, Italy, October 21–25, 1991; see also Eric D. Larson et al., "Beyond the Era of Materials," *Scientific American,* June 1986, and Robert H. Williams et al., "Materials, Affluence, and Industrial Energy Use," in Annual Reviews, Inc., *Annual Review of Energy 1987,* Vol. 12 (Palo Alto, Calif.: 1987).

10 Larson, "Trends in the Consumption of Energy-Intensive Basic Materials."

greenhouse gas would multiply threefold. If everyone in the world used as much metal, lumber, and paper as we consumers do, mining and logging—rather than tapering off as ecological health necessitates—would jump more than three-fold.[11]

The influence of the consumer class is felt strongly in regions populated mostly by the middle-income and poor classes. By drawing on resources far and near, we consumers cast an ecological shadow over wide regions of the earth. Every piece of merchandise in the retail districts of the consumer society creates its own ecological wake. A blouse in a Japanese boutique may come from Indonesian oil wells by way of petrochemical plants and textile mills in Singapore, and assembly industries in Bangladesh. Likewise, an automobile in a German showroom that bears the logo of an American-owned corporation typically contains parts manufactured in a dozen or more countries, and raw materials that originated in a dozen others.[12]

A strawberry in a Chicago supermarket in February is likely to have come from Mexico, where it might have been grown with the help of pesticides made in the Rhine Valley of Germany and a tractor made in Japan. The tractor, perhaps constructed with Korean steel cast from iron ingots dug from the territory of tribal peoples in Papua New Guinea, was likely fueled with diesel pumped from the earth in southern Mexico. At harvest time, the strawberry may have been packed in a box made of cardboard from Canadian softwood pulp, wrapped in plastic manufactured in New Jersey, and loaded on a truck made in Italy with German, Japanese, and American parts. The ecological wakes of the blouse, car, and strawberry—like the production lines themselves—span the globe.

Sadly, hard-pressed developing nations sell their ecological souls all too often in the attempt to make ends meet. Cynically playing one nation against another, manufacturing industries have segmented their production lines into dozens of countries in search of low wages, cheap resources, and lax regulations. The Philippine government, more blatant than most, ran an advertisement in *Fortune* in 1975 for the little-regulated Baatan export processing zone: "To attract companies . . . like yours . . . we have felled mountains, razed jungles, filled swamps, moved rivers, relocated towns . . . all to make it easier for you and your business to do business here."[13]

Brazil provides a vivid illustration of what transpires at the tail end of these global production lines. Burdened with an international debt exceeding $100 billion, the government has subsidized and promoted export industries. As a result, the nation has become a major exporter of aluminum, copper, gold, steel, appliances, beef, chicken, soybeans, and shoes. The consumer class gets cheaper products because Brazil is in the export business, but Brazil—most of whose citizens are middle-income—gets stuck with the tab of pollution, land degradation, and forest destruction. As of 1988, for example, 18 percent of the electricity used by all Brazilian industries went to plants producing aluminum and steel for export to industrial countries. Most of that electricity came from gargantuan

11 Worldwatch Institute estimates of world total consumption if all 5.5 billion people living in mid-1992 consumed on the levels of the consumer class assumes average consumer-class consumption of 3.5 tons of carbon emissions per capita per year as estimated from Marland et al, *CO₂, Emissions from Fossil Fuel Burning and Cement Manufacturing,* from Boden, private communication, from World Bank, *World Development Report 1991,* and from Sprout and Weaver, "1988 World Distribution of Income"; mining increase of 3.4 times estimated from annual iron and steel consumption of industrial countries of 470 kilograms per capita, compared with developing-country use of 36 kilograms per capita, from Parikh and Parikh, "Unsustainable Consumption Patterns"; logging increase estimated from industrial-country annual consumption of sawn wood per capita of 213 kilograms and developing-country use of 19 kilograms (3.3-fold), and from paper consumption of 148 kilograms and 11 kilograms respectively (3.5-fold), from ibid.

12 Auto from Robert B. Reich, *The Work of Nations: Preparing Ourselves for 21st Century Capitalism* (New York: Alfred A. Knopf, 1991).

13 Office of Promotion and Information for the Bataan Export Processing Zone, Philippines, "Remember Bataan?" advertisement in *Fortune,* October 1975.

hydroelectric dams that flooded tropical forests and displaced native peoples from their ancestral domain.[14]

The global consumer society casts a particularly long shadow over forests and soils. El Salvador and Costa Rica, for example, grow export crops such as bananas, coffee, and sugar on more than one fifth of their cropland. Export cattle ranches in Latin America and southern Africa have replaced rain forest and wildlife range. At the consumer end of the production line, Japan imports 70 percent of its corn, wheat, and barley, 95 percent of its soybeans, and more than 50 percent of its wood, much of it from the rapidly vanishing rain forests of Borneo.[15]

The Netherlands imports the agricultural output of three times as much land in developing countries as it has within its borders. Many of those agricultural imports flow to the nation's mammoth factory farms. There, millions of pigs and cows are fattened on palm-kernel cake from deforested lands in Malaysia, cassava from deforested regions of Thailand, and soybeans from pesticide-doused expanses in the south of Brazil in order to provide European consumers with their high-fat diet of meat and milk.[16]

In 1989, the European Community, Japan, and North America between them imported $136 billion worth of "primary commodities"—crops and natural resources—in excess of what they exported. Developing regions, meanwhile,

are net exporters of these goods; in the few cases in which they import a particular commodity, much of it goes to their own world-class consumers. About three fourths of developing-country imports of grains—excluding rice—fed livestock, the meat of which largely goes to urban elites.[17]

For decades, shifting tastes among the consumer class have fueled commodity booms in the tropics. Sugar, tea, coffee, rubber, palm, coconut, ivory, gold, silver, gems—each has transformed natural environments and shaped the lives of legions of workers. Today, the tastes of the consumer class retain that influence, as the wildlife trade and illegal drug production illustrate.

Each year, smugglers take millions of tropical birds, fish, plants, animal pelts, and other novelties from impoverished to wealthy lands. They take Olive Ridley and hawksbill sea turtle shells by the thousands, and pelts of jaguars and other spotted cats by the ton. Although habitat destruction is the world's leading cause of species extinction, biologists believe that more than a third of the vertebrates on the endangered species list are there primarily because of hunting for trade. That hunting is fueled by the demand of affluent consumers. Worldwide, sales of exotic wildlife exceed $5 billion a year, according to the World Wildlife Fund in Washington, D.C.[18]

High prices and fast-changing fashions can swiftly drive species to the brink of survival.

14 Debt from Julia Michaels, "Brazil to Take New Tack on Debt," *Christian Science Monitor,* June 27, 1991; electricity use from Howard S. Geller, *Efficient Electricity Use: A Development Strategy for Brazil* (Washington, D.C.: American Council for an Energy-Efficient Economy, 1991).

15 El Salvador and Costa Rica is Worldwatch Institute estimate based on FAO, *Production Yearbook 1988* (Rome: 1989), and FAO, *Trade Yearbook 1988* (Rome: 1990); Japan's imports from Jim MacNeill et al., *Beyond Interdependence: The Meshing of the World's Economy and the Earth's Ecology* (New York: Oxford University Press, 1991).

16 Netherlands National Committee for UCN/Steering Group for World Conservation Strategy, *The Netherlands and the World Ecology,* cited in World Resources Institute, World Conservation Union, and United Nations Environmental Programme, *Global Biodiversity Strategy* (Washington, D.C.: 1992).

17 MacNeill et al., *Beyond Interdependence;* grain from Alan Durning and Holly Brough, *Taking Stock: Animal Farming and the Environment,* Worldwatch Paper 103 (Washington, D.C.: Worldwatch Institute, July 1991).

18 Illegal wildlife from Debra Rose, "International Politics and Latin American Wildlife Resources," Department of Political Science, University of Florida, presented at the Sixteenth International Congress of the Latin American Studies Association, Washington, D.C., April 4–6, 1991; habitat destruction and species loss from John C. Ryan, "Conserving Biological Diversity," in Lester R. Brown et al., *State of the World 1992* (New York: W.W. Norton & Co., 1992); hunting and species extinction, and value of wildlife trade, from Sarah Fitzgerald, *International Wildlife Traffic: Whose Business Is It?* (Baltimore, Md.: World Wildlife Fund, 1989).

Peruvian butterflies sell for as much as $3,000 on the black market, and to some Asian consumers, the allegedly aphrodisiac musk from Himalayan deer is worth four times its weight in gold. Bangladesh, India, and Indonesia send 250 million Asian bullfrogs each year to Europe, where restaurants serve their legs as a delicacy. Back in Asia, the mosquitos that frogs eat have proliferated, increasing deaths from malaria, which mosquitos carry.[19]

Another token of consumer-class influence is scrolled out across 200,000 hectares of what used to be the untouched cloud forest of the Peruvian Amazon. The area, once home to a unique highland ecosystem roamed by jaguars and spectacled bears, now boasts the herbicide-poisoned heartland of the world's cocaine industry. In the upper Huallaga Valley, peasants fleeing from poverty in their mountain villages grow coca to feed the cocaine habit of urbanites in the United States and Europe. Coca growers, like farmers of any high-value export crop, spare no expense in its cultivation, plowing up steep slopes and lacing soil with chemical herbicides to maximize harvests.[20]

Processing the coca leaves compounds the ecological ruin. In 1987, Peruvian forester Marc Dourojeanni estimated that secret cocaine laboratories in the jungle spilled millions of gallons of kerosene, sulphuric acid, acetone, and toluene into the valley's watershed. And the valley's streams have since proved deadly to many types of fish, amphibians, and reptiles. Finally, the rule of drug traffickers and allied guerrilla movements has created a lawless state in which profiteering gangs log, hunt, and fish the region to its destruction.[21]

Thus from global warming to species extinction, we consumers bear a huge burden of responsibility for the ills of the earth. Yet our consumption too seldom receives the attention of those concerned about the fate of the planet, who focus on other contributors to environmental decline. Consumption is the neglected variable in the global environmental equation. In simplified terms, an economy's total burden on the ecological systems that undergird it is a function of three variables: the size of the population, average consumption, and the broad set of technologies—everything from dinner plates to communications satellites—the economy uses to provide goods and services. Generally, environmentalists work on regulating and changing technologies, and family planning advocates concentrate on slowing population growth.

There are good reasons for emphasizing technology and population. Technologies are easier to replace than cultural attitudes. Family planning has enormous human and social benefits aside from its environmental pluses. Yet the magnitude of global ecological challenges requires progress on all three fronts. Environmental economist Herman Daly of the World Bank points out, for example, that simply stopping the growth in rates of global pollution, ecological degradation, and habitat destruction—not reducing those rates, as is clearly necessary—would require within four decades a twentyfold improvement in the environmental performance of current technology. And that assumes both that industrial countries immediately halt the growth of their per-capita resource consumption, allowing the developing countries to begin catching up, and that world population no more than doubles in that period.[22]

19 Butterflies, deer, and frogs from Fitzgerald, *International Wildlife Traffic;* frogs also from Radhakrishna Rao, "India: Bullfrog Extinction," *Third World Week* (Institute for Current World Affairs, Hanover, N.H.), November 23, 1990.
20 Area and wildlife affected from Stephanie Joyce, "Snorting Peru's Rain Forest," *International Wildlife,* May/June 1990, and from James Brooke, "Peruvian Farmers Razing Rain Forest to Sow Drug Crops," *New York Times,* August 13, 1989; steep slopes and chemical herbicides from Mark Mardon, "The Big Push," *Sierra,* November/December 1988.

21 Dourojeanni quoted in Brooke, "Peruvian Farmers Razing Rain Forest."
22 Herman Daly, "Environmental Impact Identity—Orders of Magnitude" (draft), World Bank, Washington, D.C., 1991; also see Ekins, "The Sustainable Consumer Society: A Contradiction in Terms?"

Changing technologies and methods in agriculture, transportation, urban planning, energy, and the like could radically reduce the environmental damage caused by current systems, but a twentyfold advance is farfetched. Autos that go three or four times as far on a tank of fuel are feasible; ones that go 20 times as far would defy the laws of thermodynamics. Bicycles, buses, and trains are the only vehicles that can reduce the environmental costs of traveling that much, and to most in the consumer class they represent a lower standard of living. Clothes dryers, too, might run on half as much energy as the most efficient current models, but the only way to dry clothes with one twentieth the energy is to use a clothesline—another retrogressive step, in the eyes of the consumer society.

So technological change and population stabilization cannot suffice to save the planet without their complement in the reduction of material wants. José Goldemberg of the University of São Paulo and an international team of researchers conducted a careful study of the potential to cut fossil fuel consumption through maximizing efficiency and making full use of renewable energy. The entire world population, they concluded, could live at roughly the level of West Europeans in the mid-seventies—with things like modest but comfortable homes, refrigeration for food, clothes washers, a moderate amount of hot water, and ready access to public transit, augmented by limited auto use.[23]

The study's implicit conclusion, however, is that the entire world could not live in the style of Americans, with their larger homes, more numerous electrical gadgets, and auto-centered transportation. Goldemberg's scenario, furthermore, may be too generous. It would not reduce global carbon emissions by anything like the 60–80 percent that the Intergovernmental Panel on Climate Change believes necessary to stabilize the world's climate.[24]

Even assuming rapid progress in stabilizing human numbers and great strides in employing clean and efficient technologies, human wants will overrun the biosphere unless they shift from material to nonmaterial ends. The ability of the earth to support billions of human beings depends on whether we continue to equate consumption with fulfillment.

Some guidance is thus needed on what combination of technical changes and value changes would make a comfortable—if nonconsumer—life-style possible for all without endangering the biosphere. From a purely ecological perspective, the crucial categories are energy, materials, and ecosystems. . . . In each case, the world's people are distributed unevenly over a vast range, with those at the bottom consuming too little for their own good—and those at the top consuming too much for the earth's good.

23 José Goldemberg et al., *Energy for a Sustainable World* (Washington, D.C.: World Resources Institute, 1987).

24 Ibid.; carbon dioxide reductions from Intergovernmental Panel on Climate Change, "Policymakers' Summary of the Scientific Assessment of Climate Change," Report to IPCC from Working Group I, Geneva, June 1990, and from U.S. Environmental Protection Agency, *Policy for Stabilizing Global Climate* (draft) (Washington, D.C.: 1989).

Review Questions

1. How does Durning describe the consumption of materials by industrial countries such as the United States and its impact on the environment?
2. Why does Durning pick out the consumption of fossil fuels as having the most ruinous impact on the environment?
3. According to Durning, what is the effect of the consumer society on developing countries such as Brazil?

Discussion Questions

1. Is the United States consuming too much of the worlds resources? If so, what should be done about this over consumption?
2. Distinguish between a consumer and nonconsumer lifestyle. Would you be willing to be a nonconsumer? Why or why not?
3. What is a consumer society? How could such a society reduce its consumption of resources?

Famine, Affluence, and Morality

PETER SINGER

For biographical information on Singer, see his reading in Chapter 3.

In this reading, Singer begins with two moral principles. The first is that suffering and death from lack of food, shelter, and medical care are bad. He expects us to accept this principle without argument. The second principle is more controversial, and is formulated in a strong and a weak version. The strong version is that if we can prevent something bad from happening "without thereby sacrificing anything of comparable moral importance," then we should do it. The weak version is that we ought to prevent something bad from happening "unless we have to sacrifice something morally significant." It follows from those two moral principles, Singer argues, that it is a moral duty, and not just a matter of charity, for affluent nations to help starving people in countries like East Bengal.

As I WRITE THIS, in November 1971, people are dying in East Bengal from lack of food, shelter, and medical care. The suffering and death that are occurring there now are not inevitable, not unavoidable in any fatalistic sense of the term. Constant poverty, a cyclone, and a civil war have turned at least nine million people into destitute refugees; nevertheless, it is not beyond the capacity of the richer nations to give enough assistance to reduce any further suffering to very small proportions. The decisions and actions of human beings can prevent this kind of suffering. Unfortunately, human beings have not made the necessary decisions. At the individual level, people have, with very few exceptions, not responded to the situation in any significant way. Generally, speaking, people have not given large sums to relief funds; they have not written to their parliamentary representatives demanding increased government assistance; they have not demonstrated in the streets, held symbolic fasts, or done anything else directed toward providing the refugees with the means to satisfy their essential needs. At the government level, no government has given the sort of massive aid that would enable the refugees to survive for more than a few days. Britain, for instance, has given

Source: From Peter Singer, "Famine, Affluence, and Morality," *Philosophy & Public Affairs*, Vol. 1, No 3 (Spring 1972). Copyright © 1972 Princeton University Press. Reprinted with permission of Blackwell Publishing.

rather more than most countries. It has, to date, given £14,750,000. For comparative purposes, Britain's share of the nonrecoverable development costs of the Anglo-French Concorde project is already in excess of £275,000,000, and on present estimates will reach £440,000,000. The implication is that the British government values a supersonic transport more than thirty times as highly as it values the lives of the nine million refugees. Australia is another country which, on a per capita basis, is well up in the "aid to Bengal" table. Australia's aid, however, amounts to less than one-twelfth of the cost of Sydney's new opera house. The total amount given, from all sources, now stands at about £65,000,000. The estimated cost of keeping the refugees alive for one year is £464,000,000. Most of the refugees have now been in the camps for more than six months. The World Bank has said that India needs a minimum of £300,000,000 in assistance from other countries before the end of the year. It seems obvious that assistance on this scale will not be forthcoming. India will be forced to choose between letting the refugees starve or diverting funds from her own development program, which will mean that more of her own people will starve in the future.[1]

These are the essential facts about the present situation in Bengal. So far as it concerns us here, there is nothing unique about this situation except its magnitude. The Bengal emergency is just the latest and most acute of a series of major emergencies in various parts of the world, arising both from natural and from man-made causes. There are also many parts of the world in which people die from malnutrition and lack of food independent of any special emergency. I take Bengal as my example only because it is the present concern, and because the size of the problem has ensured that it has been given adequate publicity. Neither individuals nor governments can claim to be unaware of what is happening there.

What are the moral implications of a situation like this? In what follows, I shall argue that the way people in relatively affluent countries react to a situation like that in Bengal cannot be justified;

indeed, the whole way we look at moral issues—our moral conceptual scheme—needs to be altered, and with it, the way of life that has come to be taken for granted in our society.

In arguing for this conclusion I will not, of course, claim to be morally neutral. I shall, however, try to argue for the moral position that I take, so that anyone who accepts certain assumptions, to be made explicit, will, I hope, accept my conclusion.

I begin with the assumption that suffering and death from lack of food, shelter, and medical care are bad. I think most people will agree about this, although one may reach the same view by different routes. I shall not argue for this view. People can hold all sorts of eccentric positions, and perhaps from some of them it would not follow that death by starvation is in itself bad. It is difficult, perhaps impossible, to refute such positions, and so for brevity I will henceforth take this assumption as accepted. Those who disagree need read no further.

My next point is this: if it is in our power to prevent something bad from happening, without thereby sacrificing anything of comparable moral importance, we ought, morally, to do it. By "without sacrificing anything of comparable moral importance" I mean without causing anything else comparably bad to happen, or doing something that is wrong in itself, or failing to promote some moral good, comparable in significance to the bad thing that we can prevent. This principle seems almost as uncontroversial as the last one. It requires us only to prevent what is bad, and not to promote what is good, and it requires this of us only when we can do it without sacrificing anything that is, from the moral point of view, comparably important. I could even, as far as the application of my argument to the Bengal emergency is concerned, qualify the point so as to make it: if it is in our power to prevent something very bad from happening, without thereby sacrificing anything morally significant, we ought, morally, to do it. An application of this principle would be as follows: if I am walking past a shallow pond and see a child drowning in it, I ought to wade in and pull the child out. This will mean getting my clothes muddy, but this is insignificant, while the death of the child would presumably be a very bad thing.

The uncontroversial appearance of the principle just stated is deceptive. If it were acted upon, even in its qualified form, our lives, our society, and our world would be fundamentally changed. For the principle takes, firstly, no account of proximity or distance. It makes no moral difference whether the person I can help is a neighbor's child ten yards from me or a Bengali whose name I shall never know, ten thousand miles away. Secondly, the principle makes no distinction between cases in which I am the only person who could possibly do anything and cases in which I am just one among millions in the same position.

I do not think I need to say much in defense of the refusal to take proximity and distance into account. The fact that a person is physically near to us, so that we have personal contact with him, may make it more likely that we *shall* assist him, but this does not show that we *ought* to help him rather than another who happens to be further away. If we accept any principle of impartiality, universalizability, equality, or whatever, we cannot discriminate against someone merely because he is far away from us (or we are far away from him). Admittedly, it is possible that we are in a better position to judge what needs to be done to help a person near to us than one far away, and perhaps also to provide the assistance we judge to be necessary. If this were the case, it would be a reason for helping those near to us first. This may once have been a justification for being more concerned with the poor in one's own town than with famine victims in India. Unfortunately for those who like to keep their moral responsibilities limited, instant communication and swift transportation have changed the situation. From the moral point of view, the development of the world into a "global village" has made an important, though still unrecognized, difference to our moral situation. Expert observers and supervisors, sent out

by famine relief organizations or permanently stationed in famine-prone areas, can direct our aid to a refugee in Bengal almost as effectively as we could get it to someone in our own block. There would seem, therefore, to be no possible justification for discriminating on geographical grounds.

There may be a greater need to defend the second implication of my principle—that the fact that there are millions of other people in the same position, in respect to the Bengali refugees, as I am, does not make the situation significantly different from a situation in which I am the only person who can prevent something very bad from occurring. Again, of course, I admit that there is a psychological difference between the cases; one feels less guilty about doing nothing if one can point to others, similarly placed, who have also done nothing. Yet this can make no real difference to our moral obligations.[2] Should I consider that I am less obliged to pull the drowning child out of the pond if on looking around I see other people, no further away than I am, who have also noticed the child but are doing nothing? One has only to ask this question to see the absurdity of the view that numbers lessen obligation. It is a view that is an ideal excuse for inactivity; unfortunately most of the major evils—poverty, overpopulation, pollution—are problems in which everyone is almost equally involved.

The view that numbers do make a difference can be made plausible if stated in this way: if everyone in circumstances like mine gave £5 to the Bengal Relief Fund, there would be enough to provide food, shelter, and medical care for the refugees; there is no reason why I should give more than anyone else in the same circumstances as I am; therefore I have no obligation to give more than £5. Each premise in this argument is true, and the argument looks sound. It may convince us, unless we notice that it is based on a hypothetical premise, although the conclusion is not stated hypothetically. The argument would be sound if the conclusion were: if everyone in circumstances like mine were to give £5, I would have no obligation to give more than £5. If the conclusion were so stated, however, it would be obvious that the argument has no bearing on a situation in which it is not the case that everyone else gives £5. This, of course, is the actual situation. It is more or less certain that not everyone in circumstances like mine will give £5. So there will not be enough to provide the needed food, shelter, and medical care. Therefore by giving more than £5 I will prevent more suffering than I would if I gave just £5.

It might be thought that this argument has an absurd consequence. Since the situation appears to be that very few people are likely to give substantial amounts, it follows that I and everyone else in similar circumstances ought to give as much as possible, that is, at least up to the point at which by giving more one would begin to cause serious suffering for oneself and one's dependents—perhaps even beyond this point to the point of marginal utility, at which by giving more one would cause oneself and one's dependents as much suffering as one would prevent in Bengal. If everyone does this, however, there will be more than can be used for the benefit of the refugees, and some of the sacrifice will have been unnecessary. Thus, if everyone does what he ought to do, the result will not be as good as it would be if everyone did a little less than he ought to do, or if only some do all that they ought to do.

The paradox here arises only if we assume that the actions in question—sending money to the relief funds—are performed more or less simultaneously, and are also unexpected. For if it is to be expected that everyone is going to contribute something, then clearly each is not obliged to give as much as he would have been obliged to had others not been giving too. And if everyone is not acting more or less simultaneously, then those giving later will know how much more is needed, and will have no obligation to give more than is necessary to reach this amount. To say this is not to deny the principle that people in the same circumstances have the same obligations, but to point out that the fact

that others have given, or may be expected to give, is a relevant circumstance: those giving after it has become known that many others are giving and those giving before are not in the same circumstances. So the seemingly absurd consequence of the principle I have put forward can occur only if people are in error about the actual circumstances—that is, if they think they are giving when others are not, but in fact they are giving when others are. The result of everyone doing what he really ought to do cannot be worse than the result of everyone doing less than he ought to do, although the result of everyone doing what he reasonably believes he ought to do could be.

If my argument so far has been sound, neither our distance from a preventable evil nor the number of other people who, in respect to that evil, are in the same situation as we are, lessens our obligation to mitigate or prevent that evil. I shall therefore take as established the principle I asserted earlier. As I have already said, I need to assert it only in its qualified form: if it is in our power to prevent something very bad from happening, without thereby sacrificing anything else morally significant, we ought, morally, to do it.

The outcome of this argument is that our traditional moral categories are upset. The traditional distinction between duty and charity cannot be drawn, or at least, not in the place we normally draw it. Giving money to the Bengal Relief Fund is regarded as an act of charity in our society. The bodies which collect money are known as "charities." These organizations see themselves in this way—if you send them a check, you will be thanked for your "generosity." Because giving money is regarded as an act of charity, it is not thought that there is anything wrong with not giving. The charitable man may be praised, but the man who is not charitable is not condemned. People do not feel in any way ashamed or guilty about spending money on new clothes or a new car instead of giving it to famine relief. (Indeed, the alternative does not occur to them.) This way of looking at the matter cannot be justified. When we buy new clothes not to keep ourselves warm but to look "well-dressed" we are not providing for any important need. We would not be sacrificing anything significant if we were to continue to wear our old clothes, and give the money to famine relief. By doing so, we would be preventing another person from starving. It follows from what I have said earlier that we ought to give money away, rather than spend it on clothes which we do not need to keep us warm. To do so is not charitable, or generous. Nor is it the kind of act which philosophers and theologians have called "supererogatory"—an act which it would be good to do, but not wrong not to do. On the contrary, we ought to give the money away, and it is wrong not to do so.

I am not maintaining that there are no acts which are charitable, or that there are no acts which it would be good to do but not wrong not to do. It may be possible to redraw the distinction between duty and charity in some other place. All I am arguing here is that the present way of drawing the distinction, which makes it an act of charity for a man living at the level of affluence which most people in the "developed nations" enjoy to give money to save someone else form starvation, cannot be supported. It is beyond the scope of my argument to consider whether the distinction should be redrawn or abolished altogether. There would be many other possible ways of drawing the distinction— for instance, one might decide that it is good to make other people as happy as possible, but not wrong not to do so.

Despite the limited nature of the revision in our moral conceptual scheme which I am proposing, the revision would, given the extent of both affluence and famine in the world today, have radical implications. These implications may lead to further objections, distinct from those I have already considered. I shall discuss two of these.

One objection to the position I have taken might be simply that it is too drastic a revision of our moral scheme. People do not ordinarily judge in the way I have suggested thay should. Most people reserve their moral condemnation for those who violate some moral norm, such as the norm against taking another person's property. They do not condemn those who indulge in luxury instead of giving to famine relief. But given that I did not set out to present a morally neutral description of the way people make moral judgments, the way people do in fact judge has nothing to do with the validity of my conclusion. My conclusion follows from the principle which I advanced earlier, and unless that principle is rejected, or the arguments shown to be unsound, I think the conclusion must stand, however strange it appears.

It might, nevertheless, be interesting to consider why our society, and most other societies, do judge differently from the way I have suggested they should. In a well-known article, J. O. Urmson suggests that the imperatives of duty, which tell us what we must do, as distinct from what it would be good to do but not wrong not to do, function so as to prohibit behavior that is intolerable if men are to live together in society.[3] This may explain the origin and continued existence of the present division between acts of duty and acts of charity. Moral attitudes are shaped by the needs of society, and no doubt society needs people who will observe the rules that make social existence tolerable. From the point of view of a particular society, it is essential to prevent violations of norms against killing, stealing, and so on. It is quite inessential, however, to help people outside one's own society.

If this is an explanation of our common distinction between duty and **supererogation,** however, it is not a justification of it. The moral point of view requires us to look beyond the interests of our own society. Previously, as I have already mentioned, this may hardly have been feasible, but it is quite feasible now. From the moral point of view, the prevention of the starvation of millions of people outside our society must be considered at least as pressing as the upholding of property norms within our society.

It has been argued by some writers, among them Sidgwick and Urmson, that we need to have a basic moral code which is not too far beyond the capacities of the ordinary man, for otherwise there will be a general breakdown of compliance with the moral code. Crudely stated, this argument suggests that if we tell people that they ought to refrain from murder and give everything they do not really need to famine relief, they will do neither, whereas if we tell them that they ought to refrain from murder and that it is good to give to famine relief but not wrong not to do so, they will at least refrain from murder. The issue here is: Where should we drawn the line between conduct that is required and conduct that is good although not required, so as to get the best possible result? This would seem to be an empirical question, although a very difficult one. One objection to the Sidgwick-Urmson line of argument is that it takes insufficient account of the effect that moral standards can have on the decisions we make. Given a society in which a wealthy man who gives five percent of his income to famine relief is regarded as most generous, it is not surprising that a proposal that we all ought to give away half our incomes will be thought to be absurdly unrealistic. In a society which held that no man should have more than enough while others have less than they need, such a proposal might seem narrow-minded. What it is possible for a man to do and what he is likely to do are both, I think, very greatly influenced by what people around him are doing and expecting him to do. In any case, the possibility that by spreading the idea that we ought to be doing very much more than we are to relieve famine we shall bring about a general breakdown of moral behavior seems remote. If the stakes are an end to widespread starvation, it is worth the risk. Finally, it should be emphasized that these considerations are relevant only to the issue of what we should require from others, and not to what we ourselves ought to do.

The second objection to my attack on the present distinction between duty and charity is one which has from time to time been made against utilitarianism. It follows from some forms of utilitarian theory that we all ought, morally, to be working full time to increase the balance of happiness over misery. The position I have taken here would not lead to this conclusion in all circumstances, for if there were no bad occurrences that we could prevent without sacrificing something of comparable moral importance, my argument would have no application. Given the present conditions in many parts of the world, however, it does follow from my argument that we ought, morally, to be working full time to relieve great suffering of the sort that occurs as a result of famine or other disasters. Of course, mitigating circumstances can be adduced—for instance, that if we wear ourselves out through overwork, we shall be less effective than we would otherwise have been. Nevertheless, when all considerations of this sort have been taken into account, the conclusion remains: we ought to be preventing as much suffering as we can without sacrificing something else of comparable moral importance. This conclusion is one which we may be reluctant to face. I cannot see, though, why it should be regarded as a criticism of the position for which I have argued, rather than a criticism of our ordinary standards of behavior. Since most people are self-interested to some degree, very few of us are likely to do everything that we ought to do. It would, however, hardly be honest to take this as evidence that it is not the case that we ought to do it.

It may still be thought that my conclusions are so wildly out of line with what everyone else thinks and has always thought that there must be something wrong with the argument somewhere. In order to show that my conclusions, while certainly contrary to contemporary Western moral standards, would not have seemed so extraordinary at other times and in other places, I would like to quote a passage from a writer not normally thought of as a way-out radical, Thomas Aquinas.

Now, according to the natural order instituted by divine providence, material goods are provided for the satisfaction of human needs. Therefore the division and appropriation of property, which proceeds from human law, must not hinder the satisfaction of man's necessity from such goods. Equally, whatever a man has in super-abundance is owed, of natural right, to the poor for their sustenance. So Ambrosius says, and it is also to be found in the *Decretum Gratiani:* "The bread which you withhold belongs to the hungry; the clothing you shut away, to the naked; and the money you bury in the earth is the redemption and freedom of the penniless."[4]

I now want to consider a number of points, more practical than philosophical, which are relevant to the application of the moral conclusion we have reached. These points challenge not the idea that we ought to be doing all we can to prevent starvation, but the idea that giving away a great deal of money is the best means to this end.

It is sometimes said that overseas aid should be a government responsibility, and that therefore one ought not to give to privately run charities. Giving privately, it is said, allows the government and the noncontributing members of society to escape their responsibilities.

This argument seems to assume that the more people there are who give to privately organized famine relief funds, the less likely it is that the government will take over full responsibility for such aid. This assumption is unsupported, and does not strike me as at all plausible. The opposite view—that if no one gives voluntarily, a government will assume that its citizens are uninterested in famine relief and would not wish to be forced into giving aid—seems more plausible. In any case, unless there were a definite probability that by refusing to give one would be helping to bring about massive government assistance, people who do refuse to make voluntary contributions are refusing to prevent a certain amount of suffering, without being able to point to any tangible beneficial

consequence of their refusal. So the onus of showing how their refusal will bring about government action is on those who refuse to give.

I do not, of course, want to dispute the contention that governments of affluent nations should be giving many times the amount of genuine, no-strings-attached aid that they are giving now. I agree, too, that giving privately is not enough, and that we ought to be campaigning actively for entirely new standards for both public and private contributions to famine relief. Indeed, I would sympathize with someone who thought that campaigning was more important than giving oneself, although I doubt whether preaching what one does not practice would be very effective. Unfortunately, for many people the idea that "it's the government's responsibility" is a reason for not giving which does not appear to entail any political action either.

Another more serious reason for not giving to famine relief funds is that until there is effective population control, relieving famine merely postpones starvation. If we save the Bengal refugees now, others, perhaps the children of these refugees, will face starvation in a few years' time. In support of all this, one may cite the now well-known facts about the population explosion and the relatively limited scope for expanded production.

This point, like the previous one, is an argument against relieving suffering that is happening now, because of a belief about what might happen in the future; it is unlike the previous point in that very good evidence can be adduced in support of this belief about the future. I will not go into the evidence here. I accept that the earth cannot support indefinitely a population rising at the present rate. This certainly poses a problem for anyone who thinks it important to prevent famine. Again, however, one could accept the argument without drawing the conclusion that it absolves one from any obligation to do anything to prevent famine. The conclusion that should be drawn is that the best means of preventing famine, in the long run, is population control. It would then follow from the position reached earlier that one ought to be doing all one can to promote population control (unless one held that all forms of population control were wrong in themselves, or would have significantly bad consequences). Since there are organizations working specifically for population control, one would then support them rather than more orthodox methods of preventing famine.

A third point raised by the conclusion reached earlier relates to the question of just how much we all ought to be giving away. One possibility, which has already been mentioned, is that we ought to give until we reach the level of marginal utility—that is, the level at which, by giving more, I would cause as much suffering to myself or my dependents as I would relieve by my gift. This would mean, of course, that one would reduce oneself to very near the material circumstances of a Bengali refugee. It will be recalled that earlier I put forward both a strong and a moderate version of the principle of preventing bad occurrences. The strong version, which required us to prevent bad things from happening unless in doing so we would be sacrificing something of comparable moral significance, does seem to require reducing ourselves to the level of marginal utility. I should also say that the strong version seems to me to be the correct one. I proposed the more moderate version— that we should prevent bad occurrences unless, to do so, we had to sacrifice something morally significant—only in order to show that even on this surely undeniable principle a great change in our way of life is required. On the more moderate principle, it may not follow that we ought to reduce ourselves to the level of marginal utility, for one might hold that to reduce oneself and one's family to this level is to cause something significantly bad to happen. Whether this is so I shall not discuss, since, as I have said, I can see no good reason for holding the moderate version of the principle rather than the strong

version. Even if we accepted the principle only in its moderate form, however, it should be clear that we would have to give away enough to ensure that the consumer society, dependent as it is on people spending on trivia rather than giving to famine relief, would slow down and perhaps disappear entirely. There are several reasons why this would be desirable in itself. The value and necessity of economic growth are now being questioned not only by conservationists, but by economists as well.[5] There is no doubt, too, that the consumer society has had a distorting effect on the goals and purposes of its members. Yet looking at the matter purely from the point of view of overseas aid, there must be a limit to the extent to which we should deliberately slow down our economy; for it might be the case that if we gave away, say, forty percent of our Gross National Product, we would slow down the economy so much that in absolute terms we would be giving less than if we gave twenty-five percent of the much larger GNP than we would have if we limited our contribution to this smaller percentage.

I mention this only as an indication of the sort of factor that one would have to take into account in working out an ideal. Since Western societies generally consider one percent of the GNP an acceptable level for overseas aid, the matter is entirely academic. Nor does it affect the question of how much an individual should give in a society in which very few are giving substantial amounts.

It is sometimes said, though less often now than it used to be, that philosophers have no special role to play in public affairs, since most public issues depend primarily on an assessment of facts. On questions of fact, it is said, philosophers as such have no special expertise, and so it has been possible to engage in philosophy without committing oneself to any position on major public issues. No doubt there are some issues of social policy and foreign policy about which it can truly be said that a really expert assessment of the facts is required before taking sides or acting, but the issue of famine is surely not one of these. The facts about the existence of suffering are beyond dispute. Nor, I think, is it disputed that we can do something about it, either through orthodox methods of famine relief or through population control or both. This is therefore an issue on which philosophers are competent to take a position. The issue is one which faces everyone who has more money than he needs to support himself and his dependents, or who is in a position to take some sort of political action. These categories must include practically every teacher and student of philosophy in the universities of the Western world. If philosophy is to deal with matters that are relevant to both teachers and students, this is an issue that philosophers should discuss.

Discussion, though, is not enough. What is the point of relating philosophy to public (and personal) affairs if we do not take our conclusions seriously? In this instance, taking our conclusion seriously means acting upon it. The philosopher will not find it any easier than anyone else to alter his attitudes and way of life to the extent that, if I am right, is involved in doing everything that we ought to be doing. At the very least, though, one can make a start. The philosopher who does so will have to sacrifice some of the benefits of the consumer society, but he can find compensation in the satisfaction of a way of life in which theory and practice, if not yet in harmony, are at least coming together.

Endnotes

1. There was also a third possibility: that India would go to war to enable the refugees to return to their lands. Since I wrote this paper, India has taken this way out. The situation is no longer that described above, but this does not affect my argument, as the next paragraph indicates.

2. In view of the special sense philosophers often give to the term, I should say that I use "obligation" simply as the abstract noun derived from "ought," so that "I have an obligation to" means no more, and no less, than "I ought to." This usage is in accordance with the definition of "ought" given by the *Shorter Oxford English Dictionary:* "the general verb to express duty or obligation." I do not think any issue of substance hangs on the way the term is used; sentences in which I use "obligation" could all be rewritten, although somewhat clumsily, as sentences in which a clause containing "ought" replaces the term "obligation."

3. J. O. Urmson, "Saints and Heroes," in *Essays in Moral Philosophy,* ed., Abraham I. Melden (Seattle and London, 1958), p. 214. For a related but significantly different view see also Henry Sidgwick, *The Methods of Ethics,* 7th edn. (London, 1907), pp. 220–221, 492–493.

4. *Summa Theologica,* II-II, Question 66, Article 7, in *Aquinas, Selected* Political Writings, ed. A. P. d'Entreves, trans. J. G. Dawson (Oxford, 1948), p. 171.

5. See, for instance, John Kenneth Galbraith, *The New Industrial State* (Boston, 1967); and E. J. Mishan, *The Costs of Economic Growth* (London, 1967).

Review Questions

1. According to Singer, what are the moral implications of the situation that occurred in East Bengal?
2. What is Singer's first moral principle?
3. What is the second principle? Distinguish between the two different versions of this principle.
4. Explain Singer's view of the distinction between duty and charity.
5. What is the Sidgwick–Urmson line of argument? How does Singer respond to it?
6. What is the criticism of utilitarianism? How does Singer reply?
7. What are Singer's conclusions?

Discussion Questions

1. Toward the end of his essay, Singer says that it would be desirable in itself if the consumer society would disappear. Do you agree? Why or why not?
2. What does the phrase "morally significant" in the weak version of the second principle mean? See if you can give a clear definition of this crucial phrase.
3. Singer grants that "until there is effective population control, relieving famine merely postpones starvation." Is this a good reason for not giving aid to countries that refuse to adopt any measures to control population? What is your view?
4. Singer attacks the traditional distinction between duty and charity. Is there any way to save the distinction? How?
5. Is Singer a utilitarian? Why or why not?

Problem Cases

1. Hummers

(For more information see www.hummer.com., The Hummer Network, www.humvee.net. For the Sierra Club view, see www.hummerdinger.com.) The Hummer H1 is basically a civilian copy of a military jeep called the Humvee. ("Humvee" is a military term for High Mobility Multipurpose Wheeled Vehicle, that is, a fancy jeep.) The civilian Hummer H1 has the same design as the military vehicle except for the addition of a luxury interior and other creature comforts like heated seats. It is powered with a V-8 turbo-charged diesel engine, and has a full-time 4-speed automatic transmission. The list price for the 4-door wagon is $117,508. There is debate about diesel-fueled vehicles. They have better fuel efficiency than gasoline-powered cars, but they still pollute with soot and smog forming nitrogen oxides, and they do not run well in cold weather.

After the commercial success of the Hummer H1, General Motors acquired the Hummer brand name and began selling the Hummer H2, which retails for $58,325. (GM is planning to bring out a cheaper model, the Hummer H3, and truck, the Hummer H2 S.U.T.) The H2 looks like the military Humvee and the civilian H1, but it is actually a different vehicle. The H2 has the chassis of a Chevy Tahoe truck and a V-8 gasoline engine. Because it has a gross vehicle weight rating over 8500 lbs., the U.S. government does not require it to meet federal fuel efficiency regulations. GM claims it gets 13 miles per gallon, but owners say that they get about 9 or 10 miles per gallon in normal use. If we assume that the H2 gets 13 miles per gallon, then it will produce 3.4 metric tons of carbon dioxide emissions in a typical year, nearly double that of GM's Chevrolet Malibu. If one gallon of gas costs $2, then driving the H2 for one typical year (15,000 miles) will cost about $3000, and that is just the cost for the gasoline.

It is interesting that the government makes it easier for the wealthy to buy one, for the H2 is included in a tax loophole. Under President George W. Bush's new tax plan, business owners can deduct the entire cost of their $58,385 H2. If they are in the highest tax bracket, that will give them a savings of nearly $20,000.

Both the Hummers have top speeds of less than 90 miles per hour, which is slow for a high-performance car. Those who require peak performance will want to consider the 2004 Lamborghini Murcielago R-GT. This two-seater sports car has a 12-cylinder engine, and a top speed of 200 miles per hour. It gets 9 miles per gallon, about the same as the Hummer H2, but it emits 17.7 metric tons of greenhouse emissions annually. The annual fuel bill for normal driving will be about $3000, or more at higher speeds. The exact price is not available on-line (see www.lamborghini. com) but informed sources say the cost is around $200,000, not including extras.

Compare these expensive cars to the Honda Insight, which uses new gasoline-electric hybrid technology. The Honda costs about $19,000 and gets 60 mpg in the city and 66 mpg on the highway. It has an annual fuel cost of $415. (These figures come from www.fueleconomy.gov.) Based on its test crash results, The National Highway Traffic Safety Administration gives high marks to the Honda Insight's safety.

Which car do you want? Why? Explain your reasons.

Should tax breaks be provided for people who buy expensive and fuel-inefficient cars like the H1, the H2, and the Lamborghini? Why not put a special luxury tax on these cars? What is your view?

Do you really need a car? If not, you could get a sensible and reliable Trek 820 mountain bike for $249.99. (See it at www.trekbikes.com.) This bike matches or beats the off-road performance of the Hummer H1 or H2, and it is a lot easier to park. Also, you will get fewer speeding tickets than the Lamborghini driver. All things considered, isn't this a better choice? Wouldn't the world be a better place to live if more people rode bikes instead of driving cars? (See Bikes Not Bombs, www.bikesnotbombs.org. This is an organization promoting bikes as a way of achieving peace, social justice, and an environmentally sustainable mode of transportation.)

If you live in an urban area, you could do without the car and bike and just walk or ride the bus. The money you save on transportation could go to Oxfam (www.oxfam.com). Is this a good plan? Why or why not?

2. *Global Warming*

(For detailed information on global warming, see the U.S. Environmental Protection Agency Global Warming website, http://yosemite.epa.gov/oar/ globalwarming.nsf/content/index.html.) There is a consensus in the scientific community that global warming is a real phenomenon. According to the U.S. Environmental Protection Agency, the twentieth century was the hottest in the last thousand years, and the nine hottest years on record all occurred since 1987, with 1998 being the hottest year ever. Scientists estimate that during the next century, the average temperature over the whole surface of the Earth will rise some 6 degrees Fahrenheit.

Not all regions will have equal warming. Some will be hotter and drier, while others will be colder and wetter. The western United States has been in various stages of drought since 1998, with 37 percent of the land affected having severe to extreme drought. According to the U.S. Department of Agriculture, more than 75 percent of range and pastures are now classified as poor to very poor in five western states (Nebraska, Colorado, California, Wyoming, and South Dakota). The long drought has also contributed to wildfires, with more than 4 million acres burned.

In other parts of the world, there have been floods and increased frequencies of tropical storms. The Asia monsoon has become less reliable, threatening hundreds of millions of farmers in India and Asia. Current models predict the melting of the polar ice caps. When this happens, sea levels will rise, threatening the fertile delta regions of Bangladesh and Egypt, which are in low-lying areas. Homes of a third of the world's population will be flooded with water. Small islands will sink beneath the sea. Infectious diseases will increase due to the expansion of habitat for disease carriers such as mosquitoes. Many species will be unable to adapt to the climate changes and will become extinct.

The vast majority of scientists believe these climate changes are the result of rising concentrations of greenhouse gases in the Earth's atmosphere. The greenhouse gases are water vapor, carbon dioxide, nitrous oxide, methane, ozone, and chlorofluorocarbons (CFCs). CFCs are synthetic chemicals used as solvents, refrigerants, and as blowing agents for foams and packing materials. Feron is a common CFC used in refrigerators. When released into the atmosphere, these gases trap heat instead of letting it radiate out into space, the way that glass traps heat in a greenhouse. Except for the synthetic CFCs, the greenhouse gases are natural components of the atmosphere, and the greenhouse effect is a natural phenomenon. Without it, the earth would be much cooler, and human life as we know it would not be possible.

The problem is that humans have enhanced the greenhouse effect by burning fossil fuels, namely coal, oil, and natural gas. These fuels are basically stored carbon, formed millions of years ago from organic matter. Burning them returns the carbon to the air in the form of carbon dioxide. This is the gas that primarily contributes to the enhanced greenhouse effect, which in turn is producing the climate changes.

The United States is the world's biggest producer of greenhouse gases, accounting for about 20 percent of the world's greenhouse gas emissions. Specifically, the United States emits more than 5 tons of carbon per person per year, Japan and western Europe contribute about 3 tons per person per year. The numbers are much lower for China (.76 tons) and India (.29 tons).

Power plants are the largest U.S. source of greenhouse gases, producing 2.5 billion tons of heat-trapping pollution every year. Gasoline-powered automobiles are the second-largest U.S. source of greenhouse gases, pumping 1.4 billion tons into the atmosphere each year. The popularity of SUVs like the Ford Explorer and the Chevrolet Suburban does not help. The increased sales of these vehicles has caused a 20 percent increase in transportation-related carbon dioxide pollution over the last decade. Automakers have used a legal loophole to make SUVs far less fuel efficient than cars. Closing this loophole and requiring SUVs to be as fuel efficient as cars would help reduce carbon dioxide emissions.

The Kyoto Protocol was an agreement among the industrialized nations of the world to reduce greenhouse gas emissions. More than 170 nations, including the United States, signed the treaty. If the treaty had been ratified by the U.S. Congress, it would have required reduction of emissions to below 1990 levels in the years 2008 to 2012.

Critics of the agreement complained that it put restrictions only on industrial nations, and not on developing countries such as China. Another issue was whether a country was allowed to establish carbon sinks instead of reducing emissions.

In March 2001, President George W. Bush announced that the United States would withdraw from the Kyoto Protocol. The treaty was not ratified by the U.S. Congress. President Bush said that the United States would not commit to the Kyoto Protocol standards, but would fight global warming in other ways such as the development of energy-efficient technologies.

In July 2001, the European Union, Japan, Canada, Russia, Australia, and 170 other nations agreed to proceed with a revised treaty. In the revised version, the targets for emissions reduction were reduced by two-thirds from the original goals, and countries were given the option of planting carbon-absorbing forests rather than reducing emissions.

The Senate Foreign Relations Committee has passed a unanimous resolution calling on the president to either sign the revised version of the Kyoto Protocol or develop a new agreement for reducing greenhouse gases.

Do you agree that reducing greenhouse gas emissions is an important goal for the United States? If so, how should this be done? Should automobile makers be required to produce fuel-efficient vehicles that get, say, at least 20 miles per gallon? Why doesn't the country develop mass transportation systems? This would reduce pollution and reduce the traffic gridlock we see in major U.S. cities. Should the United States sign and ratify the revised Kyoto Protocol? What is your view of these issues?

3. The Arctic National Wildlife Refuge

The Arctic National Wildlife Refuge in Alaska contains 19.8 million acres of land set aside by Congress in 1980 for possible oil exploration. According to environmentalists, it is the calving ground of 129,000 porcupine caribou, which native Alaskans depend on for food. More vulnerable to habitat pressures than other animals, these caribou make a 2,000-mile annual migration, and their growth rate is less than half that of other caribou.

The refuge contains many animals besides the caribou. There are bears, ground squirrels, ptarmigans, sheep, moose, and wolves, all roaming a vast area of tundra, rivers, canyons, and broad valleys. A visitor can walk for days and never see another human or any sign of civilization.

All this will change dramatically if oil drilling is allowed, but President George W. Bush has made oil production in the Arctic National Wildlife Refuge a cornerstone of his national energy agenda. The proposal is to drill wells on 1.5 million acres of coastal plain between the ocean and the Brooks Range. This portion of the refuge is called the 1002 Area, after a section of the 1980 Alaska Land Act. It is a sprawling, treeless tundra dotted with small ponds, descending north to the ocean. According to the U.S. Geological Survey, 10 billion barrels of oil could be produced from the plain and its offshore waters. That is about what the United States consumes in eighteen months.

What are the effects of oil development? We can see these effects at the giant oil fields at Prudhoe Bay to the west of the refuge. More than 1,100 miles of pipeline and 500 miles of gravel roads link 25 production plants, seawater treatment facilities, and power plants. Commercial jets land on two 6,500-foot asphalt runways. Twenty-three gravel mines churn out material for the roads. In short, the oil development has fouled the air, water, and tundra across 1,000 miles of the North Slope.

It is doubtful that the porcupine caribou would survive this sort of oil development in the refuge. It would become another area like the Prudhoe Bay area. But the oil boom is over in Alaska without new discoveries and new developments. The Alaska pipeline now carries just 1 million barrels of crude oil a day, half its peak in 1988. Oil production in the refuge could prolong the boom. The U.S. Energy Information Agency estimates that at its peak the 1002 Area could produce at least 1 million barrels of crude oil a day.

Should oil production begin in the 1002 Area or not? Why or why not?

4. The Burning of Amazon Rain Forests

The tropical forests of the Brazilian Amazon constitute 30 percent of the world's remaining rain forests, and they are home to one-tenth of all the world's plant and animal species. Yet farmers and cattle ranchers in Brazil are burning the rain forests of the Amazon River to clear the land for crops and livestock. According to the World Wildlife Fund, an estimated 12,350 square miles have been destroyed so far (an area about the size of France), and the burning continues. Conservationists and leaders of rich industrial nations have asked Brazil to stop the destruction. They claim that if the Amazon rain forests are destroyed, more than 1 million species of plant and animal life will vanish forever. This would be a significant loss of the Earth's genetic and biological heritage. Furthermore, they are worried about changes in the climate. The Amazon system of forests plays an important role in the way the sun's heat is distributed around the Earth because it stores more than 75 billion tons of carbon in its trees. An intact acre of Amazon rain forest sequesters about 1,000 pounds of carbon dioxide annually. Burning the trees of the Amazon forests will produce a dramatic increase in the amount of carbon dioxide in the atmosphere. The trapping of heat by this atmospheric carbon dioxide—the greenhouse effect—will significantly increase the global warming trend.

Brazilians reply that they have a sovereign right to use their land as they see fit. They complain that the rich industrial nations are just trying to maintain their economic supremacy. The Brazilian government claims that the burning is necessary for Brazilian economic development, particularly when the country is struggling under a huge load of foreign debt and is in a severe economic crisis. In 1998, the government of Brazil eliminated almost all its environmental protection programs and decided to refuse $25 million in foreign donations for the programs.

Should Brazil continue burning the Amazon rain forests? If not, then what should rich industrial nations do to help Brazil?

5. Radioactive Waste

There are two main sources of radioactive waste: used fuel rods from nuclear power plants and the waste from nuclear weapons production. The world has 413 commercial nuclear reactors. The typical nuclear reactor discharges about 30 tons of irradiated fuel annually, and in 1990 the world's accumulation of used fuel was 84,000 tons. Currently, most of the used radioactive fuel is stored in large pools of cooling water alongside nuclear reactors, but this is only a short-term solution, since most of these pools were designed to hold only a few years' worth of waste. More permanent disposal sites must be found.

The radioactive waste is mostly plutonium from fifty-five years of nuclear weapons production at twenty-three sites in the United States. Information about nuclear weapons production in the former Soviet Union is not available at the moment. Currently, it seems that there is no place to store this waste safely. At the Rocky Flats Plant near Boulder, Colorado, more than 29,000 gallons of toxic chemicals are stored in two large tanks and hundreds of barrels. At the Pantex Facility in Amarillo, Texas, toxic chemicals that have been stored in a pit for twenty-six years are leaking into the town's water supply.

One plan is to build a permanent storage site at Yucca Mountain in Nevada. But after the spending of $500 million, the project is bogged down in technical and legal problems. One problem is that there are inadequate safeguards against leaking, and people living in Nevada do not want the storage site there.

A site ready to be used is the Waste Isolation Pilot Plant near Carlsbad, New Mexico. It is a deep underground storage facility carved out of salt beds 2,150 feet below the desert, and it can hold thousands of barrels of radioactive waste from nuclear weapons production. The plan is to keep the material (mostly plutonium) safely sealed away from the environment for at least 10,000 years (although the material will be dangerously radioactive for hundreds of thousands of years). Engineers at the Energy Department claim that the salt formation has a tendency to shift and that this geological pressure will seal cracks in the site, keeping the toxic wastes safely isolated inside.

Critics are not convinced that the site is safe. One problem is that there are extensive oil and gas reserves in the area, which attract drilling that might release the toxic material. There are currently 200 wells within two miles of the plant, and it is possible that a well might be accidentally drilled directly into the repository. Another problem is that the barrels could corrode. The salt beds contain pockets of water that would migrate toward heat sources such as the nuclear waste. After a few years, water could form a brine that would corrode the barrels. To keep this from happening, the Energy Department has decided to fill the empty spaces in the underground chambers with magnesium oxide, a chemical that absorbs waters. Critics doubt, however, that this is a permanent solution to the problem.

The government is ready to open the plant, but opponents argue that a 1991 injunction against burying chemical poisons still applies and that the plant should not be opened.

Should radioactive waste be stored at the New Mexico site? If not, then what should be done with it?

6. The Tongass National Forest

The Tongass National Forest is the largest national forest in the United States and the greatest temperate rain forest on the earth. It is located in Alaska's southern panhandle and covers an area slightly larger than West Virginia (about 17 million acres). It is the home of several endangered species, including the grizzly bear and the bald eagle.

The U.S. Congress has authorized the Forest Service to sign fifty-year contracts with lumber companies that build pulp mills. In return, the Forest Service sells Tongass timber at very low prices, about $2 per 1,000 feet. On the open market, the same timber would command much higher prices, over $600 per 1,000 feet. The companies claim that they will pay higher prices under proposed new contracts and that they employ 1,500 people. Critics charge that it is a sweetheart deal that subsidizes the lumber companies at a cost to the taxpayers of over $40 million a year. Worst of all, they say, the lumber companies are destroying 500-year-old trees, great stands of Sitka spruce and hemlock, and eliminating the habitat of the grizzly bears and the bald eagles.

Should the destruction of the Tongass Forest be stopped? Why or why not?

Suggested Readings

1. The Worldwatch Institute, www.worldwatch.org, provides independent research on protecting the environment and a socially just society. The World Wildlife Fund, www.worldwildlife.org., has information on endangered species. Global Issues, www.globalissues.org., covers consumption, consumerism, free trade, poverty, arms control, and other issues. Food First, www.foodfirst.org., has facts about world hunger. For more facts see Bread for the World, www.bread.org.
2. Bjorn Lomborg, *The Skeptical Environmentalist* (Cambridge: Cambridge University Press, 2001), argues that we should not worry about the greenhouse effect, pollution, and biodiversity because the world has actually improved.
3. Stuart L. Pimm, *The World According to Pimm* (New York: McGraw-Hill, 2001), disagrees with Lomborg. According to Pimm, the human consumption of the earth's resources is unsustainable. Or as he puts it, "Man Eats Planet! Two Fifths Already Gone!"
4. Edward O. Wilson, *The Future of Life* (New York: Vintage, 2003), argues if humans do not control overpopulation and wasteful consumption there will be a massive loss of plant and animal species
5. John Arthur, "Rights and Duty to Bring Aid, in *World Hunger and Moral Obligation,* William Aiken and Hugh LaFollette, eds. (Englewood Cliffs, NJ: Prentice-Hall, 1977), attacks Singer's view about giving aid to the needy and defends the right of the rich to not do this.
6. Garrett Hardin, "Living on a Lifeboat," BioScience 24 (10), pp. 561–568, argues that rich nations have no moral obligation to help poor nations, because this produces overpopulation and the run of national resources.
7. James Rachels, "Killing and Starving to Death," *Philosophy* 54, no. 208, (April 1979:159–71, argues that our duty not to let people die of starvation is just as strong as our duty not to kill them.
8. Reed F. Noss, ed., *The Redwood Forest: History, Ecology, and Conservation of the Coastal Redwoods* (Washington, DC: Island Press, 1999). This anthology of thirty-two articles describes redwood forests including flora, fauna, forest and stram ecology, conservation planning, and forest management.
9. Paul Taylor, "The Ethics of Respect for Nature," *Environmental Ethics* 3 (Fall 1981): 197–218, maintains that respect for nature requires a biocentric outlook, the attitude that all wild living things have inherent worth, and a duty to not harm wild living things.

10. Holmes Rolston III, "Duties to Endangered Species," in Holmes Rolston III, *Environmental Ethics* (Philadelphia, PA: Temple University Press, 1988), pp. 126–59, argues that we have duties to species of plants and animals because they constitute valuable forms or essences.

11. Vandana Shiva, "Women, Ecology, and Development," in *Staying Alive: Development, Ecology, and Women* by Vandana Shiva (London: Zed Books, 1988), pp. 1–13, contends that the Western development of other countries applies patriarchal principles of exploitation and domination of nature and women, with the result that forests are destroyed and women are harmed.

12. Donald VanDeVeer and Christine Pierce, *The Environmental Ethics and Policy Book* (Belmont, CA: Wadsworth, 1997), covers ethical theory, deep ecology, ecofeminism, activism, and other topics related to environmental preservation.

13. Louis P. Pojman, ed., *Environmental Ethics,* 2nd ed. (Belmont, CA: Wadsworth, 1998). This big anthology has eighty-four articles on all aspects of environmental ethics.

14. William F. Baxter, *People or Penguins: The Case for Optimal Pollution* (New York: Columbia University Press, 1974), defends the anthropocentric view that the natural environment, including animals, counts only as a means of producing human benefits; it is not an end in itself and has no value apart from humans.

15. William Godfrey-Smith, "The Value of Wilderness," *Environmental Ethics* I (Winter 1979): 309–19, argues that instrumental justifications for conservation of the wilderness fail to provide a satisfactory rationale. Instead, he proposes a holistic conception of nature based on the intrinsic value of the wilderness.

16. Bernard E. Rollin, "Environmental Ethics," in Steven Luper-Foy, ed., *Problems of International Justice* (Boulder, CO: Westview Press, 1988), pp. 125–31, maintains that sentient beings, including humans and animals, have intrinsic value and moral rights, but nonsentient things, such as rivers, forests, and species, have only instrumental value.

17. Christopher D. Stone, *Should Trees Have Standing? and Other Essays on Law, Morals, and the Environment* (Dobbs Ferry, NY: Oceana Publishers, 1996), argues that natural objects such as trees should be given legal rights and represented by legal friends who protect their interests.

18. Lily-Marlene Russow, "Why Do Species Matter?" *Environmental Ethics* 3 (Summer 1981): 103–12, argues that attempts to give species inherent value are confused. The reason species matter is that individual members of a species have aesthetic value.

19. Alastair S. Gunn, "Why Should We Care About Rare Species?" *Environmental Ethics* 2 (Spring 1989): 17–37, argues that the extermination of rare species is wrong because each species (as well as the ecological whole) has intrinsic value.

20. J. Baird Callicott, "The Search for an Environmental Ethic," in Tom Regan, ed., *Matters of Life and Death,* 3rd ed. (New York: McGraw-Hill, 1993), pp. 332–81, argues that ecocentrism, a conceptually developed version of Leopold's land ethic, is the most satisfactory environmental ethic.

21. John Passmore, *Man's Responsibility for Nature* (New York: Scribner's, 1974), maintains that we should not sacrifice art, science, or other human interests for the sake of conservation.

22. Tom Regan, ed., *Earthbound: New Introductory Essays in Environmental Ethics* (New York: Random House, 1984). This is a collection of original essays, including Alastair S. Gunn, "Preserving Rare Species," Annette Baier, "For the Sake of Future Generations," and Mark Sagoff, "Ethics and Economics in Environmental Law."

23. Karen J. Warren, "The Power and the Promise of Ecological Feminism," *Environmental Ethics* 12 (Summer 1998): 125–46. As Warren explains it, ecological feminism, or

ecofeminism, sees both the domination of women and the domination of nonhuman nature as the result of an oppressive patriarchal conceptual framework characterized by what she calls the logic of domination.

24. Margarita Garcia Levin, "A Critique of Ecofeminism," in Louis J. Pojman, ed., *Environmental Ethics,* 2nd ed. (Belmont, CA: Wadsworth, 1998), pp. 183–88, attacks Warren's ecofeminism. Levin thinks there are better explanations for the way humans treat nature than Warren's logic of domination.

25. Karen Warren and Nisvan Erkal, eds., *Ecofeminism: Women, Culture, Nature* (Bloomington, IN: Indiana University Press, 1997). This is a collection of articles that address three sets of topics: (1) empirical data about environmental racism, sexism, and classism; (2) the application of ecofeminist insights to various academic disciplines; and (3) philosophical perspectives on ecofeminism.

26. Greta Claire Gaard, ed., *Ecofeminism: Women, Animals, Nature* (Philadelphia, PA: Temple University Press, 1993). This is a collection of original articles that present a variety of ecofeminist viewpoints—for example, "Ecology and the Cult of the Romantic" and "For the Love of Nature."

27. Peter C. List, ed., *Radical Environmentalism: Philosophy and Tactics* (Belmont, CA: Wadsworth, 1993). This is a collection that includes articles on radical environmental views such as ecofeminism and deep ecology. As it is explained by Arne Naess in two articles, deep ecology starts with holism but goes on to recommend a mystical vision of the whole of nature. Also covered in the book are the tactics of radical environmental groups, such as Earth First!, that engage in nonviolent resistance called "monkey wrenching," a term taken from Edward Abbey's book *The Monkey Wrench Gang.*

28. Bill Devall and George Sessions, *Deep Ecology: Living as If Nature Mattered* (Salt Lake City, UT: Peregrine Smith Books, 1985), present a version of deep ecology that links it to religions such as Buddhism, Taoism, and Native American religion.

29. Jack Turner, *The Abstract Wild* (Tucson: The University of Arizona Press, 1996). In a series of essays about wild nature and animals, Turner calls for a radical transformation that reveals the wild earth—its mystery, order, and essential harmony.

30. George Sessions, ed., *Deep Ecology for the 21st Century* (Boston: Shambhala Press, 1995). This is a collection of articles on deep ecology, including writings by Arne Naess, the founder of the movement.

Chapter 9

War and Terrorism

Introduction

Factual Background

The history of humans is a sad chronicle of war and terrorism. Thus far there have been no nuclear or biological wars, but almost every year there has been a conventional war or an act of terrorism somewhere in the world. India and Pakistan have been fighting in the disputed area of Kashmir for over fifty years. Israel has fought several wars, and continues to fight the Palestinians on a daily basis. The Palestinians respond with suicide bombers. There was a war in Bosnia generated by ethnic differences. Saddam Hussein invaded Kuwait and the result was the first Gulf War. A short list of wars in the twentieth century includes World Wars I and II, the Korean War, the Vietnam War, and a bitter struggle in Afghanistan when Russian forces tried to invade. Iran and Iraq fought a bloody war, with Iraq being armed and supported by the United States. In 2001, U.S. and British forces attacked Afghanistan in response to the 9/11 terrorist attacks. In 2003, U.S. and British troops invaded and occupied Iraq, claiming that Iraq had weapons of mass destruction and ties to Al Qaeda, the terrorist organization responsible for the 9/11 attacks. In 2004, insurgents in Iraq continued fighting U.S. troops with casualties on both sides, and many innocent civilians were killed. (For more on the invasion and occupation of Iraq, see the first Problem Case.)

Terrorist attacks have dramatically increased in the twenty-first century. Suicide bombings, missile strikes, shootings, and other attacks have become a frequent occurrence in Iraq and Israel. Sometimes soldiers or the police are killed, but many times it is civilians who die. In 2004, Israeli missiles killed Sheik Ahmed Yassin, the spiritual leader of the militant group Hamas, which Israel claimed was responsible for terrorist bombings in Israel. In 2004, ten bombs ripped through four commuter trains in Madrid during the morning rush hour, killing nearly 200 and wounding more than 1,400. This was the deadliest terrorist attack on a European target since World War II. On September 11, 2001, nineteen terrorists hijacked four airplanes. They crashed two of the planes into the World Trade Center in New York City, destroying the twin towers. It is estimated that 3,000 people were killed. A third plane hit the Pentagon, killing nearly 200 workers. The fourth plane crashed in rural southwest Pennsylvania after the passengers overpowered the terrorists. A total of 266 people were killed on the four planes. This was the most devastating terrorist attack in U.S. history. Some compared it to the Japanese attack on Pearl Harbor that resulted in war with Japan, a war that ended shortly after Hiroshima and Nagasaki were destroyed with nuclear bombs in August 1945.

The United States produced convincing evidence that Osama bin Laden and his Al Qaeda network of terrorists were responsible for the 9/11 attacks. On September 23, 2001, bin Laden issued a statement urging his followers to remain steadfast on the path of jihad against the infidels, that is, the United States and her allies. In 2004, bin Laden had still not been captured, and he continued to issue videos declaring war against the infidels.

This was only the latest and most shocking of a series of terrorist attacks on U.S. citizens and servicemen. On October 12, 2000, a terrorist bombing killed seventeen U.S. sailors aboard the U.S.S. Cole as it refueled in Yemen's port of Aden. The United States said that bin Laden was the prime suspect. On August 7, 1998, there were car bombings of U.S. embassies in Nairobi, Kenya, and Dar es Salaam, Tanzania. More than 5,500 people were injured and 224 were killed. Once again the prime suspect was Osama bin Laden. In June, 1996, a truck bomb exploded outside the Khobar Towers in Dharan, Saudi Arabia, killing 19 U.S. servicemen and wounding hundreds of other people. Members of a radical Lebanese terrorist group, Hizballah, were indicted for the attack. On February 26, 1993, a bomb exploded in a parking garage below the World Trade Center, killing 6 people and wounding more than 1,000. Six radical Muslim terrorists were convicted and sentenced to life in prison. On April 19, 1995, a federal building in Oklahoma City was destroyed by a truck bomb. There were 168 deaths. Timothy J. McVeigh was executed for the attack and Terry L. Nichols was sentenced to life in prison. On December 21, 1998, Pam Am flight 103 exploded over Lockerbie, Scotland, killing 270 people onboard. Two Libyan intelligence officers were accused of planting a suitcase containing the bomb. One was convicted in February 2001 and the other was set free.

The Readings

A traditional and important position on war and terrorism is pacifism. Pacifism can take different forms. In the first reading for the chapter, Lackey distinguishes between four different types of pacifism: (1) the view that all killing is wrong, (2) the view that all violence is wrong, (3) the view that personal violence is always wrong, but political violence is sometimes morally right, and (4) the view that personal violence is sometimes morally permissible, but war is always morally wrong. Albert Schweitzer's position is an example of the first type of pacifism; he held that all killing is wrong because all life is sacred. Mohandas Gandhi's pacifism is an example of the second type because he opposed all violence. According to Lackey, a problem with both of these views is that sometimes killing or violence is required to save lives. For example, shouldn't a terrorist airplane hijacker be killed or restrained to prevent the hijacker from crashing the plane and killing all the passengers? The third view that condemns personal violence but allows political violence is attributed to St. Augustine. But this view has a problem with personal self-defense. Most people would agree that personal violence is justified in defense of one's life, as in the case of the terrorist airplane hijacker. The kind of pacifism that Lackey supports is the fourth view, which condemns all war as morally wrong but allows some personal violence. But this antiwar pacifism has a problem, too. Why can't some wars be justified by appealing to some great moral good such as political freedom? Certainly the Revolutionary War in America (to use Lackey's own example) is defended in this way.

Another important view on war is just war theory. Medieval Christian theologians called Scholastics originally formulated the theory, and it has been discussed ever since. The theory distinguishes between two questions about war. First, there is the question about the right to go to war, called *jus ad bellum*, or "right to war": What are the conditions that justify going to war? Second, there is the question about the right conduct in war, called *jus in bello*, or "right in war": How should combatants conduct themselves in fighting a war?

As O'Brien explains it in the second reading, then, just war theory has two components, one concerned with the right to go to war and the other with the conduct of war. Three main conditions have to be met to establish the right to go to war: (1) the war must be declared by a competent authority, (2) there must be a just cause, and (3) there must be a right intention that ultimately aims at peace. The just cause condition is subdivided into four more conditions: the substance of the just cause, the form of the just cause, the proportionality of ends and means, and the requirement of the exhaustion of peaceful remedies. The substance of the just cause is the reason for going to war, such as "to protect the innocent from unjust attack." This reason could be given to justify going to war against Germany in World War II. The form of the just cause is either defensive or offensive. Defensive wars are easier to justify than offensive ones. O'Brien notes, however, that offensive wars of vindictive justice against infidels or heretics were once permitted. (As we shall see, this is similar to the doctrine of jihad.) The requirement of proportionality has to do with general means and ends; basically the idea is that the ultimate end, such as political freedom or a democratic society, must be sufficiently good to justify the evil of warfare. (Khatchadourian in the third reading calls this the political principle of proportionality.) The fourth requirement is that going to war should be a last resort after all peaceful remedies, such as negotiation, mediation, and arbitration, have failed.

Two basic principles limit conduct in a just war, the principle of proportion and the principle of discrimination. The principle of proportion says that the intermediate military ends, such as the capture of an enemy position, must justify the means used, such as the firing of rockets. (Khatchadourian calls this the military principle of proportionality.) The principle of discrimination prohibits intentional attacks on noncombatants and nonmilitary targets. This principle is the subject of much debate, as we will see.

In the third reading, Khatchadourian applies just war theory to terrorism. He argues that all forms of terrorism (predatory, retaliatory, political, and moral/religious) are always wrong because they flagrantly violate the principles of just war theory and they violate basic human rights. They also violate the principle of necessity that forbids the wanton destruction of life and property. (O'Brien discusses this principle as one of the applications of the military principle of proportionality.) They violate the principle of discrimination because innocent people are killed or harmed. (Khatchodourian condemns the tendency of political, retaliatory, or moralistic terrorists to baselessly enlarge the circle of allegedly noninnocent people.) Acts of terrorism also violate the principle of proportion in both its political form applying to the right to go to war and its military form applying to the conduct of war. All but the moral/religious type violate a further condition of just war theory, the condition of a just cause. Finally, Khatchadourian argues that all forms of terrorism violate the fundamental human rights of the victims, including the right to autonomy, the negative right to life, and the right to be treated as a moral person.

In the fourth reading, Calhoun also applies just war theory to terrorism, but with different results than Khatchadourian's. Her focus is on political and moral/religious terrorists. Unlike Khatchadourian, she does not try to show that terrorist acts are wrong. Instead she wants to show how just war theory can be used by terrorists to defend their actions, at least to themselves and their followers, using the very same theory that democratic nations use to justify their military campaigns. Terrorists who do this see themselves as fighting a "just war." To see how they can do this, we need to look more closely at just war theory, and particularly the doctrine of double effect. How can a nation justify dropping bombs on another nation when this act results in the killing of innocent civilians? If the principle of discrimination is understood as absolutely forbidding killing innocents, then no modern war could be justified. O'Brien and Lackey both make this point in the readings. To justify killing innocents, just war theorists appeal to the Catholic doctrine of double effect. (This doctrine has already been discussed in the Introduction to Chapter 3.) The doctrine distinguishes between two effects of an action, an intended effect and one that is foreseen but not intended, a side effect. The doctrine says that as long as the intended consequence of an act is good (for example, winning a war or relief of suffering), then a bad foreseen consequence (for example, the death of innocents) is morally allowed, provided this bad consequence is not intended. Calhoun argues that terrorists can use this sort of reasoning to justify their actions, as Timothy McVeigh did when he characterized the deaths of innocent people in the Oklahoma City bombing as "collateral damage." In other words, she argues, "just war" rationalizations are available to everyone, bin Laden as well as President Bush. Terrorists can present themselves to their followers as warriors for justice, and not as mere murderers or vigilantes.

In the fifth reading, Luban discusses the new War on Terrorism, which is the result of the 9/11 attacks. According to Luban, the current fight against terrorism does not fit the traditional model of war. Instead it uses a new hybrid war-law model that combines features of the war model with a law model. The new war model allows the use of lethal force, the foreseen but unintended killing of innocents, and the capturing and killing of suspected terrorists. These are features of war. But in traditional war, the enemy can legitimately fight back, other nations can opt for neutrality, and enemy soldiers have certain rights under the Geneva Convention. The War on Terrorism rejects these features by appealing to a law model. Terrorists are criminals so they cannot legitimately fight back. Other nations cannot be neutral when it comes to illegal murder. If they harbor or aid terrorists, they are against us. Finally, terrorists are treated as enemy combatants rather than soldiers or ordinary criminals, and as such they have no rights, neither the rights of ordinary criminals nor the rights of soldiers under the Geneva Convention. There is no presumption of innocence, no right to a hearing, and they can be detained indefinitely. Even torture is allowable. So according to Luban, the War on Terrorism produces an end of international human rights because anyone identified as a terrorist has no rights. (For an example of the treatment of suspected terrorists, see the case of Jose Padilla in the Problem Cases.)

Pacifism and just war theory have dominated discussion of war and terrorism in Western thought. Both of these positions developed in the tradition of Christianity. But there is another important doctrine about war that comes from Islam and is used to justify both terrorism and war. This is the Islamic doctrine of jihad. Although the term "jihad" is often translated as "holy war," Knapp in the last reading says that this is not exactly what the term means. Literally it means struggle or striving in the path of God for a noble cause. Knapp discusses the classic and modern doctrine of jihad as it is applied to warfare. The classic view of jihad allowed defensive war against enemies of Islam, but it did not sanction the killing of all non-Muslims or even their conversion by force. He quotes the Koran (2:256): "There is no compulsion in religion." Killing of other Muslims could only be justified by classifying them as non-Muslims, e.g., as apostates or rebels. He notes that the Islamic law tradition was very hostile toward terrorism and severely punished rebels who attacked innocent victims. Modern Islamic militants have changed the doctrine of jihad. They see themselves as fighting to restore land and nations lost to Islam. The Palestinians are fighting to regain the land taken away from them by Isarel. Osama bin Laden claims that Americans are infidels occupying holy places in Saudi Arabia, namely the cities of Mecca and Medina, and fighting a war of annihiliation against Iraq, which for 500 years was the heart of an Islamic empire. But according to Knapp, the classic and modern doctrines of jihad do not condone indiscriminate killing or terrorism as practiced by suicide bombers or Al Qaeda. The Islamic militants have hijacked the doctrine of jihad to serve their own purposes.

Philosophical Issues

The readings in the chapter raise some very important issues. Can war be justified, and if so, how? Pacifists such as Schweitzer and Gandhi, who were opposed to all killing or all violence, hold that no war is ever justified. The problem with these absolutist views is that there seems to be an obvious exception, namely, killing or violence in the defense of one's life. Lackey's antiwar pacifism is not so easily dismissed. If one agrees that the killing of soldiers and civilians is a very great evil, one that cannot be balanced by goods such as political freedom, then it seems very difficult, if not impossible, to justify modern wars.

Just war theorists such as O'Brien try to justify modern wars such as World War II, but to do so they have to modify or interpret the principles of the theory. The most troublesome principle is the one about discrimination. As O'Brien says, if this principle is understood to forbid absolutely the killing of noncombatants, then it is hard to see how any modern war could be justified, since they all involved killing noncombatants. Perhaps the most graphic example was the atomic bombing of Hiroshima and Nagasaki, which killed over 200,000 innocent noncombatants. There are various ways to get around the problem. One is to deny that there are any innocent noncombatants in war; everyone in an enemy nation is a legitimate target. (Some terrorists take this position, too.) The most common way of justifying the killing of innocents, as we have seen, is to appeal to the Catholic doctrine of double effect.

There is debate about how to formulate and apply the doctrine of double effect. In the reading, O'Brien admits that the distinction between the two effects, one that is directly intended and the other, an unintended side effect, is often difficult to accept. Consider President Harry Truman's decision to bomb Hiroshima and Nagasaki. At the time, he said that his decision was based on the fact that an invasion of Japan would cost the lives of thousands of American soldiers, and he wanted to save those lives. But he surely knew that using atomic bombs on these undefended cities would result in the deaths of thousands of innocent Japanese noncombatants. Did he directly intend the killing of innocents or merely foresee this killing as an unintended consequence? Can we make the distinction in this case, and if we do, then what is the basis for the distinction?

Are acts of terrorism ever justified? As we have seen, Khatchadourian does not think so, and most pacifists would agree, with the possible exception of pacifists who forbid personal violence but allow political violence. Calhoun argues that terrorists can and do appeal to the just war theory, the very theory that Khatchadourian uses to demonstrate that terrorism is always wrong. How can just war theory be used to defend terrorism? Calhoun argues that terrorists can appeal to the doctrine of double effect. To see how this might be done, let's take another look at the doctrine as stated by Father Richard McCormick and quoted by O'Brien. McCormick says, "It is immoral directly to take innocent human life except with divine authorization." Why is the killing of innocents allowed if there is divine authorization? One explanation is that just war theory was developed by Catholic theologians to defend the holy crusades against infidels, crusades that they were believed to be commanded by God. But of course fundamentalist Muslim terrorists also believe they have divine authorization; they believe they are engaged in a holy war commanded by Allah against infidels. Thus both Christians and Muslims claim divine authorization for war and terrorism.

Now let us turn to the distinction between direct and indirect killing, which is at the heart of the doctrine of double effect. As McCormick explains it, "Direct taking of human life implies that one performs a lethal action with the intention that death should result for himself or another. Death is therefore deliberately willed as the effect of one's action." But Muslim terrorists may sincerely believe that all things happen by Allah's will, and they do not will anything, much less the death of others. They are merely submitting to the will of Allah, and Allah commands them to jihad. So they can claim that the deaths that result from their actions are not positively willed, but merely foreseen as a consequence of following Allah's commands. In other words, they are only indirectly killing innocents. It appears, then, that terrorists can attempt to justify their actions by appealing to the Catholic doctrine of double effect, at least as it is stated by McCormick.

How do we define terrorism? This is another issue discussed in the readings. Calhoun argues that there is no satisfactory definition of terrorism. The moral definition, which defines terrorism as killing or threatening to kill innocent people, is unsatisfactory because it seems to apply to every nation that has engaged in bombing campaigns resulting in the deaths of innocent children. The legal definition, which defines terrorism as illegal acts of killing or harming people, is defective because it would not apply to the reign of terror imposed by the Third Reich in Nazi Germany. Khatchadourian also rejects moral definitions that make terrorism wrong by definition, and he agrees that essentialist definitions of terrorism are inadequate. They are either too broad or too narrow. Nevertheless, Khatchadourian thinks that the vague and contested word terrorism has a core meaning that includes the idea that terrorist acts are acts of coercion or force aiming at monetary gain, revenge, a political end, or a moral/religious end. Also, he says, terrorism has a bifocal character that distinguishes it from other forms of coercion or force. That is, terrorism not only aims at killing or harming victims, it also aims at producing fear and terror in the victimized, those who are the indirect but real targets of terrorist acts.

Finally, how do we deal with terrorists? This is an issue raised by Luban. Do we treat them as enemy soldiers that have rights under the Geneva Convention, e.g., the right not to be tortured, the right to be fed, clothed, given medical treatment, and released when hostilities are over? Or are they to be considered criminals? If so, do they have the legal rights of ordinary criminals such as the presumption of innocence, the right to a trial, the right to be defended by a lawyer, the right to not testify against themselves, and the right to not be held without charges? Or are they enemy combatants who have neither the rights of soldiers nor ordinary criminals?

Pacifism

DOUGLAS P. LACKEY

Douglas P. Lackey is professor of philosophy at Baruch College and the Graduate Center of the City University of New York. He is the author of *Moral Principles and Nuclear Weapons* (1984), *Ethics and Strategic Defense: American Philosophers Debate Star Wars and the Future of Nuclear Deterrence* (1989), and *God, Immortality, Ethics: A Concise Introduction to Philosophy* (1990). Our reading is taken from *The Ethics of War and Peace* (1989).

Lackey distinguishes between four types of pacifism. There is the universal pacifist view that all killing is wrong, the universal pacifist view that all violence is wrong, private pacifism that condemns personal violence but not political violence, and antiwar pacifism that allows personal violence but condemns all wars. Lackey discusses objections to all of these views, but he seems to defend antiwar pacifism. Or at least he answers every objection to antiwar pacifism, leaving the reader with the impression that he supports this view.

1. VARIETIES OF PACIFISM

EVERYONE HAS A VAGUE IDEA of what a pacifist is, but few realize that there are many kinds of pacifists. (Sometimes the different kinds quarrel with each other!) One task for the student of

international ethics is to distinguish the different types of pacifism and to identify which types represent genuine moral theories.

Most of us at some time or other have run into the "live and let live" pacifist, the person who says, "I am absolutely opposed to killing and violence—but I don't seek to impose my own code on anyone else. If other people want to use violence, so be it. They have their values and I have mine." For such a person, pacifism is one life style among others, a life style committed

Source: Douglas P. Lackey, "Pacifism" from *The Ethics of War and Peace* by Douglas P. Lackey, pp. 6–24. Prentice Hall, Inc. Copyright 1989. Reprinted by permission of Pearson Education, Inc., Upper Saddle River, NJ.

to gentleness and care, and opposed to belligerence and militarism. Doubtless, many people who express such commitments are sincere and are prepared to live by their beliefs. At the same time, it is important to see why "live and let live" pacifism does not constitute a moral point of view.

When someone judges that a certain action, A, is morally wrong, that judgment entails that no one should do A. Thus, there is no way to have moral values without believing that these values apply to other people. If a person says that A is morally wrong but that it doesn't matter if other people do A, than that person either is being inconsistent or doesn't know what the word "moral" means. If a person believes that killing, in certain circumstances, is morally wrong, that belief implies that no one should kill, at least in those circumstances. If a pacifist claims that killing is wrong in *all* circumstances, but that it is permissible for other people to kill on occasion, then he has not understood the universal character of genuine moral principles. If pacifism is to be a moral theory, it must be prescribed for all or prescribed for none.

Once one recognizes this "universalizing" character of genuine moral beliefs, one will take moral commitments more seriously than those who treat a moral code as a personal life-style. Since moral principles apply to everyone, we must take care that our moral principles are correct, checking that they are not inconsistent with each other, developing and adjusting them so that they are detailed and subtle enough to deal with a variety of circumstances, and making sure that they are defensible against the objections of those who do not accept them. Of course many pacifists do take the business of morality seriously and advance pacifism as a genuine moral position, not as a mere life-style. All such serious pacifists believe that *everyone* ought to be a pacifist, and that those who reject pacifism are deluded or wicked. Moreover, they do not simply endorse pacifism; they offer arguments in its defense.

We will consider four types of pacifist moral theory. First, there are pacifists who maintain that the central idea of pacifism is the immorality of killing. Second, there are pacifists who maintain that the essence of pacifism is the immorality of violence, whether this be violence in personal relations or violence in relations between nation-states. Third, there are pacifists who argue that personal violence is always morally wrong but that political violence is sometimes morally right: for example, that it is sometimes morally permissible for a nation to go to war. Fourth and finally, there are pacifists who believe that personal violence is sometimes permissible but that war is always morally wrong.

Albert Schweitzer, who opposed all killing on the grounds that life is sacred, was the first sort of pacifist. Mohandas Gandhi and Leo Tolstoy, who opposed not only killing but every kind of coercion and violence, were pacifists of the second sort: I will call such pacifists "universal pacifists." St. Augustine, who condemned self-defense but endorsed wars against heretics, was a pacifist of the third sort. Let us call him a "private pacifist," since he condemned only violence in the private sphere. Pacifists of the fourth sort, increasingly common in the modern era of nuclear and total war, I will call "antiwar pacifists."

2. THE PROHIBITION AGAINST KILLING

(a) The Biblical Prohibition

One simple and common argument for pacifism is the argument that the Bible, God's revealed word, says to all people "Thou shalt not kill" (Exod. 20:13). Some pacifists interpret this sentence as implying that no one should kill under any circumstances, unless God indicates that this command is suspended, as He did when He commanded Abraham to slay Isaac. The justification for this interpretation is the words themselves, "Thou shalt not kill," which are presented in the Bible bluntly and without qualification, not only in Exodus but also in Deuteronomy (5:17).

This argument, however, is subject to a great many criticisms. The original language of Exodus and Deuteronomy is Hebrew, and the consensus of scholarship says that the Hebrew sentence at Exodus 20:23, "Lo Tirzach," is best translated as "Thou shalt do no murder," not as "Thou shalt not kill." If this translation is correct, then Exodus 20:13 does not forbid all killing but only those killings that happen to be murders. Furthermore, there are many places in the Bible where God commands human beings to kill in specified circumstances. God announces 613 commandments in all, and these include "Thou shalt not suffer a witch to live" (Exod. 22:18); "He that blasphemeth the name of the Lord . . . shall surely be put to death, and all the congregation shall stone him" (Lev. 24:16); "He that killeth any man shall surely be put to death" (Lev. 24:17); and so forth. It is difficult to argue that these instructions are like God's specific instructions to Abraham to slay Isaac: these are general commandments to be applied by many people, to many people, day in and day out. They are at least as general and as divinely sanctioned as the commandment translated "Thou shalt not kill."

There are other difficulties for pacifists who pin their hopes on prohibitions in the Hebrew Bible. Even if the commandment "Thou shalt not kill," properly interpreted, did prohibit all types of killing, the skeptics can ask whether this, by itself, proves that all killing is immoral. First, how do we know that statements in the Hebrew Bible really are God's word, and not just the guesses of ancient scribes? Second, even if the commandments in the Bible do express God's views, why are we morally bound to obey divine commands? (To say that we will be punished if we do not obey is to appeal to fear and self-interest, not to moral sentiments). Third, are the commandments in the Old Testament laws for all people, or just laws for the children of Israel? If they are laws for all people, then all people who do not eat unleavened bread for Passover are either deluded or wicked. If they are laws only for the children of Israel, they are religious laws and not moral laws, since they lack the universality that all moral laws must have.

Finally, the argument assumes the existence of God, and philosophers report that the existence of God is not easy to demonstrate. Even many religious believers are more confident of the truth of basic moral judgments, such as "Small children should not be tortured to death for purposes of amusement," than they are confident of the existence of God. For such people, it would seem odd to try to justify moral principles by appeals to religious principles, since the evidence for those religious principles is weaker than the evidence for the moral principles they are supposed to justify.

(b) The Sacredness of Life

There are, however, people who oppose all killing but do not seek justification in divine revelation. Many of these defend pacifism by appeal to the sacredness of life. Almost everyone is struck with wonder when watching the movements and reactions of a newborn baby, and almost everyone can be provoked to awe by the study of living things, great and small. The complexity of the mechanisms found in living bodies, combined with the efficiency with which they fulfill their functions, is not matched by any of the processes in nonliving matter. People who are particularly awestruck by the beauty of living things infer these feelings that life is sacred, that all killing is wrong.

Different versions of pacifism have been derived from beliefs about the sacredness of life. The most extreme version forbids the killing of any living thing. This view was allegedly held by Pythagoras, and presently held by members of the Jain religion in India. (Those who think that such pacifists must soon starve to death should note that a life-sustaining diet can easily be constructed from milk, honey, fallen fruit and vegetables, and other items that are consumable without prior killing.) A less extreme view sanctions the killing of plants but forbids the killing of animals. The most moderate view prohibits only the killing of fellow beings.

There is deep appeal in an argument that connects the sacredness of life with the wrongfulness of taking life. Even people who are not pacifists are often revolted by the spectacle of killing, and most Americans would be unable to eat meat if they had to watch how the animals whose flesh they consume had been slaughtered, or if they had to do the slaughtering themselves. Most people sense that they do not own the world they inhabit and recognize that they are not free to do with the world as they will, that the things in it, most especially living things, are worthy of respect and care. Seemingly nothing could violate the respect living things deserve more than killing, especially since much of the taking of human and nonhuman life is so obviously unnecessary.

But with the introduction of the word "unnecessary" a paradox arises. Sometimes—less often that we think, but sometimes—the taking of some lives will save other lives. Does the principle that life is sacred and ought to be preserved imply that nothing should ever be killed, or does it imply that as much life should be preserved as possible? Obviously pacifists take the former view; nonpacifists, the latter.

The view that killing is wrong because it destroys what is sacred seems to imply that killing is wrong because killing diminishes the amount of good in the world. It seems to follow that if a person can save more lives by killing than by refusing to kill, arguments about the sacredness of life would not show that killing in these circumstances is wrong. (It might be wrong for other reasons.) The more lives saved, the greater the quantity of good in the world.

The difficulty that some killing might, on balance, save lives, is not the only problem for pacifism based on the sacredness of life. If preserving life is the highest value, a value not comparable with other, non-life-preserving goods, it follows that any acts which place life at risk are immoral. But many admirable actions have been undertaken in the face of death, and many less heroic but morally impeccable actions—driving on a road at moderate speed, authorizing a commercial flight to take off, and so forth—place life at risk. In cases of martyrdom in which

people choose death over religious conversion, life is just as much destroyed as it is in a common murder. Yet, on the whole, automobile drivers, air traffic controllers, and religious martyrs are not thought to be wicked. Likewise, people on life-sustaining machinery sometimes request that the machines be turned off, on the grounds that quality of life matters more than quantity of life. We may consider such people mistaken, but we hardly think that they are morally depraved.

In answering this objection, the pacifist may wish to distinguish between *killing other people* and *getting oneself killed,* arguing that only the former is immoral. But although there is a genuine distinction between killing and getting killed, the distinction does not entail that killing other people destroys life but getting oneself killed does not. If life is sacred, life, including one's own life, must be preserved at all cost. In many cases, people consider the price of preserving their own lives simply too high.

(c) The Right to Life

Some pacifists may try to avoid the difficulties of the "sacredness of life" view by arguing that the essential immorality of killing is that it violates the *right to life* that every human being possesses. If people have a right to life, then it is never morally permissible to kill some people in order to save others, since according to the usual interpretation of rights, it is never permissible to violate a right in order to secure some good.

A discussion of the logic of rights in general and the right to life in particular is beyond the scope of this book. But a number of students of this subject are prepared to argue that the possession of any right implies the permissibility of defending that right against aggression: if this were not so, what would be the point of asserting the existence of rights? But if the possession of a right to life implies the permissibility of defending that right against aggression—a defense that may require killing the aggressor—then the existence of a right to life cannot by itself imply the impermissiblity of killing. On this view, the right to life implies the right to self-defense, including violent self-defense. It does not imply pacifism.

3. UNIVERSAL PACIFISM

(a) Christian Pacifism

Universal pacifists are morally opposed to all violence, not just to killing. Many universal pacifists derive their views from the Christian Gospels. In the Sermon on the Mount, Christ taught:

> Ye have heard that it hath been said, An eye for an eye, a tooth for a tooth:
>
> But I say unto you, that ye resist not evil: but whosoever shall smite thee on the right cheek, turn to him the other also. . . .
>
> Ye have heard it said, thou shalt love thy neighbor, and hate thine enemy. But I say unto you, Love your enemies, bless them that curse you, do good to them that hate you. . . . that ye may be the children of your father which is in heaven: for he maketh the sun to rise on the evil and on the good, and sendeth the rain on the just and the unjust. (Matt, 5:38–45)

In the early centuries of the Christian era, it was widely assumed that to follow Christ and to obey His teaching meant that one should reject violence and refuse service in the Roman army. But by the fifth century, after the Roman Empire had become Christian and after barbarian Goths in 410 sacked Rome itself, Church Fathers debated whether Christ really intended that the Empire and its Church should remain undefended. The Church Fathers noticed passages in the Gospels that seem to contradict pacifism:

> Think not that I am come to send peace on earth: I came not to send peace, but a sword.
>
> For I am come to set a man at variance against his father, and the daughter against her mother, and the daughter-in-law against her mother-in-law. (Matt. 10:34–35)

And there are several instances in the Gospels (for instance, Matt. 8:5–10) in which Jesus encounters soldiers and does not rebuke them for engaging in an occupation that is essentially committed to violence. Rather, he argues, "Render unto Caesar the things which are Caesar's; and unto God the things that are God's" (Matt. 22:21). This would seem to include military service, or at least taxes to pay for the army.

A thorough analysis of whether the Gospels command pacifism is beyond the scope of this book. The passages in the Sermon on the Mount seem to be clearly pacifist; yet many eminent scholars have denied the pacifist message. A more interesting question, for philosophy, if not for biblical scholarship, is this: If Jesus did preach pacifism in the Sermon on the Mount, did He preach it as a *moral* doctrine?

Jesus did not view his teaching as replacing the moral law as he knew it:

> Think not that I am come to destroy the law, or the prophets: I am come not to destroy, but to fulfill. . . .
>
> Till heaven and earth pass, one jot or one tittle shall in no wise pass from the law, till all be fulfilled. (Matt. 5:17–18)

Perhaps, then, the prescriptions of the Sermon on the Mount should be interpreted as rules that one must obey in order to follow Christ, or rules that one must follow in order to obtain salvation. But it does not follow from this alone that everyone has an obligation to follow Christ, and it does not follow from this alone that everyone has an obligation to seek salvation. Even Christians will admit that some people have refused to become Christians and have led morally admirable lives nonetheless; and if salvation is a good, one can nevertheless choose to reject it, just as a citizen can neglect to hand in a winning lottery ticket without breaking the law. If so, the prescriptions of the Sermon on the Mount apply only to Christians seeking a Christian salvation. They are not universally binding rules and do not qualify as moral principles.

(b) The Moral Exemplar Argument

Many people and at least one illustrious philosopher, Immanuel Kant, believe that morally proper action consists in choosing to act in such a way that your conduct could serve as an example for all mankind. (It was Kant's genius to recognize that moral conduct is *essentially* exemplary.) Some universal pacifists appeal to this idea, arguing that if everyone were a pacifist, the world would be a much better place than it is now. This is an argument that Leo Tolstoy (1828–1910) used to support the Gospel prescription not to resist evil:

> [Christ] put the proposition of non-resistance to evil is such a way that, according to his teaching, it was to be the foundation of the joint life of men and was to free humanity from the evil that is inflicted on itself. (*My Religion*, Ch. 4) Instead of having the whole life based on violence and every joy obtained and guarded through violence; instead of seeing each one of us punished or inflicting punishment from childhood to old age, I imagined that we were all impressed in word and deed by the idea that vengeance is a very low, animal feeling; that violence is not only a disgraceful act, but also one that deprives man of true happiness. . . .
>
> I imagined that instead of those national hatreds which are impressed on us under the form of patriotism, instead of those glorifications of murder, called wars . . . that we were impressed with the idea that the recognition of any countries, special laws, borders, lands, is a sign of grossest ignorance. . . .
>
> Through the fulfillment of these commandments, the life of men will be what every human heart seeks and desires. All men will be brothers and everybody will always be at peace with others, enjoying all the benefits of the world. (*My Religion*, Ch. 6)

Few would deny that if everyone were a pacifist, the world would be a better place, perhaps even a paradise. Furthermore, since the argument is essentially hypothetical, it cannot be refuted (as many nonpacifists believe) by pointing out that not everyone will become a pacifist. The problem is whether this argument can establish pacifism as a moral imperative.

One difficulty with the argument is that it seems to rely on a premise the truth of which is purely verbal. In what way would the world be a

better place if people gave up fighting? The most obvious way is that the world would be better because there would be no war. But the statement "If everyone gave up fighting, there would be no war" is true by definition, since "war" implies "fighting." It is difficult to see how a statement that simply relates the meanings of words could tell us something about our moral obligations.

A deeper problem with Tolstoy's argument is that "resist not evil" is not the only rule that would yield paradise if everyone obeyed it. Suppose that everyone in the world subscribed to the principle "Use violence, but only in self-defense." If everyone used violence only in self-defense, the same consequences would follow as would arise from universal acceptance of the rule "Never use violence." Consequently, pacifism cannot be shown to be superior to nonpacifism by noting the good consequences that would undeniably ensue if everyone were a pacifist.

(c) Gandhian Pacifism

Certainly the most interesting and effective pacifist of the twentieth century was Mohandas Gandhi (1869–1948). Though a devout Hindu, Gandhi developed his doctrine of nonviolence from elementary metaphysical concepts that are by no means special to Hinduism:

> Man as an animal is violenspirit is nt but as onviolent. The moment he awakes to the spirit he cannot remain violent. Either he progresses towards *ahimsa* [nonviolence] or rushes to his doom. (*Nonviolence in Peace and War*, I, p. 311)

The requirement not to be violent seems wholly negative; sleeping people achieve it with ease. But for Gandhi the essential moral task is not merely to be nonviolent but to use the force of the soul (*satyagraha*, "truth grasping") in a continual struggle for justice. The methods of applied *satyagraha* developed by Gandhi—the weaponless marches, the sit-downs and sit-ins, strikes and boycotts, fasts and prayers—captured the admiration of the world and have been widely copied, most notably by Martin Luther King, Jr., in his campaigns against racial discrimination. According to Gandhi, each person, by engaging in *satyagraha* and experiencing suffering on behalf of justice, purifies the soul from pollution emanating from man's animal nature:

> A *satyagrahi* is dead to his body even before his enemy attempts to kill him, i.e. he is free from the attachments of his body and lives only in the victory of his soul. (*Nonviolence in Peace and War,* I, p. 318) Nonviolence implies as complete self-purification as is humanly possible. (*Nonviolence in Peace and War,* I, p. 111)

By acting nonviolently, pacifists not only purify their own souls but also transform the souls of their opponents: "A nonviolent revolution is not a program of seizure of power. It is a program of transformation of relationships, ending in peaceful transfer of power" (*Nonviolence in Peace and War,* II, p. 8)

Though in most places Gandhi emphasizes the personal redemption that is possible only through nonviolent resistance to evil, the spiritually positive effect of nonviolence on evil opponents is perhaps equally important, since "The soul of the *satagrahi* is love" (*Nonviolence in Peace and War,* II, p. 59).

Gandhi, then, is far from preaching the sacredness of biological life. What matters is not biological life but the condition of the soul, the natural and proper state of which is *ahimsa*. The evil of violence is that it distorts and disrupts this natural condition of the soul. The basic moral law (*dharma*) for all people is to seek the restoration of their souls to the harmony of *ahimsa*. This spiritual restoration cannot be achieved by violence, but only by the application of *satyagraha*. Disharmony cannot produce harmony; violence cannot produce spiritual peace.

The "sacredness of life" defense of pacifism ran into difficulties analyzing situations in which taking one life could save many lives. For Gandhi, this is no problem at all: taking one life may save many biological lives, but it will not save souls. On the contrary, the soul of the killer will be perverted by the act, and that perversion—not the loss of life—is what matters morally.

The system of values professed by Gandhi—that the highest human good is a harmonious condition of soul—must be kept in mind when considering the frequent accusation that Gandhi's method of nonviolent resistance "does not work," that nonviolence alone did not and could not force the British to leave India, and that nonviolent resistance to murderous tyrants like Hitler will only provoke the mass murder of the innocent. Perhaps the practice of nonviolence could not "defeat" the British or "defeat" Hitler, but by Gandhi's standard the use of military force would only produce a greater defeat, perverting the souls of thousands engaged in war and intensifying the will to violence on the opposing side. On the other hand, the soul of the *satyagrahi* will be strengthened and purified by nonviolent struggle against British imperialism or German Nazism, and in this purification the Gandhian pacifist can obtain spiritual victory even in the face of political defeat.

India did not adopt the creed of nonviolence after the British left in 1948, and it is hardly likely that any modern nation-state will organize its international affairs along Gandhian lines. But none of this affects the validity of Gandhi's arguments, which indicate how things ought to be, not how they are. We have seen that Gandhi's principles do not falter in the face of situations in which taking one life can save lives on balance. But what of situations in which the sacrifice of spiritual purity by one will prevent the corruption of many souls? Suppose, for example, that a Gandhian believes (on good evidence) that a well-timed commando raid will prevent a nation from embarking on an aggressive war, a war that would inflame whole populations with hatred for the enemy. Wouldn't a concern with one's own spiritual purity in such a situation show an immoral lack of concern for the souls of one's fellow men?

Another problem for Gandhi concerns the relationship between violence and coercion. To coerce people is to make them act against their will, for fear of the consequences they will suffer if they do not obey. Coercion, then, is a kind of spiritual violence, directed against the imagination and will of the victim. The "violence" most conspicuously rejected by Gandhi—pushing, shoving, striking with hands, the use of weapons, the placing of bombs and explosives—is essentially physical violence, directed against the bodies of opponents. But if physical violence against bodies is spiritually corrupting, psychological violence directed at the will of opponents must be even more corrupting.

In his writings Gandhi condemned coercion. Yet in practice he can hardly be said to have renounced *psychological* coercion. Obviously he would have preferred to have the British depart from India of their own free will, deciding that it was in their own best interest, or at least morally necessary, to leave. But if the British had decided, in the absence of coercion, to stay, Gandhi was prepared to exert every kind of nonviolent pressure to make them go. And when Gandhi on occasion attempted to achieve political objectives by a "fast unto death," his threat of self-starvation brought enormous psychological pressure on the authorities, who, among other things, feared the riots would ensue should Gandhi die.

The Gandhian pacifist, then, must explain why psychological pressure is permissible if physical pressure is forbidden. One possible answer is that physical pressure cannot transform the soul of the opponents, but psychological pressure, since it operates on the mind, can effect a spiritual transformation. Indeed, Gandhi characterized his terrifying fasts as acts of education, not coercion. But the claim that these fasts were not coercive confuses the noncoercive intention behind the act with its predictable coercive effects; and if education is the name of the game, the nonpacifists will remark that violence has been known to teach a few good lessons in its day. In many spiritual traditions, what matters essentially is not the kind of pressure but that the right pressure be applied at the right time and in the right way. Zen masters have brought students to enlightenment by clouting them on the ears,

and God helped St. Paul to see the light by knocking him off his horse.

In addition to these technical problems, many people will be inclined to reject the system of values from which Gandhi's deductions flow. Many will concede that good character is important and that helping others to develop moral virtues is an important task. But few agree with Gandhi that the development of moral purity is the supreme human good, and that other goods, like the preservation of human life, or progress in the arts and sciences, have little or no value in comparison. If even a little value is conceded to these other things, then on occasion it will be necessary to put aside the project of developing spiritual purity in order to preserve other values. These acts of preservation may require physical violence, and those who use violence to defend life or beauty or liberty may indeed be corrupting their souls. But it is hard to believe that an occasional and necessary act of violence on behalf of these values will totally and permanently corrupt the soul, and those who use violence judiciously may be right in thinking that the saving of life or beauty or liberty may be worth a small or temporary spiritual loss.

4. PRIVATE PACIFISM

Perhaps the rarest form of pacifist is the pacifist who renounces violence in personal relations but condones the use of force in the political sphere. Such a pacifist will not use violence for self-defense but believes that it is permissible for the state to use judicial force against criminals and military force against foreign enemies. A private pacifist renounces self-defense but supports national defense.

(a) Augustine's Limited Pacifism

Historically, private pacifism developed as an attempt to reconcile the demands of the Sermon on the Mount with the Christian duty to charity. The Sermon on the Mount requires Christians to "resist not evil"; the duty of charity requires pity for the weak who suffer the injustice of the strong. For St. Augustine (354–430), one essential message of the Gospels is the good news that this present life is as nothing compared with the life to come. The person who tries to hold on to earthly possessions is deluded as to what is truly valuable: "If any man will sue thee at the law, and take away thy coat, let him have thy cloak also" (Matt. 5:40). What goes for earthly coats should go for earthly life as well, so if any man seeks to take a Christian life, the Christian should let him have it. On this view, the doctrine "resist no evil" is just an expression of contempt for earthly possessions.

But according to Augustine there are some things in this world that do have value: justice, for example, the relief of suffering, and the preservation of the Church, which Augustine equated with civilization itself. To defend these things with necessary force is not to fall prey to delusions about the good. For Augustine, then, service in the armed forces is not inconsistent with Christian values.

One difficulty for theories like Augustine's is that they seem to justify military service only when military force is used in a just cause. Unfortunately, once in the service, the man in the ranks is not in a position to evaluate the justice of his nation's cause; indeed, in many modern nations, the principle of military subordination to civilian rule prevents even generals from evaluating the purposes of war declared by political leaders. But Augustine argues that the cause of justice cannot be served without armies, and armies cannot function unless subordinates follow orders without questioning the purposes of the conflict. The necessary conditions for justice and charity require that some men put themselves in positions in which they might be required to fight for injustice.

(b) The Problem of Self-Defense

Many will agree with Augustine that most violence at the personal level—the violence of crime, vendetta, and domestic brutality, for example— goes contrary to moral principles. But most are prepared to draw the line at personal and collective self-defense. Can the obligation to be charitable justify participation in military service but stop short of justifying the use of force by private citizens, if that force is exercised to protect the weak from the oppression of the strong? Furthermore, the obligation to be charitable does not exclude acts of charity toward oneself. For Augustine, violence was a dangerous tool, best kept out of the hands of the citizens and best left strictly at the disposal of the state. Beset with fears of crime in the streets, the contemporary American is less inclined to worry about the anarchic effects of private uses of defensive force and more inclined to worry about the protection the police seem unable to provide.

For these worried people, the existence of a right to self-defense is self-evident. But the existence of this right is not self-evident to universal or private pacifists; and it was not self-evident to St. Augustine. In the Christian tradition, no right to self-defense was recognized until its existence was certified by Thomas Aquinas in the thirteenth century. Aquinas derived the right to self-defense from the universal tendency to self-preservation, assuming (contrary to Augustine) that a natural tendency must be morally right. As for the Christian duty to love one's enemy, Aquinas argued that acts of self-defense have two effects—the saving of life and the taking of life—and that self-defensive uses of force intend primarily the saving of life. This makes the use of force in self-defense a morally permissible act of charity. The right to self-defense is now generally recognized in Catholic moral theology and in Western legal systems. But it can hardly be said that Aquinas's arguments, which rely heavily on assumptions from Greek philosophy, succeed in reconciling the claims of self-defense with the prescriptions of the Sermon on the Mount.

5. ANTIWAR PACIFISM

Most people who believe in the right to personal self-defense also believe that some wars are morally justified. In fact, the notion of self-defense and the notion of just war are commonly linked; just wars are said to be defensive wars, and the justice of defensive war is inferred from the right of personal self-defense, projected from the individual to the national level. But some people reject this projection: they endorse the validity of personal self-defense, but they deny that war can be justified by appeal to self-defense or any other right. On the contrary, they argue that war always involves an inexcusable violation of rights. For such anti-war pacifists, all participation in war is morally wrong.

The Killing of Soldiers

One universal and necessary feature of wars is that soldiers get killed in them. Most people accept such killings as a necessary evil, and judge the killing of soldiers in war to be morally acceptable. If the war is fought for the just cause, the killing of enemy soldiers is justified as necessary to the triumph of right. If the war is fought for an unjust cause, the killing of enemy soldiers is acceptable because it is considered an honorable thing to fight for one's country, right or wrong, provided that one fights well and cleanly. But the antiwar pacifist does not take the killing of soldiers for granted. Everyone has a right to life, and the killing of soldiers in war is intentional killing, a deliberate violation of the right to life. According to the standard interpretation of basic rights, it is never morally justifiable to violate a basic right in order to produce some good; the end, in such cases, does not justify the means. How, then, can the killing of soldiers in war be morally justified—or even excused?

Perhaps the commonest reply to the challenge of antiwar pacifism is that killing in war is a matter of self-defense, *personal* self-defense, the right to which is freely acknowledged by the antiwar pacifist. In war, the argument goes, it is either kill or be killed—and that type of killing is killing in self-defense. But though the appeal to self-defense is natural, antiwar pacifists believe that it is not successful. First of all, on the usual understanding of "self-defense," those who kill can claim the justification of self-defense only if (a) they had no other way to save their lives or

preserve themselves from physical harm except by killing, and (b) they did nothing to provoke the attack to which they are subjected. Antiwar pacifists point out that soldiers on the battlefield do have a way of saving themselves from death or harm without killing anyone: they can surrender. Furthermore, for soldiers fighting for an unjust cause—for example, German soldiers fighting in the invasion of Russia in 1941—it is difficult to argue that they "did nothing to provoke" the deadly force directed at them. But if the German army provoked the Russians to stand and fight on Russian soil, German soldiers cannot legitimately claim self-defense as a moral justification for killing Russian soldiers.

To the nonpacifist, these points might seem like legalistic quibbles. But the antiwar pacifist has an even stronger argument against killing soldiers in war. The vast majority of soldiers who die in war do not die in "kill or be killed" situations. They are killed by bullets, shells, or bombs directed from safe launching points—"safe" in the sense that those who shoot the bullets or fire the shells or drop the bombs are in no immediate danger of death. Since those who kill are not in immediate danger of death, they cannot invoke "self-defense" to justify the deaths they cause.

Some other argument besides self-defense, then, must explain why the killing of soldiers in war should not be classified as murder. Frequently, nonpacifists argue that the explanation is found in the doctrine of "assumption of risk," the idea, common in civil law, that persons who freely assume a risk have only themselves to blame if the risk is realized. When a soldier goes to war, he is well aware that one risk of his trade is getting killed on the battlefield. If he dies on the field, the responsibility for his death lies with himself, not with the man who shot him. By assuming the risk—so the argument goes—he waived his right to life, at least on the battlefield.

One does not have to be a pacifist to see difficulties in this argument. First of all, in all substantial modern wars, most of the men on the line are not volunteers, but draftees. Only a wealthy nation like the United States can afford an all-volunteer army, and most experts believe that the American volunteer ranks will have to be supplemented by draftees should the United States become involved in another conflict on the scale of Korea or Vietnam. Second, in many cases in which a risk is realized, responsibility for the bad outcome lies not with the person who assumed the risk but with the person who created it. If an arsonist sets fire to a house and a parent rushes in to save the children, dying in the rescue attempt, responsibility for the parent's death lies not with the parent who assumed the risk, but with the arsonist who created it. So if German armies invade Russia, posing the risk of death in battle, and if Russian soldiers assume this risk and fight back, the deaths of Russians are the fault of German invaders, not the fault of the defenders who assumed the risk.

These criticisms of German foot soldiers will irritate many who served in the armed forces and who know how little political and military decision making is left to the men on the front lines, who seem to be the special target of these pacifist arguments. But antiwar pacifists will deny that their aim is to condemn the men on the battlefield. Most antiwar pacifists feel that soldiers in war act under considerable compulsion and are excused for that reason from responsibility for the killing they do. But to say that battlefield killings are *excusable* is not to say that they are morally *justified*. On the contrary, if such killings are excusable, it must be that there is some immorality to be excused.

The Killing of Civilians

In the chronicles of ancient wars, conflict was total and loss in battle was frequently followed by general slaughter of men, women, and children on the losing side. It has always been considered part of the trend toward civilization to confine the destruction of war to the personnel and instruments of war, sparing civilians and their property as much as possible. This civilizing trend was conspicuously reversed in World War II, in which the ratio of civilian deaths to total war deaths was perhaps the highest it had

been since the wars of religion in the seventeenth century. A very high ratio of civilian deaths to total deaths was also characteristic of the war in Vietnam. Given the immense firepower of modern weapons and the great distances between the discharges of weapons and the explosions of bullets or shells near the targets, substantial civilian casualties are an inevitable part of modern land war. But it is immoral to kill civilians, the antiwar pacifist argues, and from this it follows that modern land warfare is necessarily immoral.

Few nonpacifists will argue that killing enemy civilians is justifiable when such killings are avoidable. Few will argue that killing enemy civilians is justifiable when such killings are the *primary* objective of a military operation. But what about the deaths of civilians that are the unavoidable results of military operations directed to some *other* result? The pacifist classifies such killings as immoral, whereas most nonpacifists call them regrettable but unavoidable deaths, not murders. But why are they not murder, if the civilians are innocent, and if it is known in advance that some civilians will be killed? Isn't this an intentional killing of the innocent, which is the traditional definition of murder?

The sophisticated nonpacifist may try to parry this thrust with analogies to policies outside the arena of war. There are, after all, many morally acceptable policies that, when adopted, have the effect of killing innocent persons. If the Congress decides to set a speed limit of 55 miles per hour on federal highways, more people will die than if Congress sets the speed limit at 45 miles per hour. Since many people who die on the highway are innocent, the Congress has chosen a policy that knowingly brings death to the innocent, but no one calls it murder. Or suppose, for example, that a public health officer is considering a national vaccination program to forestall a flu epidemic. He knows that if he does not implement the vaccination program, many people will die from the flu. On the other hand, if the program is implemented, a certain number of people will die of allergic reactions to the vaccine. Most of the people who die from allergic reactions will be people who would not have died of the flu if the vaccination program had not been implemented. So the vaccination program will kill innocent people who would otherwise be saved if the program were abandoned. If the public health officer implements such a program, we do *not* think that he is a murderer.

Nonpacifists argue that what makes the action of Congress and the action of the public health officer morally permissible in these cases is that the deaths of the innocent, although foreseen, are not the intended goal of these policies. Congress does not want people to die on the highways; every highway death is a regrettable death. The purpose of setting the speed limit at 55 miles per hour is not to kill people but to provide a reasonable balance between safety and convenience. Likewise, it is not the purpose of the public health officer to kill people by giving them vaccine. His goal is to save lives on balance, and every death from the vaccine is a regrettable death. Likewise, in war, when civilians are killed as a result of necessary military operations, the deaths of the civilians are not the intended goal of the military operation. They are foreseen, but they are always regretted. If we do not accuse Congress of murder and the Public Health Service of murder in these cases, consistency requires that we not accuse military forces of murder when they cause civilian deaths in war, especially if every attempt is made to keep civilian deaths to a minimum.

Antiwar pacifists do not condemn the Congress and the Public Health Service in cases like these. But they assert that the case of war is different in a morally relevant way. To demonstrate the difference, antiwar pacifists provide an entirely different analysis of the moral justification for speed limits and vaccination programs. In their opinion, the facts that highway deaths and vaccination deaths are "unintended" and "regretted" is morally irrelevant. The real justification lies in the factor of consent. In the case of federal highway regulations, the rules are decided by Congress, which is elected by the people, the same people who use the highways. If Congress decides on a 55-mile-an-hour limit, this is a regulation that, in some sense, highway drivers have imposed upon themselves. Those people who die on the highway because of a higher speed limit have, in a double sense, assumed the risks generated by that speed limit: they have, through the Congress, created the risk, and by venturing onto the highway, have freely exposed themselves to the risk. The responsibility for these highway deaths, then, lies either on the drivers themselves or on the people who crashed into them—not on the Congress.

Likewise, in the case of the vaccination program, if people are warned in advance of the risks of vaccination, and if they nevertheless choose to be vaccinated, they are responsible for their own deaths should the risks be realized. According to the antiwar pacifist, it is this consent given by drivers and vaccination volunteers that justifies these policies, and it is precisely this element of consent that is absent in the case of the risks inflicted on enemy civilians in time of war.

Consider the standard textbook example of allegedly justifiable killing of civilians in time of war. Suppose that the destruction of a certain bridge is an important military objective, but if the bridge is bombed, it is very likely that civilians living close by will be killed. (The civilians cannot be warned without alerting the enemy to reinforce the bridge.) If the bridge is bombed and some civilians are killed, the bombing victims are not in the same moral category as highway victims or victims of vaccination. The bombing victims did not order the bombing of themselves through some set of elected representatives. Nor did the bombing victims freely consent to the bombing of their bridge. Nor was the bombing in any way undertaken as a calculated risk in the interest of the victims. For all these reasons, the moral conclusions regarding highway legislation and vaccination programs do not carry over to bombing of the bridge.

Nonpacifists who recognize that it will be very difficult to fight wars without bombing bridges may argue that the victims of this bombing in some sense assumed the risks of bombardment by choosing to live close to a potential military target. Indeed, it is occasionally claimed that all the civilians in a nation at war have assumed the risks of war, since they could avoid the risks of war simply by moving to a neutral country. But such arguments are strained and uncharitable, even for those rare warring nations that permit freedom of emigration. Most people consider it a major sacrifice to give up their homes, and an option that requires such a sacrifice cannot be considered an option open for free choice. The analogy between the unintended victims of vaccination and the unintended civilian victims of war seems to have broken down.

(c) The Balance of Good and Evil in War

It is left to the nonpacifist to argue that the killing of soldiers and civilians in war is in the end justifiable in order to obtain great moral goods that can be obtained only by fighting for them. Civilians have rights to life, but those rights can be outweighed by the national objectives, provided those objectives are morally acceptable and overwhelmingly important. Admittedly, this argument for killing civilians is available only to the just side in a war, but if the argument is valid, it proves that there can *be* a just side, contrary to the arguments of antiwar pacifism.

Antiwar pacifists have two lines of defense. First, they can continue to maintain that the end does not justify the means, if the means be murderous. Second, they can, and will, go on to argue that it is a tragic mistake to believe that there are great moral goods that can be obtained only by war. According to antiwar pacifists, the amount of moral good produced by war is greatly exaggerated. The Mexican War, for example, resulted in half of Mexico being transferred to American rule. This was a great good for the United States, but not a great moral good, since the United States had little claim to the ceded territory, and no great injustice would have persisted if the war had not been fought at all.

The Revolutionary War in America is widely viewed as a war that produced a great moral good; but if the war had not been fought, the history of the United States would be similar to the history of Canada (which remained loyal)—and no one feels that the Canadians have suffered or are suffering great injustices that the American colonies avoided by war. Likewise, it is difficult to establish the goods produced by World War I or the moral losses that would have ensued if the winning side, "our side," had lost. Bertrand Russell imagined the results of a British loss in World War I as follows:

> The greatest sum that foreigners could possibly exact would be the total economic rent of the land and natural resources of England. [But] the working classes, the shopkeepers, manufacturers, and merchants, the literary men and men of science—all the people that make England of any account in the world—have at most an infinitesimal and accidental share in the rental of England. The men who have a share use their rents in luxury, political corruption, taking the lives of birds, and depopulating and enslaving the rural districts. It is this life of the idle rich that would be curtailed if the Germans exacted tribute from England. (*Justice in War Time*, pp. 48–49)

But multiplying examples of wars that did little moral good will not establish the pacifist case. The pacifist must show that *no* war has done enough good to justify the killing of soldiers and the killing of civilians that occurred in the war. A single war that produces moral goods sufficient to justify its killings will refute the pacifist claim that *all* wars are morally unjustifiable. Obviously this brings the antiwar pacifist head to head with World War II.

It is commonly estimated that 35 million people died as a result of World War II. It is difficult to imagine that any cause could justify so much death, but fortunately the Allies need only justify their share of these killings. Between 1939 and

1945 Allied forces killed about 5.5 million Axis soldiers and about 1 million civilians in Axis countries. Suppose that Britain and the United States had chosen to stay out of World War II and suppose Stalin had, like Lenin, surrendered to Germany shortly after the invasion. Does avoiding the world that would have resulted from these decisions justify killing 6.5 million people?

If Hitler and Tojo had won the war, doubtless they would have killed a great many people both before and after victory, but it is quite likely that the total of *additional* victims, beyond those they killed in the war that *was* fought, would have been less than 6.5 million and, at any rate, the responsibility for those deaths would fall on Hitler and Tojo, not on Allied nations. If Hitler and Tojo had won the war, large portions of the world would have fallen under foreign domination, perhaps for a very long time. But the antiwar pacifist will point out that the main areas of Axis foreign domination—China and Russia—were not places in which the citizens enjoyed a high level of freedom *before the war began*. Perhaps the majority of people in the conquered areas would have worked out a *modus vivendi* with their new rulers, as did the majority of French citizens during the German occupation. Nor can it be argued that World War II was necessary to save six million Jews from annihilation in the Holocaust, since in fact the war did *not* save them.

The ultimate aims of Axis leaders are a matter for historical debate. Clearly the Japanese had no intention of conquering the United States, and some historians suggest that Hitler hoped to avoid war with England and America, declaring war with England reluctantly, and only after the English declared it against him. Nevertheless, popular opinion holds that Hitler intended to conquer the world, and if preventing the conquest of Russia and China could not justify six and one-half million killings, most Americans are quite confident that preventing the conquest of England and the United States does justify killing on this scale.

The antiwar pacifist disagrees. Certainly German rule of England and the United States would have been a very bad thing. At the same time, hatred of such German rule would be particularly fueled by hatred of foreigners, and hatred of foreigners, as such, is an irrational and morally unjustifiable passion. After all, if rule by foreigners were, by itself, a great moral wrong, the British, with their great colonial empire, could hardly consider themselves the morally superior side in World War II.

No one denies that a Nazi victory in World War II would have had morally frightful results. But, according to antiwar pacifism, killing six and one-half million people is also morally frightful, and preventing one moral wrong does not obviously outweigh committing the other. Very few people today share the pacifists' condemnation of World War II, but perhaps that is because the dead killed by the Allies cannot speak up and make sure that their losses are properly counted on the moral scales. Antiwar pacifists speak on behalf of the enemy dead, and on behalf of all those millions who would have lived if the war had not been fought. On this silent constituency they rest their moral case.

Review Questions

1. Characterize universal pacifists (there are two types), private pacifists, and antiwar pacifists.
2. Why doesn't Lackey accept the appeal to the Bible, or the sacredness of life, or the right to life as a good reason for accepting pacifism?
3. What is Christian pacifism and Tolstoy's argument used to defend it? Why doesn't Lackey accept Tolstoy's argument?
4. Explain Gandhi's pacifism, including *satyagraha*. What problems does Lackey raise for this view?

5. Explain Augustine's so-called limited pacifism. What problems does this view have according to Lackey?
6. State the position of antiwar pacifism. Why do antiwar pacifists believe that all wars are wrong? According to Lackey, what are the objections to antiwar pacifism, and how can antiwar pacifists reply?

Discussion Questions

1. Is Gandhi's view a defensible one? Why or why not?
2. Does the antiwar pacifist have a good reply to all the objections Lackey discusses? Are there any good objections that he does not discuss?
3. Many people think that World War II was morally justified. What does the antiwar pacifist say? What do you think?
4. According to Lackey, no great moral good was produced by the Revolutionary War in America. If America had lost this war and remained under British rule, then its history would be like that of Canada—and Canada has not suffered, he says. Do you agree? Explain your answer.

The Conduct of Just and Limited War

WILLIAM V. O'BRIEN

William V. O'Brien is professor of government at Georgetown University, Washington, D.C. He is the author of *War and/or Survival* (1969), *Nuclear War, Deterrence and Morality* (1967), *The Nuclear Dilemma and the Just War Tradition* (1986), and *Law and Morality in Israel's War with the PLO* (1991). Our reading is taken from *The Conduct of Just and Limited War* (1981).

O'Brien divides just war theory into two parts. The first, *jus ad bellum,* states conditions that should be met for a state to have the right to go to war. The second, *jus in bello,* gives principles limiting conduct in war. There are three main conditions of *jus ad bellum:* The war must be declared by a competent authority for a public purpose; there must be a just cause; and there must be a right intention that aims at peace. The condition of just cause is subdivided into four more conditions: the substance of the cause (e.g., self-defense), the form of the cause (defensive or offensive), the requirement of proportionality (the good achieved by war must be proportionate to the evil of war), and peaceful means of avoiding war must be exhausted.

Source: William V. O'Brien, *The Conduct of Just and Limited War.* Copyright © 1981 by Praeger Publishers, an imprint of Greenwood Publishing Group, Inc. Reprinted with permission of Greenwood Publishing Group, Inc., Westport, CT.

The *jus in bello* has two principles limiting conduct in war. The principle of proportion requires that the discrete military means and ends be balanced. The principle of discrimination prohibits the intentional attacks on noncombatants and nonmilitary targets.

THE ORIGINAL JUST-WAR doctrine of St. Augustine, St. Thomas, and other Scholastics emphasized the conditions for permissible recourse to war—the *jus ad bellum*. To this doctrine was added another branch of prescriptions regulating the conduct of war, the *jus in bello*. . . .

The *jus ad bellum* lays down conditions that must be met in order to have permissible recourse to armed coercion. They are conditions that should be viewed in the light of the fundamental tenet of just-war doctrine: the presumption is always against war. The taking of human life is not permitted to man unless there are exceptional justifications. Just-war doctrine provides those justifications, but they are in the nature of special pleadings to overcome the presumption against killing. The decision to invoke the exceptional rights of war must be based on the following criteria: there must be competent authority to order the war for a public purpose; there must be a just cause (it may be self-defense or the protection of rights by offensive war) and the means must be proportionate to the just cause and all peaceful alternatives must have been exhausted; and there must be right intention on the part of the just belligerent. Let us examine these criteria.

Insofar as large-scale, conventional war is concerned, the issue of competent authority is different in modern times than it was in the thirteenth century. The decentralized political system wherein public, private, and criminal violence overlapped, as well as the state of military art and science, permitted a variety of private wars. So it was important to insist that war—in which individuals would be called upon to take human lives—must be waged on the order of public authorities for public purposes. This is not a serious problem in most parts of the world today. Only states have the material capacity to wage large-scale, modern, conventional war. Two other problems do, however, exist in connection with the conditions of competent authority. First, there may be disputes as to the constitutional competence of a particular official or organ of state to initiate war. Second, civil war and revolutionary terrorism are frequently initiated by persons and organizations claiming revolutionary rights.

Most states today, even totalitarian states, have specific constitutional provisions for the declaration and termination of war. If an official or state organ violates these provisions, there may not be a valid exercise of the sovereign right to declare and wage war. In such a case the first condition of the just war might not be met. This was the charge, implicitly or explicitly, against President Johnson in the Vietnam War. Johnson never requested a declaration of war from Congress with which he shared war-making powers. War critics asserted that the undeclared war was illegal. A sufficient answer to this charge is to be found in congressional cooperation in the war effort and in the refusal of the courts to declare the war unconstitutional. . . . At this point it is sufficient to raise the issue as illustrative of the problem of competent authority within a constitutional state.

In this connection a word should be said about declaring wars. Any examination of modern wars will show that the importance of a declaration of war has diminished greatly in international practice. Because of the split-second timing of modern war, it is often undesirable to warn the enemy by way of a formal declaration. Defense measures are geared to react to hostile behavior, not declarations. When war is declared it is often an announcement confirming a condition that has already been established. Nevertheless, if a particular state's constitution does require a formal declaration of war and one is not forthcoming, the issue of competence is raised. If a public official exceeds his authority in mobilizing the people and conducting war, there is a lack of competent authority.

The second problem, however, is by far the greatest. Today, rights of revolution are frequently invoked by organizations and individuals. They clearly do not have the authority and capacity to wage war in the conventional sense. However, they do wage revolutionary war, often on an international scale. Indeed, international terrorism is one of the most pervasive and difficult problems facing the international community.

All major ideologies and blocs or alignments of states in the international system recognize the right of revolution. Usually their interpretations will emphasize the rights of revolution against others, not themselves. . . . Logically, there should be an elaborate *jus ad bellem* and *jus in bello* for revolutionary war, but development of such a doctrine has never been seriously attempted. As a result, the issues of revolutionary war tend to be treated on an ad hoc basis as special cases vaguely related to the regular categories of just war. . . .

The differences between conventional war waged by states and revolutionary war waged by rebels against states are profound. Given the formidable power of most modern governments, particularly in regard to their comparative monopoly of armed force, revolutionary rights can be asserted mainly by covert organizations waging guerrilla warfare and terrorism. The option of organizing a portion of a state and fighting a conventional civil war in the manner of the American, Spanish, or Nigerian civil wars is seldom available.

The covert, secret character of modern revolutionary movements is such that it is often hard to judge their claims to qualify as the competent authority for oppressed people. There is a decided tendency to follow the Leninist model of revolutionary leadership wherein the self-selected revolutionary elite decides on the just revolutionary cause, the means, and the circum-

stances of taking the initiative, all done in the name of the people and revolutionary justice. As a revolution progresses, the task of certifying competent authority continues to be difficult. Support for the revolutionary leadership is often coerced or given under conditions where there is not popular acceptance of the revolutionary authority of that leadership or its ends and means. Recognition by foreign powers of belligerency—or even of putative governmental powers—is an unreliable guide given subjective, politicized recognition policies.

To complicate matters, individuals and small groups take up revolutionary war tactics, principally terrorism in the form of airplane hijacking, hostage kidnapping, assassination, and indiscriminate bombing attacks. These acts are performed in the name of greatly varying causes, some of which could not be considered revolutionary. Sometimes the alleged justifications are political or ideological, but, on investigation, the real motivation turns out to be personal and criminal. Since most revolutionary movements manifest themselves in behavior difficult to distinguish from that of cranks and criminals, the task of sorting out revolutionaries entitled to acceptance as competent authorities is excruciating.

Two issues need to be resolved concerning revolutionary activity. First, insofar as treating revolutionaries as belligerents in a war and not as common criminals is concerned, the ultimate answer lies in the character, magnitude, and degree of success of the revolutionaries. If they can organize a government that carries on their war in a controlled fashion (assuming a magnitude requiring countermeasures that more resemble war than ordinary police operations), and if the conflict continues for an appreciable time, the revolutionaries may have won their right to be considered a competent authority for purposes of just war. Beyond this enumeration of criteria it seems unprofitable to generalize.

Second, concerning the authority of rebel leaders to mobilize the people by ordering or coercing individuals to fight for the revolutionary cause, the conscience of the individual takes precedence. Lacking any color of authority to govern, the rebels cannot of right compel participation in their cause. Needless to say, they will very probably compel participation by intimidation.

JUST CAUSE

. . . Authorities vary in their presentation of just cause, but it seems to break down into four subdivisions: the substance of the just cause, the forms of pursuing just cause, the requirement of proportionality of ends and means, and the requirement of exhaustion of peaceful remedies.

The substance of the just cause must, in Childress's formulation, be sufficiently "serious and weighty" to overcome the presumption of killing in general and war in particular. In Childress's approach, with which I am in essential agreement, this means that there must be a "competing prima facie duty or obligation" to "the prima facie obligation not to injure or kill others."[1] Childress mentions as "serious and weighty" prima facie obligations the following: (1) "to protect the innocent from unjust attack," (2) "to restore rights wrongfully denied," (3) "to reestablish a just order."

This is an adequate basis, reflective of the older just-war literature, for discussing the substance of just cause. Indeed, Childress is more explicit than many modern commentators who simply state that there should be a just cause. Still, it is only a beginning. It is unfortunate that modern moralists have generally been so concerned with the issue of putatively disproportionate means of modern war that they have neglected the prior question of the ends for which these means might have to be used (that is, just cause). In practical terms, this task of evaluating the substance of just cause leads inescapably to a comparative analysis of the characteristics of the polities or political-social systems posed in warlike confrontation. . . .

1 James F. Childress, "Just War Theories," *Theological Studies* vol. 39 (1978), pp. 428–435.

Even more difficult for those who would answer in the affirmative is the question whether the United States should intervene to protect a manifestly imperfect political-social order (South Korea, South Vietnam or, perhaps, that of a state such as Jordan, Saudi Arabia, or Pakistan). . . .

By comparison, the substantive just causes of the older just-war literature are almost insignificant. In the modern world the just cause often has to do with the survival of a way of life. Claims that this is so can be false or exaggerated, but they are often all too legitimate. They must be taken seriously in assessing the substance of just cause in modern just-war analyses.

However, passing the test of just cause is not solely a matter of positing an end that is convincingly just, although that is the indispensable starting point. It is also necessary to meet the tests posed by the other three subdivisions of just cause.

The forms of pursuing just cause are defensive and offensive wars. The justice of self-defense is generally considered to be axiomatic. Just-war doctrine, following Aristotle and St. Thomas as well as the later Scholastics, places great importance on the state as a natural institution essential for man's development. Defense of the state is prima facie of an essential social institution. So strong is the presumption in favor of the right of self-defense that the requirement of probable success, to be discussed under proportionality, is usually waived.

Offensive wars raise more complications. In classical just-war doctrine, offensive wars were permitted to protect vital rights unjustly threatened or injured. Moreover, in a form now archaic, offensive wars of vindictive justice against infidels and heretics were once permitted. Such wars disappeared with the decline of the religious, holy-war element as a cause of the rationale for wars. Thus, the forms of permissible wars today are twofold: wars of self-defense and offensive wars to enforce justice for oneself. As will be seen, even the second is now seemingly prohibited by positive international law. But in terms of basic just-war theory it remains an option. A war of vindictive justice wherein the belligerent fights against error and evil as a matter of principle and not of necessity is no longer condoned by just-war doctrine. . . .

Turning from the forms of just war we come to the heart of just cause—proportionality between the just ends and the means. This concerns the relationship between *raison d'état* (the high interests of state) and the use of the military instrument in war as the means to achieve these interests. This concept of proportionality at the level of *raison d'état* is multidimensional. To begin with, the ends held out as the just cause must be sufficiently good and important to warrant the extreme means of war, the arbitrament of arms. Beyond that, a projection of the outcome of the war is required in which the probable good expected to result from success is weighed against the probable evil that the war will cause.

The process of weighing probable good against probable evil is extremely complex. The balance sheet of good and evil must be estimated for each belligerent. Additionally, there should be a balancing of effects on individual third parties and on the international common good. International interdependence means that international conflicts are difficult to contain and that their shock waves affect third parties in a manner that must be accounted for in the calculus of probable good and evil. Moreover, the international community as such has its international common good, which is necessarily affected by any war. Manifestly, the task of performing this calculus effectively is an awesome one. But even its successful completion does not fully satisfy the demands of the just-war condition of just cause. Probing even further, the doctrine requires a responsible judgment that there is a probability of success for the just party. All of these calculations must be concluded convincingly to meet the multidimensional requirement of just cause.

Moreover, the calculus of proportionality between probable good and evil in a war is a continuing one. It should be made before the decision to go to war. It must then be reviewed at critical points along the process of waging the war. The best informed estimates about wars are often in error. They may need revision or replacement by completely new estimates. The *jus ad bellum* requirement of proportionality, then, includes these requirements:

There must be a just cause of sufficient importance to warrant its defense by recourse to armed coercion.

The probable good to be achieved by successful recourse to armed coercion in pursuit of the just cause must outweigh the probable evil that the war will produce.

The calculation of proportionality between probable good and evil must be made with respect to all belligerents, affected neutrals, and the international community as a whole before initiating a war and periodically throughout a war to reevaluate the balance of good and evil that is actually produced by war.

These calculations must be made in the light of realistic estimates of the probability of success. . . .

There is an important qualification to the requirement of probability of success. A war of self-defense may be engaged in irrespective of the prospects for success, particularly if there is a great threat to continued existence and to fundamental values. . . .

The last component of the condition of just cause is that war be employed only as a last resort after the exhaustion of peaceful alternatives. To have legitimate recourse to war, it must be the ultima ratio, the arbitrament of arms. This requirement has taken on added significance in the League of Nations–United Nations period. It was the intention of the nations that founded these international organizations to create the machinery for peace that would replace self-help in the form of recourse to war and limit the need for collective security enforcement action to extreme cases of defiance of international law and order. There are certainly adequate institutions of international negotiations, mediation, arbitration, and adjudication to accommodate any nation willing to submit its international disputes to peaceful settlement. Indeed, the existence of this machinery for peaceful settlement has prompted international lawyers and statesmen to adopt a rough rule of thumb: the state that fails to exhaust the peaceful remedies available before resorting to war is prima facie an aggressor. . . .

RIGHT INTENTION

Among the elements of the concept of right intention, several points may be distinguished. First, right intention limits the belligerent to the pursuit of the avowed just cause. That pursuit may not be turned into an excuse to pursue other causes that might not meet the conditions of just cause. Thus, if the just cause is to defend a nation's borders and protect them from future aggressions, but the fortunes of war place the just belligerent in the position to conquer the unjust nation, such a conquest might show a lack of right intention and change the just war into an unjust war. The just cause would have been realized by a war of limited objectives rather than a war of total conquest.

Second, right intention requires that the just belligerent have always in mind as the ultimate object of the war a just and lasting peace. There is an implicit requirement to prepare for reconciliation even as one wages war. This is a hard saying. It will often go against the grain of the belligerents' disposition, but pursuit of a just and lasting peace is an essential characteristic of the difference between just and unjust war. Accordingly, any belligerent acts that unnecessarily increase the destruction and bitterness of war and thereby endanger the prospects for true peace are liable to condemnation as violations of the condition of right intention.

Third, underlying the other requirements, right intention insists that charity and love exist even among enemies. Enemies must be treated as human beings with rights. The thrust of this requirement is twofold. Externally, belligerents must act with charity toward their enemies. Internally, belligerents must suppress natural animosity and hatred, which can be sinful and injurious to the moral and psychological health of those who fail in charity. Gratuitous cruelty may be harmful to those who indulge in it as to their victims.

Right intention raises difficult moral and psychological problems. It may well be that its tenets set standards that will often be unattainable insofar as the thoughts and feelings of belligerents are concerned. War often treats individuals and nations so cruelly and unfairly that it is unrealistic to expect them to banish all hatred of those who have afflicted them. We can, however, more reasonably insist that just belligerents may not translate their strong feelings into behavior that is prohibited by the rule of right intention. A nation may feel tempted to impose a Carthaginian peace, but it may not exceed just cause by giving in to that temptation. A nation must have good reason for feeling that the enemy deserves the full force of all means available, but the requirement to build for a just and lasting peace prohibits this kind of vengeance. The enemy may have behaved abominably, engendering righteous indignation amounting to hatred, but the actions of the just belligerent must be based on charity.

Lest this appear to be so utterly idealistic as to warrant dismissal as irrelevant to the real world, let it be recalled that the greatest enemies of the modern era have often been brought around in the cyclical processes of international policies to become trusted allies against former friends who are now viewed with fear and distrust. If war is to be an instrument of policy and not, in St. Augustine's words, a "vendetta," right intention is a counsel of good policy as well as of morality. . . .

THE *JUS IN BELLO*

In the *jus in bello* that emerged rather late in the development of just-war doctrine, two basic limitations on the conduct of war were laid down. One was the principle of proportion requiring proportionality of military means to political and military ends. The other was the principle of discrimination prohibiting direct, intentional attacks on noncombatants and nonmilitary targets. These are the two categories of *jus in bello* limitations generally treated by modern workers on just war. . . .

The Principle of Proportion

In the preceding [discussion] the principle of proportion was discussed at the level of *raison d'état*. One of the criteria of just-war *jus ad bellum* requires that the good to be achieved by the realization of the war aims be proportionate to the evil resulting from the war. When the principle of proportion is again raised in the *jus in bello,* the question immediately arises as to the referent of proportionality in judging the means of war. Are the means to be judged in relation to the end of the war, the ends being formulated in the highest *raison d'état* terms? Or are intermediate political/military goals, referred to in the law-of-war literature as *raison de guerre,* the more appropriate referents in the calculus of proportionality as regards the conduct of a war?

There is no question that the ultimate justification for all means in war lies in the just cause that is a political purpose, *raison d'état*. But there are difficulties in making the ends of *raison d'état* the sole referent in the *jus in bello* calculus of proportionality. First, relation of all means to the highest ends of the war gives little rationale for or justification of discrete military means. If all means are simply lumped together as allegedly necessary for the war effort, one has to accept or reject them wholly in terms of the just cause, leaving no morality of means. The calculus of proportionality in just cause is the total good to be expected if the war is successful balanced against the total evil the war is likely to cause.

Second, it is evident that a discrete military means could, when viewed independently on the basis of its intermediary military end (*raison de guerre*), be proportionate or disproportionate to that military end for which it was used, irrespective of the ultimate end of the war at the level of *raison d'état*. If such a discrete military means were proportionate in terms of its military end, it would be a legitimate belligerent act. If it were disproportionate to the military end, it would be immoral and legally impermissible. Thus, an act could be proportionate or disproportionate to a legitimate military end regardless of the legitimacy of the just-cause end of *raison d'état*.

Third, there is the need to be realistic and fair in evaluating individual command responsibility for belligerent acts. The need to distinguish higher political ends from intermediate military ends was acute in the war-crimes trial after World War II. It is the law of Nuremberg, generally accepted in international law, that the *raison d'état* ends of Nazi Germany were illegal aggression. But the Nuremberg and other war-crimes tribunals rejected the argument that all military actions taken by the German armed forces were war crimes per se because they were carried out in pursuance of aggressive war. The legitimacy of discrete acts of German forces was judged, inter alai, in terms of their proportionality to intermediate military goals, *raison de guerre*. This was a matter of justice to military commanders accused of war crimes. It was also a reasonable way to evaluate the substance of the allegations that war crimes had occurred.

The distinction is equally important when applied to a just belligerent. Assuming that in World War II the Allied forces were fighting a just war, it is clear that some of the means they employed may have been unjust (for example, strategic bombing of cities and the two atomic bomb attacks). It is not difficult to assimilate these controversial means into the total Allied war effort and pronounce that total effort proportionate to the just cause of the war. It is much more difficult and quite a different calculation to justify these means as proportionate to discrete military ends. Even in the absence of war-crimes proceedings, a just belligerent ought to respect the *jus in bello* standards by meeting the requirement of proportionality of means to military ends.

To be sure, it is ultimately necessary to transcend concern for the responsibility of individual military commanders and look at the objective permissibility of a military means. Thus, it may be possible and necessary to absolve a commander from responsibility for an action taken that is judged to have been disproportionate but that appeared to him to be a proportionate, reasonable military action in the light of his imperfect estimate of the situation. . . .

It would appear that analyses of the proportionality of military means will have to take a twofold form. First, any military means must be proportionate to discrete, legitimate military end. Second, military means proportionate to discrete, legitimate military ends must also be proportionate to the object of the war, the just cause. In judging the moral and legal responsibility of a military commander, emphasis should be placed on the proportionality of the means to a legitimate military end. In judging the ultimate normative permissibility, as well as the prudential advisability, of a means at the level of *raison d'état,* the calculation should emphasize proportionality to the just cause.

The focus of normative analysis with respect to a means of war will depend on the place of the means in the total pattern of belligerent interaction. Means may be divided roughly according to the traditional distinction between tactical and strategic levels of war. Tactical means will normally be judged in terms of their proportionality to tactical military ends (for example, the tactics of attacking or defending a fortified population center will normally be judged in terms of their proportionality to the military end of taking or holding the center). Strategic means will normally be judged in terms of their proportionality to the political/military goals of the war (for example, the strategy of attacking Japanese cities, first conventionally and then with atomic bombs, in order to force the surrender of Japan will be judged in terms of its proportionality to the just cause of war).

It remains clear, however, that the two levels overlap. A number of tactical decisions regarding battles for population centers may produce an overall strategic pattern that ought to enter into the highest calculation of the proportionality of a just war. The strategic decisions, on the other hand, have necessary tactical implications (for example, strategic conventional and atomic bombing of Japan was an alternative to an amphibious invasion) the conduct of which is essentially a tactical matter. The potential costs of such a tactical invasion strongly influenced the strategic choice to seek Japan's defeat by strategic bombing rather than ground conquest.

Insofar as judgment of proportionality in terms of military ends is concerned, there is a central concept appearing in all normative analyses of human behavior—the norm of reasonableness. Reasonableness must always be defined in specific context. However, sometimes patterns of behavior recur so that there are typical situations for which common models of reasonable behavior may be prescribed. In domestic law this norm is concretized through the device of the hypothetically reasonable man whose conduct sets the standard to be emulated by law-abiding persons. The reasonable commander is the counterpart of the reasonable man in the law of war. The construct of the reasonable commander is based upon the experience of military men in dealing with basic military problems.

Formulation of this experience into the kinds of working guidelines that domestic law provides, notable in the field of torts, has not advanced very far. . . . We do, however, have some instances in which this approach was followed. For example, the U.S. military tribunal in the *Hostage* case found that certain retaliatory means used in the German military in occupied Europe in World War II were reasonable in view of the threat to the belligerent occupant posed by guerrilla operations and their support by the civilian population. On the other hand, in the *Calley* case a court comprised of experienced combat officers found that Lieutenant Calley's response to the situation in My Lai was altogether unreasonable, below the standard of reasonableness expected in combat in Vietnam.[2]

---

2 [For a description of the My Lai Massacre, see the Problem Cases.]

The difficulty with establishing the standards of reasonableness lies in the absence of authoritative decisions that can be widely disseminated for mandatory emulation. In a domestic public order such as the United States, the legislature and the courts set standards for reasonable behavior. While the standards have supporting rationales, their greater strength lies in the fact that they are laid down by authority and must be obeyed. With the very rare exception of some of the post–World War II war-crimes cases, authoritative standards for belligerent conduct are found primarily in general conventional and customary international-law prescriptions. . . .

The Principle of Discrimination

The principle of discrimination prohibits direct intentional attacks on noncombatants and nonmilitary targets. It holds out the potential for very great, specific limitations on the conduct of just war. Accordingly, debates over the meaning of the *principle of discrimination* have become increasingly complex and important as the character of war has become more total. It is in the nature of the principle of proportion to be elastic and to offer possibilities for justifications of means that are truly necessary for efficacious military action. However, it is in the nature of the principle of discrimination to remain rigidly opposed to various categories of means irrespective of their necessity to success in war. It is not surprising, then, that most debates about the morality of modern war have focused on the principle of discrimination.

Such debates are vastly complicated by the opportunities afforded in the defiance of the principle of discrimination to expand or contract it by interpretations of its component elements. There are debates over the meaning of *direct intentional attack, noncombatants,* and *military targets.*

In order to discuss the problem of interpreting the principle of discrimination, it is necessary to understand the origins of the principle. The most fundamental aspect of the principle of discrimination lies in its direct relation to the justification for killing in war. If the presumption

against killing generally and war in particular is overcome (in the case of war by meeting the just-war conditions), the killing then permitted is limited to the enemy combatants, the aggressors. The exceptional right to take life in individual self-defense and in war is limited to the attacker in the individual case and the enemy's soldiers in the case of war. One may not attack innocent third parties as part of individual self-defense. In war the only permissible objects of direct attack are the enemy's soldiers. In both cases, the overriding moral prescription is that evil must not be done to obtain a good object. As will be seen, however, the literal application of the principle of discrimination tends to conflict with the characteristics of efficacious military action necessary to make the right of just war effective and meaningful.

However, it is important to recognize that the principle of discrimination did not find its historical origins solely or even primarily in the fundamental argument summarized above. As a matter of fact, the principle seems to have owed at least as much to codes of chivalry and to the subsequent development of positive customary laws of war. These chivalric codes and customary practices were grounded in the material characteristics of warfare during the medieval and Renaissance periods. During much of that time, the key to the conduct of war was combat between mounted knights and supporting infantry. Generally speaking, there was no military utility in attacking anyone other than the enemy knights and their armed retainers. Attacks on unarmed civilians, particularly women and children, would have been considered unchivalric, contrary to the customary law of war, and militarily gratuitous.

These multiple bases for noncombatant immunity were fortified by the growth of positive international law after the seventeenth century. In what came to be known as the Rousseau-Portalis Doctrine, war was conceived as being limited to what we could call today "counterforce warfare." Armies fought each other like athletic teams designated to represent national banners. The noncombatants were spectators to these struggles and, unless they had the bad fortune to find themselves directly on the battlefield, immune in principle from military attack. Attacks on noncombatants and nonmilitary targets were now prohibited by a rule of positive international law. Here again, the principle of discrimination was grounded in material facts, the state of the art and the limited nature of the conflicts, that continued to make possible its application. Moreover, the political philosophy of the time encouraged a separation of public armed forces and the populations they represented. All of these military and political supports for discrimination were to change with the advent of modern war.

At this point it is necessary to clarify the status of the principle of discrimination in just-war doctrine as interpreted in this chapter. It is often contended that there is an absolute principle of discrimination prohibiting any use of means that kill noncombatants. It is further contended that this absolute principle constitutes the central limitation of just war and that it is based on an immutable moral imperative that may never be broken no matter how just the cause. This is the moral axiom mentioned above, that evil may never be done in order to produce a good result. In this formulation, killing noncombatants intentionally is always an inadmissible evil.

These contentions have produced two principal reactions. The first is pacifism. Pacifists rightly argue that war inevitably involves violation of the absolute principle of discrimination. If that principle is unconditionally binding, a just war is difficult if not impossible to envisage. The second reaction to the claims of an absolute principle of discrimination is to modify the principle by some form of the principle of double effect whereby the counterforce component of a military means is held to represent the intent of the belligerent, whereas the countervalue, indiscriminate component of that means is explained as a tolerable, concomitant, unintended effect—collateral damage in contemporary strategic terms.

Paul Ramsey is unquestionably the most authoritative proponent of an absolute principle of discrimination as the cornerstone of just-war *jus in bello*. No one has tried more courageously to reconcile this absolute principle with the exigencies of modern war and deterrence. [But] neither Ramsey nor anyone else can reconcile the principle of discrimination in an absolute sense with the strategic countervalue nuclear warfare that is threatened in contemporary deterrence. It is possible that Ramsey's version of discrimination could survive the pressures of military necessity at levels below that of strategic nuclear deterrence and war. But the fate of Ramsey's effort to reconcile an absolute moral principle of discrimination with the characteristics of modern war should indicate the grave difficulties inherent in this effort. . . .

The question then arises whether such heroic efforts to salvage an absolute principle of discrimination are necessary. As observed above, the principle of discrimination does not appear in the just-war *jus in bello* as a doctrinally established deduction from theological or philosophical first principles. Rather, it was historically the product of belligerent practice reflecting a mixture of moral and cultural values of earlier societies. Moreover, it is significant that in the considerable body of contemporary Catholic social teaching on war, embracing the pronouncements of Pope Pius XII and his successors and of Vatican II, the principle of discrimination is not prominent in any form, absolute or conditional. When weapons systems or forms of warfare are condemned, deplored, or reluctantly condoned, the rationales are so generalized that the judgments appear to be based on a mixed application of the principles of proportion and discrimination. If anything, these pronouncements seem more concerned with disproportionate rather than indiscriminate effects.

It is a curious kind of supreme, absolute principle of the just-war doctrine that slips almost imperceptibly into the evolving formulations of the authoritative texts and then is omitted as an explicit controlling rationale in contemporary judgments by the church framed in just-war terms. Moreover, the persistent reiteration by the contemporary church that legitimate self-defense is still morally permissible should imply that such defense is practically feasible; otherwise the recognition of the right is meaningless. But, as the pacifists rightly observe, self-defense or any kind of war is incompatible with an absolute principle of discrimination.

It is my contention that the moral, just-war principle of discrimination is not an absolute limitation on belligerent conduct. There is no evidence that such a principle was ever seriously advanced by the church, and it is implicitly rejected when the church acknowledges the continued right of legitimate self-defense, a right that has always been incompatible with observance of an absolute principle of discrimination. Accordingly, I do not distinguish an absolute, moral, just-war principle of discrimination from a more flexible and variable international-law principle of discrimination. To be sure, the moral, just-war understanding of discrimination must remain independent of that of international law at any given time. But discrimination is best understood and most effectively applied in light of the interpretations of the principle in the practice of belligerents. This, after all, was the principal origin of this part of the *jus in bello,* and the need to check moral just-war formulations against contemporary international-law versions is perennial.

Such a position is in no sense a retreat from a position of maximizing normative limitations on the conduct of war. In the first place, as Ramsey's brave but ultimately unsuccessful efforts have demonstrated, attachment to an absolute principle of discrimination leads either to a finding that all war is immoral and the demise of the just-war doctrine or to tortured efforts to reconcile the irreconcilable. Neither serves the purposes of the *jus in bello.* Second, the rejection of an absolute principle of discrimination does not mean an abandonment of efforts to limit war on moral grounds. The principle of discrimination remains a critical source of both moral and legal limitations of belligerent behavior. As Tucker has observed, there are significant points of limitation between the position that no injury must ever be done to noncombatants and the position

that there are no restraints on countervalue warfare. The interpretations that follow here . . . will try to balance the need to protect noncombatants with the need to recognize the legitimate military necessities of modern forms of warfare. In this process one may err one way or the other, but at least some relevant, practical guidance may be offered belligerents. Adherence to an absolute principle of discrimination usually means irrelevance to the question of limiting the means of war or unconvincing casuistry.

In search of such practical guidance one may resume the examination of the principle of discrimination as interpreted both by moralists and international lawyers. Even before the principle of discrimination was challenged by the changing realities of total war, there were practical difficulties with the definition of *direct international attack, noncombatants,* and *nonmilitary targets.* It is useful, as a starting point for analysis, to recall a standard and authoritative exposition of the principle of discrimination by Fr. Richard McCormick.

> It is a fundamental moral principle [unanimously accepted by Catholic moralists] that it is immoral directly to take innocent human life except with divine authorization. "Direct" taking of human life implies that one performs a lethal action with the intention that death should result for himself or another. Death therefore is deliberately willed as the effect of one's action. "Indirect" killing refers to an action or omission that is designed and intended solely to achieve some other purpose(s) even though death is foreseen as a concomitant effect. Death therefore is not positively willed, but is reluctantly permitted as an unavoidable by-product.[3]

As example that is frequently used in connection with this question is the use of catapults in medieval sieges of castles. The intention—indeed, the purpose—of catapulting projectiles over the castle wall was to kill enemy defenders and perhaps to break down the defenses. If noncombatants—innocents as they

---

3 "Morality of War," *New Catholic Encyclopedia* 14 (1967), p. 805.

were called then—were killed or injured, this constituted a "concomitant effect," an "undesired by-product."

The issues of intention, act, and multiple effects are often analyzed in terms of the principle of double effect, which Father McCormick's exposition employs without invoking the concept explicitly. After centuries of inconclusive efforts to apply the principle of double effect to the *jus in bello,* Michael Walzer has proposed his own version, which merits reflection and experimental application.

> The intention of the actor is good, that is, he aims narrowly at the acceptable effect; the evil effect is not one of his ends, nor is it a means to his ends, and, aware of the evil involved, he seeks to minimize it, accepting costs to himself.[4]

It is probably not possible to reconcile observance of the principle of discrimination with the exigencies of genuine military necessity without employing the principle of double effect in one form or another. However this distinction between primary, desired effect and secondary, concomitant, undesired by-product is often difficult to accept.

It is not so hard to accept the distinction in a case where the concomitant undesired effect was accidental (for example, a case where the attacker did not know that noncombatants were present in the target area). There would still remain in such a case a question as to whether the attacker ought to have known that noncombatants might be present. Nor is it so hard to accept a double-effect justification in a situation where the attacker had reason to believe that there might be noncombatants present but that this was a remote possibility. If, however, the attacker knows that there are noncombatants intermingled with combatants to the point that any attack on the military target is highly likely to kill or injure noncombatants, then the death or injury to those noncombatants is certainly

"intended" or "deliberately willed," in the common usage of those words.

Turning to the object of the protection of the principle of discrimination—the innocents or noncombatants—another critical question of interpretation arises. How does one define noncombatants? How does one define nonmilitary targets? The assumption of separability of military forces and the populations they represented, found in medieval theory and continued by the Rousseau-Portalis Doctrine, became increasingly less valid after the wars of the French Revolution.

As nations engaged in total mobilization, one society or system against another, it was no longer possible to distinguish sharply between the military forces and the home fronts that rightly held themselves out as critical to the war effort. By the American Civil War this modern phenomenon had assumed critical importance. The material means of supporting the Confederate war effort were attacked directly and intentionally by Union forces. War in the age of the Industrial Revolution was waged against the sources of war production. Moreover, the nature of the attacks on noncombatants was psychological as well as material. Military forces have always attempted to break the will of the opposing forces as well as to destroy or scatter them. It now became the avowed purpose of military forces to break the will of the home front as well as to destroy its resources for supporting the war. This, of course, was to become a major purpose of modern strategic aerial bombardment.

To be sure, attacks on the bases of military forces have historically often been an effective strategy. But in the simpler world before the Industrial Revolution, this was not such a prominent option. When the huge conscript armies began to fight for profound ideological causes with the means provided by modern industrial mobilization and technology, the home front and consequently the noncombatants became a critical target for direct intentional attack.

The question then arose whether a civilian could be a participant in the overall was effort to such a degree as to lose his previous noncombatant immunity. Likewise, it became harder to

4 Michael Walzer, *Just and Unjust Wars* (New York: Basic Books, 1977), p. 155.

distinguish targets that were clearly military from targets, such as factories or railroad facilities, that were of sufficient military importance to justify their direct intentional attack. It is important to note that this issue arose before the great increase in the range, areas of impact, and destructive effects of modern weaponry, conventional and nuclear. What we may term *countervalue warfare* was carried out in the American Civil War not because it was dictated by the weapons systems but because the civilian population and war-related industries and activities were considered to be critical and legitimate targets to be attacked.

In World War I this kind of attack was carried out primarily by the belligerents with their maritime blockades. Above all, these blockades caused the apparent demise of the principle of noncombatant immunity in the positive international law of war. Other factors in this demise were developments that revealed potentials not fully realized until World War II (for example, aerial bombardment of population centers and unrestricted submarine warfare). In World War II aerial bombardment of population centers was preeminent as a source of attacks on traditional noncombatants and nonmilitary targets. By this time the concept of total mobilization had advanced so far that a plausible argument could be made that vast segments of belligerent populations and complexes of industry and housing had become so integral to the war effort as to lose their noncombatant immunity.

In summary, well before the advent of weapons systems that are usually employed in ways that do not discriminate between traditional combatants and noncombatants, military and nonmilitary targets, the distinction had eroded. The wall of separation between combatants and noncombatants had been broken down by the practice of total societal mobilization in modern total war and the resulting practice of attacking directly and intentionally that mobilization base. Given these developments, it was difficult to maintain that the principle of discrimination was still a meaningful limit on war. Those who clung to the principle tended to reject modern war altogether as inherently immoral because it inherently violates the principle. In the international law of war, distinguished publicists were reduced to stating that terror bombing of noncombatants with no conceivable proximate military utility was prohibited, but that the right of noncombatants to protection otherwise were unclear. . . .

Review Questions

1. O'Brien states three conditions for permissible recourse to war. What are they?
2. What problems arise in trying to satisfy the first condition?
3. How does O'Brien explain the four subdivisions of the just cause condition?
4. What are the elements of the concept of right intention, according to O'Brien?
5. Explain the principles of proportion and discrimination as O'Brien applies them to the conduct in war.

Discussion Questions

1. O'Brien says that offensive war remains an option in just war theory. When, if ever, would an offensive war be justified?
2. According to O'Brien, right intention insists that charity and love exist even among enemies. Are charity and love compatible with killing and injuring people?
3. O'Brien thinks that the bombing of Hiroshima and Nagasaki was allowed by just war theory. Do you agree? Didn't this killing of 200,000 innocent people violate the principle of discrimination?

The Morality of Terrorism

HAIG KHATCHADOURIAN

Haig Khatchadourian is emeritus professor of philosophy at the University of Wisconsin, Milwaukee. He is the author of nine books (one of them a book of poetry), including *A Critical Study in Method* (1971), *The Concept of Art* (1971), *Philosophy of Language and Logical Theory* (1995) *Community and Communitarianism* (1999), and *War, Terrorism, Genocide, and the Quest for Peace* (2003). Our reading is taken from *The Morality of Terrorism*.

Khatchadourian begins with the problem of defining terrorism. He argues that the definitions of Lackey and others are inadequate because they are too broad, or too narrow, or beg ethical issues. Instead of giving a formal definition, he says that the core meaning of terrorism includes the notion that terrorist acts are acts of coercion or force aiming at monetary gain, revenge, a political end, or a moral/religious end. So there are four types of terrorism: predatory, retaliatory, political, and moral/religious terrorism. He adds that the "bifocal character" of terrorism, the fact that it aims at both immediate victims and "the victimized," is what distinguishes terrorism from other uses of coercion or force.

Then Khatchadourian turns to the morality of terrorism. He argues that terrorism in all its forms is always wrong. It flagrantly violates three principles of just war theory: the principles of necessity, proportion, and discrimination. (The principle of proportion has two different forms, a political form applying to the right to go to war and a military form applying to the conduct of war.) In addition, all but the moralistic/religious type of terrorism violate the condition of a just cause. Finally, Khatchadourian argues that terrorism violates human rights, including the basic right to be treated as a moral person.

TERRORISM: WHAT'S IN A NAME?

WHAT TERRORISM IS or how the word should be employed is a much vexed question, and many definitions of it have been proposed. Some of the conceptual reasons for the lack of agreement on its meaning will become clearer as I proceed, but the fact that the term is almost invariably used in an evaluative—indeed, highly polemical and emotionally charged—way makes the framing of a neutral definition a difficult task. It is probably no exaggeration to say that, at present, it is as emotional a word as "war." In fact, some think of terrorism as a kind of war, and the mere mention of the word arouses similar anxieties and fears. This was particularly true at the time this was being written, against the backdrop of the Gulf War and President Saddam Hussein's repeated warnings of terrorism against American and European interests world-wide. Not surprisingly, therefore, terrorism is very widely condemned as a major evil plaguing the last decades of the Twentieth century, a century already drenched with the blood of the innocent and the noninnocent is a long series of wars, revolutions, civil wars, and other forms of violence.

Source: From Haig Khatchadourian, *The Morality of Terrorism* (New York: Peter Lang, 1998), pp. 1–38. Footnotes renumbered. Used by permission of the publisher.

The widespread condemnation of terrorism as an unmitigated evil stems in part from the fact that some of those governments or countries, political systems, or regimes, that are the main targets, particularly of state or state-sponsored political violence, use the word as a political-psychological weapon in their fight against the perpetrators and their avowed causes—for example, national liberation from foreign occupation or the overthrow of an oppressive indigenous system or regime. In fighting terrorism targeted at them, the victim groups or countries tend to indiscriminately label all their enemies as "terrorists," including those who practice the least violent kinds of protest, thus stretching the word's already loose usage and vague meaning beyond reason.[1] Despite its notorious vagueness and looseness, some overlap among the multiplicity of the word's definitions and characterizations exists. Quite a number of definitions in the literature, as well as characterizations in the media and in everyday discourse, include the idea that terrorism is the threat or the actual use of violence—the unlawful use of force[2]—directed against civilians (e.g. noncombatants in wartime) *and they alone,* sometimes with the addition of the words, *"for political* purposes." In that respect the moral philosopher Douglas Lackey's definition is typical. With wartime terrorism in mind, he writes: "What separates the terrorist from the traditional revolutionary is a persistent refusal to direct violence at military objectives. Terrorism, on this account, is the threat or use of violence against noncombatants for political purposes. In ordinary war, the deaths of civilians are side effects of military operations directed against military targets. In terrorist operations, the civilian is

the direct and intentional target of attack."[3] The same putative core of meaning occurs in other definitions I shall consider.

Although I shall argue that this and similar definitions of "terrorism" are inadequate, Lackey is right in rejecting the definition of former Vice-President George Bush's Task Force on Combating Terrorism, according to which terrorism is "the unlawful use or threat of violence against persons or property to further political or social objectives."[4] That definition, Lackey notes, is too broad, but his own definition suffers from the opposite defect, although it has the merit of not confining the victims of terrorism to civilians. Another example of a too-broad definition is the Task Force's "the threatened or actual use of force or violence to attain a political goal through fear, coercion, or intimidation."[5]

The preceding and most of the other definitions that have been proposed share a more fundamental defect, one that will be noted as we proceed.

Other proposed definitions I have examined[6] are also either too broad or too narrow, or both—a problem faced by "essentialist" definitions in general—often in addition to other defects. Some definitions are too restrictive, being limited to one form of terrorism, for example, political terrorism in the usual, restricted meaning

---

1 A notorious example, which carries this tendency to absurdity, is the late Mr. Rabin's calling the "stone children" of the Palestinian intifada "terrorists" in front of American television cameras. Mr. Rabin himself was murdered by a Jewish terrorist.

2 This is false in terrorism practiced by a ruling dictator or military junta, whenever the government's (or its military's) terrorist activities conform to (unjust) laws decreed by the dictator or junta.

3 Douglas Lackey, *The Ethics of War and Peace* (Englewood Cliffs, NJ, 1989), 85.

4 "Report of Vice-President's Task Force on Combating Terrorism," in Lackey, *Ethics,* 85.

5 Charles A. Russell et al., "Out-Inventing the Terrorist," in *Terrorism, Theory and Practice,* Yonah Alexander et al., eds. (Boulder, CO, 1979), 4. In note 2, p. 37, the authors add: "'Political' is understood in this usage to connote the entire range of social, economic, religious, ethnic, and governmental factors impacting on a body politic, stressing the notions of power and influence. The ideal definition is one that both the adherents and abhorrers of terrorism could agree upon."

6 According to Leonard B. Weinberg and Paul Davis, *Introduction to Political Terrorism* (New York, 1989), 3, more than one hundred separate definitions have been proposed by different analysts over the years. See also Harold J. Vetter et al., *Perspectives on Terrorism* (Pacific Grove, CA, 1990), 3, where it is stated that the definitions were formulated between 1936 and 1983.

of the word.[7] Still other definitions or characterizations fail because they are overtly or covertly normative (condemnatory) rather than, as definitions ought to be, neutral or nonevaluative. Former President Ronald Reagan's statement that terrorism is the deliberate maiming or killing of innocent people, and his characterization of terrorists as "base criminals," clearly beg the ethical issues.[8] A fuller definition that suffers from the same flaw among others, is proposed by Burton Leiser. Part of his definition is:[9]

> *Terrorism* is any organized set of acts of violence designed to destroy the structure of authority which normally stands for security, or to reinforce and perpetuate a governmental regime whose popular support is shaky. It is a policy of seemingly senseless, irrational, and arbitrary murder, assassination, sabotage, subversion, robbery and other forms of violence, all committed with dedicated indifference to existing legal and moral codes or with claims to special exemption from conventional social norms.

ELEMENTS OF TERRORISM

The main forms of terrorism in existence in the present-day world share at least five important aspects or elements which an adequate description of terrorism must include. They are:

1. The historical and cultural, including the socioeconomic root causes of its prevalence (e.g., the lack or loss of a homeland).

2. The immediate, intermediate and long-range or ultimate goals. Retaliation is an example of the first, while publicity is an example of the second. The regaining of a lost homeland, the acquisition or exercise of power [by a state], . . . or enforcement

of [its] authority,"[10] (which F. J. Hacker calls terrorism from above[11]), or the challenge to . . . [a state's] authority (which he calls terrorism from below) are examples of long range terrorist goals.

3. The third aspect or element consists in the forms and methods of coercion and force[12] generally resorted to to terrorize the immediate victims and to coerce[13] those who are seriously affected by the terrorism, the victimized. The latter are the individuals, groups, governments, or countries that are intimately connected with the immediate targets and who are themselves the real albeit indirect targets of the terrorist acts.[14] The forms and methods of coercion and force resorted to define the different *species* or *forms* of terrorism of any given *type*.

4. The nature or kinds of organizations and institutions, or the political systems, practicing or sponsoring the terrorism. For example, in state terrorism the terrorism is practiced by agents of a state, while in state-sponsored terrorism the terrorism is financially, militarily, or in other ways supported but not directly conducted by the sponsoring state or states.

5. The social, political, economic or military context or circumstances in which the terrorism occurs is also important and must be considered. For example, whether the

7 For example, Weinberg and Davis' definition in their *Introduction*, 3ff.

8 Quoted in Haig Khatchadourian, "Terrorism and Morality," *Journal of Applied Philosophy*, 5, no. 2 (October 1988): 131.

9 Burton M. Leiser, *Liberty, Justice, and Morals* (New York, 1979), 375. Italics in original.

10 Vetter et al., *Perspectives*, 8.

11 Frederick J. Hacker, *Crusaders, Criminals, Crazies* (New York, 1977), quoted in Vetter et al., 8.

12 I use "force" because it is morally neutral or near-neutral, unlike the more common "violence."

13 Weinberg and Davis, Introduction, 6, state: "The objective purpose of harming immediate victims is subordinate to the purpose of sending a message to some broader target population [the 'victimized']." Although this statement shows their recognition of the bifocal character of terrorism, the idea of "sending a message" is too general and vague to be of much service.

14 I borrow "immediate victim" from Abraham Edel, "Notes on Terrorism," in *Values in Conflict*, Burton M. Leiser, ed. (New York, 1981), 458.

terrorism occurs in time of peace or in wartime.[15] In the latter case, there is also an important ethical dimension in relation to terrorist violence or threats to noncombatants, just as in the case of precision "saturation" bombing of towns and cities in Twentieth century warfare. This would become incalculably more important in the case of possible nuclear terrorism.[16]

The one form of terrorism to which (1) above does not normally apply is predatory terrorism—terrorism motivated by greed. But predatory terrorism is relatively unimportant, especially for a discussion of the morality of terrorism such as the present one, since it is clearly immoral. Although seriously flawed, Leiser's definition noted earlier has the merit of incorporating several of the aspects of terrorism I have mentioned. But it fails to spell out the various sorts of causes of terrorism and makes only a passing mention of what it calls the terrorists' "political ends."[17]

DEFINING "TERRORISM"

A fully adequate characterization or formal definition of "terrorism" must be as neutral as possible and not beg the issue of the morality of terrorism in general, in addition to reflecting the five aspects or dimensions of terrorism distinguished above—notwithstanding the word's almost invariably negative connotations, particularly in the Western world. . . .

In the current literature the question of whether noninnocents can be included among the immediate victims of terrorism appears to be a very unsettled question. The absence of clarity and fixity—indeed, the ambivalence and uncertainty in current employments of the word—reflect the different users' stand on the *morality* of terrorism and the

morality, especially, of the unlawful use of force in general. These uncertainties are intimately connected with uncertainties concerning the distinction between terrorism and "freedom fighting," such as a rebellion, a civil war, an uprising, or a guerrilla war aiming, for example, at national liberation. Those who consider the harming of innocent persons an essential feature of terrorism would tend to consider "freedom fighting" as involving, *inter alia*, the maiming, killing or coercing of *non*innocents. That would allow "political assassination" to be classified as a species of "freedom fighting." Leiser states that guerrilla warfare is characterized by small-scale, unconventional, limited actions carried out by irregular forces "*against regular military forces, their supply lines, and communications.*"[18] That description would be perfectly in order provided we stipulate that the targeted soldiers are in the army of their own free will.

The preceding discussion indicates that in addition to being open textured and vague, the various current evaluative concepts of terrorism, like all other evaluative concepts, are, in W. B. Gallie's phrase, "essentially contested."[19] Yet like most vague and unsettled expressions "terrorism" has a "common core of meaning" in its different usages. This core of meaning includes the notion that terrorist acts are acts of coercion or of actual use of force,[20] aiming at monetary gain (*predatory terrorism*), revenge (*retaliatory terrorism*), a political end (*political terrorism*), or a putative moral/religious end (*moralistic/religious terrorism*).[21]

---

15 This and the next section are largely reproduced, with some stylistic and substantive changes, from my "Terrorism and Morality."

16 Cf. Joel Kovel, *Against The State Of Nuclear Terror* (Boston, MA, 1983), Robert J. Lifton and Richard Falk, *Indefensible Weapons* (New York, 1982), and Helen Caldicott, *Missile Envy, The Arms Race and Nuclear War* (New York, 1986).

17 Leiser, *Liberty, Justice and Morals*, 375.

18 Ibid., 381. Italics in original.

19 W. B. Gallie, "Essentially Contested Concepts," *Proceedings of the Aristotelian Society,* n.s., 56 (March 1956), 180ff. But Gallie maintains that a concept must have certain characteristics in addition to appraisiveness (he enumerates them on pp. 171–172) to be "essentially contested" in his sense.

20 Those who use "terrorism" as a condemnatory term would substitute "violence" for "force."

21 I borrow the categories "predatory" and "moralistic" from Edel, "Notes on Terrorism," 453. Some but not all moralistic terrorism is political terrorism, or vice versa. "Narcoterrorism" is a special subform of predatory terrorism, not a separate, additional form of terrorism. For this fundamental distinction at the heart of terrorism as a kind of use of force or violence for certain ends, I am indebted to Edel's essay.

What is absolutely essential for an adequate concept of terrorism and helps distinguish it from all other uses of force or coercion, but which most definitions I have come across lack, is what I shall call terrorism's "bifocal" character. I mean the crucial distinction between (a) the "immediate victims," the individuals who are the immediate targets of terrorism, and (b) "the victimized," those who are the indirect but real targets of the terrorist acts. Normally the latter are individual governments or countries or certain groups of governments or countries, or specific institutions or groups within a given country. The ultimate targets may also be certain social, economic or political systems or regimes which the terrorists dislike and hope to change or destroy by their terrorist activities. . . .

THE MORALITY OF TERRORISM AND A JUST WAR THEORY

Although the literature on terrorism is constantly growing, very little has been written about the morality of terrorism; perhaps because the writers take it for granted that terrorism is a scourge, always morally reprehensible and wrong: note for instance the common equation of terrorism with murder. . . .

This is not a very auspicious beginning for a moral evaluation of terrorism. From the fact that terrorist acts, including the killing of immediate victims, are prohibited in many if not all municipal legal systems, it does not follow that some or all such acts are *morally* wrong. Calling terrorist killings "murder" begs the complex ethical issues involved. . . .

Whether . . . some terrorists acts . . . are morally justified is an important question and will be discussed in relation to just war theory. . . .

The traditional conditions of a just war are of two sorts: conditions of justified going to war (*jus ad belum*) and conditions of the just prosecution of a war in progress (*jus in bello*). One of the fundamental conditions of the latter kind is that

> The destruction of life and property, even enemy life and property, is inherently bad. It follows that military forces should cause no more

destruction than is strictly necessary to achieve their objectives. (Notice that the principle does not say that whatever is necessary is permissible, but that everything permissible must be necessary). This is the principle of necessity: that *wanton* destruction is forbidden. More precisely, the principle of necessity specifies that a military operation is forbidden if there is some alternative operation that causes less destruction but has the same probability of producing a successful military result.[22]

Another fundamental condition is the principle of discrimination or noncombatant immunity, which prohibits the deliberate harming—above all the killing—of innocent persons. In "Just War Theory" William O'Brien defines that condition as the principle that "prohibits direct intentional attacks on noncombatants and nonmilitary targets,"[23] and Douglas Lackey, in *The Ethics of War and Peace,* characterize it as "the idea that . . . civilian life and property should not be subjected to military force: military force must be directed only at military objectives."[24] A third fundamental condition is the principle of proportion, as "applied to discrete military ends."[25] That condition is defined by O'Brien as "requiring proportionality of means to political and military ends."[26] Or as Lackey states it, it is the idea that "the amount of destruction permitted in pursuit of a military objective must be proportionate to the importance of the objective. This is the *military* principle of proportionality (which must be distinguished from the *political* principle of proportionality in the *jus ad bellum*)."[27]

My contention is that these three principles, duly modified or adapted, are analogically applicable to all the types of terrorism, and that

22 Douglas P. Lackey, *The Ethics of War and Peace* (Englewood Cliffs, NJ, 1989), 59. Italics in original.

23 William O'Brien, "Just-War Theory," in Burton M. Leiser *Liberty, Justice, and Morals,* 2nd ed. (New York, 1979), 39. This section is in large measure reproduced from sections III–V of Haig Khatchadourian, "Terrorism and Morality," *Journal of Applied Philosophy,* 5, no. 2 (1958): 134–143.

24 Lackey, *Ethics,* 59.

25 Ibid., 37.

26 Ibid., 30.

27 Ibid., 59. Italics in original.

they are flagrantly violated by them. Indeed, all but the moralistic/religious type of terrorism violate a further condition of just war theory. I refer to the first and most important condition of *jus ad bellum* and one of the most important conditions of a just war in general: the condition of just cause. . . .

Of the four main types of terrorism, predatory, retaliatory and nonmoralistic/religious terrorism clearly run afoul of the just cause condition, understood—in a nutshell—as the self-defensive use of force. Conceivably only some acts of moralistic and moralistic-political/religious terrorism can satisfy that condition. It is clear that the former three types of terrorism violate that condition.

Let us begin with predatory terrorism, terrorism motivated by greed. Like "ordinary" acts of armed robbery, of which it is the terrorist counterpart, predatory terrorism is a crime and is morally wrong. Both cause terror and indiscriminately hurt whoever happens to be where they strike. Indeed, hostage-taking by armed robbers in hopes of escaping unscathed by forcing the authorities to give them a getaway car or plane is an additional similarity to terrorism. It can even be regarded as predatory terrorism itself, particularly if it is systematic and not a onetime affair, since both political and moralistic terrorism tend to be systematic. . . . Even then, armed robbery involving hostage-talking, must be distinguished from the kind of armed robbery that political or moralistic terrorists may indulge in to raise money for their particular political/moralistic/religious ends.

Nonetheless, bona fide predatory (and even retaliatory) terrorism is often unsystematic; like ordinary armed robbery, it may also be a one-time thing. Some well-known terrorist airplane hijackings in the United States for monetary gain have been one-time incidents, although in all but one instance I know of, that was simply because the hijackers were apprehended!

Like predatory terrorism, retaliatory terrorism may or may not be systematic. International terrorism usually includes a systematic policy of retaliation against a hated, enemy state or its citizens. A notorious example a few years ago was the retaliatory terrorism against the United States and its interests, sponsored by Libya, Syria, and/or Iran.

More important for the present discussion, retaliatory terrorism violates, among other moral rules, the just cause condition and the principles of justice, and is consequently wrong. For what is retaliation but another (more euphemistic?) word for revenge, which is incompatible with self-defense as well as due process. That is no less true in war, if retaliatory terrorism is practiced by a country in its efforts to defend itself against aggression. For example, if an attempt is made on the life of the aggressor country's head of state by agents of the victim state in retaliation for attacks on its territory, the assassination attempt would be (a) an act of *terrorism* if it is *intended* to pressure the aggressor's military to end the aggression. But despite its *goal* and the victim's perception of it as part of its national self-defense, it remains (b) an act of retaliation, not an act of self-defense.

What I have said about predatory and retaliatory terrorism in relation to just cause applies to nonmoralistic political terrorism, to terrorism whose political goals are *not* moral. An example is when a revolutionary group commits acts of terrorism against a legitimate, democratically elected government it wants to overthrow out of lust for power.

By definition, moralistic terrorism satisfies just cause if "just cause" is interpreted broadly to mean a morally justifiable cause, for example, political terrorism strictly as part of a national liberation movement against a foreign occupier or indigenous oppressive regime. It *may* also satisfy the condition of right intention. Consequently, I shall turn to the other two conditions of just war I mentioned earlier, to ascertain whether even such terrorism can be morally justifiable.

Principle of Necessity and Terrorism

The principle of necessity states that "*wanton* destruction [in war] is forbidden. More precisely, the principle . . . specifies that a military operation is forbidden if there is some alternative operation that causes less destruction but has the same probability of producing a successful military result."[28] *Pace* Lackey, who regards it as a more precise form of the condition, it is distinct from, although closely related to, the principle that wanton destruction is forbidden in war. If a war *is* a last resort, it would follow that the destruction of life and property is necessary, not wanton. And if it is necessary, it *is* a last resort.

It is clear that predatory terrorism is always a wanton destruction of life or property, and the same is true of retaliatory terrorism; however, the concept of "last resort" is inapplicable to them. If Iran had chosen to sue the United States for compensation or reparation at the International Court of Justice at the Hague, for the shooting down an Iranian airbus during the Iraq-Iran war, that would have constituted a peaceful, nonviolent *alternative* to any terrorist retaliation against the United States Iran may have sponsored in its aftermath, such as the destruction of Pan Am Flight 103 over Lockerbie, Scotland, which some believe was instigated and financed by Iran and implemented by a notorious Palestinian terrorist. (The United States has steadfastly held Libya, and possibly Syria, responsible for that atrocity.) Logically, retaliation on the one hand and reparation, compensation, or restitution, or other peaceful ways of undoing or rectifying a wrong, are horses of very different colors.

Principle of Discrimination and Terrorism

In many acts of terrorism some or all of the immediate victims and/or victimized are innocent persons, in no way morally connected with or in any degree responsible for the wrong moralistic terrorism is intended to help rectify, hence for the physical or mental harm that the terrorists inflict on them. In predatory terrorism the immediate victims and the victimized are, almost

without exception, innocent persons. That is also often true of retaliatory terrorism, at least as far as the immediate victims are concerned. Two very tragic examples in recent memory are the hijacking of the *Achille Lauro,* and the destruction of the Pan Am plane over Lockerbie. In political and political-moralistic terrorism, whether in wartime or in time of peace, some of the immediate victims or some of the victimized are likely to be innocent persons; but some may be noninnocents, such as members (especially high-ranking members) of the military, who are morally responsible for the real or imagined wrong that triggers the terrorism.

The problem of distinguishing innocent and noninnocent persons in relation to different types and forms of terrorism, except terrorism in war, is on the whole less difficult that the much-vexed corresponding problem in relation to war. My position, *mutatis mutandis* in relation to war, simply stated, is this: (1) "Innocence" and "noninnocence" refer to *moral* innocence and noninnocence, relative to the particular acts, types, or forms of terrorism *T*. (2) Innocence and noninnocence are a matter of degree. (3) A perfectly innocent person is one who has no moral responsibility, *a fortiori,* no causal responsibility at all, for any wrong that gave rise to *T*. A paradigmatically noninnocent person is someone who has an appreciable degree of moral, hence direct or indirect causal responsibility for the wrong, triggering *T*.[29] Between that extreme and paradigmatic noninnocents there would be, theoretically, cases of decreasing moral responsibility corresponding to decreasing degrees of causal responsibility. Here the targets would be noninnocent in some but lesser degree than in paradigmatic cases of noninnocence. (4) Moral responsibility may be direct or indirect, by virtue of a person's direct or indirect role in *T*'s causation—where *T* is triggered or has its root cause(s) in some real injustice or wrong. The degree of a person's innocence may therefore

---

28 Lackey, *Ethics,* 59. Italics in original.

29 What constitutes an "appreciable degree" of moral responsibility would of course be a matter of controversy.

also vary in that way. Everyone whose actions are a proximate cause of the wrong is noninnocent in a higher degree than those whose responsibility for it is indirect. In particular cases it is always possible in principle to ascertain whether an individual is, causally, directly involved. Generally it is also actually possible, although often quite difficult, to do so in practice. Ascertaining who is indirectly responsible and who is not at all responsible is another matter. Since we are mainly concerned with the theoretical problem of the morality of terrorism, that is not too disquieting. But it is of the essence from the point of view of would-be terrorists and that of the law—unless the terrorists happen to be deranged and target innocent individuals or groups they imagine to be morally responsible for the grievances they are out to avenge or redress. Further, the very life of some individuals may depend on the potential terrorists' ability to distinguish innocent from noninnocent persons or groups. Political, retaliatory, or moralistic terrorists, driven by passion or paranoia, often baselessly enlarge, sometimes to a tragically absurd extent, the circle of alleged noninnocent persons. They sometimes target individuals, groups or whole nations having only a tenuous relation, often of a completely innocent kind, to those who have wronged their compatriots or ancestors, stolen their land, and so on. The example given earlier of terrorists striking at the high-ranking officials of governments whose predecessors committed crimes against their people, illustrates this. Another example is terrorism targeting innocent persons presumed to be guilty by association, simply because they happen to be of the same race, nationality, or religion, or enjoy the same ethnic heritage as those deemed responsible for the hurt.

An extreme, horrifying kind of justification of the targeting of completely innocent persons was brought to my attention by Anthony O'Heare.[30] It involves the justification one sometimes hears of the killing of holidaymakers, travelers, and others, in Israel and other terrorists targets,

"on the ground that . . . the very fact that they were contributing to the economy and morale of the targeted country [unwittingly] implicated them." As O'Heare comments, that defense is "a disgusting piece of casuistry." Its implications, I might add, are so far-reaching as to be positively frightening. If the travelers or holidaymakers were guilty of a crime against, say, the Palestinian people, as is claimed, then by parity of reasoning all individuals, institutions, groups or peoples, all countries or nations that have any kind of economic dealings with Israel and so contribute to its economy would likewise be guilty of a crime against the Palestinian people and so may be justifiably targeted! But then why exempt those *Arabs* who live in Israel and even those *Palestinians* residing in the West Bank or in the Gaza Strip who are employed in Israel—indeed, all those who spend any amount of money there—from guilt?

Finally, to be able to protect individuals against terrorism, law enforcement agencies as well as governments in general need to be able to protect individuals against terrorism, need to make reliable predictions about who is a likely target of known terrorist organizations. Yet in few other kinds of coercison or other uses of force is the element of unpredictability and surprise greater or the strikes more impelled by emotion and passion than in terrorism. This problem will be later taken up again in a discussion of responses to terrorism.

Principles of Proportion and Terrorism

In addition to its violation of the moral principles considered above, terrorism may appear to violate two other principles of just war theory: (1) the *political* principle of proportion of *jus ad bellum* and (2) the *military* principle of proportion of *jus in bello*. The former is stated by William O'Brien as requiring that "the good to be achieved by the realisation of the war aims be proportionate to the evil resulting from the war."[31] And "the calculus of proportionality in

---

30 Private communication to the author.

31 O'Brien, "Just-War Theory," 37.

just cause [that is, the political purpose, *raison d'etat*, "the high interests of the state"] is to the total good to be expected if the war is successful balanced against the evil the war is likely to cause."[32] Lackey describes the political principle of proportionality as stipulating that "a war cannot be just unless the evil that can reasonably be expected to ensue from the war is less than the evil that can reasonably be expected to ensue if the war is not fought."[33]

The military counterpart of the political principle is described by Lackey as the idea that "the amount of destruction permitted in pursuit of a military objective must be proportionate to the importance of the objective. It follows from the military principle of proportionality that certain objectives should be ruled out of consideration on the ground that too much destruction would be caused in obtaining them."[34]

As in the case of war, the main problem facing any attempt to apply the *political* principle of proportion to terrorism is the difficulty of reaching even the roughest estimate of the total expected good *vis-a-vis* the total evil likely to be caused by a series of connected acts of political or *moralistic/religious* terrorism. The crudest estimates of the expected good of some political-moralistic/religious cause against the suffering or death of even one victim or victimized person are exceedingly difficult to come by. And if we turn from isolated acts of political-moralistic/religious terrorism to a whole series of such acts extending over a period of years or decades, as with Arab or IRA terrorism, the task becomes utterly hopeless. For how can we possibly measure the expected good resulting from the creation of, for example, an independent Catholic Northern Ireland or a Catholic Northern Ireland united with the Irish Republic, and compare it with the overall evil likely to be the lot of the Ulster Protestants in such an eventuality or on different scenarios of their eventual

fate—then add the latter evil to the evils consisting in and consequent upon all the acts of terrorism that are supposed to help realise the desired good end? I see no possible way in which these factors can be quantified, hence added or subtracted.[35]

It seems then that we cannot ascertain whether political or moralistic/religious terrorism sometimes or always violates the political principle of proportion. However, it is a patent fact that no political or moralistic/religious terrorist movement in this century—whether Palestinian, Lebanese, Libyan, Syrian, Iranian, Irish, or Algerian—has succeeded in realizing its ultimate or overall political or moralistic objectives. Moreover, these movements have no more chance of success in the future than they have had so far. Palestinian terrorism is typical. Since, in Israel and the West, terrorism is almost synonymous with murder, it is not surprising that instead of helping the eminently just Palestinian cause, Palestinian acts of terrorism (as distinguished from Palestinian resistance, e.g. the intifada) from the very start have hurt the cause almost beyond repair. Not only has terrorism failed to win the Palestinians their human and other rights or brought them any closer to selfdetermination: it has created strong public sympathy in the West for Israel and turned public attitudes strongly against the Palestinians, or at least their leadership, and has further increased Israeli security concerns.[36] This does enable us, I think, to conclude after all that the preceding types of terrorism are indeed in serious violation of the political principle of proportion. For the result of tallying the evils of terrorist acts in human pain

32 Ibid.
33 Lackey, *Ethics*, 40.
34 Ibid., 59.

35 For the special significance of this in relation to revolutionary terrorism, see Chapter 4.
36 A personal note: My own moral condemnation of terrorism and my conviction that it was bound to hurt rather than help the Palestinian cause led me, soon after the first Palestinian skyjacking, to send an open letter to the PLO leadership. In this letter I pointed these things out and pleaded that the PLO put an end to such acts. For rather obvious reasons the Beirut publication to which I sent the letter could not publish it.

and suffering, death and destruction, against the nonexistent overall benefits leaves a huge surplus of unmitigated evil on the negative side. I refer not only to the evil inflicted by the terrorists upon their victims and the victimized but also the evil they draw upon themselves and their families by risking loss of life, limb, or liberty in ultimately futile pursuit of their dangerous and violent objectives.

We now turn to the military principle of pro-portionality—in O'Brien's words, the principle that "a discrete military means . . . when viewed independently on the basis of its intermediate military end (*raison de guerre*), must . . . be pro-portionate . . . to that military end for which it was used, irrespective of the ultimate end of the war at the level of *raison d'etat*."[37] This princi-ple, applied to discrete military means, O'Brien observes, is in line with the law of Nuremberg, which judged the "legitimacy of discrete acts of the German forces, . . . inter alia, in terms of their proportionality to intermediate military goals, *raison de guerre*. . . . It was a reasonable way to evaluate the substance of the allegations that war crimes had occurred."[38]

The present form of the principle *can* be applied, *mutatis mutandis*, to discrete acts of terrorism provided that their probable interme-diate results can be roughly assessed. For exam-ple, in evaluating the morality of the *Achille Lauro* seajacking, the short-term and intermedi-ate "political" gains the terrorists expected to receive must be weighed, if possible, against the killing of an innocent passenger and the terror-ism visited on the other passengers on board. It can be safely said that apart from the damage the seajacking did to the PLO and to the Mid-dle East peace process as a whole, whatever ben-efit the seajackers expected to reap from their acts,[39] such as publicity and the dramatization

of the plight of the Palestinians under Israeli military rule in the occupied territories, was vastly outweighed by the evils the seajacking re-sulted in.[40] More important still, the actual and not (as in O'Brien's formulation of the prin-ciple) merely the expected outcome of acts of terrorism, good and bad, must be weighed, if possible, against each other. That is, actual pro-portionality must obtain if, in retrospect, the acts are to be objectively evaluated. But to do so is precisely to assess the outcomes of the acts in terms of consequentialist criteria, and so will be left for later consideration.

The same general factors need to be weighed for the evaluation of other discrete acts of ter-rorism in relation to the military principle of proportionality; for example, the assassination of members of the Israeli Olympic team in Munich in 1972, the hijacking of TWA flight 847 in Athens, Greece, in 1985, the downing of Pan Am flight 103 over Lockerbie, Scotland, in 1989, and so on.

Terrorism and Human Rights

It can be safely said that the belief that all human beings have a (an equal) human right to life, at least in the minimal sense of a negative right to life—a right not to be unjustly or wrongly killed—is held by anyone who believes in the existence of human rights at all. That idea is also found in the United Nations *Universal Declaration of Human Rights*. Thus, Article 3 states, among other things, that "Everyone has the right to life." The importance of our ac-knowledging such a universal human right is evident: the protection of human life is the sine qua non of the individual's capacity to realize anything and everything—any and all values—a

---

37 O'Brien, "Just-War Theory," 37.
38 Ibid., 38.
39 One of the seajackers stated after being captured that the original objective was a suicide mission in Israel. That objec-tive, of course, was not realized.

40 Note that the question whether the capture, trial, and al-most certain punishment of the seajackers and others impli-cated in the act is to be judged a good or an evil to be added to one or the other side of the balance sheet, partly depends for its answer on the evaluation of the act itself as morally justified or unjustified. I say "partly depends" because the le-gal implications of the act are also relevant.

human being is capable of realizing in relation to himself or herself and others. But even if one does not acknowledge a distinct human right, a right to life as such, I believe that one is forced to acknowledge the existence of some protective norms, such as other human rights and/or principles of fairness and justice, that prohibit, except in very special circumstances, the taking of human life. For instance, justice prohibits the execution of an innocent person for a crime he or she has not committed. Or the moral protection of human life can be placed under the protective umbrella of, for example, a human right to be treated as a moral person rather than be used as an "object."

The special exceptional circumstances I have in mind are those in which the right to life is overridden by stronger moral or other axiological claims. They may include the protection of the equal rights of others, including others' right to life itself (such as in the case of soldiers sent by their country to war, to defend the lives and freedoms of their countrymen against an aggressor nation); or situations where a certain act is (1) the lesser of two evils and (2) violates no one's equal human or other moral rights, or the principles of fairness and justice. For instance, in some instances of passive or active euthanasia, or assisted suicide, such as in the case of terminal patients who are suffering unbearable physical pain (condition [1]) and the euthanasia or assisted suicide fulfils the patient's devout wish and desire to die (condition [2]). Except in such or similar exceptional cases, the deliberate or the knowing killing of innocent persons is morally wrong.

Elsewhere[41] I have argued that we must acknowledge a fundamental human right of all individuals to be treated as moral persons. Further, that that right includes an equal right of all to be free to satisfy their needs and interests, and to

actualize their potentials: that is, to seek to realize themselves and their well-being.[42] In addition, I have argued that all human beings have an equal right to equal opportunity and treatment, to help enable them to realize the aforementioned values, either as part of or as implied by the right to be treated as a moral person.

A universal negative human right to life,[43] hence a right to one's physical and mental security and integrity, can be readily derived from the right to equal treatment and opportunity as a premise, if such a right is acknowledged,[44] as a condition of the very possibility of exercising that right at all or any other moral, legal, or other kind of right or rights, including the right to be treated as a moral person as a whole. The rights to equal treatment and opportunity would be empty or meaningless in practice if not in theory if one's security is not protected. Indeed, given Thomas Hobbes' three principal causes of quarrel in human nature—competition, "diffidence" or desire for safety, and the desire for glory in the absence of the protective norm of the equal human right to life and its reinforcement by law, human existence would tend to exemplify Hobbes' State of Nature. There would be "no arts; no letters; no society; and which is worst of all, continual fear, and danger of violent death; and life of man, solitary, poor, nasty, brutish, and short."[45]

---

41 Haig Khatchadourian, "Toward a Foundation for Human Rights," *Man and World,* 18 (1985): 219–240, and "The Human Right to be Treated as a Person," *Journal of Value Inquiry,* 19 (1985): 183–195.

42 Khatchadourian, "The Human Right," passim.

43 As distinguished from a positive human right to life, which includes—over and above the right not to be physically hurt or killed—a right to a minimum standard of welfare.

44 Such a right can also be derived from John Rawls' first and second principles of justice in *A Theory of Justice* (Cambridge, MA, 1971). *Indeed, the right to equal opportunity is part of his first principle.*

45 Thomas Hobbes, "Self-Interest," in *Great Traditions in Ethics,* 5th ed., Ethel M. Albert et al., eds. (Belmont, CA, 1984), 134. Reprinted from *Leviathan.* I should add that Hobbes himself regarded self-preservation as the first law of (human) nature, and that his social contract, the creation of the "Leviathan" of civil and political society, is intended to provide, inter alia, safety and security.

It is clear that if a negative right to life is assumed, terrorists' killings of their immediate victims—unless they satisfy conditions (1) and (2) above—are always morally wrong. In reality, condition (1) may perhaps be sometimes satisfied, but condition (2) cannot ever be satisfied. In fact all types and forms of terrorism I have distinguished seriously violate the human rights of their immediate victims and the victimized as moral persons.

Treating people as moral persons means treating them with consideration in two closely related ways. First, it means respecting their autonomy as individuals with their own desires and interests, plans and projects, commitments and goals. That autonomy is clearly violated if they are humiliated, coerced and terrorized, taken hostage or kidnapped, and above all, killed. Second, consideration involves "a certain cluster of attitudes, hence certain ways of acting toward, reacting to and thinking and feeling about" people.[46] It includes sensitivity to and consideration of their feelings and desires, aspirations, projects, and goals. That in turn is an integral part of treating their life as a whole—including their relationships and memories—as a thing of value. Finally, it includes respecting their "culture or ethnic, religious or racial identity or heritage."[47] These things are the very antithesis of what terrorism does to its victims and the victimized.

In sum, terrorism in general violates both aspects of its targets' right to be treated as moral persons. In retaliatory and moralistic/religious terrorism, that is no less true of those victims or those victimized who are morally responsible in some degree for the wrong that precipitates the terrorist strike than of those who are completely innocent of it. In predatory terrorism, the terrorist acts violate the human right of everyone directly or indirectly hurt by them. For the terrorists the life of the immediate victims and their human rights matter not in the least. The same goes for the victimized. The terrorists use both groups, against their will, simply as means to their own end.[48] The matter can also be looked upon in terms of the ordinary concepts of *justice* and *injustice*. Terror directed against innocent persons is a grave injustice against them. In no case is this truer than when terrorists impute to their immediate victims or to the victimized guilt by association. It is equally true when the victims are representatives of a government one or more of whose predecessors committed large-scale atrocities, such as attempted genocide, against terrorists' compatriots or ancestors. True, the present government would be tainted by the original crimes if, to cite an actual case, it categorically refuses to acknowledge its predecessors' guilt and take any steps to redress the grievous wrongs. Similarly, if it verbally acknowledges its predecessors' guilt but washes its hands of all moral or legal responsibility to make amends to the survivors of the atrocities or their families, on the ground that it is a new government, existing decades later than the perpetrators. Yet only if the targeted representatives of the present government themselves are in some way responsible for their government's stand would they be noninnocent in some degree. Otherwise targeting them from a desire for revenge would be sheer murder or attempted murder.

Whenever the victims or victimized are innocent persons, terrorism directed against them constitutes a very grave injustice, like "punishing" an innocent person for a crime he or she has not committed. For in the present sense, justice consists in one's receiving what one merits or

---

46 Khatchadourian, "The Human Right," 192.
47 Ibid.

48 Cf. Abraham Edel's condemnation of terrorism on Kant's principle that "people ought to be treated as ends in themselves and never as means only. Terrorists necessarily treat human beings as means to the achievement of their political, economic, or social goals." Quoted by Burton M. Leiser in his introduction to the section on terrorism in his *Values in Conflict* (New York, 1981), 343.

deserves, determined by what one has done or refrained from doing.

It may be argued that some terrorist acts *may* be just punishment for wrongs committed by the immediate victims or the victimized themselves, against the terrorists or persons close to them. But first, punishment cannot be just if founded on a denial of the wrongdoer's human as well as other rights. Second, a vast difference exists between terrorist "punishment" and just legal punishment, which presupposes the establishment of guilt by a preponderance of the evidence. By definition, terrorists do not and cannot respect the legal protections and rights of the victims and the victimized, but erect themselves as judges and jury—and executioners—giving the "accused" no opportunity to defend themselves or be defended by counsel against the terrorists' allegations, let alone the possibility of defending themselves physically against their assailants.[49] This is a further corollary of the terrorists' denial of the moral and legal rights of the victims and victimized.

These strictures apply equally to terrorism from above and from below. The fact that in the former case the terrorist "organization" is the government itself or some arm of government (e.g., its secret police), and that the terrorism is practiced against those of its own citizens it considers dangerous or subversive, does not morally change the situation. It is terrorism by any other name. Such for instance was the situation in Brazil (in the 1960s), Argentina (in the 1970s), Colombia (in the 1980s), and in other Latin American countries when right-wing, anticommunist death squads killed or executed thousands of people suspected of leftist sympathies. In some countries "church and human rights organizations have been particularly hard-hit."[50]

To sum up. The discussion of the nature of terrorism prepared the way for the central question: whether terrorism is ever morally right, morally justifiable. To answer that question two kinds of ethical principles/rules were deployed, (A) applicable human rights, and (B) applicable just war principles/rules. . . . On both (A) and (B), terrorism in general, in all its various types and forms, was found to be always wrong.

Since predatory and retaliatory terrorism, like predation and retaliation in general, are patently wrong, the inquiry was focused on political and moralistic/religious terrorism, which are held by some—with apparent plausibility—to be, in certain circumstances, morally justifiable. However, it was argued that terrorism of both types is wrong, since both violate certain basic human rights and applicable just war principles or rules.

---

49 See Haig Khatchadourian, "Is Political Assassination Ever Morally Justified?" in *Assassination,* Harold Zellner, ed. (Boston, 1975), 41–55, for similar criticism of political assassination.

50 Leonard B. Weinberg and Paul B. Davis, *Introduction to Political Terrorism* (New York, 1989), 72.

Review Questions

1. How do Lackey, Regan, and Leiser define terrorism? What objections does Khatchadourian make to these definitions?
2. According to Khatchadourian, what are the five elements of terrorism?
3. What is the core meaning of terrorism, according to Khatchadourian? What distinguishes terrorism from all other uses of force or coercion?
4. Khatchadourian argues that three principles of just war theory are flagrantly violated by terrorism. What are these three principles, and why does terrorism violate them?

5. In addition, Khatchadourian argues that all but the moralistic/religious type of terrorism violate a further condition of just war theory. What is this condition and why does terrorism violate it?
6. How does Khatchadourian explain the right to life? When can this right be overridden?
7. Khatchadourian argues that terrorism violates basic human rights. What are these rights and why does terrorism violate them?

Discussion Questions

1. Does Khatchadourian succeed in proving that "terrorism, in all its types and forms, is always wrong"? For example, what about acts of terrorism by Jews in Germany during World War II?
2. The bombing of Hiroshima and Nagasaki caused the death of over 200,000 noncombatants. Was this an act of terrorism? If so, was it morally wrong? Explain your answers.
3. Given Khatchadourian's account of innocence and noninnocence, is anyone perfectly innocent? Who has no share in the moral responsibility, no causal responsibility at all, for any wrong that gives or gave rise to terrorism?

The Terrorist's Tacit Message*

LAURIE CALHOUN

Laurie Calhoun is the author of *Philosophy Unmasked: A Skeptic's Critique* (1997) and many essays on ethics, rhetoric, and war.

Like Khatchadourian in the previous reading, Calhoun applies just war theory to terrorism. Terrorism is condemned by the governments of democratic nations, who continue to engage in "just wars." But when the assumptions involved in the "just war" approach to group conflict are examined, it emerges that terrorists merely follow these assumptions to their logical conclusion. They see themselves fighting "just wars," as "warriors for justice." That is their tacit message. Accordingly, unless the stance toward war embraced by most governments of the world transforms radically, terrorism can be expected to continue over time. As groups proliferate, so will conflicts, and some groups will resort to deadly force, reasoning along "just war" lines. Because terrorists are innovative strategists, it is doubtful that measures based upon conventional military operations will effectively counter terrorism.

Source: Reprinted from *The Peace Review*. © Taylor & Francis Ltd. Used by permission of the publisher. http://www.tandf.co.uk/journals
*Editor's Note: This article was written before 9/11.

THE REFUSAL TO "negotiate with terrorists" is a common refrain in political parlance. It is often accepted as self-evident that terrorists are so far beyond the pale that it would be morally reprehensible even to engage in discourse with them. But the term "terrorist" remains elusive, defined in various ways by various parties, albeit always derogatorily. Judging from the use of the term by the government officials of disparate nations, it would seem to be analytically true that, whoever the speakers may be, they are not terrorists. "Terrorists" refers exclusively to *them,* a lesser or greater set of political actors, depending ultimately upon the sympathies of the speaker.

Government leaders often speak as though terrorists are beyond the reach of reason, but particular terrorists in particular places believe that they are transmitting to the populace a message with concrete content. The message invariably takes the following general form: *There is something seriously wrong with the world in which we live, and this must be changed.* Terrorists sometimes claim to have as their aim to rouse the populace to consciousness so that they might at last see what the terrorists take themselves to have seen. However, the members of various terrorist groups together transmit (unwittingly) a more global message. The lesson that we ought to glean from terrorists is not the specific, context-dependent message that they hope through their use of violence to convey. Terrorists are right that there is something seriously wrong with the world in which we and they live, but they are no less a party to the problem than are the governments against which they inveigh.

That the annihilation of human life is sometimes morally permissible or even obligatory is embodied in two social practices: the execution of criminals and the maintenance of military institutions. This suggests that there are two distinct ways of understanding terrorists' interpretations of their own actions. Either they are attempting to effect "vigilante justice," or else they are fighting "just wars." Because their victims are typically non-combatants, terrorist actions

more closely resemble acts of war than vigilante killings. There are of course killers who do not conceive of their own crimes along these lines, having themselves no political agenda or moral mission. Unfortunately, the tendency of governments to conflate terrorists with ordinary murderers (without political agendas) shrouds the similarity between the violent activities of factional groups and those of formal nations.

Attempts to identify "terrorists" by appeal to what these people do give rise to what some might find to be embarrassing implications. For example, to specify "terrorism" as necessarily *illegal* leads to problems in interpreting the reign of terror imposed by The Third Reich in Nazi Germany and other governmental regimes of ill repute. One might, then, propose a moral rather than a legal basis, for example, by delineating "terrorists" as *ideologically or politically motivated actors who kill or threaten to kill innocent people bearing no responsibility for the grievances of the killers.* This would imply that every nation that has engaged in bombing campaigns resulting in the deaths of innocent children has committed acts of terrorism. Faced with this proposed assimilation of nations and factions that deploy deadly force, most people will simply back away, insisting that, though a precise definition is not possible, certain obvious examples of terrorists can be enumerated, and so "terrorist" can be defined by ostension.

The governments of democratic nations harshly condemn "terrorists," but when the assumptions involved in any view according to which war is sometimes just are carefully examined, it emerges that terrorists merely follow these assumptions to their logical conclusion, given the situations in which they find themselves. While nations prohibit the use of deadly force by individuals and sub-national factions, in fact, violent attacks upon strategic targets can be understood straightforwardly as permitted by "just war" rationales, at least as interpreted by the killers. Small terrorist groups could not, with any chance of success, attack a formal military institution, so instead they select targets for their shock appeal.

While secrecy is often thought to be of the very essence of terrorism, the covert practices of terrorist groups are due in part to their illegality. The members of such groups often hide their identities (or at least their own involvement in particular acts of terrorism), not because they believe that their actions are wrong, but because it would be imprudent to expose themselves. Clearly, if one is subject to arrest for publicly committing an act, then one's efficacy as a soldier for the cause in question will be short-lived. Committing illegal acts in the open renders an actor immediately vulnerable to arrest and incarceration, but it is precisely because factional groups reject the legitimacy of the reigning regime that they undertake secretive initiatives best understood as militarily strategic. "Intelligence agencies" are an important part of modern military institutions, and secrecy has long been regarded as integral to martial excellence. Sun Tzu, author of the ancient Chinese classic *The Art of War*, observed nearly three thousand years ago that "All warfare is based on deception."

It is perhaps often simply terrorists' fervent commitment to their cause that leads them to maximize the efficacy of their campaigns by sheltering themselves from vulnerability to the laws of the land, as any prudent transgressor of the law would do. At the other extreme, suicide missions, in which agents openly act in ways that lead to their personal demise, are undertaken only when such martyrdom appears to be the most effective means of drawing attention to the cause. Far from being beyond rational comprehension, the actions of terrorists are dictated by military strategy deployed in the name of what the actors believe to be justice. The extreme lengths to which terrorists are willing to go, the sacrifices that they will make in their efforts to effect a change in the *status quo,* evidence their ardent commitment to their cause.

The common construal of war as a sometimes "necessary evil" implies that war may be waged when the alternative (not waging war) would be worse. If the military could have achieved its objectives without killing innocent people, then it would have done so. Military spokesmen have often maintained that unintended civilian deaths, even when foreseen, are permissible, provided the situation is sufficiently grave. In the just war tradition, what matters, morally speaking, is whether such "collateral damage" is intended by the actors. Equally integral to defenses of the moral permissibility of collateral damage is the principle of last resort, according to which non-belligerent means must have been attempted and failed. If war is not a last resort, then collateral damage is avoidable and therefore morally impermissible. Few would deny that, if there exist ways to resolve a conflict without destroying innocent persons in the process, then those methods must, morally speaking, be pursued. But disputes arise, in specific contexts, regarding whether in fact non-belligerent means to conflict resolution exist. To say that during wartime people *resort* to deadly force is to say that they have a reason, for it is of the very nature of justification to advert to reasons. Defenders of the recourse by nations to deadly force as a means of conflict resolution are willing to condone the killing of innocent people under certain circumstances. The question becomes: When have non-belligerent means been exhausted?

Perhaps the most important (though seldom acknowledged) problem with just war theory is its inextricable dependence upon the interpretation of the very people considering recourse to deadly force. Human fallibility is a given, so in owning that war is justified in some cases, one must acknowledge that the "facts" upon which a given interpretation is based may prove to be false. And anyone who affirms the right (or obligation) to wage war when *they believe* the tenets of just war theory to be satisfied, must, in consistency, also affirm this right (or obligation) for all those who find themselves in analogous situations. But throughout human history wars have been characterized by their instigators as "just," including those retrospectively denounced as grossly unjust, for example, Hitler's campaign. People tend to ascribe good intentions to their own leaders and comrades while ascribing evil intentions to those stigmatized by officials as "the enemy."

The simplicity of its intuitive principles accounts for the widespread appeal of the "just war" paradigm. Throughout human history appeals to principles of "just cause" and "last resort" have been made by both sides to virtually every violent conflict. "Just war" rationalizations are available to everyone, Hussein as well as Bush, Milosevic as well as Clinton. To take a recent example, we find Timothy McVeigh characterizing the deaths of innocent people in the Oklahoma City bombing as "collateral damage." The public response to McVeigh's "preposterous" appropriation of just war theory suggests how difficult it is for military supporters to admit that they are not so very different from the political killers whose actions they condemn.

The received view is that the intention of planting bombs in public places such as the Federal Building in Oklahoma City or the World Trade Center in New York City is to terrorize, and the people who do such things are terrorists. According to the received view, though some innocent people may have been traumatized and killed during the Vietnam War, the Gulf War, and NATO's 1999 bombing campaign in Kosovo, whatever the intentions behind those actions may have been, they certainly were not to *terrorize* people. Nations excuse as regrettable though unavoidable the deaths of children such as occurred during the Gulf War, the Vietnam War, and in Kosovo during NATO's bombing campaign against the regime of Slobodan Milosevic. "Terrorists" are the people who threaten or deploy deadly force for causes of which we do not approve.

Political organizations have often engaged in actions intended to instill fear in the populace and thus draw attention to their cause. But the groups that engage in what is typically labeled "terrorism" are motivated by grievances no less than are nations engaged in war. Were their grievances somehow alleviated, dissenting political groups would no longer feel the need to engage in what they interpret to be "just wars." In appropriating military rationales and tactics, terrorists underscore the obvious, that nations are conventionally assembled groups of people who appoint their leaders just as do sub-national factions. The problem with the received view is that it exercises maximal interpretive charity when it comes to nations (most often, the interpreter's own), while minimal interpretive charity when it comes to sub-national groups. The intention of a terrorist act, *as understood by the terrorist,* is not the immediate act of terrorism, but to air some grave concern, which the terrorist is attempting to bring to the public's attention. In reality, the requirement of "last resort" seems far simpler to fulfill in the cases of smaller, informal factional groups than in those involving a first-world super power such as the United States, the economic policies of which can, with only minor modifications, spell catastrophe for an offending regime. According to the just war tradition, the permissible use of deadly force is a last resort, deployed only after all pacific means have proven infeasible, and the terrorist most likely reasons along precisely these lines. Indeed, the urgency of the terrorist's situation (to his own mind) makes his own claims regarding last resort all the more compelling. A terrorist, no less than the military spokesmen of established nations, may regret the deaths of the innocent people to which his activities give rise. But, applying the "just war" approach to "collateral damage," terrorists may emerge beyond moral reproach, since were their claims adequately addressed by the powers that be, they would presumably cease their violent activities. It is because they believe that their rights have been denied that groups engage in the activities identified as "terrorism" and thought by most people to be morally distinct from the military actions of states.

Once one grants the possibility of a "just war," it seems to follow straightforwardly that political dissidents convinced of the unjust practices of the government in power ought to engage in violent acts of subversion. Factions lack the advantage of currently enshrined institutions that naturally perpetuate the very *status quo* claimed by dissidents to be unjust. Accordingly, so long as nations continue to wage wars in the name of "justice," it seems plausible that smaller groups and factions will do so as well. Many terrorist groups insist that their claims have been squelched or ignored by the regime in power. But if formal nations may wage war to defend their own integrity and sovereignty, then why not separatist groups? And if such a group lacks a nationally funded and sanctioned army, then must not the group assemble its own?

The terrorist is not a peculiar type of creature who nefariously resorts to deadly force in opposition to the demands of morality upheld by all civilized nations. Rather, the terrorist merely embraces the widely held view that deadly military action is morally permissible, while delimiting "nations" differently than do those who uncritically accept the conventions which they have been raised to believe. The nations in existence are historically contingent, not a part of the very essence of things. The terrorist recognizes that current nations came into being and transformed as a result of warfare. Accordingly, agents who, in the name of justice, wield deadly force against the society in which they live conceive of themselves as civil warriors. Terrorist groups are smaller armies than those of established nations funded by taxpayers and sanctioned by the law, but for this very reason they may feel compelled to avail themselves of particularly drastic methods. No less than the military leaders of most countries throughout history, terrorists maintain that the situations which call for war are so desperate as to require the extremest of measures.

That a terrorist is not *sui generis* can be illustrated as follows: Imagine the commander-in-chief of any established nation being, instead, the leader of a group dissenting from the currently reigning regime. The very same person's acts of deadly violence (or his ordering his comrades to commit such acts) do not differ in his own mind merely because he has been formally designated the commander-in-chief in one case but not in the other. Both parties to every conflict maintain that they are right and their adversaries wrong, and terrorist factions are not exceptional in this respect. When we look carefully at the situation of terrorists, it becomes difficult to identify any morally significant distinction between what they do and what formal nations do in flying planes over enemy nations and dropping bombs, knowing full well that innocent people will die as a result of their actions.

Most advanced nations with standing armies not only produce but also export the types of deadly weapons used by factions in terrorist actions. If we restrict the use of the term "terrorist" to those groups that deploy deadly violence "beyond the pale" of any established legal system, then it follows that terrorists derive their weapons from more formal (and legal) military institutions and industries. The conventional weapons trade has proven all but impossible to control, given the ease with which stockpiled arms are transferred from regime to regime and provided by some countries to smaller groups that they deem to be politically correct. And even when scandals such as Iran-Contra are brought to light, seldom are the culpable agents held more than nominally accountable for their actions. Leniency toward military personnel and political leaders who engage in or facilitate patriotic though illegal weapons commerce results from the basic assumption on the part of most people, that they and their comrades are good, while those who disagree are not.

In some cases, terrorists develop innovative weapons through the use of materials with non-military applications, for example, sulfuric acid or ammonium nitrate. Given the possibility for innovative destruction by terrorist groups, it would seem that even more instrumental to the perpetuation of terrorism than the ongoing exportation of deadly weapons is the support by national leaders of *the idea* that killing human beings can be a mandate of justice. Bombing campaigns serve as graphic illustrations of the approbation by governments of the use of deadly force. It is simple indeed to understand what must be a common refrain among members of dissenting groups who adopt violent means: "If they can do it, then why cannot we?"

Political groups have agendas, and some of these groups deploy violence strategically in attempting to effect their aims. Terrorists are not "beyond the pale," intellectually and morally speaking, for their actions are best understood through appeal to the very just war theory invoked by nations in defending their own military campaigns. Terrorists interpret their own wars as just, while holding culpable all those who benefit from the policies of the government with which they disagree. The groups commonly identified as "terrorists" disagree with governments about not whether there can be a just war, nor whether morality is of such paramount importance as sometimes to require the killing of innocent people. Terrorist groups and the military institutions of nations embrace the very same "just war" schema, disagreeing only about facts.

Thus we find that the terrorist conveys two distinct messages. First, and this is usually the only claim to truth recognized by outsiders, the terrorist alleges injustices within the framework of society. In many cases there may be some truth to the specific charges made by terrorist groups, and this would be enough to turn against them all those who benefit from the regime in power. But a second and more important type of truth is highlighted by the very conduct of the terrorist. Perhaps there is something profoundly misguided about not only some of the specific policies within our societies, but also the manner in which we conceptualize the institutionalized use of deadly force, the activity of war, as an acceptable route to dispute resolution.

The connotations associated with "terrorist" are strongly pejorative and, although terrorists clearly operate from within what they take to be a moral framework, they are often subject to much more powerful condemnation than non-political killers. But murderers who reject the very idea of morality would seem to be worse enemies of society than are political terrorists, who are motivated primarily by moral considerations. Why is it, then, that people fear and loathe terrorists so intensely? Perhaps they recognize, on some level, that terrorists are operating along lines that society in fact implicitly condones and even encourages. Perhaps people see shadows of themselves and their own activities in those of terrorists.

If it is true that terrorists view themselves as warriors for justice, then unless the stance toward war embraced by most governments of the world transforms radically, terrorism should be expected to continue over time. To the extent to which groups proliferate, conflicts will as well, and some subset of the parties to conflict will resort to deadly force, buoyed by what they, along with most of the populace, take to be the respectability of "just war." Military solutions are no longer used even by stable nations merely as "last resorts." Tragically, the ready availability of deadly weapons and the widespread assumption that the use of such weapons is often morally acceptable, if not obligatory, has brought about a world in which leaders often think first, not last, of military solutions to conflict. This readiness to deploy deadly means has arguably contributed to the escalation of violence in the contemporary world on many different levels, the most frightening of which being to many people those involving the unpredictable actions of factional groups, "the terrorists." But the leaders of established nations delude themselves in thinking that they will quell terrorism through threats and weapons proliferation. Terrorists "innovate" by re-defining what are commonly thought of as non-military targets as military. There is no reason for believing that terrorists' capacity for innovation will be frustrated by the construction of an anti-ballistic missile system or the implementation of other initiatives premised upon conventional military practices and strategies.

Recommended Readings

Arendt, Hannah. 1979. *The Origins of Totalitarianism.* New York: Harcourt Brace.

Calhoun, Laurie. 2002. "How Violence Breeds Violence: Some Utilitarian Considerations," *Politics,* vol. 22, no. 2, pp. 95–108.

Calhoun, Laurie. 2001. "Killing, Letting Die, and the Alleged Necessity of Military Intervention," *Peace and Conflict Studies,* vol. 8, no. 2, pp. 5–22.

Calhoun, Laurie. 2001. "The Metaethical Paradox of Just War Theory," *Ethical Theory and Moral Practice,* vol. 4, no. 1, pp. 41–58.

Calhoun, Laurie. 2002. "The Phenomenology of Paid Killing," *International Journal of Human Rights,* vol. 6, no. 1, pp. 1–18.

Calhoun, Laurie. 2001. "Violence and Hypocrisy," and "Laurie Calhoun replies [to Michael Walzer]," *Dissent,* (winter) vol. 48, no. 1, pp. 79–87. Reprinted in *Just War: A Casebook in Argumentation,* eds. Walsh & Asch, Heinle/Thomson, 2004.

Cerovic, Stanko. 2001. *Dans les griffes des humanistes,* trans. Mireille Robin. Paris: Éditions Climats.

Colson, Bruno. 1999. *L'art de la guerre de Machiavel à Clausewitz.* Namur: Bibliothèque Universitaire Moretus Plantin.

Cooper, H. H. A. 2001. "Terrorism: The Problem of Definition Revisited," *American Behavioral Scientist,* vol. 44, no. 6, pp. 881–893.

Gibbs, Jack P. 1989. "Conceptualization of Terrorism," *American Sociological Review,* vol. 54, no. 3, pp. 329–340.

Grossman, Lt. Colonel Dave. 1995. *On Killing: The Psychological Cost of Learning to Kill in War and Society.* Boston: Little Brown.

Harman, Gilbert. 2000. *Explaining Value.* Oxford: Oxford University Press.

Harman, Gilbert. 1977. *The Nature of Morality.* New York: Oxford University Press.

Holmes, Robert L. 1989. *On War and Morality.* Princeton: Princeton University Press.

Le Borgne, Claude. 1986. *La Guerre est Morte . . . mais on ne le sait pas encore.* Paris: Bernard Grasset.

Rapoport, David C. 1984. "Fear and Trembling: Terrorism in Three Religious Traditions," *The American Political Science Review,* vol. 78, no. 3, pp. 658–677.

Review Questions

1. According to Calhoun, what is the concrete message of terrorists? What is the more global message, the "tacit message"?
2. What problems does Calhoun see with the legal and moral definitions of "terrorists"?
3. How do terrorists view their actions, according to Calhoun?
4. How do military spokesmen justify "collateral damage," or the killing of innocent people, according to Calhoun?
5. What role does interpretation play in just war theory, in Calhoun's view? Why does she think that "just war" rationalizations are available to everyone, from Hussein to Bush?
6. According to Calhoun, what is the intention of the terrorist act, as understood by the terrorist?
7. Why does Calhoun believe that terrorism is best understood by appealing to the very just war theory invoked by nations defending their wars?

Discussion Questions

1. Calhoun argues that anyone can rationalize war or terrorism by appealing to just war theory. Is this true or not? Why or why not?

2. Calhoun says: "Terrorists are people who threaten or deploy deadly force for causes of which we do not approve." Do you agree? Why or why not?
3. Calhoun claims that there is hardly any moral difference between what the terrorists do and what nations such as the United States do when they drop bombs on enemy nations knowing full well that innocent people will die. Do you agree? Why or why not?

The War on Terrorism and the End of Human Rights

DAVID LUBAN

David Luban is the Frederick J. Hass Professor of Law and Philosophy at the Georgetown University Law Center. He is the author of *Lawyers and Justice* (1988), *Legal Modernism* (1994), and numerous journal articles and book chapters.

Luban argues that the current War on Terrorism combines a war model with a law model to produce a new model of state action, a hybrid war-law model. This hybrid model selectively picks out elements of the war and law models to maximize the use of lethal force while eliminating the rights of both adversaries and innocent bystanders. The result is that the War on Terrorism means the end of human rights.

IN THE IMMEDIATE aftermath of September 11, President Bush stated that the perpetrators of the deed would be brought to justice. Soon afterwards, the President announced that the United States would engage in a war on terrorism. The first of these statements adopts the familiar language of criminal law and criminal justice. It treats the September 11 attacks as horrific crimes—mass murders—and the government's mission as apprehending and punishing the surviving planners and conspirators for their roles in the crimes. The War on Terrorism is a different proposition, however, and a different model of

governmental action—not law but war. Most obviously, it dramatically broadens the scope of action, because now terrorists who knew nothing about September 11 have been earmarked as enemies. But that is only the beginning.

THE HYBRID WAR-LAW APPROACH

The model of war offers much freer rein than that of law, and therein lies its appeal in the wake of 9/11. First, in war but not in law it is permissible to use lethal force on enemy troops regardless of their degree of personal involvement with the adversary. The conscripted cook is as legitimate a target as the enemy general. Second, in war but not in law "collateral damage," that is, foreseen but unintended killing of noncombatants, is permissible. (Police cannot

Source: Luban, David, "The War on Terrorism and the End of Human Rights," from *Philosophy & Public Policy Quarterly,* Vol. 22, No. 3 (Summer 2002). Reprinted by permission of Rowman and Littlefield Publishing Group.

blow up an apartment building full of people because a murderer is inside, but an air force can bomb the building if it contains a military target.) Third, the requirements of evidence and proof are drastically weaker in war than in criminal justice. Soldiers do not need proof beyond a reasonable doubt, or even proof by a preponderance of evidence, that someone is an enemy soldier before firing on him or capturing and imprisoning him. They don't need proof at all, merely plausible intelligence. Thus, the U.S. military remains regretful but unapologetic about its January 2002 attack on the Afghani town of Uruzgan, in which 21 innocent civilians were killed, based on faulty intelligence that they were al Qaeda fighters. Fourth, in war one can attack an enemy without concern over whether he has done anything. Legitimate targets are those who in the course of combat *might* harm us, not those who *have* harmed us. No doubt there are other significant differences as well. But the basic point should be clear: Given Washington's mandate to eliminate the danger of future 9/11s, so far as humanly possible, the model of war offers important advantages over the model of law.

There are disadvantages as well. Most obviously, in war but not in law, fighting back is a *legitimate* response of the enemy. Second, when nations fight a war, other nations may opt for neutrality. Third, because fighting back is legitimate, in war the enemy soldier deserves special regard once he is rendered harmless through injury or surrender. It is impermissible to punish him for his role in fighting the war. Nor can he be harshly interrogated after he is captured. The Third Geneva Convention provides: "Prisoners of war who refuse to answer [questions] may not be threatened, insulted, or exposed to unpleasant or disadvantageous treatment of any kind." And, when the war concludes, the enemy soldier must be repatriated.

Here, however, Washington has different ideas, designed to eliminate these tactical disadvantages in the traditional war model. Washington regards international terrorism not only as a

military adversary, but also as a criminal activity and criminal conspiracy. In the law model, criminals don't get to shoot back, and their acts of violence subject them to legitimate punishment. That is what we see in Washington's prosecution of the War on Terrorism. Captured terrorists may be tried before military or civilian tribunals, and shooting back at Americans, including American troops, is a federal crime (for a statute under which John Walker Lindh was indicted criminalizes anyone regardless of nationality, who "outside the United States attempts to kill, or engages in a conspiracy to kill, a national of the United States" or "engages in physical violence with intent to cause serious bodily injury to a national of the United States; or with the result that serious bodily injury is caused to a national of the United States"). Furthermore, the U.S. may rightly demand that other countries not be neutral about murder and terrorism. Unlike the war model, a nation may insist that those who are not with us in fighting murder and terror are against us, because by not joining our operations they are providing a safe haven for terrorists or their bank accounts. By selectively combining elements of the war model and elements of the law model, Washington is able to maximize its own ability to mobilize lethal force against terrorists while eliminating most traditional rights of a military adversary, as well as the rights of innocent bystanders caught in the crossfire.

A LIMBO OF RIGHTLESSNESS

The legal status of al Qaeda suspects imprisoned at the Guantanamo Bay Naval Base in Cuba is emblematic of this hybrid war-law approach to the threat of terrorism. In line with the war model, they lack the usual rights of criminal suspects—the presumption of innocence, the right to a hearing to determine guilt, the opportunity to prove that the authorities have grabbed the wrong man. But, in line with the law model, they are considered *unlawful* combatants. Because they are not uniformed forces, they lack the rights of prisoners of war and are liable to criminal punishment. Initially, the American government declared that the Guantanamo Bay prisoners have no rights under the Geneva Conventions. In the face of international protests, Washington quickly backpedaled and announced that the Guantanamo Bay prisoners would indeed be treated as decently as POWs—but it also made clear that the prisoners have no right to such treatment. Neither criminal suspects nor POWs, neither fish nor fowl, they inhabit a limbo of rightlessness. Secretary of Defense Rumsfeld's assertion that the U.S. may continue to detain them even if they are acquitted by a military tribunal dramatizes the point.

To understand how extraordinary their status is, consider an analogy. Suppose that Washington declares a War on Organized Crime. Troops are dispatched to Sicily, and a number of Mafiosi are seized, brought to Guantanamo Bay, and imprisoned without a hearing for the indefinite future, maybe the rest of their lives. They are accused of no crimes, because their capture is based not on what they have done but on what they might do. After all, to become "made" they took oaths of obedience to the bad guys. Seizing them accords with the war model: they are enemy foot soldiers. But they are foot soldiers out of uniform; they lack a "fixed distinctive emblem," in the words of The Hague Convention. That makes them unlawful combatants, so they lack the rights of POWs. They may object that it is only a unilateral declaration by the American President that has turned them into combatants in the first place—he called it a war, they didn't—and that, since they do not regard themselves as literal foot soldiers it never occurred to them to wear a fixed distinctive emblem. They have a point. It seems too easy for the President to divest anyone in the world of rights and liberty simply by announcing that the U.S. is at war with them and then declaring them unlawful combatants if they resist. But, in the hybrid war-law model, they protest in vain.

Consider another example. In January 2002, U.S. forces in Bosnia seized five Algerians and a Yemeni suspected of al Qaeda connections and took them to Guantanamo Bay. The six had been jailed in Bosnia, but a Bosnian court released them for lack of evidence, and the Bosnian Human Rights Chamber issued an injunction that four of them be allowed to remain in the country pending further legal proceedings. The Human Rights Chamber, ironically, was created under U.S. auspices in the Dayton peace accords, and it was designed specifically to protect against treatment like this. Ruth Wedgwood, a well-known international law scholar at Yale and a member of the Council on Foreign Relations, defended the Bosnian seizure in war-model terms. "I think we would simply argue this was a matter of self-defense. One of the fundamental rules of military law is that you have a right ultimately to act in self-defense. And if these folks were actively plotting to blow up the U.S. embassy, they should be considered combatants and captured as combatants in a war." Notice that Professor Wedgwood argues in terms of what the men seized in Bosnia were *planning to do,* not what they *did;* notice as well that the decision of the Bosnian court that there was insufficient evidence does not matter. These are characteristics of the war model.

More recently, two American citizens alleged to be al Qaeda operatives (Jose Padilla, a.k.a. Abdullah al Muhajir, and Yasser Esam Hamdi) have been held in American military prisons, with no crimes charged, no opportunity to consult counsel, and no hearing. The President described Padilla as "a bad man" who aimed to build a nuclear "dirty" bomb and use it against America; and the Justice Department has classified both men as "enemy combatants" who may be held indefinitely. Yet, as military law expert Gary Solis points out, "Until now, as used by the attorney general, the term 'enemy combatant' appeared nowhere in U.S. criminal law, international law or in the law of war." The phrase comes from the 1942 Supreme Court case *Ex parte Quirin,* but all the Court says there is that "an enemy combatant who without uniform comes secretly through the lines for the purpose of waging war by destruction of life or property" would "not . . . be entitled to the status of prisoner of war, but

. . . [they would] be offenders against the law of war subject to trial and punishment by military tribunals." For the Court, in other words, the status of a person as a non-uniformed enemy combatant makes him a criminal rather than a warrior, and determines *where* he is tried (in a military, rather than a civilian, tribunal) but not *whether* he is tried. Far from authorizing open-ended confinement, *Ex parte Quirin* presupposes that criminals are entitled to hearings: without a hearing how can suspects prove that the government made a mistake? *Quirin* embeds the concept of "enemy combatant" firmly in the law model. In the war model, by contrast, POWs may be detained without a hearing until hostilities are over. But POWs were captured in uniform, and only their undoubted identity as enemy soldiers justifies such open-ended custody. Apparently, Hamdi and Padilla will get the worst of both models—open-ended custody with no trial, like POWs, but no certainty beyond the U.S. government's say-so that they really are "bad men." This is the hybrid war-law model. It combines the *Quirin* category of "enemy combatant without uniform," used in the law model to justify a military trial, with the war model's practice of indefinite confinement with no trial at all.

THE CASE FOR THE HYBRID APPROACH

Is there any justification for the hybrid war-law model, which so drastically diminishes the rights of the enemy? An argument can be offered along the following lines. In ordinary cases of war among states, enemy soldiers may well be morally and politically innocent. Many of them are conscripts, and those who aren't do not necessarily endorse the state policies they are fighting to defend. But enemy soldiers in the War on Terrorism are, by definition, those who have embarked on a path of terrorism. They are neither morally nor politically innocent. Their sworn aim—"Death to America!"—is to create more 9/11s. In this respect, they are much

more akin to criminal conspirators than to conscript soldiers. Terrorists will fight as soldiers when they must, and metamorphose into mass murderers when they can.

Furthermore, suicide terrorists pose a special, unique danger. Ordinary criminals do not target innocent bystanders. They may be willing to kill them if necessary, but bystanders enjoy at least some measure of security because they are not primary targets. Not so with terrorists, who aim to kill as many innocent people as possible. Likewise, innocent bystanders are protected from ordinary criminals by whatever deterrent force the threat of punishment and the risk of getting killed in the act of committing a crime offer. For a suicide bomber, neither of these threats is a deterrent at all—after all, for the suicide bomber one of the hallmarks of a *successful* operation is that he winds up dead at day's end. Given the unique and heightened danger that suicide terrorists pose, a stronger response that grants potential terrorists fewer rights may be justified. Add to this the danger that terrorists may come to possess weapons of mass destruction, including nuclear devices in suitcases. Under circumstances of such dire menace, it is appropriate to treat terrorists as though they embody the most dangerous aspects of both warriors and criminals. That is the basis of the hybrid war-law model.

THE CASE AGAINST EXPEDIENCY

The argument against the hybrid war-law model is equally clear. The U.S. has simply chosen the bits of the law model and the bits of the war model that are most convenient for American interests, and ignored the rest. The model abolishes the rights of potential enemies (and their innocent shields) by fiat—not for reasons of moral or legal principle, but solely because the U.S. does not want them to have rights. The more rights they have, the more risk they pose. But Americans' urgent desire to minimize our risks doesn't make other people's rights disappear. Calling our policy a War on Terrorism obscures this point.

The theoretical basis of the objection is that the law model and the war model each comes as a package, with a kind of intellectual integrity. The law model grows out of relationships within states, while the war model arises from relationships between states. The law model imputes a ground-level community of values to those subject to the law—paradigmatically, citizens of a state, but also visitors and foreigners who choose to engage in conduct that affects a state. Only because law imputes shared basic values to the community can a state condemn the conduct of criminals and inflict punishment on them. Criminals deserve condemnation and punishment because their conduct violates norms that we are entitled to count on their sharing. But, for the same reason—the imputed community of values—those subject to the law ordinarily enjoy a presumption of innocence and an expectation of safety. The government cannot simply grab them and confine them without making sure they have broken the law, nor can it condemn them without due process for ensuring that it has the right person, nor can it knowingly place bystanders in mortal peril in the course of fighting crime. They are our fellows, and the community should protect them just as it protects us. The same imputed community of values that justifies condemnation and punishment creates rights to due care and due process.

War is different. War is the ultimate acknowledgment that human beings do not live in a single community with shared norms. If their norms conflict enough, communities pose a physical danger to each other, and nothing can safeguard a community against its enemies except force of arms. That makes enemy soldiers legitimate targets; but it makes our soldiers legitimate targets as well, and, once the enemy no longer poses a danger, he should be immune from punishment, because if he has fought cleanly he has violated no norms that we are entitled to presume he honors. Our norms are, after all, *our* norms, not his.

Because the law model and war model come as conceptual packages, it is unprincipled to wrench them apart and recombine them simply because it is in America's interest to do so. To declare that Americans can fight enemies with the latitude of warriors, but if the enemies fight back they are not warriors but criminals, amounts to a kind of heads-I-win-tails-you-lose international morality in which whatever it takes to reduce American risk, no matter what the cost to others, turns out to be justified. This, in brief, is the criticism of the hybrid war-law model.

To be sure, the law model could be made to incorporate the war model merely by rewriting a handful of statutes. Congress could enact laws permitting imprisonment or execution of persons who pose a significant threat of terrorism whether or not they have already done anything wrong. The standard of evidence could be set low and the requirement of a hearing eliminated. Finally, Congress could authorize the use of lethal force against terrorists regardless of the danger to innocent bystanders, and it could immunize officials from lawsuits or prosecution by victims of collateral damage. Such statutes would violate the Constitution, but the Constitution could be amended to incorporate anti-terrorist exceptions to the Fourth, Fifth, and Sixth Amendments. In the end, we would have a system of law that includes all the essential features of the war model.

It would, however, be a system that imprisons people for their intentions rather than their actions, and that offers the innocent few protections against mistaken detention or inadvertent death through collateral damage. Gone are the principles that people should never be punished for their thoughts, only for their deeds, and that innocent people must be protected rather than injured by their own government. In that sense, at any rate, repackaging war as law seems merely cosmetic, because it replaces the ideal of law as a protector of rights with the more problematic goal of protecting some innocent people by sacrificing others. The hypothetical legislation incorporates war into law only by making law as partisan and ruthless as war. It no longer resembles law as Americans generally understand it.

THE THREAT TO INTERNATIONAL HUMAN RIGHTS

In the War on Terrorism, what becomes of international human rights? It seems beyond dispute that the war model poses a threat to international human rights, because honoring human rights is neither practically possible nor theoretically required during war. Combatants are legitimate targets; non-combatants maimed by accident or mistake are regarded as collateral damage rather than victims of atrocities; cases of mistaken identity get killed or confined without a hearing because combat conditions preclude due process. To be sure, the laws of war specify minimum human rights, but these are far less robust than rights in peacetime—and the hybrid war-law model reduces this schedule of rights even further by classifying the enemy as unlawful combatants.

One striking example of the erosion of human rights is tolerance of torture. It should be recalled that a 1995 al Qaeda plot to bomb eleven U.S. airliners was thwarted by information tortured out of a Pakistani suspect by the Philippine police—an eerie real-life version of the familiar philosophical thought-experiment. The *Washington Post* reports that since September 11 the U.S. has engaged in the summary transfer of dozens of terrorism suspects to countries where they will be interrogated under torture. But it isn't just the United States that has proven willing to tolerate torture for security reasons. Last December, the Swedish government snatched a suspected Islamic extremist to whom it had previously granted political asylum, and the same day had him transferred to Egypt, where Amnesty International reports that he has been tortured to the point where he walks only with difficulty. Sweden is not, to say the least, a traditionally hard-line nation on human rights issues. None of this international transportation is lawful—indeed, it violates international treaty obligations under the Convention against Torture that in the U.S. have constitutional status as

"supreme Law of the Land"—but that may not matter under the war model, in which even constitutional rights may be abrogated.

It is natural to suggest that this suspension of human rights is an exceptional emergency measure to deal with an unprecedented threat. This raises the question of how long human rights will remain suspended. When will the war be over?

Here, the chief problem is that the War on Terrorism is not like any other kind of war. The enemy, Terrorism, is not a territorial state or nation or government. There is no opposite number to negotiate with. There is no one on the other side to call a truce or declare a ceasefire, no one among the enemy authorized to surrender. In traditional wars among states, the war aim is, as Clausewitz argued, to impose one state's political will on another's. The *aim* of the war is not to kill the enemy—killing the enemy is the *means* used to achieve the real end, which is to force capitulation. In the War on Terrorism, no capitulation is possible. That means that the real aim of the war is, quite simply, to kill or capture all of the terrorists—to keep on killing and killing, capturing and capturing, until they are all gone.

Of course, no one expects that terrorism will ever disappear completely. Everyone understands that new anti-American extremists, new terrorists, will always arise and always be available for recruitment and deployment. Everyone understands that even if al Qaeda is destroyed or decapitated, other groups, with other leaders, will arise in its place. It follows, then, that the War on Terrorism will be a war that can only be abandoned, never concluded. The War has no natural resting point, no moment of victory or finality. It requires a mission of killing and capturing, in territories all over the globe, that will go on in perpetuity. It follows as well that the suspension of human rights implicit in the hybrid war-law model is not temporary but permanent.

Perhaps with this fear in mind, Congressional authorization of President Bush's military campaign limits its scope to those responsible for September 11 and their sponsors. But the War on Terrorism has taken on a life of its own that makes the Congressional authorization little more than a technicality. Because of the threat of nuclear terror, the American leadership actively debates a war on Iraq regardless of whether Iraq was implicated in September 11; and the President's yoking of Iraq, Iran, and North Korea into a single axis of evil because they back terror suggests that the War on Terrorism might eventually encompass all these nations. If the U.S. ever unearths tangible evidence that any of these countries is harboring or abetting terrorists with weapons of mass destruction, there can be little doubt that Congress will support military action. So too, Russia invokes the American War on Terrorism to justify its attacks on Chechen rebels, China uses it to deflect criticisms of its campaign against Uighur separatists, and Israeli Prime Minister Sharon explicitly links military actions against Palestinian insurgents to the American War on Terrorism. No doubt there is political opportunism at work in some or all of these efforts to piggy-back onto America's campaign, but the opportunity would not exist if "War on Terrorism" were merely the code-name of a discrete, neatly-boxed American operation. Instead, the War on Terrorism has become a model of politics, a world-view with its own distinctive premises and consequences. As I have argued, it includes a new model of state action, the hybrid war-law model, which depresses human rights from their peace-time standard to the war-time standard, and indeed even further. So long as it continues, the War on Terrorism means the end of human rights, at least for those near enough to be touched by the fire of battle.

Sources: On the January 2002 attack on the Afghani town of Uruzgan, see: John Ward Anderson, "Afghans Falsely Held by U.S. Tried to Explain; Fighters Recount Unanswered Pleas, Beatings—and an Apology on Their Release," *Washington Post* (March 26, 2002); see also Susan B. Glasser, "Afghans Live and Die With U.S. Mistakes; Villagers Tell of Over 100 Casualties," *Washington Post* (Feb. 20, 2002). On the Third Geneva Convention, see: Geneva Convention (III) Relative to the Treatment of Prisoners of War, 6 U.S.T. 3317, signed on August 12, 1949, at Geneva, Article 17. Although the U.S. has not ratified the Geneva Convention, it has become part of customary international law, and certainly belongs to the war model. Count One of the Lindh indictment charges him with violating 18 U.S.C. 2332(b), "Whoever outside the United States attempts to kill, or engages in a conspiracy to kill, a national of the United States" may be sentenced to 20 years (for attempts) or life imprisonment (for conspiracies). Subsection (c) likewise criminalizes "engag[ing] in physical violence with intent to cause serious bodily injury to a national of the United States; or with the result that serious bodily injury is caused to a national of the United States." Lawful combatants are defined in the Hague Convention (IV) Respecting the Laws and Customs of War on Land, Annex to the Convention, 1 Bevans 631, signed on October 18, 1907, at The Hague, Article 1. The definition requires that combatants "have a fixed distinctive emblem recognizable at a distance." Protocol I Additional to the Geneva Conventions of 1949, 1125 U.N.T.S. 3, adopted on June 8, 1977, at Geneva, Article 44(3) makes an important change in the Hague Convention, expanding the definition of combatants to include non-uniformed irregulars. However, the United States has not agreed to Protocol I. The source of Ruth Wedgwood's remarks: Interview with Melissa Block, National Public Radio program, "All Things Considered" (January 18, 2002); Gary Solis, "Even a 'Bad Man' Has Rights," *Washington Post* (June 25, 2002); *Ex parte Quirin*, 317 U.S. 1, 31 (1942). On the torture of the Pakistani militant by Philippine police: Doug Struck et al., "Borderless Network Of Terror; Bin Laden Followers Reach Across Globe," *Washington Post* (September 23, 2001): "'For weeks, agents hit him with a chair and a long piece of wood, forced water into his mouth, and crushed lighted cigarettes into his private parts,' wrote journalists Marites Vitug and Glenda Gloria in 'Under the Crescent Moon,' an acclaimed book on Abu Sayyaf. 'His ribs were almost totally broken and his captors were surprised he survived.'" On U.S. and Swedish transfers of Isamic militants to countries employing torture: Rajiv Chandrasakaran & Peter Finn, "U.S. Behind Secret Transfer of Terror Suspects," *Washington Post* (March 11, 2002); Peter Finn, "Europeans Tossing Terror Suspects Out the Door," *Washington Post* (January 29, 2002); Anthony Shadid, "Fighting Terror/Atmosphere in Europe, Military Campaign/Asylum Bids; in Shift, Sweden Extradites Militants to Egypt," *Boston Globe* (December 31, 2001). Article 3(1) of the Convention against Torture provides that "No State Party shall expel, return ('*refouler*') or extradite a person to another State where there are substantial grounds for believing that he would be in danger of being subjected to torture." Article 2(2) cautions that "No exceptional circumstances whatsoever, whether a state of war or a threat of war, internal political instability or any other public emergency, may be invoked as a justification of torture." But no parallel caution is incorporated into Article 3(1)'s non-*refoulement* rule, and a lawyer might well argue that its absence implies that the rule may be abrogated during war or similar public emergency. *Convention* *against Torture and Other Cruel, Inhuman or Degrading Treatment or Punishment,* 1465 U.N.T.S. 85. Ratified by the United States, Oct. 2, 1994. Entered into force for the United States, Nov. 20, 1994. (Article VI of the U.S. Constitution provides that treaties are the "supreme Law of the Land.")

Review Questions

1. According to Luban, what is the traditional model of war? What are its four main features? What are its disadvantages?
2. How does Luban describe the law model? How is it combined with the war model to produce a hybrid war-law approach to terrorism?
3. In Luban's view, what is the legal status of al Qaeda suspects? Do they have any rights?
4. Describe the case of the al Qaeda suspects seized in Bosnia.
5. How does Luban explain the concept of enemy combatant? How is this concept applied to Jose Padilla and Yasser Esam Harudi?
6. According to Luban what is the case for the hybrid war-law model? What is the case against it?
7. In Luban's view, what becomes of human rights in the War on Terrorism?

Discussion Questions

1. In January 2002, the U.S. military killed 21 innocent civilians in an attack on the Afganhi town of Uruzgan. Was this attack justified? Why or why not?
2. Should the Guantanamo prisoners have rights? If so, what are they? If not, why not?
3. Is it acceptable to confine suspected terrorists indefinitely with no trial?
4. Is the hybrid war-law model of the War on Terrorism acceptable? Why or why not?
5. Should torture be used to fight terrorism? Why or why not?

The Concept and Practice of Jihad in Islam

MICHAEL G. KNAPP

Michael G. Knapp is a Middle East/Africa analyst with the U.S. Army National Ground Intelligence Center in Charlottesville, Virginia. He has worked in U.S. government intelligence for over 24 years.

Knapp surveys the development of the concept of jihad in Islam. The classical view was that jihad, defined as fighting in the path of God, was restricted to defensive war against non-Muslims. Modern militant Islam has changed the concept to include

Source: Michael G. Knapp, "The Concept and Practice of Jihad in Islam," from *Parameters,* Spring 2003, pp. 82–84. Used by permission.

wars of aggression against non-Muslims. Now states such as Egypt and its neighbors that mix Islamic and European laws are considered by radicals to be non-Muslim. The radical movement has reached an extreme in the ideology of Osama bin Laden, who has twice declared war, jihad, against the United States and its allies.

"All these crimes and sins committed by the Americans are a clear declaration of war on God, his Messenger, and Muslims. . . . [T]he jihad is an individual duty if the enemy destroys the Muslim countries. . . . As for the fighting to repulse [an enemy], it is aimed at defending sanctity and religion, and it is a duty. . . . On that basis, and in compliance with God's order, we issue the following fatwa to all Muslims: The ruling to kill the Americans and their allies—civilian and military—is an individual duty for every Muslim who can do it in any country in which it is possible to do it."

— *Osama bin Laden et al., in "Declaration of the World Islamic Front for Jihad Against the Jews and Crusaders," 23 February 1998*

THE WORD "JIHAD" MEANS "struggle" or "striving" (in the way of God) or to work for a noble cause with determination; it does not mean "holy war" (war in Arabic is *harb* and holy is *muqadassa*). Unlike its medieval Christian counterpart term, "crusade" ("war for the cross"), however, the term jihad for Muslims has retained its religious and military connotation into modern times. The word jihad has appeared widely in the Western news media following the 11 September 2001 terrorist attacks on the World Trade Center and the Pentagon, but the true meaning of this term in the Islamic world (it is sometimes called the "sixth pillar" of the faith) is still not well understood by non-Muslims.

In war, the first essential is to know your adversary—how he thinks and why he thinks that way, and what his strategy and objectives are—so that you can attempt to frustrate his plans and protect the lives of your fellow citizens. Understanding how radical Muslims see jihad and are employing it asymmetrically against us can provide us with that kind of perspective.

This article will trace the development of jihad through early Islamic history into the present day, and will focus on how jihad in concept and practice has been appropriated and distorted by Muslim extremists as part of their violent campaign against the West and their own governments. Jihad as a centerpiece of radical thought is illustrated by examining the doctrines of prominent extremist groups such as Hamas and Egyptian Islamic Jihad. Misuse of the term by prominent extremist leaders, such as by Osama bin Laden and others in the quote above, is also addressed.

THE CLASSICAL CONCEPT OF JIHAD

Qur'anic and Early Legal Perspectives

Muslims themselves have disagreed throughout their history about the meaning of the term jihad. In the Qur'an (or Koran), it is normally found in the sense of fighting in the path of God; this was used to describe warfare against the enemies of the early Muslim community (*ummah*). In the *hadith,* the second-most authoritative source of the *shari'a* (Islamic law), jihad is used to mean armed action, and most Islamic theologians and jurists in the classical period (the first three centuries) of Muslim history understood this obligation to be in a military sense.[1]

Islamic jurists saw jihad in the context of conflict in a world divided between the *Dar al-Islam* (territory under Islamic control) and the *Dar al-harb* (territory of war, which consisted of all lands not under Muslim rule). The inhabitants of the territory of war are divided between "People of the Book" (mainly Jews and Christians) and polytheists. This requirement to continue jihad until all of the world is included in the territory of Islam does not imply that Muslims must wage nonstop warfare, however. Although there was no mechanism for recognizing a non-Muslim government as legitimate, jurists allowed for the negotiation of truces and peace treaties of limited duration. Additionally, extending the territory of Islam does not mean the annihilation of all non-Muslims, nor even their necessary conversion: jihad cannot imply conversion by force, since the Qur'an (2:256) states that "There is no compulsion in religion." More than a religious aim, jihad really had a political one: the drive to establish a single, unified Muslim realm justified Islam's supercession of other faiths and allowed for the creation of a just political and social order.[2]

Jihad was generally understood not as an obligation of each individual Muslim (known as *fard 'ayn*) but as a general requirement of the Muslim community (*fard kifaya*). Only in emergencies, when the Dar al-Islam comes under unexpected attack, do all Muslims have to participate in jihad. Under normal circumstances, therefore, an individual Muslim need not take part so long as other Muslims carry the burden for all of defending the realm.[3]

Other Philosophical Perspectives

This consensus view of a restricted, defensive version of jihad was contested by Muslim legal philosopher Taqi al-Din Ahmad Ibn Taymiyya (1263–1328). He declared that a ruler who fails to enforce the shari'a rigorously in all aspects, including the conduct of jihad (and is therefore insufficiently Muslim), forfeits his right to rule. Ibn Taymiyya strongly advocated jihad as warfare against both the Crusaders and Mongols who then occupied parts of the Dar al-Islam, and most important, broke with the mainstream of Islam by asserting that a professing Muslim who does not live by the faith is an apostate (unbeliever). By going well beyond most jurists (who tolerated rulers who violated the shari'a for the sake of community stability), Ibn Taymiyya laid much of the groundwork for the intellectual arguments of contemporary radical Islamists.[4]

Islamic law condemns all warfare that does not qualify as jihad, specifically any warfare among Muslims. Thus, military action against Muslims is justified only by denying them the status of Muslims (e.g., classifying them as apostates or rebels).[5] Islamic juristic tradition is also very hostile toward terror as a means of political resistance. Classical Muslim jurists were remarkably tolerant toward political rebels by holding that they may not be executed nor their property confiscated. This tolerance vanished, however, for rebels who conducted attacks against unsuspecting and defenseless victims or who spread terror through abductions, rapes, the use of poisoned arrows and poisoning of wells (the chemical warfare of this period), arson, attacks against travelers, and night attacks. In these cases, jurists demanded harsh penalties (including death) and ruled that the punishment was the same whether the perpetrator or victim was Muslim or non-Muslim.[6]

Three main views of jihad thus coexisted in pre-modern times. In addition to the classical legal view of jihad as a compulsory, communal effort to defend and expand the Dar al-Islam, and Ibn Taymiyya's notion of active jihad as an indispensable feature of legitimate rule, there was also the *Sufi* movement's doctrine of *greater jihad*. The *Sufis* (a mystical sect of Islam) understood the greater jihad as an inner struggle against the base instincts of the body but also against corruption of the soul, and believed that the greater jihad is a necessary part of the process of gaining spiritual insight. To this day, most Muslims see jihad as a personal rather than a political struggle, while physical actions taken in defense of the realm are considered the *lesser jihad*. It is not surprising, then, that disagreement over the meaning of jihad has continued into the modern era.[7]

ORIGINS OF RADICAL IDEOLOGIES

Muslim reform movements in the Middle East first acquired a sense of urgency with the arrival of European imperialism in the latter part of the 19th century. The end of colonialism and acquisition of independence by most Muslim countries after World War II accelerated this drive.

However, the massive social changes that accompanied these reforms and the simultaneous introduction of new ideas that were alien to classical Islamic tradition—such as nationalism, popular sovereignty, and women's rights—disrupted traditional ways of life and caused traumatic dislocations in these societies.[8]

Disillusionment with the path Muslim societies have taken in the modern period reached its height in the 1970s. Increasingly widespread rejection of Western civilization as a model for Muslims to emulate has been accompanied by a search for indigenous values that reflect traditional Muslim culture, as well as a drive to restore power and dignity to the community. The last 30 years have seen the rise of militant, religiously-based political groups whose ideology focuses on demands for jihad (and the willingness to sacrifice one's life) for the forceful creation of a society governed solely by the shari'a and a unified Islamic state, and to eliminate un-Islamic and unjust rulers. These groups are also reemphasizing individual conformity to the requirements of Islam.[9]

Militant Islam (also referred to as political or radical Islam) is rooted in a contemporary religious resurgence in private and public life.[10] The causes of Islamic radicalism have been religio-cultural, political, and socio-economic and have focused on issues of politics and social justice such as authoritarianism, lack of social services, and corruption, which all intertwine as catalysts. Many Islamic reform groups have blamed social ills on outside influences; for example, modernization (e.g., Westernization and secularization) has been perceived as a form of neocolonialism, an evil that replaces Muslim religious and cultural identity and values with alien ideas and models of development.[11]

Islamic militancy is still not well understood by Americans. This is partly due to the secrecy which radical Islamic groups practice to protect themselves from the authorities and from outsiders who do not share their views and aims, but also because Western public communications media frequently tend to marginalize such groups. They are dismissed as religious fanatics, anti-Western hooligans, or mindless terrorists, without making an attempt to comprehend the deep discontents that have produced these Islamic groups' violent actions or the logic of their radical cause which compels them to behave as they do.[12]

DIFFERENCES IN SUNNI AND SHI'A INTERPRETATIONS OF JIHAD

Sunni and Shi'a (Shi'ite) Muslims agree, in terms of just cause, that jihad applies to the defense of territory, life, faith, and property; it is justified to repel invasion or its threat; it is necessary to guarantee freedom for the spread of Islam; and that difference in religion alone is not a sufficient cause. Some Islamic scholars have differentiated disbelief from persecution and injustice, and claimed that jihad is justified only to fight those unbelievers who have initiated aggression against the Muslim community. Others, however, have stated more militant views which were inspired by Islamic resistance to the European powers during the colonial period: in this view, jihad as "aggressive war" is authorized against all non-Muslims, whether they are oppressing Muslims or not.

The question of right authority—no jihad can be waged unless it is directed by a legitimate ruler—also has been divisive among Muslims. The Sunnis saw all of the Muslim caliphs (particularly the first four "rightly guided" caliphs to rule after the Prophet Muhammad's death, who possessed combined religious and political authority) as legitimate callers of jihad, as long as they had the support of the realm's *ulama* (Islamic scholars). The Shi'a see this power as having been meant for the Imams, but it was wrongly denied to them by the majority Sunnis. The lack of proper authority after the disappearance of the 12th ("Hidden") Imam in 874 A.D. also posed problems for the Shi'a; this was resolved by the ulama increasingly taking this authority for itself to the point where all legitimate forms of jihad may be considered defensive, and there is no restriction on the kind of war which may be waged in the Hidden Imam's absence so long as it is authorized by a just ruler (this idea reached its zenith under Iran's Ayatollah Ruhollah Khomeini).

Both sects agree on the other prerequisites for jihad. Right intention (*niyyah*) is fundamentally important for engaging in jihad. Fighting for the sake of conquest, booty, or honor in the eyes of one's companions will earn no reward; the only valid purpose for jihad is to draw near to God. In terms of last resort, jihad may be waged only if the enemy has first been offered the triple alternative: accept Islam, pay the *jizyah* (the poll tax required for non-Muslim "People of the Book" living under Muslim control), or fight.[13]

Conditions also are placed on the behavior of combatants in jihad: discrimination of noncombatants from warriors is required, along with the prohibition of harm to noncombatants such as women, children, the disabled, monks and rabbis (unless they are involved in the fighting), and those who have been given the promise of immunity; and proportionality, meaning that the least amount of force is used to obtain the desired ends in combat.[14]

IDEAS ON JIHAD IN THE MODERN ERA

Sayyid Abu al-A'la Mawdudi (1903–1979) was the first Islamist writer to approach jihad systematically. Warfare, in his view, is conducted not just to expand Islamic political dominance, but also to establish just rule (one that includes freedom of religion). For Mawdudi (an Indo-Pakistani who agitated for Pakistan's independence from India), jihad was akin to war of liberation, and is designed to establish politically independent Muslim states. Mawdudi's view significantly changed the concept of jihad in Islam and began its association with anticolonialism and "national liberation movements." His approach paved the way for Arab resistance to Zionism and the existence of the state of Israel to be referred to as jihad.[15]

Radical Egyptian Islamist thinkers (and members of the Muslim Brotherhood) Hasan al-Banna (1906–1949) and Sayyid Qutb (1906–1966) took hold of Mawdudi's activist and nationalist conception of jihad and its role in establishing a truly Islamic government, and incorporated Ibn Taymiyya's earlier conception of jihad that includes the overthrow of governments that fail to enforce the shari'a. This idea of revolution focuses first on dealing with the radicals' own un-Islamic rulers (the "near enemy") before Muslims can direct jihad against external enemies. If leaders such as Egyptian President Anwar Sadat, for example, are not true Muslims, then they cannot lead jihad, not even against a legitimate target such as Israel. Significantly, radical Islamists consider jihad mandatory for all Muslims, making it an individual rather than a communal duty.[16]

THE USE OF JIHAD BY ISLAMIC MILITANTS

Regional Islamic Militant Groups' Perceptions

Classical Islamic criteria for jihad were based on the early unified Muslim empire. The imposition of the modern nation-state on Middle East societies, however, has made such ideas no longer applicable; this can be seen by examining contemporary Muslim militant groups' ideologies.

The Islamic Resistance Movement (commonly known as Hamas) sees its situation as similar to that of the Muslim ruler Saladin in his struggle against the Christian Crusaders, as can be seen by examining portions of its Charter. The goal of Hamas is to establish an Islamic Palestinian state in place of Israel, through both violent means (including terrorism) and peaceful political activity. Hamas argues that the current situation of the Palestinians, living under Israeli control or dispersed from their homeland, is part of an ongoing crusade by Christians to take the Holy Lands out of Palestinian hands. The loss of Palestine and the creation of Israel, the

Charter continues, were brought about by the great powers of East and West, and taken together constitute a great tragedy not only for the Palestinians but for the entire Islamic community. This, Hamas proclaims, requires jihad not in the sense of expanding the territory of Islam, but of restoring it, and to recover land rather than conquer it. Nor is it a rebellion in the classical sense; rather, this is a struggle to regain a lost portion of the territory of Islam. The Hamas Charter thus provides a uniquely Islamic rationale for *al-intifada,* the "shaking off" of illegitimate rule.[17] This language thus seems to suggest defensive jihad, rather than an offensive struggle.

Since Hamas is not acting on behalf of an established government, it must find authorization elsewhere for its struggle against not only external enemies but also so-called "Muslim" governments that collaborate with the non-Muslim powers (by cooperating with Israel or allowing the basing of Western troops on their soil). The group considers Muslim governments that cooperate with the West as ignorant of the non-Muslim nations' true intentions, or corrupt. Hamas argues that it obtains its authority to declare jihad in another way: the Western powers' invasion of Islamic territory has created an emergency situation where Muslims cannot wait for authorization other than that given directly by God, so jihad is a required duty for all conscientious Muslims.[18] This exceptional situation suspends the usual lines between parties in a relationship so that every Muslim can participate in the struggle. Hamas' Charter thus relates the current situation of Muslims to the classical period, but also marks a break with that classical past. This extraordinary situation also means a change in the nature of Muslim obligation under jihad, from a collective responsibility to extend the Dar al-Islam to a duty for each individual Muslim to restore that territory.[19]

The same pattern of thinking is present in "The Neglected Duty," a pamphlet produced by Egyptian Islamic Jihad (or EIJ, the group that assassinated Anwar Sadat in 1981). This pamphlet, the group's announced "testament," is also a clear expression of the Sunni Islamist perspective on political violence as jihad. It argues that jihad as armed action is the heart of Islam, and that the neglect of this type of action by Muslims has caused the current depressed condition of Islam in the world. EIJ attempts to communicate a sense of urgency to Muslims, who are being victimized and whose territory is being divided and controlled by non-Muslim powers. The document also seeks to justify jihad against other Muslims who, because they are ignorant of this situation, actively cooperate with the unbelievers in the name of "modernization," and are worse than rebels—they are Muslim traitors and apostates. Furthermore, fighting such unbelievers without the limits imposed if they were rebellious Muslims is justified, since they are worse than other unbelievers.[20]

"The Neglected Duty" defines the current rulers of the Muslim world (as Sadat was defined) as the primary enemies of Islam and apostates, despite their profession of Islam and obedience to some of its laws, and advocates their execution. This document is explicitly messianic, asserting that Muslims must "exert every conceivable effort" to bring about the establishment of truly Islamic government, a restoration of the caliphate, and the expansion of the Dar al-Islam, and that the success of these endeavors is inevitable.[21] "The Neglected Duty" cites a different historical analogy for this struggle than does Hamas' Charter, however: more appropriate than the threat posed by the European Crusaders was the struggle of Muslims against the Mongol invaders.

EIJ is raising an important issue connected with irregular war: the group is advocating mass resistance against an established government, and such revolution can be justified in Islam only where the ruler becomes an unbeliever through public displays of unbelief. The most significant of such acts is introduction of an innovation (*bid'ah*), which is a policy, teaching, or action that violates precedents in the Qur'an or hadith. The leadership thus loses its divinely given authority when it commits apostasy, and Muslims not only must no longer obey such a ruler, but are required to revolt and depose him.

This reference to the obligation to God for the creation and maintenance of an Islamic state and the responsibilities of Muslims serves to answer the question of authorization for militant Islamic forces.[22] "The Neglected Duty" provides further justification for armed action by arguing that Egypt, like most of its neighbors, is not an Islamic state because its constitution and laws are a mix of traditional Islamic judgments and European law codes. Imposition of such a mixed legal system (non-Islamic laws that are an "innovation") by Egypt's leaders on their subjects thus means that the nation is not part of the territory of Islam, but part of the territory of war or unbelief.[23]

Shi'a radicals have a similar perspective to their Sunni extremist "brothers in arms." Ayatollah Ruhollah Khomeini (1902–1989) contended that Islamic jurists, "by means of jihad and enjoining the good and forbidding the evil, must expose and overthrow tyrannical rulers and rouse the people so the universal movement of all alert Muslims can establish Islamic government in the place of tyrannical regimes." The proper teaching of Islam will cause "the entire population to become *mujahids* [literally "strugglers for God]." Ayatollah Murtaza Mutahhari (1920–1979), a top ideologue of the Iranian Revolution, considered jihad a necessary consequence of Islam's content: by having political aims, Islam must sanction armed force and provide laws for its use. Mutahhari deemed jihad to be defensive, but his definition includes defense against oppression and may require what international law would consider a war of aggression. For example, he endorses an attack on a country of polytheists (some Muslims see Christians as polytheists due to Christianity's belief in a God who can exist in three manifestations) with the goal simply to eliminate polytheism's evils, not to impose Islam.[24]

Another radical Shi'a perspective on the justification for jihad can be found in the words of Shaykh Muhammad Hussein Fadlallah, spiritual leader of Lebanese Hizballah. In a 1986 interview, he stated that although violence is justified only for defensive purposes and as a last resort, the contemporary situation of the people of the Middle East, in particular of Muslims, creates a scenario that breeds violence. The establishment of Israel, the dislocation of the Palestinians, and the interference of a great oppressive power (in other words, the United States) in Arab–Islamic political, economic, and social affairs leads some Muslims (e.g., militant groups) to consider themselves justified in using force to achieve their goals, and this can even sometimes lead to extreme behavior.[25] Fadlallah does clarify that terrorism (*hudna*, or violence in Arabic) is not legitimate or justified in Islam, to include the destruction of life, kidnapping, or the hijacking of airliners or ships, and suggests that militants have gone too far in the conduct of their struggle when they employ such means. Nevertheless, he concludes by informing the American people that it is up to them to improve the situation by pressing for reforms in the policies of their government.[26]

How should the West respond to Islamic militant groups? Shaykh Fadlallah suggests that the West should listen to the anger expressed by such groups. While stressing that the way to peace is through dialogue, Fadlallah said that the West must first recognize that Muslims who act in ways that are harmful to Western interests are responding to pain of their own. Islam, he added, should not be thought of as uncompromisingly hostile to the West, since militant groups do not speak for all of the community. Fadlallah adds that if the West does listen to these groups, however, it will understand that the concerns these groups have (for justice, human rights, and self-determination) are legitimate, even if their methods are excessive.[27]

Al Qaeda and Transnational Jihad: A New Twist on Old Complaints

Before his emergence as the prime suspect in the 9/11 attacks, Osama bin Laden had described his goals and grievances and the tactics of his transnational at Qaeda network in great detail in a series of statements and interviews. Taken together, these statements provide insight into an ideology that may seem abhorrent or crazy to Americans but has been carefully crafted to appeal to the disgruntled and dispossessed of the Islamic world.[28] Bin Laden's ideology, however, is really more political than religious.

At the heart of bin Laden's philosophy are two declarations of war—jihad—against the United States. The first, his *Bayan* (statement) issued on 26 August 1996, was directed specifically at "Americans occupying the land of the two holy places," as bin Laden refers to the cities of Mecca and Medina that are located in his native Saudi Arabia. Here he calls upon Muslims all over the world to fight to "expel the infidels . . . from the Arab Peninsula."[29] In his fatwa of 23 February 1998, titled "Declaration of the World Islamic Front for Jihad Against the Jews and Crusaders," which he issued along with the leaders of extremist groups in Egypt, Pakistan, and Bangladesh, bin Laden broadened his earlier edict. In the fatwa, he specifies that the radicals' war is a defensive struggle against Americans and their allies who have declared war "on God, his Messenger, and Muslims." The "crimes and sins" perpetrated by the United States are threefold: first, it "stormed" the Arabian peninsula during the Gulf War and has continued "occupying the lands of Islam in the holiest of places"; second, it continues a war of annihilation against Iraq; and third, the United States supports the state of Israel and its continued occupation of Jerusalem. The only appropriate Muslim response, according to the fatwa, is a defensive jihad to repulse the aggressor; therefore, borrowing from classical and modern Islamic scholars (because it is defensive), such a war is a moral obligation incumbent upon all true Muslims.[30]

Bin Laden's anger at the "American crusader forces" who are "occupying" his homeland stems from an injunction from the Prophet that there "not be two religions in Arabia"; the presence of foreign forces on holy soil is thus an intolerable affront to 1,400 years of Islamic tradition. In his

1996 statement of jihad, bin Laden blamed the serious economic crisis then gripping Saudi Arabia (due to falling oil prices and widespread corruption) on the presence of these Western "crusader forces." Two years later, in his 1998 fatwa, bin Laden charged that the United States was not only occupying and plundering Arabia, but was "using its bases in the peninsula as a spearhead to fight against the neighboring Islamic peoples." In bin Laden's war, the goal of expelling the "Judeo-Christian enemy" from Islamic holy lands should occur first on the Arabian peninsula, then in Iraq (which for 500 years was the seat of the Islamic caliphate), and third in Palestine, site of the Al-Aqsa Mosque in Jerusalem (which is sacred to Muslims as the place from where Muhammad ascended to heaven).[31]

Although the initial attacks associated with bin Laden occurred in Saudi Arabia, Somalia, East Africa, and Yemen, he increasingly made clear that he would bring the war to the American homeland. Al Qaeda is believed to have aided the first attack against the World Trade Center in 1993, and bin Laden told an ABC News reporter in May 1998 that the battle will "inevitably move . . . to American soil."[32] Although he appears to be fired by the religious zeal of Saudi Arabia's puritanical Wahhabi movement, bin Laden's targets have not been offending religious and cultural institutions, but political, military, and economic targets. Additionally, though he quotes selective (but incomplete) passages from the Qur'an to establish the basis for the jihad, bin Laden's motivations are really not that different from the anti-imperialistic doctrines that sustain religious and nonreligious extremist groups all over the world.[33]

In return for joining the jihad against America, bin Laden has promised his followers an honored place in paradise, in accordance with a statement in the Qur'an that "a martyr's privileges are guaranteed by Allah." Bin Laden and many of the other Islamic militant groups in the Middle East are able to draw on large numbers of enthusiastic and waiting recruits for their war against the United States—impoverished youths who are ready to die simply for the idea of jihad.

"Jihad Factories": An Enduring Legacy of Hatred

It is estimated that more than one million young men from Pakistan, Afghanistan, Central Asia, and the Muslim parts of China are attending *madrassas,* or private Islamic religious schools, every year in Pakistan. Madrassa students spend most of their day in rote memorization of the Qur'an in Arabic (this is not their native language, so few understand what they are reading) and interpreting the hadith. Only theology is taught; there is no math, science, computer training, or secular history.[34] The young men at these schools are drawn from the dire poor of the societies they come from, kept in self-contained worlds that are isolated from outside influences, and indoctrinated with a powerful, not-so-academic radical message: their highest honor and duty is to wage jihad to defend Islam from its attackers, and the United States is the chief enemy of Islam.[35]

Madrassas, which have a tradition in Pakistan that dates from colonial days of promoting political independence along with their religious teaching, fill a significant gap in the underfunded public school system by offering free tuition, room, and board. Madrassas received state funding during the Afghan War when they were used to groom the mujahedin who were being sent to fight the Soviet invaders.[36] Many of these schools were emptied in the 1990s when the Taliban needed assistance in military campaigns against its Northern Alliance foes, and many students sent to the front did not return. The graduates of these madrassas have also turned up in places like Bosnia, Chechnya, and the Kashmir, and the survivors of those conflicts have taken their battlefield experience back to their home countries where it is being put to use in jihads against their own not-Islamic-enough governments and societies.

The readiness of millions of young men trained in these schools to sacrifice their lives for Islam—and their unquestioning acceptance of anti-American and pro-Islamic extremist propaganda—will continue to be a powerful and enduring weapon against the US-led global war on terrorism, and one that bin Laden and other militants who are bent on attacking the United States and its allies can call on in the years ahead.

ACCEPTANCE OF MILITANTS' IDEAS AND METHODS IS LIMITED

The thrust of the entire jihad tradition which Islamic radicals have "hijacked" makes it clear that not everything is permissible. Although the language in the Qur'an and hadith and in other classical Muslim sources is overwhelmingly militant in many places, this is a reflection of the Muslims' world in the seventh century, which consisted initially of resistance to a variety of more powerful non-Islamic tribes and then successful military campaigns to spread the faith. Besides containing exhortations to fight, however, Islamic sacred texts have also laid out the rules of engagement for war, which (as mentioned earlier) included prohibitions against the killing of noncombatants such as women, children, the aged, and disabled. These texts also require notice to the adversary before an attack, require that a Muslim army must seek peace if its opponent does, and forbid committing aggression against others and suicide.[37] Those who are unfamiliar with the Qur'an and hadith can miss these points when confronted with the propagandistic calls to jihad of militant Islamic groups.

The actions of rebels in the classical period of Islam encountered widespread resentment and condemnation, and this strong sentiment against rebellion remains in modern Islamic thought. Most Muslims agree with the presumption in Islamic teachings on war that individuals are innocent and therefore not subject to harm unless they demonstrate by their actions that they are a threat to the safety or survival of Muslims.

On this basis, the overwhelming majority of Islamic scholars have for centuries rejected indiscriminate killing and the terrorizing of civilian populations as a legitimate form of jihad.[38] Also, at no point do Islamic sacred texts even consider the horrific and random slaughter of uninvolved bystanders that is represented by the 9/11 airliner attacks; most Muslims throughout the world were as shocked by those attacks as Americans were.

The radical message in works such as Hamas' Charter, "The Neglected Duty," and the writings of Khomeini and his fellow revolutionary Iranian Shi'a clerics nevertheless finds a lot of acceptance with contemporary Muslims. The reason is simply because of the poor socioeconomic circumstances and lack of human dignity that many Muslim peoples find themselves subject to, brought about by secular failures to attend to their problems.[39] Militant Islamic groups, exemplified by Hamas and the Palestinian branch of Islamic Jihad, have been able to use such poor conditions to their advantage. They provide social services (such as operating free or low-cost schools, medical clinics, sports clubs, and women's support groups), many of which the Palestinian Authority itself often cannot provide, to build public support and attract recruits in the occupied territories.[40]

Public statements over the last several months by some moderate Muslim religious authorities and commentators that Islamic extremists are corrupting a peaceful religious faith for their own twisted ends are encouraging. Equally positive is the growing recognition in the Muslim world both of bin Laden's lack of proper religious qualifications to issue any religious edicts that promote jihad, and his lack of success, on a strategic level, in forcing the United States to withdraw its military forces completely from Saudi Arabia or to give up its campaign against Islamic terrorism. A few prominent Muslim scholars have not only condemned the terrorist attacks upon the United States, but have declared the perpetrators of these attacks to be "suicides," not martyrs. This is significant, since Islam forbids suicide and teaches that its practitioners are sent not to paradise but to hell, where they are condemned to keep repeating their suicidal act for eternity.[41]

CONCLUSION

As described herein, jihad in Islamic thought and practice possesses a range of meanings, with Muslim radicals focusing on the physical, violent form of struggle to resist what they see as cultural, economic, military, and political assaults from outside the ummah and oppression and injustice within. So long as societal conditions within many Muslim states remain poor, with unrepresentative governments (which are seen to be propped up by the United States) that are unwilling or unable to undertake meaningful but difficult reforms, then militant Islamic groups will continue to attract recruits and financial support. In spite of logical fallacies and inconsistencies in the doctrine of jihad of radical Islamic groups, and the fact that most of the broad constituency they are attempting to appeal to does not buy into their ideology or methods, such groups nevertheless remain as significant threats to US interests everywhere in the world.

The challenge for the US government over the next several years will be to encourage and support lasting reform by Muslim states who are our allies in the Middle East, while maintaining a more balanced and fair-minded foreign policy toward all key regional players. We must also do a better job of countering the Islamic extremists' widely disseminated version of jihad, while being more persuasive that our own government—and our society—are truly not anti-Islamic. Such actions will do much to deny a supportive environment to our radical Muslim foes. For its part, the US military needs to better understand the religious and cultural aspects of our adversaries' asymmetric mindset—in this case, how Islamic militants conceive of and use jihad—to be successful and survivable in its global campaign against terrorism.

Notes

1. Bernard Lewis, *The Political Language of Islam* (Chicago: Univ. of Chicago Press, 1988), p. 72, as quoted in Douglas E. Streusand, "What Does Jihad Mean?" *Middle East Quarterly,* 4 (September 1997), 1.
2. Streusand, p. 2.
3. Ibid.
4. Emmanuel Sivan, *Radical Islam: Medieval Theology and Modern Politics* (New Haven: Yale Univ. Press, 1990), p. 101; as quoted in Streusand, pp. 2–3.
5. Fred M. Donner, "The Sources of Islamic Conceptions of War," in *Just War and Jihad: Historical and Theoretical Perspectives on War and Peace in Western and Islamic Traditions,* ed. John Kelsay and James Turner Johnson (New York: Greenwood Press, 1991), pp. 51–52, as quoted in Streusand, p. 3.
6. Khaled Abou El Fadl, "Terrorism Is at Odds with Islamic Tradition," *Los Angeles Times,* 22 August 2001.
7. Streusand, pp. 3–4.
8. Johannes J. G. Jansen, *The Neglected Duty: The Creed of Sadat's Assassins and Islamic Resurgence in the Middle East* (New York: Macmillan, 1986), pp. xi–xii.
9. Ibid., pp. xii–xiii.
10. The term "fundamentalism" is also used incorrectly in conjunction with Islam to describe this phenomenon, but this concept is really more appropriate to American Christian thought, whence it originated.
11. John L. Esposito, "Political Islam and the West," *Military Technology,* February 2001, pp. 89–90.
12. Jansen, pp. xiii–xiv.
13. Mehdi Abedi and Gary Legenhausen, eds., *Jihad and Shahadat: Struggle and Martyrdom in Islam* (Houston: Institute for Research and Islamic Studies, 1986), pp. 21–23.
14. Ibid., pp. 23–24.
15. Streusand, p. 5.
16. Sivan, pp. 16–21 and 114–16, as quoted in Streusand, p. 5.
17. John Kelsay, *Islam and War: A Study in Comparative Ethics* (Louisville, Ky.: Westminster/John Knox Press, 1993), pp. 95–97.
18. Kelsay bases his discussion on the translation by Muhammad Maqdsi, titled "Charter of the Islamic Resistance Movement (Hamas) of Palestine" (Dallas: Islamic Association for Palestine, 1990), pp. 17–18. Another translation of this document, by Raphael Israeli, is available on the Internet at www.ict.org.il/documents/documentdet.cfm?docid = 14.
19. Kelsay, *Islam and War,* p. 98.
20. Ibid., pp. 100–01.
21. Jansen, p. 162, as quoted in Streusand, p. 5.
22. Kelsay, *Islam and War,* pp. 101–02.
23. Ibid., p. 102.
24. Abedi and Legenhausen, p. 89, as quoted in Streusand, p. 6.
25. Kelsay, *Islam and War,* p. 109.
26. Ibid., pp. 109–10.
27. Quoted in Kelsay, *Islam and War,* p. 108.
28. Michael Dobbs, "Inside the Mind of Osama Bin Laden," *The Washington Post,* 20 September 2001.
29. Ibid.
30. Sohail Hashmi, "The Terrorists' Zealotry Is Political Not Religious," *The Washington Post,* 30 September 2001. For a good analysis of bin Laden's fatwa, including its historical background, see Bernard Lewis, "License to Kill," *Foreign Affairs,* 77 (November/December 1998), 14–19. The translated text of the fatwa itself is available on the Federation of American Scientists' website at www.fas.org/irp/world/para/docs/980223-fatwa.htm.
31. Dobbs.
32. Ibid.
33. Hashmi.
34. Jeffrey Goldberg, "Inside Jihad U.: The Education of a Holy Warrior," *New York Times Magazine,* 25 July 2000.
35. Indira A. R. Lakshmanan, "In Some Schools, Jihad, Anger at US Are Lessons," *Boston Globe,* 4 October 2001.
36. Ibid.
37. Teresa Watanabe, "Extremists Put Own Twist on Islamic Faith," *Los Angeles Times,* 24 September 2001.
38. Hashmi.
39. Jansen, p. 2.
40. "Islamic Groups Going for Goodwill," *Daily Progress* (Charlottesville, Va.), 18 November 1998, p. A8.
41. Bernard Lewis, "Jihad vs. Crusade," *The Wall Street Journal,* 27 September 2001.

Discussion Questions

1. What was the classical concept of jihad according to Knapp?
2. What was Ibn Taymiyya's view of jihad? By contrast, describe the Sufi doctrine of greater jihad.
3. How does Knapp explain the origin of militant or radical Islam?
4. What are the prerequisites for jihad in the view of both Sunni and Shi'a Muslims? How do the two sects disagree?
5. According to Knapp, how did the idea of jihad change in the modern era?
6. How do militant Islamic groups such as Hamas or Egyptian Islamic Jihad use the concept of jihad?
7. What are the radical Shi'a perspectives on jihad?
8. Explains Osama bin Laden's ideology.

Discussion Questions

1. Compare the classical doctrine of jihad with the just war theory. How are they different? How are they similar?
2. Knapp says that Islam is a religion of peace that has been hijacked by radicals. Do you agree? Why or why not?
3. How should the United States and allies deal with Osama bin Laden and other radicals? Explain your view.

Problem Cases

1. The Iraq War

After a long buildup, U.S. and British troops invaded Iraq in March 2003. Only two months later, in May 2003, President Bush declared combat operations over. But the fighting continued, and in April 2004, the war began again in Fallujah, a Sunni town that had been a center of anti-Americanism. The Sunni Muslim insurgents fired rocket-propelled grenades and Kalashnikovs at American troops. More than 1,300 U.S. troops responded with attack helicopters, tanks, and warplanes. In the first two weeks of April, more than 80 American soldiers and 900 Iraqi were killed, and 561 U.S. troops were wounded. Hospital workers claimed that the Iraqi dead were mostly women, children, and elderly. By the beginning of June 2004 the total number of American casualties was 812 dead and 4,637 wounded, according to the official count released by the U.S. military. Other estimates were 7,000 to 10,000 U.S. soldiers treated for illness or injury, including noncombat injury. The Iraqi casualties including civilians were estimated to be about 10,000. The total U.S. cost for the war was over a billion dollars and counting. (The source for these numbers was http://www.antiwar.com/casualties.)

What was the justification for this war? First, there was the prevention argument. In its most basic form, this is the argument that if one nation threatens another, then the threatened nation is justified in attacking the nation making the threat. The Bush administration perceived Iraq to be a potential threat to the United States and her allies, and that was the reason given for attacking. In the words of President Bush's National Security Statement (National Security of the United States of America (2002) http://www.whitehouse.gov/nsc/nss9.html), the United States must "stop rogue states and their terrorist clients before they are able to threaten or use weapons of mass destruction against the United States and our allies and friends." The problem with this statement is that Iraq did not have the alleged weapons of mass destruction or programs to develop them. According to Hans Blix, the head of the UN inspections team, the UN inspections had been effective in eliminating the weapons or programs to develop them. (See his book *Disarming Iraq* in the Suggested Readings.) Investigations by members of Congress and others revealed that the Bush administration had no solid evidence of the existence of the weapons or programs. The so-called evidence for the weapons or weapons programs, including Colin Powell's speech to the UN, can be found on the CIA website (http://www.cia.org) in the special section on the War on Terrorism. Richard A. Clark, the counterterrorism czar in both the Clinton and Bush administrations, claimed that President Bush was eager to attack Iraq from the beginning of his administration, and after the 9/11 attacks he tried to link Saddam Hussein and al Qaeda despite the lack of evidence. (See his book *Against All Enemies* in the Suggested Readings.)

But for the sake of discussion, let's assume that Iraq had the weapons of mass destruction in 2003. Would this have justified the invasion and occupation of Iraq? Perhaps, but we have to assume that Saddam Hussein would have handed these weapons over to terrorists, and risk serious reprisal. It is hard to see how that would have been in his self-interest. His reason for developing these weapons, it could be argued, was that he wanted them for self-defense. North Korea was named by President Bush as one of the nations making up the axis of evil (along with Iran and Iraq), but North Korea was not attacked by the United States because North Korea had nuclear weapons. It is not hard to see why North Korea, Iran, India, Pakistan, Israel, France, Germany, Russia, and other nations want these weapons.

The general problem with the prevention argument is that it makes it too easy to justify war. War should be the last resort, not the first thing considered. Even Henry Kissinger, surely no peacenik, acknowledged this problem when he warned against using the appeal to prevention as a universal principle available to every nation. (See Henry Kissinger, "Our Intervention in Iraq," *Washington Post* op-ed, August 12, 2002.) For example, during the cold war, the USSR was certainly threatened by the United States, which had thousands of missiles with nuclear warheads targeting Russian cities and military bases. Did this threat justify a Russian first strike? North Korea is a rogue state that actually has nuclear weapons, and may be selling them to other countries. Are we justified in attacking North Korea? Why not attack Iran, the other country in the axis of evil? For that matter, isn't Saudi Arabia a threat, since it is the country that encouraged the fundamentalist and militant religion that produced Osama bin Laden and his terrorist organization?

Second, the war was justified by the humanitarian argument that Saddam Hussein was a brutal dictator, comparable to Hitler no less, and needed to be removed from power. No doubt Saddam was an evil man, having launched aggressive wars against Iran and Kuwait, gassed thousands of Kurds, killed numerous rivals, and at least attempted to develop chemical, biological, and nuclear weapons before this was stopped by the UN inspections. But this seems to be an argument for assassination, not war. The CIA has tried to kill Fidel Castro several times because he was perceived to be evil, but the United States has not launched a massive invasion of Cuba. Why not? (The Bay of Pigs operation was not exactly an all-out military campaign like the Iraq War.) Furthermore, like the prevention argument, the humanitarian argument makes it too easy to justify war. Should we go to war against any and all counties ruled by evil men (or women)?

Third, there was the legalistic argument that war with Iraq was necessary to enforce United Nations resolutions in the face of Iraqi defiance. But France, Germany, and other member nations of the UN argued that more inspections would do the job, since Iraq was allowing them. And in the event that war was necessary, it should have been undertaken by a coalition of the member nations, and not just by the United States and Britain (although a few other nations contributed token forces.)

As the bloody occupation continued on in 2004, pundits, analysts, and journalists offered various other justifications for the war and occupation. One was the nation-building argument, the view that turning the despotic regimes in the Middle East into democracies like the United States would be a good thing. This view was attributed to Bush administration officials such as Paul Wolfowitz. But if this is such a good idea, then it would apply to nations such as Saudi Arabia, which is no democracy. Another was that the war was really an extension of the fight against al Qaeda. This justification assumed that there were close ties between al Qaeda operatives and Saddam Hussein, even though there was no evidence of this. Against this, there was the claim that the Muslim terrorists hated the secular government of Saddam Hussein. Critics of the war maintained that the real reason for the war was President Bush getting back at his father's enemy. European critics thought the war was really about oil—Americans wanted to control one of the world's largest oil reserves. They pointed to the fact that Haliburton, the company run by Dick Cheney before he became Vice President, was immediately given the contract to re-build Iraq's oil industry.

All things considered, was the Iraq war justified or not? Can you justify it using just war theory? Can you justify it some other way? Explain your view.

2. Torture at Abu Ghraib

(Reported by Seymour M. Hersh in *The New Yorker,* May 10, 17, and 24, 2004. Also see Susan Sontag, "Regarding The Torture Of Others," *The New York Times Magazine,* May 23, 2004).

The 1984 Convention Against Torture and Other Cruel, Inhuman or Degrading Treatment or Punishment defines torture as "any act by which severe pain or suffering, whether physical or mental, is intentionally inflicted on a person for such purposes as obtaining from him or a third person information or a confession." (Quoted by Sontag, p. 25) The federal criminal statute that implements the convention (Title 18, section 2340, available online at www4.law.cornell.edu/uscode/18/2340.html) defines torture as an act "intended to inflict severe physical or mental pain or suffering upon another person." Included is the threat of imminent death or the threat of severe physical pain or suffering.

By this definition, many prisoners at the Abu Ghraib prison in Iraq were tortured. There is the well-known picture of the hooded man forced to stand on a box with wires attached to his hands and neck. Reportedly he was told that he would be electrocuted if he stepped or fell off the box. Former prisoners tell stories of U.S. soldiers beating prisoners, sometimes to death. Mohammed Unis Hassan says that he was cuffed to the bars of his cell and then a female soldier poked his eye with her fingers so hard he couldn't see afterward. Now his left eye is gray and glassy and his vision is blurred. He says he saw an old man forced to lie naked on his face until he died. Other naked prisoners were threatened and bitten by attack dogs.

Some of the mistreatment involved sexual humiliation. There are photographs of naked Iraqi prisoners forced to simulate oral or anal sex. Private Lynndie England is shown giving a thumbs-up sign and pointing at the genitals of a naked and hooded Iraqi as he masturbates. In another picture, Private England is shown with Specialist Charles A. Graner; both are grinning and giving the thumbs-up sign in front of a pile of naked Iraqis, piled on top of each other in a pyramid. Another picture shows Private England leading a naked man around on a dog leash.

Many people think this humiliating treatment of the Iraqi prisoners is indefensible. But not everyone agrees. On his radio show Rush Limbaugh claimed that the humiliation was just harmless fun, similar to what goes on in college fraternities or secret societies. He said, "This is no different than what happens at the Skull and Bones initiation, and we're going to ruin people's lives over it. . . because they had a good time." (Quoted by Sontag, pp. 28–29) Certainly Private England and Specialist Graner appear to be having a good time.

One way of defending some of the mistreatment, then, is to deny that sexual humiliation is torture. Torture involves extreme physical pain. One thinks of medieval tortures such as the rack, the thumbscrew, or branding irons. But sexual humiliation doesn't involve extreme physical pain. It is just embarrassing or humiliating, like the sort of things that go on in fraternity initiation rites.

An objection to this view is that homosexual acts and public nakedness are not harmless fun in the culture and religion of Islam, but serious violations. Otherwise it would not be humiliating and demeaning. Does this imply that the sexual humiliation of Iraqi prisoners amounts to torture? What is your position?

Secretary of Defense Donald Rumsfeld adopted a similar view of the mistreatment of prisoners. According to Seymour M. Hersh, Secretary Rumsfeld approved a secret operation called Copper Green, which encouraged the use of coercion and sexual humiliation to get information about the insurgents in Iraq. Apparently Secretary Rumsfeld made a distinction between torture and coercion or sexual humiliation. Torture is the infliction of severe physical pain, and as such it is wrong and illegal. But coercion or sexual humiliation is not torture because it does not involve severe physical pain. Examples of coercion include handcuffing with flexi-cuffs which cut off circulation and cause skin lesions, solitary confinement, sensory deprivation, hooding, sleep deprivation, withholding of food and water, constant loud noise, extremes of cold or hot, and so-called stress positions such as squatting or standing with the arms lifted. One technique used by the CIA on al Qaeda detainees is water boarding, in which a prisoner is strapped down on a board, then pushed under water. Sexual humiliation includes being paraded naked outside of other cells in front of other prisoners and guards, being handcuffed naked to the bars of a cell, being forced to masturbate or engage in sodomy, being pulled around on a dog leash while naked, being put in piles of naked bodies, and so on.

Is there a clear distinction between torture and coercion or sexual humiliation? Doesn't coercion or sexual humiliation produce extreme mental pain? Is coercion or sexual humiliation morally justified if it produces no useful information? What do you think?

Suppose we grant a distinction between torture, defined as acts causing severe pain and suffering, and torture lite, as I shall call it, which supposedly causes only moderate pain and suffering. Torture lite would include sexual humiliation and the techniques of coercion listed above. Is the torture lite of prisoners morally and legally allowed? Why or why not?

A different defense of torture used by the Bush administration is to hold that every captured prisoner is an enemy combatant or terrorist having no rights. This means that the Iraqis are not soldiers protected by the Geneva Conventions or federal laws that forbid torture. Torture of enemy combatants or terrorists is justified if it yields information valuable in the War Against Terrorism.

Is torture (whether real or lite) justified if it produces life-saving information? Suppose that one of the Abu Ghraib prisoners revealed information that enabled the U.S. forces to prevent a suicide bombing. Would this information justify the mistreatment of the prisoners at Abu Ghraib? Why or why not?

The best philosophical article on torture is Henry Shue's "Torture," *Philosophy and Public Affairs* 7, 2 (Winter 1978), pp. 124–43. Shue argues that torture is morally justified in some cases. The example he uses to support his case is very relevant in today's world. Suppose a terrorist has hidden a nuclear bomb in the heart of New York City. If it is not defused it will explode and kill millions of innocent people. Is it permissible to torture the terrorist to find out where the bomb is hidden so that it can be defused? Isn't this better than letting the bomb explode? Isn't this torture justified by the principle of proportionality? Why or why not?

3. Jose Padilla

Mr. Padilla, 31, was born in Brooklyn and raised in Chicago. He served prison time for a juvenile murder in Illinois and for gun possession in Florida. He converted to Islam in prison and took the name Abdullah al Muhijir when he lived in Egypt. According to the government, he also spent time in Saudi Arabia, Pakistan, and Afghanistan.

Mr. Padilla was taken into custody by the FBI in May 2002 when he arrived from overseas at Chicago's O'Hare International Airport. Then he was held incommunicado at a Navy brig in Charleston, S.C., where he was denied access to counsel. No formal charges were brought against Mr. Padilla, but not long after his arrest, Attorney General John Ashcroft claimed that Mr. Padilla was part of a plot by al Qaeda to explode a radiological "dirty bomb."

On December 18, 2003, a federal appeals court in Manhattan ruled (2–1) that the president does not have the executive authority to hold American citizens indefinitely without access to lawyers simply by declaring them "enemy combatants." The two-judge majority decision said that the president does not have the constitutional authority as commander in chief to detain as enemy combatants American citizens seized on American soil, away from the zone of combat. Furthermore, the ruling said, citing a 1971 statue, that the detention of an American citizen under the circumstances of Mr. Padilla's case was not authorized by Congress.

On the same day as the court's decision, the Department of Justice issued a statement on the case. (The statement can be found at http://www.ssdoj.gov., and there is a link to the text of the court's decision.) The government's statement said that Padilla was associated with senior al Qaeda leaders including Osama bin Laden and that he had received training from al Qaeda operatives on wiring explosive devices and on the construction of a uranium-enhanced explosive device. The statement concluded that Jose Padilla "is an enemy combatant who poses a serious and continuing threat to the American people and our national security."

The court ordered the government to release Mr. Padilla from military custody. But he could still face criminal charges or be detained as a material witness in connection with grand jury proceedings. Do you agree with the court's decision? Why or why not?

In addition to Mr. Padilla, some 600 men of varying nationalities are being held at the Guantanamo Bay naval base in Cuba. These men were captured in Afghanistan and Pakistan during the operations against the Taliban. Like Mr. Padilla they are deemed by the U.S. government to be "enemy combatants" having no legal rights. They are not being allowed to contest their detention through petitions for habeas corpus, the ancient writ which for centuries has been used in the English-speaking world to challenge the legality of confinement.

The basic issue is whether or not the president should have the power to deny basic rights in the name of fighting terrorism. What is your view of this?

4. Fighting Terrorism

What can the United States do to prevent terrorist attacks like the September 11 assault on the World Trade Center and the Pentagon? One proposal is national identity cards, discussed by Daniel J. Wakin in *The New York Times,* October 7, 2001. According to polls taken after the attacks, about 70 percent of Americans favor such cards, which are used in other countries. French citizens are required to carry national ID cards, and they may be stopped by the police for card inspection at any time. Such cards are also required in Belgium, Greece, Luxembourg, Portugal, and Spain. Privacy International, a watchdog group in London, estimates that about one hundred countries have compulsory national IDs. Some, like Denmark, issue ID numbers at birth, around which a lifetime of personal information accumulates.

It is not clear if required ID cards would violate the U.S. Constitution. One objection is that a police demand to see the card would constitute a "seizure" forbidden by the Fourth Amendment. Another objection is that illegal immigrants would be targeted rather than terrorists. But proponents of the cards argue that they could be used to identify terrorists and protect travelers. Larry Ellison, the chief executive of the software maker Oracle, claims that people's fingerprints could be embedded on the cards and police or airport guards could scan the cards and check the fingerprints against a database of terrorists. The cards could protect airline travelers at check-in and guard against identity theft. Advocates of the cards argue that there is already a great deal of personal information gathered by private industry, any invasion of privacy caused by the ID cards would not matter much. What do you think? Are national ID cards a good way to fight against terrorism?

Another proposal is to allow suspicionless searches. In Israel, the police can search citizens and their belongings at any time without any particular cause or suspicion. These searches are conducted at shopping centers, airports, stadiums, and other public places. Citizens are also required to pass through metal detectors before entering public places. The U.S. Constitution requires police to have an objective suspicion or "probable cause" to search you, your belongings, or your car, but the Supreme Court has granted exceptions such as border searches and drunk-driving checkpoints. Why not allow suspicionless searches at public places like shopping centers, airports, and football stadiums?

Even more controversial is racial profiling. Israeli authorities single out travelers and citizens for questioning and searches based on racial profiling. Experts cite vigorous racial profiling as one of the reasons Israeli airplanes are not hijacked. The U.S. Supreme Court has not ruled on whether racial profiling violates the equal protection clause of the U.S. Constitution and has declined to hear cases on the practice. Opinions differ on what counts as racial profiling and when or if it is unconstitutional. Advocates of the practice claim that police already practice racial profiling and that it is effective in preventing crime. Critics object that it is nothing more than racism. Is racial profiling justified in the fight against terrorism?

In Canada, police are allowed to arrest and hold suspected terrorists without charges and without bail for up to ninety days. In France, suspects can be held for questioning for nearly five days without being charged and without having any contact with an attorney. Britain's antiterrorist legislation allows suspicious individuals to be detained for up to seven days without a court appearance. The new antiterrorist legislation proposed by the U.S. Congress would allow authorities to hold foreigners suspected of terrorist activity for up to a week without charges. Is this indefinite holding without charges and without bail acceptable?

Finally, in the fight against terrorism Israel has condoned assassinations or "judicially sanctioned executions," that is, killing terrorist leaders such as Osama bin Laden. The United States does not currently permit assassination, but this prohibition stems from an executive order that could be repealed, not because it is forbidden by the Constitution. Should the United States reconsider its position on assassination?

In general, are these methods of fighting terrorism acceptable to you or not? Why or why not?

5. *National Missile Defense*

National Missile Defense (NMD) is the controversial $8.3-billion missile defense shield championed by President George W. Bush and his Secretary of Defense, Donald Rumsfeld. It is an updated version of President Reagan's Strategic Defense Initiative. More than $60 billion already has been spent on the missile defense program in the last two decades.

The basic idea of NMD is appealing. Instead of ensuring peace by relying on the Cold War strategy of MAD (mutual assured destruction), where neither the

United States nor Russia can defend against nuclear attack but can destroy the other if attacked, NMD would protect the United States from missile attack with a defensive umbrella of antimissile missiles. This would give the United States an advantage over Russia or other nuclear powers not having any missile defense.

Russia is no longer seen as the main threat, even though Russia still has thousands of long-range missiles left over from the Cold War arms race. According to President Bush, the main threat to the United States comes from so-called rogue nations unfriendly to the United States such as North Korea and Iraq. In view of the September 11 attacks, the al Qaeda terrorist network of Osama bin Laden also should be considered a threat. Bin Laden has promised more terrorist attacks on the United States and has proclaimed a jihad against the United States. Even though these terrorists do not possess nuclear weapons or missiles at present (or as far as we know, they don't) it seems likely that they will acquire them in the future. Then they could hold America hostage by threatening a nuclear attack or they might launch a surprise attack on an undefended American city such as New York City or Los Angeles.

Even though it seems like a good idea, NMD has problems. There is a good chance that it would not work in an actual attack. Two out of four major missile defense tests conducted so far have failed. Critics say that trying to hit a missile with another missile is like trying to shoot down a bullet with another bullet. It is difficult, to say the least. Countermeasures such as dummy missiles or balloons could fool the defense system. Low-tech missiles, the most likely to be used, do not go in a predictable path so they would be missed by antimissile missiles.

Even if the defensive system worked perfectly, it would only defend against long-range missiles and not against nuclear weapons delivered by other means. For example, a short-range missile could be launched from a submarine just off the coast, or a weapon could be taken to its target by truck or a private shipper. The most likely scenario is that terrorists would assemble a nuclear weapon at the target and then explode it. Obviously, NMD is no defense against such terrorist attacks.

Finally, there are political problems. NMD violates the 1972 Antiballistic Missile Treaty with Russia. The treaty limits the testing and deployment of new defense systems. Russian President Vladimir Putin contends that violating the 1972 treaty will upset nuclear stability and result in a new arms race.

Given these problems and how much it will cost, is NMD a good idea? What is your position?

6. Mini-Nukes

(For more details, see Fred Kaplan, "Low-Yield Nukes," posted November 21, 2003, on http://www.slate.msn.com.)

In 1970, the United States signed the Non-Proliferation Treaty. This Treaty involved a pact between nations having nuclear weapons and nations not having them. Nations not having them promised to not develop nuclear weapons, and nations already having them promised to pursue nuclear disarmament. In 1992 the United States unilaterally stopped nuclear testing, on orders of the first President Bush, and then formalized this in 1995 by signing the Comprehensive Test Ban

Treaty. It prohibits the testing and development of nuclear weapons indefinitely, and it was signed by 186 other nations.

In 2003, the second Bush administration insisted that Iran and North Korea halt their nuclear-weapons programs, and argued that the invasion and occupation of Iraq was justified because Iraq had weapons of mass destruction or WMD, that is, chemical, biological, and nuclear weapons (or at least a nuclear weapons program). Yet at the same time, the second Bush administration was actively developing a new generation of exotic nuclear weapons including low-yield mini nukes and earth-penetrating nukes, despite the fact that the country already had 7,650 nuclear war-heads and bombs. Specifically, the Fiscal Year 2004 defense bill, passed by both houses of Congress in November 2003 did four things. First, it repealed the 1992 law banning the development of low-yield nuclear weapons. Second, the bill pro-vided $15 million to develop an earth-penetrating nuclear weapon, a bunker buster. Third, it allocated $6 million to explore special-effects bombs, for example, the neu-tron bomb that enhances radiation. Finally, the bill provided $25 million for under-ground nuclear tests.

This renewed development of nuclear weapons and testing violated the 1970 and 1995 Treaties, but the second Bush administration argued that it was necessary to do this for self-defense. The old warheads mounted on intercontinental missiles were designed to wipe out industrial complexes or destroy whole cities. But such weapons were never used, and it appeared that they had no utility. Certainly they were not effective against suicide bombers or other terrorist attacks. What was needed, it was argued, was smaller warheads that could destroy underground bunkers or WMD storage sites.

Critics argued that the U.S. development of more nuclear weapons undermined the attempt to stop similar development in other nations. If the United States needed nuclear weapons for self-defense, then why didn't other nations need them too? The fact that the United States did not attack North Korea (which had nuclear weapons) seemed to support the view that nations needed these weapons to deter attacks.

Furthermore, critics argued that mini-nukes or bunker busters were not neces-sary. Conventional weapons could do the job. The United States already had at least two non-nuclear smart bombs that could penetrate the earth before exploding. There was the GBU-24, a 2000-pound laser-guided bomb, and the BLU-109 JDAM, a 2000-pound satellite-guided bomb. Both of these bombs could be filled with incendiary explosive that will burn whatever biological or chemical agents might be stored in an underground site.

So why did the United States need to develop more nuclear weapons? Was this necessary or effective for self-defense? Explain your answer. And why did the United States continue to have 7,650 nuclear warheads and bombs? Was it ever necessary to have so many weapons? Is it necessary now? What is your view?

7. The Gulf War

(For a book-length treatment of the Gulf War, including the view of it as jihad, see Kenneth L. Vaux, *Ethics and the Gulf War* [Boulder, CO: Westview Press, 1992].) In August 1990, the Iraqi army invaded and occupied Kuwait. Although the

United States had received warnings, officials did not take them seriously. Saddam Hussein believed the United States would not intervene and apparently had received assurances to that effect. Hussein claimed that the invasion was justified because Kuwait had once been part of Iraq and because the Kuwaitis were exploiting the Rumalla oilfield, which extended into Iraq. The immediate response of the United States and its allies was to begin a ship embargo against Iraq. President George Bush, citing atrocities against the Kuwaitis, compared Hussein to Hitler. For his part, Hussein declared the war to be jihad and threatened the mother of all battles (as he put it) if the Americans dared to intervene. Iran's Ayatollah Khomeini, certainly no friend of the United States, seconded the claim of jihad, adding that anyone killed in battle would be a martyr and immediately go to paradise, the Islamic heaven.

In the months that followed, Iraq ignored repeated ultimatums to leave Kuwait. But Iraq did try to stall for time, following the Koranic teaching of "withholding your hand a little while from war" (Vaux, 1992: 71). Thousands of foreign prisoners were released, and Iraq responded positively to French and Soviet peace initiatives. At the same time, Saddam Hussein continued to call it a holy war, saying that the United States was a satanic force attacking the religious values and practices of Islam.

On January 16, 1991, after a U.N. deadline had passed, the allied forces (American, British, French, Saudi, and Kuwaiti) launched a massive day-and-night air attack on military targets in Iraq, including the capital city of Baghdad. The forty days of air war that followed was very one sided. The allied forces were able to bomb targets at will using advanced technical weapons such as radar-seeking missiles, laser-guided bombs, stealth fighters that avoided radar detection, and smart cruise missiles that could adjust their course. The Iraqi air force never got off the ground, but hid or flew to Iran. The Iraqi Scud missiles killed twenty-two American soldiers sleeping in Saudi Arabia and civilians in Israel but were mostly unreliable and ineffective. Finally, the ground war (Operation Desert Storm) lasted only 100 hours before the allied forces liberated Kuwait City. The Iraqis had more that 200,000 casualties (according to American estimates) while the allied forces sustained less than 200 casualties.

Can this war be justified using the just war theory? Carefully explain your answer. Keep in mind that some religious leaders at the time said that it was not a just war.

Was this really a jihad, as Saddam Hussein and the Ayatollah Khomeini said? Remember that Kuwait and Saudi Arabia are also Muslim countries.

Oil presented another consideration. Kuwait had about 20 percent of the world's known oil reserves at the time. Some said the war was really about the control and price of oil and argued that if Kuwait had not had valuable resources, the United States would not have intervened. (For example, the United States did nothing when China invaded and occupied a defenseless Tibet in 1949.)

8. Gandhi

Gandhi's life is beautifully portrayed in the movie Gandhi (1982), directed by Richard Attenborough, with Ben Kingsley as Gandhi. Gandhi's views on war are collected in Madadev Desai, ed., *Nonviolence in Peace and War,* 2 vols. (Ahmedalbad: Navajivan Press, 1945).

Mohandas Gandhi (1869–1948) was the most famous and effective pacifist of the twentieth century. After achieving reforms in the treatment of Hindus and Muslims in South Africa, he returned to India, where he campaigned against British rule, resulting in the departure of the British in 1948, the same year that Gandhi was killed by an orthodox Hindu.

Gandhi was a Hindu who practiced *ahimsa* (nonviolence) toward all living things. (He was considered unorthodox, however, because he rejected the caste system and did not accept everything in the Vedas, the Hindu sacred scriptures.) The concept of ahimsa originated in Jainism and was accepted by both Buddhism and Hinduism. In those religions, ahimsa is understood as not harming any living thing by actions of body, mind, or speech. In Jainism, ahimsa is practiced even with respect to plants, whereas in Hinduism and Buddhism, plants are not included, but nonhuman animals are.

The most original aspect of Gandhi's teaching and methods was what he called *satyagraha* (literally, "truth force"). Satyagraha involves ahimsa and austerities such as fasting. It is supposed to purify one's soul and transform the souls of those it is used against. In practice, the methods of satyagraha developed by Gandhi included marches, demonstrations, sit-ins, strikes, boycotts, fasts, and prayers. These nonviolent and passive methods worked well against the British and have been widely admired and copied. In the United States, Dr. Martin Luther King, Jr. (1929–1968), used similar tactics in the civil rights struggles of the 1950s and 1960s.

Gandhi's nonviolent tactics worked against the British, but would they have been effective against someone like Hitler, who was willing to kill millions of innocent people? Would they stop terrorist attacks such as the September 11 attacks? Is nonviolent resistance an acceptable alternative to war? Is it effective in fighting terrorism? Explain your answers.

Suggested Readings

1. For the official Bush administration view of the War on Terrorism and the Iraq war see the CIA website (http://www.cia.org) and the FBI website (http://www.fbi.org). Both websites are full of information and statements by officials. For pacifist views see http://www.antiwar.com and http://www.nonviolence.org. For an Arab perspective see The Institute for War and Peace Reporting website (http://www.iwpr.net).
2. Hans Blix, *Disarming Iraq* (New York: Pantheon Books, 2004). Blix was the leader of the UN weapons inspection team in Iraq. He concludes that every claim made by the Bush administration about Iraq's weapons program—the mobile biological labs, the yellowcake, the aluminum tubes—has proven to be false, and that the invasion was unnecessary.
3. Christopher Hitchens, *A Long Short War: The Postponed Liberation of Iraq* (London: Plume, 2003), argues that the U.S. invasion of Iraq liberated the Iraqis from oppression, and prevented Iraq from attacking the U.S. with nuclear weapons.
4. Richard A. Clarke, *Against All Enemies* (New York: The Free Press, 2004). Clarke was the counterterrorism coordinator in both the Clinton and second Bush administrations.

He claims that President George W. Bush was obsessed with Iraq after the 9/11 attacks, and eager to blame Iraq even though there was overwhelming evidence that al Qaeda was responsible.

5. Steve Coll, *Ghost Wars* (London: The Penguin Press, 2004), explains the history of al Qaeda in Afghanistan, including how Saudi Arabia aided the rise of Osama bin Laden and Islamic extremism.

6. Ahmed Rashid, *Taliban: Militant Islam, Oil, and Fundamentalism in Central Asia* (New Haven: Yale University Press, 2000), presents the history of the Taliban and explains their version of Islam. They believe they are God's invincible soldiers fighting an unending war against unbelievers.

7. Anthony H. Cordesman, *Terrorism, Asymmetric Warfare, and Weapons of Mass Destruction* (Westport, CT: Praeger, 2001), discusses previous commissions on terrorism, the details of homeland defense, and the risk of chemical and biological attacks.

8. Yossef Bodansky, *Bin Laden: The Man Who Declared War on America* (New York: Random House, 2001). This book is by a well-known expert on terrorism; it covers bin Laden's life and his pursuit of chemical, biological, and nuclear weapons.

9. Paul R. Pillar, *Terrorism and U.S. Foreign Policy* (Washington, DC: Brookings Institution, 2001), explains the causes of modern terrorism in countries such as Pakistan and Afghanistan and examines the new war against terrorism.

10. Peter Partner, *God of Battles: Holy Wars of Christianity and Islam* (Princeton, NJ: Princeton University Press, 1998), explains the doctrines of war in Christianity and Islam.

11. James Turner Johnson, *Mortality and Contemporary Warfare* (New Haven: Yale University Press, 1999), presents the history and development of just war theory and its application in the real world.

12. Bryan Brophy-Baermann and John A. C. Conybeare, "Retaliating against Terrorism," *American Journal of Political Science* 38, 1 (February 1994): 196–210, argue that retaliation against terrorism produces a temporary deviation in attacks but no long-term effect.

13. Dilip Hiro, *Holy Wars: The Rise of Islamic Fundamentalism* (London: Routledge, 1989), explains the development of Islamic fundamentalism found today in Iran and Afghanistan, where Islam has emerged as a radical ideology of armed warfare.

14. Ayatollah Ruhollah Khomeini, "Islam Is Not a Religion of Pacifists," in Amir Taheri, ed., *Holy Terror* (Bethesda, MD: Adler & Adler, 1987), gives a clear statement of the Islamic doctrine of holy war. According to the Ayatollah Khomeini, Islam says, "Kill all the unbelievers just as they would kill you all!"

15. R. Peters, "Jihad," in *The Encyclopedia of Religion* (New York: Macmillan, 1989), gives a scholarly account of the Islamic concept of jihad and its application to war.

16. A. Maalory, *The Crusaders through Arab Eyes* (New York: Schocken Books, 1985), covers two centuries of hostility and war between Muslim Arabs and Christian Crusaders from the West (called Franks), starting with the fall of Jerusalem in 1099. It is a depressing history of invasion, counterinvasion, massacres, and plunder.

17. Michael Walzer, *Just and Unjust Wars: A Moral Argument with Historical Illustrations* (New York: Basic Books, 1977), develops and defends just war theory and applies the theory to numerous historical cases, such as the Six-Day War, the Vietnam War, the Korean War, and World War II. He argues that the Vietnam War can be justified as assistance to the legitimate government of South Vietnam.

18. Robert L. Phillips, *War and Justice* (Norman, OK: University of Oklahoma Press, 1984), defends just war theory. He accepts two principles of the theory, the principle of proportionality and the principle of discrimination. The latter principle, however, in turn rests on the doctrine of double effect, which distinguishes between intending to kill and merely foreseeing that death will occur as an unintended consequence of an action.

19. James Johnson, *The Just War Tradition and the Restraint of War* (Princeton, NJ: Princeton University Press, 1981), explains the historical development of just war theory from the Middle Ages to the present.

20. Paul Ramsey, *The Just War: Force and Political Responsibility* (New York: Charles Scribner's Sons, 1968). This book is a collection of articles on just war theory, all written by Ramsey. He is a Christian who defends a version of the theory that has an absolute principle of discrimination against killing noncombatants. Yet having accepted this principle, he goes on to claim that the war in Vietnam was justified though it involved killing many noncombatants.

21. Paul Christopher, *The Ethics of War and Peace* (Englewood Cliffs, NJ: Prentice-Hall, 1994). This textbook covers the just war tradition, the international laws on war, and moral issues such as war crimes; reprisals; and nuclear, biological, and chemical weapons.

22. Immanuel Kant, *Perpetual Peace* (New York: Liberal Arts Press, 1957). In a classic discussion, Kant maintains that war must not be conducted in a way that rules out future peace. Perpetual peace results when democratic countries let the people decide about going to war. Kant believes that the people will always vote for peace.

23. Albert Schweitzer, *The Teaching of Reverence for Life,* trans. Richard and Clara Masters (New York: Holt, Rinehart and Winston, 1965), argues that all taking of life is wrong because all life is sacred.

24. Leo Tolstoy, *The Law of Love and the Law of Violence,* trans. Mary Koutouzow Tolstoy (New York: Holt, Rinehart and Winston, 1971), explains his Christian pacifism.

25. Mohandas K. Gandhi, "The Practice of Satyagraha," in Ronald Duncan, ed., *Gandhi: Selected Writings* (New York: Harper & Row, 1971), presents his view of nonviolent resistance as an alternative to war.

26. T. R. Miles, "On the Limits to the Use of Force," *Religious Studies* 20 (1984): 113–20, defends a version of pacifism that is opposed to all war but not to all use of force. This kind of pacifism would require one to refuse to serve in the military but would not rule out serving as a police officer.

27. William Earle, "In Defense of War," *The Monist* 57, 4 (October 1973): 561–69 attacks pacifism (defined as the principled opposition to all war) and then gives a justification for the morality and rationality of war.

28. Jan Narveson, "In Defense of Peace," in Jan Narveson, ed., *Moral Issues* (Oxford: Oxford University Press, 1983), pp. 59–71, replies to Earle. He does not defend pacifism; instead, he argues that whenever there is a war, at least one party is morally unjustified.

29. Jan Narveson, "Morality and Violence: War, Revolution, Terrorism," in Tom Regan, ed., *Matters of Life and Death: New Introductory Essays in Moral Philosophy* (New York: McGraw Hill, 1993), pp. 121–159. In this survey article, Narveson covers many different issues, including the nature and morality of violence, the right of self-defense, pacifism, just war theory, and terrorism.

30. Richard A. Wasserstrom, ed., *War and Morality* (Belmont, CA: Wadsworth, 1970), is a collection of articles on the morality of war and other issues. Elizabeth Anscombe discusses the doctrine of double effect as it applies to war. Wasserstrom argues that modern wars are very difficult to justify because innocents are inevitably killed.

31. Jean Bethke Elshtain, *Women and War* (New York: Basic Books, 1987). What is the feminist view of war? According to Elshtain, some feminists are pacifists working for world peace, whereas others want to reject the traditional noncombatant role of women and become warriors. As a result of the second position, the United States now has a higher percentage of women in the military than any other industrialized nation.

Index